Connectivity and Knowledge Management in Virtual Organizations:
Networking and Developing Interactive Communications

Cesar Camison
University Jaume I, Spain

Daniel Palacios
University Jaume I, Spain

Fernando Garrigos
University Jaume I, Spain

Carlos Devece
University Jaume I, Spain

INFORMATION SCIENCE REFERENCE

Hershey · New York

Director of Editorial Content:	Kristin Klinger
Director of Production:	Jennifer Neidig
Managing Editor:	Jamie Snavely
Assistant Managing Editor:	Carole Coulson
Typesetter:	Amanda Appicello
Cover Design:	Lisa Tosheff
Printed at:	Yurchak Printing Inc.

Published in the United States of America by
Information Science Reference (an imprint of IGI Global)
701 E. Chocolate Avenue, Suite 200
Hershey PA 17033
Tel: 717-533-8845
Fax: 717-533-8661
E-mail: cust@igi-global.com
Web site: http://www.igi-global.com

and in the United Kingdom by
Information Science Reference (an imprint of IGI Global)
3 Henrietta Street
Covent Garden
London WC2E 8LU
Tel: 44 20 7240 0856
Fax: 44 20 7379 0609
Web site: http://www.eurospanbookstore.com

Product or company names used in this set are for identification purposes only. Inclusion of the names of the products or companies does not indicate a claim of ownership by IGI Global of the trademark or registered trademark.

Library of Congress Cataloging-in-Publication Data

Connectivity and knowledge management in virtual organizations : networking and interactive communications / Cesar Camison ... [et al.], editor.

   p. cm.

  Summary: "This book analyzes different types of virtual communities, proposing Knowledge Management as a solid theoretical ground for approaching their management"--Provided by publisher.

  Includes bibliographical references and index.

  ISBN 978-1-60566-070-7 (hardvoer) -- ISBN 978-1-60566-071-4 (ebook)

  1. Virtual reality in management. 2. Knowledge management. 3. Virtual corporations--Management. 4. Information networks. I. Camison, Cesar, 1958-

  HD30.2122.C664 2009

  658.4038--dc22

                              2008020499

British Cataloguing in Publication Data
A Cataloguing in Publication record for this book is available from the British Library.

All work contributed to this book set is original material. The views expressed in this book are those of the authors, but not necessarily of the publisher.

Editorial Advisory Board

Table of Contents

Section III
Knowledge Management in Virtual Organizations

Section IV
Knowledge Management Tools

Section V
Specific Problems and Industries

Section VI
Selected Readings

Detailed Table of Contents

Section I
Building Virtual Communities for Sharing Knowledge

The first two chapters of the book place the reader in the context of virtual communities and the role that these communities play in knowledge sharing and creation. The development of virtual organizations and social networks depends on the participation and involvement of their members, and a social analysis of virtual communities and the motivation factors are crucial in any approach of virtual organization management.

The chapter analyses the growing importance of virtual communities in the creation and sharing of knowledge and their limits and ways of improvement, especially in the virtual organization context. Focusing on the role of social networks in virtual communities, the author assesses the importance of virtual organizations in promoting and nurturing social networks, and thus, virtual communities.

The chapter assesses empirically the factors that influence the members' participation in virtual communities. This study tries to shed some light on a crucial question: Which are the factors that drive professionals to participate in virtual communities and condition their involvement? Concepts like trust, past experiences and level of communication in the community and their effect on the members' participation are analysed and discussed.

Section II
Networking and Knowledge Management for Competitive Advantage

How to use networking for competitive advantage is a critical issue in knowledge demanding industries. Virtual networks offer to firms in these industries relevant information, resources, technologies and capabilities. In this section, networking is analysied as a knowledge absorptive enabler in knowlege management and as a tool for knowledge integration in strategic alliances.

Chapter III

    Cesar Camison, Universitat Jaume I, Spain
    Beatriz Forés Julián, Universitat Jaume I, Spain
    Alba Puig Denia, Universitat Jaume I, Spain

This study focuses on the increasing necessity of knowledge for organizations to be competitive, presenting a framework of proactive knowledge management tools and new organizational forms for coping with this challenge. In this new organizational structure, virtual networks are an essential component for absorbing and creating knowledge. It also describes how embeddedness in such a network can affect most of the factors identified as antecedents of absorptive capacity.

Chapter IV

    Montserrat Boronat Navarro, Universitat Jaume I, Spain
    Ana Villar López, Universitat Jaume I, Spain

This work analyses the advantages offered by virtual organizations in the problem of knowledge integration in strategic alliances. Using the Knowledge-Based View, this study ponders over the knowledge transference speed and flexibility gained when this kind of organization is used in inter-organizational alliances.

Section III
Knowledge Management in Virtual Organizations

Knowledge Management offers a solid theoretical ground for tackling some of the social and cultural problems in networking, especially those related with knowledge creation and sharing. These three chapters adopt this view for the study of virtual organizations and their possible forms of management.

Chapter V

    Mark E. Nissen, Naval Postgraduate School, USA

This study faces the knowledge management of a growing and increasingly complex virtual organization. It describes how organizational metacognition offers the potential to elucidate the key issues associated with knowledge networking and how knowledge-flow visualization can be used to diagnose dynamic knowledge patterns.

Chapter VI

    Eduardo Bueno Campos, University of Madrid, Spain
    Carlos Merino Moreno, University of Madrid, Spain
    Reinaldo Plaz Landaeta, University of Madrid, Spain

This chapter analyses the relationship between intellectual capital and knowledge strategies from a strategic management point of view. Considering the Communities of Practice as a reference for knowledge governance, this work proposes a strategic action plan for structuring the knowledge initiatives in firms.

Chapter VII

    Josep Capó-Vicedo, Universitat Politècnica de València, Spain
    José V. Tomás-Miquel, Universitat Politècnica de València, Spain
    Manuel Expósito-Langa, Universitat Politècnica de València, Spain

In this chapter, a network functioning model is proposed for the creation, transfer and sharing of knowledge in the supply chain of SMES clusters. Considering that SMES normally work and are immersed in particular geographical regions, this work analyzes the particular case of knowledge generation and sharing in SMES clusters as an essential source of competitive advantage.

Section IV
Knowledge Management Tools

These chapters consider the management tools for Knowledge Management. The first chapter presents a tool classification and evaluation of their advantages and drawbacks, and the second one the experience of development and implementation of Knowledge Management software for SME. The third chapter centers its attention on e-learning tools.

Chapter VIII

    Raquel Sanchis, Universidad Politecnica de Valencia, Spain
    José V. Tomás, Universidad Politecnica de Valencia, Spain
    Raúl Poler, Universidad Politecnica de Valencia, Spain

This chapter presents a tool classification and the characteristics searched in knowledge management systems, focusing on e-learning techniques. Choosing e-learning techniques as the most excellent method to turn explicit knowledge into tacit knowledge in the knowledge creation process, the authors present a classification of the most relevant characteristics that must be satisfied in e-learning platforms.

Chapter IX

Cesar Camison, Universitat Jaume I, Spain
Carlos Devece, Universitat Jaume I, Spain
Daniel Palacios, Universitat Jaume I, Spain
Carles Camisón-Haba, Universidad Politecnica de Valencia, Spain

This work exposes the experience of the development and use of a KM software for SMEs, and the difficulties found in the project, the results and the lessons learned. The chapter ponders the tools that must be included in any KM system to articulate basic KM procedures, tools like groupware, thesaurus, knowledge repositories and expertise maps.

Chapter X

M. Eugenia Fabra, University of Valencia, Spain
Cesar Camison, Universitat Jaume I, Spain

This chapter analyzes the progress that has been made in the quality of e-learning initiatives in the last years. Companies in knowledge intensive industries need to obtain efficiency in the administration of their training processes and this works ponders over the factors involved in achieving this efficiency like technological platforms, training materials and training methods.

Section V
Specific Problems and Industries

Networking has provoked an authentic revolution in some sectors, especially in those where the access to clients has been a determinant limitation untill the arrival of internet. The public sector and the tourism industry are two interesting exemples. Besides, some specific areas of information management are analised in a network context, such as business analytics success and decision making.

Chapter XI

Júlio da Costa Mendes, University of Algarve, Portugal

This chapter analyses how to create inter-organizational networks in a cooperative environment to pump up the advantages associated to knowledge networking in destinations and in organizations, as well as the relationships between public and private organization. The chapter is focused on how to implement inter-organizational networks for developing and maintaining an adequate environment with shared objectives and practices in tourist destinations.

This chapter assesses how governmental agencies can improve their services offered to citizens through networking and the main problems they face in doing so. An empirical research based on the perceptions of the technology managers of Spanish councils with more than 5000 inhabitants and institutional websites were carried out. The findings disclose some lessons for public managers to take into account when implementing an e-Government strategy.

This chapter proposes a framework for coping with the technical and social complexity of virtuality in business analytics which is based on the combination of Decision Sciences, Information Systems and Management. Some implications for managers interested in exploring business analytics in their organization through virtual networks are presented.

Chapter XIV

This chapter provides theoretical analysis and synthesis of how computer applications are applied in problem-solving and decision-making in the practice of real and virtual networks. It highlights the importance of knowledge management technology as a tool, offering some conclusions in its implementation, but always considering technology as another factor, and perhaps the easier one, to manage knowledge.

Section VI
Selected Readings

Chapter XVI

Cynthia T. Small, The MITRE Corporation, USA
Andrew P. Sage, George Mason University, USA

This chapter describes a complex adaptive systems (CAS)-based enterprise knowledge-sharing (KnS) model. The CAS-based enterprise KnS model consists of a CAS-based KnS framework and a multi-agent simulation model. Enterprise knowledge sharing is modeled as the emergent behavior of knowledge workers interacting with the KnS environment and other knowledge workers. The CAS-based enterprise KnS model is developed to aid Knowledge Management (KM) leadership and other KnS researchers in gaining an enhanced understanding of KnS behavior and its influences. A premise of this research is that a better understanding of KnS influences can result in enhanced decision-making of KnS interventions that can result in improvements in KnS behavior.

Chapter XVII

James G. Williams, University of Pittsburgh, USA
Kai A. Olsen, Molde College and University of Bergen, Norway

The Telecommunications Act of 1996 opened competition in the telecommunications market in the U.S. and forced the incumbent telecommunications companies to open both their physical and logical infrastructure for competitive local exchange carriers (CLECs). In this case study we focus on the problems that face a CLEC with regard to designing an information system and getting a back office system, called an operations support systems (OSS), operational in a highly competitive, complex, fast-paced market in a compressed time frame when a change in a critical telecommunications network component, namely the central office switch, is made after 75% of the system implementation was completed. This case deals with the factors that led to this change in central office switches, its impact on the IT department, its impact on the company, and the alternatives considered by the IT department as possible solutions to the many problems created by this change.

Chapter XVIII

Tor Guimaraes, Tennessee Tech University, USA

Emerging agent-based systems offer new means of effectively addressing complex decision processes and enabling solutions to business requirements associated with virtual organizations. Intelligent agents can provide more flexible intelligence/expertise and help the smooth integration of a variety of system types (i.e., Internet applications, customer relationship management, supplier network management, enterprise resources management, expert systems). This chapter presents an overview of expert systems as the most widely-used approach for domain Knowledge Management today as well as agent technology, and shows the latter as a superior systems development vehicle providing flexible intelligence/expertise and the integration of a variety of system types. To illustrate, a system developed first by using an expert system approach and then by an agent-based approach is used to identify the strengths and weaknesses of the agent-based approach. Last, the practical implications of a company adoption of agent-based technology for systems development are addressed.

Chapter XIX
Jens Gammelgaard, Copenhagen Business School, Denmark
Thomas Ritter, Copenhagen Business School, Denmark

In geographically dispersed organizations, like multinational corporations (MNCs), contextual gaps exist between senders and receivers of knowledge. Employee socialization resulting from physical proximity facilitates contextualization of the transferred knowledge. However, in MNCs most knowledge transfers take place through virtual communication media. We investigate the phenomenon of virtual communities of practice, and propose them to be efficient for individual's knowledge retrieval as participation in such communities reduces the contextual gaps between senders and receivers of knowledge. However, the organization must provide a knowledge-sharing friendly culture, and an institutional protectionism, in order to establish the required level of swift trust within the virtual community.

Preface: Knowledge Management and Virtual Organizations

ABSTRACT

In this preface, virtual organizations are described as virtual communities where the combination of social and technological characteristics makes the management of these organizations a difficult and continuously evolving challenge which still has not been completely explored. Different types of virtual communities are analysed using Knowledge Management as a solid theoretical ground for approaching their management. In the second part of the chapter, trends in virtual organization research are identified, classified, and commented upon in regards to their contribution to the state of the art as discussed in the chapters composing this book.

INTRODUCTION

With the rise of Internet and its exponential growth rate in recent years, professionals can communicate with each other via the Internet regardless of geographical distance and time. The ease of communication provided by the World Wide Web has facilitated knowledge sharing and social participation, which in turn has created a powerful type of community that breaks geographical barriers and schedule limitations and where members can share information and knowledge for mutual learning or problem solving in a virtual way. The impact of virtual organizations is increasingly pervasive, with activities ranging from economic and marketing to the social and educational (Chiu et al., 2006:1872). Thus virtual organizations are gaining importance as a new business model for online collaboration, as demonstrated by the proliferation of trading and education communities (Moor and Weigand, 2007:223).

The interest of academic and professional communities in virtual organizations is more than justified since in an "increasingly networked society, with ever more need for global and flexible ways of professional interactions, virtual organizations are natural candidates to fill collaborative gaps in traditional, hierarchical organizations" (Moor and Weigand, 2007:223). This interest has originated a stream of literature regarding the different variations of the phenomenon such as virtual organizations, virtual teams, virtual classrooms, virtual offices, virtual enterprises, virtual teamwork, etc., usually included within the general term virtual communities (VC). Nevertheless, their possibilities and how to exploit their full potential is not yet fully understood.

The motivation and reasons for participating in a virtual community in specific cases may be very varied. However, Chiu et al. (2006:1872) stress that many individuals participate in virtual communities in order to seek knowledge which may resolve problems at work. According to the BUSINESS WEEK / Harris Poll, 42 % of those involved in a virtual community say it is related to their profession.

The phenomenon of virtual communities is not new. In fact, such communities have existed for more than two decades. Nowadays, billions of users worldwide have begun to engage in knowledge sharing and social participation on the Internet through virtual communities (Hagel and Armstrong, 1997), providing a rich new field for sociologists, psychologists, and social analysts. A study developed by Horrigan, Rainie and Fox (2001) through the Pew Internet and American Life Project shows that 90 million Americans had used the Internet to contact or get information from groups, and 56% of these individuals indicated that they had subsequently joined virtual communities with which they interacted online.

Some virtual communities have gained world wide fame and are known by nearly every internet user. For example, take into consideration the following popular examples. **Usenet**, established in 1980 as a "distributed Internet discussion system," is considered the initial Internet community. Volunteer moderators and votetakers contribute to the community. The **WELL** was a pioneering online community established in 1985. The WELL's culture has been the subject of several books and articles. Many users voluntarily contribute to community building and maintenance (e.g., as conference hosts). **AOL** is the largest of the online service providers, with chat rooms which, for years, were voluntarily moderated by community leaders. It should be noted, however, that rooms and most message boards are no longer moderated. **Slashdot** is a popular technology-related forum, with articles and readers comments. Slashdot subculture has become well-known in Internet circles. Users accumulate a "karma score" and volunteer moderators are selected from those with high scores. **Wikipedia** is now the largest encyclopaedia in the world. Its editors, who voluntarily publish and revise articles, have formed an intricate and multi-faceted community.

As can be seen, there are many examples of virtual communities with their own inherent characteristics and functioning, although all of them share the capacity of creating a dynamic, world wide, easily accessible pool of knowledge. Thus, it is important to shed some light of what is considered by virtual communities and their typologies before approaching their possible potential and management in an organization.

CONCEPTUALIZATION OF VIRTUAL COMMUNITIES

Various definitions of virtual communities can be found in literature depending on the approach used in the study, but usually the social component is always underscored. For instance, Kozinets (1992) considers a VC as a "group of people who share social interactions, social ties and a common 'space'". Similarly, Smith (2002) defines VC as a "set of relationships where people interact socially for mutual benefit", and Wellman (2001) defines VC as a "social network of relationships that provide sociability support, information and a sense of belonging," which creates a sense of shared experiences and perspectives, and emotional support between people working toward similar goals.

On the other hand, from a technical point of view, a virtual community may be understood as one of the community types where the communications are computer-mediated (Koh and Kim, 2004). Hsu et al (2007:153) defines virtual community as "a cyberspace supported by information technology. It is centred upon the communications and interactions of participants to generate specific domain knowledge that enables the participants to perform common functions and to learn from, contribute to, and collectively build upon that knowledge."

Thus, a good way to conceptualize a virtual community is to consider it as a socio-technical system, a complex social system enabled by a complex set of information technologies (Preece, 2000). Following this conception, for Schubert and Ginsburg (2000), virtual communities describe "the union between individuals or organizations who share common values and interests using electronic media to communicate within a shared semantic space on a regular basis." In a similar way, Chiu et al., (2006:1873) point out that "Virtual Communities are online social networks in which people with common interests, goals, or practices interact to share information and knowledge, and engage in social interactions."

Therefore, virtual communities (VC) are socio-technical systems where their members, like in any kind of community, share social interactions and social ties in a common 'space' (De Moor and Weigand, 2007). The difference of virtual communities compared with any other kind of community is that their common space is the cyberspace and this confers a unique set of behavioural characteristics not yet completely understood. These characteristics are bound to the virtuality of the relationship. The term virtuality implies the ability of computers to represent information in ways different from reality, with new tools that allow a broad range of different people to understand complex or conceptual information and participate in exploring it. According to Bieber et al (2002:14) "Virtuality" has several implications. It indicates distance, requiring collaborators to communicate asynchronously (different time, different place). This urges for an organization (or community) structure that is flexible enough to optimize individual and group performance under new and changing conditions.

In our view, participation in Virtual Communities should involve all of these characteristics. We broadly define a Virtual Community to include anyone actively interested in, or associated with, a group formed around a particular domain of interest. Dispersed or local, the community requires electronic support to implement a continuous meta-improvement strategy in its services. Thus we parallel Mowshowitz's view of virtual organizations — "flexible organizations that actively seek flexible approaches to their own improvements." We agree with Lin et al (2007) and Lee et al (2002) defining virtual community, and identify four characteristics: (1) a virtual community is built on a computer-mediated space, called cyberspace; (2) activities in the virtual community are enabled by information technology; (3) the contents or topics of the virtual community are driven by its participants; (4) the virtual community relationship evolves through communicating among members. Similarly to Lin et al (2007), we consider that VC rest on a technology-supported cyberspace, centred upon communication and interaction of participants, and resulting in the building of a relationship.

This broad definition is not important in itself, but a declaration of intentions about how to tackle the problem under study. The combination of human relationships and technology creates a new realm where is necessary not only technical and management knowledge is necessary, but a new and not yet completely understood kind of skills to administer a new social interaction conditioned by virtuality. These aspects make Virtual Communities one of the most attractive and compelling fields of management research.

TYPES OF VIRTUAL COMMUNITIES AND THEIR ROLE IN ORGANIZATIONS

Although virtual communities have existed in some fashion for almost twenty years, it is not completely understood what reasons prompt people to use them and to share valuable information. It has to be taken into account that the members of communities are typically strangers to one another. The scholarly literature lacks of empirical work for determining the causes why people use virtual communities. Blanchard and Horan (1998) state that it is necessary to distinguish between physical based virtual communities and virtual communities of interest. It does not imply that both typologies are mutually exclusive, in fact, very often virtual communities belong to both categories.

In many cases, some communities of interest originate in an off-line context and then move to a Web site hosted by virtual community providers (portals). The members of theses communities interact with one another predominantly in cyberspace. Therefore, virtual communities should be classified as either on-line originated or off-line originated.

An example of on-line originated VC are newsgroups or various e-commerce sites, such as ebay. com, the world's online marketplace, places for buyers and sellers to come together and trade almost anything. In reference to examples of off-line originated virtual communities, we can mention on-line alumni associations or class forums in universities. Balasubramanian and Mahajan (2001) state that most on-line originated virtual communities are based on common interests and themes reinforced through computer-mediated communications.

A special case of virtual communities is the communities of practice (CoP). Pavlin (2006:136-137) and Wenger et al (2002:4) define CoPs as groups of people who share a concern, a set of problems, or a passion about a topic, and who deepen their knowledge and expertise in this area by interacting on an ongoing basis. According to Pavlin (2006:143) individuals who share common practices at a job, or job related activities, could be connected to the CoP. This type of community is different from the community of interest, community of purpose or learning community as practitioners themselves are creating and disseminating knowledge of working practices. CoP is categorized by its primary business intents; namely, to provide a forum for community members to help each other in solving everyday problems in employment, to develop and disseminate best practices, guidelines and procedures for their members to use, to organize, manage and steward a body of knowledge from which the community members can benefit, to innovate and create ideas, knowledge and practices. Thus, the structure of the CoP is based on three components (Pavlin, 2006:138): "(1) the domain as the area of knowledge that brings the community together, (2) the community as the group of people for whom the domain is relevant, and (3) the practice as a body of knowledge, methods, tools and stories that members share and develop together."

Some criteria of classification can be combined. For instance, specifically talking about CoPs, Saint-Onge and Wallace (2003) distinguish among informal, supported and structured types. The informal community of practice is self-joining, without organizational sponsor. On the contrary, supported and structured types are characterized by more intense involvement of the host organization. The competency building of such a CoP is aligned with the strategic purpose of host organization and monitoring of the management is present. Another example of CoP classification is that of Wenger et al. (2002: 76) that consider CoPs by their strategic intent to the organization. In this case, four types could be established: helping communities, best-practice communities, knowledge-stewarding communities and innovation communities. In a similar way, Pavlin (2006:143) affirms that there are many different types of CoPs serving different purposes such as problem solving, knowledge creation, sharing best practices, and so forth. This classification implies the recognition of specific problems in each CoPs beyond a common set of characteristics and consequently the necessity of different approaches in their development and governance in order to attain the dissimilar aims. For instance, in the case of knowledge creation purpose, an extremely important issue that sees knowledge as a property of the community rather than as a resource that can be generated and possessed by individuals (Brown and Duguid, 1991), the conditions and organization structure to deploy and to facilitate innovation are very complex, as in de "ba" model of Nonaka and Knoon, (1998), and a specific design and policy is necessary.

Besides the above mentioned CoPs, we can find other typologies that need a more formal approach for their development. It is the case of firms' networks. Kodama (2005:896) considers these Strategic Communities as both emergent and strategic, a collaborative, inter-organizational relationship that is negotiated and associated with creative yet strategic thinking and action in an ongoing communicative and collaborative process involving several arrangements (e.g. strategic alliances, joint ventures, consortia, associations, and round-tables) which neither depends on marked nor hierarchical mechanisms of control. From the practical aspect, Strategic Communities are a kind of informal organization with a knowledge-based foundation (Mintzberg et al., 1998) but at the same time with a strategic ignition and direction (Porter, 1980). The knowledge based view is an emergent, learning view of the community in a shared context, while the strategic view is a planning view that aims to establish a desired position in the target market. According to Kodama (2005:895-896) "it becomes most important for leaders of corporations to aggressively create strategic communities tapping on their own organizations' as well as outside contacts, including customers, in leading positions for use in innovating their own in-house core knowledge while at the same time creating new values and offering them to their customers." In this way, Interorganizational Virtual Organizations can be created (Fuehrer and Ashkanasy, 1998) as "a temporary network organization, consisting of independent enterprises (organizations, companies, institutions, or specialized individuals) that come together swiftly to exploit an apparent market opportunity."

All these classifications are related to different ways of approaching the management of Virtual Communities. Each group has its peculiarities and need a different kind of solution. This variety of classification criteria shows that a general solution cannot be applied to every Virtual Community, but each case must be studied and a specific solution must be built, knowing when past lessons can be applied and how.

To get a glimpse of the complexity of the subject, it is enough to state that in the literature there are as many classifications of VC as management areas. For instance, according to Lin et al (2007), from a sociological viewpoint, virtual communities can be classified into interest, transaction, fantasy, and relationship, while from the business viewpoint (Hagel & Armstrong, 1997), they are driven by four motivations: purpose, practice, circumstance, and interest (Bressler, 2000). In addition to all this, Wenger et al. (2002: 24-27) present the following community categorizations: big and small, long and short lived, collocated and distributed, homogeneous and heterogeneous, within and across boundaries, spontaneous and intentional, and unrecognized and institutionalized. Adding more complexity to the problem, we are obliged to consider if we are dealing with communities represented by corporate entities and non-profit organizations. (Kodama, 2005:895). We can find even mixed kinds of organization in a same VC, as the case studied by Kodama (2005:896) of a networked community in which university, hospital, private businesses and non-profit organizations take part in the advancement of virtual networking in the field of veterinary medicine.

Besides, VC can be professional societies where members participate to better understand its domain and improve the way they perform community-related tasks or they can be virtual educational communities (Bieber et al, 2002:14) where the main objective is to provide a truly interactive environment for mutual sharing and action learning. There are many kinds of professional virtual communities such as the medical professional virtual communities or the engineering networks, which view themselves as a composition of special interest groups. In the educational domain, some teachers' professional virtual communities are TappedIn (http:// www.tappedin.org). TENet (http://www.tenet.edu) or SCTNet (http:// sctnet.edu.tw). In the latter cases, the aim of the educational virtual community is to generalize the use of Internet as an innovation tool between teachers, pupils, parents, schools and institutions, that is to say, all the agents implied in the learning process. As an example, we can cite Educared, a Spanish virtual community with more than 11000 educational centres subscribed to it. Educared is a virtual learning environment that is a system that creates an environment designed to facilitate teachers in the management of educational courses for their students, especially involving distance learning. The activities developed by this kind of educational community range from extracurricular activities and knowledge about a determined topic to prizes, forums, courses, conferences, news, etc.

As it can be easily deduced, all these kinds of VC have different objectives and creation processes and need different treatment. Nevertheless, VC offer a common ground which can establish the foundation of the study of virtual organizations, since all the VC pursue the same aim— the knowledge sharing of their members.

KNOWLEDGE MANAGEMENT AND VIRTUAL COMMUNITIES

One of the main reasons to use a virtual community is to share knowledge. The members of a virtual community develop a pool of collective knowledge which transcends any individual's knowledge and it is fully accessible for all the members. If one member deals with an unfamiliar situation regarding the know-how of the organization, the members conduct a series of alternating experimentation and improvisation stages, accompanied by sharing and reflecting stories of comparable situations, which eventually leads to a solution for the problem. Therefore, Knowledge Management may be considered the most important issue in order to achieve the goals of virtual communities.

Knowledge management has been boosted in the last two decades by the tremendous IT breakthrough reached in information processing and connectivity. Although Knowledge Management has an important soft or social component, technology has functioned as an enabler that permits the exploitation of the knowledge potential of large and geographically disconnected organizations. Nevertheless, organizational practices and policies must always accompany technology, since they are the central cornerstone of any Knowledge Management initiative (Davenport and Prusak, 1998).

The potential of technological Knowledge Management tools is vast in itself, since they can not only make better use of the raw information already available, but they can sift, abstract and help to share new information, and present it to users in new and compelling ways. Nevertheless, the objectives of Knowledge Management are more ambitious, trying to influence the organizational culture, policies and procedures to lever up knowledge creation and sharing. For instance, perhaps the more popular and common tool of a Knowledge Management systems is a library for depositing the knowledge of the community. The management of this library covers such diverse issues as to sort the importance, context, sequence, significance, causality and association of the knowledge. The great advantages that can be easily reached in a community or organization by means of a digital library of multimedia documents and manuals are clear, but the inherent potential of a virtual community is greater than that related to documents management. For Bieber et al (2002), the digital repository should be expanded to support computer-mediated communications, process, workflow and decision analysis capabilities, and conceptual knowledge structures, supporting many of the everyday tasks of community members. This implies a cultural change that must be fostered to happen. In these cases, Knowledge Management theory is a good support since it explores the foundations and the variables involved in knowledge creation and sharing.

The emergence of Knowledge Management can be attributed to the high rate of job turnover among key employees, carrying with them when leaving to other firms the knowledge acquired during years of work experience. In order to solve this problem, the main aim of KM is to maximize the knowledge sharing in the organization. This knowledge can be deposited in the organization through patents, software, databases, reports, formulas, drawings, etc. In this sense, virtual organizations can take great advantage from the KM techniques since all the communication and coordination in virtual networks must be done explicitly. Following KM theory, the community's knowledge has both explicit and tacit components. Due to the special characteristics of tacit knowledge, specific policies must be articulated to tap this kind of knowledge. Since the implicit knowledge resides in the heads of the community members, special emphasis must be put in its externalization (articulating implicit knowledge into explicit documents, formulas, manuals, etc.) (Nonaka and Takeuchi, 1995). But even the explicit knowledge is not always stored so easily in the community digital repository, urging for a set of formal procedures or motivation strategies among the members of the community. Therefore, building an intranet-based store of information is not sufficient for Knowledge Management.

Exclusive virtual communication, as it happens in many virtual organizations, has a special drawback regarding Knowledge Management, since virtuality is much more limited on tacit knowledge transmission than conventional communication. The physical experience of learning by doing is not possible, restraining the socialization phase of Nonaka and Takeuchi's knowledge creation model. But this disadvantage of the virtual organizations has its positive side, since the necessity of a digital format for knowledge transmission, like text, formulas or drawings, forces the user to reflect about the explicitation of the knowledge. It must be taken into account that the key phase in knowledge creation is the "combination," where a group of experts are capable of combining their explicit knowledge in different fields and producing new knowledge. This phase needs a deep understanding of the knowledge put in place, and skills to make it explicit to the group. Here, the culture of the community and social interaction among members play a decisive role tapping out this characteristic of virtuality, and a deep understanding of the mechanism involved in knowledge creation is necessary for their correct management.

TRENDS IN VIRTUAL ORGANIZATIONS

Trends in virtual organizations have been marked by the state of the art of technology. Connectivity, compatibility and security have been big issues until now, stressing the attention on support technologies and applications for discussion or conversation, task and goal-oriented work (Stanoevska, 2002). But whereas new applications and projects are facing the most challenging technical problems like developing security architectures spanning across administrative and enterprise boundaries (Djordjevic et al, 2007:63), the social issues regarding motivation and management of the members of virtual organizations are gaining force. Technology has evolved from the initial complex to develop and install solutions to an affordable commodity, where standard systems are at hand for every company. This has caused researchers' concerns to increasingly move towards how information technologies must be used to leverage all the knowledge in the firm, not only inside the organization, but from customers, providers, competitors and government, rather the technological development. As a result, social and managerial issues like motivation, VC formal structure, control, rewards, etc are gaining interest among researchers and professionals.

Here, the interaction of both systems, the social and technical ones, has created an interesting research field. The technical system design, complex in itself, must be subordinated to the social system, but it is inevitable that the possibilities and limitations of the technology mould the organization and the social system, including goals, workflows, organizational structures and social norms.

The first thing to take into account is that fluency of communication among members of a VC depends on the goodness of the channel. Here, the limitations of the cyberspace are patent. Although the continuous improvements and breakthroughs on information technologies widen the possibilities of virtual communication at a surprising speed, most authors affirm that a virtual relationship will never reach all the hues and richness of a face to face conversation or meeting. This must be overcome by specific management policies depending on the specific communities that at the same time could range from a community with a complete lack of central control to a tight hierarchical structure in the case of some organizations. A key aspect seems to be strong and lasting interactions that bind community members in a trust relationship (Wenger et al, 2002). In this sense, Chapter I (Garrigos) *"Interrelationships Between Professional Virtual Communities and Social Networks, and the Importance of Virtual Communities in Creating and Sharing Knowledge"* and Chapter II (Flavián) *"The Role of Trust, Satisfaction, and Communication in the Development of Participation in Virtual Communities"* offers an interesting view of the problem, the second one presenting empirical data supporting the analysis.

Networking and Electronic Information as a Source of Competitive Advantage

The fast evolving and the increasingly demanding business environment has placed knowledge as a critical factor for business success. The markets, customers tastes, competitors and technology evolves so fast that promoting learning and connecting the organization to get solid information has become the new challenges for organizations. But the relationship between access to information and knowledge is not always direct, and a more complex set of variables is involved. Thus, how to use networking for competitive advantage is a critical issue. In this regard, Chapter III (Forés) *"Can Virtual Networks Encourage Knowledge Absorptive Capacity?"* analyses the effect of networking on the factors identified as antecedents of knowledge absorption and creation, and how to take advantage of the relevant business information, knowledge, resources, technologies and capabilities circulating in the virtual networks. Chapter IV (Boronat-Navarro) *"Knowledge Integration Through Inter-Organizational Virtual Organizations"* exposes the process of knowledge creation through strategic alliances using virtual collaboration.

But even more than external information management, dealing effectively with internal information poses a determinant challenge for competitiveness. Typically, about 80 % of the information used in a company is generated internally. When a firm reaches a considerable size or is dispersed geographically, even with an appropriate commitment and information sharing culture among workers, getting the exact information when necessary needs thorough planning and management. This is even more complex when the turbulence of the environment forces a continual learning and knowledge creation. This necessity is aggravated in virtual organizations, where one of the most challenging and important issues is to attain an effective and productive knowledge sharing among the members of the community or organization. The virtuality of the communication adds new difficulties to the already complex knowledge transmission, and for this reason one of the most marked trends in virtual organization is focussed on how to deal with knowledge in networks.

Knowledge Sharing in Virtual Organizations

As it has been above commented, Knowledge Management offers a solid theoretical ground for tackling some of the social and cultural problems in networking, specially those related to knowledge creation and sharing. Then, it is usual to find researches adopting this view to approach the virtual organization study. This is the case of several of the chapters proposed in this book. In Chapter V (Nissen) *"Knowledge Networks and Flows in the Virtual Organizational Context"* describes how organizational metacognition offers potential to elucidate the key issues associated with knowledge networking and how knowledge-flow visualization can be used to diagnose dynamic knowledge patterns. In Chapter VI (Bueno) *"Model on Knowledge Governance: Collaboration Focus and Communities of Practice,"* analyses the relationship between intellectual capital and knowledge strategies from a strategic management point of view. Completing these analyses of organizational networking, Chapter VII (Capó) *"Knowledge Management in SMEs Clusters"* assesses the particular case of knowledge generation and sharing in SMES clusters, proposing a network functioning model in order to improve innovation.

Besides these theoretical studies, Chapter VIII (Sanchís) *"Tools for Supporting Knowledge Management: Knowledge Internalization Through E-Learning"*, and Chapter IX (Camison) *"The Value of Virtual Networks for Knowledge Management: A Tool for Practical Development"* introduce us to the extant technical tools that would help to implement the KM practices and policies. The first one gives us a tool classification and the characteristics searched in KM, focusing in e-learning techniques. The second chapter exposes the experience of the development and use of a KM software for SMEs, and the difficulties found in the project, its results and the lessons learned. The chapter ponders the tools that must be included in any KM system to articulate basic KM procedures, tools like groupware, thesaurus, knowledge repositories and expertise maps.

But the relationship is both ways, KM theory can help to understand the social and cultural mechanism involved in virtual knowledge sharing, but at the same time, networking widens the possibilities of traditional organizational learning. Chapter X (Eugenia) *"Human Capital and E-Learning: Developing Knowledge Through Virtual Networks"* offers a review of this evolution of e-learning in the last decade.

Specific Studies

Relevant Sectors

A great advantage of networking is the access to customers and partners all over the world. This affects decisively some sectors and is provoking the complete restructuring of some industries. This book presents the analysis of two interesting sectors where government action is involved. In the first one, ione of the sectors most affected by IT is studied— tourism, which has became an attractive field for research and experimentation. Chapter XI (Mendes), *"The Development of Knowledge and Information Networks in Tourism Destinations"* analyses how to create inter-organisational networks in a cooperative environment to pump up the advantages associated with knowledge networking in destinations and in organisations, as well as the relationships between public and private organization. The chapter is focused on how to implement inter-organisational networks for developing and maintaining an adequate environment with shared objectives and practices in tourist destinations. A second chapter, Chatpter XII (de Juana) *"E-Government Challenges: Barriers and Facilitators in Spanish City Councils"* assesses how governmental agencies can offer their services to citizens through networking and the main problems these agencies face.

Relevant Problems

Finally, the last two chapters are devoted to specific problems related to information management in networking. Although the importance of networking is present in nearly every activity in business, for those areas where information is a key resource, Knowledge Management and business intelligence are unavoidable issues. For instance, Chapter XIII (Ramakrishna)*"Business Analytics Success: A Conceptual Framework and an Application to Virtual Organizing,"* proposes an interesting framework for coping with the technical and social complexity of virtuality which is based on the combination of decision sciences, information systems and management in the study of success of business analytics. Chapter XIV (Targowski) *"The Evolution from Data to Wisdom in Decision Making at the Level of Real and Virtual Networks"* contrasts the decision making problem when important information is extracted from networks and data processing, using a Knowledge Management approach to the problem.

REFERENCES

Balasubramanian, S., & Mahajan, V. (2001). The economic leverage of the virtual community. *International Journal of Electronic Commerce, 5(3),* 103-138.

Bieber, M., Engelbart, D., Furuta, R., Hiltz, S. Noll, J., Perece, J., Stohr, E., Turoff, M. & Van de Walle, B. (2002). Toward Virtual Community Knowledge Evolution. *Journal of Management Information Systems, spring, 18(4),* 11-35.

Blanchard, A. L. & Horan, T. (1998). Virtual communities and social capital. *Social Science Computer Review, 1*(3), 293-307.

Bressler, S. (2000). *Communities of Commerce: Building Internet Business Communities to Accelerate Growth, Minimize Risk, and Increase Customer Loyalty.* New York: McGraw-Hill.

Chiu, C., Hsu, M. & Wang, E. (2006). Understanding knowledge sharing in virtual communities: An integration of social capital and social cognitive theories. *Decision Support Systems, 42(3)*, 1872-1888

Davenport, T., Prusak, L. (1998). *Working Knowledge. How Organizations Manage What They Know.* Boston: Harvard Business School Press.

De Moor, A. & Weigand, H. (2007). Formalizing the evolution of virtual communities. *Information Systems*, 32(2), 223-247.

Djordjevic, I., Dimitrakos, T., Roman N., MacD. & Ritrovato, P. (2007). Dynamic security perimetes for inter-enterprise service integration. *Future Generation Computer Systems 23(4)*, pp. 633-657.

Endres, M., Endres, S., Chowdhury, S. & Alam, I. (2007). Tacit knowledge sharing , self-eficacy theory, and application to the Open Source community. *Journal of Knowledge Management, 11(3)*, 92-103.

Hagel, J. & Armstrong, A. (1997). *Net Gain: Expanding Markets Through Virtual Communities.* Boston, MA: Harvard Business School Press.

Horrigan, J. B.; Rainie, L. & Fox, S. (2001). *Online communities: networks that nurture long-distance relationships and local ties.* Washington, DC: Pew Internet and American Life Project.

Hsu, M., Ju, T., Yen, C. & Chang, C. (2007). Knowledge sharing behavior in virtual communities: The relationship between trust, self-efficacy, and outcome expectation". *International Journal of Human-Computer Studies, 65(2)*, 153-169.

Kodama, M. (2005). New knowledge cration through leadership-based strategic community—a case of new product development in IT and multimedia business fields. *Technovation,* 25(8), 895-908.

Koh, J. & Kim, Y. G. (2004). Knowledge sharing in virtual communities: an e-business perspective. *Expert Systems with Applications*, 26(2), 155-166.

Kozinets, R.V. (1992). E-tribalized marketing? The strategic implications of virtual communities of consumption. *European Management Journal, 17(3)*, 252-264.

Lin, F., & Hsueh, C. (2006). Knowledge map creation and maintenance for virtual communities of practice. *Information Processing and Management 42(2)*, pp. 551-568

Moor, A., & Weigand, H. (2007). Formalizing the evolution of virtual communities. *Information Systems, 32(2)*, 223-247.

Pavlin, S. (2006). Community of practice in a small research institute. *Journal of Knowledge Management, 10(4)*, 136-144.

Preece, J. (2000). *Online Communities: Designing Usability, Supporting Sociability.* New York, NY: John Wiley & Sons.

Saint-Onge, H. , & Wallace, D. (2003). *Leveraging Communities of Practice for Strategic Advantage.* Amsterdam: Butterworth-Heinemann.

Smith, M. (2002). Tools for navigating large social cyberspaces, *Commun. ACM, 45(4),* 51-55.

Schubert, P. & Ginsburg, M. (2000). Virtual communities of transaction: the role of personalization in electronic commerce. *Electronic Markets,* 10(1), 45-55.

Stanoevska-Slabeva, K. (2002): Toward a community-oriented design of Internet platforms. *International Journal of Electronic Commerce,* 6(3), p. 71-95.

Wellman, B. (2001). Computer networks as social networks. *Science,* 293(5537), 2031-2034.

Wenger, E. (1998). *Communities of Practice – Learning, Meaning and Identity.* Cambridge: Cambridge University Press.

Wenger, E., McDermott, R., & Snyder, W. (2002). *Cultivating Communiteis of Practice: A Guide to Manageing Knowledge.* Boston, MA: Harvard Business School Press.

Section I
Building Virtual Communities
for Sharing Knowledge

The first two chapters of the book place the reader in the context of virtual communities and the role that these communities play in knowledge sharing and creation. The development of virtual organizations and social networks depends on the participation and involvement of their members, and a social analysis of virtual communities and the motivation factors are crucial in any approach of virtual organization management.

Chapter I
Interrelationships Between Professional Virtual Communities and Social Networks, and the Importance of Virtual Communities in Creating and Sharing Knowledge

Fernando Garrigos
Universitat Jaume I, Spain

ABSTRACT

This chapter presents the interrelationships between professional virtual communities and social networks, and analyzes how, and in what ways, these communities play a crucial role in the creation and sharing of knowledge. The chapter begins by outlining how virtual communities are gaining importance in the new environment. It explains what we understand as a professional virtual community and its importance and also the relevance of social networks in today's Knowledge Management age. The study then analyses how the development of social networks is crucial to the improvement of professional virtual communities, and also how virtual organizations can promote the improvement of social networks. Finally, the study examines how virtual communities are vital as mechanisms for creating and sharing knowledge.

INTRODUCTION

The importance of information and knowledge as increasingly key aspects of competitive advantage in the activities of both individuals and organizations, is widely recognized by authors and practitioners. Modern society, based on systems of information and communication, has experienced vast changes that have affected society, industry, and "all economic entities, including people, organisations, and technologies" (Okkonen, 2007:7). Rapid progress in information and multimedia technologies, and the increasing acceptance and use of Internet, Intratet and Extranet, are paving the way for gradual innovation in diverse areas, generating flatter corporations with novel and improved communication platforms, as well as creating new business models for inter-corporation transactions of goods and knowledge, and cooperation. The new platforms are changing work practices and processes in corporate settings to support the lifestyle of individuals in their daily routines, and are also stimulating the proliferation of small offices and home offices. "New business styles based on such concepts as virtual teams and virtual community are representative of such a trend" (Kodama 2005:895).

The proliferation of network access and the rise of the Internet have facilitated the rapid growth of virtual communities (Chiu et al., 2006:1872), "as a new business model for online collaboration, as demonstrated by the proliferation of trading and education communities" (Moor and Weigand, 2007:223). Scholars such as Moor and Weigand (2007) point out that "virtual communities, such as e-business platforms and research networks, are crucial instruments for collaboration in today's networked and globalizing society" (p.244). According to these authors, "in an increasingly networked society, with ever more need for global and flexible ways of professional interactions, virtual communities are natural candidates to fill collaborative gaps in traditional, hierarchical organizations. With the advent of more user-friendly and powerful Web applications, business is also discovering the power of virtual communities" (ibid, p.223).

However, although "they could bring a lot of value and profit to the companies and most of the experiences studied have demonstrated very positive results" (Loyarte and Rivera, 2007:76), "formal research on Communities of Practice and their impact on organizations has been limited both in the way of finding results and in the research method used" (ibid, pp. 68). Similarly, Lin et al. (2007) agree that research into virtual communities, an extension of communities of practice, is still in its initial stages, and many areas remain open for researchers to investigate.

In an attempt to fill this gap, the present chapter will try to analyze the importance of virtual communities, and specifically professional virtual communities, explaining how they develop from communities of practice, and their interrelationships with social networks.

PROFESSIONAL VIRTUAL COMMUNITIES IN THE KNOWLEDGE MANAGEMENT AGE

Kalpic and Bernus (2006) state that "the pace of adoption of internet technology, especially the establishment of intranets, extranets, Web portals, etc., has created a networking potential that drives all of society and corporations to work faster, create and manage more interdependencies, and operate on global markets" (p.41). Above all, the importance of new networks is stressed in the role they play in developing Knowledge Management tools.

Perrin et al. (2007) identify "three different types of knowledge networks: technological networks (supported by technological strategy), social networks (socialization strategy), and individualized networks (personalization strategy)" (p.159) that may be related to different strategies. Their work is based on Hansen et al.'s, (1999) typology of knowledge strategies, which is the most widely supported and referenced typology and distinguishes between personalization and codification of knowledge, but with the inclusion of a third type that combines the previous two. Briefly, they distinguish: 1. technological, codification (Hansen et al., 1999), system-oriented strategy (Choi and Lee, 2003), or the technocratic school, which relies on technology and databases. Individuals make their knowledge explicit in order to transfer it via the database. According to Meroño-Cerdan et al. (2007:63), the codification strategy focuses on codifying knowledge using a "people-to-document" approach, with a heavy emphasis on information technologies. Moreover, system "orientation emphasizes codified knowledge, focuses on codifying and storing knowledge via information technology and attempts are made to share knowledge formally". 2. Personalization, related to the spatial school (Earl, 2001), and which is conceived as a human-orientation approach (Choi and Lee, 2003), designed to promote the emergence of knowledge and dependent on face-to-face contact (Hansen et al., 1999). According to Meroño-Cerdan et al. (2007), the "personalization strategy focuses on dialogue between individuals, not knowledge objects in a database. Knowledge is transferred in brainstorming sessions and one-to-one conversation", in addition, "human orientation emphasizes dialogue through social networks and person-to-person contacts, focuses on acquiring knowledge via experienced and skilled people and attempts are made to share knowledge informally" (p.63) 3. "The purpose of socialization combines both technological and personalization strategies and relies on communities of practices", or communities of practice. "People inhabiting the same knowledge space share knowledge and experience in order to improve business processes" (Perrin et al., 2007:159).

However, according to Perrin et al. (2007), "KM theory has evolved this last decade from the technological dominance to the human orienta-

tion" (p.159). For instance, when Meroño-Cerdan et al. (2007) compare the two abovementioned strategies, they find that "personalization strategy is predominant in all kinds of firms, probable due to be more feasible in first KM adoption stages"(p.70). Perrin et al. (2007) compare the use of the three strategies in 1998, 2000, 2002 and 2004, and conclude that "our results are consistent with the human and social network trend" (p.159), since although the technological strategy was predominant in 1998, "62 per cent of firms surveyed are now using a mixed strategy based on socialization"… "socialization strategy asks for the better knowledge of the "knower", the "sender" of the practice and the "receiver""(ibid, p.160).

The focus on this trend in the literature has stressed the importance of teams, communities of practice, and finally virtual communities and their human or social side, in order to enhance organizations' capability to create and share knowledge, facilitate creativity and innovate.

Meroño-Cerdan et al. (2007:62) define a team as a small number of people with complementary skills who are committed to a common purpose, set of performance goals, and approach for which they hold themselves mutually accountable (Katzenback and Smith, 1993). These authors point out that team structure facilitates the assembling, integration, and implementation of individuals' diverse knowledge and expertise at various locations, and by using their different functional knowledge, skills, perspectives, and backgrounds, they provide ideal conditions for generating new and useful products and processes. However, "formal departments, operational and project teams within an organization seem to become insufficient for prosperous creation, dissemination and utilization of knowledge. They require support of less formal communities" (Pavlin, 2006:136).

Another type of group used particularly in the KM context (Meroño-Cerdan et al., 2007), and considered as one of the most reputable (Pavlin

2006), is known as a community of practice (CoP) (Leve and Wenger, 1991; Wenger, 1999). The term "describes an activity system that includes individuals who are united in action and in the meaning that action has for them and for the larger collective" (Leve and Wenger, 1991; Loyarte and Rivera, 2007:67). Although there could be several CoPs within a organization, and most people belong to many of them, a CoP can be defined as a volunteer, or informal, group of practitioners, with common interests, values and beliefs, engaged in sharing and learning about a concern, a common set of problems, or with a passion for a certain subject, who work on the same topic but not necessarily on the same project, and who deepen their knowledge and expertise in this area by interacting on an ongoing basis (Campbell, 1999; Meroño-Cerdan et al., 2007; Pavlin, 2006:136-137; Wenger et al., 2002:4). These authors argue that CoPs are categorized by their primary business intents. They can also be considered as "social spaces of learning", that "facilitate the integration of dispersed knowledge through informal social relationships irrespective of formal intra- and inter-organizational hierarchies" (Pyöriä, 2007:18), the purpose of which is to provide a forum for community members to help each other in solving problems in employment, to build, develop, exchange and disseminate best practice, guidelines and procedures, to turn practical information into knowledge and to develop members' capabilities, and their abilities to learn. Their target is to use, organize, manage and steward a body of knowledge from which the community members can benefit, to innovate, and create ideas, knowledge and practices. Loyarte and Rivera (2007:67, 72) define communities of practice as informal entities that exist in the mind of each member, that focus on thinking together to solve problems, that help to foster a collaborative environment in which knowledge can be used to solve problems naturally and to promote and improve effectiveness, efficiency, learning and innovation. These communities last as long as their

members want them to last (Wenger and Snyder, 2000), and although frequency and formalization of collaboration vary substantially, they always make use of collaborative tools such as face-to-face meetings, or Web-enabled tools in order to facilitate interaction (Pavlin, 2006).

Finally a virtual community "includes anyone actively interested in, or associated with, a group formed around a particular domain of interest. Dispersed or local, the community requires electronic support to implement a continuous meta-improvement strategy in its services" (Bieber et al., 2002:14). A virtual community could be defined as a technology-supported cyberspace, centered on the communication and interaction of its participants and the building up of relationships among members, to generate specific domain knowledge that enables the participants to perform common functions and to learn from, contribute to, and collectively build upon that knowledge (Hsu et al., 2007:153; Lin et al., 2007). "The impact of virtual communities is increasingly pervasive, with activities ranging from economic and marketing to the social and educational" (Chiu et al., 2006:1872). However, the two most widespread types are virtual professional communities and education communities (Bieber et al., 2002:14; Moor and Weigand, 2007:223). According to Lin et al. (2007), professional communities can differ from general communities in many aspects. Members of a professional community generally share norms and values, carry out critical reflection, and continue professional dialogues with one another.

Professional virtual communities derive from or can be viewed as extended communities of practice (Bieber et al., 2002:14; Lin et al. 2007; Loyarte and Rivera, 2007:67). According to Bieber et al. (2002), "a professional society is a special kind of virtual community, in which members participate to better understand its domain and improve the way they perform community-related tasks. The virtual community of a professional society may include nonmembers and organizations and often is many times larger than the professional society's membership" (p.14). A professional virtual community aggregates and gathers together a dispersed group of people who share expertise and common interest in a specific topic and collaborate to achieve common objectives (Bressler, 2000; Hagel and Armstrong, 1997; Lin et al. 2007). Like virtual communities, communities of practice use the support of communication technologies to allow people to talk about their experiences and solve problems (Loyarte and Rivera 2007:67). However, traditional communities of practice use face-to-face interaction more frequently, and are usually intra-organizational entities, while virtual communities are inter-organizational systems.

SOCIAL NETWORKS

As pointed out above, although virtual communities are based on technological networks, the human or social part of the network plays an increasingly important role. As Pyöriä (2007) notes, "human relations are now more crucial than ever before due to the growing knowledge intensity of work and due to the deeper immersion of work organizations in information technology" (p.17).

Network analysis has developed from perspectives originating in the fields of psychology, anthropology and sociometry (Bradbury and Bergmann Lichtenstein 2000), and they have been studied extensively in the literature in these fields. In the management literature, network analysis, particularly the personal and social aspects of networks, is an increasingly relevant area of study. The ability to promote a context of psycho-social help (James 2000), the interconnections between managers and other individuals, and other aspects related to the importance of different networks are factors that are increasingly emphasized in the literature (Ellis and Mayer 2001). Its importance in the managerial literature began to grow following

the work of Granovetter (1973), who stressed "the strength of weak ties", or Bandura's (1989) Social Cognitive Theory, that highlights an individual's behavior as a product of his or her social network (Chiu et al., 2006: 1873)[1].

The relevance of human or social networks in the Knowledge Management -or intellectual capital- arena derives from the works by Grant (1996) or Nonaka (1994). Nonaka (1998, cited by Girard, 2006) suggests that "new knowledge always begins with an individual" (p.26). Social networks are essential for organizations, because "tacit-to-tacit or person-to-person knowledge transfer is the most effective way to share tacit, complex knowledge.... Person-to-person knowledge sharing is also more likely to be internalized by the receiver than, for example, person-to-document-to-person knowledge transfer" (Endres et al., 2007:94). The development of research on the social capital of organisations, one of the three main "intellectual capitals" that researchers consider in organisations together with human and structural capital (Palacios and Garrigos, 2003) also stresses this aspect. Social capital is defined as "the sum of the actual and potential resources embedded within, available through, and derived from the network of relationships possessed by an individual or social unit" (Nahapied and Ghoshal, 1998:243).

The importance of human relations and networks has recently been studied in teams, communities of practice, different alliances between enterprises and virtual organisations. In this line, Lytras and Pouloudi (2006:66) point out that "knowledge flow is a dynamic concept... that relates to the characteristic of humans to constitute teams that share a common objective and thus facilitate the exchange of knowledge". Maguire et al. (2007:41) study the importance of Knowledge Management and communities of expertise within small and medium enterprises (SMEs), arguing that "small companies... tend to rely on formal and informal networks rather than utilising publicly funded sources of support".

From their empirical research with a sample of over 200 enterprises, these authors find that SMEs tend to create tacit knowledge that "was derived from personal experience and wisdom, organically created and shared amongst individuals in the relevant department.... [and find] no evidence that a method to capture and acquire cultural knowledge has been used". However, Pyöriä (2007) states that "individual knowledge workers from "communities of practice" or professional subcultures... transcend formal and clear-cut organizational boundaries" (p.18). It is important to note that networking activities occur not only in firms, institutions or banks, or amongst lawyers and accountants (to name just a few) in a formal way (Das and Teng 1997); the formal and informal relationships between entrepreneurs, managers, organizational representatives, colleagues outside work (Paauwe and Williams 2001), personal relationships, families and other business contacts are also essential. Social relationships are important, because, according to (Hillman et al., 2000), one of the main tasks facing managers is to provide networks through their connections with the social environment. In this vein, Burt, Hogarth and Michaud (2000) argue that managers with links in separate groups are rich in the social capital of information and control the benefits associated with relationships that overcome the "structural gaps" in their information. In addition, social networks can be extended to all parts of organisations to embrace all personnel. Chiu et al. (2006:1875) report that Tsai and Ghoshal (1998) empirically justify how social capital facilitates resource exchange and production innovation within the organization, while Yli-Renko et al. (2001) examine the effects of social capital on knowledge acquisition and exploitation in young technology-based firms In addition, Wasko and Faraj (2005) examine how individual motivations and social capital influence knowledge contribution in electronic networks of practice. Kodama (2005) points out that "one of the keys to producing innovation in a knowledge based society is how

organizations can organically and innovatively network different knowledge created from the formation of a variety of SCs (strategic communities, a concept similar to relationships between firms) inside and outside the organization, and acquire the synthesizing capability through dialectical leadership they need to generate new knowledge" (p.907). Finally, according to Perrin et al. (2007: 158), "best practices... may develop through benchmarking..., learning... or by "gleaning" skills from strategic alliance partners" (Hammel and Prahalad, 1988).

What, then, are the main components of social capital? In Chiu et al. (2006:1873), Nahapied and Ghoshal (1998) define three distinct dimensions of social capital: structural (the overall pattern of connections between actors), relational (the kind of personal relationships people have developed with each other through a history of interactions), and cognitive (those resources providing shared representation, interpretations, and systems of meaning among parties). Wasko and Faraj (2005) also follow Nahapiet and Ghoshal (1998) to classify social capital in three dimensions (structural, relational, and cognitive) but do not adopt Nahapied and Ghoshal's manifestations of each of these dimensions.

To begin with the structural dimension, authors such as Chiu et al. (2006:1873) or Nahapiet and Ghoshal (1998) use the construct "social interaction ties" in order to measure this dimension of social capital. Social interaction ties are considered as channels for information and resource flows (Tsai and Ghoshal, 1998), "network ties provide access to resources" (Nahapiet and Ghosal, 1998:252), and the more social interactions undertaken by exchange partners, the greater the intensity, frequency and breadth of information exchanged (Larson, 1992; Ring and Van de Ven, 1994). In summary, Chiu et al. (2006) conclude that "strong community ties could provide important environmental conditions for knowledge exchange" (p.1875). Granovetter (1973) describes tie strength as a combination of the amount of time, the emotional intensity, and intimacy (mutual confidence), and the reciprocal services that characterize the tie. Chiu et al. (2006) state that social interaction ties represent the strength of the relationships, the amount of time spent, and frequency of communication among members of virtual communities.

To consider the relational dimension, Chiu et al. (2006:1873), again following Nahapiet and Ghoshal (1998), use the constructs of "trust", "norm of reciprocity" and "identification" to measure this dimension of social capital. According to Al-Alawi et al. (2007:23), interpersonal trust is known as an individual's or group's expectation that the promises or actions of other individuals or groups can be relied upon. Trust is a powerful mechanism in coordinating group behavior, although it has some constraining factors such as longevity, especially in the context of knowledge work teams (Pyöriä, 2007:23, 26). However, trust between co-workers is an extremely essential attribute in organizational culture (Al-Alawi et al., 2007; Hsu et al., 2007; Pyöriä, 2007), which is believed to have a strong influence on knowledge sharing (Al-Alawi et al., 2007:23). In addition, "the effectiveness of IT in actualizing KM and organizational learning is significantly dependent on sustaining trust" (Sherif, 2006:75), where trust is identified as a "key element in fostering the level of participation or knowledge sharing in virtual communities" (Chiu et al., 2006:1875). Norms of reciprocity refers to knowledge exchanges that are mutual and perceived by the parties as fair (Chiu et al., 2006:1877). Chiu et al. (2006:1875, 1877-1879) report that authors such as Dholakia, Kankanhally or Bock find that group norms have a strong effect on we-intentions (group intentions) to participate in virtual communities and that reciprocity is positively related to the usage of electronic knowledge repositories by knowledge contributors, and have a positive effect on attitude and intention to share knowledge. If we finally consider identification, according to Chiu et al. (2006), "some studies found that a sense of community...and social identity...can enhance the likelihood of members' contribution and participation in a virtual community" (pp.1875-1879).

As regards the cognitive dimension of social capital, Chiu et al. (2006:1873), again following Nahapiet and Ghoshal (1998), use the constructs "shared vision" and "shared language" to measure the cognitive dimension of social capital (see also ibid, pp. 1878-1880). In addition to these three dimensions, other social capital dimensions not considered by these authors may be the diversity and breadth of relationships, the strength of the relationships, the quality of the relationships, or the emphasis on social ties such as information from friends and families (Garrigos, 2002).

IMPORTANCE OF SOCIAL NETWORKS IN DEVELOPING VIRTUAL COMMUNITIES

According to Lin and Hsueh (2006), "learning in virtual communities can be facilitated by the transactive memory system" (p.552), which consists of three components: knowledge map (represented by knowledge objects and their dependencies); social networks (formulated by individuals, their relationships, and the strength of relationship); and mnemonic functions (which include knowledge allocation, social network updating, knowledge maintenance and collaborative knowledge retrieval). From very diverse points of view, numerous authors stress the importance of many characteristics of social networks, and in general "the human side", in order to create, maintain and develop virtual communities. Many explanations have been given for the importance of these networks. Firstly, they stress the human side, which is increasingly important to understand the functioning of virtual organisations. Secondly, because these networks are heterogeneous, they can bring new perspectives and sources of knowledge to the virtual organisations, thereby increasing knowledge creation and creativity. Thirdly, "personal and organizational networks play an important role in accessing knowledge" (Christensen, 2007:38). The fourth reason given is that the establishment of social networks can increase trust or ties, thus helping to increase knowledge sharing and enriching virtual organisations. Finally, the common identity of the members of a social network can facilitate knowledge sharing. Some of these reasons are now analysed.

Lin et al. (2007) argue that humans are social beings and tend to form groups and alliances for protection and pleasure, and due to the rapid progress of technology, the concept of community has been extended to a virtual form. However, Pyöriä (2007:25) points out that "the field of information systems has traditionally been plagued by high implementation failures because the understanding of socially situated practices in knowledge work is incomplete" (Schultze, 2000:4). According to Pyöria, (ibid, p. 26) "one of the biggest challenges of the information age is that the more deeply we are immersed in IT, and the more routine work is transferred from men to machines, the more important it is to understand the human side of work…. In this respect there is a need for research that combines perspectives from technical, behavioral and social scientific disciplines".

More specifically, Pavlin (2006:138) emphasizes the importance of communities of practice and networks, and their heterogeneity as essential instruments to increase creativity and learning. Based on the work of Wenger (1999), Pavlin states that the structure of communities of practice is grounded on three components: (1) knowledge, "the domain as the area of knowledge that brings the community together"; (2) people or "the community as the group of people for whom the domain is relevant"; and (3) experience "the practice as a body of knowledge, methods, tools and stories that members share and develop together. On this basis, Pavlin considers networks to be essential because "the number of qualified experts (managers, scientists, ICT personnel,

etc.) in a single organization (regardless of the size) may be insufficient to support the knowledge of a certain domain, that is not usually the case in a well-established network that associates the members from different organizations". According to Pavlin (2006) "acting within the same knowledge domain but from a different perspective can be an advantage for established practice. The members of our community are filling the holes in social structure between certain organizations… Networking across structural holes is clearly a form of social capital… in such a manner that competitive advantage is created for the members of the community and also for the organizations where they work. The theory of social capital emphasizes that the difference (as for example in education, occupation, employee organization) is the precondition for creativity and informal learning… we are not arguing that in the professional network the common experiences are not important, but that a "bit of difference in parity" is crucial" (p.139).

According to Christensen (2007), "without networks there is no opportunity for accessing knowledge" and similarly, "the sharing of knowledge is facilitated by some kind of personal or virtual network" (p.38). As we point out in this chapter, we believe that social and virtual communities can reinforce each other. In this vein, Christensen points out that these "networks can be maintained by formal or informal face-to-face meetings, or – the latest trend – by physical structures that do not allow individual cubicles, but emphasize transparent community spaces" (p.38).

On similar lines, Chiu et al. (2006) state that "the social interaction ties among members of a virtual community allow a cost-effective way of accessing a wider range of knowledge sources" (pp.1876-1877). Nahapiet and Ghoshal (1998) argue that "network ties influence both access to parties for combining and exchanging knowledge and participation of value through such exchange" (p.252). Furthermore, network ties provide the opportunity to combine and exchange knowledge.

Recent studies have provided empirical support for the influence of social interaction ties on interunit resource exchange and combination (Tsai and Ghoshal, 1998), knowledge sharing among units that compete with each other for market shares (Tsai, 2002), and knowledge acquisition (Yli-Renko et al., 2001).

According to Endres et al. (2007), "when individuals are embedded in a strong social network, they are motivated to more freely share knowledge (Wasko and Faraj, 2005)" (p.96). As Hsu et al. (2007:154) point out, membership of virtual organisations is open, members voluntary contribute their knowledge without receiving monetary rewards, and most members are invisible, they do not provide guarantees that others will behave as they are expected to, and there is a lack of face to face communication and legal guarantees, which makes it harder for members to share their knowledge. It therefore follows that the existence of the social network, previous to the creation of the virtual community, is crucial for it to be effective, as this is a better way of creating and sharing knowledge.

Following similar criteria, Loyarte and Rivera (2007:72) stress the importance of "Social identity theory" in order to "cultivate communities of practice". "The concept of communities of practice has in recent years become one of the most popular tools for enhancing knowledge sharing – even though no one actually knows how to practice, or cultivate, a community of practice" (Christensen, 2007:37). Loyarte and Rivera (2007) illustrate the importance of social identity theory with some examples: "open software communities (i.e. Linux, Apache, etc.) are good examples where… members are motivated and not for lucrative purposes, but because they get to nourish their esteem. People have to feel valuable and they need to trust other members (World Bank). In this sense, it can be difficult… if members feel they can lose their hierarchical power or status… in an organization change or in an innovation process" (p.72).

According to Hsu et al. (2007), the biggest challenge in fostering virtual communities is the willingness to share knowledge with other members. In this respect, two issues are involved: personal cognition, which is based on self-efficacy and outcome expectation, and social influence, based on trust. They argue that knowledge sharing is affected by trust, "an implicit set of beliefs that the other party will behave in a dependent manner… and will not take advantage of the situation" (pp.153-154). The importance of trust, in all its varieties, together with the other two variables, is crucial in the social networks literature. Hence, all the literature about trust in the social networks literature is essential to better understand the behavior of a virtual organization, as Hsu et al. (2007) point out. For instance, these authors use a social cognitive theory-based model to explore the knowledge sharing behaviors within the virtual communities of professional societies, and suggest that further research should extend their model using the social capital theory "as a broad view in exchanging and combining intellectual capital—including structural, cognitive and relational dimensions".

The study by Chiu et al. (2006) also "draws on both the Social Cognitive Theory and the Social Capital Theory to investigate the influence of outcome expectations and facets of the three dimensions of social capital on knowledge sharing in virtual communities in terms of quantity and quality" (p.1873). Chiu et al., (2006) point out that "without rich knowledge, virtual communities are of limited value… clearly, the biggest challenge in fostering a virtual community is the supply of knowledge, namely the willingness to share knowledge with other members. It is then important to explain why individuals elect to share or not to share knowledge with other community members when they have a choice" (p.1873). In order to explain this fact, they use the Social Cognitive Theory and the Social Capital Theory. They argue that "it is the nature of social interactions and the set of resources embedded within the network that sustains virtual communities. Therefore studies on virtual communities address issues related to both personal cognition and social network and should be different from the ... studies concerning computer use and internet behaviors, which focus only on personal cognition" (p.1873). In addition, they also introduce the Social Capital Theory to supplement the Social Cognitive Theory[2]. They point out, referring to Nahapiet and Ghoshal (1998), that "the Social Capital Theory suggests that the social capital, the network of relationships possessed by an individual or a social network and the set of resources embedded within it, strongly influence the extent to which interpersonal knowledge occurs"[3]. According to Chiu et al. (2006), "virtual communities differ notably from conventional organizations. There is no concrete reward system in place to reinforce the mechanisms of mutual trust, interaction, and reciprocity among individuals. However, online knowledge sharing activities cannot be successful without the active participation of online members. Lack of motivation from a knowledge contributor impedes the knowledge sharing. Under such circumstances, social capital becomes all the more important, because the resources inherent in the online social network mediate between the individuals and hence foster their intention and activeness to perform this voluntary behavior" (p.1876). Finally, the results of Chiu et al.'s (2006) study indicate that "outcome expectations and facets of social capital are helpful in explaining knowledge sharing in virtual communities"[4] (pp. 1884-1885). Hence, they conclude that "managers interested in developing and sustaining knowledge exchange through virtual communities should develop strategies or mechanisms that encourage the interaction and the strength of the relationships among members"[5] (ibid, p. 1885).

According to these measures, Moor and Weigand (2007) state that "virtual communities... are not governed by such a hierarchy, but instead should allow the interests of their members to be balanced by their unique social norms. To reduce these problems, systematic methodological support is needed for the required legitimate user driven specification process" (p.244). Hence, these authors argue that in order to improve virtual communities 1) "trust is essential for collaboration in these communities to occur" 2) "well-defined formalizations can help in the administration and facilitation of the change process, and the resolution of any breakdowns" and 3) "clear formalizations help to adapt the methodology without generating inconsistencies and incompletions" (p.244).

Finally, social networks facilitate virtual organisations because a common identity is shared between their members. In this vein, "common identity often facilitates knowledge sharing since individuals within one specialist group understand each other better than people from outside the group – they are more or less believed to possess the same absorptive capacity" (Christensen, 2007). According to this author, "apparently, a community makes it much easier to share knowledge, because people really care about their practice, are embedded in the same practice and, hence, talk the same (technical) language" (p.38).

IMPORTANCE OF VIRTUAL COMMUNITIES IN DEVELOPING SOCIAL NETWORKS, AND AS A MECHANISM TO CREATE AND SHARE KNOWLEDGE

Following the analysis of the importance of social networks for the development of virtual communities, we now demonstrate that virtual communities in today's environment are also a crucial instrument to create and maintain social networks, and a valuable system to create and share knowledge.

As Chiu et al., (2006) point out, "people who come to a virtual community are not just seeking information or knowledge and solving problems;

they also treat it as a place to meet other people, to seek support, friendship and a sense of belongingness… In other words, they attempt to develop social relationships with other people inside the community" (p.1874). From an analysis of the Business Week / Harris Poll, these authors find that 35% of people involved in a virtual community consider their community as a social group.

A further important question is how virtual communities, with the use of new technologies, can be essential instruments to codify and disseminate certain knowledge. On this point, Sherif (2006) states that "tacit knowledge is best leveraged through social interaction… whereas explicit knowledge can be codified, captured, and disseminated electronically" (p.74). Hence, virtual communities can be used by their members as a mechanism to continually obtain new knowledge from new people and at the same time, codify and select this knowledge and the social network that is of interest at each given moment. This facet is important, since authors such as Girard (2006) refer to studies where managers complain of information overload and of wasting time in locating information, thus delaying decisions because of too much information and no mechanism to select this information. According to this author, managers "dwell on information that is entertaining but not informative, or easily available but not of high quality", which becomes a major problem since "the amount of data and information available will increase in the future" (p.27) . Girard (ibid) maintains that "this mountain of unprocessed data is becoming so large that it is smothering itself and preventing its metamorphosis to knowledge. Recent research suggests that it may be quicker for scientists to repeat experiments rather than search for previous results … One wonders how organizations that invested millions of dollars in programs to manage knowledge are now discovering that their managers are less efficient than before the implementation" (p.28).

Social networks can help to avoid this problem, and the use of virtual communities can also

help in the development of these social networks, or as a mechanism to create or access the most relevant social networks for managers at each specific moment.

Social networks, more than merely the use of technology, and with them, the use of virtual organisations, is crucial, because, according to Pyöriä (2007) "technology as such is of little direct help in the process of augmenting human collaboration in knowledge work" (p.23). There is a "false conception of the utility of IT for enhancing interpersonal interaction by constructing new communication channels parallel to old ones… The true revolutionary nature of IT lies in its capacity to overcome limitations in our natural physical and mental capabilities by eliminating the need for communication"[6]. "Therefore, the elimination of useless interactions… can save time for developing its true creative strengths, which constitute the core of knowledge work. … It is in this distinctively human territory of creative problem solving and non-routine decision making where IT as such is least capable of increasing productivity" (ibid, p.24). Pyöriä (2007) stresses that "general beliefs in the communicative advantages of IT are highly overvalued… the speed with which these applications are being introduced, coupled with knowledge workers' lack of time and resources to internalize them, have resulted in a more or less chaotic situation….. for example, as numerous studies indicate, groupware and other intranet-base solutions rarely, if ever, work exactly as planned, and the systems are often used in an uncontrolled and impulsive manner" (p.26).

The debate about the importance of new technologies and Internet and whether it is useful in creating social capital is also considered by Chiu et al. (2006:1875). According to these authors "Putnam (2000) suggested that the Internet decreases social capital, while Wellmen et al. (2001) indicated that Internet use supplements social capital by extending existing levels of face-to-face and telephone contacts. Uslaner (2000) concluded that the Internet neither destroys nor creates social capital". However, these and other authors point out the importance of virtual communities to overcome these problems.

Firstly, Hsu et al. (2007) point out that the Internet facilitates the creation of professional virtual communities that enable knowledge sharing without their participants ever meeting. Hence, it facilitates the creation and development of networks. According to Djordjevic et al. (2007), virtual communities or organisations "span across organizational boundaries and enable the enactment of collaborative processes that integrate services, resources and knowledge in order to perform tasks that the virtual organizations partners could not undertake on their own" (p.634).

Kodama (2005) points out that "the dilemma faced by organizations is the need to reconcile rapid access and synthesis of relevant new knowledge, with the long time frames needed for knowledge creation and synthesis". In this vein, "Networked Strategic Communities based on deep inter-organization collaboration can offer a possible solution" (p.904). According to Kodama (2005), "knowledge, or management resources, aimed at innovation is created from SCs, a wide range of knowledge both inside and outside the company, including customers and strategic partners, is synthesized via the network, and new knowledge that never existed before is created to become a new source of competitive advantage" (p.906).

Bieber et al. (2002) state that "many researchers have observed that Knowledge Management primarily is about people and cultural change rather than technical development". They also maintain that "research on online communities concerns itself explicitly with supporting people networking together to achieve a goal. Through this networking, knowledge is created and exchanged. Technology now plays an important role by supporting activities, recording knowledge, and developing organizational memory" (p.15).

In this vein, two factors facilitate the growth of networks subsequent to the use of professional communities; the fact that participation in these communities is voluntary and involves members of different organisations, and the fact that in professional communities members are used to participating openly.

In relation to the importance of voluntary participation in virtual communities, Chiu et al. (2006) mention that "members in virtual communities differ from general Internet users in that virtual community members are brought together by shared interests, goals, needs or practices" (p.1875). With this premise, Endres et al. (2007) point out that "volunteer organizations or informal organizations outside normal firm boundaries may better facilitate fluid knowledge transfer at the individual level than within the traditional organization structure" (p.93). This fact can avoid the problem that knowledge inside closed organisations is more restricted than the knowledge found in open organisations. For instance, Endres et al. (2007) explain that "in contrast to the free and fluid flow of tacit knowledge in the Open Source community[7], knowledge sharing is often limited in organizations, especially knowledge that is complex and tacit" (p.97). In addition, Kodama (2005) points out that "the act of transcending boundaries stimulates deep, meaningful learning, which in turns opens possibilities for the generation of new knowledge" (p.904).

However, Chiu et al. (2006) mention that the character of virtual communities "begs the key question [of] whether the social capital developed in virtual communities is strong enough to stimulate members to overcome the barriers of complex knowledge sharing process and then share valuable knowledge, especially when no extrinsic reward is provided" (p.1875). Nevertheless, this problem can be avoided, according to Endres et al. (2007), because although members in virtual communities may be unpaid, a person may acquire some degree of status and may have the opportunity for financial gain based on their in-demand persona. "The reward is not formal or assured, but may be a motivator to participate" (p.98). This fact, in addition, can strengthen the social network of community members, who know each other better, following their contributions to virtual organisations.

The second important point is the open participation in professional communities. According to Lin et al. (2007), community members can communicate and collaborate as groups. Members participate in virtual communities either openly or anonymously, depending on the kind of community it is. However, Lin et al. (2007) point out that in the professional virtual community, members participate in community activities openly rather than anonymously for professional purposes. This fact can go further to facilitate the importance of these virtual communities in enhancing social networks, and to facilitate the creation and sharing of knowledge.

Examples of communities of practice and virtual communities are various. For instance, in a case study, Pavlin (2006:137) shows how a small organization was able succeed in building an extensive network of top researchers, professors, high government officials, journalists and even interested individuals who share a passion or are differently influenced by the common knowledge domain. This author also mentions that the literature presents numerous cases of communities of practice and virtual communities, mainly in large international corporations such as Ford, IBM, Airbus, British Petroleum, Cap Gemini, Ernst & Young, Clarica, Hewlett Packard, McKinsey, Mercedes-Benz, Shell Oil, Siemens, Chevron, Xerox, etc.

To summarize, with the development of Internet technology, professionals and the public at large can communicate with each other via the Internet regardless of geographical distance (Lin and Hsueh, 2006:551). However, the importance of professional virtual communities lies in

their value to create and share knowledge. For instance, according to Randeree (2006), "information systems researchers are currently looking at knowledge creation, knowledge acquisition and knowledge sharing" (p.145). Lin and Hsueh (2006) state that "the virtual community enabled by the World Wide Web (WWW) facilitates knowledge sharing and creation for communities of practice" (p.551). Hsu et al. (2007:153) point out that today, an increasing number of individuals participate in virtual communities to acquire knowledge to resolve problems at work, and that virtual communities are valuable systems that hold the key to Knowledge Management. Finally, authors such as Lin et al. (2007) study the knowledge sharing and creation process in a virtual community.

We now highlight the importance of virtual communities in creating and sharing knowledge.

Knowledge Creation

According to Sherif (2006), "knowledge creation is considered the most important of all KM processes (Lapre and Van Wassenhove, 2001)" (p.75). "Knowledge creation is concerned with the development of new organizational knowledge in the firm", although knowledge integration and exploitation can also contribute to the development of new organizational knowledge through (Nielsen, 2006:62). In the generation of knowledge, the actors translate the assembled array of tacit and explicit knowledge into a form suitable for transfer to others (Geisler, 2007:86)[8].

Sherif (2006) points out that "the general belief is that knowledge creation is an inherent trait of some organizations, an art of continuous change (Brown and Eisenhardt, 1998) that the majority of organizations may fail to imitate (Quin et al., 1996)... the majority conquer with the proposition that the process is highly tacit and cannot be captured" (p.75). However, virtual organisations can play a crucial role in the creation of knowledge.

Kodama (2005) argues that the rigidities of formal organizations make them a "poor vehicle for learning"; rather, in this situation the sources of innovation lie exclusively within firms' relationships. "Knowledge creation occurs in the context of a community that is fluid and evolving rather than tightly bound or static". "Knowledge creation is an extremely important issue that sees knowledge as a property of communities of practice..., ba..., communities of creation..., and networks of collaborating organizations... rather than as a resource that can be generated and possessed by individuals. When the knowledge base of an industry is both complex and expending, and the sources of expertise are broadly dispersed, the locus of innovation will be found in networks of inter-organizational learning rather than in individual organizations" (p.896).

Loyarte and Rivera (2007) state that "when people participate in the problem solving and share the knowledge necessary to solve the problems, it is possible to speak about the generation of knowledge in Communities of practice" (p.67). The same occurs with virtual communities. According to Pavlin (2006), the main purpose of communities of practice "is creating a platform, for supporting a structure for running the knowledge cycle (as described for example by Nonaka and Takeuchi,.....) within, among and between organizations. The community helps to disseminate and create knowledge, whilst the use (and also further creation and dissemination) of knowledge belongs to other more formal organizational structures like projects groups and teams" (p.141)[9].

Finally, Lin and Hsueh (2006), following Nonaka, point out that "organizational knowledge creation may start from the individual level via the collective (group) level to the organizational level, and sometimes reach out to the inter-organizational level", in this way, "the inter-organizational learning process facilitated by a virtual community information system constructs distributed explicit knowledge, and weaves the social networks to connect tacit knowledge owned by individuals across organizations" (p.552).

Knowledge Sharing

According to Al-Alawi et al. (2007), "the process of Knowledge Management involves several activities" (p.22). The most commonly discussed activity in the process of Knowledge Management nowadays is knowledge transfer (knowledge sharing). The sharing of knowledge is a knowledge process that has been recognized as a subject of some interest by scholars (Geisler, 2007). According to this author, "the mode of transfer of knowledge is a component of the process in which actors in the organization transfer, share, and diffuse the knowledge they possess" (p.86). Randeree (2006:153) claims that knowledge sharing involves the dissemination of information and knowledge throughout the business unit or organization. From the same point of view, Hsu et al. (2007) state that "knowledge sharing is the behavior when an individual disseminates his acquired knowledge to other members within an organization" (p.154). Virtual organisations can also help this process, since "the goal of knowledge sharing can either be to create new knowledge by differently combining existing knowledge or to become better at exploiting existing knowledge" (Christensen, 2007:37), and since they make available the use of new sources of knowledge .

Virtual communities can help in the process of sharing knowledge, both because of the importance of their social side in sharing knowledge, and also because of the fact that "knowledge is often shared with the help of the technology" (Wenger, 1999; Perrin et al., 2007:159). According to Lin and Hsueh (2006), "in the Internet era, explicit knowledge exists generally in hypertext on the Web or texts on the Intranet.... In order to shorten the learning cycle, an individual can exploit the experience of others to enlarge his or her experiences, which can be carried out by sharing explicit knowledge on the Internet". "Besides, well-structured knowledge objects reveal the relationship among knowledge, and reduce information overloading on knowledge sharing and creation" (p.552) . In addition, according to Randeree (2006) "knowledge sharing is as much of a people issue as it is technological". In this way, "technology can act as both a facilitator and a control mechanism to protect knowledge", and "firms see benefits to sharing knowledge and establish motivational approaches and communication mechanisms to share knowledge" (p.153). In addition, Endres et al. (2007) argue that there is an "inherent co-occurrence of informal and formal social networks in organizations... In a given organization, tacit-to-tacit knowledge sharing may occur in some groups but not in others. In addition, some informal, strong social networks that effectively transfer knowledge may be embedded in otherwise formal structures" (p.100). Hence, the use of technological and social sides can complement and strengthen the process of knowledge sharing.

Christensen (2007:38) identifies five problems in the literature inherent in organizational knowledge sharing: (1) the "stickiness" of knowledge, that refers to the epistemologically different faces of knowledge (mainly tacit versus explicit knowledge); (2) the absence of a common identity between the people who are trying to share this knowledge, a fact that hinders the knowledge sharing process; (3) the lack of any relation between the receiver and sender of knowledge; (4) a lack of willingness to share knowledge, an issue that mainly "deals with social dilemmas...as the trade of commons, and the power of possessing knowledge"; (5) and the lack of knowledge about knowledge[10].

Hsu et al. (2007) state that "prior research has highlighted the various factors that affect an individual's willingness to share knowledge, such as costs and benefits, incentive systems, extrinsic and intrinsic motivation, organization climate and

management championship" (p.154). In the same vein, different authors have created models that emphasize the importance of various variables in the sharing of knowledge.

For instance, Al-Alawi et al. (2007:25-26) create a model including certain cultural factors that influence knowledge sharing, specifically: trust, communication between staff, information systems, reward system, and organization structure. According to their results, "trust, communication, reward system and organization structure all received strong literature support. However, information systems/technology received mixed support" (ibid, p.39). They state that "the relationship that proved to exist between knowledge sharing and trust communication, information systems, reward system and organization structure indicates the importance of such factors as prerequisites of the success of knowledge sharing" (ibid, p.37), and recommend and suggest some ways of emphasizing these aspects in the firm.

Lin et al. (2007) conducted a three-phase study on a teachers' virtual community in order to understand the knowledge flows among community members from different organisations. The objective of their study was to identify essential factors in individual, group, organization, and environmental contexts, which affect knowledge sharing and creation in the professional virtual community. Specifically, their model categorizes these factors as environmental, information technology, project, organizational, group and individual contexts, and defines the process of knowledge sharing and creation by the sequence of causal conditions[11], action/interaction strategies, and consequences (at the individual, group and organizational level)[12].

Finally, according to (Chiu et al., 2006), "some studies... suggested that individuals would share knowledge within virtual communities with the expectation of enriching knowledge, seeking support, making friends, etc. Butler et al... suggested that the primary reason for individuals to share knowledge is their expectation of being seen as skilled, knowledgeable or respected. Other studies suggested that individuals share knowledge with the expectation of helping the virtual community to accumulate its knowledge, continue its operation, and grow..." (p.1875)

However, literature and empirical studies that thoroughly address the problem are scarce; in addition, according to Lin et al. (2007), few studies have addressed the knowledge sharing and creation processes successfully by collecting data from commercial companies, and further research is therefore necessary.

CONCLUSION

The development of new technologies and information and communication systems, the expansion of network access, and the rise of the Internet have led to the proliferation of new business styles based on information and knowledge. This trend has facilitated the growth in importance of the construction of strong social networks and advances and effective professional virtual communities as a mechanism that can enhance competitive advantage for organisations.

Professional virtual communities can be conceived as an evolution of teams, and communities of practice, that combine a technological and a human orientation. The technological side is crucial to promote communication and to cross organizational borders in order to enhance knowledge creation and sharing capabilities, while the human and social side, which has emerged as the most important, stresses the relevance of social and informal relationships as a source of creativity and innovation.

With the increasing relevance of the human side, the understanding of social networks, as a source and as a consequence of the development of virtual communities, is stressed by the literature. Network analysis has developed from perspectives in the fields of psychology, anthropology

and sociometry, and is an increasingly relevant issue in the literature of management because of the importance of individuals and their social relations and cultural aspects related to networks such as ties, trust, sense of community, shared vision or the existence of diverse relationships inside and outside the enterprise, to generate and share knowledge.

In the same vein, social networks, and all aspects related to their development, are crucial to developing virtual communities. Social networks can facilitate learning, collaboration, knowledge sharing and creation in virtual communities. The main aspects explaining the importance of networks in virtual communities are: the fact that they stress the importance of the human side of these communities; the importance of heterogeneity of networks to bring new perspectives and sources of knowledge to virtual communities, which increase knowledge creation and creativity; their importance because of their role in accessing crucial or tacit knowledge; and because of the importance of increasing trust, ties, motivation, willingness, and a common identity, facts that contribute to increasing the creation and sharing of knowledge.

However, virtual communities are also important in the development and maintenance of social networks and as an essential mechanism or valuable system for creating and sharing knowledge in today's technological society. In this way, virtual communities are essential places to meet other people with different perspectives, to seek support, friendship, and a sense of belonging, and in summary, to develop social relationships with other individuals. They are useful mechanisms to obtain a constant flow of new knowledge from new people, and essential instruments to codify and disseminate different knowledge, avoiding information overload and wasting time by their members in the search for selecting information. They are essential mechanisms to create or access the most relevant social network for managers or other professionals at each given moment, gaining more time to develop its true creative strengths. In addition, they can help to eliminate limitations in our natural physical and mental capabilities. The use of new technologies by virtual communities also helps to extend existing levels of face-to-face and telephone contacts, maintaining and developing social interactions, and facilitating the creation and development of networks across organizational boundaries, and collaboration among their members. They help to integrate services, resources and knowledge in order to perform tasks that the members of virtual communities could not undertake on their own, supporting people networking together to achieve a goal. The voluntary participation, and the shared interests, goals, needs or practices of virtual organizations members, together with the open participation of the professional members, enhance social networks, as well as facilitating the creation and sharing of knowledge.

If we turn to the importance of virtual communities in creating and sharing knowledge, creation is promoted by the open, voluntary and fluid character of virtual organisations, because through them, individuals can access broadly dispersed sources of expertise, and because they act as a platform that supports the running of the knowledge cycle, helping to combine different sources of ideas. In addition, the sharing process is encouraged as virtual organisations help to make available the use and exploitation of existing knowledge or new sources of knowledge. By combining the social side with the motivational approaches, with the help of technology that facilitates the communication and control of knowledge, the sharing of knowledge is promoted. In this vein, all the above-mentioned processes in virtual communities facilitate the common identity of their members, the relationships between the senders and receivers of knowledge, the communication and information systems, the trust and motivation to share knowledge, and the knowledge of knowledge, facilitating knowledge sharing.

FUTURE RESEARCH DIRECTIONS

This chapter has highlighted the relationships between virtual communities and social networks, and how they can enhance each other's development. Furthermore, the importance of virtual communities to create and share knowledge has been expounded. However, further research is necessary: firstly theoretical research that can complement and develop the ideas suggested in this chapter; and secondly, empirical research to develop hypotheses and test them with data from a range of virtual communities.

ACKNOWLEDGMENT

The authors acknowledge financial support from Fundació Caixa Castelló-Bancaixa (P1 1A2006-10), and Generalitat Valenciana (GV/2007/100).

REFERENCES

Al-Alawi, A.I., Al-Marzooqi, N.Y., & Mohammed, Y.F., (2007). Organizational culture and knowledge sharing: critical success factors. *Journal of Knowledge Management, 11* (2), 22-42.

Bandura, A. (1989). Social Cognitive Theory. In R. Vasta (Ed.), *Annals of Child Development* (pp. 1-60). Greenwich, CT: Jai Press LTD.

Bieber, M., Engelbart, D., Furuta, R., Hiltz, S. Noll, J., Perece, J., Stohr, E., Turoff, M., & Van de Walle, B. (2002). Toward virtual community knowledge evolution. *Journal of Management Information Systems, spring, 18* (4), 11-35.

Bradbury, H., & B.M. Bergmann Lichtenstein (2000). Relationality in organizational research: Exploring the space between. *Organization Science, 11*(5). 551-564.

Bressler, S.E. (2000). *Communities of Commerce: Building Internet Business Communities to Ac-*

celerate Growth, Minimize Risk, and Increase Customer Loyalty. New York: McGraw-Hill.

Brown, S.L., & Eisenhardt, K.M. (1998). *Competing on the Edge: Strategy as Structured Chaos.* Boston, MA.:Harvard Business School Press.

Burt, R.S., R.M. Hogarth, & C. Michaud (2000). The social capital of French and American managers. *Organization Science 11*(2),123-147.

Campbell, A. (1999). Knowledge management in the Web enterprise: exploiting communities of practice. In P. Jackson,. (Ed.), *Virtual Working: Social and Organisational Dynamics* (pp. 21-32). London, UK: Routledge.

Chiu, C., Hsu, M., & Wang, E. (2006). Understanding knowledge sharing in virtual communities: An integration of social capital and social cognitive theories. *Decision Support Systems, 42,* 1872-1888.

Choi, B., & Lee, H. (2003). An empirical investigation of KM styles and their effect on corporate performance. *Information and Management, 40*(5), 403-417.

Christensen, P.H. (2007). Knowledge sharing: moving away form the obsession with best practices. *Journal of Knowledge Management, 11*(1), 36-47.

Djordjevic, I., Dimitrakos, T., Roman N., Mac D., & Ritrovato, P. (2007). Dynamic security perimeters for inter-enterprise service integration. *Future Generation Computer Systems, 23,* 633-657.

Earl, M (2001). Knowledge management strategies: toward a taxonomy. *Journal of Management Information Systems, 16*(1), 215-233.

Ellis, N., & R. Mayer (2001). Inter-organisational relationships and strategy development in an evolving industrial network: Mapping structure and process. *Journal of Marketing Management, 17,* 183-222.

Endres, M., Endres, S. Chowdhury, S., & Alam, I. (2007). Tacit knowledge sharing , self-eficacy theory, and application to the open source community. *Journal of Knowledge Management, 11*(3), 92-103.

Garrigos, F. (2002). *Análisis del Papel Contingente De La Percepción Directiva Sobre El Desempeño Empresarial: Un Estudio En El Sector Hotelero.* Doctoral Thesis. Castellón, Spain: Universitat Jaume I.

Geisler, E. (2007). A typology of Knowledge Management: strategic groups and role behavior in organizations. *Journal of Knowledge Management, 11*(1), 84-96.

Girard, J.P. (2006). Where is the knowledge we have lost in managers?. *Journal of Knowledge Management, 10*(6), 22-38.

Granovetter, M. (1973). The strength of weak ties. *American Journal of Sociology, 78*(6), 1360-1380.

Grant, R.M. (1996). Towards a knowledge-based theory of the firm. *Strategic Management Journal 17*(10), 109-122.

Hagel, J., III, & Armstrong, A.G. (1997). *Net Gain: Expanding Markets Through Virtual Communities.* Boston, M.A.: Harvard Business School Press.

Hamel, G., & Prahalad, C.K (1988). *When Competitors Collaborate.* London, UK: London Business School.

Hansen, M., Nohria, N., & Tierney, T. (1999). What's your strategy for managing knowledge?. *Harvard Business Review, March-April,* 106-116.

Hillman, A.J., Jr. A.A. Cannella, & R.L. Paetzold (2000). The resource dependence role of corporate directors: Strategic adaptation of board composition in response to environmental change. *Journal of Management Studies, 37*(2), 235-255.

Hsu, M., Ju, T., Yen, C., & Chang, C. (2007). Knowledge sharing behavior in virtual communities: The relationship between trust, self-efficacy, and outcome expectation. *International Journal of Human-Computer Studies*, 65, 153-169.

James, E.H. (2000). Race-related differences in promotions and support: Underlying effects of human and social capital. *Organization Science*, *11*(5), 493-508.

Kalpic, B., & Bernus, P (2006). Business process modeling through the knowledge management perspective. *Journal of Knowledge Management*, *10*(3), 40-56.

Katzenbach, J.R., & Smith, D.K (1993). The discipline of teams, *Harvard Business Review*, *17*(2), 111-120.

Kodama, M. (2005). New knowledge creation through leadership-based strategic community—a case of new product development in IT and multimedia business fields. *Technovation*, *25*, 895-908.

Larson, A. (1992). Networks dyads in entrepreneurial settings: a study of governance of exchange relationships. *Administrative Science Quarterly*, *37*(1), 76-104.

Lave, J., & Wenger, E. (1991). *Situated Learning: Legitimate Peripheral Participation*, New York, NY: Cambridge University Press.

Lapre, M., & Van Wassenhove, L. (2001). Creating and transferring knowledge for productivity improvement in factories, *Management Science*, *47*(10), 1311-1325.

Lin, F. & Hsueh C. (2006). Knowledge map creation and maintenance for virtual communities of practice. *Information Processing and Management*, *42*, 551-568.

Lin, F., Lin, S., & Huang, T. (2007). Knowledge sharing and creation in a teachers' professional virtual community. *Computers & Education*, xxx. Article in press.

Loyarte, E., & Rivera, E. (2007). Communities of practice: a model for their cultivation. *Journal of Knowledge Management 11*(3), 67-77.

Lytras. M.D., & Pouloudi, A. (2006). Towards the development of a novel taxonomy of knowledge management systems form a learning perspective: an integrated approach to learning and knowledge infrastructures. *Journal of Knowledge Management*, *10*(6), 64-80.

Maguire, S., Koh, S.C.L, & Magrys, A. (2007). The adoption of e-business and knowledge management in SMEs. *Benchmarking. An International Journal*, *14*(1), 37-58.

Meroño-Cerdan, A.L., Lopez-Nicolas, C., & Sabater-Sánchez, R. (2007). Knowledge management strategy diagnosis from KM instruments use. *Journal of Knowledge Management*, *11*(2), 60-72.

Moor, A., Weigand, H. (2007). Formalizing the evolution of virtual communities. *Information Systems*, *32*, 223-247.

Nahapiet, J., & Ghoshal, S (1998). Social capital, intellectual capital, and the organizational advantage. *The Academy of Management Review*, *23*(2), 242-266.

Nielsen, A. P. (2006). Understanding dynamic capabilities through knowledge management. *Journal of Knowledge Management*, *10*(4), 59-71.

Nonaka, I. (1994). A dynamic theory of organizational knowledge creation. *Organization Science*, *5*(1), 14-37.

Okkonen, J. (2007). Democracy in management – the new coming of MBO via organisational dialogue. *Benchmarking: An International Journal*, *14*(1), 7-21.

Paauwe, J., & R. Williams (2001). Seven key issues for management development. *The Journal of Management Development, 20*(2), 90-105.

Palacios, D., & Garrigós (2003). Validating and measuring IC in the biotechnology and telecommunication industries. *Journal of Intellectual Capital, 4*(3), 332-347.

Pavlin, S. (2006). Community of practice in a small research institute. *Journal of Knowledge Management, 10*(4), 136-144.

Perrin, A., Rolland, N., & Stanley ,T. (2007). Achieving best practices transfer across countries. *Journal of Knowledge Management, 11*(3), 156-166.

Pyöriä, P. (2007). Informal organizational culture: The foundation of knowledge workers' performance. *Journal of Knowledge Management, 11*(3), 16-30.

Putnam, R. (2000). *Bowling Alone: The Collapse and Revival of American Community.* New York: Touchstone.

Quin, J.B., Anderson, P., & Finkelstein, S. (1996). Managing professional intellect: Making the most of the best, *Harvard Business Review, 72*(2), 71-81.

Randeree, E. (2006). Knowledge management: securing the future. *Journal of Knowledge Management, 10*(4), 145-156.

Ring, P., & Van de Ven, A. (1994). Development processes of cooperative interorganizational relationships. *Academy of Management Review, 19*(1), 90-118.

Saint-Onge, H , & Wallace, D (2003). *Leveraging Communities of Practice for Strategic Advantage.* Amsterdam, Netherland: Butterworth-Heinemann.

Schultze, U. (2000). A confessional account of an ethnography about knowledge work. *MIS Quarterly, 24*(1), 3-41.

Sherif, K. (2006). An adaptive strategy for managing knowledge in organizations. *Journal of Knowledge Management, 10*(4), 72-80.

Tsai, W. (2002). Social structure of "coopetition" within a multiunit organization: coordination and intraorganizational knowledge sharing. *Organizational Science, 13*(2), 179-190.

Tsai, W., & Ghoshal, S. (1998). Social capital and value creation: an empirical study of intrafirm networks. *Academy of Management Journal, 41*(4), 464-476.

Uslaner, E. (2000). Social capital and the Net. *Communications of the ACM, 43*(12), 60-65.

Wasko, M., & Faraj, S. (2005). Why should I share? Examining social capital and knowledge contribution in electronic networks of practice. *MIS Quarterly, 29*(1), 35-57.

Wellman, B., Quan-Haase, A., Witte, J., & Hampton, K. (2001). Does the Internet increase, decrease, or supplement social capital? Social networks, participation, and community commitment. *American Behavioral Scientist, 45*(3), 437-456.

Wenger, E. (1999). *Communities of Practice. Learning, Meaning and Identity.* Cambridge. Boston, MA: Cambridge University Press.

Wenger, E.C., & Snyder, W.M. (2000). Communities of practice; the organizational frontier. *Harvard Business Review, 78*(1), 139-145.

Wenger, E., McDermott, R., & Snyder, W. (2002). *Cultivating Communities of Practice: A Guide to Managing Knowledge.* Boston, MA: Harvard Business School Press.

Yli-Renko, H., Autio, E., & Sapienza, H. (2001). Social capital, knowledge acquisition, and knowledge exploitation in young technology-based firms. *Strategic Management Journal, 22*(6), 587-613.

ENDNOTES

[1] According to Bandura (1989) and Chiu et al. (2006), "The Social Cognitive Theory argues that a person's behavior is partially shaped and controlled by the influences of social network (i.e., social systems) and the person's cognition (e.g., expectations, beliefs)…" "Through close interactions, individuals are able to increase the depth, breadth, and efficiency of mutual knowledge exchange" (pp. 1874-1873). In addition, Lytras and Pouloudi (2006) point out that "Behavioral change… enlightens the way in which individuals transform their behavior according to feedback they gain from participation in bigger social construction" (p.68).

[2] Chiu et al. argue that "Social Cognitive theory is limited in addressing what components are within a social network and how they influence an individual's behaviour"

[3] Hence, as Chiu et al. (2006:1875) state, "according to the Social Cognitive Theory, the question—why do individuals spend their valuable time and effort on sharing knowledge with members in virtual communities, should be addressed from the perspectives of both personal cognition and social network".

[4] "Facets of social capital positively relate to the quantity of knowledge sharing or the quality of knowledge shared by members…. Outcome expectations can contribute to knowledge sharing to some extent, but it is the social capital factors (e.g. social interaction ties, trust, norm of reciprocity, identification, shared language and shared vision) that lead to greater level of knowledge sharing in terms of quantity or quality…social interaction ties were significant predictors of individuals' knowledge sharing in terms of quantity".

[5] For instance, "holding face-to-face meetings or seminars.. as a way of enhancing the social interaction ties among members.. or providing personal message boards and blogs as tools for enhancing online communication and interaction among members".

[6] According to this author, (ibid, p.24) "the efficient use of IT simply enables the automation of routine tasks and helps us to avoid useless communication…is the only way to win more time for collaborative problem-solving and other tasks that resist "the logic of the binary code""

[7] "The purpose of the "Open Source" software community is essentially knowledge sharing and collaboration… the goal … is to develop, distribute, redistribute, and share source code of software that benefits individuals and organizations, with no discrimination and with restricted licensing (www.opensource.org) Software developed with a General Public License creates the freedom for people to copy, study, modify and redistribute software. It forbids anyone to forbid others to copy, study, modify and redistribute the software"… .According to this organisation (ibid, p.98), well-known Open source projects include the Linux operating system, Apache server software, Python coding language, and OpenSSL system secure communication software.

[8] Geisler's paper proposes a model that links the generation of knowledge with its users. These process or "four modes or stages of knowledge processing are: generation, transfer, implementation and absorption" (ibid, pp.90-91).

[9] According to this author, communities of practice, such as the virtual organisation, can link members to the strategic knowledge domain of the organization, develop core organisational competency through collaboration and learning, provide common development needs, distribute functional expertise, facilitate cross-generational and cross functional exchange of knowledge

(Saint-Onge and Wallace, 2003:36-91), "CoP can present a toll of alignment in organizations, a forum for problem solving, center for knowledge creation, type of corganizational infrastructures" (Saint-Onge and Wallace, 2003:71).

10 According to Christensen (2007)... "the five problems are caused by either social dilemmas or knowledge dilemmas"; the two first represent knowledge dilemmas caused by the epistemologically different faces of knowledge, such as tacit knowledge making it somewhat difficult to both identify and transfer knowledge, while the other three are "social dilemmas caused by the behaviour, or misbehaviour – of persons" (p.38).

11 At an individual level (active asking for help, habit of cooperation, propensity to share, perception of communication media) and group level (group roles, knowledge creation roles, group norms, cohesiveness, and leadership style).

12 Their study revealed that different strategies, including collaboration strategies, using IT strategies, and knowledge sharing and creation strategies, led to different consequences. In addition, they identified phenomena of knowledge flow discontinuities, and designated possible causes which contribute to these discontinuities, proposing the concept of the knowledge buckle (based on the SECI model put forward by Nonaka, which views knowledge creation as a spiralling process of interactions between explicit and tacit knowledge, and the study by Lin et al. which traces knowledge flows (or the knowledge buckle) among socialization, externalisation and combination activities) to address these problems and to gain insight into the knowledge sharing and creation process.

Chapter II
The Role of Trust, Satisfaction, and Communication in the Development of Participation in Virtual Communities

Luis V. Casaló
University of Zaragoza, Spain

Carlos Flavián
University of Zaragoza, Spain

Miguel Guinalíu[1]
University of Zaragoza, Spain

ABSTRACT

The rapid growth of virtual communities has created a new interest in researchers. Indeed, understanding these communities is especially relevant because it may allow for the obtaining of valuable information (e.g. needs of particular groups of people). In this respect, this work tries to explore which factors motivate individuals to take part of a virtual community since participation is one of the most important variables for the development and sustainability of virtual communities. More specifically, we analyze the effects of trust in a community, satisfaction with previous interactions and the communication level of the members' intentions to participate in a given virtual community. The data (obtained through an online surveys made to members of several virtual communities) show that trust in a virtual community had a positive and significant effect on members' participation in a virtual community. In addition, we found that satisfaction with previous interactions and the level of communication in a community significantly increased the level of trust in that virtual community.

INTRODUCTION

The Internet has come out as a new medium for social activities (Kim *et al.*, 2004) that favours the connection among individuals and organizations (Pitta *et al.*, 2005). Indeed, consumers are increasingly turning to computer-mediated communication in order to get information on which to base their decisions (Kozinets, 2002). They are using several online formats to share ideas and contact other consumers who are seen as more objective information sources (Kozinets, 2002). These online interactions have motivated the creation of social groups in the Internet that have been traditionally called virtual communities (Rheingold, 1993).

The importance of virtual communities for marketers is continuously increasing since relationships between consumers may influence brand choice (Wind, 1976) or the election of a specific service (Pitta *et al.*, 2005). In addition, these online communities provide a great opportunity to understand the members likes, dislikes, needs, behaviours or concerns (Ridings *et al.*, 2002; Pitta *et al.*, 2005). However, there is still a lack of studies that analyze empirically which are the main precursors of consumer's participation in these virtual communities. In fact, although the concept of virtual community is almost as old as the concept of Internet (Flavián and Guinalíu, 2005), little is known about what motivations induce people to participate in virtual communities (Ridings *et al.*, 2002). Therefore, this study is designed to identify some of the factors that influence the members' intentions to participate in a virtual community. More specifically, following the trust-commitment theory (Morgan and Hunt, 1994), we firstly consider that to participate actively in a virtual community, an individual will need to trust first in that virtual community and in its members. Secondly, we also consider that a general satisfaction in the previous interactions with the virtual community and a higher communication quality

in the community may increase the level of trust placed in a virtual community.

Taking into account the previous considerations, this work is structured as follows. Firstly, we carry out an in-depth review of the relevant literature concerning the concept of virtual community and the variables included in the study. Secondly, we formalize the hypothesis. Then, we explain the process of data collection and the methodology employed. Lastly, the main conclusions of the work are discussed and the future research is presented.

CONCEPTUAL BACKGROUND

The Virtual Community

Many definitions on the concept of the virtual community have appeared in the literature but, traditionally, this concept has been defined from a social point of view (Li, 2004). In line with this perspective, the concept of virtual community is firstly defined by Rheingold (1993) as a social group that is originated in the Internet when people discuss in this communication channel. Similarly, Ridings *et al.* (2002) expose that a virtual community is a group of people with a common interest that interact regularly in an organized way over the Internet. Thus, the Internet provides the infrastructure for enhancing the development of these communities since it is possible to overcome the space and time barriers to interaction that exist in traditional communities (Andersen, 2005). In addition, the justification to the exponential expansion of virtual communities is found in the advantages generated by these communities. In this respect, Hagel and Armstrong (1997) point out that virtual communities can help to satisfy four types of consumer needs: sharing resources, establishing relationships, trading and living fantasies.

Among all the typologies of virtual communities, this work focuses on virtual brand communities. To be precise, a brand community is a set of individuals who voluntarily relate to each other for their interest in some brand or product (Muniz and O'Guinn, 2001). Furthermore, these authors point out that a brand community is characterized by three core components:

- *Consciousness of kind.* It refers to the feeling that binds every individual to the other community members and the community brand (e.g. the passion for drinking a Coke) and it is determined by two factors: (1) legitimization, the process of establishing a difference between true and false members, that is, those who have opportunist behaviours and those who do not; and (2) opposition to other brands. For instance, community members of open source software communities have a strong feeling against firms selling proprietary software, especially the Microsoft Corporation (Bagozzi and Dholakia, 2006).

- *Rituals and traditions.* These are processes carried out by community members who help to reproduce and transmit the community meaning in and out of the community. Members relate to each other with the memory of major events in the history of the brand and they usually share a common set of values and certain behaviors, such as a specific language or way of dressing.

- *Sense of moral responsibility.* This reflects the feelings that create moral commitment among the community members. As a result of moral responsibility, there are two types of fundamental actions: (1) integration and retention of members, which guarantees the community survival (e.g. by spreading bad experiences suffered by those individuals who chose a different brand); and (2) support in the correct use of the brand (e.g. by shar-

ing information about product properties). Thus, these communities provide consumer support with the ongoing use of the product (Pitta *et al.*, 2005).

More specifically, we focus attention on virtual brand communities since these communities have a great relevance for marketers. The reason behind this interest is threefold. Firstly, virtual brand communities can affect their members' behaviour (Muniz and O'Guinn, 2001) since individuals can use these communities to inform and influence fellow consumers about products, brands or organizations (Kozinets, 2002). Secondly, virtual brand communities may help to identify the needs and desires of particular individuals or groups of people (Kozinets, 2002). Lastly, active participation in virtual brand communities may favour higher levels of individuals' loyalty to the brand around which the community is developed (Koh and Kim, 2004) since a key aspect of membership and participation in these communities is the ongoing purchase and use of the brand products (Algesheimer *et al.*, 2005).

Active Participation

Participation in a virtual community is a crucial element to guarantee the community survival (Koh and Kim, 2004). To be precise, the level of participation is a key factor to perpetuate the brand community (Algesheimer *et al.*, 2005) since higher participation means a higher level of involvement with the community. Indeed, due to the participation in the activities carried out in the virtual community, members can share information and experiences, which are key aspects in order to develop the group cohesion. In addition, it is important to note that some authors (e.g. Algesheimer *et al.*, 2005) state that participation in the virtual community activities also promotes the members' identification with the community and, as a consequence, the value of the community is increased. Wikipedia (http://www.wikipedia. org/), MyCoke (http://www.mycoke.com) or Youtube (http://youtube.com), where millions of people use to participate frequently in, are clear instances of how virtual communities may be developed thanks to the community participation, in terms of interactions among members and contributions to the community.

In this work, according to the recommendations of Koh and Kim (2004), we consider the following factors to measure the individual's participation in a virtual community:

- The effort to stimulate the virtual community,
- The value of the comments posted in order to help other community members,
- The excitement with which an individual posts messages and responses in the community, and
- The motivation to interact with other community members.

Antecedents of Participation in a Virtual Community

Trust

The concept of trust has often been associated with the achievement of long lasting and profitable relationships (e.g. Anderson and Narus, 1990; Dwyer *et al.*, 1987). Indeed, this is the consequence of the role of trust in decreasing the uncertainty of a relationship. Thus, the importance of trust in the context of virtual communities is even greater since individuals perceived a higher risk in online relationships (Harris and Goode, 2004). In this respect, Ridings *et al.* (2002) state that trust may help to decrease the uncertainty of the relationships between the individual and the other community members. More specifically, the importance of trust in this

context is based on some special characteristics of virtual communities (Ridings *et al.*, 2002). For instance, the lack of face-to-face contact in virtual communities increases the perceived risk of the relationship between the individual and the community members. In addition, there is no guarantee that the other members will behave as they are expected to (e.g. they can provide other members e-mail addresses to external organizations without permission). Therefore, trust serves to decrease the perceived risk of relationships in a virtual community and its management must be a crucial aspect for the organization that creates the virtual community.

Traditionally, the concept of trust has been analyzed from a cognitive point of view (e.g. Morgan and Hunt, 1994). From this perspective, trust may be defined by three types of beliefs which refer to the levels of competence, honesty and benevolence, as perceived by the individual (e.g. Mayer *et al.*, 1995). In the context of virtual communities, which are always centred on a specific mutual concern, *competence* refers to the ability of the community members with respect to that mutual interest (Ridings *et al.*, 2002). In turn, *honesty* is the belief that the second party (the other community members) will keep their word, fulfil their promises and be sincere (Gundlach and Murphy, 1993; Doney and Cannon, 1997). Finally, *benevolence* reflects the belief that one of the parties is interested in the well-being of the other. Thus, in the context of virtual communities, benevolence refers to the expectation that community members will have the intention and the desire to help, support and care for the other members of the virtual community (Ridings *et al.*, 2002). Taking into account the previous considerations, we propose that the concept of trust in a virtual community may be considered as a multidimensional construct formed by three different dimensions: honesty, benevolence and competence in the virtual community.

Satisfaction

Satisfaction can be defined as an affective condition that results from a global evaluation of all the aspects that make up a relationship (Severt, 2002). More specifically, satisfaction can be divided into two distinct perspectives (Geyskens *et al.*, 1999). On the one hand, the first perspective considers satisfaction as an affective predisposition sustained by economic conditions. On the other hand, the second perspective, known as non-economic satisfaction, considers the concept using more psychological factors, such as a partner fulfilling promises or the ease of relationships with the aforementioned partner.

In this project, we will concentrate on the psychological perspective of satisfaction (Shankar *et al.*, 2003). From this point of view, satisfaction is considered as a global evaluation or attitude made by the individual about the behaviour of the other virtual community members resulting from the interactions produced by both parties in the relationship. Therefore, satisfaction is not the result of a specific interaction, but that of a global evaluation of the relationship history between the parties. With each new interaction the individual's perception is fed by new information, which is the information that determines the level of satisfaction at any given time.

Communication

In general, communication can be defined as the formal and informal distribution of significant and updated information (Anderson and Narus, 1990). Furthermore, communication between the parties has been considered as a key element in the existence of a relationship (e.g. Bendapudi and Berry, 1997; Crosby and Stephens, 1987). Indeed, Duncan and Moriarty (1998) propose that communication is a human activity that joins people and generates relationships. In addition, several authors have noted that quality of communication is more important than quantity and, consequently,

effective communication implies that both parties must be committed to the communication processes (Chiou *et al.*, 2004).

In the context of virtual communities, communication is especially relevant since the existence of a virtual community is directly based on postings and their responses made by the community members (Ridings *et al.*, 2002). More specifically, according to these authors, the speed and frequency of response when an individual posts a message can be considered as key elements of the communication in the community since they allow the creation of conversation. However, communication must be also effective; that is, responses must be valuable for the individual that posts a message. If responses have no value, the individual will not be motivated to participate in that virtual community.

FORMULATION OF HYPOTHESES

Although the relationship between satisfaction and trust in a virtual community has not been analyzed yet, some authors have considered that satisfaction has a positive effect on trust in the context of business to consumer relationships through the Internet (e.g. Bauer, 2002). In addition, as suggested by the Disconfirmation of Expectations Model (e.g. Spreng and Chiou, 2000), satisfaction reflects the degree to which expectations generated on previous occasions have been met. If we focus attention on how satisfaction with a virtual community has been generated, we can see that the first phase consists of individuals having certain expectations with regard to the trustworthiness of the other virtual community members. Then, they perceive whether the expectations are met or not. If they are met, individuals will feel satisfied and more confident, since they will feel that the other community members are trustworthy and capable of meeting its commitments. Following the previous considerations, we propose our first hypothesis:

Hypothesis 1: *Greater user satisfaction is directly and positively related to greater trust in a virtual community.*

Traditionally, communication has been considered as a major antecedent of trust and proximity feelings between the parties in a relationship (e.g. Morgan and Hunt, 1994; Anderson and Narus, 1990). Indeed, Morgan and Hunt (1994) state that communication helps to solve conflicts between the parties, which favours the development of affective reactions such as trust (Kumar *et al.*, 1995). More specifically, communication promotes trust since it improves the environment by aligning perceptions and expectancies (e.g. Anderson and Weitz, 1989; Morgan and Hunt, 1994).

In the online context, many researchers have proposed that a higher communication quality between the parties produces higher degrees of trust (McIvor *et al.*, 2002). In a similar way, the perceived level of communication in a community, which is represented by the repeated interactions over time between the community members, may increase the levels of trust placed in that virtual community. In this way, trust in a virtual community is built thanks to these repeated interactions among the virtual community members. Therefore, if an individual posts several messages and there are no responses, trust in other community members will not arise and consequently, following the trust transfer process in the online context (Stewart, 2003), trust in the whole community will not be developed either. Therefore, we propose our second hypothesis:

Hypothesis 2: *A higher communication quality in a virtual community is directly and positively related to greater levels of trust placed in that community.*

Traditionally, several authors have considered that trust determines the nature of a relationship (e.g. Gefen, 2000). Indeed, following the trust-commitment theory (Morgan and Hunt, 1994), a relationship in which both parties trust each other generates enough value so that the parties will be committed to the relationship (e.g. Garbarino and Johnson, 1999). This greater value generated by trust is the consequence of the role of trust in decreasing the uncertainty of a relationship. In fact, trust means that one of the parties involved in a relationship will think that the other party will not exploit its vulnerabilities (Corritore *et al.*, 2003). Therefore, the decrease of the perceived risk in either a transaction or a relationship is an important result derived from the process of trust building (Mitchell, 1999). In this way, individuals' commitment and participation in a relationship will only be possible if they trust the other party.

In addition, if we focus attention on virtual communities, trust may also help to favour integration of members and to increase interactions among them (Ridings *et al.*, 2002). Indeed, trust is a crucial factor when individuals face relationships without having complete information regarding the other party (Hawes *et al.*, 1989), as it may be the case of virtual communities since an individual does not usually have much information about all the other community members (Ridings *et al.*, 2002). In these cases, trust serves to decrease the degree of information asymmetry that exists between partners (Batt, 2003). Thus, taking all these considerations into account, it is reasonable to think that trust in a virtual community and in its members may be a major precursor of the individuals' intentions to participate in a virtual community. Thus, we propose our last hypothesis:

Hypothesis 3: *Greater levels of trust placed in a virtual community are directly and positively related to greater levels of participation in that virtual community.*

DATA COLLECTION

Data were collected thanks to a Web survey using Spanish-speaking members of several virtual communities. More specifically, we select the open source software (OSS) as the mutual interest around which virtual communities must be developed since: (1) there are a great number of OSS virtual communities, and (2) OSS communities are a clear instance of virtual brand communities as the three core components of a brand community are present in OSS communities (Bagozzi and Dholakia, 2006). In addition, the analysis of the OSS communities is especially relevant in order to study the behaviour of virtual community members since OSS is developed thanks to the collaboration and interaction among members inside the communities.

To obtain the responses, several posts were included on heavy traffic Websites, e-mail distribution lists and well-known electronic forums. The selection of the Websites to promote the research was founded on: (1) the level of awareness among the Spanish-speaking users of OSS, (2) traffic level and (3) availability. This method of collecting the data, which is consistent with the recent practice in the online context research (e.g. Bagozzi and Dholakia, 2006; Steenkamp and Geyskens, 2006), generated 215 valid questionnaires (atypical cases, repeated responses and incomplete questionnaires were controlled). Thus, according to the specific characteristics of the population and the great number of virtual communities analyzed, we consider that our sample may be representative of the Spanish-speaking members of OSS virtual communities.

Besides, it is important to note that subjects were allowed to choose the OSS virtual community to analyze, as the objective of this project was to understand the behaviour of the virtual community members, regardless the OSS product around which the community was developed. However, it was a pre-requisite that the subject was registered as a member of that OSS virtual community. More specifically, subjects had to respond to several questions about their levels of satisfaction, participation and trust in the virtual community they had selected as well as about the perceived level of communication that exists in that virtual community. All questions were measured on a seven-point Likert scale.

MEASURES VALIDATION

The process of validation included the following stages:

Content and Face Validity

Scale development was based on the review of the most relevant literature on relationship marketing and the recent advances in e-marketing (see Table 1).

From the literature review an initial set of items was proposed but, due to the lack of valid scales adapted to the context of virtual communities, it was necessary to adapt the initial scales. This adaptation had the objective of guaranteeing the face validity of the measurement instruments. Face validity is defined as the degree that respondents judge that the items are appropriate to the targeted construct and is habitually confused with content validity. Nevertheless, content validity is the degree to which items correctly represent the theoretical content of the construct and it is guaranteed by the in-depth literature review undertaken. Face validity was tested through a variation of the Zaichkowsky method (1985), whereby each item is qualified by a panel of experts as "clearly representative", "somewhat representative" or "not representative" of the construct of interest. In line with Lichtenstein et al. (1990) an item was retained if a high level of consensus was observed among the experts.

Table 1. Content validity

Variable	Adapted from
Participation	Koh and Kim (2004); Algesheimer *et al.* (2005)
Trust	Kumar *et al.* (1995); Doney and Cannon (1997); and Roy *et al.* (2001)
Communication	McMillan *et al.* (2005); and Chiou *et al.* (2004)
Satisfaction	Brockman (1998); Servet (2002); and Smith and Barclay (1997)

Exploratory Analysis of Reliability and Dimensionality

The validation measuring process started with an initial exploratory analysis of reliability and dimensionality (Churchill, 1979; Anderson and Gerbing, 1988). The Cronbach alpha indicator was used to assess the initial reliability of the scales, considering a minimum value of .7 (Cronbach, 1970; Nunnally, 1978). The item-total correlation was used to improve the levels of the Cronbach alpha, considering a minimum value of .3 (Nurosis, 1993). All items were adjusted to the required levels.

Secondly, we proceeded to evaluate the unidimensionality of the proposed scales by carrying out a principal components analysis. Factor extraction was based on the existence of eigenvalues higher than 1. In addition, it was required that factorial loadings were higher than .5 points and a significant total explained variance. Only one factor was extracted from each scale: satisfaction, communication, benevolence, honesty, competence and participation.

Confirmatory Analysis of Dimensionality

With the aim of confirming the dimensional structure of the scales and to allow for a rigorous test of convergent and discriminatory validity, we used the Confirmatory Factor Analysis (Steenkamp and Geyskens, 2006). That is, we included all individual-level constructs in a single confirmatory factor model. More specifically, we employed the statistical software EQS version 6.1, and we chose Robust Maximum Likelihood as the estimation method, since it affords more security in samples which might not present multivariate normality. In addition, we followed the criteria proposed by Jöreskog and Sörbom (1993):

- The weak convergence criterion means eliminating indicators that do not show significant factor regression coefficients (t student > 2.58; p = .01).
- The strong convergence criterion involves eliminating non-substantial indicators; that is, those indicators whose standardized coefficients are lower than .5.
- Finally, we also eliminated the indicators that least contribute to the explanation of the model, taking $R^2 < .3$ as a cut-off point.

These recommendations allow us to obtain acceptable levels of convergence, R^2 and model fit (Chi-square = 425.910, 155 d.f., p< .001; Bentler-Bonett Normed Fit Index =.834; Bentler-Bonett Nonnormed Fit Index =.881; Comparative Fit Index (CFI) =.903; Bollen (IFI) Fit Index =.905; Root Mean Sq. Error of App. (RMSEA) =.073; 90% Confidence Interval of RMSEA (.062, .083)).

Finally, in order to confirm the existence of multidimensionality in trust, we developed a Rival Models Strategy (Hair *et al.*, 1999; Anderson and Gerbing, 1988). In this strategy, we compared a second order model in which the construct is measured by various dimensions with a first order model in which all the items formed only one factor. Results showed that the second order model fits much better than the first. This implies that trust placed in a virtual community is a multidimensional construct formed by three dimensions: honesty, benevolence and competence.

Composite Reliability

Although the Cronbach alpha indicator is the most frequent test to assess reliability, some authors consider that it underestimates reliability (e.g. Smith, 1974). Consequently, the use of composite reliability has been suggested (Jöreskog, 1971), using a cut-off value of .6 (Nunnaly and Bernstein, 1994). The results were satisfactory.

Construct Validity

Construct validity was assessed by considering two types of criteria: convergent and discriminatory validity:

- *Convergent validity.* This shows if the items that compose a determined scale converge on only one construct. This was tested by checking that the factor loadings of the confirmatory model were statistically significant (level of .01) and higher than .5 points (Sanzo *et al.*, 2003). Results showed that all the indicators loaded significantly (p < .001) and substantively (all factor loadings went beyond .5) on their proposed constructs, providing evidence of convergent validity of the measures (Steenkamp and Geyskens, 2006).

- *Discriminatory validity.* This verifies if a determined construct is significantly distinct from other constructs that are not theoretically related to it. We tested discriminatory validity in two ways: Firstly, we checked that the correlations between the variables in the confirmatory model were not higher than .8 points. Secondly, we checked that the value

Table 2. Discriminatory validity

PAIR of constructs	Correlation	95% Confidence Interval	
COMMU-SAT	.302*	.1648	.4392
COMMU-HON	.293*	.14404	.44196
COMMU-BENEV	.368*	.22296	.51304
COMMU-COMP	.589*	.44984	.72816
COMMU-PARTI	.202*	.055	.349
SAT-HON	.615*	.47192	.75808
SAT-BENEV	.501*	.34224	.65976
SAT-COMP	.115	-.04572	.27572
SAT-PARTI	.419*	.28376	.55424
HON-BENEV	.705*	.60896	.80104
HON-COMP	.345*	.19996	.49004
HON-PARTI	.223*	.06424	.38176
BENEV-COMP	.283*	.13796	.42804
BENEV-PARTI	.271*	.11224	.42976
COMP-PARTI	.173	-.0132	.3592

Note: (*) expresses that coefficients are significant at the level of .01.

1 did not appear in the confidence interval of the correlations between the different variables. Results showed an acceptable level of discrimination (see Table 2) since all pairs of constructs satisfied both criteria.

RESULTS

To test the hypotheses we develop a structural equation model. Figure 1 shows the results corresponding to hypotheses 1 to 3. Results reveal the acceptance of these hypotheses to a level of .01. Similarly, the model fit showed acceptable values (Chi-square = 282.923, 74 d.f., p< .001;

Bentler-Bonett Normed Fit Index = .847; Bentler-Bonett Nonnormed Fit Index = .886; Comparative Fit Index (CFI) = .909; Bollen (IFI) Fit Index = .910; Root Mean Sq. Error of App. (RMSEA) = .083; 90% Confidence Interval of RMSEA (.069, .097); normed Chi-square = 3.823).

It was also notable that consumer trust in a virtual community could be explained at a very high level (R^2 = .55) by the direct effects of only two variables: satisfaction with previous interactions and the level of communication in the community. In addition, this model also allow us to partially explain the members' intentions to participate in a virtual community (R^2 = .16).

Figure 1. The structural equation model

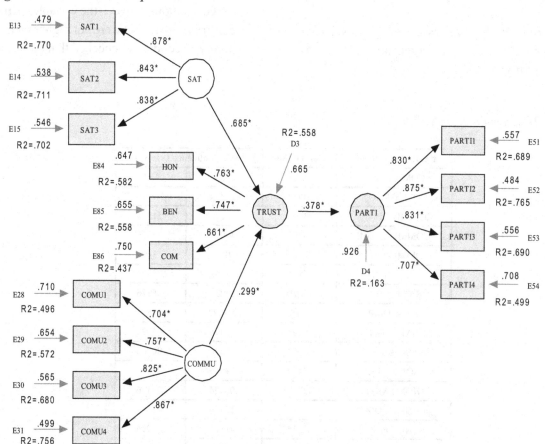

Note: (*) expresses that coefficients are significant at the level of .01.

CONCLUSION AND MANAGERIAL IMPLICATIONS

From a marketing point of view, the importance of virtual brand communities is continuously increasing due to the fact that individuals making product and brand elections are frequently using these online formats in order to get information on which to base their purchase decisions (Kozinets, 2002). In addition, some authors have considered that virtual communities may help to understand the needs and desires of particular groups of people (Ridings *et al.*, 2002; Kozinets, 2002) and that participation in a virtual brand community may foster consumer loyalty to the brand around which the community is developed (Andersen, 2005; Algesheimer *et al.*, 2005; Muniz and O'Guinn, 2001). Therefore, the analysis of these communities is especially relevant. However, most of the works on virtual communities have been conducted at the conceptual level (Koh and Kim, 2004) and, as a consequence, there is still a lack of studies that empirically analyze which are the drivers of participation in a virtual community. Thus, with the aim of moving on this topic, this study investigates some of the antecedents of individuals' participation in a virtual community.

First of all, results have shown that trust placed in a virtual community may increase the levels of participation in that community. Therefore, trust may be a crucial aspect to guarantee the virtual community survival since it favours individuals' participation and, consequently, both group cohesion and consciousness of kind can be fostered. Secondly, we have also found positive and significant effects of satisfaction in the previous interactions with the virtual community and perceived communication quality in the community on the trust placed by an individual in a virtual community. These results have allowed us to clearly explain the concept of trust placed in a virtual community ($R^2 = .55$).

These results are especially relevant for managers due to the fact that they offer some keys in order to foster participation in a virtual community, which may lead to an increase in consumer loyalty to the brand around which the community is developed (Koh and Kim, 2004). Indeed, the high costs every company has to face in order to win new customers make it increasingly necessary to reinforce the ties established with current customers. Thus, this study offers some alternatives in order to increase consumers' loyalty by promoting their participation in a virtual brand community. More specifically, to enhance consumers' participation in virtual communities, firms should:

- Promote communication and group cohesion in the community in order to encourage interactions among community members. To do that, it would be a good idea to carry out actions that may increase the consumers' commitment to the virtual community (e.g. organizing meetings among the community members, asking them for suggestions, etc.), and

- Satisfy in the virtual community some of the consumers' needs (e.g. offering detailed information about products or making special offers to virtual community members). Indeed, the virtual brand community should be created according to its members' needs, and not with those of the company which promotes it (Flavián and Guinalíu, 2005). Thus, individuals will perceive that they can satisfy their needs and demands in the virtual community and, consequently, they will be motivated to participate in the community. Finally, to guarantee the sustainability of the virtual community, the evolution of its members' needs and interests should be constantly analyzed (Wang et al., 2002).

Following these recommendations, trust between consumers and the virtual community will be built and therefore, it will be easier to turn community visitors into members, members into contributors, and contributors into evangelists of the community and the brand around which the community is developed. Consequently, consumers will probably develop greater emotional feelings and loyalty to that brand.

FUTURE RESEARCH

First of all, it is important to note that the survey was answered exclusively by Spanish-speaking members of open source software virtual communities. Thus, to generalize the results of this research, we should repeat the study using a wider sample of consumers. Specifically, the sample should represent a greater diversity of nationalities. At the same time, it would be interesting to carry out a new validation of our model using a greater variety of virtual communities.

Secondly, it would be a good idea to analyze in more detail the precursors of participation in a virtual community in order to explain this variable to a greater extent. In fact, perceived control, privacy, familiarity or identification with the community may also influence the level of consumers' participation in a virtual community.

Finally, an interesting route to extend this research would be to analyze the effects on consumer behaviour associated to the consumers' participation in virtual communities, since most of the studies focused on the virtual communities outcomes have been carried out from a conceptual point of view. More specifically, it would be useful to carry out a quantitative assessment of the impact of virtual communities in consumer loyalty, trust and commitment to the brand around which the community is developed, due to the fact that loyalty is a major objective for most of the organizations (Andreassen, 1999) and trust and commitment are key factors in order to establish successful long-term oriented relationships (Morgan and Hunt, 1994).

REFERENCES

Algesheimer, R., Dholakia, U.M., & Herrmann, A. (2005). The social influence of brand communities: Evidence from European car clubs. *Journal of Marketing, 59*(3), 19-34.

Andersen, P.H. (2005). Relationship marketing and brand involvement of professionals through Web-enhanced brand communities: The case of Coloplast. *Industrial Marketing Management* (34), 39-51.

Anderson, J., & Gerbing, D. (1988). Structural modeling in practice: A review and recommended two-step approach. *Psychological Bulletin, 103*(3), 411-423.

Anderson, J.C., & Narus, J.A. (1990). A model of distribution firm and manufacturer firm working partnerships. *Journal of Marketing, 54*(1), 42-58.

Anderson, E. & Weitz, B. (1989). The use of pledges to build and sustain commitment in distribution channels. *Journal of Marketing Research* (29), 18-34.

Andreassen, T.W. (1999). What drives customer loyalty with complaint resolution? *Journal of Service Research, 1*(4), 324-332.

Bagozzi, R.P. & Dholakia, U.M. (2006). Open source software communities: A study of participation in linux user groups. *Management Science, 52*(7), 1099-1115.

Batt, P.J. (2003). Building trust between growers and market agents. *Supply Chain Management: and International Journal, 8*(1), 65-78.

Bauer, H. H., Grether, M., & Leach, M. (2002). Building customer relations over the Internet. *Industrial Marketing Management* (31), 155-163.

Bendapudi, N. & Berry, L.L. (1997). Customer's motivations for maintaining relationships with service providers," *Journal of Retailing, 73*(1), 15-35.

Brockman, B. (1998). The influence of affective state on satisfaction ratings. *Journal of Consumer Satisfaction, Dissatisfaction and Complaining Behavior* (11), 40-50.

Chiou, J.S., Hsieh, C.H., & Yang, C.H. (2004). The effect of franchisors' communication, service assistance, and competitive advantage on franchisees' intentions to remain in the franchise system. *Journal of Small Business Management, 42*(1), 19-36.

Churchill, G. A. (1979). A paradigm for developing better measures for marketing constructs. *Journal of Marketing Research, 16*(1), 64-73.

Corritore, C.L., Kracher, B., & Wiedenbeck, S. (2003). On-line trust: Concepts, evolving themes, a model. *International Journal of Human-Computer Studies, 58*(6), 737-758.

Cronbach, L.J. (1970). *Essentials of psychological testing*, New York: Harper and Row.

Crosby, L., & Stephen, N. (1987). Effects of relationship marketing on satisfaction, retention, and prices in the insurance industry. *Journal of Marketing Research* (24), 404-411.

Doney, P., & Cannon, J. (1997). An examination of the nature of trust in the buyer-seller relationship. *Journal of Marketing, 61*(2), 35-51.

Duncan, T., & Moriarty, S. (1998). A communication-based marketing model for managing relationships. *Journal of Marketing* (62), 1-13.

Dwyer, F. R., Schurr, P. H., & Oh, S. (1987). Developing buying-seller relationships. *Journal of Marketing* (51), 11-27.

Flavián, C., & Guinalíu, M. (2005). The influence of virtual communities on distribution strategies in the Internet. *International Journal of Retail & Distribution Management, 33*(6), 405-425.

Garbarino, E., & Johnson, M.S. (1999). The different roles of satisfaction, trust, and commitment in customer relationships. *Journal of Marketing, 63*(2), 70-87.

Gefen, D. (2000). E-commerce: The role of familiarity and trust. *OMEGA: The International Journal of Management Science* (28), 725-737.

Geyskens, I., Steenkamp, J., & Kumar, N. (1999). A meta-analysis of satisfaction in marketing channel relationships. *Journal of Marketing Research, 36*(2), 223-238.

Gundlach, G.T., & Murphy, P.E. (1993). Ethical and legal foundations of relational marketing exchanges. *Journal of Marketing, 57*(4), 35-46.

Hagel, J. III, & Armstrong, A.G. (1997). *Net Gain: Expanding markets through virtual communities.* Boston, MA: Harvard Business School Press

Hair, J.F. Jr., Anderson, R.E., Tatham, R.L., & Black, W.C. (1998). *Multivariate data analysis.* Prentice Hall.

Harris, L.C., & Goode, M.M.H. (2004). The four levels of loyalty and the pivotal role of trust: A study of online service dynamics. *Journal of Retailing* (80), 139-158.

Hawes, J.M., Mast, K.E., & Swan, J.E. (1989). Trust earning perceptions of sellers and buyers. *Journal of Personal Selling and Sales Management* (9), 1-8.

Jöreskog, K. (1971). Statistical analysis of sets of congeneric tests. *Psychometrika* (36), 109-133.

Jöreskog, K., & Sörbom, D. (1993). *LISREL 8 structural equation modeling with the SIMPLIS command language.* Scientific Software International, Chicago-Illinois.

Kim, W.G., Lee, C., & Himstra, S.J. (2004). Effects of an online virtual community on customer loyalty and travel product purchases. *Tourism Management* (25), 343-355.

Koh, J., & Kim, D. (2004). Knowledge sharing in virtual communities: An e-business perspective. *Expert Systems with Applications* (26), 155-166.

Kozinets, R.V. (2002). The field behind the screen: Using netnography for marketing research in online communities. *Journal of Marketing Research, 39*(1), 61-72.

Kumar, N., Scheer, L., & Steenkamp, J.B. (1995). The effects of supplier fairness on vulnerable resellers. *Journal of Marketing Research 32*(1), 42-53.

Li, H. (2004). Virtual community studies: A literature review, synthesis and future research. In *Proceedings of the Americas Conference on Information Systems*, New York, August 2004.

Lichtenstein D.R., Netemeyer R.G., & Burton S. (1990). Distinguishing coupon proneness from value consciousness: An acquisition—transaction utility theory perspective. *Journal of Marketing, 54*(3), 54– 67.

Mayer, R., Davis, J., & Shoorman, F. (1995). An integrative model of organizational trust. *Academy of Management Review, 20*(3), 709-734.

McIvor, R., McHugh, M., & Cadden, C. (2002). Internet technologies: Supporting transparency in the public sector. *The International Journal of Public Sector Management, 15*(3), 170-187.

McMillan, K., Money, K., Money, A., & Downing, S. (2005). Relationship marketing in the not-for-profit sector: An extension and application of the commitment-trust theory. *Journal of Business Research* (58), 806-818.

Mitchell, V. (1999). Consumer perceived risk: Conceptualisations and models. *European Journal of Marketing, 33*(1/2), 163-195.

Morgan, R., & Hunt, S. (1994). The commitment -trust theory of relationship marketing. *Journal of Marketing, 58*(3), 20-38.

Muniz, A., & O'Guinn, T.C. (2001). Brand communities. *Journal of Consumer Research* (27), 412-432.

Nunnally, J.C. (1978). *Psychometric theory*. Mc-Graw-Hill, 2 ed., New York.

Nunnaly, J.C., & Bernstein, I.H. (1994). *Psychometric theory*. McGraw-Hill, New York.

Nurosis M.J. (1993). *SPSS. Statistical data Analysis*, Spss Inc.

Pitta, D.A., & Fowler, D. (2005). Online consumer communities and their value to new product developers. *Journal of Product & Brand Management, 14*(5), 283-291.

Rheingold, H. (1993). *The virtual community: Homestanding on the electronic frontier*. New York: Addison-Wesley.

Ridings, C.M., Gefen, D., & Arinze, B. (2002). Some antecedents and effects of trust in virtual communities. *Journal of Strategic Information Systems* (11), 271-295.

Roy, M., Dewit, O., & Aubert, B. (2001). The impact of interface usability on trust in Web retailers. *Internet Research: Electronic Networking Applications and Policy, 11*(5), 388-398.

Sanzo, M., Santos, M., Vázquez, R., & Álvarez, L. (2003). The effect of market orientation on buyer-seller relationship satisfaction. *Industrial Marketing Management, 32*(4), 327-345.

Severt, E. (2002). *The customer's path to loyalty: A partial test of the relationships of prior experience, justice, and customer satisfaction*. Doctoral Thesis, Faculty of the Virginia Polytechnic Institute and State University (EEUU), 2002.

Shankar, V., Smith, A., & Rangaswamy, A. (2003). Customer satisfaction and loyalty in online and offline environments. *International Journal of Research in Marketing* (20), 153-175.

Smith, K.W. (1974). On estimating the reliability of composite indexes through factor analysis. *Sociological Methods & Research* (2), 485-510.

Smith, J., & Barclay, D. (1997). The effects of organizational differences and trust on the effectiveness of selling partner relationships. *Journal of Marketing* (61), 3-21.

Spreng, R. A., & Chiou, J. (2002). A cross-cultural assessment of the satisfaction formation process. *European Journal of Marketing, 36*(7/8), 829-839.

Steenkamp, J.B.E.M., & Geyskens, I. (2006). How country characteristics affect the perceived value of a Website. *Journal of Marketing, 70*(3), 136-150.

Stewart, K.J. (2003). Trust transfer on the World Wide Web. *Organization Science, 14*(1), 5-17.

Wang, Y., Yu, Q., & Fesenmaier, D.R. (2002). *Defining the virtual tourist community: Implications for tourism marketing. Tourism Management,* (23), 407-417.

Wind, Y. (1976). Preference of relevant others in individual choice models. *Journal of Consumer Research, 3*(1), 50-57.

Zaichkowsky, J.L. (1985). Measuring the involvement construct. *Journal of Consumer Research, 12*(4), 341-352.

ENDNOTE

[1] Authors are grateful for the financial support received from the Spanish Ministry of Science and Technology (SEC2005-4972; PM34; AP2005-2823); the Aragón Goverment (S-46) and Fundear.

Section II
Networking and Knowledge Management for Competitive Advantage

How to use networking for competitive advantage is a critical issue in knowledge demanding industries. Virtual networks offer to firms in these industries relevant information, resources, technologies and capabilities. In this section, networking is analysied as a knowledge absorptive enabler in knowlege management and as a tool for knowledge integration in strategic alliances.

Chapter III
Can Virtual Networks Encourage Knowledge Absorptive Capacity?

Cesar Camison
Universitat Jaume I, Spain

Beatriz Forés Julián
Universitat Jaume I, Spain

Alba Puig Denia
Universitat Jaume I, Spain

ABSTRACT

Organisations are finding it more difficult to keep abreast with the pace of change. The continuous rise of business opportunities and the increase in global competition demands a capability to acquire, assimilate, transform and apply external critical knowledge to renew and reconfigure existing capabilities and knowledge, and to innovate. Developing this dynamic capability requires, in turn, new proactive Knowledge Management tools and new organisational forms. This chapter presents a framework in which virtual networks constitute more flexible new organisational structures to absorb and create knowledge. It also describes how embeddedness in such a network can affect most of the factors identified as antecedents of absorptive capacity. In addition, it evidences the important role of the firm's relational capabilities in taking advantage of the relevant business information, knowledge, resources, technologies and capabilities circulating in the virtual networks.

INTRODUCTION

In the current business environment, characterised by intense global competition, rapid technological advancements, innovative managerial practices and increased pressure in demand, the importance of knowledge as a critical resource for firms' competitive advantage is widely recognised (Teece, 1998). This knowledge allows firms to create and sustain competitive advantages through, for example, management innovations, product innovations and process innovations.

Firms can generate knowledge internally by investing in the development of distinctive competences related, for instance, to R&D activities. However, because of their limited size, some firms can barely sustain all the structural costs involved in developing the necessary knowledge and capabilities internally to innovate and compete at an international level.

In addition, authors such as Chang (2004) and Phene, Fladmoe-Lindquist and Marsh (2006) find that firms operating in turbulent and unstable environments cannot be self-sufficient in creating knowledge, due to the tremendous risk it entails.

In a context where innovations are incremental or related to previous technologies, organisations can be confident of the internal development of knowledge without exposing themselves to high risks, since these kinds of technological changes are related to the firm's existing experience. However, in dynamic environments in which rapid changes and radical technological innovations occur, firms should be able to acquire external information, by focusing on the adoption of a strategy that emphasises the exploration rather than the exploitation of knowledge (March, 1991).

Similarly, Shan and Song (1997) suggest that firms in industries characterised by rapid technological change will find their competitive advantage eroded if they rely solely on internally existing knowledge and capabilities.

According to the dynamic capability view of the firm (Teece, Pisano and Shuen, 1997), in a changing operating environment, superior performance depends on the ability to recognise critical changes and knowledge and on the processes of renewing the firm's knowledge base and capabilities.

In this scenario, the mechanism for the creation and development of internal knowledge must be combined and complemented with the mechanism for the absorption of external sources of knowledge (Veugelers, 1997; Teece, Pisano and Shuen, 1997; Lowe and Taylor; 1998; Oltra and Flor, 2003). Firms should therefore manage two learning processes: an internal and an external learning process.

Despite the importance that information and external knowledge has for firms, its identification, acquisition and, above all, its implementation is a far from simple process (Veugelers, 1997). Consequently, organisations need to invest time and effort in developing their absorptive capacities (Kim, 1998). An increasing number of companies recognise that their competitive advantages are derived from knowledge resources that are deeply rooted in social relationships with other companies (Koka and Prescott, 2002; Uzzi and Lancaster, 2003).

Recent studies show how a firm's embeddedness in networks formalised in different organisational forms such as joint ventures (Vermeulen and Barkema, 2001), business alliances (Kumar and Nti, 1998; Ahuja, 2000; Lane et al., 2001; Chen, 2004), technology licences (Atuahene-Gima, 1992), and cooperation agreements with public and private research centres like universities and technology institutes (Meyer Krahmer and Schmoch, 1998) are increasingly used as knowledge sources to complement internal R&D activities that favour external knowledge absorption processes. As the market demands a shorter response time to environmental changes and a greater adaptation to varying customer needs, there is a growing awareness of the need for new flexible cooperation structures.

In this vein, authors such as Zimmermann (1997) and Rodríguez and Ranguelov (2004) argue that although traditional cooperation agreements between firms provide an adequate organisational strategy to operate in a competitive context, the dynamism and turbulence of the current context render virtual structures an appropriate alternative strategic choice to attend to the changing needs of the market and transcend the limitations of the company.

In light of the above arguments, the main aim of this work is to develop a theoretical model that can explain the advantages of the company's integration in a virtual network in order to stimulate its capacity to absorb external knowledge. The present chapter is structured as follows. First, the concept of absorptive capacity is analysed. Second, the main factors identified by the literature that affect a firm's absorptive capacity are reviewed. Third, a brief review of the literature on the virtual network is presented. Embeddedness in a virtual network is suggested as an important determinant of absorptive capacity and most of its antecedents. Fourth, the importance of investment in and development of relational capabilities to efficiently take advantage of the integration in a virtual network is highlighted. Finally, conclusions and the most relevant implications of the study are presented.

CONCEPTUALISATION OF EXTERNAL KNOWLEDGE ABSORPTIVE CAPACITY

In 1989, Cohen and Levinthal defined the absorptive capacity of a firm as its ability to recognise the value of new, external information, assimilate it, and apply it to commercial ends. They sustain the idea that a firm's ability to acquire knowledge from its external environment is a by-product of its own R&D. As a result of this work, R&D began to be considered as a key player in organisational learning.

The authors revised their original definition, based on industrial organisation (IO) economics, in 1990, and developed a more extensive explanation of the construct with a greater emphasis on the processes underlying this type of organisational learning.

Cohen and Levinthal again modified their definition of absorptive capacity in 1994, adding that this capability not only enables the firm to exploit new external knowledge, but also allows it to predict the nature of future technological advances more accurately.

Since the appearance of these three definitions, framed in the context of technological knowledge, surprisingly few review articles have revised the definition of the absorptive capacity concept (e.g., see Van den Bosch, Volberda, & De Boer, 1999, and Zahra & George, 2002). Hence, the absorptive capacity construct has been applied to a great variety of areas in organisational research according to the specific needs of each study, without considering the previous state of the literature. However, contributions by Lubatkin (1998), Dyer and Singh (1998) Van den Bosch, Volberda y de Boer (1999) Zahra and George (2002) and Lane, Koka and Pathak (2006) should be highlighted.

The relative absorptive capacity construct proposed by Lane and Lubatkin (1998) essentially differs from that of Cohen and Levinthal (1989) in the context of their analysis. Whereas Cohen and Levinthal (1989) take the firm as their unit of analysis to study absorptive capability, Lane and Lubatkin analyse the capacity of a "student firm" to absorb knowledge from a "teacher firm".

Contemporaneous with the previous authors, Dyer and Singh (1998) view absorptive capacity as "an iterative process of exchange" leading to "relational rents"—supranormal profits that are jointly generated and shared by the collaborative partners.

Van den Bosch, Volberda and de Boer (1999) consider new aspects of the absorptive capacity construct related to the firm's knowledge environment. Thus, Van den Bosch, Volberda and de Boer (1999) suggest that Cohen and Levinthal's implicit feedback loop (absorptive capacity→learning→new absorptive capacity) is mediated by the environment in which a firm competes and by its success in coping with that environment.

Zahra and George (2002) reconceptualise the construct as a set of organisational routines and strategic processes by which firms acquire, assimilate, transform and exploit external knowledge in order to produce a dynamic organisational capability. The traditional three-dimensional model introduced by Cohen and Levinthal (1989) is thus reformulated to include a fourth dimension: transformation capability.

These authors further suggest that these dimensions can be integrated in two complementary components:

a. Potential absorptive capacity (PACAP), which comprises knowledge acquisition and assimilation capabilities, and
b. Realised absorptive capacity (RACAP), which includes knowledge transformation and exploitation capabilities.

Finally, based on an exhaustive review of the main published papers on absorptive capability, Lane, Koka and Pathak (2006) define the construct as the firm's ability to utilise externally held knowledge through three sequential learning processes: (1) explorative learning; (2) transformative learning; and (3) exploitative learning.

This latter definition once again alludes to Cohen and Levinthal's (1989) three classical dimensions. Nevertheless, it is our view that transformation capability should be separated from assimilation capability, since each one is based on routines and processes of a different nature in the organisation. We firmly believe that

the specification of Zahra and George (2002) is an improvement on that put forward by Cohen and Levinthal (1990), and hence, we use their specification in this chapter.

Dimensions of Absorptive Capacity

According to Zahra and George's (2002) definition and following our own interpretation, there are four different but complementary dimensions of absorptive capacity: acquisition, assimilation, transformation and exploitation. These four elements must progress chronologically.

Acquisition is defined as the ability to recognise, value and acquire the external knowledge that is critical to a firm's operations (Lane and Lubatkin, 1998; Zahra and George, 2002). Hamel (1991) defines the acquisition of new specialised knowledge as the motivation for establishing inter-organisational collaborations. This capacity develops the "intelligence generation" function in the organisation, introduced by Liao, Welsch and Stoica (2003).

Assimilation refers to the firm's capacity to absorb external knowledge. It can also be defined as the routines and processes that allow the firm to understand, analyse, interpret and include information from external sources (Szulanski, 1996; Zahra and George, 2002).

Transformation refers to the firm's ability to develop and refine routines that facilitate the transfer and combination of existing knowledge with newly acquired and assimilated knowledge. The main objective of this ability is to find out how to adapt or reconfigure the new knowledge to the reality and specific needs of the organisation (Zahra and George, 2002). Transformation can be achieved by adding or deleting knowledge, or interpreting existing knowledge in a different way (Kogut and Zander, 1992; Van Den Bosch, Volberda, and de Boer, 1999).

Exploitation refers to a firm's ability to apply new external knowledge commercially to achieve organisational objectives (Lane and Lubatkin,

1998). It can also refer to the routines that allow firms to refine, extend, and leverage existing competences or create new ones by incorporating acquired and transformed knowledge into its operations (Tiemessen, Lane, Crossan and Inkpen, 1997; Zahra and George, 2002).

ANTECEDENTS OF ABSORPTIVE CAPACITY

Factors affecting a firm's absorptive capacity can be theoretically categorised as internal or external. The most important internal factors include prior knowledge base, diversity of backgrounds, organisational culture, organisational structure, strategic orientation, Knowledge Management systems, age, size and financial resources. The

internal factors are necessary, but not enough to determine a firm's absorptive capacity[2].

In the present study, the internal factors are ignored in favour of a focus on the specific effects that virtual networks exert on external factors affecting a firm's absorptive capacity, due to the scarcity of studies linking them with integration in a virtual network, or of studies examining external factors as antecedents of absorptive capacity.

The external knowledge environment is crucial to absorptive capacity. A knowledge-creating company operates in an "open-system" in which it constantly interacts with its outside environment by exchanging knowledge (Nonaka and Takeuchi, 1995). This knowledge may be in the form of new technologies and capabilities, which improve the firm's absorptive capacity.

External factors presented in the previous literature as determinants of absorptive capacity

Table 1. External factors that affect a firm's absorptive capacity

Degree of environmental turbulence or variability	Grant (1996); Van den Bosch, Volberda and de Boer (1999); Liao, Welsch and Stoica, (2003); Warner (2003)
Level of spillovers (externalities)	Cohen and Levinthal (1990); Huselid (1995); Zander and Kogut, (1995); Henderson and Cockburn (1996); Veugelers (1997); Nieto and Quevedo (2005)
Existence of technological opportunities	Cohen and Levinthal (1990); Nieto and Quevedo (2005)
Characteristics of knowledge in other companies	Cohen and Levinthal (1990); Kogut and Zander, (1992); Nonaka, (1994); Von Hippel (1994); Zander and Kogut (1995); Szulanski (1996); Lane and Lubatkin (1998); Simonin (1999)
Geographical distance	Szulanski (1996); Santoro and Gopalakrishnan (2001); Koschatzky (2002)
Cultural diversity	Mowery, Oxley and Silverman (1996); Lane and Lubatkin (1998); Simonin (1999); Hofstede (1999); Gupta and Govindarajan (2000); Lane, Salk and Lyles (2001)
External knowledge mechanisms	Lei and Hitt (1995); Veugelers and Cassiman (1999); Shenkar and Li (1999); Dyer and Nobeoka (2000); Zahra and George (2002)
Position in the knowledge networks	Nonaka and Takeuchi (1995); Arthur and Defillippi (1994); Powell, Koput and Smith-Doerr, (1996); Deeds, Decarolis, and Coombs (2000); Oliver (2001); Erramilli, Agarwal and Dev (2002)

include the degree of environmental turbulence or variability, level of externalities, existence of technological opportunities, characteristics of knowledge in other companies, geographical distance, cultural diversity, external knowledge mechanisms and position in the knowledge networks.

Most of these external factors will be explained in depth in the section that considers how they are affected by the integration in a virtual network. It is important to highlight that the relations between these external factors are not mutually exclusive.

EMBEDDEDNESS IN VIRTUAL NETWORKS

The dynamic, global and knowledge intensive business environment, a complex array of technologies, fast-changing needs of the market, short product life cycles, more demanding customers, market structures where preferences are segmented and markets that extend beyond national boundaries, among other aspects, demand a rapid response from organisations (e.g. see Quinn, 1992; Cravens, Piercy and Shipp, 1996; Gummesson, 1994). Hence, agility, understood as the capability to flexibly adapt the organisation in order to cope with the unanticipated business environment, is considered a key feature in contending with global competitiveness.

Management scholars and practitioners agree that knowledge resources surpass physical and financial resources as drivers of firm competitive advantages and performance in such a hypercompetitive environment. Zahra and George (2002) stress that knowledge offers the capability to generate, extrapolate and infer new knowledge and information. Knowledge creation always requires more knowledge, which makes it increasingly diversified. Cumulativeness makes creation more collective, as no one can master all the domains of science. Thus, the task of effectively absorbing,

disseminating and exploiting external knowledge resources becomes an important agenda item for organisational managers.

Firms no longer operate as stand-alone entities, but create networks of customers, suppliers, distributors, engineers, service providers and partners, in order to tap into relevant business information, complementary competences, technologies, knowledge, practices and resources (see e.g. De Michelis 2001; Chesbrough, 2003; Evans and Wolf, 2005). Collaboration is even possible with actual or potential competitors which provides an excellent opportunity for co-opetition (Brandenburger and Nalebuff, 1996), and furthermore, effective value creation.

These networks can also facilitate: (1) renewal and upgrading of existing resources and capabilities; (2) reduction of risk and transactional costs; (3) gains in flexibility to cope with the rapidly changing and intensely competitive marketplace; (4) development of the skills and resources needed to identify and move innovations quickly to commercial success (Cravens and Piercy, 1994); (5) achievement of the operating economies and efficiencies essential to offer value to customers, stockholders, and other stakeholders (Cravens and Piercy, 1994), and (6) new marketplace access and improvement of the firm's competitive position (e.g. Child and Faulkner, 1998). As a result, the locus of working, learning, innovation and competition shifts from structures inside the firm to structures that emphasise external relationships.

At the societal level, these changes create a networked economy which requires different strategies that go too far beyond the internal strategies for the creation and management of knowledge. At this point, it should be noted that any reference made to knowledge includes not only technological or scientific knowledge, but also other types of business-related knowledge, such as managerial techniques, marketing expertise and manufacturing know-how.

In a networked economy, a node represents a unique repository of knowledge, whereas a link represents economic and strategic ties that enable knowledge flows between the nodes (Jarvenpaa and Tanriverdi, 2003). The breadth of the firm's internal and external networks determines its ability to absorb, create and leverage knowledge. The external networks comprise customers, suppliers, partners, competitors and other stakeholders in the firm that influence a firm's absorptive capacity.

These networks are giving rise to a variety of new organisational forms. Three forces drive the proliferation and virtualisation of a firm's networks. First, information technologies and telecommunications make it possible to coordinate work across time and space boundaries. Physical location, buildings, and distribution channels become transparent and less important as interactions between customers and the firm shift from physical channels to the Internet and much of the back-end work at the firm is done by information technology.

The convergence between the ongoing revolutions in telecommunications and information technologies, besides providing a delocalisation of transactions which become space and time independent, also allows a radical increase in the number of agents that form a community, a virtually unlimited increase in the number of connections and therefore in the potential size of the community, and a increment in speed of information transmission which takes place at the speed of electronic communication. In this sense, virtual networks create an endless communication of "one with one" (through electronic mail), "one with many" (through a personal Web page or a electronic conference), "many with one" (through an electronic diffusion) and the most relevant communication of "many with many" (through a on-line debate forum or a chat room).

Second, firms' products, services and processes are becoming more knowledge intensive. Almost all physical products carry some coded knowledge or service element. In addition, many products are being digitised and traded via virtual media. Therefore, a firm's value-creating process and products appear increasingly less tangible and more virtual to outsiders (Jarvenpaa and Tanriverdi, 2003).

Third, the rising globalisation of competences and production have increased the need and the opportunities to reach global markets and utilise global resources, establishing relationships with actors with diverse cultural backgrounds and interests, in order to be competitive. Although a great number of organisational forms can help to compete globally, virtual networks allow firms to interact with other organisations rapidly and flexibly and to remain independent.

The literature contains abundant definitions of virtual networks (e.g. Cravens and Piercy, 1994; Goldman, Nagel and Preiss, 1995; Hedberg, Dahlgren, Hansson and Olve, 1997; Sieber, 1997; Jägers, Jansen and Steenbakkers, 1998; Venkatraman and Henderson, 1998; DeSanctis and Monge, 1999; Passiante and Andriani, 2000; Franke, 2002; Saabeel, Verduijn, Hagdom and Kumar, 2002).

In light of these conceptualisations, the following definition of this organisational configuration is proposed:

A virtual network is a network of several independent organisations collaborating to reach a common strategic goal, exploit an opportunity for business and sustain competitive advantages through cooperation and the creation and sharing of complementary resources and capabilities. While similar in several aspects to traditional organisational cooperation, virtual networks involve more flexible and extensive inter-organisational relationships that are produced via information and communication technologies (ICT).

The virtual network is sometimes called the "virtual organisation", so named because it has a long-term orientation with the objective of adapting to meet the needs of segmented market structures (Cravens and Piercy, 1994). Nevertheless, the virtual network's temporal dimension is always determined by the characteristics of the opportunity to be exploited. Virtual networks make possible technically egalitarian interactive communication, in that they are devices which operate at the same level in a network architecture. As no one company dominates in the virtual network model because everyone has the same weight and importance in the network, it is a more democratic and participatory model.

The main behaviours of virtual networks may be identified as:

a. Horizontal collaboration across an independent structure, which is replacing traditional vertical hierarchies (Zenger and Hestley, 1997);

b. Organisation of production and transaction grounded on intermodality and complementarity rather than substitution, based on the assumption that the best way to handle risk and uncertainties is to share them by leveraging capabilities and resources from many players (Passiante and Andriani, 2001).

These processes allow companies to reduce transactional costs, coordination costs and the complexity of traditional forms of organisation. While virtual networks may exist in physical-asset intensive industries, they are more important for and prominent in small and medium-sized enterprises (SMEs) and enterprises operating in high-technology and science-based sectors (e.g. computers, semiconductors, pharmaceuticals and biotechnology), where technological requirements exceed the skills and resources of the core organisation.

INTERACTIONS BETWEEN EMBEDDEDNESS IN VIRTUAL NETWORKS AND ABSORPTIVE CAPACITY

As pointed out above, many internal and external factors have been identified in the literature as antecedents of a firm's absorptive capacity. Although there is a vast literature that recognises virtual networks as organisational structures potentially able to strengthen an organisation's capabilities to accumulate, transfer and apply external knowledge, few empirical or even theoretical studies directly examine the relationships between the two constructs.

A firm's integration in a virtual network facilitates the joint development of new ideas, skills, and knowledge, and the sharing of in-house resources, experience, technologies, knowledge and best practices, on any topic, project or problem in any field of operation between a firm's employees and between employees from different organisations across disciplinary, spatial, time, and cultural boundaries regardless of physical presence, location and size.

The information and communication tools that encourage employees to directly share experience-based knowledge with their co-workers can be of two types:

a. Synchronous (in real time) communication tools (video-conferences, Web chat, chat systems such as the Internet Relay Chat, computer conferences, debate forums, wikis, WWW-based phone systems, mobile telephony, audio-conferencing, workflow tools, peer-to-peer file sharing, instant messaging, newsgroups), that allow informal and spontaneous communication; and

b. Asynchronous (in delayed time) communication tools (electronic mail, Weblogs, FTP, directories, document archive, USENET, shared databases, "data warehouse", "data mining"; Web pages; intelligence searching; electronic journals).

Moreover, interactions are nourished with documents, bibliographic references or graphic Webs, examples, experiences and ideas that on the one hand make them more dynamic, and on the other, more systematic.

The availability of all these communication technologies facilitates the organisation, contextualisation and analysis of large quantities of raw data and frees up time to analyse the information innovatively and creatively. Chat rooms are examples of collaborative learning spaces where the wealth of interchange surpasses expository information models, since their members interact not only individually by asking for or contributing information, but also by setting up relationships for debate, argumentation and confrontation of ideas and knowledge.

Virtual networks also provide systems and tools that allow employees to constantly question the best way to carry out their tasks and solve problems, create and manage multidisciplinary workgroups effectively, gather employees' suggestions and proposals, as well as to support the decision-making process. Employees can use this common area of collaboration to shorten the time it takes to e-mail documents, revise them, and send them back. Workers use their colleagues as a readily available, trustworthy source of technical-professional information and guidance.

Table 2 shows each of the functions that a virtual network performs to stimulate the processes of absorption and accumulation of external knowledge as well as some examples of information and communication tools that can be used to support them.

Moreover, not only does a company's integration in a virtual network have advantages in terms of new knowledge, but it also leads to improvements in employee training, organisational structure (Jarvenpaa and Tanriverdi, 2003) and even organisational culture and the reduction of the geographical and cultural distances between companies.

In the following section, we explore how the company's integration in a virtual network affects the development of its capacity to absorb external knowledge through the direct effect it has on most of the external factors that determine this absorptive capacity. The external factors studied are: degree of environmental turbulence, level of environmental externalities, existence of technological opportunities, characteristics of knowledge in other companies, geographical distance and cultural diversity.

External Factors

Degree of Environmental Turbulence

Environmental turbulence has an influence on how the company adapts to the environment (Duncan, 1972). The degree of turbulence is defined by the existence of high levels of change in the key environmental variables (Dess and Beard, 1984; Glazer and Weiss, 1993) such as consumer preferences, number of new consumers, the number of new products, number and position of competitors, market size, use of technology and regulations.

Environmental turbulence creates threats for companies. Firms operating in turbulent environments that do not want to lose their competitive advantages are expected to increase their capacities of acquisition, assimilation and posterior dissemination of the acquired external knowledge (Van den Bosch, Volberda, and de Boer, 1999; Grant, 1996; Liao, Welsch and Stoica, 2003). Therefore, high degrees of change in the industry will encourage companies to increment their absorptive capacity.

Some of these changes are due to rapid transformation of industries, globalisation, and new information and communication technologies. Virtual networks have developed an information economy where the exchange of information and services has increased more rapidly than physical

Table 2. Main functions of virtual networks in the development of a firm's absorptive capacity

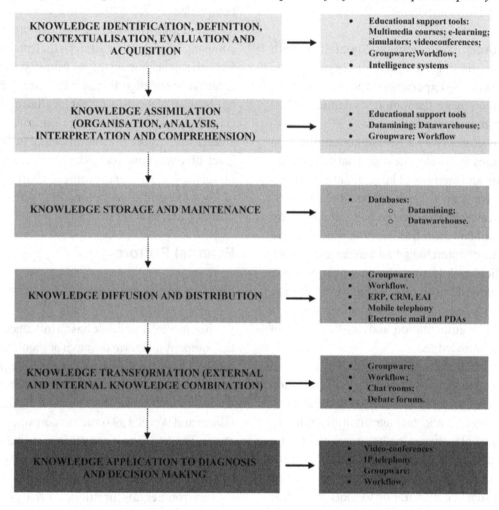

goods. Nevertheless, physical goods are being digitised, as they are becoming increasingly knowledge intensive.

The growth of information has therefore both been stimulated by virtual networks and encouraged their spread. The major flows of information produce an increase in the segmentation of consumers' preferences and introduce new product markets and new competitors into markets, among other aspects, which change firms' competitive environments and force them to sustain a continuous learning system and innovate.

Level of Environmental Externalities

The difficulties the firm faces in appropriating all the results derived from its innovative effort produces a volume of knowledge that other organisations can acquire and use without having to assume any external cost (Zander and Kogut, 1995). This mass of public knowledge comprises the knowledge externalities or *spillovers* (Nieto and Quevedo, 2005).

Many of the studies on this issue have pointed out that while the existence of externalities accelerates the technological advance in the industry, it also discourages a firm from investing in its own R&D, thus affecting absorptive capacity (Spence, 1984; Henderson and Cockburn, 1996; Nieto and Quevedo, 2005).

However, authors such as Huselid (1995) and Veugelers (1997) state that the firm's access to external knowledge is not cost exempt. Companies have to invest in R&D and develop sufficient expertise internally in order to capture and use the results of external research and to be able to sustain or create competitive advantages in an industry where innovation, the main source of these advantages, can be acquired easily.

Bearing in mind that absorptive capacity is often a by-product of firms' internal R&D activities (Cohen and Levinthal, 1989, 1990) and according to the results obtained in works such as Becker and Peters (2000), it is assumed that the greater the level of environmental externalities, the greater the company's incentive to invest in its absorptive capacity will be. Despite this indirect effect, the level of externalities also has a direct influence on absorptive capacity, since it allows the organisation's knowledge base to grow.

Virtual networks increase transparency in business processes, as different firms are able to communicate and exchange knowledge without major difficulty through the Internet and through access to a central database. This intensive information exchange improves technological spillovers (Krugman, 1991) and, as a consequence, the firm's incentives to develop its absorptive capacity.

Existence of Technological Opportunities

Research has shown that technological advances are more easily obtained in some industries than in others, since advances in relevant scientific and technological knowledge take place at a different pace in each industry (Nieto and Quevedo, 2005). The concept used in the literature to reflect the

potential for technological progress in different industries is that of technological opportunity. According to Cohen and Levinthal (1990), technological opportunity represents the costs a company bears to achieve a normalised unit of technical advantage in a certain sector.

Technological opportunity has two dimensions. The first consists of the quantity of technological knowledge, external to the sector or to the industry (for example, in universities and research centres), that can be acquired. The second dimension is the degree to which a new knowledge unit improves the technological performance of the production processes or the products and, therefore, of the company's profits.

A growth in technological opportunities increases the incentives to invest in R&D which, as a result, produces an increment in the absorptive capacity of companies that want to sustain or obtain competitive advantage. On the other hand, the existence of technological opportunity affects absorptive capacity directly through the improvement in the capacities to identify and value external knowledge.

As with the level of environmental externalities, ICTs also facilitate the emergence of technological opportunities, as they increase transparency in the information and knowledge generated by agents and organisations that are external to the virtual network. The firm's access to this information through the extranet enables it to increase its knowledge base and consequently its absorptive capacity.

Characteristics of Knowledge on Other Companies

A critical dimension of knowledge that raises barriers to its transfer and absorption is its tacitness (Von Hippel, 1994; Nonaka, 1994; Kogut and Zander, 1992; Zander and Kogut, 1995; Szulanski, 1996; Simonin, 1999). Reed and DeFillippi (1990) define tacitness as the implicit and noncodifiable accumulation of skills that results from learning by doing. Tacit knowledge is highly personal, deeply rooted in experiences, processes, actions and in complex organisational routines which cannot easily be codified and transmitted in a formal, systematic language or representation (Szulanski, 1996; Simonin, 1999).

Other barriers to knowledge transfer are its complexity and specificity. Complexity refers to the number of interdependent technologies, routines, individuals, and resources linked to a particular knowledge or asset. Specificity is defined as "the ease with which an asset can be redeployed to alternative uses and by alternative users without loss of productive value" (Williamson, 1990). Therefore, the more explicit (easy to codify), simple and generic the external knowledge, the easier its absorption will be.

Although the transfer of tacit, complex and specific knowledge could be regarded as incompatible with distant collaboration, this is not necessarily the case. The transfer of tacit knowledge may be facilitated by the use of information and communication technologies. These technologies also demonstrate properties such as facilitating the remote coordination of complex research projects (Passiante and Andriani, 2000; Gallié and Guichard, 2002).

According to Passiante and Andriani (2000) applications like video-conferencing (desktop video) and room-based video-conference enhance the learning mechanism related to the conversion from tacit to tacit knowledge. In fact, video-conferencing facilitates brainstorming camps, informal meetings, detailed discussion, sharing experiences between product developers and customers, which can also take place if people are not co-located. On the other hand, e-mail, WWW-based phone systems, groupware shared databases, consulting, collaboration tools, chat systems, computer conferences, and workflow tools allow firms to articulate tacit knowledge into explicit concepts.

Gallié and Guichard (2002), quoting Foray (2000), identify three elements of ICTs in the codification process:

- By encouraging the evolution of printing techniques (computers and printers, graphics, software, etc.), ICTs reduce the cost of codification for easily codified knowledge;
- By motivating the creation of new computer languages (for instance artificial intelligence, E-mail, groupware shared databases, collaboration tools, and workflow tools), thus elevating the modelling capacity for complex phenomenon, they allow us to contemplate the possibility of codifying increasingly complex knowledge (for example, expert knowledge);
- As they become the physical support of a worldwide network, ICTs increase the economic value of codification, as the production of codified knowledge is strongly stimulated by virtual networks.

In light of the above, it may be posited that the usage of ICTs increases transparency and ease of transferring and absorbing complex, specific and tacit knowledge.

Geographical Distance

Geographical distance, or physical distance between partners sharing and transferring knowledge, also represents an obstacle to effectiveness in knowledge absorption processes. Distance increases the cost and time that partners need to invest to establish contacts and interchange information (Santoro and Gopalakrishnan, 2001). Trust is not easily maintained through distant collaboration. More misunderstandings can occur at a distance, as the context in which the remote team works is unfamiliar to their distant colleagues.

However, Rocco, Finholt, Hofer and Herbsleb (2001) conclude that distant workers are not as disadvantaged in terms of communicating their reliability and competence as they are in terms of communicating emotional openness. In other words, there is not a great difference between local and long distance relationships in reading cues associated with cognitive trust.

For example, attributions of reliability may be reinforced as easily by a prompt e-mail reply or a telephone call (i.e. as in geographically distributed teams) as by a prompt visit in response to a note left on an office door (i.e. in a local team). In a similar vein, judgements of competence are based on the correct execution of tasks that depend on the worker's skills and not on his or her location.

Other studies such as those by Walther (1996; 1997) and Bos, Olson, Olson and Wright (2002) show that computer-mediated communication does not differ from face-to-face communication in terms of the capability of social information exchange, but rather in terms of a slower rate of transfer. As technologies are richer in terms of immediacy of feedback, and the available channels incorporate new tools like video and audio for interpreting communication cues, virtual networks may perform more effectively in terms of fostering trust (Daft and Lengel, 1986). Hence, ICTs, in their diversity, offer firms answers to the many obstacles of remote collaboration, by reducing the importance of face-to-face interactions.

Cultural Diversity

Cultural diversity is the degree of dissimilarity between the partner's business nationalities, values and language, as well as business practices, organisational structures, institutional heritage and organisational cultures (Simonin, 1999; Hofstede, 1999).

Generally, cultural diversity increases the difficulties and challenges firms face to absorb and transfer knowledge, due to the fact they have to invest more time in communication, in compatible routine design and in the development of common management systems (Mowery, Oxley and Silverman, 1996).

Thus, the greater the differences between firms involved in the knowledge transfer process, in corporate, national, organisational and professional terms, the more problems the firm will have in communicating and absorbing the transferred knowledge.

A firm's embeddedness in a virtual network stimulates the building of a common identity through the combination of collective and individual interests. In other organisational structures, identity is devoted to formulating general value systems and trying to convince the members and stakeholders to identify themselves with these value systems. However, if one focuses only on attitudes of commitment, the result is often somewhat superficial and unreliable (Rasmussen and Wangel, 2007).

Virtual networks make it easier for firms to create a transient, boundaryless, lateral, flat, team-based, computer mediated, flexible and dynamic structure which involves, empowers and motivates all the social actors to create and share knowledge, to take responsibilities themselves and to initiate corrections or changes in the procedures of the virtual network. Hence, this structure provides nodes to create a common identity and solve most cultural problems quickly and without time restrictions.

RELATIONAL AND SOCIAL CAPABILITIES

According to Jarvenpaa and Tanriverdi (2003), although virtual networks can be "strong structures" for handling complex information, they are frequently "weak structures" for managing and providing support for social relationships in the network. Thus, virtual networks critically depend on the quality of these relationships.

To benefit from the integration in a virtual network, a firm should develop network, socialisation and relational capabilities that eliminate internal resistances to change and promote knowledge and resource sharing. Virtual networks depend heavily on these relational capabilities, because an essential part of their competitiveness depends on the process of building and integrating capabilities in the various "nodes".

Researchers have to learn how to adapt the very wide range of communication patterns to the nature of their object; these communication patterns may be very traditional or high-tech, formal or informal, synchronous or asynchronous, written or oral.

Specifically for technical collaboration, the interacting nodes must also enhance their knowledge bases through new technical and organisational capabilities while simultaneously creating and agreeing on the very knowledge by which the enhancement is interpreted and judged (Rasmussen and Wangel, 2007). Particularly, firms should develop applications that enhance sharing of data and visualisations, and applications that allow remote use of important instruments and facilities.

However, while adapting communication patterns and developing common technical and organisational capabilities are important, the survival of the virtual network also depends heavily on trust between the collaborating units (Mohr and Spekman, 1994; Dahlstrom and Nygaard, 1995; Simpson and Mayo, 1997).

The partners in a virtual network must share their knowledge in order to be able to collaborate, while at the same time safeguarding their own business interests. How these continuously active tensions between cooperation and competition are handled depends on the levels of trust.

Without trust, there is no shared vision and no collaborative relationships, merely arm's length transactions. Trust is important for three reasons. First, it allows firms to reduce the uncertainty associated with virtual knowledge, which is enabled as well as limited by information technology. Trust may reduce this uncertainty by providing what is expected from collaborators.

Second, virtual networks have many different stakeholders with different motivations. These interests are bound to conflict as conditions and opportunities change. Trust is crucial in avoiding or managing conflicts, settling disputes, and sustaining relationships. Trust reduces the likelihood that other parties will behave opportunistically in times of conflict by introducing social obligations, often called social capital, external to the particular transaction.

Third, virtual networks are limited by the very technology that spawned them. Computer-mediated communication and information systems limit trust-building opportunities, as they provide more anonymous access. When people are limited to purely virtual forms of communication, social relationships may not strengthen and frequently deteriorate over time. Weakened social relationships increase the temptation to engage in hit-and-run behaviour, which sows the seeds for distrust between parties. Distrust in one part of the network connection can quickly spread to other parts of the network.

However, authors such as Rocco, Finholt, Hofer and Herbsleb (2001), Walter (1996, 1997) and Bos, Olson, Olson and Wright. (2002) demonstrate that far from discouraging social information exchange, ICTs encourage organisations to increase frequency of contacts, engage in recurrent business transactions and an intense exchange of information, communication and interaction, thereby calling into question the position outlined above.

Previous experience at managing collaboration through networks is a crucial asset to assure the formation of a visible trust between partners. Organisations with experience in multiple ties to others should develop better protocols for exchanging information and resolving disputes (Powell, 1998; Rasmussen and Wangel, 2007). This experience would help to integrate the tasks distributed across the network or create motivation to share knowledge across the barriers caused by a lack of face-to-face clues and cultural differences, ensuring that contributors receive a fair share of the rewards that are generated.

Other important elements that influence virtual networks are the level of mutual commitment

(Mohr and Spekman, 1994; Geyskens, Steenkamp, Scheer and Kumar, 1996; Sarkar, Echambadi, Cavusgil, and Aulakh, 2001; Dahlstrom and Nygaard, 1995) and relational norms such as flexibility, solidarity, mutuality and conflict harmonisation.

Flexibility implies a willingness on the part of the organisation to adapt to the terms of interchange before unforeseen events or changing circumstances (Heide and John, 1992). Solidarity implies the mutual expectation that the inter-organisational relationship has a high value, and determines behaviours managed specifically towards its maintenance (Heide and John, 1992). Mutuality determines the attitude of accepting that the success of each party depends on that of the other, expressing a feeling of joint responsibility (Cannon, Achrol and Gundlach, 2000). Finally, conflict harmonisation reflects the degree to which there is a spirit of mutual agreement on the cooperative aims (Cannon, Achrol and Gundlach, 2000).

CONCLUSIONS AND IMPLICATIONS

In the current changing environment, the ability to sense and seize new opportunities (Teece, 2000) and to build and reconfigure knowledge-based assets is crucial for the firm's long-term competitiveness and survival. If a firm concentrates solely on strengthening existing capabilities, there is a risk that its core capabilities will harden into core rigidities (Leonard-Barton, 1992).

Absorptive capacity is revealed as one of the most important organisational dynamic capabilities, as no single firm can cope independently with the complexity and risks of rapidly changing environments, or possess all the necessary skills and resources to stay on top of all areas of progress and bring significant innovations to the market.

Absorptive capacity refers to the dynamic capacity that allows value creation through the development of external knowledge acquisition,

assimilation, transformation and exploitation capabilities. In other words, absorptive capacity is the result of the combination of internal and external learning.

In recent years, the firm's embeddedness in virtual networks has gained prominence as a powerful management tool and as an opportunity to facilitate corporate learning and knowledge creation and sharing, through novel ways of expounding ideas, and fast and easy access to skills and resources.

Virtual networks favour a participative and collaborative culture in which the objective is to create a "sharing experience" rather than an "experience which is shared". These networks are especially appropriate when the knowledge required is dispersed between many specialists who have to provide a coordinated solution to a complex problem (Quinn, Anderson and Finkelstein, 1996).

The proliferation of this new flexible and decentralised inter-organisation structure is explained by the convergence of technological innovations in computing and telecommunications. Multiplication of agents and connections, and time and space independence constitute the four key features of the new network operating systems.

Despite its importance, the literature to date has not articulated the unique features of virtual networks that may lead to the development of absorptive capacity. This chapter attempts to fill this theoretical gap by determining the Internet-based drivers for facilitating the way firms communicate, share and create a common knowledge to sustain or create competitive advantages. Special attention is given to the relationship between virtual networks and external factors affecting absorptive capacity. The chapter ends with a section underlining the importance of developing trust and relational capabilities to take advantage of the firm's integration in a virtual network.

The academic implications of the study lie in the conceptual framework of absorptive capacity and virtual networks that the research provides. The conceptual reviews carried out may serve as a guideline for managers in organisational configuration and in identifying the key elements to sustain and create new competitive advantages in changing environments.

REFERENCES

Ahuja, G. (2000). The duality of collaboration: inducements and opportunities in the formation of inter-firm linkages. *Strategic Mangement Journal*, 21(3), 317-343.

Arthur, M.B., & Defillippi, R.J. (1994). The boundaryless career: A competency-based perspective. *Journal of Organizational Behavior*, *15*(4), 307-324.

Atuahene-Gima, K. (1992). Inward Technology Licensing as an Alternative to Internal R&D in New Product Development: A Conceptual Framework. *Journal of Product Innovation Management*, *9*(2), 156-167.

Becker, W., & Peters, J. (2000). *Technological Opportunities, Absorptive Capacities and Innovation*. Paper presented at the Eighth International Joseph A. Schumpeter Society Conference, Centre for Research in Innovation and Competition (CRIC), Manchester.

Bos, N., Olson, J., Olson, G., & Wright, Z. (2002). Effects of four computer-mediated communications channels on trust development. In *Proceedings of the SIGCHI conference on Human factors in computing systems: Changing our world, changing ourselves. Confidence and Trust* (pp. 237-288). New York: Association for Computing Machinery Press.

Brandenburger, A.M., & Nalebuff, B.J. (1996). *Co-opetition*. New York: Doubleday.

Camisón, C., & Forés, B. (2007). *Factores antecedentes de la capacidad de absorción de cono-cimiento: un estudio teórico*. Paper presented at the XXI AEDEM Annual Congress, Madrid.

Cannon, J.P., Achrol, R.S., & Gundlach, G.T. (2000). Contracts, norms, and plural form governance. *Journal of the Academy of Marketing Science*, *28*(2), 180-194.

Chang, C. (2004). The Determinants of Knowledge Transfer through Strategic Alliances". *Academy of Management Proceedings*, pp. H1-H6.

Chesbrough, H. W. (2003). *Open Innovation: The New Imperative for Creating and Profiting from Technology*. Harvard Business School Press.

Child, J. & Faulkner, D. (1998), *Strategies of co-operation. Managing alliances, networks, and joint ventures*. New York: Oxford University Press.

Cohen, W.M., & Levinthal, D.A. (1989). Innovation and learning: The two faces of R&D. *Economic Journal, 99*, 569-596.

Cohen, W.M., & Levinthal, D.A. (1990). Absorptive capacity: A new perspective on learning and innovation. *Administrative Science Quarterly, 35*, 128-152.

Cohen, W.M., & Levinthal, D.A. (1994). Fortune favours the prepared firm. *Management Science, 40*, 227–251.

Cravens, D. W., Piercy, N. F., Shipp, S.H (1996). New Organizational Forms for Competing in Highly Dynamic Environments: the Network Paradigm. *British Journal of Management, 7*, 203-218.

Cravens, D.W., & Piercy, N.F. (1994). Relationship marketing and collaborative networks in service organizations. *International Journal of Service Industry Management, 5*, 39-53.

Daft, R.L., & Lengel, R.H. (1986). Organisational information requirements, media richness and structural design. *Management Science, 32*(5), 554-571.

Dahlstrom, R., & Nygaard, A. (1995). An exploratory investigation of interpersonal trust in new and market economies. *Journal of Retailing, 71*(4), 339-361

de Michelis, G. (2001). Cooperation and Knowledge Creation. In I. Nonaka & T. Nisiguchi (Ed.), *Knowledge Emergence. Social, Technical and Evolutionary Dimensions of Knowledge Creation* (pp.124-144). Oxford: Oxford University Press.

Deeds, D.L., Decarolis, D., & Coombs, J. (2000). Dynamic capabilities and new product development in high technology ventures: An empirical analysis of new biotechnology industry. *Journal of Business Venturing, 12*, 31–46.

DeSanctis, G., & Monge, P. (1999). Introduction to the special issue: communication processes for virtual organizations. *Organization Science, 10*(6), 693-703.

Dess, G., & Beard, D. (1984). Dimensions of Organizational Task Environments. *Administrative Science Quarterly, 29*(1), 52-73.

Duncan, R. B. (1972). Characteristics of organizational environments and perceived environmental uncertainty. *Administrative Science Quarterly, 17*, 313-327.

Dyer, J.H., & Nobeoka, K. (2000). Creating and managing a high-performance knowledge-sharing network: The Toyota case. *Strategic Management Journal, 21*, 45–367.

Dyer, J.H., & Singh, H. (1998). The relational view: Cooperative strategy and sources of inter-organizational competitive advantage. *Academy of Management Review, 23*(4), 660-679.

Erramilli, M.K., Agarwal, S., & Dev, C.S. (2002). Choice between non-equity modes: An organizational capability perspective. *Journal of International Business Studies, 33*, 223–242.

Evans, P., & Wolf, B. (2005). Collaboration rules. *Harvard Business Review, July–Aug*, 1–10.

Foray, D. (2000). *L'économie de la connaisance.* París: La Découverte.

Franke, U.J. (2002). The competence-based view on the management of virtual Web organizations. In U.J. Franke (Ed.), *Managing virtual Web organizations in the 21st century: issues and challenges* (pp. 1-27). London: Idea Group Publishing.

Gallié, E.P., & Guichard, R. (2002). *The impact of ICT sophistication on geographically distant networks: the case of space physics as seen from France.* Paper presented at the Workshop TIC et réorganisation spatiale des activités économiques, Brest.

Geyskens, I., Steenkamp, J.E.M., Scheer, L.K. & Kumar, N. (1996). The effects of trust and interdependence on relationship commitent: a trans-atlantic study. *International Journal of Research in Marketing, 13*, 303-317.

Glazer, R., & Weiss, A. (1993). Marketing in Turbulent Environments: Decision Processes and the Time-Sensitivity of Information. *Journal of Marketing Research, 30*(November), 509-521.

Goldman, S., Nagel, R., & Preiss, K. (1995). *Agile competitors and virtual organizations.* New York, Van Nostrand Reinhold.

Grant, R.M. (1996). Prospering in Dynamically-Competitive Environments: Organizational Capability as Knowledge Integration. *Organization Science, 7*(4), 375-387.

Gummesson, E. (1994). Service Management: An Evaluation and the Future. *International Journal of Service Industry Management, 5*(1), 77-96.

Gupta, A., & Govindarajan, V. (2000). Knowledge flows within MNCs. *Strategic Management Journal, 21*, 473-496.

Hedberg, B., Dahlgren, G., Hansson, J., & Olve, N. G. (1997). *Virtual Organizations and Beyond: Discover Imaginay Systems.* Chichester, UK: John Wiley & Sons.

Heide, J.B., & John, G. (1992). Do norms matter in marketing relationship?. *Journal of Marketing,* **56**, 32-44.

Henderson, R., & Cockburn, I. (1996). Scale, Scope, and Spillovers: The Determinants of Research Productivity in Drug Discovery. *RAND Journal of Economics, 27*(1), 32-59.

Hofstede, G. (1999). *Culturas y Organizaciones. El Software Mental. La Cooperación Internacional y su Importancia para la Supervivencia.* Madrid: Alianza Press.

Huselid, M.A.(1995). The impact of human resource management practices on turnover, productivity, and corporate. *Academy of Management Journal, 38*(3), 635-643.

Jägers, H., Jansen, W., & Steenbakkers, W. (1998). Characteristics of virtual organizations. In P. Sieber & J. Griese (Ed.), *Organizational virtualness* (pp. 65-76). Bern: Simona Verlag Bern.

Jarvenpaa, S.L., & Tanriverdi, H. (2003). Leading virtual knowledge networks. *Organizational Dynamics, 31*(4), 403-412.

Kim, L. (1998). Crisis construction and organizational learning: Capability building in catching-up at Hyundai Motor. *Organization Science, 9*(4), 506-521.

Kogut, B., & Zander, U. (1992). Knowledge of the firm, combinative capabilities, and the replication of technology. *Organization Science, 3,* 383-397.

Koka, B., & Prescott, J. (2002). Strategic Alliances As Social Capital: A Multidimensional View. *Strategic Management Journal, 23,* 795–816.

Koschatzky, K. (2002). Networking and knowledge transfer between research and industry in transition countries: empirical evidence from the Slovenian Innovation System. *Journal of Technology Transfer, 27*(1), 27-38.

Krugman, P. (1991). Increasing returns and economic geography. *The Journal of Political Economy, 99,* 483-499.

Kumar, R., & Nti, K. (1998). Differential Learning and Interaction in Alliance Dynamics: A Process and Outcome Discrepancy Model. *Organization Science, 9*(3), Special Edition: *Managing Partnerships and Strategic Alliances,* 356-367.

Lane, P.J., & Lubatkin, M. (1998). Relative absorptive capacity and interorganizational learning. *Strategic Management Journal, 19,* 461-477.

Lane, P.J., Salk, J.E. & Lyles, M.A. (2001). Absorptive Capacity, Learning, And Performance In International Joint Ventures. *Strategic Management Journal, 22*(12), 1139–1161.

Lane, P.L., Koka, B. & Pathak, S. (2006). The reification of absorptive capacity: a critical review and rejuvenation of the construct. *Academy of Management Review, 31*(4), 833-863.

Lei, D, & Hitt, M. A. (1995). Strategic restructuring and outsourcing: The effect of mergers, acquisitions and LBOs on building firm skills and capabilities. *Journal of Management, 21,* 835–859.

Leonard-Barton, D. (1992). Core capabilities and core rigidities: A paradox in managing new product development. *Strategic Management Journal, 13*(Summer special number), 111–125.

Liao, J., Welsch, H., & Stoica, M. (2003). Organizational Absorptive Capacity and Responsiveness: An Empirical Investigation of Growth-Oriented SMEs'. *Entrepreneurship: Theory & Practice, 28*(1), 63-86.

Lowe, J., & Taylor, P. (1998). R&D and technology purchase through licence agreements: complementary strategies and complementary assets. *R&D Management, 28*(4), 263-278.

March, J.G. (1991). Exploration and exploitation in organizational learning. *Organization Science, 2,* 71-87.

Meyer-Krahmer, F., & Schmoch, U. (1998). Science-based technologies: university-industry interactions in four fields. *Research Policy, 27*(8), 835-851.

Mohr, J.J., & Spekman, R.(1994). Characteristics of partnership success: partnership attributes, communication behaviour, and conflict resolution techniques. *Strategic Management Journal, 15*, 135-152.

Mowery, D.C., Oxley J. & Silverman, B.S. (1996). Strategic alliances and interfirm knowledge transfer. *Strategic Management Journal, 17*(Winter special number), 77–91.

Nieto, M., & Quevedo, P. (2005). Variables estructurales, capacidad de absorción y esfuerzo innovador en las empresas manufactureras españolas. *Revista Europea de Dirección y Economía de la Empresa, 14*(1), 25-44.

Nonaka, I., & Takeuchi, H. (1995). *The Knowledge-Creating Company: How Japanese Companies Create the Dynamics of Innovation.* New York: Oxford University Press.

Nonaka, I. (1994). A dynamic theory of organizational knowledge creation. *Organization Science, 5*, 14-37.

Oliver, A.L. (2001), Strategic alliances and the learning lifecycle of biotechnology firms. *Organization Studies, 22*, 467–489.

Oltra, M. J., & Flor, M. (2003). The impact of Technological Opportunities and Innovative Capabilities on Firms. *Creativity & Innovation Management, 12*(3), 137-144.

Passiante, G., & Andriani, P., (2000). Modelling the learning environment of virtual knowledge networks: some empirical evidence. *International Journal of Innovation Management, 4*(1), 1-31.

Phene, A., Fladmoe-Lindquist, K. & Marsh, L. (2006). Breakthrough innovations in the U.S. biotechnology industry: the effects of technological space and geographic origin. *Strategic Management Journal, 27*(4), 369-388.

Powell, W.W. (1998). Learning from collaboration: knowledge and networks in the biotechnology and pharmaceutical industries. *California Management Review, 40*(3), 228–240.

Powell, W.W., Koput, K.W. & Smith-Doerr, L. (1996). Interorganizational collaboration and the locus of innovation: Networks of learning in biotechnology. *Administrative Science Quarterly, 41*, 116–145.

Quinn, J. B. (1992). *Intelligence Enterprise.* New York: Free Press.

Quinn, J.B., Anderson, P. & Finkelstein S. (1996). Managing professional intellect: making the most of the best. *Harvard Business Review, 74*(2), 71-80.

Rasmussen, L.B., & Wangel, A. (2007). Work in the virtual enterprise – creating identities, building, trust, and sharing knowledge. *AI & Soc, 21*, 184-199.

Reed, R., & DeFillippi, R.J. (1990). Causal Ambiguity, Barriers to Imitation, and Sustainable Competitive Advantage. *Academy of Management Review, 15*(1), 88-102.

Rocco, E., Finholt, T.A., Hofer, E.C., & Herbsleb, J.D.(2001). *Out of sight, short of trust.* Paper presented at the Conference of the European Academy of Management, Barcelona, Spain.

Rodríguez, A., & Ranguelov, S. (2004). Knowledge Networks: A Key Element for University Research and Innovation Process. *The ICFAI Journal of Knowledge Management, 2*(4), 78-85.

Saabeel, W., Verduijn, T.M., Hagdom, L., & Kumar, K. (2002). A model of virtual organisation: a structure and process perspective. *Electronic Journal of Organizational Virtualness, 4*(1), 1-16.

Santoro, M.D., & Gopalakrishnan, S. (2001). Relationship Dynamics between University Research Centers and Industrial Firms: Their Impact on Technology Transfer Activities. *Journal of Technology Transfer, 26*, 163-171.

Sarkar, M.B., Echambadi, R., Cavusgil, S.T., & Aulakh, P.S. (2001). The influence of complementary compatibility and relationship capital on alliance performance. *Journal of the Academy of Marketing Science, 29*(4), 358-373.

Shan, W., & Song, J. (1997). Foreign Direct Investment And The Sourcing Of Technological Advantage: Evidence From The Biotechnology Industry. *Journal of International Business Studies, 28*(2), 267-284.

Shenkar, O., & Li, J. (1999). Knowledge Search in International Cooperative Ventures. *Organization Science, 10*(2), 134-143.

Sieber, P. (1997). Virtual organizations: static and dynamic viewpoints. *Virtual-organization. net, Newsletter, 1*(2), 3-9.

Simpson, J.M., & Mayo, D.T. (1997). Relationship management: a call for fewer influence attempts?. *Journal of Business Research, 39*, 209-218.

Spence, M. (1984). Cost reduction, competition, and industry performance. *Econometrica, 52*, 101-122.

Szulanski, G. (1996). Exploring internal stickiness: Impediments to the transfer of best practice within the firm. *Strategic Management Journal, 17*, 27-43.

Teece, D.J. (1998). Capturing value from knowledge assets: The new economy, markets for know-how, and intangible assets. *California Management Review, 40*(3), 55-79.

Teece, D.J. (2000). Strategies for managing knowledge assets: the role of firm structure and industrial context. *Long Range Planning, 33*, 35-54.

Teece, D.J., Pisano, G., & Shuen, A. (1997). Dynamic capabilities and strategic management. *Strategic Management Journal, 18*, 509-533.

Tiemessen, I., Lane, H.W., Crossan, M., & Inkpen, A.C. (1997). Knowledge management in international joint ventures. In P. W. Beamish & J. P. Killing (Ed.), *Cooperative strategies: North American perspective* (pp. 370–399). San Francisco: New Lexington Press.

Uzzi, B., & Lancaster, R. (2003). Relational embeddedness and learning: the case of bank loan managers and their clients. *Management Science, 49*(4), 383-399.

Van den Bosch, F.A.J., Volberda, H.W., & de Boer, M. (1999). Coevolution of firm absorptive capacity and knowledge environment: Organizational forms and combinative capabilities. *Organization Science, 10*, 551-568.

Venkatraman, N., & Henderson, J.C. (1998). Real strategies for virtual organizing. *Sloan Management Review*, Autumn, 33-48.

Vermeulen, F., & Barkema, H. (2001). Learning through acquisitions. *Academy of Management Journal, 44*, 457–476.

Veugelers, R., & Cassiman, B. (1999). Make and buy in innovation strategies: Evidence from Belgian manufacturing firms. *Research Policy, 28*, 63–80.

Veugelers, R. (1997). Internal R&D expenditures and external technology sourcing. *Research Policy, 26*, 303-315.

Von Hippel, E. (1994). Sticky information and the locus of problem solving: Implications for innovation. *Management Science, 49*, 429-439.

Walther, J. (1996). Computer-mediated communication: Impersonal, interpersonal and hyperpersonal Interaction. *Communication Research, 23(*1), 3-43.

Walther, J. (1997). Group and interpersonal effects in international computer-mediated collaboration. *Human Communication Research, 19*, 50-88.

Warner, A. (2003). Buying Versus Building Competence: Acquisition Patterns in the Information and Telecommunications Industry 1995–2000. *International Journal of Innovation Management, 7*(4), 395–415.

Williamson, O. (1990). *Comparative economic organization: The analysis of discrete structural alternatives.* Working paper presented at the law and economics workshop, the University of Michigan.

Zahra, S. A., & George, G. (2002). Absorptive capacity: A review, reconceptualization, and extension. *Academy of Management Review, 27*(2), 185-203.

Zander, U., & Kogut, B. (1995). Knowledge and the speed of the transfer and imitation of organizational capabilities: An empirical test. *Organization Science, 6*, 76-92.

Zenger, T.R., & Hestley, W.S. (1997). The disaggregation of corporations: selective intervention, high-powered incentives and molecular units. *Organisation Science, 8*(3), 209–222.

Zimmerman, F. O. (1997). Structural and managerial aspects of virtual enterprises. In *Proceedings of the European Conference on Virtual Enterprises and Networked Solutions - New Perspectives on Management, Communication and Information Technology* (pp. 7-10). Germany: Paderborn.

ADDITIONAL READING

Ahuja, G. (2000). Collaboration Networks, Structural Holes and Innovation: a Longitudinal Study. *Administrative Science Quaterly, 45*, 425-455.

Alavi, M. (1994). Computer-mediated collaborative learning: an empirical evaluation. *MIS Quarterly, 18*(2), 159-174.

Barabasi, A-L. (2002). *Linked: The New Science of Networks.* Persues Publishing.

Bultje, R., & Van Wijk, J. (1998). Taxonomy of virtual organisations, based on definitions, characteristics and typology. *Virtual-organization. net, Newsleter 2*(3), 7-21.

Caloghirou, Y., Kastelli, I., & Tsakanikas, A. (2004). Internal capabilities and external knowledge sources: complements or substitutes for innovative performance. *Technovation, 24*(1), 29-39.

Ciborra, C.U., & Andreu, R. (2001). Sharing knowledge across boundaries. *Journal of Information Technology, 16,* 73-81.

Daghfous A. (2004). Absorptive Capacity and the implementation of Knowledge-Intensive Best Practices. *SAM Advanced Management Journal,* pp.21-27.

Eng, T-Y. (2004). Implications of the Internet for Knowledge Creation and Dissemination in Clusters of Hi-tech firms. *European Management Journal, 22*(1), 87-98.

Fosfuri, A., & Tribó, J.A. (2008). Exploration the antecedents of potential absorptive capacity and its impact on innovation performance. *Omega, 36,* 173-187.

Hughes, J.A., O'Brien, J., Randall, D., Rouncefield, M., & Tolmie, P. (2001). Some 'real' problems of 'virtual' organization. *New Technology Work Employ, 16*(1), 49-64.

Jansen, J., Van Den Bosch, F., & Volberda, H. (2005). Managing Potential and Realized Absorptive Capacity: How Do Organizational Antecedents Matter?. *Academy of Management Journal, 48*(6), 999-1015.

Jarvenpaa, S., & Leidner, D. (2002). Communication and trust in global virtual teams. *Organization Science, 10*(10), 791-815.

Kogut (2000). The network as knowledge: Generative rules and the emergence of structure. *Strategic Management Journal, 21*, 405-425.

Lenox, M., & King, A. (2004). Prospects For Developing Absorptive Capacity Through Internal Information Provision. *Strategic Management Journal, 25*, 331–345.

Martínez, M.T., Fouletier, P., Park, K.H., Favrel, J. (2001). Virtual enterprise: organisation, evolution and control. *International Journal of Production Economics, 74*, 225-238.

Matusik, S., & Heeley, M. (2005). Absorptive Capacity in the Software Industry: Identifying Dimensions that Affect Knowledge and Knowledge Creation Activities. *Journal of Management, 31*, 549-572.

McEvely, B., & Zaheer, A. (1999). Bridging ties: A source of firm heterogeneity in competitive capabilities. *Strategic Management Journal, 20*, 1133-1156.

Nooteboom, B., Van Haverbeke, W., Duysters, G., Gilsing, V., & Van den Oord, A. (2007). Optimal cognitive distance and absorptive capacity. *Research Policy, 36*, 1016-1034.

Robins, J.A., Tallman, S., & Fladmoe-Lindquist, K. (2002). Autonomy and dependence of international cooperative ventures: an exploration of the strategic performance of U.S. ventures in Mexico. *Strategic Management Journal, 23*, 881-901.

Van den Bosch, F., Van Wijk, R., & Volberda, H. (2003). Absorptive capacity: antecedents, models and outcomes. In the M. Easterby-Smith and M.A.

Lyles (Ed.), *The Blackwell Handbook of Organizational Learning and Knowledge Management* (pp.278-301). Malden, MA: Blackwell.

Weisenfeld, U., Olaf, F., Alan, P., & Klaus, B. (2001). Managing technology as a virtual enterprise. *R & D Management, 31*(3), 323-334.

Wenger, E. (1999). *Communities of practice, learning, meaning and identity.* US: Cambrige University Press.

Zaheer, A., & Geoffrey G. B. (2005). Benefiting from Network Position: Firm Capabilities, Structural Holes, and Performance. *Strategic Management Journal, 26*, 809-825.

Wellman, B., & Gulia, M. (1999). Virtual communities as communities: Net surfers don't ride alone. In the M.A. Smith and P. Kollock (Ed.), *Communities in cyberspace* (pp. 167–194). London: Routledge.

ENDNOTES

[1] This research was supported by four grants from the Spanish Ministry of Science and Technology and Feder (European Fund for Regional Development) (SEC 2003-01825/ECO), General Direction of Research and Technology Transfer of Valencian Generalitat (ACOMP06/240), IVIE project OGI099/1 Program of Grants for Research in Economics 2006) and R+D Valencian Plan from Valencian Generalitat (project GV/2007/075).

[2] To study this internal factors in depth, see research by Camisón and Forés (2007).

Chapter IV
Knowledge Integration Through Inter-Organizational Virtual Organizations

Montserrat Boronat Navarro
Universitat Jaume I, Spain

Ana Villar López
Universitat Jaume I, Spain

ABSTRACT

In this study we adopt an inter-organizational view to examine virtual organizations. Thus, we understand this phenomenon as a strategic agreement between organizations that collaborate and coordinate their work through information technologies. This dimension adds greater flexibility to the strategic alliance, which in turn is beneficial for the integration of knowledge. In high technology industries, inter-organizational virtual organizations add further advantages to this option of knowledge integration through strategic alliances because of the importance of speed and flexibility. We put forward a series of propositions, following an initial approximation to this phenomenon through the combination of the strategic alliances, virtual organizations and the knowledge-based view literatures.

INTRODUCTION

Progress in information and communication technologies has led to the development and increasing importance of virtual organizations. There are various definitions of this term. Greis

and Kasarda (1997) recognize a common factor in all definitions: that a virtual organization is a related group of companies formed to enable collaboration toward mutually agreed on goals. One of the main features of virtual organizations is that people are linked not by face-to-face relationships but by sharing information through electronic networks (Weber, 2002); hence virtual organizations are associated with an intense use of computer networks and information technologies to support cooperation. Moreover, adaptability, flexibility and the ability to react quickly to changes in the market are properties that are usually assigned to virtual organizations (Grabowski and Roberts, 1999).

We adopt an inter-organizational view to examine virtual organizations. Thus, we understand this phenomenon as a strategic agreement between organizations that collaborate and coordinate their work through information technologies. This last dimension lends greater flexibility to the strategic alliance, which in turn is beneficial for the integration of knowledge.

According to the knowledge-based view (Nonaka, 1994; Nonaka and Takeuchi, 1995; Grant, 1996; Spender, 1996), knowledge integration is one of the main capabilities that organizations must possess in today's markets. In some industries, such as biotechnology, that need to integrate different bases of specialized expertise, the sources of knowledge are distributed across a great variety of organizations. Strategic alliances are an option that may solve problems of speed or cost in these cases.

Hence, in this chapter we draw on the knowledge-based view and strategic alliances literatures to identify advantages that inter-organizational virtual organizations may have in the creation of knowledge.

The study begins with an overview of virtual organizations and their properties. We then review the idea of strategic alliances and networks as a way of integrating knowledge, explaining their advantages and placing special emphasis on the case of strategic alliances in which the main aim is the joint creation of knowledge between partners and not simply the appropriation of this knowledge by one of the members of the agreement. In the following section, we argue that inter-organizational virtual organizations add

more advantages to this type of alliance because of these special features. The latter two sections include some propositions, and the chapter closes with our conclusions.

VIRTUAL ORGANIZATION

Since the concept of virtual organization was introduced by Mowshowitz (1986) and popularized by Davidow and Malone (1992), it has become increasingly used in management theory and, in particular, in the information systems literature. An initial approach to this term suggests that a virtual organization is a geographically distributed organization whose members are bound by a long-term common interest, and who communicate and coordinate their work through information technologies (Ahuja and Carley, 1999). Computers and information technologies favour the linking of corporate processes (Davidow and Malone, 1992) and the shift towards virtual organizations entails fundamental changes in managing daily operations and coordination tasks.

According to some authors (e.g. Kasper-Fuehrer and Ashkanasy, 2003), there are two approaches to studying virtual organizations, depending on the unit of analysis: the intra-organizational view, in which virtual organization is a collaboration of business units within an organization, or the inter-organizational view, in which different organizations collaborate to form a cooperative agreement. We focus on the second approach since our interest lies in the integration of knowledge through various firms.

Virtual organizations use information technologies such as electronic mail to share information and coordinate their work, and this characteristic enables a group to create and sustain its identity without a shared physical setting (Ahuja and Carley, 1999). The structure of a virtual organization allows a high degree of flexibility, competitiveness and cost efficiency (Fitzpatrick and Burke, 2000). In line with the inter-organizational approach, we consider a virtual corporation as a temporary network of independent companies linked by information technology to share skills and costs or to accomplish other specific objectives (Byrne, 1993). Other definitions exist, but all of them share the idea that a virtual corporation involves a loosely related group of companies formed to enable collaboration toward mutually agreed on goals (Greis and Kasarda, 1997).

Technology allows sharing and communication of information, but virtual organizations also need a high level of trust between individuals involved in the network. As Daniels (1998) states, a cultural network that links people together is perhaps more important than the technology network on its own. Thorne (2004) reflects on some important characteristics of this type of organization: flow of information, permeable internal and external boundaries, shifting work responsibilities, shifting line of authority, and work practices which are more about communication and information than about any material structure. A key feature of virtual alliances or networks is their high degree of adaptability and flexibility (Grabowski and Robert, 1999; Weber, 2002), essential if they are to respond quickly to changes in today's markets.

STRATEGIC ALLIANCES AS A SOURCE OF KNOWLEDGE INTEGRATION

Strategic Alliances

Strategic alliances may be an important source of the distinctive competencies that are at the root of competitive advantages (Ireland, Hitt andVaidyanath, 2002). The knowledge-based view (KBV) has acquired particular weight in strategic alliance research. This approach has highlighted knowledge and learning capabilities as the most valuable assets that partners can obtain or create through strategic alliances. The special-

ized literature has also generally accepted that distinctive competencies in knowledge creation and learning through strategic alliances have a positive effect on business performance (Emden, Yaprak and Cavusgil, 2005; George et al., 2001; Shrader, 2001; Dyer and Singh, 1998; Simonin, 1997; Powell, Koput and Smith-Doerr, 1996).

The aim of strategic alliances may be to develop necessary resources or capabilities jointly or to gain access to them when other partners have complementary and valuable assets (Hamel, Doz and Prahalad, 1989; Buckley and Casson, 1988). Access to certain resources or capabilities lacking in the cooperating companies is an important underlying factor in the establishment of strategic alliances (Ireland, Hitt and Vaidyanath, 2002; Harrison et al., 2001; Rothaermel, 2001; Das and Teng, 2000; Gulati, 1999; Dyer and Singh, 1998; Madhok and Tallman, 1998; Eisenhardt and Schoonhoven, 1996; Glaister and Buckley, 1996; Grant, 1996; Mitchell and Singh, 1996; Crossan and Inkpen, 1994).

Firms decide to stablish a strategic alliance when they find themselves in a vulnerable strategic position because they need resources or capabilities that cannot be developed internally at a reasonable cost in a reasonable time (Das and Teng, 2000), or cannot be achieved through an exchange on the market (Eisenhardt and Schoonhoven, 1996) because there are no organized markets in which they can be acquired, or because these capabilities can be learned or assimilated through cooperation (Ireland, Hitt and Vaidyanath, 2002; Cohen and Levinthal, 1990). Companies that need particular assets that they cannot efficiently transfer on markets or develop internally will seek alternative means of obtaining them. Strategic alliances appear especially attractive as they are a fast, flexible method and also involve a much lower commitment in terms of cost and resources than other possible options such as mergers.

Environmental uncertainty in today's markets and rapidly changing technologies need quick responses, which are more easily achieved through the establishment of strategic alliances than in isolation (Dodgson, 1993).

Through the extension and combination of the partner firms' assets, strategic alliance partners are able to learn by establishing valuable assets that can lead to sustainable competitive advantages, and therefore to economic rents (Ireland, Hitt and Vaidyanath, 2002; George et al., 2001; Shrader, 2001; Dyer andSingh, 1998; Simonin, 1997; Powell, Koput and Smith-Doerr, 1996). In this way, companies can create greater value through cooperation than that which they could generate by acting independently.

Alternatives in the Integration of Knowledge

Integration of knowledge is a capability that may be developed in the context of a strategic alliance.

According to the knowledge-based view, organization is a distributed system of knowledge (Tsoukas, 1996). Kogut and Zander (1992) advance the idea that the justification for the existence of organizations lies in the frame that these provide– like social communities of actions constructed on organizational principles, which cannot be provided by isolated individuals. The creation and transference of knowledge occurs efficiently within the organization (Kogut and Zander, 1992). Therefore, the main aim of organizations and the reason for their existence is the integration of knowledge (Grant, 1996). This is due to the fact that knowledge is stored in the individuals in the shape of specialized knowledge, which allows the creation of new knowledge to advance.

Nevertheless, progress in the creation of value through processes of transformation of knowledge into new products and services requires a combination of more than one type of specialized knowledge. Individuals have limits to make this knowledge integration.. Integration into the

market is also problematic, due to difficulties in appropriating explicit knowledge by means of market contracts, or in transference of tacit knowledge, since it requires specific transactions associated with major investments.

The organization has also been considered as a community of practice where collective knowledge is absorbed (Brown and Duguid, 1991; Lave and Wegner, 1992). This is also similar to the notion proposed by Tsoukas (1996) in which the organization is a distributed system of knowledge. This author believes that it is a distributed system, not only because it is diffused in the organization, but also because it is indeterminate. The evolution of the system cannot advance, and moreover, it is dependent on the context. Nonaka, Toyama and Nagata (2000) also argue that continuous creation of knowledge is the main aim of an organization.

Nevertheless, this approach proposes that strategic alliances and networks also constitute a mechanism for integration of knowledge (Grant, 1996). Grant (1996) justifies the existence of strategic alliances and networks in the creation of knowledge, in some situations. The first of these refers to the transference of explicit knowledge that is not absorbed in specific products, and therefore, cannot be transferred across the market, yet due to uncertainty over its use and sources, neither can it be efficiently created internally. Secondly, an efficient utilization of knowledge requires a correspondence between knowledge and how it can be used, that is to say, how it develops firms' products (Grant, 1996).

When the company's knowledge base does not match its product portfolio, or when uncertainty surrounds the relation between the two, collaboration between organizations will be an efficient mechanism for the integration of knowledge (Grant, 1996). This is because collaboration enables specialized knowledge to be utilized, since different organizations with different knowledge bases may find it easier to apply this specialized knowledge and also find more connections between new knowledge and products that can be developed through this knowledge. The third situation that justifies collaboration in this context is when the speed of innovation is an important factor in competition. In rapidly changing environments, collaboration provides a faster way of innovating (Grant, 1996).

The importance of the time factor means internal development is not viable and the acquisition and merger option can turn out to be more expensive than alliances as there is a high degree of uncertainty over what is being acquired (Deeds and Rothaermel, 2003; Lambe and Spekman, 1997). The appropriation or imitation of tacit knowledge, such as technological know-how, is practically impossible mainly because there are no organized markets in which firms can acquire it, and because of the causal ambiguity and social complexity on which knowledge is based. In these conditions, strategic alliances are the main vehicle through which the company can access and internalize external knowledge (Das and Teng, 2000; Kogut, 1988). This value increases when the competencies are heterogeneous among the companies taking part in the agreement (Sakakibara, 1997). Grant (1996) indicates that, under certain circumstances, strategic alliances are the most effective option for integrating knowledge. One situation is- the case where the speed with which the company extends its knowledge is a fundamental issue in creating competitive advantage. Another situation is the case where there is a lack of fit between the knowledge the company has and its product portfolio.

Even if the knowledge the firm needs could be obtained through an exchange in the market, it may be that its value deteriorates notably because it is embedded in either organizational routines or other assets possessed by the organization from which it is difficult to separate (Madhok and Tallman, 1998; Pucik, 1988). One characteristic of organizational know-how is precisely its cumulative nature, and the exchange of know-how among

companies requires long-term relationships to be established (Kogut and Zander, 1992).

Organizations in today's markets need innovation as well as flexibility and efficiency, but they also concentrate their resources on core capabilities. Therefore, self-sufficiency is increasingly difficult (Inkpen, 1996).

Grant (1996) postulates this idea when he states that flexibility is one of the characteristics essential to the integration of knowledge if it is to be capable of creating competitive advantage. Flexibility in the integration of knowledge is the degree to which a firm accesses additional knowledge and re-shapes existing knowledge (Grant, 1996), and it is one of the most important factors for the development of capabilities in hyper-competitive environments. In the search for this flexibility, advantages can be found in integration through collaboration with other organizations in some competitive industries such as biotechnology, since they allow access to a wider range of relations between knowledge and its possible applications. Therefore, collaboration provides a mechanism that will facilitate knowledge integration.

The justification of the superiority of alliances over the market and over a single organization is therefore determined by the existence of imbalances between knowledge and its application, that is to say, products (Grant, 1996). Nevertheless, rather than conditioning efficiency of knowledge creation through inter-organizational collaboration to the situations proposed by Grant (1996) and Grant and Baden-Fuller (2004), we agree with Powell, Koput and Smith-Doerr (1996) that, in rapidly changing environments and in industries with particularly fast technological development, the specialized knowledge necessary to make innovations is distributed across a great variety of organizations. It is difficult for an isolated organization to have all the necessary capabilities to innovate continuously.

This is more evident in high technology industries, where the knowledge needed to produce innovations rapidly and effectively is rarely found in a single, isolated firm. Hence, cooperation arises between companies as a mechanism that increases organizational learning and knowledge (Powell, Koput and Smith-Doerr, 1996; Hamel, 1991; Dogson 1993). Therefore, we propose that organizational collaboration is a mechanism which facilitates knowledge creation in certain circumstances. This idea is shared by some authors who contend that organizational performance and differences between companies cannot be understood nowadays without considering the collaboration and social networks in which they are situated. Gulati, Nohria and Zaheer (2000) analyze how the incorporation of strategic collaboration enriches discussion in different areas of strategic research. Our proposition suggests that external knowledge development through collaboration complements rather than substitutes internal knowledge integration (Powell, Koput and Smith-Doerr, 1996).

Therefore, we put forward the following proposition:

Proposition 1. *In rapidly changing and hyper-competitive environments, knowledge sources are distributed across organizations and the establishment of strategic alliances will provide a superior mechanism that enables the generation of knowledge creation capabilities.*

Specific Learning Alliances

On the other hand, knowledge-related strategic alliances may be established in order to acquire knowledge from the partner or to jointly develop new knowledge. We agree with Grant and Baden-Fuller (2004) when they argue that strategic alliances will be more positive to all of the partners if their aim is to share diverse frameworks of specialized knowledge. Knowledge is distributed between different entities (Powell, Koput and Smith-Doerr, 1996) and the collaboration between them will favour learning (Levinthal and March, 1994). Learning in collaboration will depend on sharing knowledge and also on sharing dynamic capabilities that allow it to be used and exploited (Powell, Koput and Smith-Doerr, 1996).

Alliances whose chief aim is learning have been termed *learning alliances* (Lane and Lubatkin, 1998; Khanna, Gulati and Nohria, 1998). In this type of alliance, the process of establishing and implementing the alliance will be more important than the final result, since this process presents an opportunity for mutual learning (Khanna, Gulati and Nohria, 1998), rather than acting as a passive receptor of the partner's capabilities (Hamel et al., 1989). Joint knowledge creation in the alliance will provide common benefits to partners, as opposed to the private benefits that will be only derive from copying partners' skills for later application in individual operations (Khanna, Gulati and Nohria, 1998). These authors propose the concept of common benefits as those that every alliance partner accumulates from the collective application of the learning that organizations obtain as a consequence of forming part of an alliance (Khanna, Gulati and Nohria, 1998: 195). Hence, they implicitly recognize the joint creation of knowledge, or at least, that both partners learn.

We therefore believe that the purpose of the alliance should be to create new knowledge together, and not to absorb the partner's knowledge. New knowledge arising from the alliance has not previously existed for either of the partners (Phan and Peridis, 2000). This line of research is still in its first stages, since it differs from studies that analyze alliances as a way of accessing the partner's knowledge. These studies do not specifically address the joint creation of knowledge. One of the few studies in this line is by Phan and Peridis (2000) who compare research into acquiring knowledge to single-loop learning, whereas, for new knowledge to be created, double-loop learning should take place.

Double loop or second order learning (Argyris and Schon, 1978, 1996) also changes the paradigms on which organizational thought is based. For this type of learning to occur in alliances, the mental models partners use to resolve problems or to interpret conclusions must be changed. It provides a new way of drawing conclusions and of resolving conflicts in the alliance and therefore, of creating knowledge that will be new for the partners. Lubatkin, Florin and Lane (2001) follow a similar view. They study reciprocal learning, taking as their unit of analysis the two organizations that collaborate on a project rather than only one of the firms. The partners therefore become interdependent. These authors assimilate this type of learning to the concept of double loop learning proposed by Argyris and Schon (1978).

Nevertheless, cooperation across strategic alliances is an organizational learning process through which companies internalize competencies from their partners (Kale, Singh and Permutter, 2000) or configure new knowledge together. It is not unusual to find companies that only take part in strategic alliances to gain access to their partners' knowledge, but make no attempt to integrate this knowledge into their own operations. Therefore, we do not deny the existence of strategic alliances in which the main aim is the transference, acquisition or absorption of knowledge. The type of company that acts in this way may even make up the most numerous group. Lubatkin, Florin and Lane (2001) propose a typology of these types of alliances in which learning is the principal objective, depending on how tacit the knowledge the alliance attempts to create or acquire is, and on how difficult the governance of the alliance is. Reciprocal learning alliances are one of the proposed types: they are characterized by low levels of difficulty in governance and the creation of tacit knowledge. This is the type of alliance in which our interest lies, since our area of study concerns markets characterized by hyper-competition and rapid change. The same authors also argue that this type

of alliance will become more common as a result of global competition, the convergence of technologies and the need to develop capabilities more rapidly. In these circumstances, the absorption of the partner's knowledge, which may frequently be unfamiliar to the firm attempting to absorb this knowledge, may be a slow process.

Therefore, our second proposition is:

Proposition 2. *In environments that demand rapid innovations, all partners in alliances based on the joint creation of knowledge will perform better than those in alliances in which the aim is to absorb knowledge from one of the organizations.*

KNOWLEDGE INTEGRATION THROUGH INTER-ORGANIZATIONAL VIRTUAL ORGANIZATIONS

We now turn to virtual organizations and the advantages this form of virtual collaboration may have in the integration of knowledge.

Information and communication technology is the essential enabler of virtual organizations, defined as a conglomerate of firms that collaborate in a strategic alliance (Kasper-Fuehrer and Ashkanasy, 2004). This technology allows greater flexibility, which is an important characteristic to obtain competitive advantage in dynamic environments. Following the arguments of some authors (e.g., D'Aveni, 1994) who claim that traditional organizational designs such as functional structures are too rigid in today's hyper-competitive markets, new inter-organizational structures need more dynamic and flexible ways of organizing. New information and communication technologies have the particular attributes to support the virtuality of these inter-organizational structures (Scholz, 1996), and add dynamism and flexibility. Temporal and distance barriers can easily be jumped with the use of these new technologies (Byrne et al., 1993; Mowshowithz, 1994; Goldman et al., 1995), which also facilitate global collaboration by allowing organizations to cross distance barriers (Byrne et al., 1993).

As stated above, compared to the option of internal development, strategic alliances are a fast and flexible means to develop new resources, such as knowledge, and have lower costs than other options such as mergers. All of these advantages multiply in the context of inter-organizational virtual organizations, since they have the same properties as a strategic alliance, but with greater flexibility and reduced temporal and spatial barriers.

If strategic alliances are the most effective option to integrate knowledge when speed is a fundamental issue in creating competitive advantage (Grant, 1996), the case of inter-organizational virtual organizations may be even more beneficial. This idea is embraced in our next proposition.

Proposition 3. *Inter-organizational virtual organizations contribute to increase flexibility in the collaboration between organizations and therefore they are superior to other options in the integration of knowledge in rapidly changing and hyper-competitive environments.*

Furthermore, one of the properties of knowledge integration that Grant (1996) explains is flexibility or the degree to which an organization accesses additional knowledge and reconfigures its existing knowledge. Since flexibility is an essential feature of knowledge integration, it must be present in the case of alliances in which the main objective is the creation of knowledge.

In the context of a changing knowledge environment, flexibility is a requirement for the integration of knowledge (Van den Bosch, Volberda and de Boer, 1999) since this context demands that firms have different types of knowledge that are distributed across companies. Through collaboration, organizations can easily create a network between different blocks of knowledge

and gain access to a wider application of this knowledge (Grant, 1996). Inter-organizational virtual organizations facilitate this access because they reduce temporal and spatial barriers.

Individuals from different organizations working together must be also trained to deal with their partners' diverse organizational cultures. This training also enables individuals to break out of the mental prisons that prevent them from adopting an innovative attitude because of an organization's strong identity and values. In this vein, Van den Bosch, Volberda and de Boer (1999) state that a strong culture makes flexibility for knowledge absorption more difficult, a perspective we adopt in the integration of knowledge from different organizations. Furthermore, strong cultures can cause - "xenophobia" (Ouchi, 1981). The wide range of knowledge necessary to create innovations in hyper-competitive environments could be constrained by this strong organizational culture.

In the case of strategic alliances, cultural boundaries must be relaxed in order to deal with other partners. Introducing features from inter-organizational virtual organizations is beneficial to the day-to-day working with different organizational cultures. The reasoning here is that individuals become used to the way other organizations do things if communication and information technologies connect these daily operations easily, without considering spatial barriers.

Therefore, we make the following proposition:

Proposition 4. *Flexibility in the integration of knowledge is facilitated by inter-organizational virtual organizations due to their easy access to global collaboration without temporal and spatial barriers.*

CONCLUSION

This study examines virtual organizations from an inter-organizational point of view. Connections between organizations may be easier through the new communication and information technologies. Employees carry out their daily operations with other organizations without concern for spatial barriers. We apply this idea to strategic alliances since we define virtual organizations as a network of independent companies linked by information technology to share skills and costs or to accomplish specific objectives (Byrne, 1993). In this vein, we argue that the virtual factor may provide strategic alliances with certain advantages, specifically in alliances whose main purpose is knowledge integration.

Knowledge integration is one of the main capabilities that organizations must possess in today's markets (Grant, 1996). Organizations pertaining to high technology industries need to accelerate the speed with which they introduce innovations in the market in order to survive in hyper-competitive environments. Nevertheless, sources of knowledge are often distributed across a great variety of organizations. We propose that strategic alliances are a superior mechanism that enables the creation of new knowledge in this type of environment. We also argue that the advantage could be even greater in the case of alliances in which the main aim is the joint creation of knowledge, as compared to other kinds of agreements in which one partner absorbs knowledge from other partners. Common benefits to all of the partners may be higher if their objective is mutual learning and creating new knowledge (Khanna, Gulati and Nohria, 1998) as a consequence of being part of the alliance because of the distribution of expertise across organizations.

In high technology industries, inter-organizational virtual organizations add further advantages to this option of knowledge integration through strategic alliances because of the importance of speed and flexibility. Moreover, one of the properties or dimensions in the integration of knowledge according to Grant (1996) is the flexibility or the degree in which an organization accesses additional knowledge and reconfigures its existing knowledge. We also argue that inter-organizational virtual organizations facilitate this knowledge reconfiguration because they reduce temporal and spatial barriers.

Implications for managers concern the option of considering this kind of inter-organizational virtual agreement as an alternative and an opportunity to integrate knowledge faster than in isolation. This is an important strategic decision that they should bear in mind. Where their organizations participate in this type of collaboration, they should also consider changing the way daily operations are undertaken, and the fact that these changes can have both positive and negative effects.

Our study has some limitations derived from its theoretical nature. We cannot confirm and generalize our arguments without testing the propositions through an empirical study. A deeper analysis is therefore required in order to prove whether the advantages of strategic alliances over other alternatives consist of superior forms of organizing in the case of knowledge integration in high technology industries and whether including the virtual dimension in these linkages adds even more advantages. Further research should also extract and contrast the true, specific characteristics of inter-organizational virtual organizations as compared to traditional strategic alliances and what their possible strengths may be. However, this is an initial approach to the phenomenon from a point of view in which we combine strategic alliances, virtual organizations and knowledge-based view literatures.

REFERENCES

Ahuja, M.K., & Carley, K.M. (1999). Newtork structure in virtual organizations. *Organization Science,* 10 (6), 741-757.

Argyris, C., & Schön, D. (1978). *Organizational learning: a theory of action perspective.* Mass: Addison-Wesley, Reading.

Argyris, C., & Schon, D. (1996). *Organizational learning II. Theory, method and practice.* Mass: Addison-Wesley, Reading.

Brown, J.S., & Duguid, P. (1991). Organizational learning and communities-of-practice: toward a unified view of working, learning, and innovation. *Organization Science,* 2 (1), 40-57.

Buckley, P.J., & Casson, M. (1988). A theory of cooperation in international business. In F.J. Contractor, & P. Lorange (eds.), *Cooperative strategies in international business* (pp. 31-54). Lexington: Lexington Books.

Byrne, J. (1993). The virtual corporation. *Business Week,* 8, 98-102.

Cohen, W.M., & Levinthal, D.A. (1990). Absorptive capacity, a new perspective on learning and innovation. *Administrative Science Quarterly,* 35 (1), 128-152.

Crossan, M.M., & Inkpen, A.C. (1994). Promise and reality of learning through alliances. *The International Executive,* 36 (3), 263-274.

D'Aveni, R. (1994). *Hypercompetition: Managing the Dynamics of Strategic maneuvering.* Free Press, New York.

Das, T.K., & Teng, B. (2000). A resource-based theory of strategic alliances. *Journal of Management,* 26 (1), 31-61.

Davidow, W., & Malone, M. (1992). *The virtual corporation: structuring and revilatizing the corporatin for the 21st Century.* New York: Harper Collins.

Daniels, M. (1998). Focussing in a fuzzy world: trading in the networking world. *Journal of Information System,* 24 (6), 451-456.

Dyer, J.H., & Singh, H. (1998). The relational view, Cooperative strategy and sources of inter-organizational competitive advantage. *Academy of Management Review,* 23 (4), 660-679.

Eisenhardt, K.M., & Schoonhoven, C.B. (1996). Resource-based view of strategic alliance formation, Strategic and social effects entrepreneurial firms. *Organization Science,* 7 (2), 136-150.

Emden, Z., Yaprak, A., & Cavusgil, S.T. (1998). Learning from experience in international alliances, antecedents and firm performance implications. *Journal of Business Research,* 58 (7), 883-892.

Fitzpatrick, W.M., & Burke, D.R. (2000). Form, functions, and financial performance realities for the virtual organization. *SAM Advanced Management Journal,* 65 (3), 13-22.

George, G., Zahra, S.A., Wheatley, K.K., & Khan, R. (2001). The effects of alliance portfolio characteristics and absortive capacity on performance. A study of biotechnology firms. *Journal of High Technology,* 12, 208-226.

Glaister, K.W., & Buckley, P.J. (1996). Strategic motives for international alliance formation. *Journal of Management Studies,* 33 (3), 301-332.

Grabowski, M., & Roberts, K.H. (1999). Risk mitigation in virtual organizations. *Organization Science,* 10, 704-721.

Grant (1996). Prospering in dynamically-competitive environments: organizational capability as knowledge integration. *Organization Science,* 7, 375-387.

Grant, R. M., & Baden-Fuller, C. (2004). A knowledge accessing theory of strategic alliances. *Journal of Management Studies,* 41(1), 61-85.

Greis, N.P., & Kasarda, J.D. (1997). Enterprise logistics in the information era. *California Management Review,* 39 (3), 55-78.

Gulati, R. (1999). Network location and learning, the influence of network resources and firm capabilities on alliance formation. *Strategic Management Journal*, 20, 397-420.

Gulati, R., Nohria, N., & Zaheer, A. (2000). Strategic networks. *Strategic Management Journalk,* vol. 21, n.3, 203-217.

Hamel, G. (1991). Competition for competence and interpartner learning within international strategic alliances. *Strategic Management Journal*, vol. 12, 83-103.

Hamel, G., Doz, Y.L., & Prahalad, C.K. (1989).Collaborate with your competitors and win. *Harvard Business Review,* 67 (1), 133-139.

Harrison, J.S., Hitt, M.A., Hoskisson, R.E., & Ireland, R.D. (2001). Resource complementarity in business combinations, extending the logic to organizational alliances. *Journal of Management,* 27, 679-690.

Inkpen, A.C. (1996). Creating knowledge trough collaboration. *California Management Review,* 39 (1), 123-140.

Ireland, R.D., Hitt, M.A., & Vaidyanath, D. (2002). Alliance management as a source of competitive advantage. *Journal of Management*, 28 (3), 413-446.

Kale, P., Singh, H., & Perlmutter, H. (2000). Learning and protection of proprietary assets in strategic alliances, Building relational capital. *Strategic Management Journal*, 21, 217-237.

Kasper-Fuehrer, E.C., & Ashkanasy, N.M. (2004). The interorganizational virtual organization. *International Studies of Management and Organization,* 33 (4), 34-64.

Khanna, T., Gulati, R., & Nohria, N. (1998). The dynamics of learning alliances: Competition, Cooperation, and relative scope. *Strategic Management Journal*, vol. 19, n.3, 193-212.

Kogut, B. (1988). Joint ventures: theoretical and empirical perspectives. *Strategic Management Journal*, 9 (4), 319-333.

Kogut, B., & Zander, U. (1992). Knowledge of the firm, combinative capabilities, and the replication of technology. *Organization Science*, 3 (3), 383-397.

Lave, J. and Wenger, E. (1992). *Situated Learning: Legitimate Peripheral Participation.* Mass: Harvard U. Press.

Lane, P.J., & Lubatkin, M. (1998). Relative absorptive capacity and interorganizational learning. *Strategic Management Journal*, 19 (5), 461-477.

Madhok, A., & Tallman, S. (1998). Resources, transactions and rents, managing value through interfirm collaborative relationships. *Organization Science*, 9 (3), 326-339.

Mitchell, W., & Singh, K. (1996). Survival of business using collaborative relationships to commercialize complex goods. *Strategic Management Journal*, 17, 169-195.

Mowshowith, A. (1986). Social dimensions of office automation. In M. Yovitz, *Advances in Computers (v.25)*. New York: Academic Press.

Nonaka, I. (1994). A dynamic theory of organizational knowledge creation. *Organization Science,* 5 (1), 14-37.

Nonaka, I., & Takeuchi, H. (1995). *The knowledge-creating company.* New York: Oxford University Press.

Nonaka, I., Toyama, R., & Nagata, A. (2000). A firm as a knowledge creating entity: a new perspective on the theory of the firm. *Industrial and Corporate Change*, 9 (1), 1-20.

Ouchi, W.G. (1981). *Theory Z: How American business can meet the Japanese challenge.* Reading, MA: Addison-Wesley.

Powell, W.W., Koput K.W., & Smith-Doerr, L. (1996). Interorganizational collaboration and the locus of innovation, networks of learning in biotechnology. *Administrative Science Quarterly*, 41 (1), 116-145.

Pucik, V. (1988). Strategic alliances, organizational learning and competitive advantage: the HRM agenda. *Human Resource Management*, vol. 27, n. 1, 77-94.

Rothaermel, F.T. (2001). Incumbent's advantage through exploiting complementary assets via interfirm cooperation. *Strategic Management Journal*, 22, 687-699.

Sakakibara (1997). Heterogeneity of firm capabilities and cooperative research an development: an empirical examination of motives. *Strategic Management Journal*, vol. 18, n. 6, 143-165.

Shrader, R.C. (2001). Collaboration and performance in foreign markets, the case of young high-technology manufacturing firms. *Academy of Management Journal*, 44 (3), 45-60.

Simonin, B.L. (1997). The importance of collaborative know-how, an empirical test of the learning organization. *Academy of Management Journal*, 4 (5), 1150.

Spender, J.C. (1996). Making knowledge the basis of a dynamic theory of the firm. *Strategic Management Journal*, 17 (Winter Special Issue), 45-62.

Tsoukas, H. (1996). The firm as a distributed knowledge system: a constructionist approach. *Strategic Management Journal*, 17 (Winter Special Issue), 11-25.

Van den Bosch, F.A.J., Volberda, H.W., & de Boer, M. (1999). Coevolution of firm absortive capacity and knowledge environment: organizational forms and combinative capabilities. *Organization Science*, 10 (5), 551-568.

Weber, M.M. (2002). Measuring supply chain agility in the virtual organization. *International Journal of Physical Distribution & Logistics Management,* 32 (7), 577-590.

ENDNOTE

[a] The present study is part of a wider research project, which has received financial support through a grant (SEC2003-01825/ECO) from the Spanish Ministry of Science and Technology and FEDER (European Fund for Regional Development) and from the Valencian Institute of Economic Research (Convocatoria de a yudas a la investigación 2006).

Section III
Knowledge Management in Virtual Organizations

Knowledge Management offers a solid theoretical ground for tackling some of the social and cultural problems in networking, especially those related with knowledge creation and sharing. These three chapters adopt this view for the study of virtual organizations and their possible forms of management.

Chapter V
Visualizing Knowledge Networks and Flows to Enhance Organizational Metacognition in Virtual Organizations

Mark E. Nissen
Naval Postgraduate School, USA

ABSTRACT

In today's increasingly networked world of organizational practice, information and computer technologies are enabling people and organizations to collaborate ever more virtually (i.e., even when distributed temporally and geographically). Despite the clear and many advantages enabled by the virtual organization, this increasingly common virtual organizational form is very demanding in terms of Knowledge Management. The key problem is that many otherwise knowledgeable people and organizations are not fully aware of their knowledge networks, and even more problematic, they are not aware that they are not aware. Thus organizational metacognition (e.g., an organization knowing what it knows) offers the potential to elucidate the key issues associated with knowledge networking in the virtual organization. The research described in this chapter builds upon a stream of work to understand and harness dynamic knowledge and organization for competitive advantage, with a particular emphasis upon knowledge networks and flows in the virtual organizational context.

INTRODUCTION

In the increasingly networked world of organizational practice today, information and computer technologies are enabling people and organizations to collaborate ever more closely, even when distributed temporally and geographically. Indeed, organizations themselves are becoming increasingly virtual (e.g., see Davidow and Malone, 1992; Wong and Burton 2000): forming across formal organizational boundaries, national borders, cultures, specializations and time zones to collaborate on the accomplishment of projects that require specific mixes of expertise that the various participants possess (e.g., see Nissen, 2007).

Shekhar (2006) reviews substantial literature on virtual organizations, including a variety of definitions: "a temporary network of independent companies" (Byrne, 1993), "a bundle of competencies [. . .] pulled together to deliver a value" (Donlon, 1997), "an opportunistic alliance of core competencies" (Goldman et al., 1995), "an ever-varying cluster of common activities in the midst of a vast fabric of relationships" (Davidow and Malone, 1992), "a way of structuring, managing and operating dynamically" (Mowshowitz, 1997), and "organization in which workers are not physically but electronically connected" (Fulk and DeSanctis, 1995). Common among these is a focus on competencies and activities that are combined and managed at a distance (e.g., electronically), beyond the authority of a single organization (e.g., independent companies), and that involve dynamic interrelationships between participants (e.g., temporary network). This leads to (p. 468) a working definition that is suitable for our purposes here: *"...any organization with non-co-located organizational entities and resources, necessitating the use of virtual space for interaction between the people in these entities to achieve organizational objectives."*

By accessing, linking and coordinating the competencies and activities of multiple organizations, the virtual organization is able to increase the scope of its endeavors without the need to invest in and grow the requisite expertise internally. This can be particularly important in knowledge-intensive competitive arenas, in which opportunities are ephemeral, but the tacit knowledge required to seize such opportunities requires years if not decades to accumulate. Whereas a single firm,

for instance, which lacked such tacit knowledge, would be unable to take advantage of a knowledge-intensive opportunity within the time allowed by competitive pressure, this firm could team with one or more others, which had accumulated the requisite knowledge, and compete. Hence the virtual organization offers potential advantages in terms of the speed with which organizations can respond to ephemeral opportunities. Additionally, by teaming with one or more other firms, the resulting virtual organization would distribute the cost and risk of pursuing such opportunity effectively among each of the participating firms. Hence the virtual organization offers potential advantages also in terms of the cost and risk associated with responding to ephemeral opportunities.

Despite the clear and many advantages enabled by the virtual organization, however, this increasingly common, virtual, organizational form is inherently very demanding in terms of Knowledge Management (KM). This is the case in particular where knowledge-intensive opportunities are pursued: the same access to and integration of knowledge across participants that offers potential for competitive advantage to the virtual organization also requires identification, organization, sharing and application of such knowledge from different organizations. This serves to exacerbate a well-known KM problem that is severe even within single organizations (e.g., see Kogut and Zander, 1992; Szulanski and Winter, 2002). The problem exacerbation is even more pronounced where the key knowledge required to be access and shared across organizations is tacit: tacit knowledge is notably "sticky" (von Hippel, 1994), appropriable (Grant, 1996) and difficult to codify, substitute or imitate (Saviotti, 1998). Hence to realize the potential opportunities enabled by virtual organizations, its inherent and exacerbated KM demands must be met.

Knowledge networking becomes critically important in this context of the virtual organization. The term networking implies that the diverse chunks of knowledge are linked together—even loosely and informally—so that they can be identi-fied, accessed, integrated and applied across the various organizational participants. In order to do this in a timely manner (i.e., the central point of the virtual organization), participants must develop the means to identify and access the knowledgeable people, processes and technologies that are distributed across both time and space as well as organizational members. The problem is, many otherwise knowledgeable people and orga-nizations are not fully aware of their knowledge networks. Although the knowledge is networked, the people who need to identify and access such knowledge do not understand the corresponding knowledge network sufficiently well to utilize it. This can undermine any potential advantages sought through virtual organization. Even more problematic, knowledgeable people and organiza-tions are not aware that they are not aware. Hence participants in a virtual organization may not even realize the need for or importance of learning about the knowledge network. In essence, such virtual organization does not know what it knows, and does not know that it does not know.

Organizational metacognition focuses on an organization learning and knowing what it knows. Investigation of this phenomenon offers potential to elucidate the key issues associated with knowledge networking in the virtual orga-nization. The research described in this chapter builds upon a stream of work to understand and harness dynamic knowledge and organization for competitive advantage, with a particular emphasis upon knowledge networks and flows in the virtual organizational context. Specifically, we draw from emerging knowledge-flow theory and techniques to model and visualize knowledge networks and flows, and we leverage recent fieldwork to illus-trate the potential of enhancing organizational metacognition through visualization of knowledge networks and flows. This chapter makes a research contribution through articulation of a powerful and expressive theoretical framework with high applicability to the investigation of KM in virtual organizations. It also illustrates the use and util-ity of such framework through application in the field. In turn this leads to a practical contribution by demonstrating how the leader or manager can turn to organizational metacognition in his or her organization to learn to know and use the corresponding knowledge networks.

BACKGROUND

This section draws heavily from Looney and Nissen (2007) to provide background informa-tion pertaining to organizational metacognition. Metacognition implies thinking about thinking or knowing about knowing. In the field of cogni-tive psychology, metacognition has been studied for some time (e.g., see Metcalf and Shimamura, 1994), but its investigation has been limited ex-clusively to the individual level of analysis. How-ever, understanding the concepts and principles that are important for Knowledge Management (KM), at the enterprise level, requires rising above this individual level of analysis. For instance, concepts such as *organizational cognition* (Lant and Shapira, 2001), *organizational memory* (Stein and Zwass, 1995; Walsh and Ungson, 1991), and *organizational learning* (Argyris and Schon, 1978; Levitt and March, 1988) rise above such individual-level study accordingly, and address phenomena such as *cognition, memory* and *learning* at the organization level directly. This work implies that there is more to organizational cognition, memory and learning than the sums of the cognitions, memories and learning of the individual people who work in an organization (cf. Simon, 1991). For instance, Nelson and Win-ter (1982) and Weick and Roberts (1993) make convincing arguments about how organizational routines and like patterns of collective action re-flect knowledge beyond the sum of the individuals engaged in the routines.

Further, scholars have succeeded in building upon and leveraging individual-level concepts and principles to inform and guide organization-level conceptualization and understanding. Work on absorptive capacity (Cohen and Levinthal, 1990) provides an exemplar. For instance, an individual-level principle such as, *the more that one knows about a topic, the easier it is for him or her to learn about that topic*, is applied convincingly at the organizational level, and empirical support (see Nissen, 2006b) in terms of firms entering competitive arenas at different times (e.g., one firm gets a head start) provides some evidence regarding the utility of this approach.

Hence organizational memory and organizational learning can be viewed as more than simple metaphors for individual-level cognitive behaviors envisioned to take place at the organizational level. Rather, organizational memory and organizational learning are viewed through this lens as organization-level phenomena directly. A substantial part of the KM literature ascribes to this view, and the research described in this chapter is viewed best as extending such literature to address metacognition as an organization-level phenomenon. Building upon individual-level metacognition (e.g., as with absorptive capacity noted above), we interpret organizational metacognition to mean an organization knowing what an organization knows. With a great part of organizational knowledge—particularly experience-based tacit knowledge—resident within networks of people and organizations, this is where we look for evidence and effects of organizational metacognition in the enterprise.

KNOWLEDGE-FLOW ANALYSIS AND VISUALIZATION

Nissen (2006a) describes the concept *knowledge flows* in terms of dynamic knowledge, and indicates that it subsumes similar concepts such as *knowledge conversion, transfer, sharing, integration, reuse* and others that depict changes, movements and applications of knowledge over time. Drawing directly from Nissen (2007), we organize this discussion into four parts: (1) knowledge uniqueness, (2) knowledge flows, (3) knowledge dimensions and visualization, and (4) knowledge-flow analysis.

Knowledge Uniqueness

In this characterization, *knowledge* is conceptually distinct from *information, data* and *signals*: knowledge enables direct action (e.g., decisions, behaviors, work); information provides meaning and context for action (e.g., decision criteria, behavioral stimuli, work settings); data answer context-specific questions (e.g., How much profit is expected by selecting Alternative A? Who says that we should honor our commitments to the workers? How many industrial accidents have occurred so far this year?); and signals transmit detectable events across physical space (e.g., light patterns from pages in a book, sound waves from voices in a room, voltage differences across cables in a computer network).

Many scholars (e.g., Davenport and Prusak, 1998; Nissen et al., 2000; von Krogh et al., 2000) conceptualize a hierarchy of knowledge, information, and data. As illustrated in Figure 1, each level of the hierarchy builds upon the one below. For example, data are required to produce information, but information involves more than just data (e.g., need to have the data in context). Similarly, information is required to produce knowledge, but knowledge involves more than just information (e.g., it enables action). We operationalize the irregular shape of this hierarchy using two dimensions—*abundance* and *actionability*—to differentiate among the three constructs.

Briefly, data lie at the bottom level, with information in the middle and knowledge at the top. The broad base of the triangle reflects the abundance of data, with exponentially less information available than data and even fewer chunks of knowledge in any particular domain. Thus, the width of the shape at each level reflects decreasing abundance in the progress from data to knowledge. The height of the shape at each level reflects actionability (i.e., the ability to take appropriate action, such as a good decision, effective behavior or useful work). Converse to their abundance, data are not particularly powerful for supporting action, and information is more powerful than data are, but knowledge supports action directly, hence its position at the top of the shape.

Notice that we position tacit knowledge "above" its explicit counterpart in this figure. Tacit knowledge is characterized widely as being very rich in terms of enabling action, whereas explicit knowledge represents often a diluted formalization of its tacit counterpart, with many properties and behaviors that are similar to those of information (see Nissen, 2006a for elaboration). Further, unlike explicit knowledge, which must by definition be formalized, articulated or otherwise made explicit (e.g., via books, graphs, charts, software), and hence is somewhat limited in abundance, tacit knowledge accumulates naturally (e.g., through direct experiences and observations of people), and is quite abundant. This is the basis for the irregular shape depicted in the figure.

Knowledge Flows

In terms of knowledge flows (e.g., movements of knowledge across people, organizations, places and times), the two connected knowledge hierarchies depicted in Figure 2 illustrate some key concepts. On the left side, we see a producer's or source's knowledge hierarchy, and on the right side, we see a knowledge consumer's or receiver's hierarchy. Both of these knowledge hierarchies conform to the characterization above (e.g., abundance vs. actionability, layers building upon one another, distinct concepts, irregular shape). The producer hierarchy includes an arrow pointed downward (i.e., from knowledge, through information, to data), and the consumer hierarchy includes an arrow pointed upward. This depicts

Figure 1. Knowledge hierarchy (adapted from Nissen 2006b)

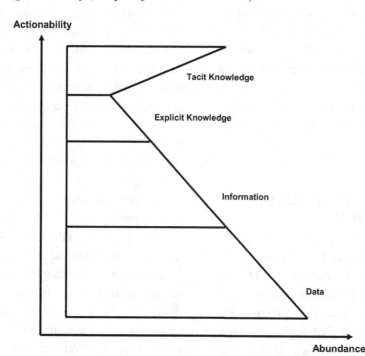

Figure 2. Knowledge flows (adapted from Nissen 2006b)

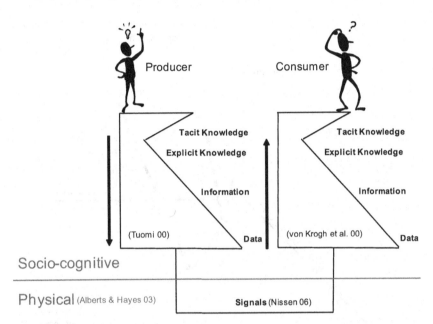

the relative direction of knowledge as it flows from producer to consumer.

Specifically, following Tuomi (2000), the producer utilizes existing knowledge to create information, which is used in turn to produce data, which are transmitted via signals across some physical space. Then, following von Krogh et al. (2000), the consumer interprets the data from signals, develops information through incorporation of meaning and context, and finally develops actionable knowledge through some learning mechanism. Of course, the directionality of arrows can reverse (i.e., a "producer" can become a "consumer," and vice versa), and multiple knowledge hierarchies can participate simultaneously, but this provides a phenomenological description of how knowledge flows. Notice that only signals are involved with flows across physical space; following Alberts and Hayes (2003), flows of data, information and knowledge take place in the socio-cognitive domain.

Knowledge Dimensions and Visualization

Figure 3 depicts a multidimensional space to visualize dynamic knowledge flows. Briefly, the vertical axis represents the dimension *explicitness*, which characterizes the degree to which knowledge has been articulated in explicit form. This dimension draws from the Spiral Model (Nonaka, 1994), and includes a binary contrast between tacit and explicit knowledge. The horizontal axis represents the dimension *reach*, which characterizes the level of social aggregation associated with knowledge flows. This dimension draws from the Spiral Model also, and includes several ordinal categories of social aggregation (e.g., individual, group, organization). The third axis represents the dimension *life cycle*, which characterizes the kind of activity associated with knowledge flows. This dimension represents an extension to the Spiral Model (see Nissen, 2002), and includes several

Figure 3. Multidimensional knowledge-flow visualization (adapted from Nissen 2006b)

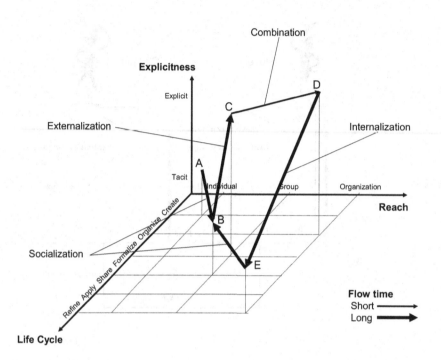

nominal categories of life cycle activity (e.g., create, share, apply). Together, these axes combine to form a three-dimensional space. We include the fourth dimension *flow time,* which pertains to the length of time required for knowledge to move from one coordinate in this three-dimensional space to another. This dimension represents an extension to the Spiral Model also, and includes a binary contrast between relatively long (i.e., slow) and short (i.e., fast) knowledge flows. Because visualization in four dimensions does not come naturally to most people, we use arrows of different thickness (e.g., thick for slow flows, thin for fast flows) when delineating various knowledge-flow vectors.

For instance in the figure, these four dimensions are used to visualize the kinds of patterns associated with the Spiral Model. Each vector in this loop corresponds to one of four knowledge-flow processes articulated in the model

(i.e., *socialization, externalization, combination, internalization*). We begin at Point A, representing tacit knowledge created by an individual. The socialization flow (A-B) reflects a movement of tacit knowledge across the reach dimension to the group level. The externalization flow (B-C) reflects a movement from tacit to explicit knowledge at this group level. The combination flow (C-D) reflects in turn a movement of explicit knowledge across the reach dimension to the organization level. In terms of flow time, notice that we use a thinner arrow to represent this combination flow, as only explicit knowledge—which is not as "sticky" as tacit knowledge is (see von Hippel, 1994 Nissen et al., 2000)—is involved. Penultimately, the internalization flow (D-E) reflects a movement from explicit to tacit knowledge at this organization level. Finally, we include a (reverse) socialization flow from Points E to B (i.e., tacit knowledge moving from the organization to the group level) to complete the one loop. Clearly, myriad other knowledge flows can be represented in this manner, but this single loop is representative of the technique, and it provides an illustration of how the four knowledge dimensions can be integrated into a single figure for flow visualization.

Knowledge-Flow Analysis

Finally, knowledge-flow analysis utilizes the multidimensional visualization space from above. To re-iterate, *knowledge* does not represent a single, monolithic concept. Different kinds of knowledge (e.g., in various parts of the multidimensional knowledge-flow space) have different properties and behaviors. Indeed, one can identify at least 96 (2 levels of *explicitness* x 4 levels of *reach* x 6 levels of *life cycle* x 2 levels of *flow time*) theoretically distinct kinds of knowledge, each potentially with its own, unique set of properties and behaviors. Hence the position of a particular knowledge flow within this multidimensional space would appear to be important, and such position can be used for knowledge-flow analysis.

For instance, notice that all but one of the knowledge-flow vectors represented in Figure 3 are depicted using relatively thick lines to designate long flow times (i.e., slow flows), and that all such vectors involve flows of tacit knowledge. Drawing from knowledge-flow principles (see Nissen, 2006b), we understand that "sticky," tacit knowledge flows relatively slowly, and that such flows are constrained generally to individuals, dyads and small groups. Take, for example, the kind of trial-and-error learning associated generally with experience-based knowledge; it takes people years, and even decades, to master certain domains via experience, and learning such experience-based, tacit knowledge represents largely an individual endeavor.

However, as noted above, tacit knowledge is very rich in terms of enabling action, with many actions (e.g., riding a bicycle, negotiating a contract, conducting qualitative research) de-pendent upon experience-based tacit knowledge for effective performance. Hence tacit knowledge flows tend to be limited to a specific portion of the multidimensional space depicted above (i.e., the tacit end of *explicitness,* the individual range of *reach*, and the long end of *flow time*), but it is rich in terms of enabling action. Alternatively, explicit knowledge flows have contrasting properties and behaviors: they flow relatively quickly and broadly, yet become diluted, and are limited in terms of enabling action (e.g., consider attempting to ride a bicycle, negotiate a contract, or conduct qualitative research based *solely* upon reading a book about the subject; i.e., with no direct experience to develop tacit knowledge).

If one is interested in moving knowledge from one part of the multidimensional space to another, then one has multiple possible paths for the corresponding knowledge flows to follow. Consider the multidimensional knowledge-flow space depicted in Figure 4. Say that some individual creates new, tacit knowledge (e.g., how to accomplish some useful action), and that the organization is interested in such new knowledge being applied, quickly, organization-wide, say by 100 people who are separated across both time and space in a virtual organization. In the figure, such knowledge would have to flow from Point A to Point B. Consider, however, that such path may be infeasible: the organization may not have a process that enables such tacit knowledge to flow—quickly and directly—from an individual to 100 geographically and temporally distributed people. This is depicted in the figure by the symbol "RIDGE" that blocks such a direct flow.

Instead, we illustrate two, alternate flow paths that the organization could consider. One reflects a thick, curved path that stays within the tacit plane, and which appears to go around the ridge (labeled "Tacit path"). Remaining within the tacit plane as such, this knowledge flow would be relatively slow, but it would retain its richness in terms of enabling action. The corresponding organizational processes could include a series along the lines of: the individual learns (e.g., via trial and error) to apply the new knowledge; then shares such tacit knowledge (e.g., via mentoring) with a small group of colleagues; who participate in turn to mentor other small groups (e.g., in various communities of practice).

Alternatively, the organization could choose instead to formalize the tacit knowledge (e.g., in terms of a classroom course). This formalization is represented by Point C, and is depicted by a relatively thick vector (labeled "tacit-to-explicit path") to indicate slow knowledge flow (e.g., known well through abundant knowledge-formalization research in artificial intelligence), which appears to go over the ridge. Nonetheless, at this point above the tacit plane, the formalized knowledge has been made explicit, and hence can be shared broadly and quickly with many people in the organization (e.g., taking the course). This is represented by Point D, and is depicted by a relatively thin vector to indicate fast knowledge flow. Still, people taking the course would need to internalize the knowledge, and to have it become tacit, before being able to apply it effectively at Point B. Noting the relatively thick arrow depicting

the corresponding knowledge-flow vector, such internalization represents a relatively slow process (e.g., few people emerge from a formal training course as "masters" of the subject studied). Moreover, some question remains as to whether this knowledge—even after being internalized and applied as such—would retain the same degree of action-enabling richness as that flowing along the other path (i.e., within the tacit plane).

Hence one can trade off the relative speed, breadth and dilution of knowledge flowing along this latter, tacit-to-explicit path against the comparatively slow and narrow but rich knowledge flows within the tacit plane. Of course, many other, alternate paths are possible too, and each pair of coordinate points within this multidimensional space offers its own unique set of alternate paths and corresponding tradeoffs. The key is, we have the ability to characterize and visualize a diversity of knowledge flows—taking account of the different properties and behaviors corresponding to various positions within the multidimensional space—and we have a graphical and analytical technique to compare alternate knowledge flows in the organization. This equips us to examine

Figure 4. Best knowledge-flow path analysis (adapted from Nissen 2006b)

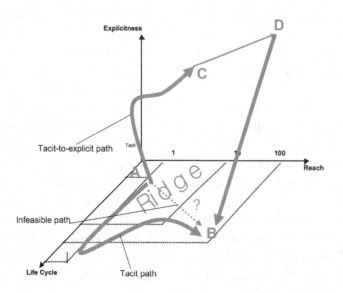

how multidimensional knowledge-flow analysis and visualization can enhance organizational metacognition.

ILLUSTRATION THROUGH FIELDWORK

The focal organization in this study is involved with military planning. The organization is virtual, in that it is comprised of people from multiple, different, formal organizations, who come together—as individuals, groups and whole organizational units—temporarily to accomplish a set of common objectives. Details of the organization can be found in Looney and Nissen (2006).

Research Design

For background, we draw heavily from Looney and Nissen (2006) to summarize the basics of the research design. We designed a qualitative study in the field, through which we immersed ourselves in the organization, processes, people and technology involved with the 2005 Trident Warrior experiment at sea (Woods, 2005). Trident Warrior represents a series of annual field experiments in which military organizations from multiple nations participate collectively in exercises—on land, at sea and in the air—utilizing operational warships and other military weaponry in realistic-yet stylized scenarios. The experimentation series has been the platform for early examination and assessment of novel tactics, techniques, procedures and technologies, set in a "floating laboratory" environment that is manned by real military professionals performing real military activities using real military equipment and methods. Hence results have excellent external validity and generalizability beyond the experimental setting.

The setting for this study covered a ten-day military field experiment, during which we conducted

direct observations and multiple interviews, and administered surveys. The setting provided a high level of fidelity to observe the planning process directly. One of the authors is a Navy Commander, with substantial experience in this domain, which provided both insight and access to the organization and its people and processes. During the experiment, we were allowed unfettered access to observe all planning events. Additionally, we conducted seven extensive interviews with key planning process leaders and executives; four of those interviews were tape recorded and transcribed. We also administered multiple qualitative surveys, and supplemented our observations with dozens of informal conversations. Other sources of data included archival data regarding details of the planning process. All of this data collection was performed in an effort to corroborate what had been observed directly, as well as provide additional insights and perspectives on the planning process, and in particular to investigate the phenomenon *organizational metacognition* in the context of the knowledge network associated with this virtual organization.

Planning Process

The planning process requires integration of knowledge and expertise from across the organization. From a KM perspective, the planning process is focused predominately on *work* flows—producing plans for military operations—without incorporating much opportunity for *knowledge* flows through the organization. Through discussion with planning group members, we observed that they were largely unaware of what people in different organizations knew. Hence they experienced difficulty incorporating knowledge and expertise from throughout the virtual organization. This situation can be visualized via knowledge-flow patterns. For instance, following Nissen (2006b), such patterns have been shown to identify pathological knowledge clumping, clotting and hemorrhaging in the organization. This enables us to provide a diagnostic view of dynamic organizational knowledge, which can shed light on the virtual organization's metacognitive state.

To illustrate in Figure 5, we characterize the key planning knowledge flows through the virtual organization. The diagram in the figure includes the same dimensional axes and layout as outlined above, but here it includes the pattern observed for the planning knowledge flows. In describing this pattern, we begin with an oval shape, set within the tacit plane of the figure, labeled "Individual OP4 work." This depicts the cyclic flow of knowledge associated with an individual with "OP4" knowledge who performs and learns from his or her work in the organization (i.e., plotted at the "Individual" level along the *reach* axis). It represents cyclic interaction between knowledge application (i.e., using knowledge to accomplish work; plotted at the "apply" point along the *life cycle* axis) and creation (i.e., learning from work performance; plotted at the "create" point along the *life cycle* axis). Each individual with such OP4 knowledge would be expected to have a flow similar to this one, and indeed, each distinct kind of knowledge

could be represented as such. This represents the accumulation of planning knowledge by an individual in the virtual organization.

A similar, oval-shape, cyclic pattern set within the tacit plane is labeled "Group teamwork," which reflects this same, repetition-based, doing-learning pattern, but at the group level (i.e., plotted at the "Group" level along the *reach* axis); that is, similar to the manner in which an individual will likely learn through individual work, a group of people is likely to learn through teamwork as a group, and the longer that a (functional) group works together, the greater such group-level learning is likely to be. This represents the accumulation of planning knowledge by the planning group in the virtual organization.

Now for the diagnostics, a two-headed arrow *should* connect these two, cyclic knowledge-flow patterns, and drawing from Nonaka (1994), such arrow would be labeled "Socialization." This would mirror the socialization flow noted above in the Spiral Model, and would be plotted at the "share" point along the *life cycle* axis. It would depict the manner in which—in a "healthy" vir-

Figure 5. Observed planning knowledge flows

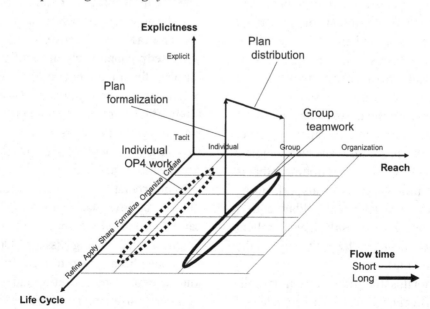

tual organization—an individual would learn to become part of a group, and how a group would learn from the individuals who comprise it. In this observed virtual organization, however, there is no "socialization" vector connecting this individual knowledge flow with the group-level flows of the virtual planning group. Hence the planning group as a whole fails to incorporate the OP4 knowledge, *principally because members were not aware of the OP4 expertise resident within the planning group.*

Returning to the figure, notice how a vertical arrow rises from the oval, group teamwork flow in the tacit plane. It depicts the formalization of group planning knowledge in terms of a formalized, explicit plan (e.g., a planning document), and is plotted at the "formalize" point along the *life cycle* axis. The arrow representing this plan-formalization knowledge flow is depicted using a thinner arrow than those used to depict the other flows. This represents a relatively faster (i.e., shorter *flow time*) flow, for once the group has socialized and learned from its members, and has worked as a planning team, formalization of a particular plan can be accomplished relatively quickly. Another, relatively thin arrow labeled "Plan distribution" stems from this vertical arrow, and depicts the relatively rapid flow of such explicit planning knowledge (e.g., via a planning document) across the organization (i.e., plotted at the "Organization" level of *reach*). At this point, the planning knowledge is explicit, and has been disseminated organization-wide.

In the observed virtual organization, problematically, the associated plan lacked the required breadth of knowledge and expertise that could have been provided by members possessing OP4 knowledge. Through visual examination of this figure, we identify a systemic pathology associated with the pattern of knowledge flows: the knowledge flows do not enable the incorporation of OP4 knowledge into the group planning process. Alternatively, had the people in the virtual planning organization been aware that the orga-

nization possessed OP4 knowledge—that is, had the organization known what it knew—it could have revised its planning process to incorporate members with OP4 knowledge. Indeed, had the people been exposed to the diagram illustrated in Figure 5, they may have been able to see—directly, just as the reader of this chapter can—how the disconnected knowledge flows would cause problems with the planning work. This sheds some light on the issue of organizational metacognition: by visualizing the key knowledge flows through a virtual organization, one can become aware of what the organization knows, and one can leverage such organizational metacognition to intervene in pathological work processes such as the planning effort illustrated above.

CONCLUSION

In the increasingly networked world of organizational practice today, information and computer technologies are enabling people and organizations to collaborate ever more virtually (i.e., even when distributed temporally and geographically). Despite the clear and many advantages enabled by the virtual organization, however, this increasingly common, virtual, organizational form is very demanding in terms of Knowledge Management. The key problem is, many otherwise knowledgeable people and organizations are not fully aware of their knowledge networks, and even more problematic, they are not aware that they are not aware.

In this chapter, we describe how organizational metacognition offers potential to elucidate the key issues associated with knowledge networking in the virtual organization. We build upon a stream of work to understand and harness dynamic knowledge and organization for competitive advantage, with a particular emphasis upon knowledge networks and flows in the virtual organizational context. Drawing upon recent fieldwork pertaining to military planning, we illustrate how knowledge-flow visualization can be used to diagnose pathological, dynamic knowledge patterns in a virtual organization, and articulate how exposing members of the affected organization to such visualization techniques—as an organizational metacognitive enhancement—offers potential for them to intervene to cure such pathological condition.

This chapter makes a research contribution through articulation of a powerful and expressive theoretical framework with high applicability to the investigation of KM in virtual organizations. The knowledge-flow framework for analysis and visualization can be applied to myriad other organizations—conventional and virtual alike—and offers substantial room for extension. For instance, the largely qualitative nature of its principal dimensions (i.e., *explicitness, reach, life cycle*) highlight opportunity to develop more powerful scales (esp. of the interval and ratio types), and as such, the largely heuristic nature of knowledge-flow analysis to date offers potential to be extended to incorporate numerical analysis and possibly even optimization.

The chapter also illustrates the use and utility of the knowledge-flow framework through application in the field. Whereas a great many theoretical frameworks never see or support application, this knowledge-flow framework supports direct observation of organizational metacognition in the field, and it enables practical use to diagnose structural, knowledge-network and -flow problems within the virtual military organization. In turn this leads to a practical contribution by demonstrating how the leader or manager can turn to organizational metacognition in his or her organization to learn to know and use the corresponding knowledge networks. The practicing leader or manager can use the study reported in this chapter to guide analysis, diagnosis and treatment directly in his or her organization, essentially leveraging the benefits of state-of-the-art research to extend the state of the practice in a different application domain. Much more research along these lines

will need to be accomplished, of course, for we are only just beginning to realize the potential of organizational metacognition. Nonetheless, even as such, the potential is compelling.

FUTURE RESEARCH DIRECTIONS

As noted above, much more research along the lines of this investigation will need to be accomplished. Three directions appear to be particularly promising at present. First, we note above how the powerful and expressive theoretical framework has high applicability to the investigation of KM in virtual organizations, and how the knowledge-flow framework for analysis and visualization can be applied to myriad other organizations—conventional and virtual alike. Extending this investigation to address other organizations represents a straightforward and natural direction for future research.

Second, we note above also how more powerful scales (esp. of the interval and ratio types) need to be developed for the knowledge-flow model's principal dimensions (i.e., *explicitness, reach, life cycle*). Such scales would enable quantitative measurement of diverse knowledge flows. This could help research along these lines to advance from descriptive and explanatory toward prescriptive and normative theory, and offers potential to be extended to incorporate numerical analysis and possibly even optimization. Pushing the level of our knowledge and understanding toward such theory, analysis and optimization represents a challenging but exciting direction for future research.

Third, using the knowledge-flow framework articulated in this chapter, connections to and conceptualization of *organizational metacognition* may offer great leverage to understand virtual organizations better. Metacognition has proven to be conceptually powerful in psychology, and it offers great promise in the domain of organizations—particularly virtual organizations. We have only just begun such conceptualization here. Hence future research directions are wide open at present.

REFERENCES

Alberts, D.S. & Hayes, R.E. (2003). *Power to the Edge* Washington, DC: CCRP.

Argyris, C. & Schon, D.A. (1978). *Organizational Learning* Reading, MA: Addison-Wesley.

Byrne, J. (1993), "The virtual corporation", Business Week, pp. 36-41.

Cohen, W.M. & Levinthal, D.A. (1990). Absorptive Capacity: A New Perspective on Learning and Innovation. *Administrative Science Quarterly,* 35, 128-152.

Davenport, T.H. & Prusak, L. (1998). *Working Knowledge: How Organizations Manage what they Know* Harvard Business School Press: Boston, MA.

Davidow, W.H. & Malone, M.S. (1992). *The Virtual Corporation* New York, NY: Harper Business.

Donlon, J.P. (1997). The virtual organization. *Chief Executive* 125, 58-66.

Fulk, J. and DeSanctis, G. (1995). Electronic communication and changing organizational forms. *Organization Science* 6(4), 1-13.

Grant, R.M. (1996). Toward a Knowledge-Based Theory of the Firm. *Strategic Management Journal* 17, Special Issue: Knowledge and the Firm, 109-122.

Kogut, B. and Zander, U. (1992). Knowledge of the Firm, Combinative Capabilities, and the Replication of Technology. *Organization Science* 3(3), 383-397.

Lant, T. & Shapira, Z. (2001). *Organizational Cognition: Computational and Interpretation* Mahwah, NJ: Lawrence Erlbaum Associates.

Levitt, B. & March, J.G. (1988). Organizational Learning. *Annual Review of Sociology,* 14, 319-340.

Looney, J.P. & Nissen, M.E. (2006). Computational Modeling and Analysis of Networked Organizational Planning in a Coalition Maritime Strike Environment. In *Proceedings* 2006 Command and Control Research and Technology Symposium, San Diego, CA.

Looney, J.P. & Nissen, M.E. (2007). Organizational Metacognition: the Importance of Knowing the Knowledge Network. In *Proceedings* Hawaii International Conference on System Sciences, Waikoloa, HI.

Metcalf, J. & Shimamura, A. (Eds.). (1994). *Metacognition: Knowing about Knowing* Cambridge, MA: MIT Press.

Mowshowitz, A. (1997). Virtual organization. *Communications of the ACM* 40(9), 30-7.

Nelson, R.R. and Winter, S. (1982). *An Evolutionary Theory Economic Change* Cambridge, MA: Harvard University Press.

Nissen, M.E. (2007). Knowledge Management and Global Cultures: Elucidation through an Institutional Knowledge-Flow Perspective. *Knowledge and Process Management* 14(3), 211-225.

Nissen, M.E. (2006a). Dynamic Knowledge Patterns to Inform Design: A Field Study of Knowledge Stocks and Flows in an Extreme Organization. *Journal of Management Information Systems*, 22(3), 225-263.

Nissen, M.E. (2006b). *Harnessing Knowledge Dynamics: Principled Organizational Knowing & Learning* Hershey, PA: Idea Group Publishing.

Nissen, M.E. (2002). An Extended Model of Knowledge-Flow Dynamics. *Communications of the Association for Information Systems,* 8(18), 251-266.

Nissen, M.E., Kamel, M.N. & Sengupta, K.C. (2000). Integrated Analysis and Design of Knowledge Systems and Processes. *Information Resources Management Journal,* 13(1), 24-43.

Nonaka, I. (1994). A Dynamic Theory of Organizational Knowledge Creation. *Organization Science,* 5(1), 14-37.

Saviotti, P.P. (1998). On the Dynamics of Appropriability, of Tacit and of Codified Knowledge. *Research Policy* 26, 843-856.

Shekhar, S. (2006). Understanding the virtuality of virtual organizations. *Leadership & Organization Development Journal* 27(6), 465-483.

Simon, H.A. (1991). Bounded Rationality and Organizational Learning. *Organization Science* 2, 125-134.

Stein, E.W. & Zwass, V. (1995). Actualizing Organizational Memory with Information Systems. *Information Systems Research,* 6(2).

Szulanski, *G.* and Winter, S. (Jan 2002). Getting it right the second time. *Harvard Business Review* 80(1), 62-69.

Tuomi, I. (1999). Data is More than Knowledge: Implications of the Reversed Knowledge Hierarchy for Knowledge Management and Organizational Memory. *Journal of Management Information Systems,* 16(3), 103-117.

von Hippel, E. (1994). 'Sticky Information' and the Locus of Problem Solving: Implications for Innovation. *Management Science,* 40(4), 429-439.

von Krogh, G., Ichijo, K. & Nonaka, I. (2000). *Enabling Knowledge Creation: How to Unlock the Mystery of Tacit Knowledge and Release the Power of Innovation* New York, NY: Oxford University Press.

Walsh, J.P. & Ungson, G.R. (1991). Organizational Memory. *Academy of Management Review,* 16(1), 57-91.

Weick, K.E. & Roberts, K.H. (1993). Collective Mind in Organizations: Heedful Interrelating on Flights Decks. *Administrative Science Quarterly,* 38, 357-381.

Woods, R. (2005). *Trident Warrior Experiment Series,* Unpublished briefing by Space and Naval Warfare Systems Command (SPAWAR); http://enterprise.spawar.navy.mil/UploadedFiles/TridentWarriorExperimentSeries.pdf .

Chapter VI
Model on
Knowledge–Governance:
Collaboration Focus and
Communities of Practice

Eduardo Bueno Campos
University of Madrid, Spain

Carlos Merino Moreno
University of Madrid, Spain

Reinaldo Plaz Landaeta
University of Madrid, Spain

ABSTRACT

The aim of this chapter is to deepen the concept of 'Communities of Practice' (CoPs) from the under-standing of a reference framework for knowledge governance, stressing the grey area which distinguishes such governance from the traditional term 'Knowledge Management,' since knowledge governance means not just the management of such assets but also their creation and development, which generates a richer and more appropriate meaning or sense. Without entering into exhaustive referential analyses, we attempt to offer the reader a practical approach which allows structuring an action plan that, in this case, will be explicated for the field of CoPs. Identification and measurement of assets based on informa-tion and knowledge and the processes carried out towards its improvement create the convergence of the dynamic of intellectual capital and the afore-mentioned knowledge governance as complementary subjects for an appropriate exploitation and monitoring of the impact which the organizational fostering of this strategic-reality has on business.

VALUATION OF ORGANIZATIONAL INTANGIBLE ASSETS

The strategic approach of businesses in the current economy has an important part related with certain support processes linked to analysis tasks corresponding to dynamic processes of decision making, as an attempt to diminish the risks inherent to such processes. In this sense, such argument on intelligent or learning-capable organizations (Senge, 1990) gains a high value for the extraction of information and the creation of both appropriate internal and external knowledge.

This approach insists on the importance of basic resources for strategic management focused on the couple information-knowledge (Itami, 1987; Vassiliadis *et al.*, 2000) and on derived individual and organizational learning. In this case, corporative philosophy should create the necessary atmosphere to recognize the value of intangible assets, very close to the understanding of the theory of resources and abilities, which does not only take into account those resources related with the tangible field but also those linked to non-physical elements located in the organizational 'roots' (1).

Obviously, it arises a requirement around a model or scheme of analysis; firstly, for the identification and measurement of such typology of assets, and also to facilitate a structured framework of reflection and analysis, an area covered by the intellectual-capital approach (Itami & Roehl, 1991; Grant, 1991; Bontis, 1999; Bueno & Salmador, 2000; Ordoñez, 2000).

This thematic area of intangible assets—which we could qualify as emerging if study cases are observed, although it is has been historically tackled in organizational literature within the field of the theory of resources and abilities (Wernerfelt, 1984; Barney, 1991; Grant, 1991; Peteraf, 1993)— had already collected, in different ways, contributions which helped to the valuation of non-tangible assets.

The basic models of intellectual capital (2) are generally structured by three basic components (IADE-CIC, 2003). Firstly, human capital—where attitudes, competency and abilities are analysed developing a profile to identify and measure knowledge from an individual viewpoint. On the other hand, structural capital (3) —responsible for knowledge diagnosis of organizational nature (Nonaka & Takeuchi, 1995; Brown & Duguid, 1991 and 1998; Teece, 1998 and 2000; Nonaka *et al.*, 2000; Tsoukas & Vladimirou, 2001)— considers aspects such as organizational design, reported culture and processes, and also a technology reality related with efforts in I+D such as tools and results which facilitate and make knowledge tangible (Brooking, 1996).

Finally, relational capital—which is explained by knowledge and information flows derived from the framework of alliances directly related with business processes (customers, suppliers, etc.) or involved with the social environment (4) (Nahapiet & Ghosal, 1996).

However, measurement only lacks of sense without a sustainable exertion allowing the analysis of different initiatives developed to improve the stock of intellectual capital. Such initiatives are processes related with the idea of 'knowledge in action' (Davenport & Prusak, 1998), creating a requirement of a holistic model integrating different alternatives and options, and also avoiding the common error linked to the consideration of strategic plans for knowledge governance or management just as a mere accumulations of initiatives. This accumulative approach creates difficulty and complexity in understanding certain dimensions and interactions among assets, generates chaos and includes contradictions among different programmes.

The result of such intellectual capital is centred on a 'photograph' (Bontis, 1999) as a traditional balance showing the status of the basic intangible assets identified by the organization; however, this approach may present a double objective —that is, the improvement of internal management and external communication through the information for stakeholders about a more complete organizational reality (5).

The general argument of 'knowledge in action' is traditionally linked to 'knowledge governance or management', processes which develop intellectual capital looking for improving the results of the initial measurement scheme. In this sense, there is a basic difference between intellectual capital and knowledge governance, bearing in mind a static or dynamic perspective, respectively.

However, the need for a complete exercise of management beyond the traditional financial-accountant approach creates an emerging line for the development of new areas within the structure of organizational responsibilities with a specific demand of abilities.

COLLABORATION APPROACH WITHIN KNOWLEDGE GOVERNANCE

Organizations consider in their strategies those factors to which they recognize significant value contributions (Barney, 1991; Grant, 1991; Peteraf, 1993), certainly measurable or at least as presumptions. This initial argument means the possibility of different strategic approaches according to business orientation or awareness showed by the organization towards the relevance of the different types of assets it owns.

In Figure 1 it is observed a distinct evolution and evidence towards the consideration of knowledge as a key asset (6), as an organizational value—that is, as a resource to which a significant contribution is recognized openly.

Without deepening into the theoretical framework associated to the concept of knowledge, this resource owns a characteristic linked to its intangibility which is that of enriching through the exchange among the large agents owning it (Nonaka, 1994; Nonaka & Takeuchi, 1995; Grant, 1996; Kogut & Zander, 1992 and 1996; Spender, 1996; Tsoukas, 1996), which implies the consideration of certain transference and exchange schemes as means supporting its advance and development.

Individual knowledge is transformed and is the base of the collective since it is transmitted through oral, written, encoded, sign, etc. language.

Figure 1. Evolution of the economic paradigms (Source: Gorey & Dobat (1996) and Bueno & Salvador (2000))

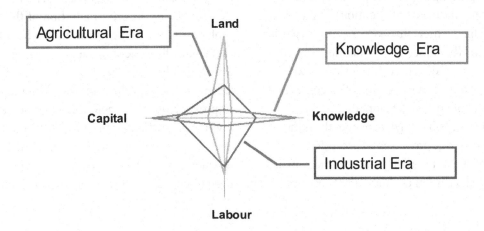

For Spender (1996), Von Krogh & Ross (1995) and Cook & Brown (1999), among others, social knowledge is not merely the sum of individual knowledge, but something else, different from that, which is especially important for organization survival and development in the long run.

This transference pattern means that individual knowledge is enriched in the process of exchange and transmission adding a contextual dimension to it, which gives it organizational value. In this sense, individual knowledge is idiosyncratic by nature and owns strong links to the organizational context in which it is developed. Knowledge transference, from this perspective, is necessarily social and conclusively outdistances from the schemes of electronic transference of data and information.

Social knowledge is built up from networks of agents creating a system of relations which facilitates, fosters and allows that individual knowledge is transferred and, at the same time, enriched, giving rise to social or organizational knowledge. It is precisely in this point where we can identify the difference between Knowledge Management and governance. In the first, management occurs around an explicit and encoded object or entity which we call, usually in a wrong manner, knowledge, when in fact it is data or information. In the latter, we rather talk about a system of relations among agents governed by a series of guidelines, norms and rules regulating, leading and guiding knowledge flows or processes. In this system, the centre of attention is the subject of knowledge, which involves a more organic viewpoint of the concept —contemplating in a clear manner its different dimensions: explicit and tacit— and its relation with the context in which it is created and developed.

From a viewpoint of governance, thinking of guiding knowledge processes transcends the very meaning of the expression. Many authors insist that knowledge, in an abstract sense, cannot be managed (Drucker, 2001). Knowledge, as we have already mentioned, lies in people and responds to mental models of behaviour intrinsic to the very nature of individuals. At most, we can induce certain behaviours in subjects. It is possible to give them tools and competences to exercise and develop their mental and cognitive abilities with the aim of increasing their knowledge stock and use. From this viewpoint, and in the field of cognitive processes, each individual will build patterns of social behaviour linked to processes of understanding, assimilation, learning and application of new knowledge (Bueno, 2005).

In the sense of the contributions by Foss (2006), this knowledge governance is close to a double level —micro (individual) and macro (collective), where it is important to consider not just tools, but also those attitudes and motivations which come into play in this reality of behaviours.

These processes are endogenous by nature and, therefore, they do not admit norms, rules and external intervention. A pedagogical method for learning, for instance, is nothing more than an instrument or tool to facilitate learning. However, its effectiveness will depend, deep down, on the individual's ability, interest and motivation for learning. We can induce or favour behaviours and stimulate processes; however, the governance of what-is-known is a subject concerning the individual him/herself and depends on his/her context (Cook & Brown, 1999).

Organizations are increasingly giving more importance to the administration of their intangible assets and to the forms in which such assets contribute to generate business value (Bueno, 2003). In this sense, the processes of professional learning and development are oriented at the improvement of competences for innovation, allowing their articulation in organizational models and systems which in turn become differentiating elements to achieve competitive positioning in markets. This knowledge approach adopts an open and systemic viewpoint of the organizational processes —in which interactions, relations and collaboration processes act as channels for new-knowledge transmission and assimilation (Plaz & Gonzalez, 2005).

From this viewpoint, an ontological approach of knowledge centred on the governance of processes of social relations emerges. It is in this context that the transference of knowledge flows takes place, causing expressions of knowledge organization, codification and specification in the form of organizational records. It is this way how relations and relational capital, for instance, constitute key sources of organization enrichment and a means to keep the dynamic of knowledge renovation (Bueno, 2005).

This approach has recently distinguished between individual knowledge and the creation (development), management or governance of organizational knowledge (Nonaka, 1994 and 1995; Bueno & Plaz, 2005). Such distinction is important since it focuses the discussion on Knowledge Management at the level of organizational system and its management.

Knowledge management or administration places the debate in the field of governance of the exchange flows and key organizational processes which increase the value of intangible assets. In this sense, talking about organization implies referring to the system of relations and connexions allowing the interaction of agents and individuals, and that knowledge flows —as a part of such process— are produced in the same directions of such interaction. It is important to stand out that Knowledge Management —considered from this viewpoint and with a sense of governance— means the definition of policies, guidelines, channels, proceedings and resources to create optimum conditions for fostering, channelling, catalysing and promoting such flows of organizational knowledge.

PROPOSAL OF FRAMEWORK MODEL FOR KNOWLEDGE GOVERNANCE

Talking about organizational-knowledge governance and development therefore means creating support structures for the processes of interaction individual-individual, individual-organizational system, and organizational system-organizational system. These structures facilitate knowledge flows and allow at the same time leaving a trace or record. This record is the result of specifying tacit knowledge to convert it into explicit codes leading to the definition of routines of organizational behaviour and progressively acquiring an own identity.

Organizational culture is nothing but the historic trace of individual behaviours grounded on a collective expression. Stating that an organization owns a determined working culture makes us date back to and look for —in its founders and previous leaders— those behaviours which have been progressively modelled and have become in reference and standard.

These processes are initiated through relations and interactions among knowledge agents or subjects from a determined viewpoint or strategic thought, given a context of reference which incardinates the process of knowledge. Information technologies are only the catalyser to facilitate collaboration among subjects and propose knowledge exchange as a common resource, which —once it is developed by action of practice— will be transformed from explicit into tacit, and from individual into social.

Without this conviction, at least in its top-down version (7), it is very complex to face —moving away from the approach of simple fashion— a scheme aimed at a more appropriate way to tackle knowledge, or more precisely, the so-called knowledge governance (Plaz & Gonzalez, 2005), than just management, given that this term should gather those tasks related to creation and development.

Going back to the argument on knowledge governance, such governance is obviously configured from a structure of processes acting as drivers of the business in question, assuring the exploitation of all organizational knowledge —an aspect which doubtlessly should be imbricated with a system of organizational intelligence (8) acting as a supplier of informative inputs for the recycling and updating of the organization's knowledge base (Vassiliadis *et al.*, 2000; Merino, 2004). The dynamics of creation of value occur around the tasks of internal transference of tacit and explicit knowledge, as well as around those tasks of incorporation of external knowledge or that created by other agents, generating learning cycles which build up the new knowledge within a process of transformation of essential competences which generate intangible or intellectual-capital assets (see Figure 2), as Bueno (2002) proposes in the new conception of the company as an economic system based on knowledge.

Accompanying this overall framework and prior to tackling the projection of the model of knowledge governance on the role of transference and collaborative approaches, it should be stood out the need to aligning such structure with a series of business objectives which allow clarify-

ing, visualizing and understanding the returns or impacts involved in knowledge valuation and acting in consequence. Those returns, beyond a short-term period, will adjust to the context of the organization, looking for action lines adapted to its level of organizational and technological maturity, considering a set of possible key factors for success (Plaz & Gonzalez, 2005).

At the same time, the achievement of results will require an appropriate scheme of measures which allow an appropriate evaluation not just of those variables of a finalist nature for business, but also of the statistics associated with the afore-mentioned chain of knowledge creation, development and management.

For both analysis and fixation of objectives and the reality of these processes linked to knowledge governance, we may use the dynamic of a balanced scorecard (Kaplan & Norton, 1992) and even for more specific themes, like the support for the control panel, several instruments such as the model of the European Foundation for Quality Management (EFQM) or the models of intellectual capital (10) can be used.

Undoubtedly, the action on knowledge governance should pursue the improvement of the organization's intellectual capital as a way to

Figure 2. Company as a system based on knowledge (Source: Bueno, 2002)

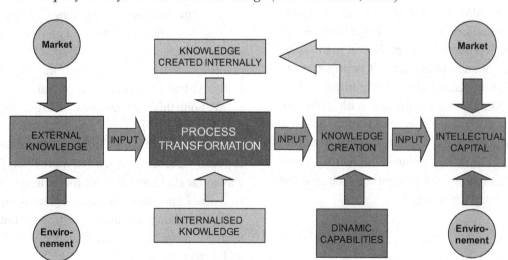

get to know the suitability of the actions aimed at putting into practice a strategy in the line of knowledge valuation (see Figure 3).

The approach of processes which shapes the model of knowledge governance makes clear an action loop (Bueno & Plaz, 2005; Nonaka, 1991 and 1994; Kogut & Zander, 1992; Blumentritt & Johnston, 1999; Shin *et al.*, 2001; Alavi & Leidner, 2001; Staples *et al.*, 2001; Zahra & George, 2002; Argote *et al.*, 2003; Zack, 2003) around the dynamics of understanding, register, storage (Walsh & Ungson, 1991; Davenport & Prusak, 1998; Teece, 2000; Staples *et al.*, 2001; McGrath & Argote, 2002), diffusion (Davenport & Prusak, 1998; Szulanski, 2000), use and improvement of information and knowledge, where the organization should consider the way of putting it into practice or value, already counting on a traditional approach based on certain support departments —namely, documentation centres, system departments, training units, quality areas, etc.— whose mission is clearly positioned in relation to the afore-mentioned loop.

In any case, it would be convenient to integrate the set of dynamics specified in a modelled framework which allows visualizing, in a complete manner, the reach of knowledge governance in order to be able to face its display properly. In this case, literature revision (Gupta & Govinda-rajan, 2000; Alavi & Leidner, 2001; Shin *et al.*, 2001; Staples *et al.*, 2001; Zack, 2003; Argote *et al.*, 2003; among others) describes a wide range of references which partially raise the different

viewpoints of the afore-mentioned knowledge governance, losing a reference of holistic sense. The configuration of this model joins the dynamic of the afore-mentioned loop and the stages which achieve its alignment with the key strategy and factors of the business, apart from the corresponding evaluation of impacts (see Figure 4).

All this is included within a scheme characterized by complexity, given that the 'act or fact of knowing' is complex in itself, as well as the different knowledge processes (flows), given their diversity and functionality, which justify understanding governance as an action aimed at guiding such complexity.

This decrease in the terms alluding knowledge government allows translating its conceptual framework into a series of action lines recognized by all organizations and that, therefore, own a history, a record, programmes and tools which in many cases merely lack of integration; that is, a model for knowledge governance is not about accumulating programmes. These action lines are centred on the afore-mentioned organizational intelligence, expert management, communication, quality, learning-training, I+D and documental management, and on the strategies/mechanisms briefly described next:

- Organizational intelligence is an action line which pursues the configuration of an alert system for the organization (Escorsa & Maspons, 2001; Kurtyka, 2003; Almeida *et al.*, 2003). The activities linked to techno-

Figure 3. Improvement of intellectual capital (Source: Personal compilation)

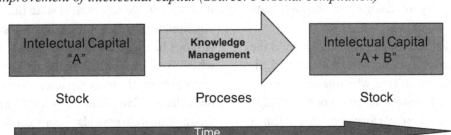

Figure 4. Knowledge-governance model (Source: Bueno & Plaz (2005) and personal compilation)

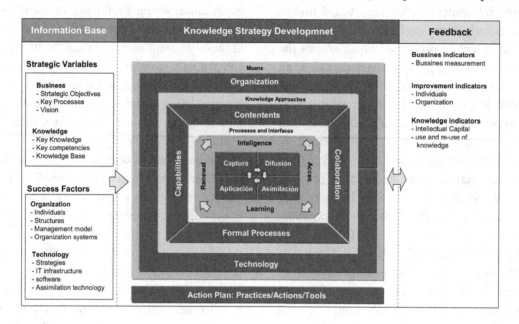

logical vigilance, competitive intelligence, benchmarking, etc., are practices recognized within this kind of action.

- Expert management is a mechanism mainly based on collaborative approaches, networks, communities of practice, etc., where knowledge exchange, especially that of tacit knowledge, becomes a key objective.

- Communication, strategy based on the information about the organization's abilities, resources, results, etc., where communication models, existing channels, etc., play essential roles (Davenport & Prusak, 1998; Szulanski, 2000).

- Content management is centred on the systems allowing appropriate tackling and accessibility to documents through data bases.

- Individual learning —bearing in mind the dynamics of training, offer and demand, attendance and on-line, which generate cycles (Nonaka & Takeuchi, 1995) of knowledge recycling where performance of the learnt concepts is an important objective.

- Organizational learning is an action line based on the development of exchange and collaboration areas where the concept of communities in practice may favour knowledge register in organizational memory and the improvement of its degree of advance when shaping thematic groups of interest (Easterby-Smith & Lyles, 2003), and

- Innovation and improvement is centred on the organization's efforts on I+D and the obtained results (Zack, 1999). Thus, those dynamics favouring creativity, incentives and recognition are an important part of this strategy.

Once the breadth of knowledge governance is observed, we can clearly state that the central positioning of collaboration dynamics in this matter goes further than the documental approaches which have characterized the first stages of the strategies of those companies concerned with Knowledge Management, in which great efforts for digitalization have also been raised. As a result, we have come to the subsequent replacement of *knowledge stock* by *knowledge flow*.

Once we have reached this point, and from the double dimension (see Figure 5) which intersects between the loop and the action lines, it is important to emphasize the enriching effect on coordination and individual and organizational learning derived from a collaborative working approach.

Therefore, transference and exchange dynamics appear as recipes of high strategic interest from the couple collaboration-communication, where we can reflect, design and explore areas, channels and subject matters.

From the field of collaboration, the main axes of action are centred, on one hand, on the creation of appropriate areas—attendance or virtual—which facilitate sharing ideas and documents, and, on the other hand, on establishing a culture prone to share, in which leadership, awareness and recognition exertion become key elements for its operation.

Therefore, the phenomenon of transference as a communication process influenced by a set of causal contingencies or variables of contextual nature —so that we have to take into account the attitudes, competency and abilities of the emitter and receiver agents, and the existence, on one hand, of a wide range of messages (information and knowledge) with a comprehensive and available approach of added value and, on the other hand, of the appropriate channels for their transmission according to the nature of such messages with the aim of eliminating or avoiding, as much as possible, mechanic, semantic and contextual noises and interferences. Regarding the latter, message is linked to the information and the knowledge we attempt to transfer, both if it is of documental or tacit nature, all set in a specific cultural context.

Thus, from the beginning, in spite of counting on a significant value offer, it may occur that the set of resources and abilities of the emitter or receiver may benefit or limit the process. This

Figure 5. Field of action for knowledge governance (Source: personal compilation)

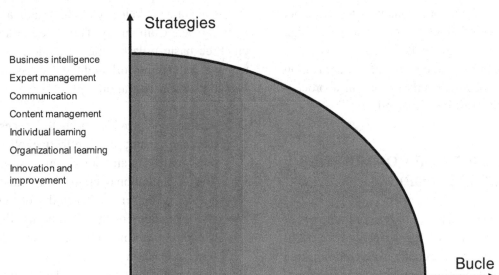

way, it should be emphasized that it would be more interesting to count on a motivated and capable emitter with a first-level offer, since —to a large extent— a relevant number of requirements are not found in the vanguard of knowledge.

To sum up, we attempt to reach understanding between both extremes of the transference process, for which the channel or means should be adjusted to the nature of knowledge —whether it is explicit or tacit, intellectual or collective, since each of them will raise specific and different requirements.

Active and passive communication may also be taken into account, bearing in mind those mechanisms which allow the message to reach its addressee (systems of selective information diffusion) or, on the contrary, others needing willingness from the addressee in order to achieve the objective of communication (e.g., notice-boards), according to the dimensions characterizing knowledge (epistemological, ontological, systemic and strategic), which leads to the design of different operative programmes of management of knowledge processes, according to the LICI index (Level of Information, Complexity and Imagination) of the transferred knowledge (Bueno, 2002).

Among all options occurring nowadays on the subject of collaboration, it is to stand out communities of practice as a concept of high strategic interest, given its linkage to an area of specific knowledge and interest for organization which includes collaboration within a process from which a result is expected.

THE CONCEPT OF COMMUNITIES OF PRACTICE (COP)

The purpose of existence of the communities of practice (Wenger, 2001; Wenger & Sneyder, 2000) is oriented towards the creation of a common area for individual meeting in order to interact in benefit of the generation, exchange and assimilation of experiences around specific application areas with clearly defined objectives.

This common area should use, on one hand, the cycle of knowledge reception, diffusion, assimilation and renovation in the organizational data base, structuring the experiences and facilitating its members' searches and contributions. This way, we can apply to CoP, as an agent, the whole model of knowledge governance from the viewpoint of both the loop and the seven defined strategies (see Figure 6).

On the other hand, it should also facilitate the relation among community members beyond mere information exchange, which is the only way to make non-specified knowledge appear in reports of formal nature. This exchange dynamic is only possible if mission and objective internalization occurs within the context of the community, since that internalization would facilitate the flow of the interaction cycle which will favour cohesion among its members.

A consolidated community of practice represents the natural place we turn to when we need to seek for advice or raise requests linked to its field. The development of practice and attention to requests raised to the community facilitates the replication of experiences in order to dynamize and accelerate the velocity of the organizational learning cycle. Community of Practice is grounded on three basic pillars which provide it with a management framework and the necessary support tools for its operation:

- Technology provides with the necessary tools and means to create effective collaboration areas from an operational viewpoint.
- The organizational environment and the necessary culture to meet the objectives and necessities of the community, the organization and its individuals, in order to achieve an identity and generate policies and appropriate management plans grounded on a solid base of training, awareness (com-

Figure 6. Knowledge processes (Source: Personal compilation)

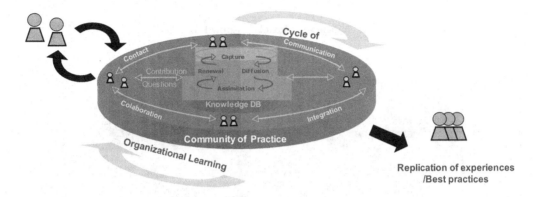

THE PROCESS OF CREATION AND DEVELOPMENT OF A COP

munication) and motivation (incentives and recognitions), and

- The management model through which the rules of the game are established, the definition of flows and work processes, identification of actors (roles), knowledge types and their associated taxonomy.

In this sense, Figure 7 shows the relations of these three components with the community, as well as its linkage with the expected impact at the level of individuals, organization, business and the community itself, fields which lead to visualize the different returns which may be derived of an approach of CoPs.

Therefore, monitoring of practice in the community is carried out through indicators linked to four dimensions —namely, people, group, organization and business— which allow measuring the impact of the results, the generated and seized know-how and, through that, establishing strategies of impulse/monitoring which contribute to the creation of improvements and the alignment of objectives and actions.

The creation of a CoP may be mainly linked to two approaches:

1. A push one, declared by the organization, in which practices structuring the community are decided and chosen by headship, involving a previous exercise of strategic reflection, and
2. A pull one, whose approach is based on providing resources and support to those groups developing a certain successful collaboration labour within the organization.

Obviously, success expectancy of both options may turn out to be very unequal, especially if we bear in mind the predisposition to collaboration showed by both alternatives. In any case, the process goes through a series of stages (see Figure 8):

- **Stage 1—Identification:** It is linked to the strategic priorities of the organization, which may be originated from the previously-mentioned push and pull viewpoints.

Figure 7. Overall approach of CoP (Source: Personal compilation)

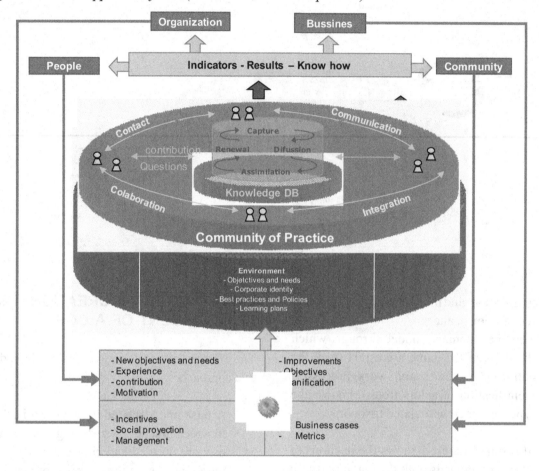

- **Stage 2—Design:** The generation of a model which adjusts to collaboration necessities; that is, identifying the processes developed in its area and their fundamental requirements.
- **Stage 3—Construction:** Articulation of the preliminary organizational structure of the community, with its defined and necessary objectives, roles, responsibilities, and resources. In this case, the institutionalization of the CoP may be achieved through the formal recognition of its existence and certain responsibilities within the practice in question.
- **Stage 4—Implementation:** Turning on of a functional model through the generation of

an area or platform supporting collaboration, an aspect in which non-area criteria prevail nowadays.
- **Stage 5—Growth:** Development of an extensive approach of the communities involving a higher number of people and, therefore, exceeding the idea of the organization's preliminary structure. In this sense, preliminary stages can entitle the role of 'observer' as an agent which shows interest in becoming a part of the CoP in the future. This expansion clearly impacts in the ambiguity of the organizations' limits, and
- **Stage 6—Improvements:** Establishment of a self-diagnosis policy, consolidating the

benefits which it contributes to the community, especially through the generation of an organized set of indicators.

FINAL REFLECTION

Through the approach of Communities of Practice we make clear important benefits which enable the identification of opportunities for growth and development of an organizational culture centred on the seizing of talent and continuous improvement. Among the most obvious general benefits of this approach we can emphasize the following:

1. Boast a structured and common data base containing relevant information for the different projects and activities carried out in the organization in the context of the influence areas of the CoPs.

2. Count on technological resources which allow creating new virtual areas of collaborative work for the generation and construction of documents in an asynchronic and ubiquitous manner, facilitating the exchange of documents and opinions among group members without depending on attendance meetings.

3. This interaction will work to generate —in real time— a record of all documents generated by the group, which may be consulted.

4. Facilitate and accelerate the processes of generation of records and work around the conclusions and commitments established in a meeting, and

5. Boast instruments and platforms which facilitate assessment processes of suppliers and the creation of a common data base on suppliers, an interface which optimize the actions of diffusion and access to informa-

Figure 8. Process of creation of a CoP (Source: Personal compilation)

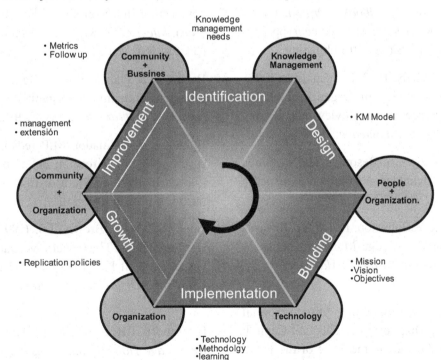

tion on suppliers, and registers (records) of the result of relevant indicators for CoPs in order to facilitate the activities related to benchmarking.

Therefore, given the concept of CoP, the pillars on which its turning-on is grounded, and the general process which may act as a roadmap, we have come to meet a specific reality as a tool which —from a collaborative viewpoint— insists on the approach of the knowledge-governance model, making a proper use of transference and exchange dynamics, which is the aim of this chapter.

REFERENCES

Alavi, M. & Leidner, D.E. (2001). Review: Knowledge Management and Knowledge Management Systems: Conceptual Foundations and Research Issues. *MIS Quarterly, 25*, 107-136.

Almeida, P.; Phene, A. & Grant, R. (2003). Innovation and Knowledge Management: Scanning Sourcing and Integration. In M. Easterby-Smith & M.A. Lyles (eds.), *Handbook of Organizational Learning and Knowledge Management* (pp. 356-371). Oxford, UK: Blackwell Publishing.

Argote, L.; McEvily, B. & Reagans, R. (2003). Managing Knowledge in Organizations: An Integrative Framework and Review of Emerging Themes. *Management Science, 49*, 571-582.

Barney, J.B. (1991): Firm Resources and Sustained Competitive Advantage: A Comment. *Journal of Management, 17*(1), 99-120.

Blumentritt, R. & Johnston, R. (1999). Towards a Strategy for Knowledge Management. *Technology Analysis and Strategic Management, 11*, 287-300.

Bontis, N. (1999). Managing Organizational Knowledge by Diagnosing Intellectual Capital: Framing and Advancing the State of the Field.

International Journal of Technology Management, 18, 433-462.

Brown, J.S. & Duguid, P. (1991). Organizational Learning and Communities of Practice: Towards a Unified view of Working, Learning and Innovation. *Organization Science, 2*, 40-57.

Brown, J.S. & Duguid, P. (1998). Organizing Knowledge, *California Management Review, 40*, 90-111.

Bueno, E. (2005). Fundamentos epistemológicos de dirección del conocimiento organizativo: Desarrollo, medición y gestión de intangibles. *Economía Industrial* [Spanish Ministry for Industry, Tourism y Trade], *357*, 13-26.

Bueno, E. (2003). Enfoques principales y tendencias en dirección del conocimiento (Knowledge Management). In R. Hernández (ed.), *Dirección del conocimiento: Desarrollos teóricos y aplicaciones* (pp. 21-54). Trujillo, Spain: Ediciones La Coria.

Bueno, E. (2002). Dirección estratégica basada en conocimiento: Teoría y práctica de la nueva perspectiva. In P. Morcillo & J. Fernández Aguado (eds.), *Nuevas claves en la Dirección Estratégica* (pp. 91-166), Madrid: Ariel.

Bueno, E. & Plaz, R. (2005). Desarrollo y Gobierno del Conocimiento Organizativo: Agentes y procesos. *Boletín Intellectus, 8*, 16-23.

Bueno, E. & Salmador, M.P. (eds.) (2000). Perspectivas sobre Dirección del Conocimiento y Capital Intelectual. Madrid: Instituto Universitario Euroforum Escorial.

Cook, S.D.N. & Brown, J.S. (1999). Bridging Epistemologies: The Generative Dance between Organizational Knowledge and Organizational Knowing. *Organization Science, 10*(4), 381-400.

Davenport, T.H. & Prusak, L. (1998). *Working Knowledge. How Organizations What They Know.* Harvard, US: Harvard Business School Press.

Drucker, P. (2001): The Next Society. *The Economist*, November 3rd, 3-22.

Easterby-Smith, M. & Lyles, M.A. (Eds.) (2003). *The Blackwell Handbook of Organizational Learning and Knowledge Management*. Oxford: Blackwell.

Escorsa, P. & Maspons, R. (2001). De la Vigilancia Tecnológica a la Inteligencia Competitiva. *Financial Times*. Madrid: Prentice Hall.

Foss, N. (2006): The Emerging Knowledge Governance Approach: Challenges and Characteristics, DRUID Working Paper, no. 06-10.

Gorey R.M. & Dovat D.R. (1996). *Managing on the Knowledge Era*. New York: Harper and Row.

Grant, R.M. (1996) Toward a Knowledge-based Theory of Firm. *Strategic Management Journal*, *17*, 109-122.

Grant, R.M. (1991). A Resource Based Theory of Competitive Advantage: Implications for Strategy Formulation. *California Management Review*, *33*(3), 114-135.

Gupta, A.K. & Govindarajan, V. (2000). Knowledge Management's Social Dimension: Lessons from Nucor Steel. *Sloan Management Review*, fall issue, 71-80.

IADE-CIC (2003). *Modelo de medición y gestión del capital intelectual: Modelo Intellectus*. Madrid: Universidad Autónoma de Madrid: CIC-IADE.

Itami, H. (1987). *Mobilizing Invisible Assets*. Boston, Harvard University Press.

Itami, H. & Roehl (1987). *Mobilizing Invisible Assets*. Cambridge, MA: Harvard University Press.

Kaplan, R.S. & Norton, D.P. (1992). The Balanced Scorecard Measures that Drive Performance. *Harvard Business Review*, *70*(1), 71-79.

Kogut, B. & Zander, U. (1992). Knowledge of the Firm, Combinative Capabilities and the Replication of Technology. *Organization Science*, 3, 383-397.

McGrath, J.E. & Argote, L. (2002). Group Processes in Organizational Contexts. In M.A. How & R.S. Tindale (eds.). *Blackwell Handbook of Social Psychology*. Oxford, UK: Blackwell.

Merino, C. (2004). La Inteligencia Organizativa como Dinamizador del Capital Intelectual. *Revista Puzzle*, *3*(14), 4-10.

Nahapiet, J. & Ghoshal, S. (1998). Social Capital, Intellectual Capital, and the Organizational Advantage. *Academy of Management Review*, *23*, 242-266.

Nonaka, I. (1991). The Knowledge-creating Company. *Harvard Business Review*, *69*, 96-104.

Nonaka, I. (1994). A Dynamic Theory of Organizational Knowledge Creation. *Organization Science*, *5*(1), 14-37.

Nonaka, I. & Takeuchi, H. (1995). *The Knowledge-Creating Company: How Japanese Companies Create the Dynamics of Innovation*. New York: Oxford University Press.

Nonaka, I.; Toyama, R. & Cono, N. (2000). SECI, Ba and Leadership: A Unified Model of Dynamic Knowledge Creation. *Long Range Planning*, *33*, 5-34.

Ordoñez, P. (2001). Relevant Experiences on Measuring and Reporting Intellectual Capital in European Pioneering Firms. In N. Bontis & C. Cheng (eds.) *World Congress on Intellectual Capital Reading*. New York: Butterworth-Heinemann.

Peteraf, M.A. (1993). The Cornerstone of Competitive Advantage: A Resource-Based View. *Strategic Management Journal*, 14, 179-191.

Plaz, R. & González, N. (2005). La gestión del conocimiento organizativo: dinámicas de agregación de valor en la organización. *Economía Industrial, 357,* 41-62.

Senge, P. (1990). *The Fifth Discipline: The Art and Practice of the Learning Organization.* New York, Doubleday Currency.

Shin, M.; Holden, T. & Schmidt, R.A. (2001). From Knowledge Theory to Management Practice: Towards an Integrated Approach. *Information Processing and Management, 37,* 335-355.

Spender, J.C. (1996). Making Knowledge the Basis of a Dynamic Theory of the Firm. *Strategic Management Journal, 17,* 45-62.

Staples, D.S.; Greenaway, K. & Mckeen, J. (2001). Opportunities for Research about Managing the Knowledge-based Enterprise. *International Journal of Management Reviews, 3,* 1-20.

Szulanski, G. (2000). The Process of Knowledge Transfer: A Diachronic Analysis of Stickiness. *Organizational Behaviour and Human Decision Processes, 82,* 9-27.

Teece, D.J. (1998). Research Directions for Knowledge Management. *California Management Review, 40,* 289-292.

Teece, D.J. (2000). Strategies for Managing Knowledge Assets: The Role of Firm Structure and Industrial Context. *Long Range Planning, 33,* 509-533.

Tsoukas, H. (1996). The Firm as a Distributed Knowledge System: A Constructionist Approach. *Strategic Management Journal, 17,* 11-25.

Tsoukas, H. & Vladimirou, E. (2001). What Is Organizational Knowledge? *Journal of Management Studies, 38,* 973-993.

Vassiliadis, S.; Seufert, A.; Back, A. & Von Krogh, G. (2000). Competing with Intellectual Capital: Theoretical Background. Institute for Information Management and Institute of Management, University of St. Gallen.

Walsh, J.P. & Ungson, G.R. (1991). Organizational Memory. *Academy of Management Review, 16,* 57-91.

Wenger, E. (2001). *Comunidades de práctica aprendizaje, significado e identidad.* Barcelona: Paidós.

Wenger, E.C. & Sneyder, W. (2000) Communities of Practice: The Organizational Frontier. *Harvard Business Review, 78*(1), 139-145.

Wernerfelt, B. (1984). A Resource-Based View of the Firm. *Strategic Management Journal, 5,* 171-180.

Von Krogh, G. & Ross, J. (1995). *Organizational Epistemology.* New York: MacMillan and St Martin's Press.

Zack, M. (1999). Developing a Knowledge Strategy. *California Management Review, 41,* 125-145.

Zack, M. (2003). Rethinking the Knowledge-Based Organization. *MIT Sloan Management Review,* summer issue, 67-71.

ENDNOTES

[1]   It is important to consider not just the aspect of resource and ability property but also their availability —that is, the existence of an external offer of added value, frequently within the area or environment in which the organization is located.

[2]   In the line of the model EFQM, intellectual-capital models propose a set of factors for reflection on organizational intangible assets.

[3]   Due to management criteria, structural capital is composed by organizational capital and technological capital, where the first establishes a set of structural and

non-technological factors and the second establishes all those elements linked to the use of technology and the results of innovation (intellectual and industrial property).

4   In the case of public organizations, social capital is related with the task of public service. This consideration may transfer social capital to structural capital, since it is shaped as a nucleus which legitimizes the organization's labour.

5   In this case, the interest towards intellectual capital is oriented at better information for investors and other stakeholders who may be found within certain levels of technical or economic relations with the organization.

6   Knowledge should be emphasized as a strategic key of the current economy, embodied in a person, transferred to the organization or social group according to real or moral contracts, and valued as a productive resource and dynamic competence.

7   Where it is necessary to raise an appropriate management style articulated on the base of a leadership, awareness, etc. exercise which permeates the organization's culture.

8   Systems turning around the concept of corporate radar, as an antenna which feeds the organization on information and basic knowledge.

9   Instrument which favours organizational diagnosis according to a series of key criteria looking for certain fields of improvement and strengthens, and

10   Tool for reflection and report on the organization's intangible assets, in its side of identification and measurement.

Chapter VII
Knowledge Management in SMEs Clusters

Josep Capó-Vicedo
Universitat Politècnica de València, Spain

José V. Tomás-Miquel
Universitat Politècnica de València, Spain

Manuel Expósito-Langa
Universitat Politècnica de València, Spain

ABSTRACT

This chapter highlights the necessity of establishing relationships with other companies and external agents in order to empower the creation and diffusion of knowledge, through factors such as innovation. Likewise, the influence of geographical and territorial factors will be studied in the context of this economy. SMES normally work and are immersed in particular geographical regions so this chapter will analyze the particular case of knowledge generation and sharing in SMES clusters as an essential source of competitive advantage. A new organizational form will be suggested in order to make possible the creation, transfer and sharing of knowledge in supply chain of SMES clusters. In this sense, a network functioning model is finally proposed.

INTRODUCTION

In recent years, the balance between knowledge and resources has changed so dramatically in the developed economies that the former has become the most decisive factor in relation to standard of living. Knowledge has become even more important than traditional resources such as land, machinery and work. However, the existence of economic systems based on small and medium enterprises (SMES) represents an important barrier for transition to take place from traditional economies to those based on knowledge.

It is important to distinguish between the individual and the organizational level of competences. The individual competences are necessary, but not sufficient, for organizational competence. A high level of organizational competence requires mechanisms to facilitate the conversion of individual, or tacit knowledge, into explicit organizational knowledge, as can be seen in some of the most important Knowledge Management models, particularly in Nonaka and Takeuchi's (1995).

But, besides the organizational level itself, the importance of the external sources of competence and knowledge must be borne in mind, especially in the case of the SMES, which lack the potential, size and resources to be self-sufficient in this area. It is extremely important to establish the necessary mechanisms to acquire new competences and knowledge from outside sources. These range from the recruitment of staff to the interaction with other organizations such as, consultants, clients and suppliers, other firms, universities or research centres, training organizations, banks or public administrations.

For these companies, cooperation with others of their same size or larger is a strategic alternative that allows them to take benefit of the competitive advantages of the companies with which they have decided to associate themselves. If these agreements are carried out among a large number of companies, they can knit a lattice of relationships that create compact networks through the links established.

In order for this configuration to take place, the existence of an environment which guarantees a series of factors that allows for this configuration and Knowledge Management among the participant companies becomes necessary. In the particular case of SMES, the fact that the companies are located in a certain territory can favour greater product specialization, greater flexibility

and a considerable increase in competitiveness. The grouping in function of a group of abilities, knowledge, technologies or markets, can be a catalyst that impels the innovative process in companies. In this case, the existing implicit knowledge in a territory plays a vital role, by means of the establishment of mechanisms of collaboration and participation, formal or informal, of the different public and private agents of the territory.

This chapter will analyze the particular case of SMES located in a certain territory, forming clusters or industrial districts. Firstly, a brief literature review about Knowledge Management at an inter-organizational level will be carried out. The particular case of industrial districts of SMES will be dealt with, studying the importance of the network concept in order to improve the Knowledge Management process at this level. A new organizational form, based on the Virtual Enterprise will be lastly suggested in order to make Knowledge Management possible in this specific case. A dynamic knowledge network will be proposed, represented within a mechanical analogy, in order to better understand the Knowledge Management process.

RELATION BETWEEN KNOWLEDGE MANAGEMENT AND THE ORGANIZATIONAL AND ENVIRONMENTAL CONTEXTS

There is a strong interrelation between knowledge and the organizational and environmental contexts, since it is precisely in this area that knowledge will be generated, so that their features will have an influence on the way in which it is created, transmitted and used.

Each specific context will require a different form of Knowledge Management, as well as different support systems for this management. This becomes even more evident when we go outside the limits of a simple organization and talk about inter-organizational Knowledge Management. We may find it necessary to form a relationship or deal with organizations whose experience, languages and contexts are very different from our own, and therefore also with their Knowledge Management systems, which may not be perfectly "compatible" with ours. This will mean new organizational ideas will be necessary for businesses, and also an environment of trust and collaboration between enterprises to facilitate the creation and distribution of knowledge.

Knowledge management will therefore involve (besides distinguishing between the various types of knowledge, such as tacit and explicit, individual and collective, and the means by which it is transmitted) thinking about the interdependence that exists between knowledge and the organizational context (Ciborra and Andreu 2001).

Brief Literature Review

Most of the existing literature on Knowledge Management in an inter-organizational context refers to horizontal relationships between two or more partners, while very few authors deal with vertical relationships between suppliers and clients, i.e., in the supply chain. In any case, most of the results obtained from horizontal relationships are perfectly valid for the vertical type.

Whatever the kind of relationship established, the studies carried out indicate that a large number of inter-organizational relationships are unsuccessful. Consequently, many of the studies into collaboration between enterprises aim at trying to discover the reasons for these failures, as well as the factors that are vital to success.

From another vantage point, Ding and Peters (2000) indicate that to achieve effective innovation businesses must form relationships with other enterprises. To be precise, collaborative inter-organizational networks increase the capacity for innovation of the enterprises that compose them, since they facilitate the transmission of knowledge from one company to another. The same authors review the existing literature on Knowledge Management and conclude that the practices in this field vary from one enterprise to another. This, they conclude, facilitates the flows of knowledge and at the same time permits innovation, providing that these collaborative networks are created and managed correctly.

Another analysis of inter-organizational Knowledge Management was carried out by Levy *et al.* (2003) where they introduced the term "co-opetition" to show that both co-operation and competition could take place at the same time, as for example in the case of SMES grouped in clusters. This term includes the transfer of knowledge that could be vital to achieve a competitive advantage for the SMES, by means of using the knowledge gained by co-operation to compete in the market. Levy *et al.* create a work context based on the theory of games to analyze the transfer of knowledge between organizations through "co-opetition". This study centers on the SMES, since they consider that these kind of enterprises are good knowledge generators but cannot or do not know how to properly utilize it.

In another study, Grant (2001) indicates that the key to efficiency in the integration of individual knowledge into the production of goods and services lies in creating mechanisms that avoid learning costs. He suggests that if each individual has to learn what all the others know, the benefit of specialization is lost. In the case of strategic links between enterprises, he states that in many cases the interest is in gaining access to the knowledge of the other partners rather than in acquiring new knowledge. Such access permits a better utilization of resources based on knowledge, which is advantageous for the business when there is uncertainty as to technological change, for example.

Grant (2001) also indicates that there are occasions when better integration and diffusion of knowledge are achieved by collaborating with another enterprise rather than by internal collaboration (as in the case of the supply chain of

Toyota, or in the SME networks of the north of Italy, for example). This is due to the fact that between different enterprises informal relationships are usually created, based on common interests and the will to share experiences, which is much more effective than the more formal processes of the enterprise when knowledge is integrated and transferred.

Apostolou et al. (2003) talk about creating networks of knowledge in the field of the Extended Enterprise, indicating that both innovation and competitive advantage increase through the creation and exploitation of knowledge chains.

Besides research already mentioned, Knowledge Management papers at an inter-organizational level, that focus on certain sectors, can be found; in the construction sector, Bresnen and Marshall (2000), Cushman (2001) or Egbu and Botterill (2001) can be mentioned; Apostolou et al. (1999) analyze the development and use of cooperation tools, based on the Internet, to facilitate the transmission of knowledge through distinct organizations that form part of the wood and furniture sector.

Lastly, some authors that propose models for Knowledge Management at an inter-organizational level can be found, such as Nonaka et al. (2000) or Ciborra and Andreu (2001). These authors start from intra-organizational Knowledge Management models to later study their applicability outside their own organization.

Environmental Factors

In the previous section, the importance in the literature of the environment and of the organizational context for knowledge creation and transmission at an inter-organizational level has been analyzed. In short, the importance of creating new organizational forms, by means of which this process is facilitated, has been mentioned.

In order for this configuration to take place, the existence of an environment which guarantees a series of factors that allows for this configuration and Knowledge Management among the participant companies becomes necessary. This environment should constitute a true business ecosystem that guarantees the following points (Camarinha-Matos, 2002); Trust building, Common interoperability, ontology and distributed collaboration infrastructures, Agreed business practices, Sense of community and Sense of stability.

This is especially important in the case of SMES since, because of their characteristics (lack of resources, lack of defined managerial strategies), they have difficulties in thinking about innovation and Knowledge Management.

In this particular case, the fact that the companies are located in a certain territory can favour greater product specialization, greater flexibility and a considerable increase in competitiveness. The grouping in function of a group of abilities, knowledge, technologies or markets, can be a catalyst that impels the innovative process in companies. In this case, the existing implicit knowledge in a territory plays a vital role, by means of the establishment of mechanisms of collaboration and participation, formal or informal, of the different public and private agents of the territory.

Theories on endogenous growth point to knowledge generation and technological innovation as the true drivers of local (or regional) strategic change. These factors, as opposed to the simple accumulation of capitals, conclude in the innovation of products and processes.

Various authors have made similar propositions from different fields: Sabel (1992); Porter (1994); Sweeney (1987), Pyke and Sengenberger (1990), Benko and Lipietz (1994), Becattini (1990), Bagnasco, (1977), Brusco (1982), Cagmani (1992).

Therefore, the competitive advantage of the economies and firms seems to reside mainly in their innovation capacity. This corresponds to "know-how" which is, in fact, one of the aspects of the tacit knowledge. It should be considered also that both knowledge dimensions could be effective only if they are supplemented with other factors linked with economic development: physical, social, and organizational assets.

If we keep in mind, as Scott (1989) points out that "the quality of life of the inhabitants of a territory come, ultimately, from the competitiveness of the firms located there, that is to say, of the capacity of those to produce and sell their products and services to the world, with positive economic results in a sustained way", it seems that the measures implemented to develop Knowledge Management and generation of the firms located in a territory and concentrated around a cluster would contribute to the improvement of the quality of life of the citizens.

In the European case, the preponderance of SMES in the economy represents a barrier to the transition from the traditional economies to those based on knowledge. In this sense, it should not be forgotten that the limited resources of the SMES do not favour their managers or owners in dealing with the processes of strategic change, absolutely necessary in the current scenarios of the new global economy.

This circumstance is also reflected in the management patterns followed by most SMES that tend to deal with more short-term problems rather than focus on strategies in the short and medium term. Thus it could be said that SMES tend to adopt a reactive more than a proactive attitude to changes in the environment.

In relation to technological change, the EIMS study (European Commission, 1996) points out that the traditional SME tends to deal with it as a contingency, something that appears suddenly and needs to be negotiated if it cannot be avoided, more than as an opportunity (Dankbaar, 1998). Today, after a technologically stable era, many of these companies face radical and rapid changes in their productive processes: digitalization, new systems of the production, etc. A more critical fact is the rejection of the managers of SMES (and especially those in the South) to face the problems of technology in a proactive way. This fact has to be kept in mind by the Public agencies of Innovation when promoting Programs of technology transfer to the SMES.

Equally, SMES tend to value more the information coming from its own environment as the already mentioned EIMS study points out. Also it should be taken into account that not only technical information and knowledge can be a barrier to innovation. Again the EIMS studies point out that commercial technological information is a demand in the innovative process of the SME.

In parallel, these problems are more acute in certain territories (the intermediate regions) at a distance from the centres of information (mainly located in urban areas) or where the IT culture has not yet been extended.

The clustering strategy consists in the monitoring of the main economic agents of a territory with the purpose of facilitating them information about their optimum success alternatives.

These policies are harvesting excellent results in some of the most dynamic regions in the world, with an industrial district profile, when it has been applied to networks of SMES: the Emilia Romagna in Italy, Scotland in UK, Arizona, the Silicon Valley, highway 128 in Boston, New Zealand, Catalonia and the Basque regions in Spain, Finland, etc.

The firms of these advanced clusters adopt coordinated strategic change decisions starting from the mutual knowledge of their possibilities. And, in function of them, carry out managerial cooperation activities when designing projects and carrying out developments, which due to their span could reach at individual level with difficulty, being SMES.

For the above reasons, the development of specific tools is required to systematize the formulation of clustering strategies and to find the know-how which will empower the local systems of innovation and, with them, the decisive factors of the territorial competitiveness.

The recovery of the marshallian theory on industrial districts by Becattini (1987; 1989), starts from the parallelism of the polarized localization of SMES, registered in Italy in the decades of the 70s and the 80s, and the industrial reality of the textile and metallurgists industrial districts existing in Great Britain in the XIX century. The direction that seems to take the technological change of the last half a decade, in the measure that facilitates the delocalization of the production and the quick transport of goods, seems to renovate the initial conditions foreseen by Alfred Marshall (1919) for sustaining industrial districts, facilitating the proliferation of small specialized companies that work jointly in well defined areas and with certain outputs in a market open to international competition.

The cluster approach derives from the model of Porter (1990), which tries to explain why some nations attain sustained higher levels of productivity. Here the relevant questions appear to be: a) which environmental factors at national or regional level propitiate the development of competitive industries at international level?; and (b) Which are the governing bodies best suited to activate these factors? Porter recurs here to his known diamond model.

The strategic school has brought an alternate view on the cluster structure view (Porter, 1990). According to this school of thought, firm performance will be dependent on its favourable position within the structural competitive forces (bargaining power, rivalry, barriers to entry, etc.). A second strategic school of thought (Dyer and Singh, 1998) has recurred to the resource-based view of the firm (Barney, 1991; Rumelt, 1984, Wernerfelt, 1984) to propose that firm competitive advantage may draw from inter organizational relationships: interfirm relation- specific assets, knowledge sharing routines, complementary resources and capabilities and effective governance. This theory links the cluster approach with technology absorption capacity and Knowledge Management. A third school of thought devel-

ops these concepts by adding certain elements: building the knowledge repository, the interfirm relationships such as firm leadership, and the global cluster connections.

KNOWLEDGE MANAGEMENT IN SMES NETWORKS

Existing Knowledge Management models will be applicable to SMES provided that the companies involved fulfil certain conditions. These conditions can be summed up in one; companies must establish relationships in such a way that a dynamic network is established in which learning barriers are eliminated so that knowledge can flow freely from one to another.

Another point to be considered is if the environment in which the companies operate will have a big influence on their Knowledge Management system. If there is to be a positive interaction between different companies and a knowledge interchange and creation process is to be produced, a series of requisites must be fulfilled that include similarity of systems of management, culture, language, objectives, etc. that do not always occur between two companies in a relationship.

That is to say, all the components of each value chain must give their total commitment to creating a climate of cooperation and mutual trust. This is only possible with a durable and stable collaboration in which both partners are equals, so that links are developed and knowledge is exchanged in what is known as knowledge networks. This approach is very close to the concept of the "industrial atmosphere" of the Marshallian industrial districts.

It could be described the qualities that companies must have to be successful in the knowledge-based economy. These qualities are of special importance in the case of the SMES since, if they do not occur it will be impossible to generate, acquire, transfer and combine knowledge among them in such a way as to produce satisfied customers.

These general requisites are based on the need for an organizational structure in the SMES, encouraging cooperation between businesses in networks and clusters, the latter being especially important for localities and regions. The key to gaining competitive advantages in the knowledge-based economy lies in the capacity of companies and other organizations to acquire and absorb knowledge and exploit it to develop new products and processes and to learn from the best practices. It is therefore important, among other factors, to strengthen links with other companies and organizations by establishing inter-organizational networks.

Unquestionably, in the end, the directors of the SMES will have to realise that they will be able to generate more value for their companies within a network than in going it alone. Therefore a change of mentality is necessary and a new business culture must be created in which the exchange of knowledge is facilitated in such a way that the tacit knowledge possessed by their employees can be shared and utilised by the entire organization.

Within the necessary organizational changes in the SMES there are two important possibilities for cooperation, which are not mutually exclusive and could even be regarded as complementary; cooperation within a geographic region (clusters) and cooperation among businesses (networks).

Cooperation in a Geographic Region

The world we live in has become a global economy in which the use of ICT and advanced logistics enables relations to be established between businesses in any part of the world. Nevertheless, in order to establish successful inter-organizational relations or alliances it is important to be able to count on the so-called business ecosystems (Camarinha-Matos, 2002), i.e. on environments favourable to networks of businesses that use similar strategies and practices, where there exists mutual trust among the companies involved, as

well as an atmosphere of community and stability. Such favourable ecosystems or environments can be found for instance in the form of networks of specialised companies, concentrated in certain localities in a large number of advanced countries (Italy, Spain, etc.) in the form of clusters or industrial districts.

The fact that businesses can be concentrated geographically in the form of clusters is a key factor for the SMES in their evolution towards the knowledge-based economy. Some companies are finding out that they can get more benefit from their organizational knowledge, even increasing their competences, within an interactive cluster that possesses informal inter-business links favourable to the creation and transfer of knowledge.

The study of clusters is not new, but goes back to the Marshallian concept of industrial districts. When transport costs were still high and raw materials were the most expensive cost item, businesses tended to gather around zones with abundant natural resources or around big cities. Nowadays, firms tend to stay close to one another, in search of a reserve of trained workers and specific local infrastructures.

Porter (1998) asserts that clusters can be an important source of a sustainable competitive advantage. The firms that compose the cluster can obtain economies of proximity, for example, and even obtain economies of scale through the specialization of the individual companies, joint purchase of raw materials, etc. On this aspect, as regards the range of knowledge, the proximity of institutes, universities, etc., these are proving to be more important factors than the mere fact of being in a geographical cluster.

Another important factor in clusters is the fact that, although it may sound paradoxical, the grouping of businesses is of great importance, in spite of the advances in the ICT, since the correct assimilation of tacit knowledge and innovation needs an environment of cooperation and mutual trust among people, who are more easily reachable in such circumstances. Regarding this aspect, the

ICT have not yet been able to achieve better results in the exchange of knowledge (not information) than interpersonal relations.

Interorganizational Networks as Source of Knowledge and Innovation

Innovation varies significantly among firms (Cohen and Levinthal, 1990; Dosi, 1988) and it is probably the best indicator of the creation of value (Hitt et al., 1996). Innovation refers to the conversion of knowledge into new products, services or processes to be introduced on the market (or the introduction of significant changes into existing ones).

More specifically, innovation and firms' capacity to innovate can be associated with the capacity to combine and exchange knowledge resources (Kanter, 1988; Kogut and Zander, 1992). Resources in networks include information, products and personnel, as well as support for these resources. Moran and Ghoshal (1996) have argued that new sources of value are generated by means of new exploitations of resources, and more particularly through new ways of exchanging and combining resources. Either way, since the pieces of knowledge to be combined may reside in different parties, the exchange of information becomes a requisite for combination and thus for knowledge creation (Cabrera and Cabrera, 2002)

Undoubtedly, knowledge and innovation come both from internal and external sources, yet in the recent strategy and innovation literature a great deal of emphasis has been placed on determinants that are external to the firm. These factors refer to the positive externalities firms receive in terms of knowledge from the environment in which they operate (Van Waarden, 2001). More specifically, interorganizational relationships create opportunities for knowledge acquisition and exploitation (Dyer and Singh, 1998; Lane and Lubatkin, 1998).

As the embeddedness perspective argued, access to external innovation sources is associated with the characteristics of the interactions of the firm with other actors in the social networks.

Territorial Interorganizational Networks

Proximity can be expected to shape social networks by producing a dense structure and strong ties. Therefore, firms benefit from efficiency by exploiting existing opportunities through sharing high quality information and tacit knowledge as well as through cooperative exchange. If geographical dispersion prevents or hinders the generation of routines and redundancies of the interactions, face-to-face interactions between actors induce the frequency and redundancy of the ties (McEvily and Zaheer, 1999). In short, proximity provides frequent, repeated, non-marked, informal contacts, all of which facilitate strong ties and the density of the network of ties.

However, one of the primary concerns for researchers is how to generate the growth of cluster development within the context of dynamic innovation systems. Lock-in is part of the positive as well as the negative story of clusters because it is the capability to innovate within exclusive networks that provides the key that locks in learning capacity. Grabher (1993) referred to the risk of lock-in and group-thinking, particularly when the cluster has to cope with external changes. Only when that learning has been superseded and new knowledge is not absorbed does lock-in become a problem (Cooke, 2002).

As we understand it, cluster membership produces far more than a proximity effect for firms. Cluster firms enjoy a number of relations which are unavailable to external firms. In terms of structural holes, we know about the existence of local institutions within the cluster that act as intermediary agents by providing contacts with external, otherwise unconnected, "actors" belonging to very different circles.

In the context of territorial networks we suggest that, rather than creating this portfolio of ties internally, firms can use external parties (but which are still within the cluster network) to connect themselves to disperse and weakly tied networks. Among possible third parties, we focus on local institutions.

We can conceptualize that as bridging social capital. Individual and organizations with geographical proximity forms groups that determine attitudes, beliefs, identities and values. At the same time to form part of a group determine access to resources, opportunities and power. It may have a high social capital within the group (bonding social capital) which helps members, but they may be excluded from other groups (they lack bridging social capital). It can be distinguished two types of social networks, bonding social capital as reinforcement of homogenous groups whereas bridging social capital as bonds of connectedness that are formed across diverse social groups (Putnam's, 2000).

In conclusion firms must participate in multilevel networks in order to be provided by knowledge and information required for innovation process. In the following section we analyze different interorganizational networks.

THE MOST IMPORTANT TYPOLOGIES OF INTERORGANIZATIONAL RELATIONSHIPS

In recent years many studies have been on the subject of interorganizational cooperation. In this chapter we will follow the classification proposed by Trienekens and Beulens (2001) in which they distinguish vertical relationships in the Value Chain and the Supply Chain, from horizontal relationships in the business background including the theory of networks of businesses engaged in the same industry.

As has been mentioned in the introduction, the SMES will have to make changes in the form of their organizations and of doing business in order to evolve and adapt themselves to a knowledge-based economy. These changes will have to include the creation of interorganizational cooperation. The most usual type of cooperation will be an association with its own suppliers and clients or cooperation with other companies in the same sector or geographical region.

Bearing this in mind, in the following sections we will concentrate on two specific typologies of interorganizational relationships proposed by Trienekens and Beulens (2001), which respond to the needs of the SMES. A detailed analysis will be carried out of the Supply Chain and of Networks following the system proposed by Lazzarini et al. (2001).

The latter authors point out that these two types of analysis have been traditionally considered in the literature as two distinct approaches to interorganizational cooperation. In one the supply chain is usually defined as a set of organized sequential vertical transactions in the different stages of the creation of value. This involves flows of information, materials and resources among the member companies in the different stages of production. In the other, the network analysis is usually directed towards horizontal relationships among companies and other organizations active in the economy, belonging to a specific industry or sector, although it can also refer to vertical relationships.

Although both approaches underline the importance of the interdependence of companies and the way in which interorganizational relationships can bring competitive advantages, they have still not been integrated. Lazzarini et al.(2001) came near to it when they proposed the concept of a *netchain*, which will be explained in detail later. This chapter will also try to unify these two theoretical approaches to interorganizational cooperation.

In the following section we will take a more detailed look at these two approaches in the particular case of the SMES.

Analysis of the Supply Chain

In this section we will summarize the characteristics and tendencies of the first of these approaches.

The Supply Chain is an approach to interorganizational relationships based on the successive stages of the creation of value in a vertical structure of business companies. Lazzarini et al. (2001) identify three principal sources of value in this type of organization:

- **Optimization of production and operations:** The concept of Supply Chain Management (SCM) originated in logistics although it was later amplified to include interorganizational relationships inside and among companies. SCM includes the coordination and control of the flows of information, finance and materials among the members of the chain (Simchi-Levi et al. 2000). The SCM models aim to achieve the optimization of production and operations as the key source of value for the chain as a whole.

- **Reduction of transaction costs:** If efficient relations are established in the Supply Chain the costs of the transactions carried out between members can be reduced.

- **Acquisition of value within the chain:** The constituent companies of the SC can acquire value from innovations in other parts of the chain.

The Supply Chain can be defined as "The network of organizations that are involved, through upstream and downstream linkages, in the different processes and activities that produce value in the form of products and services in the eyes of the ultimate consumer" (Christopher, 1992).

It will be observed that this definition changes the traditional concept of client-supplier based on a simple commercial operation to the concept of the client-supplier chain belonging to Total Quality. To be exact, we can speak of a chain where every enterprise is the client of the preceding link and supplier to the next, and where each time a enterprise acts as supplier it must satisfy the requirements demanded by the client, who will have given the supplier a clear description of his needs.

In this context, **the Supply Chain Management** (SCM) is none other than the management system that controls this supply chain; which cannot be the traditional authoritarian system but must be founded on the involvement and commitment of all the members of the chain in a common project, which is the satisfaction of the final consumer. The objective must be to seek the common good of all members of the chain, so that the profits are distributed among all its members, as against the traditional model in which each member seeks to make a profit for himself alone.

With regard to its principal characteristics, it must be remembered that the correct SCM must ensure that all operations are carried out as efficiently and effectively as possible, increasing quality and customer satisfaction at the lowest possible price. Therefore, the correct SCM is that which unites and maintains the ties among all the processes and parts of the chain.

All the activities involved in the production of any goods or services and their distribution to final consumers should be combined in a continuous process. The SC is not a chain of separate businesses, but is rather a network of multiple relationships. Management of the supply chain offers the opportunity to capture the synergy inside and among companies and implies a new form of managing businesses and also relationships with the other members of the chain (Lambert et al. 1998). In this way, quality, efficiency and efficacy are improved. Thus, a network must be formed to transmit information and knowledge among the members of the chain.

Among the tendencies detected the most important is the change in the conception of the Supply Chain itself. The traditional SC began with production and ended with sales to consumers. In this process, the consumer had very little say: the whole operation was concentrated on the products that flowed through the different stages and logistic channels, and the manufacturers were the ones who controlled characteristics and volumes. The big mistake in this approach was in the lack of flexibility in the offer of products that really met the consumers' needs and expectations.

Nowadays, the client or consumer is becoming the principal element in the Chain, and we now talk of the *Demand Chain* (DC), which consists in a circular process flowing from the mind of the consumer to the market. This means that businesses have to think again about their role in the SC, taking on new functions and responsibilities and accepting the global concept of the DC. In a DC products may be developed at any point and by any of the participants in the SC, thus all the members must have a very good idea both of the consumer and the demand. In this context, the efficient interchange of information and knowledge becomes indispensable.

For this, the development of new organizational structures is necessary as a consequence of the design and integration of a strategic project in the SC. These new strategic structures will have to serve as a base for the operation of new functions, competences and reconfigurations with clients; in effect, to mobilise the personnel of the enterprise around the strategic structure of the Network.

The real situation that we find is that, in many cases, the different firms that participate in a supply chain do not have more contact with each other than is strictly necessary for the operation of the chain, such as communicating termination dates, problems, etc., so that there is never any real coordination or interchange of information and knowledge.

There must be an organizational structure that eliminates the barriers to the creation, transference and diffusion of knowledge, while at the same time satisfying the above mentioned requirements,

especially that of actively including the client in the Supply Chain *(Demand Chain)*.

This means the aim of the Supply Chain must be to regard itself as one single organization in which economies of scale and responses to competitive strategies can be obtained. This would involve a high degree of cooperation and integration among the member companies.

When the various objectives of the chain have been defined as regards satisfying clients' needs, the utilization of resources and the low cost of optimization, the facilitation of operational activities related to production, distribution and delivery can then become the principal objective of the integration of the supply chain. The key factor will be to create more value than the competition by utilising the competitive advantages offered by each of the members in the chain.

One of the initial responses to the need to restructure the companies can be found in Network Organizations. Each member of the network carries out certain functions and it is necessary that somebody coordinates and integrates these operations. Normally, the dominant enterprise is the one that acts as coordinator of the value creating process.

In the following section, we will go into a detailed study of the structural models of network organizations.

Network Analysis

In the Introduction has been mentioned the need for the creation of cooperation among SMES in order to face the challenges of the knowledge-based economy. With regard to this cooperation we have just seen the type that occurs between one enterprise and others in its supply chain and detected the need for this chain to be configured as an organization in the form of a network.

In this section we will examine a second approach to possible interorganizational relationships among the SMES; this is the network or virtual organization and can be structured either vertically or horizontally. This approach must be understood as totally complementary to the preceding.

Network analysis is an approach to the analysis of cooperation among companies, which has increased greatly in recent years, especially in the form of virtual organizations, which we will now examine.

The analysis of this type of organization gives three principal sources of value (Lazzarini et al., 2001).

- **Social structure:** The theoretical approaches to network analysis agree on the importance of the social structure (interpersonal relationships and the individual positions of the members of the network) on behaviour and results, both individually and collectively.
- **Learning:** There are two principal types of learning, with different consequences from the point of view of creation of value. If independent agents or groups develop "local" knowledge and each one specialises in a certain field of knowledge, this results in a diversity of knowledge beneficial for the creation of value and opportunities for innovation. On the other hand, if the efforts are directed towards developing joint specific knowledge "collective" specialization occurs, which can even be harmful in the medium and long term.
- **Generation of external economies in the network:** This source of creation of value happens if the benefits of adopting a new technology or working relationship increase in proportion to the number of participants. In this case benefits are produced for the companies in the network as a result of the total increase in value.

Next we will deal with the concept of network or virtual organizations as well as with their principal types and most important characteristics.

Virtual Organizations

The application of the term "virtual" to the new forms of organization sometimes mixes different viewpoints. Thus, Hammer and Champy (1993) speak of virtual teams, Davidow and Malone (1992) of a virtual corporation, Benjamin and Wigand (1995) of a virtual chain, and Upton and McAfee of a virtual factory, among others.

The term "virtual organization" was first suggested by Davidow and Malone in 1992, referring to market-oriented organizations, i.e. those able to respond immediately to clients' needs. It is structured as a group of value chains with relationships among suppliers, clients, competitors, other organizations and the enterprise itself.

In 1993, the magazines *Fortune, Business Week* and *The Economist* wrote articles, the first on February 8, including the term "Modular Corporation", the second, on the same date, referring to "Virtual Corporation" and the third, two days previously, had remarked that the global enterprise had died and that the new model of enterprise had to concentrate fundamentally on a) a few basic or nuclear activities, a concept that had already been proposed by Prahalad and Hamel (1990), these activities consist of the fundamental business of the enterprise and are also called the *Core Business* and b) the search for networks through agreements or partnerships to carry out the rest of the activities that complete the value chain of the enterprise.

Virtual organizations appear as a response to changes in the working background (specialization, adaptability, opportunity, optimization of cost structures, etc.), i.e. in the areas where companies must concentrate in order to offer a satisfactory response to the needs of their clients.

TYPOLOGIES OF THE MOST SUITABLE NETWORK ORGANIZATIONS FOR THE SITUATION OF THE SMES

Now that the concept of the virtual network organization has been briefly introduced with its various approaches, we will give a more detailed examination the typologies of the principal networks in the literature on interorganizational associations best suited to the situation of the SMES, the Extended Enterprise and the Virtual Enterprise.

The SMES normally form two types of basic interorganizational relationship; vertically, with suppliers and clients, i.e. with members of their supply chain, and horizontally, with other companies in the same area.

The typology of the Extended Enterprise covers the first case, since it is an "extension" or evolution of Supply Chain Management with a central or "dominant" enterprise.

The concept of the Virtual Enterprise goes further and can include both vertical and horizontal relationships in a climate of mutual trust without "dominant" companies. This is the case which most interests us for the subject of this chapter and the one to which we will therefore give most attention.

The Extended Enterprise

The term "Extended Enterprise" is frequently used to describe a high degree of interdependence among organizations that participate in the same business (Browne and Zhang, 1999). It is an extension of Supply Chain Management. As we concluded in the section on this philosophy of management, to be precise, it tends to direct the supply chain towards network structures in the form dealt with in this section.

The most important characteristics of the Extended Enterprise (EC) are as follows:

- **The existence of a dominant enterprise**, which extends its influence to the other members of the supply chain:

- **The establishment of alliances or cooperation with other members of the SC;** this cooperation is based on mutual agreement and long-term commitment to share resources, rewards and risks. The ultimate objective is to work together to achieve greater added value than each would achieve by working alone. Each of the participants therefore has the opportunity to work and specialize in the fields in which it works best. This type of association is usually established with key suppliers or with intermediaries.

- **Management philosophy.** Although in the US alliances are established between members, the fact that there is a dominant enterprise normally means that this enterprise unilaterally imposes its management philosophy. This means there is strong integration in operational and tactical terms but weak in terms of strategy integration.

- **Increase in value added to final product/ service.** The product is oriented towards the final consumer *(Demand Chain)* with the aim of delivering a product or service with the maximum possible added value by means of achieving competitive advantages through the configuration of the Extended Enterprise.

- **Combined capital of participating companies.** In the US the capital (human, operational, technological, etc.) of the members of the SC is combined, although only partially. This is because the dominant enterprise forcibly extends its capital to include that of the other partners, over which it achieves control.

Virtual Enterprise

Here we will examine another concept of network organization, the Virtual Enterprise. This model is more advanced than that dealt with in the previous section, and is more appropriate for the aims of this chapter since it does not necessarily include a dominant enterprise but involves relationships based on mutual trust and the creation of value for the network as a whole.

The Virtual Enterprise can be considered as a particular evolution of network organizations in which the participants attempt to establish a form of management and organization more "democratic or federal" with regard to the management of the flows of information, goods, decisions and control.

Nowadays, production processes are no longer carried out by one enterprise; we normally find that various companies cooperate in a network where each member is a node that adds value to the product. According to Martinez et al. (2001) the principal objective of the Virtual Enterprise is to allow a group of companies to rapidly develop a common work environment and to manage the resources of each one of them so as to achieve a series of common objectives.

The model of the Virtual Enterprise was developed from the simplest organizational forms, such as those mentioned in the previous section. The Virtual Enterprise is given support by evolution in the TIC, the evolution of the global market and new concepts in strategic alliances among companies.

Since modern markets demand ever faster response times and more flexibility with regard to clients' needs there is a growing necessity for new and more flexible forms of cooperation in network organizations. In this context, the Virtual Enterprise appears as a structural response based on flexibility, adaptability, opportunity and optimization of cost structures, in such a way that the resulting group can respond efficiently and profitably to clients' needs.

All the definitions of the VC agree that it is a network of cooperating companies all of which act as nodes and contribute what they can do better than the others *(Core Business)*. From the clients' point of view they all belong to the same enterprise. The result is the optimum cost structure. Each time there is a market opportunity the VC is configured. Thanks to open system structures and the use of TIC, communications are quickly established and the configuration is created in real time.

This need for rapid configuration means that information and knowledge flow horizontally through the network nodes. All potential participants in the VC must have free access to the background information so as to be able to take decisions and form knowledge networks.

NEED OF A NEW ORGANIZATIONAL STRUCTURE

All the above mentioned conditions can be ultimately united in only one; SMES must establish relations among each other in such a way that a dynamic network is created, in which learning barriers are eliminated, so that knowledge can flow freely throughout the network.

In order to do this, it is important, among other factors, to strengthen ties, through the establishment of inter-organizational networks. The need for this collaboration is due to two main factors; one is the fact that mechanisms must be established to ensure that the tacit knowledge held by the members of the enterprises is suitably used and developed; the other is the fact that competition is changing and SMES must learn to work together in order to obtain economies of scale and to be able to use new technologies. SMES must change their mentality and create a new business culture in which the exchange of knowledge is encouraged, so that the tacit knowledge possessed by their employees can be shared and utilized by the whole supply chain.

Total implication from all of the agents is necessary, creating a climate of collaboration and mutual confidence. This is only possible by means of more stable and durable relationships, where equal relations are established. A dynamic network may be created by developing links. So, an organizational structure that eliminates barriers is necessary to the creation, transference and diffusion of knowledge. In this context, concepts related with the Virtual Enterprise (VE) will help us to define the needed organizational model.

The Virtual Enterprise model has been considered as one of the most advantageous methods for SMES, due to the short-term nature of the alliances that arise (alliances created for each particular project).

The current definitions in the literature consider VE as networks of collaborating companies. Each company is a node which makes a contribution about what it knows best (its Core Competence) to the network. Every time that a market opportunity arises, the VE is configured. Each member of the network will establish good communication with the others and with the environment outside the network. It is crucial for cooperation to understand the activities of others, which will provide a context for the node's own activity. The most important aspect of a VE is the mutual trust among its members.

The need for flexibility and a fast-changing organization implies that information has to flow through the network's nodes. All members in the VE should have access to the information to be able to take the right decisions. This reinforces the idea of collaboration; neither leaders nor followers exist.

The most representative nodes in a project would be the following:

- **Initiator node:** The initiator is the node which is responsible for starting the configuration of the network.

- **Operational nodes:** Each of these nodes will provide a complementary core competence to the Virtual Enterprise.
- **Integrator node or Project Manager Node:** This node will coordinate, unify and manage the operational nodes. It will be made up of different members of all the other nodes. It will act as an interface with the rest of the nodes.

These nodes will organize themselves to create a flexible and dynamic structure that will allow the network to exchange and share knowledge. Figure 1 represents the required configuration.

The Integrator or Project Manager Node will be carried out by the Project Manager and a person in each node included in the network. The leadership of the project will be exercised by different nodes, depending on the phase of the project. The aim is to obtain a balance of power among the nodes.

Each person of the Project Manager Node will be part of a change team of his own node. The change team should be formed by people of different hierarchic levels and disciplines. They will work as facilitators, allowing the horizontal and vertical knowledge transmission.

The advantage of this configuration is that, for each new project, a different network will be created, on the basis of the nodes' characteristics.

Figure 1. Principal nodes of the VE

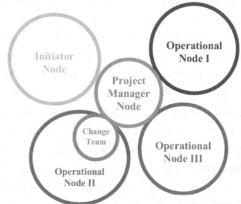

PROPOSAL OF A DYNAMIC KNOWLEDGE NETWORK

To explain the process of creation and transmission of knowledge in SMES networks, a mechanical analogy is proposed; each node of the VE can be seen as a cog that rotates at a given speed. This speed represents the level of organizational knowledge that this node possesses at a particular moment. If the Virtual Enterprise is represented, we would have the following (Figure 2).

All the nodes have been represented with the same size, which means that they all have to turn at the same speed for the right system performance. The fundamental requirements of a dynamic network are that its members have all the same importance and they all have access to the knowledge network. The Project Manager Node will be the system's motive cog, because in this node the interaction among all of the agents occurs, and so creation, transmission and utilization of knowledge.

If new knowledge is created in the project's framework, the knowledge level of the network will vary, which will be represented in the mechanical analogy as acceleration.

Nevertheless, it does not necessarily imply that the dynamic network reaches a new equilibrium point, corresponding to the new velocity. In fact, acceleration can be temporary, returning the network to the initial velocity if each member of the Project Manager Node is not able to transfer that knowledge to its respective node (Project-to-Business -P2B- transfer) when the project finishes.

The change team will become, once the project has finished, the motive cog. They will be the facilitators of a new equilibrium point of the cog, if they are able to turn that new tacit or explicit knowledge into organizational knowledge. These teams should be working continuously so as to get into learning dynamics. At the same time, it has to be able to convert the new knowledge generated into organizational knowledge.

Figure 2. Representation of the VE

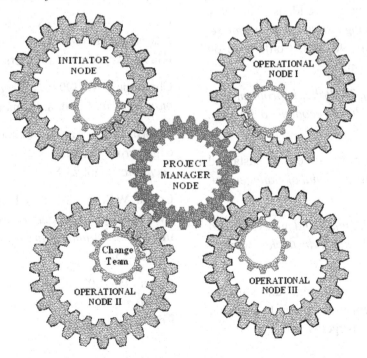

CONCLUSION

In this chapter, the knowledge generation process in SMES has been analyzed. A new organizational form based on the Virtual Enterprise has been suggested in order to make the creation, transfer and sharing of knowledge possible in this case, and a knowledge network model has been proposed, represented within a mechanical analogy, in order to better understand the knowledge creation and transfer process.

We have looked first at the chief conditions and requisites for achieving real Knowledge Management in this special case of SMES. We have arrived at the conclusion that collaboration must be established between chain members, in the form of inter-organizational networks, to encourage the exchange and the creation of knowledge. In this, a fundamental factor is that there must be mutual confidence among the members and similarity in the way of thinking.

REFERENCES

Apostolou, D., Mentzas, G. & Maas, W. (2003). *Knowledge Networking in Extended Enterprise.* Espoo, Finland: ICE, 9th. Int. Conference on Concurrent Engineering.

Bagnasco, A. (1977). *Tre Italie: la problematica territoriale dello sviluppo economico italiano.* Bolonia: Il Mulino.

Barney, J (1991). Firm resources and sustained competitive advantage. *Journal of management,* 17 (1), 99-120.

Becattini, G. (1987). *L'unitá d'indagine / Mercato e forze locali: Il distretto industriale.* Bolonia: Il Mulino.

Becattini, G. (1990). The marshallian industrial district as a socio-economic notion. In Pyke, F., Becattini, G. & Sengenberger, W. (Eds.), *Industrial Districts and Local Economic Regeneration,* Geneva: International Institute for Labor Studies.

Benko, G. & Lipietz, A. (1994). *Las regiones que ganan.* Valencia: Ed. Alfons el Magnànim.

Bresnen, M. & Marshall, N. (2000). Building partnerships: case studies of client-contractor collaboration in the UK construction industry. *Construction Management and Economics,* 18: 819-832.

Browne, J. & Zhang, J. (1999). Extended and Virtual Enterprises: Similarities and differences. *International Journal of Agile Management Systems,* 1(1), 30-39.

Brusco, S. (1982). The Emilian model: Productive descentralisation and social integration. *Rev. Cambridge Journal of Economics,* 6.

Cabrera, A. & Cabrera, E. (2002). Knowledge-sharing dilemmas. *Organization Studies,* 23(5), 687-710.

Camagni, R. P. (1992). Development Scenarios and Policy Guidelines for the Lagging Regions in the 1990s. *Regional Studies,* 26(4).

Camarinha-Matos, L.M. (2002). *Collaborative Business Ecosystems and Virtual Enterprises.* Kluwer Academic Publishers.

Christopher, M. (1992). *Logistics and supply chain management.* London: Pitman Publishing.

Ciborra, C.U. & Andreu, R. (2001). Sharing knowledge across boundaries. *Journal of Information Technology,* 16: 73-81.

Cohen, W.S., & Levinthal, D.A. (1990). Absorptive capacity: A new perspective on learning and innovation. *Administrative Science Quarterly,* 35, 128-152.

Cooke, P. (2002). *Knowledge economies. Clusters, learning cooperative advantage.* London: Routledge

Cushman, M. (2001). *Action research in the UK construction industry - the B-Hive Project*. IFIP 8.2, Boisit USA.

Dankbaar, B. (1998). Technology Management in technology contingent SMES. *International Journal of Technology Management*, 15(1-2), 70.

Davidow, W.H. & Malone, M.S. (1992). *The Virtual Corporation: Structuring and Revitalising the Corporation for the 21st Century*. Harper Collins Publishers.

Ding, H.B. & Peters, L.S. (2000). Inter-firm knowledge management practices for technology and new product development in discontinuous innovation. *International Journal of Technology Management*, 20(5-8): 588-600.

Dosi, G. (1988). Sources, procedures and microeconomic effects of innovation. *Journal of Economic Literature, 26*, 1120-1171.

Dyer J.H. & Singh, H. (1998). The relational view: Cooperative strategy sources of interorganisational competitive advantage. *Academy of Management Review*, 23, 660-679.

Egbu, C. & K. Botterill (2001). *Knowledge Management and Intellectual Capital: Benefits for project based industries*. CoBRA.

Grabher, G. (1993). The weakness of strong ties: the lock-in of regional development in the Ruhr area, in G. GRABHER, (Ed.). *The embedded Firm: on the Socioeconomics of Industrial Networks*. London: Routledge.

Grant, R.M. (2001). Knowledge and Organization, Nonaka, I. and Teece, D.J. (eds) (2001): *Managing industrial knowledge: Creation, transfer and utilization*. London: Sage.

Hammer, M. & Champy, J. (1993). *Reengineering the corporation: A manifesto for business revolution*. New York: Harper Collins.

Hitt, M.A., Hoskisson, R.E., Johnson. R.A. & Moesel, D.D. (1996). The Market for Corporate Control Firm Innovation. *Academy of Management Journal*, 36, 1084-1119.

Kanter, R.M. (1988). When a thous flowers bloom: Structural, collective, social conditions for innovation in organizations, in B. M. STRAW, L. L. CUMMINGS (Eds). *Research in organizational behavior*, 169-211. Greenwich, CT: JAI Press.

Kogut, B. & Zander, U. (1992). Knowledge of the firm, combinative capabilities, the replication of technology. *Organization Science*, 3, 383-397.

Lambert, D., Cooper, M. & Pugh, J. (1998). Supply Chain Management. *International Journal of Logistics Management*. 9(2), 1-19.

Lane, P.J. & Lubatkin, M. (1998). Relative absorptive capacity interorganisational learning. *Strategic Management Journal*, 19, 461-477.

Lazzarini, S.G., Chaddad, F.R. & Cook, M.L. (2001). Integrating supply chain and network analyses: the study of netchains. *Journal on Chain and Network Science*, 1(1), 7-22.

Levy, M., Loebbecke, C. & Powell, P. (2003). SMES, co-opetition and knowledge sharing: the role of information systems. *European Journal of Information Systems*, 12(1), 3-17.

Martínez, M.T., Fouletier, P., Park, K.H. & Favrel, J. (2001). Virtual enterprise: organisation, evolution and control. *International Journal of Production Economics,* 74.

McEvily, B. & Zaheer, A. (1999). Bridging ties: A source of firm heterogeneity in competitive capabilities. *Strategic Management Journal*, 20, 1133-1156.

Moran, K. & Ghoshal, S. (1996). Value Creation by Firms. *Academy of Management Best Paper Proceedings*, 41-45.

Nonaka I. & Takeucki H. (1995). *The Knowledge-creating Company: How Japanese Companies Create the Dynamics of Innovation.* New York: Oxford University Press.

Nonaka, I., Toyama, R. & Cono, N. (2000). SECI, Ba and Leadership: a Unified Model of Dynamic Knowledge Creation. *Long Range Planning*, 33: 5-34.

Porter, M.E. (1980). *Competitive Strategy: Techniques for Analysing Industries and Competitors.* New York: Free Press.

Porter, M.E. (1990). The competitive advantage of nations. *Harvard Business Review*, March-April 1990.

Porter, M. E. (1994). The role of location in competition. *Journal of the Economics of Business*, 1(1).

Porter, M.E. (1998). *On Competition.* Harvard Business School Press.

Prahalad, C.K. & Hamel, G. (1990). The Core Competence of the Corporation. *Harvard Business Review*, 86.

Putnam, R. (2000). *Bowling alone: the collapse and revival of American community.* New York: Simon and Shuster.

Pyke, F. & Sengenberger, W. (1992). *Industrial districts and Local Economic Regeneration.* Geneve: International Institute for Labour Studies.

Rumelt, R.P. (1984). The evaluation of business strategy, in Glueck, W.F., (ed) *Business policy and strategic management*, New York: Mc Graw Hill.

Sabel, Ch. (1992). Studies Trust: Building New Forms of Cooperation in a Volatile Economy. In Pyke, F. & Sengenberger, W. (Ed.) *Industrial Districts and Local Economic Regeneration.* Geneve: International Institute for Labour Studies, International Labour Office.

Scott, B. R. (1989). Competitiveness: Self Help for a Worsening Problem. *Harvard Business Review*, 67 (4), 115 - 121.

Simchi-Levi, D., Kaminski, P. & Simchi-Levi, E. (2000). *Designing and Managing the Supply Chain: Concepts, Strategies, and Case Studies.* New York: McGraw-Hill.

Sweeney, G. (1991). Technical culture and the local dimension of entrepreneurial vitality. *Entrepreneurship and Regional Development*, 3.

Trienekens, J.H. & Beulens, A.J.M. (2001). Views on inter-enterprise relationships. *Production Planning & Control*, 12(5), 466-477.

Van Waarden, F. (2001). Institutions innovation: the legal environment of innovating firms. *Organization Studies*, 22 (5), 765-795.

Wernerfelt, B. (1984), A resource based view of the firm. *Strategic Management Journal*, 5(2), 171-178.

Section IV
Knowledge Management Tools

These chapters consider the management tools for Knowledge Management. The first chapter presents a tool classification and evaluation of their advantages and drawbacks, and the second one the experience of development and implementation of Knowledge Management software for SME. The third chapter centers its attention on e-learning tools.

Chapter VIII
Tools for Supporting Knowledge Management:
Knowledge Internalization Through E-Learning

Raquel Sanchis
Universidad Politécnica de Valencia, Spain

José V. Tomás
Universidad Politécnica de Valencia, Spain

Raúl Poler
Universidad Politécnica de Valencia, Spain

ABSTRACT

This chapter presents a general overview of the relationships between information and communications technologies (ITCs) and the process of Knowledge Management (KM). ITCs through KM tools support the processes to obtain, use and exploit, create and discover, capture, organize and classify, and share and disseminate knowledge. In literature, many classifications of KM tools are defined but problems like bad structures and lacks of understanding have caused the definition of a structured and integrated classification of KM tools. The importance of obtaining knowledge is the reason to analyze KM tools classification in order to obtain profitable information to select the most appropriate one. E-learning techniques have been chosen as the most excellent method to turn explicit knowledge into tacit knowledge (internalization process), therefore a description of this technique will be developed. But the process of selecting the most suitable e-learning platform is difficult; hence a classification of the most relevant characteristics that will guide users will be defined.

INTRODUCTION

The increasing importance of knowledge is modifying the ways to manage organizations to obtain optimal results. Knowledge is a very important resource for any organization in order to preserve its cultural patrimony, to learn new things and to create new methods to solve new problems. It is a fundamental resource for organizations, and human resources are important players because they are the owners of the individual knowledge. Knowledge is an intangible asset, and its nature makes it difficult to manage. One of the most important challenges of organizations is to develop techniques, tools and oriented methods to create, obtain, assimilate, manage and apply the knowledge.

Currently, a great amount of organizations have understood that one of its strategic objectives, is to manage the knowledge with the creation and development of Knowledge Management (KM) technologies and tools to support this process. But the main problem is that Knowledge Management is a trendy concept, but its understanding is poorly applied in real cases. Knowledge has meant and means a challenge of great dimensions for organizations.

Organizations need a new approach of their organizational culture, and information and communication technologies (ICTs), support the activities associated to KM process in order to promote the generation of new competitive advantages. The applications of ICTs to KM process, cause the creation of KM tools. A great amount of tools classified as KM tools exist, but this rich variety and volume of tools have caused that several authors have performed numerous classifications of them. These categorizations try to describe and organize KM tools and their associated technologies. But problems like, bad structures and lack of understanding, appear within these frameworks. Tools, those are very different due to its conceptualization and functionality, are included in the same group. This fact produces serious incoherencies. Moreover, many of these classifications are presented as a simple list of KM tools without any type of connection. KM tools are in continuous evolution, but the classifications found in literature, do not allow integrating new tools that will be developed in the future.

Therefore, it is necessary to define a classification that resolves these problems. Within the project titled 'Integration of Business Processes, Knowledge Management and Decision Support Tools in Supply Chain of Industrial SMEs (GNOSIS)', research project financed by the InterMinisterial Commission of Science and Technology (CICYT) with reference number DP2002-01755, a study about KM tools has been developed. The results generated in the framework of this project are a classification of KM tools, within a well defined framework, the knowledge creation cycle adapted from Skyrme (1999) and the well-known cycle of Nonaka and Takeuchi (1995), in order to provide an integrated and structured view.

The development of this framework has enabled to establish an organized structure of KM tools. And one of our main objectives is focused on the internalization as a process to turn explicit knowledge into tacit knowledge, in order to apply their tacit knowledge to achieve their goals. If knowledge is explicit but it is not internalized, will not be incorporated into one's self', and this process is indispensable to make an optimal use of it. Therefore, taking this hypothesis as a starting point, we will focus on the obtaining stage through e-learning techniques as a KM tool that has the power of communication, organization, management and training.

Firstly, our intention is to make readers, familiarize with the basic concepts of e-learning. A brief state-of-the-art on e-learning will be exposed, which will treat from the pedagogical and technological perspective.

After discussing the advantages and disadvantages of e-learning, a classification of the most relevant characteristics to select the optimal configuration of the e-learning platform will be explained. In this section, e-learning characteristics have been integrated within an adapted e-learning cube (Garlasu et al., 2005) in which three dimensions are included. E-learning characteristics have been classified according to the content, infrastructure and e-services dimensions as a guide to make the selection easier.

THE ROLE OF INFORMATION AND COMMUNICATION TECHNOLOGIES (ICTS) IN KNOWLEDGE MANAGEMENT (KM)

Several authors have proposed many definitions for the term knowledge. Since old times, classical authors have tried to find and reach a consensus on the concept of knowledge. Currently, several definitions exist; being one of the most recognized the one developed by Nonaka and Takeuchi (1995). Knowledge has two points of view in their definition, the static one, which aims to a 'justified true belief' and the dynamic perspective that points out 'the dynamic human process of justification of the personal beliefs that searches the truth'.

Knowledge can be considered as the distillation of information that has been collected, classified, organized, integrated, abstracted and value added. Knowledge is at a level of abstraction higher than the data, and information on which it is based and can be used to deduce new information and new knowledge. When considering knowledge it is usually in the context of human expertise used in solving problems (Hasman, 1995). In general, the first intention to manage knowledge is to generate technical solutions for a problem that has a great factor of human dependency. Therefore, it is important to compensate and equilibrate both perspectives.

Tsui (1999), explains that it does not exist a single definition of KM universally accepted, although most of the definitions aim to the acquisition and dissemination of knowledge in order to improve the skills of the human resources and in general, the advantages of a global entity. Malhotra, (1997) explains that **KM** essentially embodies organizational processes that seek synergistic combination of data and information processing capacity of information technologies, and the creative and innovative capacity of human beings.

The first definition of **KM** is focused on the skills of human resources, whereas the second one links the capacity of information technologies and the capacity of human beings. In this sense, these two capacities cause controversy among the research community. Many researchers (Davenport and Prusak, 1998; Nonaka and Takeuchi, 1995; Anand *et al.*, 1998) strongly criticize the excessive importance of technology. They consider that a successful KM performance does not only depends on information and communication technologies (ICTs) although they facilitate the KM process. The aforementioned authors explain that ICTs do not manage knowledge on their own, but they support KM in each of its phases. Trend (2000) explains that ICTs provide the framework, but not the content. The content remains in the individuals. ICTs facilitate KM process, but ICTs on their own are incapable of extracting knowledge from a person's brain. Several authors (Brown and Duguid, 1998; Silver, 2000; Roberts, 2000; Delclós, 2003; and Chua, 2004) agree and state that **ICTs** work as enabler for KM process. And we also support this statement due to KM depends fairly heavily on ICTs but ICTs only play the role of enabler.

Therefore, **ICTs** are the key factor to support the identification and acquisition of knowledge and it can be viewed as turning data into information and forming information into knowledge. It is largely regarded as a cyclic process involving various activities (Nonaka, 1991). We must draw our attention to the differences of these concepts, because they are dependent on each other. In next figure, we could see the interconnection among them:

Figure 1. Differences between data, information and knowledge

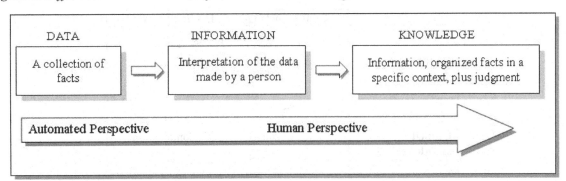

The level of human involvement increases when we advance in the previous figure. ICTs impact especially on the first two dimensions and contribute to facilitate the generation of third one, but computers are suitable to manage data, less suitable for information and much less for knowledge. Therefore, KM focuses the attention on human resources as processor of symbols to generate new meanings and processes in an organization, but ICTs are necessary to support and achieve this goal.

The applications of **ICTs** to the KM process, cause the creation of KM tools. Ruggles (1997) and Carvalho and Araújo (2002) define **KM tools** as a kind of software that supports any of the three basic KM processes (Davenport and Prusak, 1998): generation, codification and transfer. But cycles of KM have more basic KM processes. Therefore, we define KM tools as the instruments that support all the activities related to KM in all the phases of the whole cycle. These tools allow promoting, organizing and enabling the process of KM in order to improve the decision making. Currently, the fact to understand the meaning and application of ICTs, is the key factor to avoid committing a conceptual error. This error is to confuse the establishment of a KM system, like an activity exclusively related to ICTs as we mentioned previously. Therefore, the objective of a KM tool, is not to manage the knowledge, but facilitate the implementation of

the KM process, that is, to generate the frame and structure based on the use of ICTs. They can also be used to clarify suppositions, to accelerate the communication, to obtain tacit knowledge and to construct to behaviors or conducts files, as well as, to catalogue them (Grantham and Nichols, 1993).

A KM tool will show its utility through the interaction of the people who use it. In many cases, these tools could automate certain types of tasks in the areas based on knowledge. But in general, the role of KM tools, is purely an enabler to lead the activities based on knowledge. They are designed to facilitate the work load and to allow that the resources are applied in an effective way to the most suitable tasks. That is the reason why a classification of these tools is necessary in order to clarify the description, structure and organization of them and their associated technologies.

THE CLASSIFICATION FRAMEWORK

KM tools classification has been developed according to two cycles. Nonaka and Takeuchi (1995), and Skyrme (1999) approaches have been used as the basis of the development of the framework. It is very important to establish the framework and the context in which the integration of KM tools could be developed in a suit-

Figure 2. Creation knowledge model (Nonaka & Takeuchi, 1995).

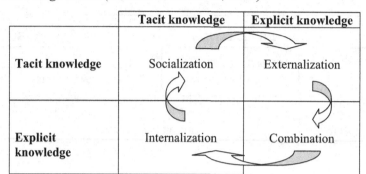

	Tacit knowledge	Explicit knowledge
Tacit knowledge	Socialization	Externalization
Explicit knowledge	Internalization	Combination

Figure 3. Adapted cycle of Skyrme (1999)

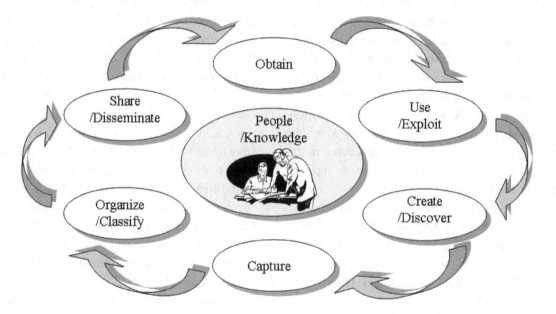

able way. The choice of these two cycles, is due to they cover all the stages in which knowledge could be found. Moreover, these two cycles are well-known and for that reason, it will be very easy to understand the classification.

Nonaka and Takeuchi (1995) present their cycle where knowledge creation is obtained by the relationship of tacit and explicit knowledge. Tacit knowledge is defined as the knowledge that remains in the minds of people. This type of knowledge is difficult to formalize or explain to others. Explicit knowledge is formal knowledge that is easy to communicate between individuals and groups and it is simple to gain access of it.

The creation knowledge model is divided into four stages where tacit knowledge is turned into explicit and vice versa:

- Socialization is a process of converting tacit knowledge into tacit knowledge, sharing experiences between people.

- Externalization is a process of conversion tacit knowledge into explicit concepts (conceptual knowledge) through the use of metaphors, analogies, or models.
- Combination is the conversion of explicit knowledge from a number of sources into explicit knowledge by techniques like reasoning, programming, data mining, and information exchange through formal information systems.
- Internalization is a process to convert explicit knowledge into tacit knowledge by means the know-how.

The other cycle is proposed by Skyrme (1999) whose goals are to obtain, create and disseminate knowledge (this cycle has been adapted). It includes all the phases where knowledge is manipulated, through the definition of a set of actions that operate on the tacit and explicit knowledge. This cycle, that has been personalized, is divided into the following stages:

- **Obtaining knowledge:** The necessary knowledge (explicit) is obtained of the knowledge repositories through search engines or any other search and selection tool. It is also possible to obtain knowledge directly (tacit) through the interaction among people communicating experiences, training sessions, etc.
- **Use and exploitation of knowledge:** Knowledge is used like a part of the work process. It is refined and developed.
- **Creation and discovery of knowledge:** Use and exploitation of the knowledge allow obtaining new knowledge, through its creation or through its discovery.
- **Capture of knowledge:** The existing tacit knowledge located in the brains of people within an organization, which has been developed during the work process, can be captured and codified to convert it into explicit knowledge in order to use it later.
- **Organization and classification of knowledge:** The explicit knowledge obtained, must be organized and classified in the knowledge repositories of the company through organizational taxonomies. Whereas, the captured tacit knowledge, as well as the

Figure 4. Methodology used to classify the different KM tools (Tomás et al., 2004).© 2008 Raquel Sanchis. Used with permission.

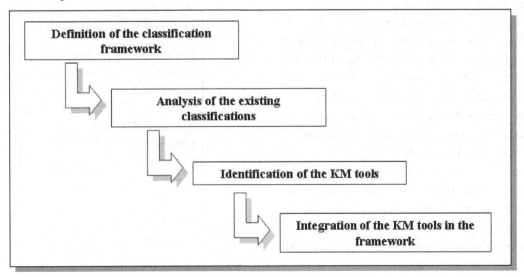

created or discovered one, must be also organized and classified on the basis of these taxonomies.

- **Sharing and dissemination knowledge:** The knowledge is shared or disseminated in order to get competitive advantages of it. This knowledge will be the starting point for the creation process again. It is regarded as a cyclic process.

METHODOLOGY AND ANALYSIS OF KM TOOLS

There exist a great amount of tools classified like KM tools, that is for example, Groupware or Artificial Intelligence. This rich variety and volume of tools have caused that several authors have performed numerous classifications of KM tools (Pávez, 2000; Grau, 2001; Tyndale, 2002; Carvalho and Araújo 2002; Wise, 2002). These categorizations try to describe and organize the tools and their associated technologies. But problems like, bad structures and lack of understanding, appear within these frameworks. Tools, those are very different due to its conceptualization and functionality, are included in the same group. This fact produces serious incoherencies. Therefore, it is necessary to define a classification that resolves these problems.

Within the project titled 'Integration of Business Processes, Knowledge Management and Decision Support Tools in Supply Chain of Industrial SMEs (GNOSIS)', research project financed by the InterMinisterial Commission of Science and Technology (CICYT) with reference number DP2002-01755, a study about support tools of the knowledge board has been developed.

One of the project's objectives focuses on studying different KM tools that are available currently on the market in order to classify them according to its nature and characteristics. Therefore, the main goal is to develop a KM

tools classification to structure the current set of tools and technologies, in order to enable a logical comprehension of them. The definition of a methodology is necessary in order to organize and configure **KM tools** classification. The methodology begins with the definition of the KM tools classification framework. This framework serves as the connection of the tools with the context of KM. Nonaka and Takeuchi (1995), and Skyrme (1999) approaches have been used to define the framework in order to develop a suitable KM tools classification, as we can see in the previous section.

Once the framework has been established, the analysis and assessment of the existing KM tools classifications will be performed considering their suitability, deficiencies and advantages. Later, the identification of different tools will be developed and the result will be the elaboration of a complete directory. Finally this directory will

Table 1. The most representative KM tools (Tomas, et al., 2004).). © 2008 Raquel Sanchis. Used with permission.

Search Engines
Intelligent Agents
Personalized Information Distribution
Knowledge Maps
Simulation Tools
Artificial Intelligence Systems
Decision Support Tools
Conceptual Map Tools
Data Mining- Text Mining
Data Warehousing.
Visual Representation Data Tools
E-Learning Platforms
Collaborative Tools
Workflow
CRM
Modelling tools
Taxonomies management Tools

be integrated within the framework to facilitate the understanding of the different KM tools.

Throughout the process of analysis, five **KM tools** classifications have been studied. A general overview of these classifications is presented in order to deepen profitable information of the researches that have been performed:

- Pávez (2000) classified the KM tools according to their uses. But this categorization lacks the necessary integration of the framework what produces an obstacle to a suitable understanding of the different types of tools.
- Grau (2001) presented a simple classification of KM tools. One of the main results of this research is that the analysis is made of more than 70 market tools; therefore this study adds a great amount of information.
- Tyndale (2002) elaborated a broad classification of KM tools. The categorization

is made according to the tools antiquity and the different phases of the knowledge (creation, organization, distribution and application).

- Carvalho and Araújo (2002) developed an interesting classification of KM tools fitted within the Nonaka and Takeuchi's knowledge cycle.
- Within the European Project titled WISE, IST-2000-29280, a "Review of Knowledge Management tools" (Wise, 2002) is presented and it establishes a KM tools classification. This framework lacks a suitable nexus with KM, although an exhaustive study of different market KM tools is developed.

After an exhaustive analysis of the previous classifications, as well as a study of the current market tools, a set of the most representative tools within the KM field, have been defined:

Figure 5. Tools classification according to knowledge creation life cycle (Tomás et al., 2004).© 2008 Raquel Sanchis. Used with permission.

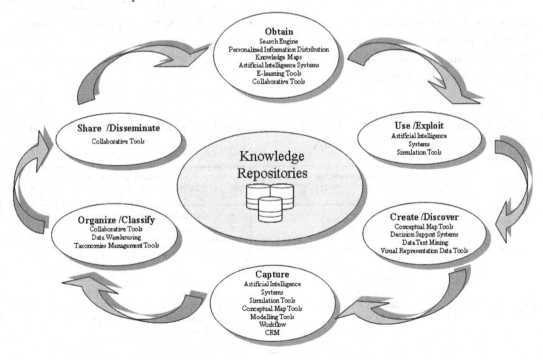

This set of tools describes groups of technologies that help and support KM processes. Most of the studies developed, finishes at this point, like a simple list of KM tools. In order to provide the maximum understanding and comprehension of **KM tools** , our research focused the attention on the integration of each tool within two cycles: the knowledge creation cycle adapted from Skyrme (1999) and the well-known cycle of Nonaka and Takeuchi (1995).

The previous analyses were based on only one framework and some conceptual characteristics and integration properties were ignored. For example, the collaborative tools foment the knowledge dissemination. Therefore, the necessity to fit these tools within the stages of socialization, externalization and combination; is crucial. For that reason, the analysis according to both cycles, is completely obligatory, in order to achieve the accomplishment of this study. Finally, this analysis allows creating macro-types of KM tools in order to get a better understanding of their functionalities and applications.

For the Knowledge Creation Cycle, the classification is focused on:

- Tools to obtain knowledge.
- Tools to use and exploit knowledge.
- Tools to create and discover knowledge.
- Tools to capture knowledge.

- Tools to organise knowledge.
- Tools to disseminate knowledge.

The following scheme shows the generic **KM tools** framework related to the knowledge creation cycle. Each one of the different types defined, integrate into its role in the KM process.

The figure shows a new actor within the framework of KM tools, knowledge repositories. These elements, cannot be consider tools, due to their morphology and functionalities, but they play a fundamental role within the general process of KM. The explicit knowledge is based on several knowledge repositories. The costs of the information storage devices have decreased too much, that is why organizations are able to store great amounts of critical information in an easy way, and make it available to their users through corporative networks.

According to the knowledge conversion life cycle describedd by Nonaka and Takeuchi, the classification of **KM tools** presents:

- Tools to support the externalization.
- Tools to support the combination.
- Tools to support the internalization.
- Tools to support the socialization.

Table 2. Tools classification according to the knowledge conversion life cycle (Tomas et al., 2004).).© 2008 Raquel Sanchis. Used with permission.

	Tacit knowledge	Explicit knowledge
Tacit knowledge	Socialization • Collaborative Tools • Knowledge Maps	Externalization • Collaborative Tools • Artificial Intelligence Systems • Simulation Tools
Explicit knowledge	Internalization • Search Engine • Intelligent Agents • Personalized Information Distribution • E-Learning Tools	Combination • Collaborative Tools • Data Mining • Text Mining • Visual Representation Data Tools • Conceptual Map Tools • Decision Support System

In this table, tools are classified in order to improve their understanding and contextualization within KM.

Once the identification of the different KM tools is developed, this classification could be used now and in the future. Technologies are in continuous evolution, but this classification allows integrating new tools that will be developed in the future.

Every phase of the cycles is extremely important in order to complete the whole cycle. But we start from the premise that people need the internalization as a process to convert explicit knowledge into tacit knowledge, in order to apply their tacit knowledge to achieve their goals. If knowledge is explicit but it is not internalized, will not be incorporated into one's 'self', and this process is indispensable to make an optimal use of it.

Therefore, taking this hypothesis as a starting point, we will focus on the obtaining stage according to knowledge creation life cycle or in the transition of explicit knowledge into tacit one, by means of the **internalization process**. In both stages, we can observe the coincidence of e-learning tools as techniques that have the power of communication, organization, management and training. **E-learning platforms** are one of the most excellent support methods to convert explicit knowledge into tacit knowledge, because learning provides intellectual knowledge that is the key to take actions and achieve results. With learning and without application, the objectives cannot be reached.

The rapid development of ICTs has enabled new methods to communicate and learn. Barriers as time, geographic distance, etc, have been solved by means the use of ICTs. In this sense, e-learning is a new form for managers and educators to deliver high quality training material and overcome barriers. For that reason, a study of the e-learning technique will be developed in next section.

KNOWLEDGE INTERNALIZATION THROUGH E-LEARNING

Learning is the development and acquisition of knowledge or capability through study, read, experience and understanding. It is a gradual activity that has influence, guides and causes long-term changes in the potential behaviour and personality. Potential behaviour describes the expected to become or be behaviour of an individual (not actual behaviour) in a situation in order to accomplish a goal. Therefore, the process of learning is an increase in the skills for effective action. Personal, group, and organizational learning can all be measured by the outcomes that result from effective action.

The fast growth of ICTs makes feasible to define and create new ways of education, learning and training. Many years ago the new way of learning was based on computer based training (CBT) which used primary CD and local area networks as information medium. Currently, this term has evolved to e-learning through the use of Internet, Wide World Web and learning management systems (LMS) that have fundamentally altered the practice of distance teaching and learning. In the past, trainers had to either find the time to develop their own classroom or workshop materials. With e-learning, all the work is done for users and it is possible to print-on-demand as many courses as users need when users need them. In the array of learning tools available, e-learning is an important, upcoming learning tool.

The concept **e-learning**, also called Online learning, networked learning, electronic learning, Internet-based learning and Web-based learning, is a general term that relates to all training material that is delivered with the assistance of a computer. Delivery of e-learning could be via CD, Internet, or shared files on a network. Generally, CBT and e-learning are synonymous, as we have seen previously, but CBT is the older term, dating from the 1980s. And the term e-learning evolved from CBT with the maturation of the Internet, CDs, and DVDs.

E-learning applications are generally built around the interactive multimedia. Learners see text, graphics and animations in e-learning courses. Other mediums that may be present primarily include video and sound. There is usually a feedback mechanism built in for users to respond. This could be through the keyboard, the mouse, or through the microphone. The instructional approach varies widely from having plain multiple-choice questions to complex simulations. E-learning applications could be developed in any field or area, with any nature of content and performance outcomes. Moreover, e-learning is very helpful to build cognitive skills, procedures, facts, conceptual knowledge and to convert the explicit knowledge into tacit knowledge. It has been extraordinarily successful in the field of soft skills, management, leadership, interrelationship management, etc... But e-learning present problems with psychomotor skills due to users need practice. Although, e-learning is not capable to teach these skills, it provides critical knowledge components related to these capabilities.

It is very important to give the right design and technology. Therefore, a classification of the most relevant characteristics t configure an optimal e-learning platform will be developed in next section.

E-learning is naturally suited to distance and flexible learning, but can also be used in conjunction with face-to-face teaching, in which case the term blended learning, defined as the combination of multiple approaches to learning, is commonly used. Another concept related to e-learning that has obtained great popularity is m-Learning. This term includes the ability to learn everywhere at every time without permanent physical connection to cable networks. This can be achieved by the use of mobile and portable devices such as PDA, cell phones, portable computers and Tablet PC. They must have the ability to connect to other computer devices, to present educational

information and to realise bilateral information exchange between the users and the instructor (Georgiev, 2004).

Nowadays, the tendency of e-learning as an optimal process to train, is growing up. Increasingly, organizations are adopting online learning as the main delivery method to train employees (Simmons, 2002). E-learning provides flexibility because it offers learners with increased choice, convenience, and personalization. In particular, flexible learning provides learners with choices about where, when, and how learning occurs. For those participants who have others commitments, e-learning facilitate the communication between them, great adaptability to their needs, the ability to work at users own pace and more variety in learning experience with the use of multimedia and non-verbal presentation of training material. E-learning provides attendants with opportunities to access information and expertise, contribute ideas and opinions, and correspond with other learners and mentors.

For learners, online learning knows no time zones, and location and distance are not an issue. In synchronous e-learning, trainer and users are involved in the course, class or lesson at the same time (synchronized). Web conferencing is an example of synchronous e-learning. Participants can log on with an instructor and interact with participants at multiple facilities or locations. In asynchronous e-learning, trainer and users are involved at different times (not synchronized, or asynchronous). Some of the training material can be paused and reversed for watching again, so many times, that the attendants need in order to get a better understanding of the contents of the e-learning material. It is also very profitable for organizations with distributed and constantly changing personnel. In this case, e-learning has huge benefits when compared with organizing face-to-face classroom training.

But there are several researchers of different fields (ICTs, Psychology...) that critic e-learning arguing that this process is not longer educational in the highest philosophical sense. Nonaka (1991) recognized face-to-face communication as the most efficient method to increase the benefits of collaborative knowledge. E-learning is characterized by the lack of face-to-face interaction with a trainer, what confer isolation feeling of users. But, in this case, it would be interesting to use blended learning, alternation of e-learning training with face-to-face classrooms, to solve this problem. Moreover, e-learning techniques provide several options to motivate human interactions through Web-conferencing programs, chats, forums, e-mail, etc… Therefore, we consider that this technique is very suitable; because it enables to learn the field or area users have chosen and reinforce ICTs skills.

E-LEARNING PERSPECTIVES

There are four fundamental pedagogical perspectives which historically have had an important influence on the approach to computer based pedagogy, distance education and continue to provide guiding principles for the pedagogy of **e-learning**:

- The Cognitive perspective focuses on the cognitive processes involved in learning as well as the way the brain works.

Greitzer (2002) outlined a set of cognitive principles to guide the creation of learning applications. These principles are stimulating semantic knowledge, manage cognitive load, problem-centered, interactive and frequent and varied practice.

The foundation for the design and implementation of these principles is the notion of interaction elements, which form the basis of student-centered/active learning approach. Interaction elements are basic objects for engaging the learner through ideas, problem-solving activity, or interaction. By associating specific

Figure 6. The adapted three e-learning dimensions (Garlasu et al., 2005).).© 2008 Raquel Sanchis. Used with permission.

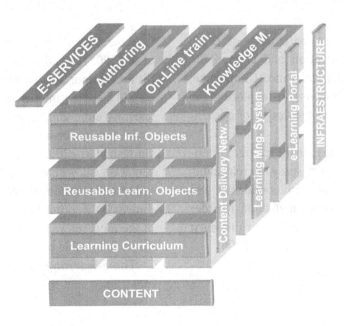

Table 3. Organizations promoting standards on e-learning

Airline Industry CBT Committee (AICC)	Focus on standards for airline training e.g. tests, lessons, modules, etc.	www.aicc.org
EDUCAUSE Institutional Management System Project (IMS)	Vendor group working to build standards for e-learning based on work of AICC	www.imsproject.org
Advanced Distributed Learning (ADL)	US Federal government initiative. Development of SCORM	www.adlnet.org
Alliance of Remote Institutional Authoring and Distribution Network for Europe (ARIADNE)	An industry association focusing on e-learning standards issues	www.ariadne-eu.org
IEEE Learning Technology Standards Committee (IEEE LTSC)	Accredits the standards for the US that emerge from the other groups	ieeeltsc.org
ISO/IEC JTC1 SC36 (ITLET)	IT for Learning, Education and Training	
Advanced Learning Infrastructure Consortium (ALIC)	Japanese Consortium for promotion of e-leaning technology and infrastructure	www.alic.gr.jp
E-Learning Consortium Japan (eLC)	Vendor/User company working to promote e-learning business and technology	www.elc.or.jp

learning objectives with interaction elements, the instructional designer can transform them into learning objects that transcend their original purpose and enable their re-use by other courses that call upon the same or similar learning objectives (Greitzer, 2003).

- The Emotional perspective focuses on the emotional aspects of learning, like motivation, engagement, fun, etc.

Keller (1983) synthesized existing research on psychological motivation and created the ARCS model (Attention, Relevance, Confidence, Satisfaction) as a framework to exploring the emotional components in the design of e-learning applications.

It is very important to gain the learner's attention, assuring that what they study has relevance, allowing them to proceed with confidence, and having the outcome provide satisfaction. In order to achieve all these components, e-learning must be more fun, more gamelike (Quinn, 2006).

- The Behavioural perspective focuses on the skills and behavioural outcomes of the learning process. Role-playing and application to on-the-job settings.
- The contextual perspective focuses on the environmental and social aspects which can stimulate learning. Interaction with other people, collaborative discovery and the importance of peer support as well as pressure (Black and McClintock, 1995).

Apart from the previous perspectives, Garlasu et al., (2005) considers the content perspective as the most important one. But two new dimensions should be taken into account to construct the e-learning cube and these are infrastructure and e-services dimensions. The **e-learning** cube of Garlasu et al. (2005) is a 4x4x4 graphical representation, but we have adapted it to a 3x3x3 representation with the most relevant elements of each dimension in order to develop the classification of the most relevant characteristics to configure the most suitable e-learning platform.

The **e-learning dimensions** are the following:

The Content Dimension

One of the main properties related to the content dimension is the reusability of it. But this reusability is necessary not only from the content point of view but also from the interoperability point of view, as the ability of using e-learning content in different e-learning platforms. There are some organizations that support standards:

The content dimension consists of the following elements:

- **Reusable information objects (RIO):** Also called reusable content objects (RCO). RIO are self-enclosed chunks of information built around an objective addressed to learning. These objects are tagged with metadata describing its characteristics, purpose and relationships with other objects. As defined by Clark (1989), a RIO is a concept, fact, procedure or principle.
- **Reusable learning objects (RLO):** Are generally mini-lessons, able to be assigned as a unit for a learning management system (LMS). A learning object involves an organisation of knowledge elements, learner guidance, performance and feedback. In other words they are not single media files, but can stand alone as learning opportunities. A RLO is based on a single objective derived from a specific job task. The RLO approach has resulted in successful implementations (Clark, 2002)
- **Learning curriculum:** Joints together RLOs into a larger hierarchy. It can also be expressed as an educational program customized to the learner. The most typical learning curriculum structure in: Curriculum, Unit, Module, Lesson/Chapter (RLO) and Section (RIO).

The E-Services Dimension

This dimension is referred to the provision of learning services provided via the Internet and its main elements are:

- **Authoring:** Building the RLOs and placing them on a server is not enough, the RLOs must be combined through authoring into a structured learning curriculum. An authoring tool helps in the creation a final application merely by linking together objects, such as a paragraph of text, an illustration, a video, etc. This material could be delivered via synchronous or asynchronous learning.
- **Online training:** It is an essential part of an e-learning strategy, simply providing RLOs is not enough to achieve the objective of a efficient learning. Online training eliminated well known computer bases training (CBT) disappointments: unfit content, unauthentic learning, etc.).
- **Knowledge management:** Supports the creation, archiving and sharing valued information, expertise and insight within and across communities of interest. A KM strategy provides a common approach for managing information.

The Infrastructure Dimension

The e-learning infrastructure is the technological capabilities to deliver and manage e-learning. Its main elements are the following:

- **Content delivery network:** Is the system of computers networked together across the Internet that cooperate transparently to deliver content to end users.
- **Learning management system:** Is a software application or Web-based technology used to plan, implement, and assess a specific learning process. Typically, a learning management system provides an instructor

with a way to create and deliver content, monitor users' participation, and assess users' performance. A learning management system may also provide users with the ability to use interactive features such as threaded discussions, video conferencing, and discussion forums.

- **E-learning portal:** Is in effect a gateway into an area containing training and reference materials. It is a Web frame which will provide users with an array of e-learning and collaborative tools enabling them to seek on-line help, chat together, post questions and of course access learning courseware.

These three dimensions and their associated elements, will be used as the framework to classify the most important characteristics to configure the e-learning platform.

E-LEARNING PLATFORMS CHARACTERISTICS

One of the main goals is to select the most suitable **e-learning platform** according to the most relevant characteristics. The selection process is a difficult task, therefore a classification of the most important characteristics have been integrated in the adapted e-learning cube (Garlasu et al., 2005) in order to provide an integrated and structured classification to facilitate the choice. The classification is organized trough the three **e-learning dimensions** of the e-cube and within each dimension, characteristics haven been categorized as follows:

The Content Dimension

Reusable Information Objects (RIO) and Reusable Learning Objects (RLO)

- **Scalability:** The ability to adapt according to the number of students, performance, etc.

- **Standards support:** The systems support the use of standards like SCORM, AICC, etc.
- **Interoperability:** The product could be integrated in other platforms.
- **Web compatibility:** The product is compatible with the Web technology (MP3, real audio, avi, quicktime, gif, 3d, java, etc.).
- **Ease of integration:** The platform enables to download files or show links to existing files or Web pages.
- **Extensibility:** The platform could be upgraded with a stable life cycle.

Learning Curriculum

- **Learning schema:** The planning to follow the course.
- **Index creation:** The creation of a course index or table of contents to summarise the information.
- **Glossary:** An alphabetical list of technical terms in some specialized field of knowledge with the definitions for those terms.
- **Course objectives:** The possibility to present the curriculum intentions, goals and targets.
- **Courses, workshops and services:** The offer of courses, workshops and training material.
- **Learning paths:** Instructors should be able to define individual student learning paths.

The E-Services Dimension

Authoring

- **Synchronous collaborative learning:** Users should synchronously communicate and collaborate though the use of tools like chats, videoconferencing, etc.
- **Asynchronous collaborative learning:** Users should asynchronously communicate

and collaborate though the use of tools like e-mail, forums, etc.

- **Course download/Offline Working:** The opportunity to download the complete course (or partially) in order to work offline.

- **Asynchronous tutorship:** The realization of asynchronous tutorships (by e-mail, forums, etc.).

- **Synchronous tutorship:** The realization of synchronous tutorships (by chat, audio-conferencing, videoconferencing, shared blackboard, etc.).

- **Course development interface:** An easy and intuitive interface for the development of the course.

- **Offline development:** The possibility to develop and manage in an offline interface.

- **Resource administration:** The administration of different resources as documents, images, URLs, etc.

- **Statistics/reports:** The generation of access statistics, accessed pages, times, etc..

On-Line Training

- **Moderation functionalities:** The platform should allow that one member could become a moderator-instructor with the capabilities to create, modify and take part in the course.

- **Online capabilities:** The information should be enabled in the platform using online facilities.

- **Course announcements:** Users should be informed about issues of interest.

- **Tutor-student agenda:** The integration of the agendas of students and instructor.

- **Access tracking:** The tutor should track the accesses and times made by each user.

- **Online registration:** The facilities to enrol student via Web.

- **Online Technical support:** An online technical support via Web, e-mail or phone

in order that students receive the necessary technical assistance.

Knowledge Management

- **Private annotations:** The possibility to take down private comments, remarks, observations... made by the student.

- **One to one – mail and one to many – mail:** The communication between a student and other student and also between a student and a group of students in order to share knowledge.

- **Students tracking:** Instructors should be able to track the learner's progress and learners should be able to be informed of their own progress.

- **Required knowledge:** The definition of the advanced technical skills and competences required to follow or build the course.

- **Electronic marks and certification:** The property to develop a system of electronic marks and certifications (digital certificates of course completion, e-diplomas, etc.).

- **Collaboration knowledge development:** The evaluation of the progress of the knowledge acquired by the students.

- **Knowledge assessment:** Through exams with different options like multiple choice, matching, randomization, examination time, management of online self-evaluate questionnaires...

- **Result based actions:** The realization of different actions based on the results obtained by each student.

The Infrastructure Dimension

Content Delivery Network

- **Discussion forums:** Informal modes of learning - peer interaction. Forums provide an efficient space to conduct discussions and argumentations about a topic and thus to build a common knowledge on a subject.

- **Upload capabilities:** The chance for file uploading by the student in order to exchange information.
- **Chat room:** On-line text-based communication between students.
- **Shared blackboard:** The communication and interaction mechanism between game logic components hosted among teachers and students.
- **Standard Web browser:** A standard client program that initiates requests to a Web server and displays the information that the server returns.
- **Different operating systems support:** The client platform should be supported by different operating systems (Windows, MacOS, Linux, Unix…).
- **Backup:** Copying or saving data to a different location in case of loses or damage of information.
- **Multiple instructor support:** Multiple instructors could maintain and update a single course.
- **Working group selection:** Organization of different working groups.
- **Material assignment:** The instructor could assign a specific course material to a students group.

Learning Management System (LMS)

The most relevant and popular Open Source LMS with its main characteristics are presented, in order to facilitate the choice:

- **Moodle:** http://moodle.org/
  Moodle is an open-source virtual learning environments (VLE) that is very similar in many respects to the course management components of the major commercial VLEs.
- **Claroline:** http://www.claroline.net/
  Claroline is an Open Source software based on PHP/MySQL. It is a collaborative

learning environment allowing teachers or education institutions to create and administer courses through the Web. The system provides group management, forums, document repositories, calendar, chat, assignment areas, links, and user profile administration on a single and highly integrated package. Claroline is translated in 28 languages and used by hundreds of institutions around the world. The software is released under Open Source licence (GPL). Downloading and using Claroline is completely free of charge.

- **ATutor:** http://www.atutor.ca/
  ATutor is an Open Source Web-based learning content management system (LCMS) designed with accessibility and adaptability in mind. Administrators can install or update ATutor in minutes. Educators can quickly assemble, package, and redistribute Web-based instructional content, easily retrieve and import prepackaged content, and conduct their courses online. Students learn in an adaptive learning environment.
- **Ilias:** http://www.ilias.uni-koeln.de/ios/index-e.html
  ILIAS is an Open Source learning management system, offered free of charge, for developing and realizing Web-based e-learning. ILIAS allows efficient creation of courses and course materials. It offers standardized tools and templates for the learning and working process including integrated navigation and administration.
- **eConf:** http://econf.sourceforge.net/
  eConf is an open source e-learning software, written in Java. It allows to easily record Web sessions and has been used to record multiple computer science courses. eConf is an add-on to an HTTP proxy that is able to capture the Web pages shown during the session and the voice of the presenter. The audio and the Web pages are then synchronized to allow the students to listen to the recorded course. The current release of

eConf is built on top of the W3C's Jigsaw proxy but any other proxy may be used.

- **Colloquia:** http://www.colloquia.net/
Colloquia is a peer-to-peer learning management and groupware system, supports and encourages self-organising groups, provides asynchronous group and personal conversation facilities, allows personal information to be shared between participants, allows learning and other online resources to be referenced and accessed, has an inbuilt Web browser, runs on all Java enabled platforms.

- **CHEF:** http://www.chefproject.org.
The *CHEF* project, an initiative by the University of Michigan to create an extensible platform for online collaboration, is one of the four learning management environments being combined in the Sakai Project of the University of Michigan, Indiana University, MIT, and Stanford. One of the preconfigured toolsets that comes with CHEF allows for the creation of a course worksite. A course worksite allows for online or Web-based management of a course. This includes online resources, scheduling, discussion forums and assignments.

- **Fle3:** http://fle3.uiah.fi/
Fle3 is a Web-based learning environment. To be more specific Fle3 is server software for computer supported collaborative learning (CSCL). Fle3 is Open Source and Free Software released under the GNU General Public Licence (GPL). The licence is protecting your freedom to use, modify and distribute Fle3.

- **EduPlone:** http://edplone.net/index_ html?cl=en
Eduplone products melt together the enterprise content management system plone with leading didactic models and standards and also plone based dayta platform. Uniting these theories, technologies and methodologies strengthens the competencies in the conference- and implementation network, advances the innovation power and supports standardisation. Everyone – author, teacher or student – gets a personal folder in the portal and will be able to place or create own material in this secured environment.

- **LON-CAPA:** http://www.lon-capa.org
LON-CAPA is an Open Source freeware distributed learning content management and assessment system. LON-CAPA is a full-featured, Web-based course management system similar to commercial systems.

E-Learning Portal

- **Security and authentication:** The platform should include encryption algorithms in the authentication processes.

- **Other technologies:** The platform could be installed without the use of other software products.

- **Word/Image searching:** A tool to facilitate the word or sentence and images searching.

- **Printing facilities:** The users could print pages or frames of the course they are working in.

- **Interface quality:** An easy and intuitive interface, customised to the necessities of the students.

- **Private annotations made by the author:** The function that supports private comments made by the author.

- **Access restrictions:** The feasibility to define restricted access in a part of the course or different access types per student.

- **User Id and password:** The customized authentication information composed of a string of characters that enables students to access the platform.

- **Access rights:** The authority to restrict or enable the access to users, authors or instructors.

- **Multi-language support:** The possibility to use different languages in the platform configuration.

The classification of these characteristics integrated within the three dimensions of the adapted e-learning cube of Garlasu et al. (2005), provides a summary to choose those that are suitable for the configuration of the e-learning platform. This classification can be used as a guide to take into account the most relevant characteristics of the e-learning platform.

CONCLUSION

Currently the rich variety and volume of KM tools have caused that several authors have performed numerous classifications of them. But bad structures and lack of understanding appear within these classifications. Tools, those are very different due to its conceptualization and functionality, are included in the same group. This fact produces serious incoherencies. Moreover, many of these classifications are presented as a simple list of KM tools without any type of connection. KM tools are in continuous evolution, but these classifications do not allow integrating new tools that will be developed in the future. Therefore, it has been necessary to define a classification that resolves these problems. KM tools have been classified within the framework of two KM Cycles, in order to provide an integrated and structured view.

The development of this classification has enabled to establish an organized structure of KM tools. We have focused our attention on the KM tools that support the internalization process as the process to convert explicit knowledge into tacit knowledge. The previous classification has helped us in order to know which our alternatives were. E-learning techniques have been chosen as the optimal way to obtain knowledge and to turn explicit into tacit knowledge. At this point the main

challenge has been to select the most advantageous e-learning platform according to the most relevant characteristics. As the selection process is a hard task, we have proposed a classification in order to facilitate the choice. Therefore, e-learning characteristics have been integrated within the three dimensions of e-learning cube (adapted from Garlasu et al., 2005): content, infrastructure and e-services in order to guide users to choose the most suitable e-learning configuration.

FUTURE RESEARCH DIRECTIONS

The future research aims to two main objectives. Firstly, once the identification of the different KM tools has been developed and described, the goal is to maintain this classification in order to be used now and in the future. Technologies are in continuous evolution therefore, this classification will be continuously updated so as to integrate new tools that will be developed in the future.

Secondly, the attention is focused on the process of knowledge internalization through e-learning. In this case, our goal is to apply all the e-learning characteristics defined in this chapter in order to choose the optimal e-learning configuration. The integration of the e-learning characteristics within the three dimensions of content, infrastructure and e-services will guide users to choose the most suitable e-learning platform.

REFERENCES

Anand, V., Manz, C.C. & Glick, W.H. (1998). An organizational memory approach to information management. *Academy of Management Review*, 23(4), 796-809.

Black, J. & McClintock, R. (1995). An Interpretation Construction Approach to Constructivist Design. In B. Wilson (Ed.), *Constructivist learning environments*. NJ: Englewood Cliffs.

Braden R. (1989). RFC 1122: Requirements for Internet Hosts: Communication Layers. *Information Sciences Institute (ISI) at University of Southern California*. Retrieved September 15, 2007, from http://www.isi.edu/in-notes/rfc1122.txt

Brown, J. & Duguid, P. (1998). Organizing Knowledge. *California Management Review*, 40(3), 90-111.

Carvalho, R. & Araújo, M. (2002).Using information technology to support knowledge conversion processes. *Information Research, 7*(1).

Clark, R. (1989). *Developing Technical Training: A Structured Approach for the Development of Classroom and Computer-Based Instructional Materials*. Reading, MA: Addison-Wesley

Clark, R. (2002). *Putting Learning Standards into Practice. ASTD E-learning Hanbook.* McGraw Hill.

Chua, A. (2004). Knowledge management system architecture: a bridge between KM consultants and technologists. *International Journal of Information Management*, 24, 87-98.

Davenport, T. & Prusak, L. (1998). *Working Knowledge: how organizations manage what they know*. Boston, Harvard Business School Press.

Delclós, M. (2003). Una herramienta para la productividad. *Automática e Instrumentación*, 343.

Garlasu, D., Dumitrache I., & Mihai A. (2005). A new approach for e-learning in collaborative networks. *Proc. of 6th Conference on Virtual Enterprises. Collaborative Networks and Their Breeding Environments* (pp. 243-248). New York: Springer

Georgiev, T., Georgieva, E., & Smrikarov, A. (2004, June). M-Learning - a New Stage of E-Learning. Paper presented at International Conference on Computer Systems and Technologies - CompSysTech'2004, Rousse, Bulgaria.

Grantham, C.E. & Nichols, L.D. (1993). *The digital workplace: Designing groupware platform.* New York: Van Nostrand-Reinhold Grau, America.

Grau, A. (2001). Herramientas de Gestión del Conocimiento. Retrieved February 19, 2007, from http://www.gestiondelconocimiento.com/documentos2/america/herramientas.htm

Greitzer, F. L. (2002). A cognitive approach to student-centered e-learning. Proceedings Human Factors and Ergonomics Society 46th Annual Meeting, (pp. 2064-2068).Baltimore, Maryland, USA.

Greitzer FL, DM Rice, SL Eaton, MC Perkins, RT Scott, and JR Burnette. (2003). A Cognitive Approach to e-learning. *In Proceedings of the Interservice/Industry Training, Simulation, and Education Conference (I/ITSEC)*. Orlando, Florida.

Hasman, A., Albert, A., Wainwright, P., Klar, R., & Sosa, M. (Ed.) (1995). *Education and Training for Health Informatics in Europe: State of the Art - Guideline - Applications.* Amsterdam, Netherlands: IOS Press.

Keller, J. (1983). Motivational Design of Instruction. In Reigeluth, C. (Ed.). *Instructional-design theories and models: an overview of their current status*. Mahwah, NJ: Lawrence Erlbaum.

Malhotra, Y. (1997). Knowledge management in Inquiring Organizations, in the *Proceedings of 3rd Americas Conference on Information Systems*. Philosophy of Information Systems Mini-track (pp. 293-295). Indianapolis.

Nonaka, I. (1991). *The knowledge creating company*. Massachusettes: Harvard Business Review.

Nonaka, I., & Takeuchi, H. (1995). *The Knowledge-creating Company: How Japanese Companies Create the Dynamics of Innovation*. New York: Oxford University Press.

Pávez, A. A. (2000). Modelo de implantación de gestión del conocimiento y tecnologías de la información para la generación de ventajas competitivas. Retrieved April 1, 2007, from http://www.gestiondelconocimiento.com/documentos2/apavez/gdc.htm

Quinn, C.N. (2006). Making It Matter to the Learner: E-motional e-learning. *Practical Applications of Technology for Learning*. Retrieved January 13, 2007, from http://www.quinnovation.com/eMotional-eLearning.pdf

Roberts, J. (2000). From know-how to show-how: Questioning the role of information and communication technologies in knowledge transfer. *Technology Analysis and Strategic Management*, 12(4), 429-443.

Ruggles, R. (1997). *Knowledge management tools*. Oxford: Butterworth-Heinemann.

Silver, C.A. (2000). Where technology and knowledge meet. *Journal of Business Strategy*, 21(6), 28-33.

Simmons, D. E. (2002). The forum report: E-learning adoption rates and barriers. In A. Rossett (Ed.), *The ASTD e-learning handbook* (pp. 19-23). New York: McGraw-Hill.

Skyrme, D.J. (1999). *Knowledge networking. Creating the collaborative enterprise*. Oxford: Butterworth-Heinemann.

Tomás, J.V., Poler, R., Capó J., & Expósito, M. (2004, September). *Las herramientas de gestión del conocimiento*. Una visión integrada. Paper presented at Congreso de Ingeniería de Organización, Leganés, Spain.

Trend (2000). La gestión del conocimiento. La herramienta del futuro. *Trend Management*, 2(3), 83-107.

Tsui, E. (2000). Exploring the KM toolbox. *Knowledge Management*, 4.

Tyndale, P. (2002). A taxonomy of knowledge management tools: origins and applications. *Evaluation and Program Planning 25* (2), 183-190.

WISE Consortium. (2002). Deliverable D1.3: Review of KM Tools. IST-2000-29280, Web-enabled Information Services for Engineering. Retrieved March 26, 2002, from http://www-eurisco.onecert.fr/Wise/Publication/WISEReviewKMtoolsVA4.pdf

ADDITIONAL READING

Bock, G. & Marca, D. (1995). *Designing Groupware*. New York, McGraw-Hill.

Car A.A. (2005). Global Perspectives On E-Learning: Rhetoric And Reality. Sage Publications.

Cohen, E. B. & Nycz, M. (2006). Learning Objects and E-Learning: an Informing Science Perspective. Interdisciplinary Journal of Knowledge and Learning Objects, 2.

Colace, F., DeSanto, M. & Vento, M. (2003). Evaluating On-line Learning Platforms: a Case Study. In Proceedings *36th Hawaii International Conference on System Science*. Hawaii: IEEE Press

Conole G. & Oliver, M. (2006). Contemporary Perspectives in E-learning Research (Themes, Methods And Impact on Practice). Routledge.

Choo, C.W., Detlor, B. & Turnbull, D. (2000). *Web Work: Information Seeking and Knowledge Work on the World Wide Web*. Dordrecht, Kluwer Academic Publishers.

Choo, C.W. (1998). *The Knowing Organization*. Oxford University Press.

De la Rica, E. (2000). *Marketing en internet y e-business*. Madrid, Anaya Multimedia.

Dixon, N. (2000). *El conocimiento común*. Oxford University Press.

Ewt, N. & Ewc, C. (2005). Evaluation of knowledge management tools using AHP. *Expert Systems with Applications, 29*(4), 889-899.

Graf, S. & List, B. (2005). An Evaluation of Open Source E-Learning Platforms Stressing Adaptation Issues. In Proceedings of the *Fifth IEEE International Conference on Advanced Learning Technologies (ICALT'05)*, (pp. 163 – 165). Washington: IEEE Computer Society.

Housel, T. & Bell, A. (2001). *Measuring and Managing Knowledge*. New York, McGraw-Hill.

Hughes, G. & Hay, D. (2001). Use of concept mapping to integrate the different perspectives of designers and other stakeholders in the development of e-learning materials. *British Journal of Educational Technology 32* (5), 557–569.

Kamara, J.M., Anumba C.J., & Carrillo, P.M. (2002). A clever approach to selecting a knowledge management strategy. *International Journal of Project Management*, 20, 205-211.

Lindvall, M., Rus, I. & Suman, S. (2002). *Technology Support for Knowledge Management*. Paper presented at 4th International Workshop on Learning Software Organizations (LSO'02). Chicago, Illinois, EEUU.

Ordóñez, P. (2004). Knowledge flow transfers in multinational corporations: knowledge properties and implications for management. *Journal of Knowledge Management, 8*(6), 105-116.

Pérez-Soltero, A. (1997). Modelo para la representación de una memoria organizacional utilizando herramientas computacionales de Internet. Doctoral dissertation, University of Monterrey, Mexico.

Poler, R. (2006). Deliverable D10.3. Training courses on Interoperability. *IST-1-508011: Interoperability Research for Networked Enterprises Applications and Software (INTEROP)* Retrieved March 2, 2007, from http://interop-noe.org/backoffice/deliv/D10.3/

Poler, R. & Sanchis, R. (2006). Deliverable D10.4. Dissemination of courses on Interoperability. Version 1. *IST-1-508011: Interoperability Research for Networked Enterprises Applications and Software (INTEROP)* Retrieved April 5, 2007, from http://interop-noe.org/backoffice/workspaces/Reviewers/documents/M36/dtg10.4/

Poler R., & Tormo G. (2003, November). Business Process Integration, Knowledge Management and Decision Support Tools in Supply Chain of Industrial SMEs. Paper presented at CONex, Donostia.

Rory, C. (2000). La gestión del conocimiento. La herramienta del futuro. *Trend Management, 2* (3), 83-107.

Shenk, D. (1998). *Data smog: Surviving the information glut*. San Francisco, Harper.

Sunassee N. N., & Sewry, D.A.(2002). A Theoretical Framework for Knowledge Management Implementation. *Proceedings ACM International Conference Proceeding Series; Vol. 30.* (pp. 235 – 245). Port Elizabeth, South Africa.

Vernadat, F.B. (1996). *Enterprise modelling and integration: principles and applications*. Chapman & Hall.

Zander, U., & Kogut, B. (1995). Knowledge and the speed of the transfer and imitation of organizational capabilities: an empirical test. *Organization Science, 6*, 76-92.

Chapter IX
The Value of Virtual Networks for Knowledge Management:
A Tool for Practical Development

Cesar Camison
Universitat Jaume I, Spain

Carlos Devece
Universitat Jaume I, Spain

Daniel Palacios
Universitat Jaume I, Spain

Carles Camisón-Haba
Universidad Politécnica de Valencia, Spain

ABSTRACT

In this chapter we describe a practical tool useful to managing knowledge in the firm. It has already been introduced and tested in several firms and we have obtained good conclusions about its performance. In this chapter, we combine the modules of the software application with the theoretical functions of Knowledge Management principles. We also develop a list of indicators to measure the effect of implementing SoftKnow in a firm. This is useful to have an economic impact of the introduction of a practical tool based on Knowledge Management. After reading this chapter we think the managers' perceptions of this type of tool will change, since they will able to assimilate all the impacts and applications of the tool.

KNOWLEDGE ECONOMY: CHALLENGES FOR COMPANY COMPETITIVENESS

In the era of business transition, the effective management of knowledge is proposed as a strategy that exploits organizational intangible assets. Knowledge management (KM) with no doubt could be considered as one of the hottest research topics of the past decade (Kalpic and Bernues, 2006: 40), the birth of KM, which occurred in the early 1990s, grew from recognition of how difficult is to deal with complexity in an environment of ever increasing competition spurred by technology and the demands of sophisticated customers.

"Advance towards the knowledge society is unstoppable, verified by the emergence of knowledge workers. As just one example, during the XX century in USA, knowledge workers, defined as employees working mainly with information - managers, salesmen, clerks, professionals, technicians - have increased from 17% to 59%, while, at the same time, blue-collar workers have dropped from 83% to 31%. Thomas Stewart (1997), editor of Fortune, places the historic point of inflection in 1991, when, for the first time, investment by US firms in information technologies exceeded investment in production plants and equipment." (Camisón, 2000: 1)

It is not surprising that knowledge has become the main factor in value creation modern society. However, knowledge is by no means an unknown variable, as it has always been present in firms and in economic activities. Intelligence, understanding, talent, skills and learning have always been essential components in innovation and success. Just as an anecdote, Aristotle Onassis rightly said that "the secret of any business is to know something that nobody else knows".

While knowledge has been identified as the competitive advantage of the future, its wide-spread bad management is worrying. McKinsey's recent study among 6000 executives in 77 firms shows that knowledge and skills are the worst managed assets in organizations. Only 23% of the executives stated that their firms got to attract talented managers, and only 10% got to retain the best professionals. The waste of the knowledge owned by organizations has a direct affect on costs, as it can lead to duplicating tasks or repeating past failures (which could be avoided by simply using experience learned in the past), wasting the time and money invested. The expression "reinvent the wheel" perfectly illustrates the absurdity of this behaviour. Concerning this poor use of knowledge, we might mention studies demonstrating that between 20% and 30% of firms' resources of are squandered on "reinventing the wheel"; or as Lew Platt, executive of Hewlett Packard, said: "If we knew what we know, we would be three times more profitable," (Boshyk, 1999: 7). This perception leads to the statement that only the tip of the iceberg (one eleventh) of human talent is managed. The rest of the knowledge, still "under water", is the great challenge, the copious source of value creation.

David Skyrme, co-author of the study *Creation of the firm based on knowledge*, considers that no big firm has effective information management or widespread Knowledge Management practices. There is a poor capitalization of ideas and creativity, and knowledge is lost in staff turnover, as well as unexploited knowledge assets. Some firms even buy expert services they already possess simply because they are not informed about what they know. In fact, *CIO Magazine* recently said that the participants in the knowledge economy presently are probably a minority of companies rich in knowledge and in knowledge experts, as opposed to a large majority of companies whose Knowledge Management is so awkward that they need help to enter this battle.

The effective introduction of Knowledge Management in organizations raises a series of diverse problems (Rastogi, 2000; Dibella and

Nevis, 1998; Revilla, 1996). In summary, the reasons that make Knowledge Management so difficult to implement are conceptual, organizational, cultural and technological.

The management of knowledge is difficult, first, because of the complexity and inaccessibility of knowledge itself as an asset. Unlike tangible assets, intangible assets based on knowledge present problems of identification and representation, heightened when the knowledge is so fragmented that it is not known where it resides, or when the knowledge is so complex that it is practically inaccessible.

It is worth outlining two more technological obstacles. Firstly, the cost and the time needed to implement the technology supporting Knowledge Management systems. SAP, a company specializing in more traditional ERP software, estimates that the implementation of its system in a medium-size company costs between €90,000 and €180,000, and this does not take into account costs deriving from the adjustment of the organization's system, which can significantly increase the final price. The Lotus Notes solution for big companies can exceed €280,000. The second problem is that this kind of system can generate so much information and data that these can limit or damage executives' clarity of perception, ideas and decision-making ability.

Knowledge management is a new advance in business management, progressing in its development thanks to big pioneering companies (Skandia, BBV, Finanzia, Ericsson, Bankinter, etc.). Until now, the companies dedicated to developing information systems related to Knowledge Management have only had big corporations in mind. Illustratively, one of these prominent software companies (Meta 4) specifically declares that its target clients are companies with annual sales of above 600 million euros. This trend is not an insuperable obstacle that prevents the application of this management innovation to SMEs, taking into account, of course, the difference in size. Nevertheless, it is important to eliminate the reticence present in SMEs on this issue, probably motivated because software companies developing KM systems have until now dedicated all their efforts to big corporations. In addition, it must be borne in mind that management ideas originating in the context of big companies are not directly applicable to SMEs by merely reducing their scale. It is necessary to endow the SMEs with tools for self-diagnosing their Knowledge Management needs and to create systems adapted to their particular strategic, organizational, human and technological features.

The managerial perception of knowledge needs in SMEs is mainly related to efficiency aspects in operations and processes. When the managers' vision of IT investments is not strategic but operational, the results of the technological innovation are always effective but they are also limited. In this context, it is common to think that Knowledge Management in companies is equivalent to having an advanced management application, or, better still, an ERP. Taking into account the magnitude of investment necessary in a system of this kind, top managers are often overwhelmed: "After having implemented the ERP, our IT investment in Knowledge Management is covered in mid-term." This is a phrase that is often heard today. The dominant feeling in many organizations, after covering this phase, is that they have reached a cul-de-sac. This conviction is simultaneously developed with a long process of difficult and almost always controversial implementation, in view of the deep and extensive changes in work processes forced by the new computer system.

The lack of a strategic approach guiding the investment in technology leads to the tool deciding the course of the organizational innovation, when the theoretical prescription is precisely the opposite.

This vision corresponds to an outdated concept: that the environment is basically stable, needs for information are going to remain unchanged and the investment to meet them will be useful for a long time. This managerial concept is deeply wrong. Uncertainty and change dominate the managerial environment of any industry, constantly renewing requirements for knowledge that executives must control in order to compete. Traditional computer systems, even the more holistic ones such as ERPs, can affect the efficiency of the company, providing new functions that will allow delivery times, stocks or financial costs to be cut. But these management tools rarely improve innovation in organizations. The value added by a KM system relies on the incorporation of strategy in IS and competitive intelligence systems. An ERP system will usually achieve a logical transition from a "chaotic" state to a structured and ordered system dealing with the storage and handling of information and access to it, but the organization will remain a long way from having knowledge. In the practice, the organization will have data that, when transformed and compiled, turns into information, vital in the daily business activities, but which is not enough in itself to lead innovation processes. In order to access strategically valuable knowledge, SMEs need to invest in systems and technologies capable of feeding managers with the intelligence necessary for them to stand out from competition. The essential nutrient in this knowledge derives from the processes of comparing, weighing, simplifying, focusing and evaluating the accumulated information. To tackle this challenge, new Knowledge Management systems must be developed and combined with the suitable human resources policies.

One of the areas where SMEs are weaker is in knowledge of markets and competitors. This fact is a consequence of their low sensitivity to the world that surrounds them, their centripetal trend to concentrate efforts in operational areas, neglecting systematic strategic analysis of the industry and of environmental changes. However, necessary knowledge about a rival company, a potential customer, a partner or a future stakeholder can be a determining factor in the development of their business.

Another problem lays on the scope of KM. According to Maguire et al. (2007:40) different authors have different perspectives on the technology scope of KM. Some authors include workflow, document control, e-mail, intranets, extranets, e-business, CRM, data mining and business intelligence. Other authors follow a narrower perspective including only the technology which directly affects the functions of KM.

DEVELOPMENT OF KNOWLEDGE MANAGEMENT SOLUTIONS FOR VALENCIAN FIRMS

The need for this change in managers' perceptions of KM systems triggered the creation in 2000 of the *Research Group for Investigation on Strategy, Knowledge Management, Innovation and Organizational Learning* (GRECO) at the Universitat Jaume I. The group's aim was the development of different projects to help local companies achieve better competitive conditions for penetrating the knowledge society.

The first step in this direction was the contract signed with the Ministry of Industry and Trade of the Generalitat Valenciana (regional government), as part of the "Networks of Intermediate Organisations for Innovation Support" program of IMPIVA (Valencian SME Institute) forming part of the Initiative for SME Managerial Development, to run the project called *Knowledge Club: Approaches, Tools, Platforms and Applications for Knowledge Management in SMEs*. It was a two-year project (2000-2001), which led to the creation of an informal group of companies (interested in organizational learning, intellectual capital, Knowledge Management and innovation) that served as a debating forum and laboratory in this field, and that took the name of the *Club for Knowledge Management, innovation and Organizational Learning of the Valencian Community (GENOMA)*. This Club has carried out different activities since then, bringing together more than 70 organizations, including a selected group of leading Valencian Community companies. This experiment was a pioneering one in Spain, as two other projects operating at the time had quite different characteristics: Euroforum Escorial was exclusively based on big companies, and Cluster Conocimiento in the Basque Country was an organization tied to the implementation of public policy. The Club is a private initiative for the competitive development of knowledge practices in a Community and for the design of a strategy helping to extract all the knowledge potential to benefit the competitiveness of companies in any industry. Its vision is become a **leading organization for the development of Knowledge Management and Innovation in the Valencian Community**, contributing opportunities for learning, exchange of experiences and knowledge among all agents in the organization in order to improve the competitiveness of companies in any business.

Three types of actions were undertaken in order to determine the present state of Knowledge Management of Valencian SMEs, as well as specifying the criteria and directives that any Knowledge Management system should meet to be easily implemented in any SME. First, the gathering of qualitative information during the first phase of the project, prior to the design of the Knowledge Management model, was carried out by 5 dynamic groups with the SMEs participating in the project, held throughout June and July 2002. These meetings were made up of a total of 32 specialists from different companies, together with the project team. In addition, a Delphi study of external experts was carried out in order to identify the Knowledge Management tools most suitable for specific managerial contexts. The experts' panel included university researchers in the area under study, members of the public administration, and managerial professionals from top companies in order to gather both managerial and theoretical opinions. After the qualitative study, some quantitative studies were carried out

in a representative sample of SMEs in the Valencian Community. The quantitative studies were carried out on a sample of 401 companies from the Valencian Community. The sample selection was guided by the desire to reach a significance of ± 95.5% in the SME population of the Valencian Community, with an error of ± 5%.

One of the conclusions of the work meetings and the empirical studies developed as part of GENOMA was the need to develop a Knowledge Management model, with its subsequent operationalization based on IT and with the following goals:

1. To respond effectively to the Knowledge Management needs of Valencian Community companies, presenting a reference system for them.
2. To cognitively support the processes of improving learning and innovation capacities in SMEs.
3. To stimulate distribution and managerial application of the tools for strategic management and innovation management based on knowledge.
4. To offer updated and global information. The system should be orientated towards meeting managers' needs for information for the adoption of strategic decisions, encouraging the application of a strategic management approach based on knowledge.
5. To develop a polyvalent system, useful as platform for SME in any industry, capable of supporting subsequent developments in specific sectors.

With this mission in mind, the model and the operative technical solution should be an application destined for document and Knowledge Management in the company, as management must not only consider the already codified and structured explicit knowledge, in any format, in the company's databases, but also the tacit knowledge hoarded by its people.

In our view, similarly as Wright et al. (2004) consider, a Knowledge Management systems must be leaned on two practices. First, a knowledge repository that makes information contextually available (Markus, 2001), managing social networks to facilitate awareness of, and access to, specialists (McDonald and Ackerman 1998). Second, a more informal forum where employees can exchange ideas and work products via enterprise groupware applications.

Besides, this system would allow that knowledge and information deposited in the corporate Intranet to be shareable by all members of the organization, as well as people outside (clients, suppliers, etc.), with the necessary safety filters, in order to improve efficiency in the performance of tasks and processes, as well as the reputation and the competitiveness of the company.

The generic solution needed for Knowledge Management was conceived as the hypertext organization of Nonaka and Takeuchi (1995), where knowledge-based layers are introduced in parallel with the business functional structure, without any kind of re-engineering. This knowledge layer is supported by a technical system combined with the appropriate Human Resources policies. The functioning and contribution of every member of the organization to this knowledge layer cannot be left to chance, so formal procedures and recognition must be introduced in the organization. A virtual network therefore runs in parallel with the daily activities of the organization, supporting them without interfering.

The innovation potential of such a virtual network has been demonstrated in many instances, as in the case of OSS development. Although some restrictions must be considered regarding the size of the community involved, the lessons learned in the motivation issues and the formal structures in the evaluation and consolidation of the ideas contributed are very valuable (Ahuja, 2000). The reticence of employees to share their knowledge can be perfectly well overcome, as the "private-collective" innovation model in

OSS development has proved (von Hippel and von Krogh, 2003.)

In this respect, two different "virtual spaces" were considered necessary in the Knowledge Management system. First, an informal space where the debate about new ideas and practices is unrestricted, and the informal acknowledgement and praise of colleagues drive the motivation to contribute. Secondly, a formal database, where the knowledge generated throughout the organization is incorporated into formal documents backed up by managers and experts in each field. This second "virtual space" of consolidated knowledge will guide business activities in form of procedures, routines, formulas, manuals, etc. The recognition of these formal contributions must go beyond the signature of the author of the documents. Tangible incentives must be introduced, such as promotion or financial rewards. Besides, in this model, the role of the knowledge reviewer is crucial. Knowledge maps of the organization must be traced. The identification of the experts in each field brings, as well as the explicit recognition of these professionals, the responsibility to help and advise the members of the community when their services are required.

Aware that the success of a system depends on its actual usage (Devaraj and Kohli, 2003), the research team included different technical characteristics in the design of the model that facilitate the implementation of organizational policies and norms supporting the sense of community. This includes the identification of the contributions of each member of the organization and the use and assessment of each knowledge unit in the system.

GRECO and GENOMA had been working in this conceptual model of Knowledge Management from 2002 to 2005, through the development of the application **KnowSoft for Knowledge Management**. The model offers the following features:

- Firstly, the system allows the company to manage the knowledge stored in its routines and processes, both when it is codified and recorded in some material support and when it is still only possessed by an employee. In this second case, the system offers a way for the members of the company to make explicit and deposit any tacit knowledge in any knowledge area (clients, suppliers, markets, processes, tasks). This can then be brought together and classified to be made available to any other member who may need it later.

- The second basic feature of the program is related to documentary management: the system allows the storage, management and distribution of all kinds of documents (catalogues, invoices, forms, reports) in any format. The application also offers an efficient response to documentary management needs deriving from management system certification processes, as it is adapted to the latest versions of the standards ISO 9000 and ISO 14000.

- The application also offers a platform that supports the controlled search, extraction and distribution of documentation and knowledge, as well as workflows and collaborative resources among its users.

The most outstanding characteristics of the system are as follows:

- KnowSoft is a computer solution applicable to any company, regardless of its size and technological and organizational architecture.

- The system is easily accessible for any user through the company's network, allowing the centralization and rationalization of files in the server. It is an open system, configurable into an Intranet / Extranet, which lies in a secure, centralized repository, fully manageable from a browser. The technological platform that supports the computer system has been designed so it can be fully integrated into the corporate Intranet and into an Internet environment.

- Safe access outside and inside of the organization by means of a "login" and "password" system. By means of this system it is possible to unequivocally identify any user of the system and guarantee the privacy of the data owned by the users and by the company.

- Restricted access to the different functions of the application, depending on the type of user and work group. When a document or knowledge is introduced in the system, it can be marked as free access for any user, or its use can be restricted to only certain users or work groups. Depending on the security level assigned to users, they will be able to access certain functions, documents and knowledge.

Security and confidentiality are guaranteed by the creation of work groups inside the company and three user levels: system manager, group manager and user. The tasks of the system manager are to create and delete users and work groups, as well as to introduce the fields that define the knowledge units (processes, instructions, types of documents and locations). The group managers are responsible of administering the knowledge units, the tasks and the contacts of their field, as well as the bulletin board and definition of the key words of the thesaurus. The users have unrestricted access to the fields in which they have been authorized to work, as well as full access to the communication modules, although for the creation or modification of knowledge units they need the approval of the group expert.

- Fully compatible with the corporate Intranet and with any pre-existing database implementation, like an outer layer on the existing information systems, promoting advanced information handling and its integration, without need to modify the previous IS structure of the organization.

- Robustness of documents, with access from any terminal and without duplication.
- Advanced search engine for documents and internal knowledge organization.
- Creation of common language and terminology in the organization, facilitating codification and searches of knowledge and documentation.
- Remote and secure access via the Web for search and retrieval of information in the corporate database.
- It allows communication and coordination of tasks and agendas among workers, even those located in different geographical areas, through *groupware* modules.
- Scalable application, with modules adjustable to the company's needs and with the possibility of including new modules developed ad hoc.
- A solution that needs simple installation with a few minimal requirements for easy access working with any browser (Explorer 5.5 or above, Netscape 6.0 or above, Opera 7.11 or above).
- The software that has been used for operationalizing the model consists of existing free software tools on the market, with an open and scalable architecture. Specifically, the program was developed using PHP language with some JAVA components. The system is fully compatible with different operating systems (Windows, Linux and Unix) as well as with a Web environment. The application is compatible with the following database systems: MySQL and Server and any other system through ODBC. The only additional needs for running the application are an Apache Server, the database MySQL, and the LINUX operating system. The needs for investment are therefore very small as the application uses free access software,

although it is always advisable to use compiled solutions.

- Economical solution. The base price of the system is 1.500 euros. Customization of the program for information searching and reading generated by other programs and ad hoc development of other functions has an initial cost of 42 euros / hour. A maintenance service is offered by telephone or internet, with an annual cost per application of 250 euros.

SoftKnow solution for the Knowledge Management includes different spaces and services. The Document Space, the Best Practices Space and the Experts' Directory are tools for codifying, storing and searching knowledge. Groupware tools, on the other hand, are aimed at improving communication and coordination between the users.

- **Documentary space.** This storehouse provides the necessary tools for recording, cataloguing, searching and filing documents, as well as extensibility more suitable for the development of new solutions from the basic services. The idea is to reflect the common life-cycle of documents, from their creation, passing through different levels of approval up to the establishment of search taxonomy. Documents can only be released, removed or modified by the author and the group managers to which they are assigned.

We would like to emphasize that the application allows both procedures and quality handbooks deriving from the certification process under the series of ISO procedures to be checked and released. Every document preserves all its versions through a log file of modifications.

The documents obtained from quality process certification result in the design of a **map and tasks process** for the company, which constitutes the basis of the hierarchical tree for the whole system.

- **Best practices space.** The best practices space tries to establish a common framework to facilitate the sharing of experiences in general and, particularly, practices increasing organizational efficiency. The best practices space allows the capture, registration, cataloguing and reinforcement of best practices arising directly from the operation of the business (Wenger, McDermott and Snyder, 2002.). On one hand, by means of follow-up services, it seeks to identify best practices on the basis of measuring performance and successes. The Knowledge Management systems must be capable of identifying "gaps" in the map of organizational knowledge. When certain individuals significantly outperform others, it is a sign that there exists a better practice that could be shared. In addition, the workflow tools allow the creation of applications based on processes to ensure that the practices are generally continued and measured.

The deposit and the administration of knowledge are carried out very simply, from four modules:

Knowledge units. This is the main tool for capturing, storing and later accessing the knowledge deposited in the system. Through this module knowledge units are created, supported and eliminated. It is therefore the place where knowledge resides, accessible for every employee. This presentation makes the management of the knowledge dynamic, valuing the incorporation and the maintenance of a knowledge unit, depending on its usefulness. First of all, it must be said what it is understood by knowledge units. These units can be any kind of document where exists relevant information and this information has been organized by establishing context, has been refined by discovering relationships, has been

abstracted and synthesized (Muthusamy, 2005). This implies a big difference between the treatment necessary for managing data and knowledge units. Whereas in data warehouse the processing techniques play the main role due to great amount of data, in Knowledge Management the focus is centred in experts, and the introduction of a single unit in the system is a meditated action that needs a process of reflection. The responsibility of the validity and usefulness of knowledge in the system repository falls on the experts shoulders, and the system can only facilitate the process proposing some standard fields or parameters that will help in the contextualization and identification of the knowledge.

Considering this philosophy, the implementation of the knowledge repository was designed as follows: The deposit, removal or modification of knowledge units can only be carried out by the knowledge area manager or the group managers to which a unit belongs. Every knowledge unit consists of several parameters, as we can see from the information collection screen included in Figure 1. When a knowledge unit is introduced, it must compulsorily be associated with a series of key words (predefined in the Thesaurus) that outline the topics to which it refers. Every knowledge unit will also store a reference to the author of the unit, as well as the mention (from drop-down menus) of the area of knowledge, the business procedures, processes, products or services associated with this knowledge unit, type of document (text, drawing, video, spreadsheet, etc.) and the office or premises where the unit was generated or can be used (Wiig, 1993). Besides these standard parameters, a specific company would need some other fields depending on the business activities where it is involved.

The search of the knowledge units can be made by each of its fields or any combination of them. The search output offers a list of knowledge units that satisfy the search conditions established.

Thesaurus. When an user non expert in a field consults a knowledge unit some problems may

Figure 1. Introduction of knowledge units in SoftKnow

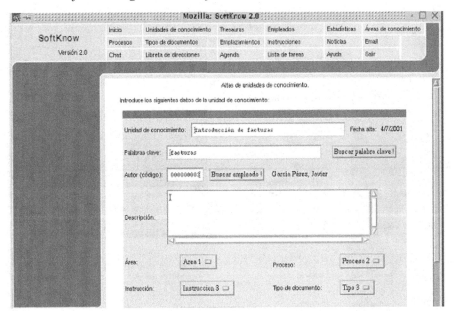

arise in its understanding, most of them related to semantic non-interoperability (Pundt and Bishr, 2002). This phenomenon occurs because describing an item thematically is a subjective procedure, and due to semantic heterogeneities and different terminologies and conceptualizations (Proko-piadou et al., 2004). To overcome this problem the thesaurus is a powerful tool. This consists of a dictionary of key words defining the content of a knowledge unit or document. It facilitates the organization of the contents and the later retrieval of knowledge, imposing a common language in the organization so that the contents are organized appropriately and do not fragment in extend.

Data sharing between different information communities or simply different people, requires a common universe of discourse that is based on a consensus concerning the semantics of the data (Pundt and Bishr, 2002). The semantic used in the classification of knowledge units contributes strongly to the organization of information. For Prokopiadou et al. (2004), a thesaurus accom-

plishes the following objectives in a Knowledge Management system: (1) establish descriptive terminology, (2) guide the end-user to an efficient pathway towards high-quality information retrieval, (3) organize information and knowledge. These objectives can be achieved by establishing a descriptive and controlled interrelated terminology.

In the programme, this is implemented as follows: the system insists on the definition of key words when a new knowledge unit is created or when a new document is established, after consultation the drop-down list with the existing ones. At the same time, the introduction of new terms in the thesaurus must be backed by the permission of the area expert. Although the thesaurus can be consulted partially for each knowledge area, to avoid misunderstandings, the same term cannot be used in different knowledge areas with different meanings. Figure 2 reproduces the information collection screen.

Figure 2. Thesaurus in SoftKnow

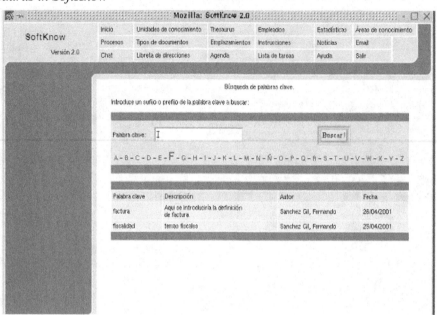

- *Knowledge areas.* We can define different areas of knowledge which will group the firm knowledge. It is therefore a way of organizing and setting up the contents. At the same time, because each area has an expert or manager who validates and is responsible of the information in it, this classification acts like an experts map. Being an area expert is an explicit recognition and implies that the expert will be the first to ask by the rest of employees when finding a difficulty in the understanding of a knowledge unit. Besides, the validation and continuous updating of the knowledge can be a time consuming task, and this must be taken into account in the experts's schedule planning and accordingly rewarded.

  This recognition would help to break the "resistance to be known as an expert" (Desouza, 2002), one of the main cultural problems in knowledge transference. Nevertheless, the knowledge areas are more than this. From a strategic approach of Knowledge Manage-

ment, the definition of the knowledge areas in the firm is emphasizing and prioritizing those areas of knowledge that need more attention strategically for the future of the company (Wiig, 1993), so their establishment must be thoroughly pondered decision.

- *Statistics module.* The purpose of this module is to provide information for assessing the performance of the knowledge units deposited by users in the system. Among other data, it provides information related to the number of consultations of every knowledge unit and the number of these units introduced and consulted by every user. An example of the information that can be compiled can be seen in Figure 3. More information can be added to these parameters, like the mean of the valuation done by the users. This kind of statistics are essential in the implementation of some aspects of skills and competence management systems (Dingsoyr et al., 2005), a powerful human resource policy to overcome some of the cultural barriers found in Knowledge Management. Besides, the analysis of the statistics may answer some strategic questions such as which are the areas where more training is needed, which is the knowledge more valuable for the firm or who are the employees who give to the firm the most valuable knowledge.

- **Directory of experts.** A Directory service represents a place of unification providing order and structure to the objects and items defined in the corporation. In the directory, information is stored on each and every member of the company's staff (white pages), and on their skills, curricular information, areas of expertise (yellow pages). On the basis of these services, other richer solutions can be provided, such as communities of knowledge, when experts are found with singularly excellent knowledge in a certain

area and can for part of the community. The system also allows the skills, competences and areas of expertise of the staff to be monitored, facilitating the periodic review of the performance and achievement of aims.

The management of the staff of the company for these purposes begins with the collection of information carried out from the "User" paragraph, planning the users' profiles and establishing the privileges they enjoy in the management of the system. The expert search is carried out using the same key words assigned to the knowledge units.

- **Groupware tools.** When an Intranet is designed for Knowledge Management, it is also important to provide it with a few functions for the team work and for horizontal and vertical communication (Desouza, 2002). The modules of tool groupware that we have incorporated into SoftKnow are:

Figure 3. Statistics in SoftKnow

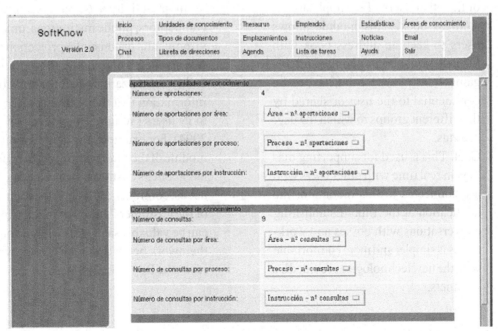

- E-mail. Though this functionality can be met by other means, we consider it a good idea to integrate it into the program so its management is easier and it is adapted to the requirements of the users. It allows the sending of e-mail messages from the different accounts users have given in compatible mail servers with POP3/SMTP/IMAP from any point on Internet.
- Task planning module (WorkFlow). This allows management of an individual list of tasks, or additions by those with permission (managers and experts), affecting other users' lists of tasks. The module is easy to use, working graphically and intuitively.
- Collective Agenda. Users can manage their own agenda, assigning meetings, trips, bank holidays, etc. Not all the events on a user's agenda are visible to all staff because the user is able to make private appointments with complete privacy. Managers and experts have the opportunity to make additions that can affect the agendas of the other users of the application.
- Address book. This module allows users to keep an address book with information about people and organizations. These contacts can be confidential to the user or shared by the different groups to which the user belongs.
- Chat. This is used for supporting dialogs in real time with other users who are connected to this module of the application at the time. Establishing conversations with bosses and workmates is simpler and more comfortable with the new technologies provided by Intranets.

- Notice board. This allows the exchange of ideas in an informal way between communities interested in the same area of knowledge.
- Discussion forums. These allow users to communicate asynchronously in order to debate on topics of interest and, particularly, to answer frequently asked questions. As the forum can be seen by all users, when a user answers a question, this answer is also available to the other Intranet users.
- FAQ Paragraph (Frequently Asked Questions). The discussion forums and the FAQ paragraph are particularly interesting because of the extent to which they are disseminated, because the answers are noticeable and because the knowledge is distributed to all users.
- **Information module about the company's external agents.** Though an Intranet is created particularly to manage information and knowledge about the users' own company, we must not forget the importance of certain external agents of special interest because of their activities (suppliers, customers, competitors, public institutions, unions, environmental or consumer protection organisations, etc.). This module allows the storage and systematization of all the non-strategic information that the company offers freely to its users (Wright, Jindanuwat and Todd, 2004). For example, the compilation in this module of the information that the company has about its customers (purchasing profile, needs, contracts, invoicing, location, profile of the customers' heads of purchasing, etc.) can be valuable sales staff who can organize their work better around it (Dingsoyr, Djarraya and Royrvik, 2005).

IMPLEMENTATION OF THE SOFTKNOW MODEL: RESULTS

Implementation Methodology

The implementation of the different modules making up TALISMAN consists of the following steps:

- Presentation of the product, definition of requirements and procedures of installation at the company.
- Definition and adjustment of the tools, the procedures and the working methods to implement the tools.
- Identification of the company's needs in order to define the practical applications to develop in each of them.
- Preparation of the plan of technical work and training development. This includes the definition of a calendar, a working plan with the companies for the implementation of the tools in the companies and a plan of practical application and training development. The customization of the model has allowed the accommodation of the contents and processes of Knowledge Management with the aims and interests of every collaborating SME, starting with specifying the knowledge that is valid for management and which takes priority.
- Running the processes and procedures defined in the model. This has consisted of the integration into the SME's management processes and systems of the action criteria deriving from Knowledge Management.
- On-site training and continuous tele-training using the Intranet from the project. The viewpoint adopted with implementation attempts not only to implement the system but also to train the organisations in running it, so that the computer system is installed at the company along with staff training in the methodology and tools. In every SME, a

person was selected to be trained as manager of the Knowledge Management system. In addition, even during the testing phase of the Web project, the operators provided constant assistance with the system by means of e-mail.

The implementation calendar was developed during October and November 2002, at a pace of 10-12 days per company. Implementation is concluded when the full integration of the action criteria deriving from the system occurs in the strategic management processes and systems of every company and when the executives are aware of the knowledge flows that the system offers in their decision-making process. The system has been installed in a network of 17 companies associated with GENOME, working perfectly both at service companies (consultancy, engineering companies, computer applications industry and energy services) and manufacturers (ceramics, footwear, marble, construction material and cardboard).

Indicators of the Effect of the Results of Implementing SoftKnow

After the installation of the system, we have carried out a final implementation audit which allows us to check the efficiency of the running of the action criteria defined and implemented for Knowledge Management at every company, and this audit reports information that allows us to gradually adapt the level of implementation of Knowledge Management at the SME. The experience we have accumulated in the practical application of SoftKnow's confirms the practical utility of our work.

The SoftKnow solution has allowed the quality of the document management and knowledge to be noticeably improved in the company. Some indicators support the following results:

- The accessibility of information collected as well as the capacity of interpretation of the knowledge by executives has risen remarkably thanks to better organization and access to the contents.
- Staff access to the updated documentation and to explicit knowledge in real time has grown by 88%.
- The internal communication of ideas and knowledge has grown by 60% (measured in terms of transaction numbers) thanks to the use of chat, opinion forums and the notice board).
- Staff knowledge about management best practices internally compiled and related to their tasks reaches 100% of the staff.
- The growth of the sharing of tacit knowledge among staff is shown by the fact that 40% of the staff have already voluntarily deposited knowledge in the system, a rate of increase of 15 points / year.
- The internal organization of work has progressed, with 80% of meetings already coordinated with Groupware instruments, such as the collective agenda.

CONCLUSION

SoftKnow is a computer innovative application, which contributes original solutions to overcome the restrictions that prevent or harm Knowledge Management:

- It can be purchased and implemented at an affordable price for any organization. The implementation of an intranet for Knowledge Management is an economical solution because its price does not exceed the sum of €12,000.
- The product is designed from the beginning satisfactorily meet the current trend of basing Knowledge Management systems on platforms that work with Internet technol-

ogy. It allows the handling of both explicit and documentary knowledge and the tacit knowledge hoarded by people.

SoftKnow is a powerful and complete tool applicable to any organization that wants to rationalize and to improve its Knowledge Management. The practical applicability of the tool has been positively confirmed with its practical operation in the networks of the companies taking part in the project.

In this sense, the Softknow experience undermines the conviction that Knowledge Management systems can significantly leverage firm knowledge only in big companies (more than 200 employees) (Davenport and Prusak, 1998). The advantages are clear for firms where a frequent direct contact among employees is not possible, although there are few members, as in firms geographically disperse or an itinerant sales force. Nevertheless, even for those companies with few employees in a single premise, the sharing of knowledge among staff has doubled. The knowledge repository system allows to store any kind of information, from text to draws, and any size, from complex procedures to simple tips for a determined task, and when the use of information in the business and the complexity of the tasks reach a relative high level, the knowledge repository and retrieval system has improved considerably the accessibility and use of information in all the firms.

And important conclusion extracted during the implantation of the systems in the different firms is that an explicit firm policy on relevant information deposit and distribution must be stated. Besides, organizational routines systematising the information deposit by the employees in different formats such as documents, reports, procedures and formulas must be established (Davenport et al., 1992). Although some employee training is always necessary for the correct use of any programme, the easy and intuitive use of SoftKnow permitted a full commandment of the application in only two days of training, nevertheless, the final usage of the programme depends on the CEO's support and breeding of an information-share culture.

Regarding the difficulties found during the adaptation of the programme to the different firms involved in the project, the general purpose of the application made the implantation relatively easy. From a technical point of view, the use of internet technology smoothed the problems found in local applications, the installation being only necessary in the server. During the customization, the major adjustments were realized in the unit knowledge stored and retrieval module. In some firms, keeping track of the different versions of documents and their evolution during time was mandatory, so in these cases the system stored all versions of any knowledge unit with their related fields. In other firms, new fields were introduced in the date base for knowledge units storage and retrieval. Besides the common fields recommended by Wiig (1993) such as author, date, reviewer, key words, department, product, technology, office, kind of document or task, some sectors demanded other crucial information in the process of search and retrieval, such as client, client place, official procedure, etc. No major modifications were necessary besides this module.

The biggest difficulties were found during the introduction of the firms present information into the system. The exacting identification and classification of the information during the knowledge unit deposit made impossible the automatic migration of the current information to the knovasoft datebase. This demanded a considerable effort during the manual introduction of the most relevant information of the company to make the program operative.

As a general conclusion we can say that the objective of a non-aggressive and cheap implantation was attained by means of a Web-based, compact, simple maintenance, standard technology program. The independence of the system with other applications of the firm smoothened the introduction of Softknow. Nevertheless, this independence may produce a disadvantage de-

pending on the application purpose. Following the hypertext model of Nonaka (Nonaka and Takeuchi, 1995), the conception of SoftKnow as a system where the relevant knowledge of the firm is introduced following a strict process of expert validation permits to separate the management knowledge system from the daily fast data generation during the business activities. This does not prevent the workers' consulting and use of the firm knowledge in any moment for their daily task at the independent knowledge layer created by SoftKnow,

ACKNOWLEDGMENT

The authors acknowledge financial support from Fundació Caixa Castelló-Bancaixa (P1 1A2006-10), and Generalitat Valenciana (GV/2007/100).

REFERENCES

Ahuja, G. (2000). The duality of collaboration: Inducements and opportunities in the formation of inter-firm linkages. *Strategic Management Journal, 21*(3), 317-343

Boshyk, Y. (1999). *Beyond knowledge management: how companies mobilise experience.* Financial Times, 8 February, pp.12-13.

Camisón, C. (2000). La empresa valenciana ante la sociedad del conocimiento: situación actual y retos de futuro. *Revista Valenciana de Estudios Autonómicos,* (32), 3-28.

Davenport, T.H., Eccles, R.G., & Prusak, L. (1992). Information politics. *Sloan Management Review,* 34(1), 53-65.

Davenport, T., & Prusak, L. (1998). *Working knowledge: How organizations manage what they know.* Harvard Business School Press.

Desouza, K.C. (2002). Barriers to effective use of knowledge management in software engineering. *ACM 46*, 1.

Devaraj, S., & Kohli, R. (2003). Performance impacts of information technology: Is actual usage the missing link? *Management Science, 49*(3), 273-289.

Dibella, A.J., & Nevis, E.C. (1998). *How organization learn: An integrated strategy for building learning capability.* Jossey-Bass. Inc. California.

Dingsoyr, T., Djarraya, H. K., & Royrvik, E. (2005). Practical knowledge management tool use in a software consulting company. *Communications of the ACM, 48*(12), 96-100.

Kalpic, B., & Bernues, P. (2006). Business process modelling through the knowledge management perspective. *Journal of Knowledge Management, 10* (3), 40-56.

Maguire, S., Koh, S.C., & Magrys, A. (2007). The adoption of e-business and knowledge management in SMEs. *Benchmarking, an International Journal, 14*(1), 37-58.

Markus, M. L. (2001). Toward a theory of knowledge reuse: Types of knowledge reuse situations and factors in reuse success. *Journal of Management Information Systems, 18*(1), 57-93.

McDonald, D. W., & Ackerman, M.S. (1998). Just talk to me: A field study of expertise location. In *Proceedings of the 1998 ACM Conference on Computer Supported Cooperative Work* (CSCW).

Muthusamy, S. K., Palanisamy, R., & MacDonald, J. (2005). Developing knowledge management systems (KMS) for ERP implementation: A case study from service sector. *Journal of Services Research*, pp. 66-92.

Nonaka, I., & Takeuchi, H. (1995). *The knowledge-creating company: How Japanese companies create the dynamics of innovation.* New York: Oxford University Press.

Prokopiadou, G., Papatheodorou, C., & Moschopoulos, D. (2004). Integrating knowledge management tools for government information. *Government Information Quarterly, 21*(2), 170-198.

Pundt, H., & Bishr, Y. (2002). Domain ontologies for data sharing: An example from environmental monitoring using field GIS. *Computers and Geosciences, 28*, 95–102.

Rastogi, P.N. (2000). Knowledge management and intellectual capital: The new virtuos reality of competitiveness. *Human Systems Management, 19*.

Revilla, E. (1996). *Factores Determinantes del Aprendizaje Organizativo. Un Modelo de Desarrollo de Productos.* Club Gestión de Calidad, Madrid.

Stewart T.A. (1997). *Intellectual capital: The new wealth of organizations.* New York: Doubleday Currency.

Von Hippel, E., & von Krogh, G. (2003). Open source software and the private-collective innovation model: Issues for organization science. *Organization Science, 14*(2), 209-223.

Wiig, K.M. (1993). *Knowledge management foundations, thinking about thinking: How people and organizations create, represent and use knowledge.* Schema Press, Arlington Texas.

Wright, W. F., Jindanuwat, N., & Todd, J. (2004). Computational models as a knowledge management tool: A process model of the critical judgments made during audit planning. *Journal of Information Systems, 16*(1), 23-33.

ADDITIONAL READINGS

Bowman, C. (2001). Tacit knowledge: Some suggestions for operationalization. *Journal of Management Studies, 38*(6), 811-829.

Bontis, N., Crossan, M.M., & Hulland, J. (2002). Managing an organizational learning system by aligning stocks and flows. *Journal of Management Studies, 39*(4), 437-469.

Brown, J., & Duguid, P. (1998). Organizating knowledge. *California Management Review, 40*(3), 90-111.

Cook, S.D., & Brown, J.S. (1999). Bridging epistemologies: The generative dance between organizational knowledge and knowing. *Organization Science, 10*(4), 381-400.

Cook, S.D., & Yanow, D. (1993). Culture and organizational learning. *Journal of Management Inquiry, 2*(4), 373-390.

Foss, N.J. (1996). Knowledge-based approaches to the theory of the firm: Some critical comments. *Organization Science, 5*(7), 470-476.

Goh, S., & Richards, G. (1997). Benchmarking the learning capacity of organizations. *European Management Journal, 15*(5), 575-583.

Hu, Y.S. (1995). The international transferability of the firm's advantages. *California Management Review, 37*(4), 73-88.

Huber, G. (1991). Organizational learning: The contributing processes and the literatures. *Organization Science, 2*(1), 88-115.

Jérez, P., Céspedes, J., & Valle, R. (2005). Organizational learning capability: A proposal of measurement. *Journal of Business Research, 58*(6), 715-725.

Kim, D.H. (1993). The link between individual and organizational learning. *Sloan Management Review*, pp. 37-50.

Kogut, B., & Zander, U. (1992). Knowledge of the firm, combinative capabilities, and the replication of technology. *Organization Science, 3*(3), 383-397.

Kogut, B., & Zander, U. (1996). What firms do? Coordination, identity and learning. *Organization Science, 7*(5), 502-518.

Kogut, B., & Kulatilaka, N. (2001). Capabilities as real options. *Organization Science, 12*(6), 744-758.

Lähteenmäki, S., Toivonen, J., & Mattila, M. (2001). Critical aspects of organizational learning research and proposals for its measurement. *British Journal of Management, 12*(2), 113-119.

Lant, T.K., & Mezías, S.J. (1992). An organizational learning model of convergence and reorientation. *Organization Science, 3*, pp. 47-71.

Lei, D., Hitt, M.A., & Bettis, R. (1996). Dynamic core competence through meta-learning and strategic context. *Journal of Management, 22*(4), 549-569.

Lei, D., Slocum, J.W., & Pitts, R.A. (1999). Designing organizations for competitive advantage: The power of unlearning and learning. *Organizational Dynamics, 37*(3), 24-38.

Levitt, B., & March, J. (1988). Organizational learning. *American Review of Sociology, 14*, pp. 319-340.

March, J.G. (1991). Exploration and exploitation in organizational learning. *Organization Science, 2*(1), 71-87.

McGill, M.E., & Slocum, J.W. (1993). Unlearning the organization. *Organizational Dynamics, 22* (2), 67-79.

Miner, A.S., & Mezías, S.J. (1996). Ugly duckling no more: Past and futures of organizational learning research. *Organization Science, 7*(1), 88-99.

Montes, J.M., Pérez, S., & Vázquez, C. (2006). Managing knowledge management: The link between culture and organizational learning. *Journal of Knowledge Management* (forthcoming).

Nevis, E.C., Dibella, A.J., & Gould, J.M. (1995). Understanding organizations as learning systems. *Sloan Management Review, 36*(2), 73-85.

Nicolini, D., & Meznar, M.B. (1995). The social construction of organizational learning: Concepts and practical issues in the field. *Human Relations, 48*(7), 727-746.

Nonaka, I. (1988). Creating organizational order out of chaos: Self-renewal in Japanese firms. *California Management Review, 30*(3), 57-73.

Nonaka, I. (1991). The knowledge-creating company. *Harvard Business Review, 69*(6), 96-104.

Nonaka, I . (1994). A dynamic theory of organizational knowledge creation. *Organization Science, 5*(1), 14-37.

Nonaka, I., Byosiere, P., Borucki, C., & Konno, N. (1994). Organizational knowledge creation theory: A first comprehensive test. *International Business Review, 3*(4), 337-351.

Nonaka, I., Toyama, R., & Knno, C. (2000). SECI, ba and leadership: A unified model of dynamic knowledge creation. *Long Range Planning, 33*(1), 5-34.

Schein, E.H. (1993). How can organizations learn faster? The challenge of entering the green room. *Sloan management Review*, winter, pp. 85-92.

Tsang, E.W.K. (1997). Organizational learning and the learning organization: A dichotomy between descriptive and prescriptive research. *Human Relations, 50*(1), 73-89.

Ulrich, D., von Glinow, M.A., & Jick, T. (1993). High-impact learning: Building an difussing, learning capability. *Organizational Dynamics, 22*(2), 52-66.

Von Krogh, G., Nonaka, I., & Ichijo, K. (1997). Develop knowledge activists. *European Management Journal*, 15(5), 475-483.

Zollo, M., & Winter, S.G. (2002). Deliberate learning and the evolution of dynamic capabilities. *Organization Science, 13*(3), 339-351.

Chapter X
Human Capital and E-Learning:
Developing Knowledge Through Virtual Networks

M. Eugenia Fabra
University of Valencia, Spain

Cesar Camison
Universitat Jaume I, Spain

ABSTRACT

Companies are increasingly conscious of the fact that the achieving of their objectives, together with the improvement of their competitive advantages, depends on the appropriate management of the human factor. The dynamism and strong competition that characterize the business world make it increasingly necessary to introduce a system of human resources to allow the exploiting of the knowledge and skills of both people and teams, thus encouraging their learning capacity. In this context, e-learning is becoming established as a flexible and quick way of improving the acquiring of knowledge and skills within a company. The rapid growth and expansion of e-learning, together with the failure of some of its projects, has made the development of various assessment approaches a necessity. Given the importance of this aspect, the aim of this study is to analyze the progress that has been made in the quality of e-learning initiatives.

INTRODUCTION

Globalization, rapid technological innovation, and deregulation in certain sectors have been changes that have had a strong impact on the structure of the markets, and have consequently caused changes to the business environment. Some of these changes are connected to the shifting of the basis of competitive success. The physical, financial, and even technological assets that were a source of differentiation in the industrial economy are no longer sufficient, as they tend to be available to all under equal conditions. In contrast, people and the way in which they are managed are becoming more and more important.

The literature insists on the fact that human resources constitute the most valuable asset and the most difficult to imitate, mainly because most of their characteristics are tacit and complex (Wright, et al, 1994; Boxall, 1996; Kamoche, 1996). The reserve of human capital in a company thus becomes one of the main stimulators of its competitive advantage, and depends on the strategic management of these human resources in order to develop and maintain them (D'Aveni, 1999)

In this context it can be said that a system of human resources that allows companies to exploit the existing knowledge of people and teams, thus encouraging their learning capacity, is what is necessary (Koch and McGrath, 1996; Kamoche and Mueller, 1998). In dynamic environments, indeed, the company's skill in learning faster than its competitors may be the only sustainable source of competitive advantage (Stata, 1989; McGill and Slocum, 1993: Nevis et al, 1995; Lei, Slocul and Pitts, 1999). In the words of Nonaka and Takeuchi (1995), the only companies that will be successful are those that consistently create new knowledge, disseminate it throughout the company, and rapidly incorporate new technologies and products.

For the Resources and Skills Theory, knowledge is consolidated as one of the most important strategic resources that the company has with which to achieve a sustainable competitive advantage. Faced with this situation, companies are becoming aware of the importance of the development of human capital as an element generating organizational knowledge, together with organizational learning as an essential part of the development of this knowledge.

The literature gives various definitions of learning. Montes, Pérez, and Vázquez (2002)

define it as the dynamic process of the creation, acquisition, and integration of knowledge aimed at the development of recourses and skills that allows a company to improve its operations. Martínez, Ruiz, and Ruiz (2001) refer to it as the process allowing individuals and/or companies to acquire knowledge or skills based on a certain concept, or how to make a certain thing or why this is done, transforming the information that reaches them into knowledge through the said learning process.

There are various ways at the disposal of companies in which their employees can acquire knowledge. Itami and Roehl (1987) show two:

- Professional practice where employees can acquire knowledge through their experience, having conversations with colleagues or managing company information.—Continuous training to eliminate lack of knowledge and provide with new skills to the human resources.

The part placed by new information and communication technologies in the process of the creation of knowledge is that of introducing alternatives into the information transformation cycle. According to Nonaka (1991), in the data-information-knowledge cycle the last named factor is the result of the efficient management of the other two dimensions. The importance of new technologies is above all their effect on data and information accessibility, this contributing to the creation of the third. As we make process in the knowledge generation cycle the degree of human participation increases as it is consolidated as an information processor (Daveport, 1999). New technologies are therefore necessary tools but are not enough for the service that people need (Sáez Vacas, 1991). The following figure shows the differences among data, information and knowledge.

Figure 1. Data-information-knowledge (Source: J.L. Lara (2000), © 2008 MaEugenia Fabra and Cesar Camisón. Used with permission.)

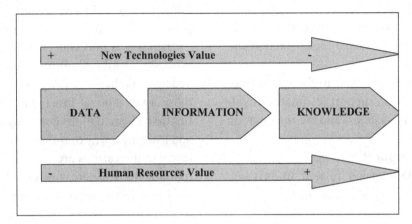

Data	Information	Knowledge
Easy observations of the reality. - Easy to capture - Easy to structure - They can be counted - Easy to communicate	Data with pertinence and intention. - It has to be analyze - It needs a common consent about its meaning - It needs the human intervention	Valuable information - Difficult to structure - Difficult to obtain by new technologies - Tacit - Difficult to communicate

E-LEARNING: NEW LEARNING PARADIGM

The presence of new technologies in the learning of the members of the company leads to the appearance of the concept of e-learning. Rosenberg (2001) show that e-learning refers to the use of Internet technologies to deliver a broad array of solutions that enhance knowledge and performance. The author establishes it is based on three fundamental criteria:

- E-learning is networked, which makes it capable of instant updating, storage/retrieval, distribution and sharing of instruction or information.

- It is delivered to the end-user via a computer using standard Internet technology.
- It focuses on the broadest view of e-learning solutions that go beyond the traditional paradigms of training

Khan, Badrul H. (1997, 2001), presents e-learning as a phenomenon with several dimensions (Figure 2):

- **Pedagogical:** Referred to training, their objectives, contents, organization, methodology and didactic strategies.
- **Technological:** Dimension which try to analyze technological resources, hardware and software.

- **Interface design:** Dimension which is important to ensure the communication among the participants.
- **Evaluation:** Dimension where it is possible to analyze the participant's satisfaction and the process quality.
- **Management:** Dimension related to technological platform support (estimates, royalties, security systems) and the information distribution.
- **Resource support**
- **Ethical:** Dimension related to privacy, contingency plagiarism plan, etc.

E-learning takes the form of a new learning concept that uses a methodology that is practical and flexible as far as the spatial and time possibilities of the individual are concerned. However, its application is not without difficulties as this requires a cultural change in both workers and management, together with an investment in technical infrastructure that will only be recovered if the training objectives are clear and have been adapted to the needs of the company.

The introduction of e-learning into a company facilitates the creation of spaces of communication, knowledge, and collaboration, and also assists the learning process by means of training. In a context in which employees need to adapt to changes by constantly renewing their knowledge, continuous training as a form of learning is being consolidated as an essential part of the personal and professional development of the worker.

Jornet, Suárez, and Perales (2001) define continuous training as instruction aimed at employees with the objective of improving their personal training and thus favoring workers' promotion or adapting human resources to the changes in production processes that occur within certain sectors or companies. According to Marcelo (2002), it is the sum of the acts of training carried out by the companies or the workers and their respective organizations, which are aimed at improving skills and workers' qualifications so as to reconcile increased competitiveness within the company with the social, professional, and personal development of the workers.

Training is thus consolidated as a permanent process with a double aim: learning and teaching. Teaching is the increasing or maintaining of all those organizational, functional, and specific abilities to the benefit of the company and the worker, and learning a way of transferring what has been learnt to the various areas of performance of the individual, thus increasing quality of life and the worker's performance from when he/she enters to when he/she leaves the company.

Aguilar et al (2007) suggests seven stages in the learning process:

- **Documentation:** First stage where the organizational, functional and specified competences identification and registration take place in order to obtain a framework which can be compared with the next stage necessities.
- **Necessities findings:** This stage pretends to identify the knowledge and skills which employees have to compare them with the organizational competences identified before. The differences can be considered as learning necessities.
- **Fit:** Stage where learning necessities and competences must be fit to reduce the differences between them.
- **Learning planning** where it is important to define objectives, resources, contents, methodology, etc.
- **Learning execution**
- **Quality and benefit evaluation**
- **Improvement plan.** In this stage it is possible to find systems mistakes in time in order to correct them.

In this process, e-learning offers clear advantages:

- E-learning provides flexibility because it offers learners with choice about where, when and how learning occurs.
- E-learning facilitates the adaptability between participants and their needs. When the learners have others commitments, it offers the ability to work at users own space.
- E-learning provides attendants with opportunities to access information and expertise contribute ideas and opinions, and correspond with other learners and mentors.
- E-learning material can be paused and reversed for watching again if it is necessary.
- E-learning offers the possibility of bring up to date the contents.

However, many e-learning initiatives are not living up to expectations because they have not been developed as part of a business strategy to satisfy the company's real needs.

The need to ensure the effectiveness of these initiatives has led to the need for drawing up assessment models suitable for the training objective and the various contexts in which it occurs. Various solutions have been developed in an attempt to address the concern for quality in e-learning from socioeconomic, technological, educational, methodological, and psychological perspectives. Up to now no single factor has managed to fulfill the requirements of this extremely complicated environment.

TRENDS TO ANALYZE THE QUALITY OF E-LEARNING

In general terms two trends can be mentioned in relation to the practices carried out in order to analyze the quality of e-learning. It is a case of a partial approach concentrating on training, training materials, technological platforms, or the cost-profit ratio; and secondly a overall approach that follows two trends, namely standard and total quality assessment systems, and systems based on benchmarking (Table 1).

PARTIAL APPROACH TO ANALYZE THE QUALITY OF E-LEARNING

Training Assessment

In the case of training, the process of quality analysis concentrates on the assessment of a specific training action. In order to do so the level of compliance with objectives, the improvement of the training action itself, and the return percentage of the investment made are taken into account. Belanguer and Jordan (2000) identify three main models in the assessment of training actions, which come from a set of variables that interact as factors predicting success in e-learning.

- **System model:** This shows the existence of a set of variables that interact as fac-

Table 1. Trends

Partial Approach	Overall Approach
Training assessment	Total quality assessment system
Training materials assessment	
Technological platforms assessment	Benchmarking
Cost-profit ratio assessment	

tors predicting the success of e-learning. These variables are: 1) institutional characteristics, related to the company's ability to introduce e-learning actions (aims of the company, the infrastructure supporting the action, the economic capacity), 2) the characteristics of those receiving the training, i.e. their interests, expectations, and skills (self-sufficiency, personal time administration, computer skills, attitude to technology, problem-solving ability), 3) the characteristics of the course or capacity of the e-learning system (course teaching/learning methodologies), and 4) the characteristics of distance learning or the need to create new models to adapt users to the new environments.

Two important aspects of this model must be emphasized. In the first place, it concentrates on the capacity of the company to introduce e-learning rather than training actions in themselves. Secondly, it is important to show that it is the only model that attaches attention to the worker as a factor in the success or failure of the activity. In the literature however the user has already been mentioned as an aspect of the success of the activity (Richarson, 2001; Ramussen and Davidson ,1996).

• Model of the five assessment levels of Marshall and Shriver (en McArdle,1999). Its special feature is that is concentrates on five levels of action, the aim of which is to ensure the worker's knowledge and skills. These levels are: (1) teaching, which analyses the teacher's capacity to project himself/herself in on-line training by means of the technological medium (e-mail, chat, the virtual classroom), making use of communicative skills that are appropriate to this environment; (2) course materials analyzed by the student in accordance with their level of difficulty, pertinence, interest, or effec-

tiveness; (3) contents; (4) course modules; and (5) transferring the learning that aims to determine the degree in which e-learning allows the participants to transfer the knowledge acquired to their job.

• Four-level model by Kirkpatrick (1994). This is orientated towards the assessment of the effect of a certain e-learning activity by means of four levels: (1) participants' reaction in questionnaires, or in a more qualitative way in discussion groups; (2) the learning achieved that aims to check the level of knowledge or skills acquired by means of validated and viable performance tests (Mantyla, 2000). Kirkpatrick (1999) recommends the use of a quasi-experimental methodology as a strategy to be able to establish the effectiveness of the course in an objective manner. Other authors consider that this assessment should be used as feedback to improve the course rather than to seek its effectiveness (Rosenberg, 2001), (3) The level of transfer reached that detects whether the skills acquired during training are being applied to the work environment and whether they are maintained over time (improved performance of the task, faster, fewer errors, a change of attitude). The most frequently used instruments or strategies are observation, interviews of supervisors, and the self-assessment of workers (Pineda, 2002), and finally (4) the impact or effect on the results in economic terms (increased sales, greater productivity, fewer errors, quality of service, fewer claims).

Despite the fact that these models contribute lines of analysis for the assessment of e-learning, none of them explain clearly either the assessment indicators, the assessment standards, or the ways and means of obtaining evidence from each of the elements assessed (Rubio, 2002). Moreover, the indicators reflect end-of-course assessment and not a continuous process leading to the improvement of quality.

Training Materials Assessment

In the assessment of materials, multimedia materials or educational software stand out. Those experiences related to the assessment of multimedia materials have concentrated on the analysis of needs, of the input, of the process, of the product, and/or of the results. The display developed for the assessment of the product orientated towards certifying material quality and/or facilitating decision-making in its selection is particularly noteworthy (Rubio, 2003). Cabero (2001:451-455) identifies three types of assessment with regard to technological environments (assessment of the characteristics of the environment, the comparative assessment of another environment, and the didactic assessment of the environment), and three assessing agents (producers, experts, and users).

The following table shows some initiatives that aim to design instruments to measure quality for the assessment of technological materials for education.

Instruments aiming to establish a series of criteria so that the assessor can certify the quality of the materials also exist. These include the instrument promoted by the European Academic Software Award (Baumgartner and Payr, 1997), which refers to the following criteria: exactness,

relevance, scope, interaction, learning, use, navigation, documentation, interfaces, using the computer, adaptability, and innovation.

Technological Platforms Assessment

The need for virtual platforms in order to develop didactic materials has given rise to the proliferation of integrated platforms known as virtual platforms or integrated learning environments (Roman, 2001). These are tools used for the creation, management, and distribution of training activities on the Internet; in other words these are applications that facilitate the creation of teaching-learning environments by integrating didactic materials and tools of communication, collaboration, and educational administration.

All the virtual platforms are built on one of the follow platform systems types:

- Content management systems which have as their primary goal the efficient and effective sharing of documents, images and other data resources. It can be almost infinitely flexible in terms of broad content manipulation.
- Collaborative portal systems which are built for community building and afford powerful interactive communication.

Table 2. Technological materials assessment

Project	Description
Instructional Management Systems Project (http://ims.org),	It is integrated by American computing multinationals and learning Institutions. It defines technological standards
Promoting Multimedia Access Education and Training in European Society" (http://www.perseus.tufts.edu)	It evaluates multimedia materials quality
Software quality model(Mendoza et al., 2001)	It evaluates software quality
E-CumLaude proyect (Rodríguez et al., 2001)	It evaluates multimedia materials quality
Educative materials evaluation method (Galvis, 2000)	
SAMIAL (Navarro, 1999)	It evaluates materials quality

- Web publishing systems which are designed to make it easy for teachers and students to post and share information via Web.

Since the technological platforms constitute the technical base on which the design and implantation of e-learning is based and developed, the best alternative selection process is a difficult task. The first stage is to analyze information about the different learning management systems. The most popular are mentioned below:

- **WebCT:** Software which offers techniques to develop training material for e-learning.
- **Digital think:** It offers an Internet solution which combine appropriate contents with instruments to assess the quality of learning.
- **ATutor is an Open Source Web-based learning content management system (LCMS)** designed with accessibility and adaptability in mind. Administrators can install or update ATutor in minutes. Educators can quickly assemble, package, and redistribute Web-based instructional content, easily retrieve and import prepackaged content, and conduct their courses online. Students learn in an adaptive learning environment.
- **Moodle:** It is an open-source virtual learning environments (VLE) that is very similar in many respects to the course management components of the major commercial VLEs.
- **Lotus learning management system:** This a support for troubleshooting problems which allows anyone with a personal computer and Internet access to enroll in Web-based courses.
- **Claroline:** It is an Open Source software based on PHP /MySQL. It is a collaborative learning environment allowing teachers or education institutions to create and admin-

ister courses through the Web. The system provides group management, forums, document repositories, calendar, chat, assignment areas, links, and user profile administration on a single and highly integrated package. Claroline is translated in 28 languages and used by hundreds of institutions around the world. The software is released under Open Source license (GPL). Downloading and using Claroline is completely free of charge.
- **Colloquia:** It is a is a peer-to-peer learning management and groupware system which supports and encourages self-organizing groups, provides asynchronous group and personal conversation facilities, allows personal information to be shared between participants and allows learning and other online resources to be referenced and accessed. It has an inbuilt Web browser, runs on all Java enabled platforms.
- **eConf:** It is an open source e-learning software, written in Java. It allows to easily record Web sessions and has been used to record multiple computer science courses.

As far as the quality of the technological platforms is concerned, Rubio (2003) affirms that a quality platform is one that is stable, reliable, tolerant of faults, standard in the introduction of contents, flexible, current, and intuitive for user interaction.

Some of the initiatives that have led to the drawing up of quality models are established in the following table, (see Table 3).

According to the European Network on Intelligent Technologies for Smart Adaptive Systems, it is still necessary to establish and agree on criteria at a European level in order to assess the quality of technological platforms and virtual campuses.

Financial Assessment

Financial assessment tries to value to what extent the improvement of skills and knowledge deriving from learning affects business results.

Table 3. Technological platform assessment

Project	Description
Cybernetic Model for Evaluating of Virtual Learning Environments (Britain y Liber, 1999)	It analyzes the relationship among resources assigned to negotiation, coordination, organization and adaptation
Quality Standards on the Virtual Campuses (http://www.vup.org/standards/),	It evaluates user' interface, software, licenses and accessibility
ACTIONS Bates Model (1999),	It values advantages and disadvantages of a technological platforms considering costs, teaching and learning, interactivity and use facility, organizational issues, novelty and speed

The introduction of an e-learning solution makes no sense if there is no return on the investment made. To assess this return rate, we have used the ROI, which is the ratio obtained from dividing the profits obtained by the cost produced. It is hard to calculate the ROI because of the difficulty in measuring profits deriving from learning. According to Horton (2001), the most productive benefits of training are the most intangible and difficult to quantify (satisfaction, initiative, and leadership, and the skills of the people making up the company), while the most operative, although they give results in the short term, are due to the result of mechanical knowledge (increased productivity, time-saving).

The importance of the ROI as an assessment instrument lies in not attributing the benefits deriving from the improvement of skills and knowledge exclusively to training, but in being able to consider how this improvement affects the economic results of a company, which makes it an instrument to control efficiency and effectiveness in the application of investments.

OVERALL APPROACH TO ANALYZE THE QUALITY OF E-LEARNING

Total Quality Assessment System

Quality management is distinguished by its complete overall approach; it is an organized strategy and a management methodology that makes all members of a company participate with the essen-tial aim of continuously improving its efficiency, effectiveness, and functionality.

In words of Gonzalez (2000) introducing a total quality assessment system depends on the follow principles:

- Process oriented to satisfy the user's needs and expectations.
- Continuous improvement in order to get the established objectives
- Process quality as a way to get the product quality
- Errors prevention instead of error supervision
- Leadership, work as a team and agility to communicate the information.

Two quality management tools have been generated on these principles:

- ISO standards, which are international rules deriving from a European Union decision with the aim of constituting a model for guaranteeing quality in the designing, development, production, installation, and after-sales service of a company. These rules require an organization to define and plan its procedures and document them correctly, check their attitude, and guarantee that they have been controlled and checked.

To apply ISO standards to e-learning projects, W. Van de Berghe (1997) proposes the following:

- The EFQM (European Foundation for Quality Management) model, which is consolidated as a model that aims to analyze all the elements making up the mechanism of a company (leadership, policies and strategies, the people involved, collaboration and resources, processes, results). The objective of the EFQM is therefore to stimulate and help European companies to take part in improvement activities that make their relation with their clients and employees, their social impact, and their business results completely satisfactory.

The application of the EFQM model to e-learning means that certain equivalents must be taken into account (Álvarez, 1998).

Benchmarking

Both ISO standards and the EFQM model are assessment tools frequently used in companies. They are however closer to administration models than to learning processes, as they highlight aspects of organizational management, client satisfaction, or the cost-profit ratio (Mateo, 2000; Barberá, 2001).

Barberá (2001) proposes the following indicators for assessing e-learning: (1) the scenario in which it occurs; (2) the proposals of the participants involved in the process (motivation, objective, cognitive demands); (3) instructional agents; (4) intervention and educational interaction; and (5) knowledge building.

Most of these dimensions are included in benchmarking, which can be defined as a sustained, rigorous, reliable, and continuous process that is orientated towards specific parameters. It basically consists of making a comparison with companies of either the same sector (whether they are competitors or not) or a different sector so as to adopt practices that can improve organizational performance. Assessment by means of benchmarking in e-learning aims to offer tools and indicators to improve actions starting from observation, comparison, and cooperation based on good practice.

CONCLUSION

Knowledge has become one of the differential values of the company, capable of giving competitive advantages, which has meant that companies conscious of the importance of their

Table 4. Application ISO standard to e-learning projects (Source: Van de Berghe, W. (1997), © 2008 MaEugenia Fabra and Cesar Camison. Used with permission.

ISO	Application to e-learning
Supplier	Institution which offers training
Customer	Participants in the e-learning course
Product	Course. Program
Executive Council	Directors Committee
Design	Technological platform
Purchases	Acquisition of materials and services (licenses, software, hardware)
Process	Learning
Inspection	Evaluation
Calibration	Assessment systems validation.

Table 5. Application EFQM model to e-learning

EFQM	Application to e-learning
Customer	User, learner
Professional	Teacher
Results	Improve the acquiring of knowledge and skills within a company.

human capital invest more time, effort, and money in training (Bassi and Van Buren, 1999). This recognition of the value of knowledge, together with the development of new information technologies (Mantyla, 2000; Salas and Cannon-Bowers, 2001) has given rise to the appearance and development of e-learning.

E-learning eliminates the frontiers of space and time, makes the participants in the training the centre of the learning process, and allows the dissemination of the learning of others, of their experiences, and of their practices.

However, some companies with an e-learning infrastructure have not managed to increase efficiency in the administration of their training processes, and neither have they developed the necessary skills in the workers in order to achieve their strategic business objectives.

Implementing an e-learning strategy means not only investing in technology but also involves an effort for all the participants intervening in knowledge and learning, so that (1) e-learning becomes the transmission of knowledge and not only of information, and (2) there is a suitable alignment between learning and organizational strategy.

Only when e-learning is placed at the disposal of the needs of the company will new technologies bring their potential to the creation of knowledge within the company.

In this context the assessment of the quality of e-learning initiatives becomes an essential factor to bear in mind before, during, and after the putting into practice of the project. In order to do so various perspectives and solutions have been developed on this subject, some more economicist in nature, others from the world of management, others technological, and others pedagogical. Up to now however, none of these alone has managed to cover all the variables and factors influencing the success of an e-learning project.

FUTURE RESEARCH DIRECTIONS

It is clear that e-learning initiatives are beneficial if they are developed as part of a business strategy to satisfy the company's need. So, researchers are convinced to create a separate debate about ways of improving the quality of e-learning.

What is the really meaning of "quality of e-learning"? What are the current and future challenges quality and standardisation of e-learning? What are the difficulties and the opportunities, and where can hidden potential be released? Is it possible and positive that e-learning was a part of the philosophy of the organization? Those are some questions that can be important to answer in the area of quality progress.

This article try to examine the main tends to analyse quality of e-learning but it insists that none of these alone has managed to cover all the variables and factors influencing the success of an e-learning project. So researchers are concerned about the need to develop a generally recognised standard which leads to certification of e-learning provision: An outline of the main requirements for the formulation of such a standard can be summarised in the key words "participation, transparency, degree of familiarity and acceptance, openness adaptability and scalability harmonization and integration integrated methodology quality awareness and measurability. Moreover, they agree to accept the following guidelines as objectives for futures quality actions:

- Learners must play a key part in determining the quality of e-learning services.
- Quality must play a central role in education and training policy.
- Quality must not be the preserve of large organisations-
- Support structures must be stabilised to provide competence, service –oriented assistance for organisations` quality development.
- Open quality standards must be further developed and widely implemented.
- Interdisciplinary quality research must become established in future as an independent academic discipline.
- Research and practise must develop new methods of interchange.
- Quality development must be designed jointly by all those involved.
- Appropriate business models must be developed for services in the field of quality

The quality of e-learning is been considered as a part of another important subject that is the culture of quality. From the strategic to the operational level, quality needs to become a feature of personal and organizational actions. So, more and more, researchers are working in order to provide a framework for quality of e-learning , lines to improve it and guides to develop a generally accepted certificates and procedures.

REFERENCES

Álvarez, M. (1998). *El liderazgo de la Calidad Total*. Madrid: Escuela Española. S.A.

Aguilar Bustamante, M.C., Martínez, A., Fandiño, A. & Fajardo, S.C. (2007). A retrospective vision of the formation process in the organizations. *Revista Diversitas: Perspectivas en Psicología, 3 (1) ,*151-174.

Barberá, E. (2001). *La incógnita de la educación a distancia*. Barcelona: Editorial Horsori, S.L.

Bassi, L.J. & Van Buren, M.E. (1999). Valuing investments in intellectual capital. *International Journal of Technology Management, 18,* 414-432.

Baumgartner, P. & Pays, S. (1997). *Methods and practice of software evaluation. The case of the European Academic Software Award.* Proceeding of ED-MEDIA 97. ED-TELECOM 97, ACCE.

Belanguer, F. & Jordan, D.H. (2000). *Evaluation and Implementation of Distance Learning. Technologies, tools and techniques*. London: Idea Group Publishing.

Boxall, P. (1996). The strategic HRM debate and the resource-based view of the firm. *Human Resource Management Journal, 6(3),* 59-75

Cabero, J. (2001). La evaluación e investigación sobre los medios de enseñanza. In J. Cabero, *Tecnología Educativa. Diseño y utilización de medios de enseñanza*. Barcelona: Ediciones Paidós Ibérica, S.A., 447-490.

D'Aveni, R.A. (1994). *Hyper-Competition: Managing the dynamics of strategic manoeuvring*. New York: Free Press.

Davenport, T. (1999). *Ecología de la Información*. Oxford University Press,

Horton, W. (2001). *Evaluating e-learning*. California. ASTD (American Society for Training and Development).

Horton, W. (2000). *Designing Web-Based Training*. New York: John Wiley

Itami, H. & Roehl, T.W. (1987). *Mobilizing invisible assets.* Harvard University Press, Cambridge.

González, T. (2000). Evaluación y gestión de la calidad educativa. In T. González (coord.): *Evaluación y gestión de la calidad educativa. Un enfoque metodológico.* Málaga: Ediciones Aljibe, 49-80.

Jornet, J., Suarez, J. & Perales, M.J. (2001). Evaluación de la Formación Ocupacional y Continua. *Revista de Investigación Educativa, 19 (2).*

Kamoche, K. (1996). Strategic Human Resource Management within a resource-capability view of the firm. *Journal of Management Studies, 33,* 213-233.

Kamoche, K. & Mueller, F. (1998). Human Resource Management within a Resource-Capability View of the Firm. *Journal of Management Studies, 33 (2),* 213-233.

Khan, Badrul, H. (eds.) (2007). *Flexible learning in an information society.* Hershey, P.A.: Information Science Publishing.

Kirkpatrick, D.L. (1999). *Evaluación de acciones formativas: los cuatro niveles.* Barcelona: EPISE-Barcelona: Edicions Gestió 2000, S.A.

Koch, M.J. & McGrath, R.G. (1996). Improving labor productivity: human resource management policies do matter. *Strategic Management Journal, 17,* 335-354.

Lara, J.L. (2000). *Diez respuestas a las preguntas más frecuentes sobre gestión del conocimiento.*

Lei, D., Slocum, J.W. & Pitts, R.A. (1999). Designing organizations for competitive advantage: the power of unlearning and learning. *Organizational Dynamics, 37 (3),* 24-38.

Mantyla, K. (2000). Evaluating Program Success. En K. Mantyla, *Distance Learning Yearbook* (pp. 259-287). New York: McGraw-Hill,

Marcelo, C. (2000). Formación, empleo y nuevas tecnologías. In C. Marcelo (coord), D. Puente, M.A. Ballesteros & A. Palazón. *E-learning-Teleformacion, Diseño, desarrollo y evaluación de la formación a través de Internet* (pp. 9-18). Barcelona: Ediciones Gestión 2000, S.A.

Martínez, I; Ruiz, J. & Ruiz, C. (2001). *Aprendizaje organizacional en PYMES.* Paper presented at the XI ACEDE National Congress, Zaragoza.

Mateo, J. (2000). La evaluación del profesorado y la gestión de la calidad de la educación. Hacia un modelo comprensivo de evaluación sistemática de la docencia. *Revista de Investigación Educativa, 18 (1),* 7-34

McArdle, G.E. (1999). *Training Design and Delivery.* Alexandria: V.A. American Society for Training and Development

McGill, M.E. & Slocul, J.W. (1993). Unlearning the organization. *Organizational Dynamics, 22 (2),* 67-79.

Montes, J.M., Pérez, S. & Vázquez, C.J. (2002). *Influencia de la cultura organizativa sobre el aprendizaje: Efectos sobre la competitividad.* Paper presented at XII ACEDE National Congress, Palma de Mallorca.

Nevis, E.C., Dibella, A.J. & Gould, J.M. (1995). Understanding organizations as learning systems. *Sloan Management Review, 36 (2),* 73-85.

Nonaka, I. (1991). The Knowledge-Creating Company. *Harvard Business Review, 69 (6),* 96-105.

Nonaka, I. & Takeuchi, H. (1995). *The Knowledge Creating Company: How Japanese Companies Create the Dynamics of Innovation. Oxford University Press, Nueva York*

Pineda, P. (2002). Formació, transferència i avaluació: un triangle complex. *Revista Econòmica de Catalunya, 44,* 79-89.

Ramussen, K. & Davidson, G.V. (1996). *Dimensions of learning styles and their influence on* performance in hypermedia lessons. CD-ROM Proceedings from the annual ED-MEDIA/ED-TELECOM conference. Article n° 385.

Richarson, J. (2001). An evaluation of Virtual Learning Environments and their learners: do individual differences effect perception of virtual learning environments. Interactive. *Educational Multimedia*, 3.

Rosenberg, M. (2001). *E-learning: Estrategias para transmitir conocimiento en la era digital.* Bogotá: McGraw-Hill Intramericana.

Rubio, M.J. (2003). Enfoques y modelos de evaluación del e-learning. *Revista electrónica de Investigación y Evaluación Educativa, Relieve,* 9 (2).

Sáez Vacas, F. (1991). La sociedad informatizada: Apuntes para una patología de la técnica, Claves de la Razón Práctica. *Colección Impactos. Ed. Funesco*

Van De Bergue, W. (1997). *Aplicación de las Normas ISO 9000 a la enseñanza y la formación. Interpretación desde una perspectiva europea.* Luxemburgo: CEDEFOP.

Van Slyke, C., Kittner, M. & Belanguer, F. (1998). *Identifying Candidates for Distance education: A telecommuting perspectiva.* Proceedings of the America's Conferencie on Information Systems (pp. 666-668). Baltimore

Wright, P.M., McMahan, G.C. & McWilliams (1994). Human resources and sustained competitive advantage: a resource based perspective. *The International Journal of Human Resource Management,* 5,301-326

ADDITIONAL READING

Alton, C & Wing L. (2007). Quality assurance in online education: The Universitas 21 Global

approach. *British Journal of Educational Technology 38 (1)*, 133–152

Barbera, E. (2004). Quality in virtual education environments. *British Journal of Education Technology 35 (1)*, 13-20.

Belanger, F. & Jordan, D.H. (2000). *Evaluation and Implementation of Distance Learning: technologies, tools and techniques.* London: Idea Group Publishing.

Bates, A.W. (1999). Research and Evaluation. In A.W. Bates. *Managing Technological Change*, 198-210. California: Jossey-Bass.

Baumgartner, P. $ Payr, S. (1997). *Methods and practice of software evaluation. The case of the European Academic Software Award.* Proceedig of ED-MEDIA 97 & ED-TELECOM 97, AACE.

Berk, J. (2003). Learning Measurment: It's Not How Much You Train, But How Well. *The E-learning Developer' Journal*, 11, 1-8

Cashion, J. & Palmieri, P. (2002). *Evaluation of Quality in On-line Learning.* TAFE School of Social Sciences. Swinburne University of Technology. From http://www.tafe.swin.edu.au/ncver/

Clark, R. (2002). *Putting Learning Standards into Practice.* ASTD E-learning Hanbook. McGraw Hill.

Davies, G. & Stancey, E. (2003). *Quality education a distance.* Kluwer Academy Publishers. This book contains the papers presented at the working conference on Quality Education

Ehlers, U.D., Goertz, L & Hildebrant, B. (2005). Use and dissemination of quality approaches in European e-learning. A study by the European Quality Observatory. Cedefop Panorama series, 116.

Frydenberg, J. (2002). Quality Standards in e-learning: A matrix of analysis. *International*

Review of Research in Open and Distance Learning, 3,2.

Jara, M. & Mellar, H. (2006). Exploring the mechanism for assuring quality of e-learning courses in UK higher education institutions. *European Journal of Open Distance and E-learning.*

Kamara, J.M., Anumba C.J., & Carrillo, P.M. (2002). A clever approach to selecting a knowledge management strategy. *International Journal of Project Management*, 20, 205-211.

Keller, J. (1983). Motivational Design of Instruction. In Reigeluth, C. (Ed.). *Instructional-design theories and models: an overview of their current status.* Mahwah, NJ: Lawrence Erlbaum.

Lockee, B., Moore, M. & Burton, J. (2002). Measuring Success: Evaluation Strategies for Distance Eduaction. Educase Quaterly, 1, 20-26.

Manju K. Ahuja & Kathleen M. Carley (1992). Network structure in Virtual Organizations. *Journal of computer- Mediated Communication, 3, 4.*

Massy, J. (2002). Quality and e-learning in Europe. Bizmedia.

Oliver, M. (1998) (Ed.) Innovation in the Evaluation of Learning Technology. London. University of North London.

Ordóñez, P. (2004). Knowledge flow transfers in multinational corporations: knowledge properties and implications for management. *Journal of Knowledge Management*, 8(6), 105-116.

Rubio, M.J. (2003). Enfoques y modelos de evaluación del e-learning. *Relieve,9,2*, 101-120

Skyrme, D.J. (1999). *Knowledge networking. Creating the collaborative enterprise.* Oxford: Butterworth-Heinemann.

Stata, R. (1989): Organizational learning: the key to management innovation. *Management Review,30,1,* 63-74.

Stufflebeam, D.L. (2000). *The CIPP model for evaluation.* In Stufflebeam, D.L., Madaus & G.F., Kellaghan, T. (ed.): Evaluation Models. Boston.

Tsvetozar Georgiev, T., Georgieva, E., & Smrikarov, A. (2004). *E-Learning, a New Stage of E-Learning. Paper* presented at International Conference on Computer Systems and Technologies - CompSysTech'2004, Rousse, Bulgaria.

Van De Berghe, W. (1997). *Aplicación de las Normas ISO 9000 a la enseñanza y la formación. Interpretación desde una perspectiva europea.* Luxemburgo. CEDEFOP.

Section V
Specific Problems and Industries

Networking has provoked an authentic revolution in some sectors, especially in those where the access to clients has been a determinant limitation untill the arrival of internet. The public sector and the tourism industry are two interesting exemples. Besides, some specific areas of information management are analyised in a network context, such as business analytics success and decision making.

Chapter XI
The Development of Knowledge and Information Networks in Tourism Destinations

Júlio da Costa Mendes
University of Algarve, Portugal

ABSTRACT

This chapter looks to analyse new paradigms in the relationship between public and private organisations towards tourism destinations. It proposes new approaches for increased performance both at the competitive and the organisational level. Based on the literature review, this chapter suggests new organisational forms of being and interaction directed at increased customer needs and growing competitiveness on the tourism industry. The development of public-private partnerships and knowledge networking in destinations and in organisations are issues also addressed. Furthermore, the implementation of inter-organisational networks in a cooperative environment is important in developing and maintaining an adequate environment with shared objectives and practices in tourist destinations.

INTRODUCTION

Globalisation has had a decisive impact on the changing environment and one in which nowadays economies are facing. This fact has stimulated growing interest from researchers who have turned their attention to issues of globalisation, the digital era, innovation and Knowledge Management.

The rise of the so-called New Digital Economy, characterised by the spread of new information and communication technologies, has provoked over recent years a revolution in the world of business and more specifically in tourism, causing changes in corporate strategies and organisational structures.

For the majority of countries, the tourism sector represents an important service industry, socioeconomically significant for hosting regions. This is not only related to dynamic sector growth but also to the multiple effects generated by globalisation to other sectors of the economy.

Nowadays, tourism organisations face a dynamic and uncertain environment that require flexible and fast results essential to changing businesses. This, linked to the need for cooperation between the various actors in the value chain of the tourist destination, has generated the onset and development of several inter-organisational networks, aimed at improving competitiveness of destinations and involved organisations.

Developing a climate of cooperation in tourist destinations implies firstly that actors are aware that they belong to a chain where their performance complements and contributes to the value of the tourist experience. The introduction of programmes and integrated projects, common visions, cooperative agreements and collaboration between public and private entities based on the pursuit of greater global objectives, is a networking reality for tourism destinations.

The interactive process of close and coherent collaboration between all actors and organisations, public and private, at the regional, national and even international scale, is of central importance for competitiveness in tourist destinations. This creates synergies for networking providers and allows the development of a common vision towards tourism building based on concerted efforts from involved parties.

Based on the review of the literature focused on the concepts of tourism destination and virtual knowledge and information networks, the paper intends to discuss, in theoretical terms, the benefits of the establishment of partnerships and cooperation networks between public and private tourism organisations, contributing for the development and implementation of improvement competitiveness strategies in tourism destinations.

To the effect, the paper begins by clarifying the tourism destination concept and characterizing the kind of consumption product that consubstantiates the tourism experience. Than, it discusses the need for new approaches in terms of tourism destination management, assuming that the main objective of the Destination Management Organisations is to maximize the synergies of the value chain, ensuring high levels of satisfaction for tourists as much as stakeholders. Finally, it suggests that the constitution of partnerships and the sharing of knowledge and information between the tourism sector organisations is a strategic issue for the competitiveness of the tourism destinations and, in that sense, it must be an object of the greatest attention from the Destination Management Organisations intending to succeed in terms of performance.

TOURISM DESTINATION

Tourism destination is closely linked to new experiences and associated memories. Although a composite unit representing a region's supply, it is considered a paradigmatic example of virtual organisation.

As a setting comprising economic, cultural and social activities, the tourism destination has come to be understood as a product on offer, and thus the public institutions responsible for that destination and the regional tourism organisations operating within that destination see themselves as obliged to establish a set of facilities and actions that ensure the best possible positioning in a highly competitive market when it comes to attracting tourists (Beerli & Martin, 2004)

The studies carried out by Butler (1980), Gunn (1993), Laws (1995) and Pearce (1989) regard tourism destination as a system containing a number of components such as attractions, accommodation, transport and other services and facilities. The tourism destination generally comprises different types of complementary and competing organisations, multiple sectors, facilities and an array of public/private linkages that create a diverse and highly fragmented structure (Pavlovich, 2003).

The complexity of the system arises from the interactive environment and complementarity that characterises the relations that develop between the different types of service providers and their acting influence. Under a complex system of the provision of services, with product and services being provided simultaneously by different units of an organisation, or different organisations, involved agents should interact efficiently, so that no situation contributes negatively on the global tourist experience.

Given the close and complementary inter-relationships established between the different types of industry organisations, it becomes important to ensure efficient coordination of flow of information between organisations of the sector (Bouncken, 2000; Hope & Muhlemann, 1998; Smith, 1994; Pizam, 1991).

In this sense, besides the organic structure embodied, the tourism destination develops its activity essentially through the pursuit of common objectives and strategic implementation grounded on a Web of relations and contacts with organisation of the sector. The destination must be considered as a whole – a system with inputs and outputs (Tinsley & Lynch, 2001).

The Composite Product

The global or composite product, by definition is an interactive product that results from the total supply made available to tourists. Structurally, it is a product developed around a combination of experiences which are central to the expectations and overall assessment by customers. In this sense, it can be analysed as "an intangible composite of many interrelated components" (Pizam, Neumann & Reichel, 1978: p. 316) or as a combination of rendered and used services in a dynamic, multifaceted environment, domestic or international, where controversial issues and conflicting interests are always present (Silva,

1991; Papadopoulos, 1989; Guibilato, 1983).

Klein (2000) considers that the tourist product is the destination and the process that results from the overall experience of tourists, while the subproducts are transports, excursions, food and drink, accommodation, entertainment and services, as well as the respective management. The same point of view is held by Silva, Mendes & Guerreiro (2001) and by Rita (1995) among others.

The value chain joins actors and consumers, representing a chain link to an experience that the tourist classifies in terms of satisfaction and value. Managing the chain and maximising the value of experiences of customers by interacting with several chain links is a task which transcends the sectorial boundaries of industry. The break of a chain link, disfunctionality, an ill-established contact or an unpleasant surprise may result negatively in terms of tourist satisfaction and contribute toward a negative image of the destination. The "halo effect" can still occur, which means that satisfaction or dissatisfaction with one of the components leads to satisfaction or dissatisfaction with the total tourist product (Weiermair, 2000a,b; Stauss & Weinlich, 1997; Brathwaite, 1992; Pizam *et al.*, 1978).

Once the value is added at each level of the production process, it becomes important to understand to some degree of certainty how the tourist production chain for a specific destination or destination package will combine to produce added value for the different types of consumers and market segments. The tourists, in consuming the destination-product, look to obtain the greatest value for the least effort which assumes the maximum destination competitiveness (Martín, 2000; Huete, 1994; Smith, 1994; Weiermair, 1994).

Tourism Experience

The leisure and tourism experience has been described as an "a subjective mental state felt by participants" (Otto & Ritchie, 1996, p.166). While products are fungible and services intangible, the value of the experience remains in the memory of individuals investing in the event. For intangible services, the experiences are regarded as events that commit people in a particular manner and, as such, are memorable. While the supply of services ends with the experience of visitors to a destination, it begins before arrival and ends with memories and future visit plans (Pine & Gilmore, 1999; Commission Européenne, 1999).

Various authors refer to the composite product associating it to the complex experience that the tourist has from the moment he or she leaves the place of residence until the moment he or she returns home (Silva *et al.,* 2001; Davidson & Maitland, 1997; Smith, 1994; Papadopoulos, 1989; Buckley, 1987).

For consumers that deal with a number of meetings during a stay, it is the sum of services that is at the origin of forming perceptions and not the specific products or isolated meetings of services. Regardless of the evaluation or perception of specific quality of subproducts, tourists assess the tourism experience as a whole. This suggests that what is consumed and evaluated in a holistic manner should also be produced and managed holistically (Weiermair, 2000a; Fayos-Solá & Moro, 1995; Gummesson, 1994; Brathwaite, 1992).

The process by which the tourist perceives and recollects a destination travel experience is complex and multifaceted precisely because there are a significant number of involved actors in the experience. Consequently, complete destination experience results from a wide combination of individual experiences by tourists, separated in time and space. In conceptual terms, the tourist experience consists in the continuous flow of services related and integrated, and which are acquired during a limited period of time, most often in different geographical areas.

Most businesses that supply tourist products or services do so in the form of a package which includes a combination of physical items, services;

interactions that a tourist experiences at different occasions and holds in perceived memory his or her tourist experience. Increasingly, how these packages are conceived and operated influence the experience of tourists at the destination (Albrecht & Zemke, 2002; Kandampully, 2000; Denmann, 1998; Ritchie & Crouch, 1997; Haywood, 1993; Michaud, Planque & Barbaza, 1991).

Research in service marketing recognises that, although the performance of services is supported by tangible goods, in the case of tourism, what is actually bought by tourists is an experience, that is, an array of interactions, interpersonal relations that result from various contacts established between service providers and tourists during the period spent at the destination (Frochot & Hughes, 2000; Kandampully, 2000; Ritchie & Crouch, 2000; Weiermair, 2000a).

During his or her stay, the tourist consumes not only reality but also representations and symbols of reality, asserting what Lutz & Ryan (1993, p.356) refer to as the rise of "consumption aesthetics". In this sense, trying to attribute rationalism to the tourist experience may confuse the reason behind tourist motivation and behaviour, more so when there is an awareness that emotions and confusion that tourists reveal are part and parcel of the tourist phenomenon (Ryan, 1995).

In this sense, the experience is embodied around a combination of emotions, experiences, in essence a holistic product, which has significant implication in terms of repositioning the supply of tourism destinations. On the other hand, it is clear that the tourist embarks on this experience with knowledge and demand levels increasingly more developed, resulting from comparisons with past experience, greater awareness to details, through communication and informal messages, word of mouth, etc.

The paradigm of experimental vision analyses the experience consumption as "a subjective fundamental level of knowledge with a variety of symbolic meaning, hedonistic responses and aesthetic criteria (...) focused on caring answers by each person, including, though not limited to, fantasies, sentiments and enjoyment" (Otto & Ritchie, 1995, p. 38).

The experience is affected by a vast set of factors, many of which are not directly related with the purchase of a specific product. It is the combination of inherent factors in terms of context and satisfaction of each of the purchased services, consumed throughout the unfolding holistic experience, which determines the overall level of tourist satisfaction. The quality of the experience is generally recognised as a more subjective measure, while quality service is often obtained in more objectively. While quality of service focuses generally on a specific service commitment, the quality of the experience includes a larger combination of commitments. A more comprehensive concept and greater temporal horizon on the quality context of the experience tends to highlight the hedonistic component of the relation that visitors establish with the tourist destinations (Ritchie & Crouch, 1997).

The tourists look to obtain working benefits that are symbolic and experiences through activities and services that make up the tourist experience. In fact, the tourist experience is a continuum moment of truth, the quality of which is reached only when reality coincides with consumer expectations. But consumers are different; possessing different expectations transforms the concept of quality into one that is relative. Quality cannot be regarded in a singular manner rather it is diverse composed by different market segments (Vega, Casielles & Martín, 1995; Bordas, 1994).

The tourist experience is thus consolidated around a vast set of components offered by several organisations with different objectives and form of operation. Service suppliers should recognise that satisfaction of visitors with organisation is influenced by several pre-arrival and post-arrival services. The success of the destination product depends on the provision of the right combination of components to satisfy the demands of visitors, requiring coordination, cooperation and partnerships.

From the management point of view of Destination Management Organisations, it is clear that it is impossible to control many of the factors that contribute to a destination quality experience. On the other hand, the skills and possibilities of actors and operators controlling these factors are diverse and distinct; some of which are by separate organisations, other not yet controlled. This can compromise the standards promised or proposed in campaigns affecting how tourists experience their stay.

Competitiveness of Tourism Destinations

Competitiveness is one of the central concerns by tourist destination managers. Improving performance levels of tourist destinations in order to meet stakeholder expectations, adapted to accommodate sustaining needs related to environment, heritage and culture of hosting regions, constitutes a challenge and an investment for most Destination Management Organisations.

The challenges for organisational management and other local or regional virtual systems are today particularly high. In the case of tourist destinations, they are expected to react clearly and intelligently, to act simultaneously according to plans, to reinforce identity and added supply value, to conceive alliances for coordinated and cooperative networking actions, stressing product quality and culture service. Analysis, planning, implementation and control of programs intended to influence the visiting customer choice, especially before arriving at the destination, strategy selection, and destination marketing plans, represent the importance given to competitiveness of tourist destinations (Leoni, 1999; Ridley, 1995; Middleton, 1994).

The issue is even more relevant when there is an awareness that "tourism is a highly decentralized industry consisting of enterprises different in size, location, functions, type of organization, range of services provided and methods used to market and sell them. In addition, a variety of trade associations, co-operative institutions and official or semi-official organisations at the local, regional and national and international level play an important role in the industry "(Schmoll, 1997, p.30).

Most of these organisations are small-scale, constituting an added challenge for Destination Management organisers who among others should assume a dynamic or facilitating role in the process of formalising cooperation in the entrepreneurial sector. "Networking is also important for small and medium-sized enterprises, in that it offers a way of combining advantages such as flexibility, with economies of scale which networks offer" (Corvelo, Moreira e Carvalho, 2001, p. 23).

The performance of the tourist destination benefits greatly if based on knowledge sharing and long-life learning and innovation. Maximising information flows for all those involved is essential to consolidate the learning process of involved actors (Klein, 2000; EFQM 1999). The need to learn, to generate greater value and differentiate supply constitutes nowadays a key component for competing systems. The competitive advantage is gained only by bringing together the knowledge, expertise, capital and other resources of the various tourism organizations (Fayall & Garrod, 2004).

NEW ORGANISATIONAL AND MANAGEMENT PARADIGMS IN THE CONTEXT OF TOURISM DESTINATIONS

In this environment of great complexity, instability and uncertainty, organisational changes have been regarded as one of the main vehicles in structuring and exploring the new world of business (Toledo & Loures, 2006). The advent of the information era has made many of the fundamental assumptions of the industry obsolete and the more boundaries lessen the more involved corporate strategies and identity change. New organisational forms are possible because information technology has the capacity to modify the traditional space-time interaction (Schultze & Boland, 2000).

The virtual reality, or the process of virtual reality, possesses two main characteristics that facilitate its use on organisations. Detachment of the here and now according to Lévy (1996), an organisation which virtualises itself, deterritorialises itself, becoming "non-present". Customers can contact organisations virtually, regardless of where they may be as long as they possess access to a computer and modem. The second characteristic stated by the author is the passing from the interior to the exterior and the exterior to the interior, suggesting that there are no longer limits, place and time commix.

Virtual organisation appears as an organisational model of the 21st century, sustained by a radical change of classical organisational concepts and work division. Previous research suggests that virtual organisations tend to be non-hierarchical (Goldman, Nagel & Preiss, 1995; Beyerlein, Johnson & Beyerlein, 1994; Camilus, 1993; Mills 1991) and decentralised (Baker 1992). Researchers have found that network structures explain organisational behaviour better than formal structures (Krackhard & Hanson 1993; Bacharach & Lawer 1980).

The concept of virtual organisations can be understood as a form of cooperation between businesses and organisations, thus becoming true dynamic cooperation networks, which through the use of new information and communication technology have as objectives increasing competitiveness of network partners and enabling exploration of new market opportunities. The components of this new organisational form essentially develop from partnerships, response capacity in terms of market demands, quality of products and services rendered and greater awareness and environmental responsibility (Tapscoot & Caston, 1993).

This strategic option which consists in supervising the running and organisation of business for virtualisation is one of the options being followed by organisations that seek sustainable competitive advantages. In recent literature, virtual organisations are presented as success models, suggesting that ultimately virtual reality represents innovation, a widening of the corporate value chain, better information flows and corporate decision-making (Toledo & Loures, 2006).

There is a proliferation of terms used to define emerging "new organisations": agile organisations, network organisations, virtual organisations, extended enterprises, knowledge enterprises, learning organisations and smart organisation (Carbo, Molina & Davila, 2003; Aladwani, 2002; Baker, Georgakopoulos, Schuster & Cichocki, 2002; Bradner 2002; CastelFranchi 2002; Merali, 2002; Ricci, Omicini & Denti, 2002; Shumar & Renninger, 2002; Inkpen & Ross, 2001; Burnett 2000; Devine & Filos 2000; Filos & Banaham, 2000; Frenkel, Afsaermanesh, Garita & Hertzberger, 2000; Goranson 2000; Molina & Flores 2000; Mundim & Bremer, 2000; Riempp 1998;).

According to Devine & Filos (2000), a virtual organisation is a collection of geographically-distributed and operating entities that may or may not be culturally diverse and use information and communication technologies supported by lateral and dynamic relationships for coordinated action needs.

On the other hand, Frenkel *et al.*, (2000), considers that virtual organisations should be seen as a group collaboration of self-governing and existing organisations, who share expertise, skills and resources in order to achieve a common product or service..

Molina & Flores (2000) define virtual organisations as temporary networks of independent organisations connected through information technology who share skills, facilities and business processes with the aim of responding to specific market demand.

Finally, Ricci *et al.*, (2002) argue that virtual organisations occur as a response to consumer needs and a temporary assemblage of self-governing and possibly heterogeneous organisations, conceived to provide flexibility and adaptability to the frequent changes that characterise business scenarios.

We are therefore before a new organisational format that exceeds the physical boundaries of organisations in a process that includes complex relationships with partners, customers, suppliers and the market (Mowshowitz, 1997). The paradigm of virtual or network organisations assumes the presence of various service providers, operating autonomously and flexibly, though directed in the same direction as a result of a common culture, an information management system. This allows information sharing of crucial business information and an infrastructure in charge of controlling and developing the overall management process of the tourist destination (Martín, 2000; Valles, 1999; McHugh, Merli & Wheeler, 1995; Gummesson, 1994).

The main challenges that these types of organisations face involve maintaining the balance between people and culture, maintaining the organisation in tune to processes, information and technology, and finally issues related to leadership in a new organisational structure format. Basic technologies supporting virtual organisations include the Internet and the World Wide Web, telecommunications, electronic mail, groupware such as Lotus Notes and video conferencing. It is important to note that understanding the technology is not enough.

According to Strausak (1998), there are currently two different approaches of virtual organisations. The first identifies the virtual organisation as a business that relies more heavily on information and communication technology than on physical presence in order to interact and drive their businesses. The attribute "virtual" is used to define an organisational logic, where boundaries of time, geographical space, organisational units and information access are less important, while the use of communication technologies is considered highly useful. (Siebert 2000; Zimmerman, 2000; Kluber, 1998).

The second approach considers virtual organisation as a network of independent organisations that possess a temporary characteristic through the use of information and communication technologies, in this way gaining greater competitive advantage.

Regardless of the first or second approach, there are several motives that can prompt organisations to opt for a virtual solution. These include the sharing of resources and skills, the need to innovate, to divide risks, the need to reduce costs, market access, agility, better productivity, quality and competitiveness (Lipnack, 1993).

Given this, incorporating both approaches need to be considered in order to provide a more consistent and operational concept in practical terms. In fact, both perspectives complement each other and it difficult to separate the two. The virtual organisation reflects both internally, when assuming a new structural form and more importantly when assuming a new form of thinking and positioning in the business world and relationally as with other sector and non sector organisations. The logic behind this process of strategic redirection of organisations has no defined boundaries and, as such, the concept should be assumed in a flexible and wide-ranging manner, interrelating internal changes to new relational and interacting forms in the surrounding environment.

To implement the virtual organisational concept, Les Pang (2001) recognises that there are a set of good practices that should be considered by all those that have a mission to impel organisations towards this new paradigm by: fostering cooperation, trust and empowerment; ensuring that each partner contributes to an identifiable strength or asset; ensuring skills and competences are complementary and not overlapping; ensuring that partners are adaptable; ensuring that contrac-

tual agreements are clear and specific on roles and deliverables; not replacing face-to-face interaction entirely, provide training which is critical to team success; recognising that it takes time to develop a team; ensuring that technology is compatible and reliable; and, providing technical assistance that is competent and available.

In terms of the virtual organisations concept application to the specific context of tourism, it is argued that the new organisational paradigm be grounded on four fundamental pillars: cooperation, innovation, flexibility and knowledge. The first pillar is represented in terms of inter-organisational networking and in the sharing of resources and know-how. The second is essentially related to promoting creativity between organisations and the search of new solutions for business management problems. The third involves adapting organisations to the surrounding environment and to quick solutions to environmental changes. Lastly, knowledge is a fundamental requirement which upholds the concept of "learning organisation" and what it entails in terms of sharing and free information access.

This new organisational structure, which should be undertaken and lead by the Destination Management Organisations, will have as a mission to promote the creation of new value systems and a new culture in the relationship between stakeholders. The restructuring of organisational and architectural models will give rise to the development of new management paradigms both at the organisational and tourist destination management levels.

A new managerial style is required because of the special issues one must face in an inter-organisational environment. As Tapscoot (1995) states, interactive multimedia technologies and the information highway contribute to a new economic order based on human intelligent networks. According to this author, it is possible to foresee the document and paper circuits as well as traditional forms of running businesses.

So that the Destination Management Organisation can begin the prepare the future and the transition for these new organisational and management paradigms, it becomes important to rethink its role in terms of considering how actors are influenced, redefining a vision intended for the destination, re-equating aspects of technical and logistic order of cooperation networks, identifying benefits of various technologies that support virtual organisations and lastly, considering new forms of operation in terms of partner relationships and managements and stakeholders in the field of tourist destination.

In this context, and considering that the tourism sector essentially comprises small and medium enterprises, it is crucial that tourism destination management directors assume leadership in the process of change and, from the first moment, create a basis for active participation from the majority of stakeholders. Besides following through with mega projects and the involvement of small and medium enterprises in this process, it is important to make entrepreneurs and managers aware of the advantages in knowledge and information sharing based on commitment with new forms of greater and continued cooperation in tourist destinations.

THE COOPERATIVE ENVIRONMENT IN TOURISM DESTINATIONS

In a growing scenario of competitiveness and for reasons related to the need to overcome the specific difficulties or pursuit of common objectives at the tourist destination level, it has become common practice to create ways to cooperate inter-organisationally in tourist destinations. The "relational" perspective is particularly relevant in the tourism industry, as groupings of organisations cluster together to form a destination context.

Bjork and Virtanen (2005) consider that the necessity of well functioning co-operation networks is well articulated in the tourism literature, whether in terms of destination marketing (von Friedrichs Grangsjo, 2002), destination planning (Jamal & Getz, 1995; Ladkin & Betramini, 2002) or development of tourism partnerships (Selin & Chavez 1995).

Different forms of inter-organizational relations (e.g., co-ordination, network, collaboration, partnership, cooperation) have started to receive growing attention in recent years from researchers worldwide as a means of finding solutions to resource management and destination development problems (Augustyn & Knowles, 2000; Bramwell & Lane, 2000; Hall, 2000; Selin, 2000; Timothy, 1998; Jamal & Getz, 1995; Selin & Myers, 1995; Benson, 1975).

These forms of inter-organisational cooperation in tourist destinations are all the more necessary when there is a clear understanding that objectives can only be fulfilled with the effort and participation of all destination actors and organisations. In this context, the involvement of organisations with partnerships is increasingly greater, going beyond traditional organisational boundaries in order to achieve consumer needs more rapidly (Glendinning, 2003; Austin, 2002, Bradner, 2002; Molina & Flores, 2000; Riempp, 1998).

According to Pearce (1989), tourist organisations can better achieve their objectives when they are able to coordinate the activities of the vast participants who contribute towards to composite product and the tourist experience. Watkins and Bell (2002, p.20) believe that "the experience of co-operation was described as stimulating more business through working together to share information and engage in joint activities".

Collaboration can be regarded as a process of shared decision-making among key stakeholders regarding future issues. Joint decision-making is important for all those parties having an interest or stake in tourism destinations (Gray, 1985). Usually, what arises from these cooperative projects are cooperation and formal agreements established by the organisations involved and the

191

common objective that justifies and polarises joint efforts. What is equally relevant is to understand the expectations, objectives and benefits that the managers wish to obtain in exchange.

Wang & Fesenmaier (2005) identified four broad issues related to collaboration in the area of marketing, which can be adopted for the tourism case: the precondition construct, which delineates the economic, social, and environmental conditions for alliance and network formation; the motivation construct which attempts to explain why organisations choose to enter into strategic alliances and networks to achieve their specific goals; the stage construct which captures the dynamics of collaborative process and the outcome construct which attempts to describe the consequences of collaborative activities.

This type of inter-organisational cooperation should rely on some degree of virtuality in order to offer greater ease and response to market changes, stakeholders and unexpected alterations, besides repercussions in the performance of involved organisations, profitability level productivity and quality of rendered services. Actors should recognise and understand that cooperation facilitates the introduction of change, enabling strategic direction for organisations, stimulating and facilitating learning for all, developing business interaction and providing better relationship between actors.

It is important, however, not to lose sight that cooperative effort is based on a relationship of interests, costs and expected benefits. It can be assumed then that as a question of principle, the synergy effects that are created as a combination should reverberate in better organisational performance. This reflects a need to analyse information and monitor systems that support the evaluation process of performance results, whether in terms of organisational networks whether in terms of determining the reciprocal impact established between both levels of decision-making.

The development and consolidation of these types of tourist destination networks should begin to by interiorising in the set of actors the need to adopt new management paradigms based on a culture of chain relationships, driven by quality principles and entrepreneurial excellence in the entire region. Given the developing processes, whether in terms of costs or benefits, it is important to comprehend that from the first moment, the advantages to be gained by each participant will be greater if there is an awareness that businesses will continue to compete with one another in line with the less or more advanced cooperative ties established.

The climate of cooperation and collaboration between the various actors represents significant importance for a sustained global vision of the tourist product. The development of partnerships, especially between the public and private sector, constitutes one of the more effective formulas for the development of tourist destinations and the exploration of local resources, as well as the key for destinations to offer quality products (Buhalis, 2000; Leoni, 1999; Manente & Furlan, 1998; Ritchie & Crouch, 1997; Wanhill, 1995).

Participation and engagement in a tourism network relies on favourable behavioural disposition influenced by the individual participant's attitude and, more specifically, his or her values. From an integrated management perspective, what is sought is a balanced development of behaviour, attitude, equipment and other facilities to satisfy consumer and stakeholder requirements in the service sector. Increasingly, tourist destination competitiveness and the image of countries and regions, that represent tourist destinations and providers of quality service, depend essentially on the creative capacity of people, introduction of new technologies, the use of new processes and new organisational forms (Gibson, Lynch & Morrison, 2005; Sancho, 1993).

According to Yuksel and Yuksel (2005), factors critical for the success of inter-organizational relations which include recognising a high degree of interdependence in the planning and managing of the domain/project; recognising individual and/or mutual benefits to be derived from the collaborative process; understanding that decisions arrived at will be implemented; including key stakeholder groups; appointing legitimate convenors to initiate and facilitate community-based collaboration; and, formulating aims and objectives. Some of these key tasks of Destination Management Organisations are related with the need to conciliate diverging interests of the different actor, with balance and satisfaction of the relevant needs of stakeholders (industry professionals, clients, suppliers and society in general), with the adoption of strategies that incorporate ethical principles based on sustainability and regional development (Silva *et al.*, 2001; Davidson & Maitland, 1997; O'Neill, Watson & Mckenna, 1994).

In order to achieve these objectives, it is strategically important that organizations and leaders possess the necessary skills to motivate and involve all those interested in an integrated vision of destination and common projects that result from a social contract allowing for a coordinated, responsible and beneficial performance for all (Laszlo, 1999).

There are several major types of environmental forces that lead to interaction among potential partners. Some of the reasons more frequently referred to in the literature as reasons for the construction and development of networks in tourism are: crises – which direct energies of potential partners towards a specific problem (Croitts & Wilson, 1995; Fosler & Berger, 1982); existing networks which introduce members of a potential partnership to each other (Fyall & Garrod, 2004); visionary leadership - which is embodied in an individual as opposed to a group (Fyall, Callod & Edwards, 2003; Gray, 1985); economic and technological change in which individual organizations are not able to compete successfully by acting alone (Wahab & Cooper, 2001; Poon, 1993) and finally the existence of a third party convener, providing a forum or opportunity for interaction (Hall, 1999).

DEVELOPMENT OF INTER-ORGANISATIONAL NETWORKS IN TOURISM DESTINATIONS

As World Tourism Organisation recognised in the 2000 report, two key forces, globalisation and technology, are transforming the tourism sector into a dynamic economic force that has never been possible before. New forms of organisations arise in different cultural contexts, adapting to the new information era and witnessing a point of historical discontinuity (Castells, 1996).

Due to the need of exceeding specific difficulties or proceeding with common objectives at the destination level, the creation of public-private partnerships has become a common practice. This fact has been widely recognized by the tourism literature, which emphasises the substantial importance of networks and partnership for tourism sector (Costa, 1996). In spite of the popularity of partnerships, few empirical investigations have been done in order to explain the processes occurred whenever these interactions are implemented (Selin & Chavez, 1995).

The need for the cooperation at a destination is inevitable, given the recognised importance of the cooperation networks integrated in the analysis of the production systems of goods and services. However, and according to Framke (2001), only in marketing-driven organisations has cooperation reached its meaning. Also, according to this author, the cooperation theme at the tourism level has not been properly investigated, mainly where its meaning is concerned and the importance of the relationship between tourism enterprises.

According to Easton (1992), a network can be defined generically as a model or metaphor which describes a generally high number of linked entities. Van de Ven and Ferry (1980) regards a network as a complete pattern of relationships between organisations that act with a view towards common objectives. Networks can be observed as a set of ties and social relationships that unite organizations (Lundgren, 1995), as a specific type of relation linking a set of persons, objects or events (Knoke & Kuklinski, 1983) or a set of actors that control resources and perform activities (Hakansson & Snehota, 1995; Hakansson & Johanson, 1992).

The Scottish-Scandinavian Discussion Group (2001), referred to in Gibson, Lynch, and Morrison (2005) regard a network as belonging to a set relationships between individuals acting in an organisational and/or private capacity to achieve a particular purpose. Such networks may be of three types: formal – a formalised set of actors who interact in the context of identified aims; semi-formal – a formalised set of actors who interact in the context of identified aims, and informal – a set of actors who meet mainly for social purposes but also exchange information which has instrumental (business) value.

In essence, the tourism virtual networks are characterised by a variety of participants that transcend organisational boundaries and structures (Mars, 1998; Rhodes, 1997; Howlett and Ramesh, 1995) and are recognised as stimulators of inter-organizational coordination of policies (Selin & Myers, 1998; Costa, 1996). Dredge (2006, p 269), believes that "networks operate within and around tourism's formal organisations, between industry actors, different government agencies and civil society to provide an important forum for the development and communication of interests and strategies."

"A networking organisation appears as a form of inter-entrepreneurial organisation able to overcome some of the inherent market and hierarchical restrictions, whether from the point of view of reduced transaction costs, whether from the decrease of diseconomies of scale, though, more importantly as another form of inter-entrepreneurial relationship with individual virtues that surpass these benefits and belong to domains that are nowadays essential: innovation, learning and knowledge." (Corvelo et al., 2001, p 76.)

Network theory assumes that "relationships do not occur within a vacuum of dyadic ties, but rather in a network of influences, where a firm's stakeholders are likely to have direct relationship with one another" (Rowley, 1997, p. 980) and, nowadays, plays a critical role in determining the way planning and management solutions are designed (Miguéns e Costa, 2006).

The need to learn, in order to generate greater differentiated value, becomes in reality one of the crucial issues of the competing system. In this sense, and as recognised by Corvelo *et al.* (2001, p. 78), "networking, through the arrangement and type of commitment between actors, there is a more favourable environment in terms of satisfaction of needs since no imposed obstacles are encountered from hierarchical rigidity, nor sporadic or more distant market relationships." Corvelo *et al.* (2001, p. 78) assert yet that, "in fact networking works as a last measure, as a privileged system of creation and exploration of value because this is constructed and generated as a "constellation" in the sense that economies of scale are not only considered together with the supply of production variety, but as greater customisation, given the set of distinctive skills from markets which and unattainable through individual network actors, act so as a group and in a synergetic manner."

The impacts that tourism provokes in the environmental, cultural and societal systems require that the construction and the development of networks be developed through holistic approaches, framed in wider and multidimensional contexts, where besides business profitability and purely economic visions be considered aspects of social responsibility of all involved parties.

According to Helgensen (1995), the organisational architecture in the form of a network is recommended based on the following reasons: (1) the context in which firms currently operate is characterised by a high level of change, in the face of growing innovation and complexity; (2) the assertion of globalisation from markets and original technology to worldwide distribution of value and wealth; (3) the needs of specialising in skills and focusing on the specific links in the value chain; (4) the shortening of the life cycle of products and technologies; (5) the need to place products in the market, more speedily, less costly and of higher quality; (6) the increase in cost and risk, associated to the development of new products.

The performance of the tourist destination is maximised when based on the sharing of knowledge and a culture of continued learning and innovation. Maximising information flows for all those involved is essential in order to consolidate the learning process of involved actors. As such, "networks are best seen as primarily a cultural phenomena, that is, as sets of meanings, norms and expectations usually linked with behavioural correlates of various kinds"(Curran, Jarvis, Blackburn & Black, 1993). In this context, setting up partnerships, especially between the public and private sectors, constitute one of the more efficient formulas for the development of tourist locations and the exploration of local resources, as well as the key for destinations to offer quality products (Buhalis, 2000; Leoni, 1999; Manente & Furlan, 1998; Ritchie & Crouch, 1997; Wanhill, 1995).

Another possible form of prompting and institutionalizing cooperation between the actors in tourist destinations would be through the creation of "holonic networks". The concept, introduced by McHugh *et al.* (1995), looks to bring a new form of being and response from organizations based on establishing communication platforms, the exchange of information and efficient response to market needs. This new operational concept in the service chain is based on a process of business reengineering, centred on customer satisfaction and the success of organizations in a competitive environment, has been applied successfully in the tourism destination context and meets the needs of cooperation between actors organizations and other regional entities.

The concern with customers is the focal point of the holonic system. Holonic organisational networks share common objectives, and uses total quality as well as other management techniques so that all participants work towards greater level of customer satisfaction (McHugh *et al.*, 1995).

The holonic network can be described as a group of organizations that act in an integrated form and are organically linked. The following characteristics of the network include: (1) the network not organizationally hierarchical, (2) each business or *holon* containing whole network characteristics and identical to others, (3) being dynamically balanced, (4) auto-regulated, (5) open access and exchange of information, (6) an evolutionary network in constant interaction with the environment, and (7) a knowledge network and auto-learning.

Each organisation, with its specific set of skills, is referred to as a *holon*. For the tourism case and through a set of competences, the network assumes a specific arrangement, known as virtual organisation whose purpose is to manage each business opportunity observed in the market and in this way contribute to better performance and service of each organisation of the tourist destination.

As already mentioned, the fundamental concept associated to a network of information sharing is the creation of a network of contacts between the different parties for the sharing of knowledge, experience and practice, and information dissemination (electronic or personal) in order to improve competitiveness, sustainability and quality of activities and products. Finally, information sharing networks in tourist destinations can: (1) promote and develop an interactive dynamic system in constant evolution between agents, public or private, involved in the tourist sector, (2) help the different actor to plan and manage activities in a coordinated and efficient manner, (3) develop *benchmarking* systems, (4) promote cooperation and development of partnerships between actors, (5) develop good practices and lines of action for integrated quality management, and (6) to offer support and manage information sharing with other institutions.

The cooperation lays in a relationship between expected interests, costs and benefits, and synergism should reflect on the best performance of organisations. This thought leads to the need of analysing the information and monitoring systems which will support the evaluation process of the expected performance results, in terms of the partnership and organisations as well as in terms of the study of mutual impacts established between both decision levels. Different organisations, with different organisational cultures will inherently have different views on how a network should be managed and developed (Allen, Colligan & Finnie, 1999).

CONCLUSION

From the literature review we can infer that the constitution of information and knowledge networks should be seen as a strategic issue for the greater part of public and private organisations. The tourism sector is no exception and the development of ways of virtual cooperation in the tourism destinations, no doubt constitutes a challenge to overcome.

In effect, without this kind of interaction and commitment structures between the organisations in a specific tourism region, it becomes hard for a Destination Management Organisation to, efficiently, manage the value chain and take responsibility in terms of the tourism destination's global performance

On the other hand, it is noted that the virtual networks' characteristics are perfectly adequate for the structure that the Destination Management Organisations must develop with the remaining stakeholders in order to ensure the fulfilment of goals and the competitive positioning facing other competitors.

Tourism destinations currently face challenges and problems that require quick decision making and a collective effort to adapt to a constantly changing reality. Times are changing, whether in terms of organisational arrangement and new attitudes in the relationship of actors in tourist destinations, whether in terms of vision and pursuits by destination management organisations.

The development of processes for continued improvement of global performance and competitiveness of tourist destination, aims above all to redirect tourist activity to adopt new management paradigms based on a culture of network relations guided by principles of sustainability, quality and entrepreneurial excellence. The cooperation and collaborative environment between actors is of crucial importance in order to achieve a sustained global vision of the tourist product.

This chapter presents an overview of research concerned with destination competitiveness, the concept of virtual organisations, cooperative environments, new organisational and management paradigms and the development of inter-organisational cooperation networks.

Based on a theoretical framework the chapter contributes to enlighten the applicableness of the virtual networks concept in a tourism destination context. All the while, it highlights the need and the opportunity the Destination Management Organisations have to assimilates and implement this kind of structures and strategies leading to a news organisational and management paradigms.

It must be admitted that the chapter has the limitations inherent to a reflection developed only around the theoretical knowledge on the subject. Furthermore, the chapter doesn't consider the specificities that characterize and differentiate the coastal tourism destinations from the urban and rural ones. The entrepreneurial fabric that supports each of these kinds of tourism destinations is substantially different; witch may imply different formats of partnerships to be established between stakeholders.

In terms of future research, several possibilities must be considered. First of all, it is important to reinforce the theoretical knowledge framework on the cooperation between public and private organisations of the tourism sector, as much as the research on costs, benefits, expectations and the other aspects of the virtual partnerships from management process in the tourism destinations.

The paper also stimulates the development of empirical research in different kinds of tourism destinations, promoting comparison between formats, methodologies, good practices and results of the implementation of virtual networks between organisations in a cooperative environment of tourism destinations.

REFERENCES

Aladwani, A. M. (2002). An empirical examination of the role of social integration in sytem development projects. *Information Systems Journal*, 12(4), 339-353.

Albrecht, K., & Zemke, R. (2002). *Serviço ao Cliente – A Reinvenção da Gestão do Atendimento ao Cliente*, Rio de Janeiro, Editora Campus.

Allen, D., Colligan, D. & Finnie, A. (1999). Trust, power and inter-organizational information systems: The case of the electronic trading community translease. *The 7th European Conference on Information Systems* (pp. 834-849). Copenhagen, Denmark: Copenhagen Business School.

Augustyn, M. M., & Knowles, T. (2000). Performance of tourism partnerships: A focus on York. *Tourism Management*, 21, 341-351.

Austin, J. E. (2002). *Meeting the Collaboration Challenge Workbook: Developing Strategic Alliances Between Nonprofit Organizations and Businesses*. New York: Peter F. Drucker Foundation for Nonprofit Management.

Bacharach, S., & Lawler, K.(1980). *Power and politics and organizations*. San Francisco, CA: Jossey-Bass.

Baker, D., Georgakopoulos, D., Schuster, H. & Cichocki, A. (2002). Awareness provisioning in collaboration management. International Journal of Cooperative Information Systems, 11(1-2), 145-173.

Baker, W. E. (1992). The network organization in theory and practice. In Nohria, N. and R. Eccles (Eds.), *Networks and Organizations*. (pp 397-429). Boston, MA: Harvard Business School Press.

Benson, J. K. (1975). The inter-organizational network as a political economy. *Administrative Science Quarterly*, 20(2), 229-249.

Beyerlein, M., Johnson, D. & Beyerlein, S. (1994). *Theories of self-managing work teams (Advances in Interdisciplinary Studies of Work Teams)*. Stamford, CT: JAI Press.

Beerli, A., & Martin, J. D. (2004). Tourists'characteristics and the perceived image of tourist destinations: a quantitative analysis – a case study of Lanzarote, Spain. *Tourism Management*, 25(5), 623-636.

Bjork P. & Virtanen H. (2005). What Tourism Project Managers Need to Know about Co-operation Facilitators, *Scandinavian Journal of Hospitality and Tourism*, 5(3), 212-230.

Bordas, E. (1994). La Calidad de los Servicios Turísticos: De la Teoria a la Prática, *WTO Seminar on "Quality - A Challenge for Tourism"* (pp. 133-159). Madrid: World Tourism Organization.

Bouncken, R. B. (2000). The Effect of Trust on Quality in the Culturally Diverse Tourism Industry, *Journal of Quality Assurance in Hospitality & Tourism,* 1(3), 85-104.

Bradner, E. (2002). Computer mediated communication among teams: what are "teams" and how are they "virtual"?. In C. & D. FISHER

(Eds). *From UseNet to CoWebs: interacting with social information spaces* (pp. 135-152). London: Springer-Verlag.

Bramwell, B., & Lane, B. (2000). Collaboration and partnership in tourism planning. In B. Bramwell, & B. Lane (Eds.), *Tourism collaboration and partnerships: Politics, practice and sustainability* (pp. 143-158). Clevedon, Uk: Channel View Publications.

Brathwaite, R. (1992). Value-Chain Assessment of the Travel Experience, *Cornell Hotel and Restaurant Administration Quarterly*, 33(5), 41-49.

Buckley, P. J. (1987). Tourism - an economic transactions analysis, *Tourism Management*, 8(3), 190-194.

Buhalis, D. (2000). Marketing the competitive destination of the future, *Tourism Management,* 21(1), 97-116.

Burnett, G., (2000). Information exchange in virtual communities: a typology. *Information Research*, 5(4). Retrieved January 18, 2007, from http://informationr.net/ir/5-4/paper82.html.

Butler, R., (1980). The concept of a tourist area cycle of evolution: implications for management of resources. *Canadian Geographer* 24(1), 5-12.

Camillus, J. (1993). Crafting the competitive corporation: Management systems for the future organizations. In P. Lorange, B. Chakravarthy, J. Roos, & A. Van De Ven (Eds), *Implementing strategic process: Change, learning, and cooperation* (pp. 313-328). Oxford, Uk: Blackwell.

Carbo, J., Molina, J. M. & Davila, J. (2003). Trust management through fuzzy reputation. *International Journal of Cooperative Information Systems*, 12(1), 135-155.

CastelFranchi, C. (2002). The social nature of information and the role of trust. *International Journal of Cooperative Information Systems*, 11(3-4), 381-403.

Castells, M. (1996). The Information Age: Economy, Society, and Culture. Volume I: *The Roise of the Network Society*. Oxford: Blackwell

Commission Européenne (1999). *Pour un tourisme urbain de qualité – La gestion integrée de la qualité (GIQ) des destinations touristiques urbaines*. Bruxelles: Commission Européenne.

Costa, C. (1996). Towards the Improvement of the Efficiency and Effectiveness of Tourism Planning and Development at the Regional Level – Planning and Networks. The case of Portugal. Unpublished doctoral dissertation, University of Surrey, Guildford.

Corvelo, S., Moreira, P. S. & Carvalho, P. S. (2001). *Redes Interorganizacionais*. Lisboa: Inofor.

Croitts, J. C. & Wilson, D. (1995). An integrated model of buyer-seller relationship in the international travel trade. *Progress in Tourism and Hospitality Research*, 1(2), 125-140.

Curran, J., Jarvis, R., Blackburn, R., & Black, S., (1993). Networks and small firms: constructs, methodological strategies and some findings. *International Small Business Journal* 11(2), 13-25.

Davidson, R. & Maitland, R. (1997). *Tourism Destinations*. London: Hodder & Stoughton Educational.

Denmann, R. (1998). *Integrated quality management of rural tourist destinations*. Paper presented at the European Tourism Forum of the Austrian Presidency of the Council of the European Union and the European Commission, Mayrhofen.

Devine, M. & Filos, E. (2000). Erastos. Virtual teams and the organisational gravepine. In Kluwer Academic Publishers (Ed.), *International Federation for Information Processing; Working Conference on Infrastructures for Virtual Organisations*, Florianopolis.

Dredge, D. (2006). Policy networks and the local organisation of tourism. *Tourism Management*, 27(2), 269-280.

Easton, G. (1992). Industrial Networks: A Review. In B. Axelsson & G. Easton (Eds.), *Industrial Networks: A new View of Reality*, London: Routledge.

EFQM (1999). *Eight Essentials of Excellence*, Brussels: European Foundation for Quality Management.

Fayos-Solá, E. & Moro, J. R. (1995). Calidad Ecoturística para el Desarrollo Sostenible, *Conferencia Mundial de Turismo Sostenible* (pp. 33-42). Islas Canarias.

Filos, E. & Banahan, E. (2000). Will the organization disappear? The challenges of the new economy and future perspectives. In Kluwer Academic Publishers *(Eds.), International Federation for Information Processing; Working Conference on Infrastructures for Virtual Organisations*, Florianopolis.

Fosler, R., & Berger, R. (1982). Public-private sector partnership in American cities: Seven case studies. Lexington: Heath.

Framke, W. (2001). The Destination: a problematic concept. IPaper presented at the *10th Nordic Tourism Research Conference*, Vasa, Finland.

Frenkel, A., Afsarmanesh, H., Garita, C. & Hertzberger, L. (2000). Supporting information access rights and visibility levels in virtual enterprises. In Kluwer Academic Publishers *(Ed.), International Federation for Information Processing; Working Conference on Infrastructures for Virtual Organisations*, Florianopolis.

Frochot, I. & Hughes, H. (2000). Histoqual: the development of a historic houses assessment scale, *Tourism Management*, 21(2), 157-167.

Fyall, A., & Garrod, B. (2004). *Tourism marketing: A collaborative approach.* Cleveland: Channel View Publications.

Fyall, A., Callod, C. & Edwards, B. (2003). Relationship marketing: The challenge for Destinations. *Annals of Tourism Research*, 30 (3), 644-659.

Gibson, L., Lynch, P. A. & Morrison, A. (2005). The Local Destination Tourism Network: Development Issues, *Tourism and Hospitality Planning & Development*, 2(2), 87-99.

Glendinning, C. (2003). Breaking down barriers: integrating health and care services for older people in England. *Heath Policy*, 65(2), 139-151.

Goldman, S., Nagel, R., & Preiss, K. (1995). *Agile competitors and virtual organizations: Strategies for enriching the customer.* New York: Van Nostrand Reinnhold.

Goranson, H. T. (2000). Infrastructure for the advanced virtual enterprise: a report using a Brasilian-based example. In Kluwer Academic Publishers (Ed.), *International Federation for Information Processing; Working Conference on Infrastructures for Virtual Organisations*, Florianopolis.

Gray, B. (1985). Conditions facilitating interorganizational relations. *Human Relations*, 38(10), 911-936.

Guibilato, G. (1983). *Economie Touristique*, Suisse: Delta & Spes.

Gummesson, E. (1994). Service Management: An Evaluation and the Future. *International Journal of Service Industry Management*, 5(1), 77-96.

Gunn, C., (1993). Tourism Planning. London: Taylor & Francis.

Hakansson, H. & Johanson, J. (1992). A model of industrial networks. In B. Axelsson & G. Easton (Eds.) *Industrial Networks: A New View of Reality*, (pp. 28-34), London: Routledge.

Hakansson, H. & Snehota, I. (1989) No business is an island: The network concept of business strategy. *Scandinavian Journal of Management*, 5(3), 187-200.

Hall, C. M. (2000). Rethinking collaboration and partnership: A public policy perspective. In B. Bramwell, & B. Lane (Eds.), *Tourism collaboration and partnerships: Politics, practice and sustainability* (pp. 143-158). Clevedon, Uk: Channel View Publications.

Hall, C. M. (1999). Rethinking collaboration and partnership: A public policy perspective. *Journal of Sustainable Tourism*, 7(3/4), 274-289.

Haywood, K. M. (1993). The Price-Value Relationship: Perspective and Definitional Issues. *World Travel and Tourism Review*, 3, 213-217.

Helgensen, S. (1995). *The Web of Inclusion: Building an Organization for Everyone*. Currency Doubleday.

Hope, C. A. & Muhlemann, A. P. (1998). Total quality, human resource management and tourism. *Tourism Economics*, 4(4), 367-386.

Howlet M. & Ramesh, M. (1995). *Studying public policy: policy cycles and policy subsystems*. Toronto: Oxford University Press.

Huete, L. M. (1994). Factores que infuyen en la calidad del producto, In World Tourism Organization (Ed.), *WTO Seminar on Quality - A Challenge for Tourism* (pp. 53-55). Madrid.

Inkpen, A. & Ross, J. (2001). Why do some strategic alliances persist beyond their useful life?. *California Management Review*, 44(1), 132-148.

Jamal, T. & Getz, D. (1995). Collaboration theory and community tourism planning. *Annals of Tourism Research*, 22(1), 186-204.

Kandampully, J. (2000). The impact of demand fluctuation on the quality of service: a tourism industry example. *Managing Service Quality*, 10(1), 10-18.

Klein, R. (2000). EU activities to improve the quality of European tourist products, In *Workshop on Quality in Tourism: from Patterns to indicators*. Faro: Universidade do Algarve.

Kluber, R. A. (1998).A framework for virtual organizing. In Sieber, P. & Griese J. (Eds), *Organizational Virtualness. Proceedings of the VoNet* – Workshop (pp. 9-24). Bern: Simona Verlag Bern.

Knoke, D., & Kuklinski, J. (1983). *Network Analysis*.Beverly Hills: Sage.

Krackhard, D. & Hanson, J. (1993). Informal networks: The company behind the chart. *Harvard Business Review,* 71(4), 104-111.

Ladkin, A. & Bertramini, A. M. (2002). Collaborative tourism planning: Case study of Cusco, Peru. *Current Issues in Tourism*, 5(2), 71-93.

Laws, E., (1995). Tourism Destination Management: Issues, Analysis and Policies. London: Routledge.

Lazlo, G. P. (1999). Implementing a quality management program- three Cs of success: commitment, culture, cost. *The TQM Magazine*, 11(4), 231-237.

Leoni, P. (1999). *La città ospitale*, Paper presented at the International Conference "From Destination to Destination Marketing and Management", Venice.

Les Pang (2001). Understanding Virtual Organizations. *Information Systems Control Journal*, 6.

Lévy, P. (1996). *O que é o virtual*, São Paulo: Editora 34.

Lipnack, J. S. (1993). *Rede de Informações*. Rio de Janeiro: Makron Brooks.

Lundgren, A. (1995). *Technological Innovation and Network Evolution*. London: Routledge.

Lutz, J. & Ryan, C. (1993). Hotels and the businesswoman - An analysis of businesswomen's perceptions of hotel services. *Tourism Management*, 14(5), 349-356.

Manente, M. & Furlan, M. (1998). Quality in the Macroeconomics System of Tourism. *Revue de Tourisme*, 2, 17-28.

Mars, D. (1998). *Comparing policy networks.* Buckinghan: Open University Press.

Martín, D. (2000). Metodología de Calidad en Turismo, in Turismo: comercialización de productos, gestión de organizaciones, aeropuertos y protección de la naturaleza. In Tirant lo Blanch (Ed.), *II Congreso Universidad y Empresa, Turismo: comercialización de productos, gestión de organizaciones, aeropuertos y protección de la naturaleza* (pp. 429-447), Benicasim.

McHugh, P., Merli, G. & Wheeler III, W. (1995). Beyond *Business Process Reengineering – Towards the Holonic Entreprise.* Chichester: John Wiley & Sons.

Merali, Y. (2002). The role of boundaries in knowledge process. *European Journal of Information Systems*, 11(1), 47-60.

Michaud, J.-L., Planque, V. &. Barbaza, Y. (1991). Tourisme qualitatif - Ses Conditions et ses Chances Futures sur le Plan Economique, Social et Ecologique. In AIEST (Ed.), *41ème Congrès de l'Association International d'Experts Scientifiques du Tourisme* (pp. 63-78), Mahé, Seychelles.

Middleton, V. T. (1994). The marketing and Management of Tourism destinations: research directions for the next decade, In AIEST (Ed.) *44ème Congrès de l'Association International d'Experts Scientifiques du Tourisme* (pp. 115-141), Vienne, Austria.

Miguéns, J. & Costa, C. (2006). Tourism Network: new methodologies, potential approach to tourism analysis. In School of Management, University of Surrey (Ed.), Proceedings of *Cutting Edge Research in Tourism: New directions, Challenges and Applications*, School of Management, University of Surrey, UK.

Mills, D. (1991). *Rebirth of the corporation.* New York: John Wiley and Sons, Inc.

Molina, A. & Flores, M. (2000). Exploitation of business opportunities: the role of the virtual enterprise broker. In Kluwer Academic Publishers (Ed.), *International Federation for Information Processing; Working Conference on Infrastructures for Virtual Organisations*, Florianopolis.

Mowshowitz , A. (1997). *Virtual organization.* Communications of the ACM. 40(9), 30-37.

Mundim, A. P. & Bremer, C. F. (2000). Design of a computer-supported cooperative environment for small and medium enterprises. In Kluwer Academic Publishers *(Ed.), International Federation for Information Processing; Working Conference on Infrastructures for Virtual Organisations*, Florianopolis.

O'Neill, M. , Watson, H. & Mckenna, M (1994). Service Quality in the Northern Ireland Hospitality Industry. *Managing Service Quality*, 4(3), 36-40.

Otto, J. E. & Ritchie, J. R. (1996). The service experience in tourism. *Tourism Management*, 17(3), 165-174.

Otto, J. E. & Ritchie, J. R. (1995). Exploring the Quality of the Service Experience: A Theoretical and Empirical Analysis. *Advances in Services Marketing and Management*, 4, 37-61.

Papadopoulos, S. I. (1989). Greek Marketing Strategies in the European Tourism Market. *The Service Industries Journal*, 9(2), 297-314.

Pavlovich, K. (2003). The evolution and transformation of a tourism destination network: the Waitomo Caves, New Zealand. *Tourism Management*, 24(2), 203-216.

Pearce, D., (1989). Tourism Development. New York: Longman.

Pine II, B. J. & Gilmore, J. H. (1999). *The Experience Economy – work is theatre & every business a stage*, Boston: Harvard Business School Press.

Pizam, A. (1991). The Management of Quality Tourism Destinations, In AIEST (Ed.) *41ème Congrès de l'Association International d'Experts Scientifiques du Tourisme* (pp. 79-87), Mahé, Seychelles.

Pizam, A., Neumann, Y. &. Reichel, A. (1978). Dimensions of Tourist Satisfaction with a Destination Area, *Annals of Tourism Research*, 5(3), 314-322.

Poon, A. (1993). Tourism, technology and competitive strategies. UK: Cab International.

Rhodes, R. A. (1997). *Understanding governance: policy networks, governance, reflexivity and accountability.* Buckingham: Open University Press.

Rita, P. (1995). O Turismo em Perspectiva: Caracterização e Tendências do Mercado Internacional. *Revista Portuguesa de Gestão*, II/III, 7-18.

Ricci, A., Omicini, A. & Denti, E. (2002). Virtual enterprises and workflow management as agent coordination issues. *International Journal of Cooperative Information Systems*, 11(3-4), 355-379.

Ridley, S. (1995). Towards a new business culture for tourism and hospitality organizations. *International Journal of Contemporary Hospitality Management*, 7(7), 36-43.

Riempp, G. (1998). *Wide area workflow management:* creating partnerships for the 21st century. London: Springuer-Verlag London.

Ritchie, J. R. B. &. Crouch, G. I. (2000). The competitive destination: a sustainability perspective. *Tourism Management,* 21(1), 1-7.

Ritchie, J. R. B. &. Crouch, G. I. (1997). Roles and contributions to destination competitiveness, In AIEST (Ed.), *47th Congress of the Association*

International d'Experts Scientifiques du Tourisme (pp. 117-139), Cha-Am, Thailand.

Rowley, T. J. (1997). Moving beyond dyadics ties: a network theory of stakeholder influences. *Academy of Management Review*, 22(4), 887-910.

Ryan, C. (1995). Learning about tourists from conversations: the over - 55s in Majorca, *Tourism Management*, 16(3), 207-215.

Sancho, A. (1993). Calidad Y Educación: Un reto para el Sector Turístico. *Estudios Turísticos*, 119/120, 23-28.

Schmoll, G. (1977). *Tourism Promotion. Marketing Background, Promotion Techniques and Promotion Planning Methods.* London: Tourism International Press

Selin, S. (2000). Developing a Typology of Sustainable Tourism Partnerships. In B. Bramwell, & B. Lane (Eds.), *Tourism collaboration and partnerships: Politics, practice and sustainability* (pp. 143-158). Clevedon, Uk: Channel View Publications.

Selin, S, & Chavez, D. (1995). Developing an evolutionary tourism partnership model, *Annals of Tourism Research*, 22(4), 844-856.

Selin, S., & Myers, N. (1995). Correlates of partnership effectiveness: the coalition for unified recreation in the Eastern Sierra. *Journal of Recreation Administration,* Winter, 13(4), 37-46.

Selin, S. & Myers, N. (1998) Tourism marketing alliances: member satisfaction and effectiveness attributes of a regional initiative. *Journal of Travel and Tourism Research*, 7, 79-94.

Silva, J. A. (1991). *O Turismo em Portugal – Uma Análise de Integração Micro-Macroecómica*, Unpublished doctoral dissertation, Universidade Técnica de Lisboa, Lisboa, Portugal.

Silva, J. A., Mendes, J. & Guerreiro, M. M. (2001). A Qualidade dos Destinos Turísticos: dos Modelos aos Indicadores. *Revista Portuguesa de Gestão,* III(1), 65-81.

Smith, S. L. (1994). The Tourism Product, *Annals of Tourism Research,* 21(3), 582-595.

Schultze, U., Boland, R. J. (2000). Place, space and knowledge work: a study of outsourced computer systems administrators. *Accounting Management and Information Technologies,* 10(3), 187-219.

Shumar, W. & Renninger, K. A. (2002). On conceptualizing community. In K. Renninger & W. Shumar (Ed.) *Building virtual communities: learning and change in cyberspace.* Cambridge: Cambridge University Press.

Siebert, P. (2000). Virtual organizations: static and dynamic viewpoints. *VoNet: The Newsletter.*

Stauss B. &. Weinlich, B. (1997). Process-oriented measurement of service quality. *European Journal of Marketing,* 31(1), 33-55.

Strausak, N. (1998). Resumée of Vo Talk. In Sieber, P & Griese J. (Eds). *Organizational Virtualness. Proceedings of the VoNet* – Workshop (pp. 9-24), Simona Verlag Bern.

Tapscoot, D. &. Caston, A. (1993). *Paradigma Shift,* McGraw-Hill.

Tapscoot, D. (1995). *The Digital Economy,* Richard D. Irwin.

Timothy, D. J. (1998). Co-operative tourism planning in a developing destination. *Journal of sustainable Tourism,* 6(1), 52-68.

Tinsley, R., & Lynch, P. (2001). Small tourism business networks and destination development. *International Journal of Hospitality Management,* 20(4), 367-378.

Toledo, L. A., & Loures, C. A. (2006). Organizações Virtuais. *Cadernos EBAPE. BR.* IV(2), 1-17.

Wabad, S., & Cooper, C. (2001). *Tourism in the age of globalization.* London: Routledge.

Wang, Y., & Fesenmaier, D. (2005). Towards a theoretical framework of collaborative destination marketing. In *Proceeding of the 36ʰ travel and tourism research association annual conference.* New Orleans, USA.

Wanhill, S. (1995). Some Fundamentals of Destination Development. *Revista Portuguesa de Gestão,* II/III, 19-33.

Watkins, M. & Bell, B. (2002). The experience of forming business relationships in tourism. *International Journal of Tourism Research,* 4(1), pp. 15-28.

Weiermair, K. (2000a) Tourist's perceptions towards and satisfaction with service quality in the cross-cultural service encounter: implications for hospitality and tourism management, *Managing Service Quality,* 10(6), 397-409.

Weiermair, K. (2000b) Quality Assessment and Measurement in Tourism: Issues and Problems, Paper presented at the *Workshop Quality in Tourism: from Patterns to Indicators,* Universidade do Algarve, Faro, Portugal.

Weiermair, K. (1994) Quality Management in Tourism: Lessons from the Service Industries? In AIEST (Ed.) *44éme Congrès de l'Association International d'Experts Scientifiques du Tourisme* (pp. 93-113), Vienne, Austria.

WTO (2000). Global Tourism Forescast to the Year 2000 and Beyond : The World, WTO, Madrid.

Valles, D. M. (1999). Calidad en los Servicio. Una aproximación metodológica. *Estudios Turísticos,* 139, 15-33.

Van de Ven, A. H. & Ferry, D. L. (1980). *Measuring and Assessing Organizations.* New York, John Wiley.

Vega, A. V. R., Casielles, R. V. & Martín, A. M. D. (1995). La Calidad Percibida Del Servicio en Establecimientos Hoteleros de Turismo Rural. *Papers de Turisme,* 19, 17-33.

Von Friedrichs Grangsjo, Y. (2002). Marketing equilibrium in entrepreneurial cluster: An idea of a dynamic relationship between co-operation , competition and institutions. Paper presented at the 11th Nordic Symposium in Tourism and Hospitality Research, Goteborg, Sweden.

Zimmermman, F. (2000). *Structural and Managerial Aspects of Virtual Entreprises*. University of Bamberg, Business Information Systems, Germany. Retrieved May 7, 2000, from http://www. seda.sowi.uni-bamberg.de/persons/zimmermann. html

Yuksel, A. & Yuksel, F. (2005). Managing relations in a learning model for bringing destinations in need of assistance into contact with good practice. *Tourism Management*, 26(5), 667-679.

Chapter XII
E–Government Challenges:
Barriers and Facilitators in Spanish City Councils

E. Claver-Cortés
University of Alicante, Spain

S. De Juana-Espinosa
University of Alicante, Spain

J. J. Tarí
University of Alicante, Spain

ABSTRACT

Government agencies are being pressed to become more efficient. For this reason, e-government strategies result from the expectations from society to be able to use Internet technologies as a strategic means of communications and relationship with its public sector, virtualising the delivery of public services. The aim of this chapter is to identify the main barriers and facilitators affecting the deployment of e-government, and to classify them into dimensions that may help researchers and practitioners to identify and better understand these factors. A literature analysis and empirical research based on the perceptions of the technology managers of Spanish councils with more than 5000 inhabitants and institutional Websites were carried out. The findings disclose some lessons for public managers to take into account when implementing an e-government strategy. However, the ultimate challenge seems to be in the hands of the politicians of the council, who are responsible for developing these e-government strategies.

INTRODUCTION

Organisations from around the globe are actively exploring opportunities and challenges brought about by the Internet and e-business. This is not limited to private sector companies. Public institutions are also facilitating and shaping the development of infrastructure and services and experimenting with new ways of information and services delivery via electronic channels (Govindarajan and Gupta, 2001; Phan, 2003; Li, 2006). In this respect, Knowledge Management tools like Websites or intranet databases usually allow for the provision and canalisation of information and documents for internal activities along the public sector value chain and delivery of public services (Prokopiadou *et al.*, 2004). The better the knowledge base upon which public policies are built, the more likely they are to succeed (Brigdman and Davis, 2004).

The question is, how does Internet really affect local administrations? By enabling local e-government strategies. This is the logical answer to such a trivial question, but there is more than meets the eye. The key word is "enabling": not every council actually succeeds, even if the expenditure is the same. An e-government strategy is a fundamental element in modernising the public sector, because it does not only provide a wide variety of information and a form of interaction between public sector organisations, business and citizens, but also improves the performance of government organisations and the welfare of citizens (Ebrahim and Irani, 2005).

Therefore, e-government practices must be regarded as tools for creating added value to public products and services, thus increasing governmental efficacy, efficiency, transparency and security. The latter two are even more important considering the virtual side of these practices. For that reason, it seems crucial to analyse the importance of the design of successful e-government practices according to the principles of strategic management and organisational change, as do private firms regarding e-business initiatives.

According to the existing literature, there are many factors that affect the success of e-government (Bueno García, 2002; Hackney and Jones, 2002; ICMA, 2002; Holden, 2003; Li, 2003; Barca and Cordella, 2004; Eyob, 2004; Vishanth and Jyoti, 2004). These are known as e-government facilitators and barriers, for they might help achieving success in the design and implementation of the council's e-government strategy, but they can also create difficulties. City councils face the challenge of learning to recognize such factors and implementing whatever measures are needed to overcome or deploy them, depending on their influence.

These factors may be of different natures: social (e.g. employees' attitudes toward technology, society's perception of e-government practices, legal issues); political/institutional (e.g. political will, hierarchy and division of labour, workflow management); or infrastructural (e.g. availability or lack of finance, skilled personnel and technology) (Joia, 2004). The role that each factor plays in the definition of e-government success will depend on how public governments approach them, which is why barriers and facilitators are essentially the same elements from opposite perspectives.

This chapter explores the facilitating and barrier factors that, ultimately, shape the formulation and implementation processes of strategic e-government, focusing on the point of view of local government. The objectives of this chapter are to identify the main barriers and facilitators affecting the deployment of e-government, and to classify them into dimensions that may help researchers and practitioners to identify and better understand these factors.

To do so, both theoretical and empirical analysis are carried out, in order to overcome the lack of specific studies about this topic, as Al-Sebie and Irani (2003) have mentioned. Indeed, most current research on e-government, particularly regarding local government, consists in the description of individual, limited initiatives, avoiding theoretical frameworks that may provide them with a solid foundation (Becker *et al.*, 2003). It is essential thus to compare what academics and practitioners have to say in the matter of local e-government, in order to bridge the gap between what has been written and what is done (Ho *et al.*, 2003).

Quantitative empirical data were obtained from the experience of e-government practitioners. A quantitative survey was sent to every municipality in Spain over 5000 inhabitants that has an official portal. This survey consisted in a Web-based questionnaire sent to the Chief Technological Officer (CTO) of the city council or, should this position not exist, to the person in charge of information systems issues. The degree of importance given to the literature-based barriers and facilitating factors is measured with a Likert scale and a factor analysis. These quantitative findings express respondents' impressions on the presence of these factors and the initiatives that are enforced to deal with them. The findings established three types of barriers and facilitators, with an emphasis on political issues as triggers of local e-government success.

The layout of this chapter is as follows. The next section addresses the academic arguments, whereas the third one presents the methodology employed. The fourth section discusses these findings. The chapter concludes with some suggestions aiming at a better comprehension of the local e-government phenomenon, as well as the future research lines that stem from this project.

LITERATURE REVIEW

Internet is nowadays considered as a cost-effective means for public information and services management and supply, as shown by the numerous successful e-business experiences of private firms (Govindarajan and Gupta, 2001; Phan, 2003). The new added value of the public sector comes from the transformation of the old impersonal bureaucratic organisation into an interactive model that prizes two-way communication and service customisation (Claver *et al.*, 2005). This is the foundation for the different e-government strategies that are being developed and implemented in public administrations everywhere. Their effects vary in nature and intensity depending on the addressee of such practices and the type of governmental body that enforced them.

E-government refers to the provision of internal administration services to its external environment, which is related directly with the need for internal transparency of the public organisation. E-government is, simply stated, a chance for public organisations to detect and fulfil the needs of their stakeholders more efficiently, and a means to promote a conscience of goodness regarding the development of information technologies (IT) (Claver *et al.*, 2006). For a thorough discussion on the definition of this term, a prime work would be that by Al-Sebie and Irani (2003).

Citizens increasingly question government' positions and decisions (or lack thereof), and demand authorities to disclose their information sources. As Carr (1996) has pointed out, taking a strategic view of the public interest is not easy. It requires a coordinated effort to understand the economic consequences of civic pressures, to avoid or mitigate costs by appeasing the public, gaining new income by serving the public interest, and influencing or even changing the public's views. This is supported by Ebrahim and Irani (2005), in their hypothesis that every e-government initiative planning must formulate its IT strategies in the light of the business models and technology solutions that deliver in government policy.

The measures devised for e-government implementation should be deployed according to a prior analysis of the internal and external environment. Generally, these measures will be influenced by the municipality's IT budget and the users' expectations, as proposed by the stakeholder approach (Scott *et al.*, 2004).

One stakeholder group that draws particular attention is that of public human resources. According to Clift (2003) and MCYR and MAP (2003), it is of the utmost importance that there should be a good leadership policy that provides human resources with the necessary motivation to carry out these implementation measures. Accordingly, new managerial positions have been created with the aim of improving performance in departments traditionally neglected like that of Human Resource Management itself or IT, especially at local levels (Harris, 2002).

On the constructive side, Criado and Ramilo (2001) disclose the following factors that may lead e-government strategies towards success:

- A certain level of interest and will from the politicians regarding the project;
- The ability of politicians and managers to gather resources and assistance inside and outside the organisation;
- Appropriate legal support;
- A good strategic planning that takes into account the actual needs of the municipality;
- And a cultural change towards the values and principles of the information society rather than keeping to the traditional bureaucratic model.

In relation to the latter, there are some authors who support the introduction of private sector practices to ensure the changes in the organisational values. This philosophy is known as New Public Management (NPM). Two NPM elements relate directly to the success of e-government: human resource management policies and quality management programmes.

Regarding the new human resource management policies, public sector organisations carry them out as a result of the need for qualified personnel who are able to accept the working principles and values of the new economy (White and Hutchinson, 1996). Public sector workers may respond positively to an initiative they perceive as contributing to the organization's mission. Human resource managers may thus encourage the deployment of a wide Knowledge Management programme associated with the organizational goals and missions of the e-government strategy (Yao *et al.*, 2007). Riege and Lindsay (2006) have shown that the concept of Knowledge Management is not new to the public sector, and these initiatives have always been integrated in government strategy and planning. The difference lies in whether Knowledge Management has been used purposely for the improvement of the delivery of public services or if it is inborn in the organization's workflows.

In relation to quality management programmes, their objective is to achieve excellence in the provision of e-services (Teicher *et al.*, 2002; McAdam and Walker, 2004). They are usually based on the ISO 9000 standard, or on quality models such as the EFQM model. They may take the shape of public service charters or excellence awards. These programmes have a greater effect when impelled from the inside of the public organisation, since they act as a self-motivating force (Irani *et al.*, 2003). Nevertheless, they may face financial and institutional handicaps that may jeopardise their outcomes (Dewhurst *et al.*, 1999).

Koh *et al.* (2006) are of the opinion that a key to ensure success is to promote the evaluation of the e-service and of e-government strategic principles by the stakeholders (citizens, employees and businesses). Every public service involves a very wide range of relationships between policymakers and stakeholders, and continuous collaboration and communication between them potentially provides a cost-effective way of obtaining good or better quality knowledge for a bigger impact on policy and service provision (Riege and Lindsay, 2006). For that reason, advertising the supplied e-services supplied and gathering the stakeholders' opinions and demands through a thorough Knowledge Management system are two of the most relevant facilitating factors.

For Janssen *et al.* (2006), one of the most relevant facilitating factors is the design of a customer-oriented Website, which will provide a number of organisational, strategic and operational benefits. This includes a usable interface design, self-explanatory and friendly, so that users maximize their efficiency in terms of time and money while carrying out their transactions (Pieterson *et al*, 2005).

Finally, Hurst (1997) draws attention to the effect that trust and collaboration relationships between public sector organisations have on the strategic development of e-government. Furthermore, this author stresses the importance of the gap between those who make decisions (politicians) and those who carry them out (public servants), under the premise that the maintenance of formalities and the objectivity that theoretically feature public organisations may place constraints upon their adaptability. Also, governmental organisations must develop the ability to harmonise the political wishes of the political leader, the IS political goals of the organisation and the vision of the project manager (often a public servant). Without the joint force of these three positions, it will not be possible to develop an adequate vision of the concept of local e-government, a basic requirement for success from a strategic management point of view.

Table 1 shows a summary of all the facilitating factors discussed up to this point.

Similarly, there are several hindering factors that have been analysed by many researchers. According to Eyob (2004) and the ICMA research (2002), the main barriers for the development of a successful e-government strategy are the scarcity of technological, financial and human resources (the latter in terms of qualifications). Funding is a major issue, especially if it comes from higher level institutions (ICMA, 2002). Nevertheless, the actual endowment of resources within local governments will largely depend on their bestowed political value, so that their importance as barriers is associated to political leadership, or lack thereof. A good example of these political barriers would be the Spanish Administrative Procedure and Legal System Act, passed in 1958 and still in force. Indeed, some political leaders may be afraid of the changes that e-government entails, even of losing power, thus becoming a real threat for its success (Ebrahim and Irani, 2005). However, this fear can be overcome by making politicians aware of the benefits that e-government may provide.

Other authors have found that the organisational barriers are the need for public sector organisations to change their organisational culture, management strategy communication between departments and business processes to adapt to the new strategies and values of e-government (McClure, 2000; Li and Steveson, 2002; Riege and Lindsay, 2006). Besides, changes in

Table 1. Facilitating factors

A capable formal project manager in the council	Financial resources for the provision of IT infrastructure	Political awareness of the importance of IT projects
A joint rationalisation process of the internal workflows	Data Protection Laws and other legal support	Political commitment and leadership
A well designed information system	Authentication devices for privacy and security	Strategic consideration of e-government policies
Acknowledgment of need for support from higher institutions	Knowledge of stakeholders' requirements	Trust and collaboration between public workers
E-services advertising	Qualified human resources	Customer oriented portal
Usability of council's Website	Quality management programs	

the internal workflow may be necessary to make the city council's administration run smoothly (Waisanen, 2002).

Ebrahim and Irani (2005) have considered that the most important barriers are rooted in the implementation of an adequate IT infrastructure for a user's experience of easy and reliable electronic access to government. On the whole, they agree with Bonham *et al*. (2001) and McClure (2000) on the fact that governments consider a lack of technical infrastructure as a significant barrier to the development of public sector organisations' capabilities to provide online services and transactions. All of these technology-related barriers increase the operational costs of e-government implementation. Among them, the most remarkable are the high cost of IT professionals and consultancies, the cost of installation, operation and maintenance of e-government systems, and the cost of training and system development.

Among other barriers that relate to IT, one of the most frequently cited is the security and privacy of the transactions. Indeed, an e-government strategy might be considered successful only when all the stakeholders are comfortable using the applications and means to carry out electronic transactions with the councils. Therefore, investing in security matters is a necessary but not sufficient condition for the success of the e-government strategy (Layne and Lee, 2001; Belanger and Hiller, 2006) and the confidentiality of personal data and other sensitive information (Bonham *et al*, 2001; Ebrahim and Irani, 2005).

Li (2003) and Norris *et al*. (2001) concur in identifying the human factor barriers as the greatest, since those related to technology can be easily overcome with money. The shortage of IT skills affects both the provision and the implementation of e-government services, from the supply and demand sides respectively, and therefore should be tackled from both points of view. This barrier increases its effect with the degree of development of the e-government portal, which is necessary to enhance the effectiveness of

e-government strategies (Moon, 2002). This has led many public sector organisations to offer IT training courses for citizens and public workers, and to recruit already qualified personnel from the private sector.

Finally, the European Union has also addressed this issue (European Union, 2007), by creating a project which aims to collect further information about barriers relating to e-government stakeholders. A project team has identified seven key categories of barriers that may block or restrain progress on e-government, derived from literature reviews and the analysis of the experience and knowledge of the project's partners (Oxford Internet Institute, gov3, CRID and the University of Murcia) and several experts and stakeholders. These categories are the following:

1. **Leadership failures:** Lack of political will, poor strategic vision and planning, poor understanding of e-government by senior management.
2. **Financial inhibitors:** Lack of research and development and innovation funding, costs of developing, implementing and maintaining e-government, costs of providing multiple channels, etc.
3. **Digital divides and choices:** Skill gaps between different sectors of society, failures to develop and implement e-government services that meet citizens' needs.
4. **Poor coordination:** Lack of coordination between local and regional government institutions, government departments failing to agree on common procedures to provide shared networked e-government services, etc.
5. **Workplace and organisational inflexibility:** Departmental "turf wars", inadequate skills training, failure to learn from good practice …
6. **Lack of trust:** The "Big Brother" fear, anxieties over liability for online content, intrinsic "cybertrust" tensions, etc.

Table 2. Barriers

Specific software for public management programmes	Disregard for e-government advantages	Strong belief in the power of technology by itself
Cost of IT infrastructure	Employees' resistance to change	Scarcity of financial resources
Complexity of public work processes and bureaucracy	Lack of motivation and involvement (political will)	Scarcity of qualified personnel
Citizens do not demand e-services	Digital analphabetism	Unsuitable legislation
Decisions are made by politicians instead of IT professionals	Politicians' lack of knowledge about e-government's benefits	

7. **Poor technical design:** Difficulty in accessing and using public services, incompatibilities between newer e-government systems and older "legacy" systems, failure to implement global standards, etc.

A summary of the barrier factors addressed in this section is shown in Table 2.

RESEARCH METHODOLOGY

Spain ranks 10 in the world e-government rankings by country (Lee *et al.*, 2006), just behind Japan and above Australia, and holds the 5th position in services provided electronically (Cap, Gemini, Erst and Young, 2002). Therefore, it is a quite well-developed country in terms of e-government, and its practitioners have a certain degree of knowledge on the topic. This ensures that the findings of the research are good enough for establishing conclusions from which many other countries may benefit. As for local governments as subjects of study, it is a known fact that they have a tendency to be early adopters of new technologies, because they are closer to the communities they serve (Neff, 2007).

An electronic questionnaire was sent to the 960 councils that met two requirements at the time of the research: having an official Website (or considered as such by the council), and a population over 5000 people (according to the 2004 national census). If there was a former site, now extinct, or if the council had published its Website after the survey had been launched, these municipalities were not considered suitable for our purposes. Even though this is not a required instrument for e-government policies, it is believed that it is a must because, although almost every city council has an e-mail address, not all of them have a Website, so that only a certain percentage have consciously taken a step forward towards their integration into the new economy.

The Web-based questionnaire was addressed to the CTO of the city council or, if there was not such a post, to the person in charge of IS issues. Other researchers have also relied on the practical knowledge that CTOs have regarding the implementation of e-government strategies, like Ward (2006), and their role as key players in transformation of public services has recently been highlighted by the SOCITM (UK Society of Information Technology Management) (SOCITM, 2006).

A total of 165 questionnaires were answered (rate of response: 17.2%). In 47% of the surveyed councils, it was the CTO himself/herself who answered the questionnaire. The rest of the surveyed municipalities did not have a CTO position in their hierarchy; in 29% of those cases the questionnaire was answered by a computer qualified expert, 7% of the questionnaires were answered by people holding political posts, and the rest of answers were provided by other civil servants in administrative positions. There was no significant relationship found between the position of the person who answered the research and the level of e-maturity of the municipality.

CTOs were presented with the two lists of factors shown in tables 1 and 2, on a Likert scale, and they were asked to value their impact on e-government success from 1 (none) to 5 (very strong). For the following steps, only those items which had a 3 or more for average value in the pretest were taken into account. The final lists of items passed Cronbach's alpha test for internal consistency (0.800 for barriers and 0.836 for facilitators).

A principal components factor analysis was carried out in order to establish the suitable number of groups of barriers and facilitators, to see whether common answering patterns could be found that would allow for a better interpretation of the findings. This is a statistical approach that can be used to analyze interrelationships among a large number of variables and to explain these variables in terms of their common underlying dimensions (factors), providing one unique solution so that the original data can be reconstructed from the results. It involves finding a way of condensing the information contained in a number of original variables into a smaller set of dimensions (factors) with a minimum loss of information (Hair *et al.,* 1995). It looks at the total variance among the variables, so the solution generated will include as many factors as there are variables, although it is unlikely that they will all meet the criteria for retention.

First, the correlations matrices were studied and it was verified that the data were suitable for the validation of the instrument: the Kaiser-Meyer-Olkin Measure of Sampling Adequacy presented an index of 0.812 for the facilitators and 0.784 for the barriers, which are considered good for carrying out factor analyses. As for the number of factors that can be extracted from the correlations matrices, the determinants of the matrices were very close to zero, indicating that

the number of factors is smaller than the number of items in the instrument for both.

In order to choose the number of factors, the following indices were examined: the variance explained by each factor, the sedimentation graph, the *eigenvalues* greater than 1 and the total variance explained by the instrument. Following the criterion that the total variance explained by all factors is greater than 60% of the total, the principal components analysis indicates the possibility of three factors for both facilitators and barriers. According to the criterion of *eigenvalues* greater than 1, three factors emerge in the instrument, and this is confirmed with the sedimentation graphs. Correlations between the factors were non-existent for both sets of questions.

Second, a hierarchical analysis was carried out in order to classify the participant municipalities in groups according to their perception of these barriers and facilitators, and their initial centres, which would be used in order to perform a non-hierarchical analysis and thus obtain a higher fit of the results. The final analysis was validated through the analysis of the variance in one factor (Hair *et al.,* 1995). In the hierarchical analysis, Ward's method and the square Euclidean distance were used to minimize the differences within the cluster, analysing the dendogram and the change in the agglomeration coefficient, and the validation was verified. Through the combined usage of these methods, it was observed that three groups would be an acceptable number for both sets of factors. From the k-means analysis with four groups, the characteristics of each group should be derived, together with the differences among them. The real scalar values have been used when performing the subsequent analysis.

RESULTS AND DISCUSSION

First, the facilitating factors are ranked, and the most remarkable positions are discussed. The barrier factors are similarly displayed. The final part of this section deals with the results of the cluster analysis.

Factor Analysis: Facilitators

Table 3 shows a summary of the final items deemed as positive influences for local e-government strategies, their literature sources, their value (mean) and classification according to nature. The parameter "Item value" refers to the degree of effect that such a factor has on e-government success, according to the perceptions of the municipal CTOs (1: none at all; 5: very strong). Only those that ranked over 3 were taken into account in the analysis.

The most relevant factor is the political leadership commitment to the e-government strategy, followed by having qualified human resources who make the most of IT applications and provide e-public services. The role of politicians is definitely the most important, because it is their tacit (e.g. endowment of resources) and explicit (e.g. signs of support and public services sup-

ply) behaviour that enhances e-government at local levels. The competences and commitment of public workers are likewise significant in the correct development of e-government strategies, especially if the required technical competences are found within the organisation.

The third place goes to a usable and friendly Website, followed closely by the availability of financial resources, which relates to the ability of the city council to obtain external funding for e-government strategies. The Web page is the main interface between the public organisation and its customers, both internal (employees) and, first and foremost, external (citizens and businesses). It adds value directly to the provision of e-services and may be a great hindrance if the first contact was not satisfactory.

The lower positions are held by NPM related elements: quality management programmes and changes in workflow and decision-making processes. The former may owe its place to the scarcity of these programmes among city councils; therefore those CTOs that have not implemented any of

Table 3. Ranking of the most relevant facilitating factors

FACILITATORS	MAIN AUTHORS	ITEM VALUE	FACTOR CLASSIFICATION
1-Political leadership and commitment	Criado and Ramilo (2003); Moon *et al* (2005)	4.36	3- Institutional
2-Qualified human resources	White and Hutchinson (1996); Scott *et al.* (2004); Yao *et al* (2007)	4.15	2- Infrastructural
3-Usability of Website	Pieterson *et al* (2005); Janssen *et al.* (2006)	4.08	1- Social
4-Availability of financial resources (from external programmes)	Criado and Ramilo (2003)	4.07	2- Infrastructural
5-Acknowledgment of e-government benefits by political statements	Hurst (1997); Moon *et al* (2005)	4.03	1- Social
6- E-Government explicit strategic planning	Criado and Ramilo (2003); Ebrahim and Irani (2005)	3.99	1- Social
7- IT infrastructure availability	Ebrahim and Irani (2005)	3.99	2- Infrastructural
8-Designation of a formal project manager	Harris (2002)	3.94	3- Institutional
9-Quality management models application	Dewhurst *et al* (1999); Teicher *et al* (2002); Irani *et al* (2003)	3.61	1- Social
10-Changes in decision making processes towards less bureaucracy	Hurst (1997); Criado and Ramilo (2003)	3.43	3- Institutional

these practices do not have a full understanding of the effect of quality management strategies. This contradicts the literature, but it is expected to change with time. The latter may respond to the pervasive redtape of Spanish public organisations, strictly ruled by administrative laws that clash more often than not with leaner workflows.

The three top facilitators, coincidentally, are the epitomes of the three factors found with the factor analysis, which have been named considering the nature of their components:

- **Institutional facilitators (Factor 1):** Political leadership and commitment, Designation of a formal project manager and Changes in decision-making processes towards less bureaucracy. The elements contained in this factor are characterised by a strong influence of politics and power structures within the public organisation. The denomination follows Joia's taxonomy, since the contents are similar (Joia, 2004).
- **Infrastructural facilitators (Factor 2):** Qualified human resources, IT infrastructure availability and Availability of financial resources (from external programmes). This factor is made up of the availability and access of the city council to financial, human and technological resources. It includes those infrastructural aspects of the public organisation related to the management of resources.
- **Social facilitators (Factor 3):** Usability of Website, Acknowledgment of e-government benefits by politicians, E-government explicit strategic planning and Quality management models application. It is composed of elements related to the management of the different stakeholders' interests regarding the formulation and implementation of the local e-government strategy.

In sum, those public organisations that wish to build competitive advantages for e-govern-

ment strategies, should exploit strengths based on three pillars: political commitment (institutional), adequate infrastructures and a coherent set of organisational behaviours that may conform a tangible body for those stakeholders that are still wary of e-government.

Factor Analysis: Barriers

Table 4 follows the same layout as Table 3, and it shows that most barriers resemble a negative picture of the facilitating elements. Again, only those that ranked over 3 were taken into account in the analysis.

Once again, the most important barrier is the political will, or lack thereof in this case, which confirms the importance of politicians in the final performance of e-government. Such hierarchical structures need the approval of top management for every stage in the work process (unless ruled by law in a task normalisation of sorts), which leads to bottle-necks and inefficiencies. Nevertheless, this is a double-edged razor because political commitment not only is necessary but can become sufficient in most cases.

Actually, one of the main causes for this lack of commitment is the second barrier. Fear of changes is usually fuelled by misinformation, and in many instances the person holding political power does not have a proper background about e-government's meaning and benefits. Therefore, this lack of knowledge will reinforce the previous barrier.

Tied in second place are the barriers related to financial sources. These can be considered from diverse points of view. On the one hand, some respondents believed that the financial handicaps were the most important ones, since e-government strategies required large amounts of money for purchasing and implementing technology, training human resources, etc. On the other hand, the impact of financial issues can be dismissed considering the outcomes of local e-government, because, as the saying goes, "where there's a will,

Table 4. Ranking of the most relevant barriers

BARRIERS	MAIN AUTHORS	ITEM VALUE	FACTOR CLASSIFICATION
1- Lack of political will	Clift (2003); Criado and Ramilo (2003); European Union (2007)	4.12	1- Institutional
2-Politicians' lack of knowledge on e-government's benefits	Ebrahim and Irani (2005)	3.93	1- Institutional
3- Scarcity of financial resources	ICMA (2002); Eyob (2004); European Union (2007)	3.93	2- Infrastructural
4- Scarcity of qualified human resources	Norris *et al* (2001); Li (2003); Eyob, (2004)	3.90	2- Infrastructural
5- Cost of IT infrastructure availability	Bonham *et al* (2001); Ebrahim and Irani (2005)	3.62	2- Infrastructural
6- Complexity of public work processes and bureaucracy	McClure (2000); Li and Stevenson, (2002); Waisanen (2002)	3.43	3- Social
7- Decisions are made by politicians instead of IT professionals	Li and Stevenson, (2002)	3.42	1- Institutional
8- Employees resistance to change due to lack of knowledge	Norris *et al* (2001); Li (2003)	3.36	3- Social
9- Citizens do not demand e-services	Koh *et al* (2006); European Union (2007)	3.33	3- Social
10- Unsuitable legislation	Criado and Ramilo (2003)	3.09	3- Social

there's a way", and therefore money barriers are just a by-product of the political ones.

The same could be said regarding human related barriers. These are also the least tangible sources of threat, and therefore the most difficult to tackle. The allocation of resources within local institutions belongs mostly with the political levels, although they are not the ones to put these modernisation strategies into practice, which leads to many negative implications for the expected performance.

A proposed solution to the shortage of IT skilled public workers would be to carry out IT outsourcing practices, so that training and qualifications are not an issue regarding the obtention of professional outcomes. Several authors support this proposal, such as Kakabadse and Kakabadse (2001), although they have encountered a certain reluctance to follow this suggestion among the most controlling public managers, who prefer to keep public-related tasks within the council's organisation chart. Chen and Perry (2003) have shown that some local governments may have a quite obsolete notion of public procurement,

which does not allow for strategic thinking of this area, thus hindering the evolution towards higher levels of e-government.

The cost of IT infrastructures holds a surprising fifth position, at least considering the importance given to this barrier in the literature. Technology is a tangible resource that can be bought, and it would be the CTO who designs the IT system, subject to the approval of the politician signing the bill. Consequently, this half-way position evidences the real importance of technology: there are other restrictions that play a bigger role in improving e-government's performance.

Taking a look at the least important barriers, Spain's unsuitable legislation on e-government comes in the penultimate position because of the rapid advances that Spain has been making in this area since 2001. Thus, it is acknowledged, but its importance is decreasing.

The last element, the lack of use of e-services, is a by-product of security and privacy issues. IT departments in public sector organisations should be aware of security and privacy being critical in two ways. On the one hand, to provide correct delivery of public e-services and to comply with the legal requirements regarding data protection; and, on the other hand, to build users' confidence and trust on e-government services. Besides, it seems that this outcome is very specific of local government, since higher institutions seem to have overcome this handicap quite successfully, as is the case of the Spanish Inland Revenue (see http://www.agenciatributaria.com) or Social Security (http://www.tgss.es).

The three barrier factors found with the factor analysis have been also been categorised according to their elements:

- **Institutional barriers (Factor 1):** Lack of political will, Politicians' lack of knowledge on e-government's benefits, and decisions made by politicians instead of IT professionals. The institutional barriers refer to the problems posed by the public institution itself, the politicians and the decision-making processes. These barriers influence directly the culture and system of values of the organisation, permeating throughout its levels and thus affecting e-government in a holistic manner.
- **Infrastructural barriers (Factor 2):** Scarcity of financial resources, scarcity of qualified human resources and cost of IT infrastructure availability. As with the facilitators, this factor is made up of the availability and access of the city council to financial, human and technological resources; therefore this factor includes those infrastructural aspects of the public organisation related to the management of resources.
- **Social barriers (Factor 3):** Complexity of public work processes and bureaucracy, Resistance to change due to lack of knowledge, Citizens do not demand e-services and Unsuitable legislation. This factor includes the elements related to the relationship mechanisms between the city council and its

stakeholders, i.e. its employees, its citizens, and society at large. That is why it is characterised as "social", because it deals with human–related problems (Joia, 2004).

In brief, the weaknesses of the municipalities' e-government strategies come essentially from political aspects and the availability of resources, especially human resources. Actually, both strengths and weaknesses are very similar in meaning, while the difference lies on the specific weight. The effects from having to gain access to something you do not have are much more negative than to have it available but not using it. This is particularly the case in the case of public sector organisations, where hierarchy rules over need in many cases. Nevertheless, the strong influences that the organisational culture has on the informal structure play a very important role when considering these barriers. For that reason, it seems that a municipality's weaknesses suffer from a greater causal ambiguity than its strengths, which are of a more generalist and less sustainable character.

Cluster Analysis

The cluster analysis showed four groups of significantly different municipalities (see Table 5 and Figure 1); according to their impression of the above mentioned barners and faciliators.

A number of conclusions can be extracted from Table 5 and Figure 1. For instance, it can be seen that the smallest group (number 2) is, in general terms, the most cautious, since the mean values for all the factors are the lowest, whereas the bigger groups, 3 and 4, show mostly the highest values for all factors. So, it would seem that there are few municipalities that have not given much thought to the possible handicaps and keys for success when implementing their e-government strategies.

Another finding is the almost complete coincidence of values given to the institutional

Table 5. Cluster analysis

Factors	Group 1 n=30	Group 2 n=12	Group 3 n=49	Group 4 n=1	Chi squared	p value
Infrastructural barriers	4,347	2,341	3,32	4,255	12,502	0,004
Institutional barriers	3,533	3,333	3,354	4,425	41,712	0,000
Social barriers	2,883	2,25	3,408	3,484	59,554	0,000
Infrastructural facilitators	4	3,042	3,7791	4,194	73,211	0,000
Institutional facilitators	4,447	3,222	4,194	4,5484	33,544	0,000
Social facilitators	3,4	2,778	3,917	4,575	47,838	0,000

Figure 1. Perceptions of municipalities

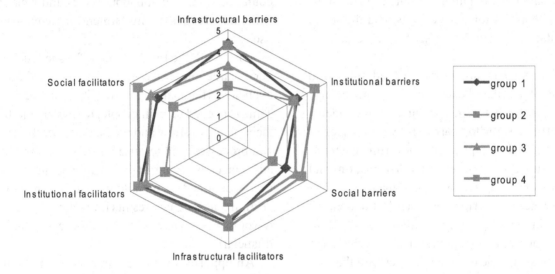

barriers (except group 4), which means that there is a common perception of the vast effects that politicians and organisational issues have on the outcome of local e-government. Moreover, the values of the social barriers and facilitators are the most disparate among the groups, reinforcing the idea that there are socially-related intangible sources of classification.

In the end, a cross-variable analysis found no common features among the members of the groups, from a demographic point of view (population, number of employees within the city council, number of employees in the IT department, geographical location, party in power, etc.).

In conclusion, the groups are based only on common intangible aspects like political atmosphere, personal relationships between the CTO and the politicians, willingness of the CTO towards e-government, or the importance given to the information society in the municipality.

CONCLUSION

This research has contributed to an understanding of e-government challenges at municipal levels, by studying the comprehensive literature about barriers and facilitators for e-government success. Also, this chapter attempts to bridge the gap between theory and practise of e-government at a local level, by using these elements in a factor analysis. This empirical analysis has found that Spanish city councils regard three types of requirements for a satisfactory implementation of e-government strategies. These are the institutional factors, mainly political leadership and commitment, which are the most relevant, as a whole; the structural facilitators, which play a differential role in the success of local e-government, and portray human resources as the most valuable assets for city councils; and the social facilitators, which do not seem to be crucial in this matter.

The barriers are more affected by causal ambiguity, so that the degree of importance may vary greatly between particular city councils. Nevertheless, the top barrier is by far the lack of political will to implement e-government strategies, supported by several other institutional factors such as IT Knowledge Management. The infrastructural barriers are tainted by this political unwillingness, specially the allocation of financial resources and the investment in technology. The most significant social barriers are the lack of use of e-government applications by citizens and public workers.

A cluster analysis was carried out to show groups of councils according to their perception of the influence of the aforementioned factors. The councils were classified in four categories, which reflected their approach to e-government. Groups 3 and 4, incidentally the bigger ones, are the most conscious of these effects, both positive and negative, whereas group 2 is represented by the most cautious councils.

After analysing these factors and discussing their roles, there are a few highlights that e-government implementers may find of interest. First, work processes must be restructured to make the most of IT and to reduce production and coordination costs, duplication costs and red tape. This way, Knowledge Management policies can be successfully implemented within the council,

since information will flow smoothly along the public value chain. The adoption of these policies will drive the needed change in organizational culture.

Second, it is undeniable that an appropriate technological infrastructure is necessary, as seen in the literature section. However, a good outsourcing policy and a sufficient budget may overcome this barrier easily. It is the use of this infrastructure that poses the difficulties for the councils, since technophobia issues and lack of skills may render the investment in technology useless.

Last of all, the third resource for success is a very scarce one: time, even if it has not shown explicitly in the analysis or in the literature section. Time is needed to train people, to implement the technology, to study and redesign the workflows and processes, and to raise awareness about the advantages of going digital. Unfortunately, the new economy does not allow room for time; everything must deliver results immediately or else it would be seen as a waste of resources (mainly financial).

An opportunity for researchers would be to revise this classification employing other taxonomies or statistical methodologies. Nevertheless, the priorities shown in this chapter are sensible as they come from the perspective of the practitioners themselves. Also, since this study relied primarily on local government CTOs' opinions, who represent only one group of stakeholders, future researchers might consider whether citizens are of the same opinion, as well as other council staff. Particularly, an interesting line of thought would be to examine how much influence the different actors (CTOs, politicians, citizens) bear in guiding the strategic orientation of local e-government policies.

Moreover, another area for future research would be to link this classification to the performance of the council. This could be done once the e-government strategies have been implemented for a sufficient period of time in which these effects become noticeable.

Finally, as has been said, the interpretations of these results will benefit greatly from a qualitative analysis of the results by confronting this data with several known e-government experts.

REFERENCES

Al-Sebie, M. & Irani, Z. (2003). E-Government: Defining Boundaries and Lifecycle maturity. In *Proceedings of the 3rd European Conference on e-government*, (pp. 19-29) Ireland: Trinity College of Dublin,.

Barca, C. & Cordella, A. (2004). Seconds out, round two: Contextualising e-government projects within their institutional milieu – A London local authority case study. In *ECIS: The European Information Systems Profession in the Global Networking Environment*, Turku, Finland.

Becker, J.; Algermissen, L. & Niehaves, B. (2003). Implementing e-government Strategies. A procedural model for process oriented e-government projects. In K. Soliman (Ed.), *Proceedings of the 2003 International Business Information Management Conference (IBIMA): "E-Business and organisations in the 21st Century"*, El Cairo, Egypt.

Bellanger, F., & Hiller, J.S. (2006). A framework for e-government: privacy implications. *Business Process Management Journal, 12* (1), 48-60.

Bonham, G., Seifert, J. & Thorson, S. (2001). The transformational potential of e-government: the role of political leadership, In *Proceedings of the 4th Pan Euroepan International Relations Conference*, Kent, UK.

Byrne, J. & Davis, G. (1998). *The Australian Policy Handbook*. Sydney, Australia: Allen & Unwin, 3rd edition.

Bueno García, O. (2002). Modernización de la AAPP, líneas estratégicas para la e-Administración. Retrieved from http://www.lawebmunicipal.com

Cap, Gemini, Erst & Young. (2002). Summary Report: Web-based Survey on Electronic Public Services. Results of the second measurement. Retrieved from http://europa.eu.int/information_society/eeurope/ benchmarking

Carr, N.G. (2006). The Sixth Force: Strategy and the Public Interest. Retrieved from http://www. nicholasgcarr.com/digital_renderings/archives/ the_sixth_force_strategy.shtml

Chen, Y.C. & Perry, J. (2003). Outsourcing for e-government. Managing for success. *Public Performance and Management Review, 26* (4), 404-421

Claver-Cortés, E., de Juana-Espinosa, S. & González, R. (2005). Local e-government strategies in Spain: an empirical survey. In *Proceedings of the 2005 BAM Conference*, Oxford, UK.

Claver-Cortés, E., de Juana-Espinosa, S. & Tari, J. (2006). e-government maturity at Spanish local levels. In *Proceedings of the 2006 EMCIS Conference*, Alicante, Spain.

Clift, S. (2003). *Public Network On-line Information Exchange in Pursuit of Public Service Goals*. OCDE E-Government Project.

Criado Grande, J.I. & Ramilo Araujo, M.C. (2003). E-Government in practice. An analysis of Web site orientation to the citizens in Spanish municipalities. *The International Journal of Public Sector Management, 126* (3), 191-218.

Dewhurst, F., Martínez Lorente, A.R., & Dale, B.G. (1999). TQM in public organisations: an examination of the issues. *Managing Service Quality, 9*(4), 265-273.

Ebrahim, Z. & Irani, Z. (2005). E-government adoption: architecture and barriers. *Business Process Management Journal, 11* (5), 589-611.

European Union (2007). Breaking barriers to e-government. Retrieved from http://www.egov-barriers.org

Eyob, E. (2004). E-Government: breaking the frontiers of inefficiencies in the public sector. *Electronic Government, 1*(1), 107-114

Janssen, M., Gortmaker, J. & Wagenaar, R.W. (2006). Web service orchestration in public administration: challenges, roles and growth stages, *Information Systems Management, 23* (2), 44-55.

Govindarajan V. & Gupta, A. (2001). Strategic innovation: a conceptual road map. *Business Horizons, 44* (4), 3-12.

Hackney, R.A, & Jones, S. (2002). Towards e-government in the Welsh (UK) Assembly: an information systems evaluation. In *Proceedings of the ISOne World Conference*, Las Vegas, US.

Hair, J., Anderson, R., Tatham, R.; & Black, W. (1999). *Multivariant Analysis*. Boston, US: Prentice Hall, 5°ed.

Harris, L. (2002). The future for the HRM function in local government: everything has changed-but has anything changed?. *Strategic Change, 11*, 369-378.

Ho, V.Y., Ang, S. & Straub, D. (2003). When subordinates become IT contractors: persistent managerial expectations in Outsourcing. *Information Systems Research, 14* (1), 66-86.

Holden, S.H. (2003). The new e-government equation: ease, engagement, privacy and protection. *The Council for Excellence in Government*. Retrieved from: http://www.excelgov.org

Hurst, D.K. (1997). When it comes to real change, too much objectivity may be fatal to the process. *Strategy and Leadership, 25*, 7-11.

ICMA (2002). e-government survey. Retrieved from: http://www.icma.org.

Irani, Z., Khoumbathi, K., & Themistocleous, M. (2003). Conceptual Model for the Adoption of Enterprise Application Integration in Healthcare Organizations. In *Proceedings of the America's Conference on Information Systems,* Tampa (Florida), US.

Joia, L.A. (2004). Developing Government-to-Government enterprises in Brazil: a heuristic model drawn from multiple case studies. *International Journal of Information Management, 24* (2), 147-166.

Kakabadse, A. & Kakabadse, N. (2001). Outsourcing in the public services: a comparative analysis of practice, capability and impact. *Public Administration and Development, 21* (5), 401-413.

Koh, C.E., Prybutok, V.R., Ryan, S., & Ibragimova, B. (2006). The importance of strategic readiness in an emerging e-government environment. *Business Process Management Journal, 12* (1), 22-33.

Layne, K. & Lee, J. (2001). Developing fully functional E-Government: A four stage model. *Government Information Quarterly, 18*(2), 122-136.

Lee, S., Tan, X. & Trimi, S. (2006). Current practices of leading e-government countries. *Communications of the ACM, 48* (10), 99-104.

Li, F. (2003). Implementing E-Government strategy in Scotland: current situation and emerging issues. *Journal of Electronic Commerce in Organizations, 1* (2), 44-65.

Li, F. (2006). *What is e-Business? How the Internet transforms organisations*. Oxford, UK: Blackwell.

Li, F. & Stevenson, R. (2003). Implementing e-government strategy in Scotland: current situation and emerging issues. In *Proceedings of the 2nd European Conference on e-government*, Oxford, UK.

McAdam, R. & Walker, T. (2004). Evaluating the best value framework in UK local government services. *Public Administration and Development, 24* (3), 183-196.

McCLure, D. (2000). Electronic government: federal initiatives are evolving rapidly but they face significant challenges. Retrieved from: http://www.gao.gov/new.items/a200179t.pdf

MCYT & MAP (Ministerio de Ciencia y Tecnología & Ministerio de Administración Pública) (2003). Plan de Choque para el Impulso de la Administración Electrónica en España. Retrieved from http://www.csi.map.es/csi/pdf/plan.pdf

Moon, M.J. (2002): The evolution of E-Government among municipalities: Rhetoric or reality?. *Public Administration Review, 62* (4), 424-433.

Moon, M.J. & Norris, D.F. (2005). Does managerial orientation matter? The adoption of reinventing government and e-government at the municipal level. *Information Systems Journal, 15* (1), 43-60.

Neff, D. (2007). Local wireless networks- a prerequisite for the future. *Public Management, 89* (2), 10-14.

Norris, D.F.; Fletcher, P.D. & Holden, S.H. (2001). *Is your local government plugged in? Highlights of the 2000 electronic government survey.* Maryland, US: International City/County Management Association (ICMA) and Public Technology, Inc. (PTI).

Phan, D.D. (2003). E-business development for competitive advantages: a case study, *Information & Management, 40*, 581-590.

Pieterson, W., Ebbers, W., & Van Dijk, J. (2005). The opportunities and barriers of user profiling in the public sector. In *Proceedings of the 2005 EGOV,* Copenhagen, Denmark.

Prokopiadou G., Paptheodorou C. & Moschopoulos D. 2004. Integrating knowledge management tools for government information. *Government Information Quarterly, 21*, 170-198.

Riege, A. & Lindsay, N. (2006). Knowledge management in the public sector: stakeholder partnerships in the public policy development. *Journal of Knowledge Management, 10* (3), 24-39.

Scott, M.; Golden, W. & Hugues, M. (2004). Implementation strategies for e-government: a stakeholder analysis approach. In *Proceedings of ECIS: The European Information Systems Profession in the Global Networking Environment,* Turku, Finland.

SOCITM (2006). Modern public services: a role for change. The CIO as agent of transformation. Retrieved from: http://www.socitm.gov.uk/socitm/Services/Socitm+Insight/News/Role+of+CIO.htm

Teicher, J.; Hughes, O. & Dow, N. (2002). E-Government: a new route to public sector quality. *Managing Service Quality, 12* (6), 384-393.

Vishanth, W. & Jyoti, C. (2004). Exploring e-government: challenges, issues and complexities. In *Proceedings of the European and Mediterranean Conference on Information Systems (EMCIS),* Tunisia, Tunez.

Waisanen, B. 2002. The future of E-government: Technology fuelled management toll. *Public Management, 84* (5), 6-9.

Ward, M. (2006). Information Systems Technologies: a public-private sector comparison. *The Journal of Computer Information System, 46* (3), 50-56.

White, G. & Hutchison, B. (1996). Local Government. In Farnham D. Hortorn (eds.), *Managing People in the Public Services* (pp. 185-224). Basingstoke: Macmillan Press.

Yao, L.J., Kam, T.H.Y & Chan, S.H. (2007). Knowledge sharing in Asian public administration sector: the case of Hong Kong. *Journal of Enterprise Information Management, 20* (1), 51-69.

Chapter XIII
Business Analytics Success:
A Conceptual Framework and an Application to Virtual Organizing

Hindupur Ramakrishna
University of Redlands, USA

Avijit Sarkar
University of Redlands, USA

Jyoti Bachani
University of Redlands, USA

ABSTRACT

The chapter presents a conceptual framework that identifies technological and organizational factors that impact the success of business analytics (BA) use in organizations in general and virtual organizations in particular. The framework explores BA success through three business disciplines: Decision sciences (DS), information systems (IS), and management. We believe that BA success comes from proper interaction between the three disciplines. Though the concept of BA has been around for a long time in business literature, its full potential use has not been realized in organizations for a variety of reasons. The information and communication technologies (ICT) that have made virtual organizations, and flattening of the world possible have also created a better infrastructure/environment for use of BA by providing the capability to collect massive amounts of data and by providing easier-to-use analytic tools. Currently, BA is being touted as the next information technology (IT) capability that will generate considerable value including competitive advantage to businesses. In this chapter we present and discuss our framework, discuss its viability through existing examples of BA success, and finally apply the framework to a special emerging context in organizations, virtual organizing. Implications of this framework for identifying and filling research gaps in this area and implications for managers interested in exploring BA use in their organizations are presented.

INTRODUCTION

Though the history of organizational/managerial decision-making is long, its movement from "decision-making as an art" to "decision-making as a science" is more recent. Parallel, and sometimes independent, developments in three fields have aided this evolution. Management theory focused on the typologies and processes of decision-making and the behavioral aspects (Henderson & Nutt, 1980; Kepner & Tregoe, 1965; Mintzberg *et al*, 1976; Simon, 1977; Tydeman *et al*, 1980)—the softer side. Decision Sciences (DS) as a field was formally defined in the early 1970s, and the field included the work done in management theory and extended it through the use of quantitative techniques—the harder side. Though quantitative techniques, mathematical and statistical, were available for use by organizations and managers, their use was not widespread due to the lack of availability and ease-of-use of the tools and data necessary for quantitative analysis. A parallel development in information systems (IS) that made the necessary tools and data available, and easier to use by most managers, made it possible for organizations to capture/collect/access massive amounts of data regarding the organizational processes and analyze them for decision-making through the use of quantitative analysis.

Business analytics (BA)—the use of analytic techniques (driven by data and quantitative analysis) for organizational/managerial decision-making, a new term that has been coined recently—is a result of the parallel developments in the three disciplines, Management, DS, and IS. History of analytic techniques and data to improve organizational decision-making can be traced to the 1960s to the development of the first decision support systems (DSS) (Power, 2001, 2002, and 2004). Analytics has also been defined to be a subset of business intelligence (BI). BI includes both data access and reporting, and analytics. More formal definitions of BI and its essential components can be found in Negash and Gray (2003). The terms "data mining" and "business analytics" have also been used interchangeably in the literature (Kohavi, Rothleder, and Simoudis, 2002) to indicate the general process of investigation and subsequent analysis of data to identify the existence of new and meaningful trends.

Relatively few formal definitions of BA exist in the literature. Davenport and Harris (2007) define analytics as "the extensive use of data, statistical and quantitative analysis, explanatory and predictive models, and fact-based management to drive decisions and actions." Davenport & Harris further state that the "analytics may be input for human decisions or may drive fully automated decisions." While data access and reporting help businesses understand "what happened," and "what actions are needed," analytics helps them to understand "why is this happening," "what if these trends continue," and perhaps forecast "what will happen next" (Davenport & Harris, 2007).

Prior work related to the Management, IS, and DS aspects of BA is extensive in each area. Success in decision-making and problem-solving (including success of different phases) and its relation to different problem-solving methods and individual and group behavior has been studied extensively in the Management literature. Data collection, storage, and access issues have been addressed extensively in IS literature. Extensive work on building a variety of quantitative models exists in DS (sometimes also referred to as Management Science or Operations Research) literature. Some literature also exists that integrates two disciplines – for example, group decision support systems (GDSS) work that integrates Management and IS aspects of BA. Davenport's (2006) work is the first attempt to link explicitly the three disciplines critical to BA success. Davenport identified three key attributes for organizations to be analytically competitive – (1) widespread use of modeling and optimization, (2) an enterprise approach, and (3) senior executive advocates. In the same work, the author argues that organizational success in BA can result if analytics-minded leaders actively recruit analytically competent people who are proficient in the use of technology and can decide "when to run the numbers."

Though some case-based evidence exists, Davenport's (2006) work represents the only instance in the literature which hints that BA success results from an optimal blend of competence in several business disciplines. However the inter-relationship between the disciplines towards the achievement of business analytics success has not been explicitly developed in his research. For BA to be used extensively in organizations and for it to succeed in providing value to organizations, it is important to build and test a conceptual model of BA success – a model that links relevant DS, IS, and Management factors (the independent variable set) to BA success (the dependent variable set). We believe that BA success is derived not only from understanding factors in each discipline but also from a good understanding of the relevant intersections/interactions of the three aspects of BA (DS, IS, and Management).

From our review of the literature, it is clear that BA use in organizations is currently limited. Some factors that may have contributed to this are (1) a lack of specialized skill in quantitative modeling both at an individual and organizational level, (2) limited/restrictive IT infrastructure, often with the lack of enterprise-wide support for IT initiatives necessary for BA implementation, and (3) lack of an organizational culture that can successfully engineer a company-wide shift in decision-making paradigm. In addition, there is a clear lack of metrics of BA success that may have prevented companies from linking measures of BA success to their strategic goals or establish a connection between BA-related activities undertaken and financial outcomes achieved (Ittner and Larcker, 2003). Further, failures of BA initiatives in organizations have not been documented in the academic literature. Overall it is fair to say that BA success and the factors/actions that lead to it are not well understood.

The primary objective of this chapter is to develop and present a framework for BA success. We argue that BA success lies at the intersection of three disciplines (1) decision sciences, (2) information systems, and (3) management. Though a considerable body of literature, and some case-based evidence, exists in different business disciplines as it pertains to BA, prior work has mostly been discipline-specific and not well integrated. We are building our framework based mostly on prior research in the three distinct business disciplines—three different components that are needed for BA success in organizations: (a) basic quantitative modeling and analysis needs with respect to data, tools, models, and interfaces, (b) IT infrastructure needs toward the support and successful implementation of BA technologies, and (c) top-down commitment to make analytics central to strategy coupled with an organizational culture that supports and rewards skillful use of data-driven analysis for the purpose of organizational decision-making. Clearly a one-to-one correspondence between each previous component (a), (b), and (c) and broader business domains of DS, IS, and Management, respectively, is intuitively apparent. If we take one or more of the disciplines/components away, BA success will be compromised. Data and models are key to quantitative analysis. But without adequate IT support, it is not possible to store large-scale data and run computationally intensive algorithms that provide modeling horsepower. An enterprise with access to data, models, and IT infrastructure will not be "BA successful," however, in the absence of top-level commitment for measuring, testing, and evaluating quantitative evidence for decision-making purposes.

Another unique contribution of this work is the application of our framework to virtual organizing. This application is cognizant of the fact that decision-making in businesses today is increasingly distributed in time and space. The increased use of group-based problem-solving

(Davenport, 2006) and virtual teams (Jessup and Valacich, 2007) poses challenges and provides opportunities in each discipline that is a part of our BA success framework. We apply our model to virtual environments and explore several benefits of virtualization and also identify challenges which result due to the ability to span time and space.

The chapter is organized as follows: (1) we present some discussion/review of literature on BA and in the three disciplines as they relate to BA, (2) we present our framework, its development, description of the framework, and its application/implications for research and practice, (3) we present the application of the framework to virtual organizing and justification for the application, and (4) we present some conclusions.

RELATED RESEARCH/ DEVELOPMENTS

In order to develop a conceptual framework for BA success it is important first to understand developments in BA and related fields in the past few decades. In this section, we explore the developments in BA use in organizations and developments in the three fields/disciplines that are believed to have an impact on BA success: management, DS, and IS.

Business Analytics

As we have noted earlier, Davenport and Harris (2007) state that business analytics is a subset of BI. They define BI as "a set of technologies and processes that use data to understand and analyze business performance." According to Davenport and Harris, BI includes (1) data access and reporting, and (2) analytics. While data access and reporting includes tools such as standard reports, ad hoc reports, queries, and alerts, analytics includes tools such as optimization, predictive modeling, forecasting, and statistical analysis.

Davenport & Harris suggest that the degree of intelligence increases as analytics complements data access and reporting.

The terms "data mining" and "business analytics" have also been used interchangeably in the literature (Kohavi, Rothleder, & Simoudis, 2002) to indicate the general process of investigation and subsequent analysis of data to identify the existence of new and meaningful trends. Like Davenport, Kohavi *et al.* identify data collection, storage, and processing as issues pertinent to analytics and state that mined data is used extensively by business organizations that employ analytics for everyday operations.

Over the last few years groundbreaking analytics-based systems such as online reservations (at American Airlines), predictive maintenance (at Otis Elevator), and revenue management systems (at Marriott International to determine the optimal price of guest rooms) have become more and more common. The fact that analytics can be applied to many business processes to add value and gain competitive advantage has been demonstrated by organizations like Amazon.com, Harrah's, Capital One, and the Boston Red Sox, which have dominated their respective domains by employing analytics for key strategic decision-making purposes.

Davenport and Harris (2007) have identified analytical competitors in a variety of industries, including consumer products, telecommunications, financial services, pharmaceuticals, transport, retail, hospitality and entertainment, airlines, and e-commerce. The same work also mentions the use of analytics by various levels of government – national, state, and local, for crime prevention, predictive modeling of contagious diseases, resource (gas, oil, minerals, etc.) optimization, and fraud detection. In fact sales, marketing, supply chain optimization, and fraud detection are several areas identified by Kohavi *et al* (2002) that routinely use business analytics. The same authors have mentioned that organizations in financial, retail, manufacturing, utilities, and telecommunications sectors increasingly want their field personnel to have access to BA information through wireless devices. Apte *et al.* (2002) state that industries that have derived benefits from data mining include insurance, direct mail marketing, telecommunications, retail, and healthcare.

A summary of several successful BA applications is tabulated in Table 1. Each specifically describes the nature of the application, and tools, techniques, methodologies, or paradigms employed by the respective organization, and BA success measures used.

A detailed list of several other business functions with scope for application of business analytics, description of the exact nature of usage of analytics (for example in capacity planning, demand-supply matching, location analysis, reducing inventory and preventing stock-outs, etc. toward the effective management of supply chains), and corresponding examples from industry can be found in Davenport (2006).

Davenport and Harris (2007) provide the only instances when organizations have not been particularly successful in spite of adopting BA. These organizations are both prominent players in the US aviation industry – United Airlines and American Airlines. Davenport and Harris postulate that two factors have prevented these airlines from succeeding with their analytical strategies – (a) their analytics support an obsolete business model, far superior versions of which have been adopted by their competitors, and (b) other airlines too have adopted BA since airline industry data has become more readily available from associations and external providers.

The BA literature is replete with examples of BA success. Several such examples are tabulated earlier in Table 1. In some instances, analogous metrics of BA success have been used. For example, market share at Harrah's, earnings per share and return on equity at Capital One, market capitalization at Progressive have been used as surrogates for revenue. Negash and Gray state

that ROI analysis is frequently necessary for BI projects and list statistics related to ROI figures for given levels of investment. Davenport and Harris (2007) contains similar statistics. Sports teams have often used number of games /titles won or reduction in player injuries as metrics of analytics success. Revenue increase (or cost reduction) is a commonly used (and intuitive) metric of BA success; however, our research did not yield any consistent metrics of business analytics success across industries in different sectors.

Davenport *et al.* (2001) introduced a model for building analytic capability in organizations. The authors discussed the contextual factors in the model (a particular business strategy, a particular set of skills and experiences, a particular set of culture and organizational structure, and a particular set of technology and data capabilities) and also constructed a decision tree for implementing analytical capability. The authors also presented a framework that identifies and articulates the primary success factors which are required to develop broad organizational capabilities for transforming electronic data into knowledge and then into business results.

Luecke (2006) cites several characteristics shared by organizations that routinely make good decisions. These include but are not restricted to employees who recognize behavioral traps that lead to bad decisions, decision-makers who understand their roles and possess skills their roles require, development of a number of feasible decision alternatives, availability of an array of decision-making tools and processes, and overall people who are dedicated to improving decision quality. Along similar lines, Davenport (2006) outlines the characteristics and practices at analytics-driven organizations and describes some of the very substantial changes that other organizations must undertake to compete on analytics turf. These changes include a top-down commitment to make analytics central to strategy, abundant use of complex data and statistical analysis, significant investment in technology, and

Table 1. Examples of successful BA applications in industry

Example #	Organization (Reference)	Specific BA Application	Methodology/Paradigm Employed	BA success measures
1	Capital One (Davenport, 2006; Davenport and Harris, 2007)	Maximized the likelihood that (a) potential customers will sign up for credit cards, and (b) they will actually pay back Capital One once they sign up.	Simulates more than 30,000 scenarios each year with different interest rates, incentives, direct mail advertising, and several other variables of interest	Customer retention has increased by 87% and the cost of acquiring a new account has decreased by 83% over a period of time.
2	Netflix (Davenport and Harris, 2007)	Endeavored to match buying patterns with customer behavior; also in deciding what to pay for the distribution rights of DVDs.	Hired mathematicians who developed algorithms and subsequently computer codes to "define clusters of movies, connect customer movie rankings to the clusters, evaluate thousands of ratings per second, and factor in current Website behavior – all to ensure a personalized Webpage for each visiting customer".	Has grown from $5 million in revenues in 1999 to $1 billion in 2006.
3	Progressive (Davenport, 2006; Davenport and Harris, 2007)	Profitably insured high risk customers, a constituent that competitors would otherwise ignore blindly assuming that these customers are "loss-making".	Closely analyzed data to categorize customers into several narrow clusters, each characterized by age, college education, previous accident history, credit scores, etc. in order to rank them as high versus low risk, and then employed regression analysis to identify factors that closely define losses a particular cluster of customers produces.	Market capitalization doubled during the 2003-2007 period to $23 billion.
4	Marriott International (Davenport, 2006)	Established an analytical system for optimal pricing of guest rooms, conference facilities, and catering.	Pioneered the concept of revenue management, in which an analytical model computes and maximizes actual revenues as a percentage of optimal rates that could have been charged to customers; also developed a system to optimize offerings such as price discounts to frequent customers.	Actual revenues when computed as a percentage of optimal rates increased from 83% to 91%; annual profit increased by $86 million in 2004.
5	Harrah's Entertainment (Davenport and Harris, 2007)	Developed the ability to use real-time data to make decisions on their business processes right down to individual machines where their patrons are gaming.	This is achieved by changing the odds based on the behavior of patrons that are analyzed as soon as they use the Harrah's card. The incentives required to bring these patrons into the casino and to keep them playing can be manipulated based on exact data collected from their card usage.	Increased market share from 36% to 43% between 1998 and 2004.

continued on following page

Table 1. continued

6	Proctor and Gamble (Camm *et al,* 1997)	Successfully redesigned North American supply chain by integrating production, sourcing, and distribution functions.	A group of about 100 analysts from several organizational functions such as operations, supply chain, sales, marketing, etc. worked in tandem. For example, sales and marketing analysts supplied data on opportunities for growth in existing markets to analysts who design supply and distribution networks.	Reduced number of North American plants by almost 20% thereby saving over $200 million in pretax costs per year in the mid 1990s.
7	Sears, Roebuck and Company (Weigel and Cao, 1999)	Tremendously improved their technician dispatching and home-delivery business.	Employing an analytically powerful vehicle routing and scheduling system within a geographic information systems (GIS) based framework to run its delivery and home service fleets more efficiently.	Achieved $9 million in one-time savings and over $42 million in annual savings; were able to consolidate vehicle dispatch facilities by more than 50%.
8	Deere and Company (Davenport and Harris, 2007)	Attempted to reduce inventory and complexity by eliminating product configurations that were difficult to produce and sell.	Worked with academic collaborators and successfully optimized configurations of products on two product lines.	Profits on the two lines increased by 15% due to 30-50% reduction in the number of product configurations.

executives' unswerving commitment to change the way employees think, work, and are treated. Davenport (2006) further outlines four factors in defining analytical competition. These are (a) distinctive capability, (b) enterprise-wide analytics, (c) senior management commitment, and (d) large scale ambition. Davenport and Harris (2007) add that it would be a "huge mistake" to call analytics a happy marriage between analytical tools and information technology (IT). The authors argue that "human and organizational aspects" of analytics distinguish the successful exponents of BA in various industries. The hint that BA success stems from an optimal blend of *(i)* distinctive analytics-friendly management style with *(ii)* analytical tools, and *(iii)* IT is unmistakable. However the fact that *(i)*, *(ii)*, and *(iii)* each represent one key business discipline has not been explicitly stated in any existing literature. Moreover the current literature also lacks a conceptual framework of BA success.

In summary, though BA is a newly defined field, it is clear that research in BA-related fields such as DSS, BI, data mining, etc. have been around for many decades. There have been many successful (and some unsuccessful) applications reported in the literature. The applications have been in diverse organizational functions and in diverse industries. In addition, we can speculate that there must have been many unreported BA failures. As the field is fairly new, academic research that assists in developing a good understanding of factors that contribute to BA success (or failure) are scarce (Negash & Gray, 2003), and the evidence from most existing research is anecdotal. While the exact metrics of business analytics success can be industry specific, our review of the literature reveals that understanding of factors and/or disciplines, which combine to generate BA success, is limited. Several examples of BA applications in industry have been documented, and frameworks for classifying organizations competing on analytical turf exist. However, a good understanding of what contributes to BA success, as well as metrics of BA success, is fuzzy and almost non-existent in the literature.

Management Factors for BA Success

The field of management has explored managerial/organizational decision-making, one of the core activities of management as identified by Mintzberg (1973), from multiple perspectives. They include: (1) the idea of rational decision-making that first originated in neo-classical economic theories, (2) the concept of bounded rationality and decision-making as "satisficing" as opposed to optimizing, (3) the garbage can model of decision-making. Management literature has also dealt with many aspects of managerial decision-making. The behavioral theory of the firm focused research on the managerial behaviors and

their impact on organizations (Cyert & March, 1992). The pros and cons of individual versus group decision-making and the phenomenon of groupthink have been identified (Janis, 1972). The individual biases in decision-making (Kahneman *et al*, 1982) and the importance of framing the decisions have been studied. The importance of politics was highlighted by Allison and Zelikow's (1999) study of the Cuban Missile Crisis and the different ways decisions were made in that situation. The roles of other organizational factors, (e.g. technology or organizational structure) on managerial decisions have also been investigated (Lawrence and Lorsch, 1967; Scott, 2003; Thompson, 1967, 2003; Woodward 1975). The behaviorists have questioned the standard rational model of economics, and bounded rationality is now widely accepted as an alternative assumption for explaining managerial behaviors (Simon 1997).

In the meantime, progress in the fields of IS

Figure 1. Business analytics adoption matrix

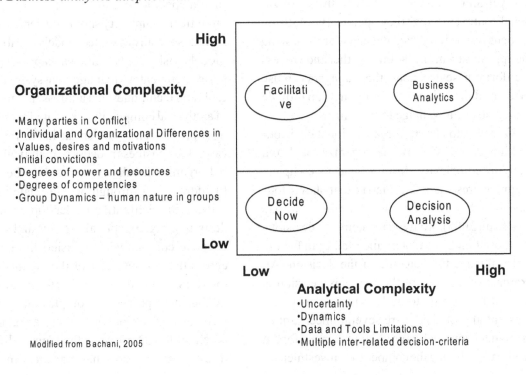

Modified from Bachani, 2005

and DS led to better tools, techniques, models, and computational power to allow managers to be increasingly scientific and rational in their decision-making. Evolutionary economics and the theory of the firm were becoming the basis for newer management theories. Together, these changes led to the present situation, when we consider that it is imperative to take a joint look across management, DS and IS, in order to really understand the impact of managerial decision-making on organizational success.

Firms with managers who know how to deploy IS resources well were better positioned toward (hard) evidence-based decision-making (Ayers, 2007). Thus, IS offered competitive advantage to these firms. According to the resource-based view of the firm, organizations achieve competitive advantage by securing inimitable and scarce resources (Barney, 1991). With increasing automation and affordable technology, IS is available to all firms as a resource, but only a handful are able to deploy it in a manner that creates competitive advantage. The differentiation comes from having managers who know how to play their decisional role well and are allowed to do so by the organizational context in which they operate. By choosing to focus on the important decisions and knowing the appropriate information to gather and process to inform these decisions, the managers can use IS to build the unique capability that can provide a competitive advantage to their firms.

One way to classify organizational decision-making contexts is by the organizational and analytic complexity, from simple to complex. Figure 1 presents a 2x2 matrix that shows four possible different decision-making contexts (Bachani, 2005). Analytically complex decisions are those that have a lot of uncertainty in factors that influence the outcome of the decision. An example of an analytically complex decision is when a firm needs to build a new factory at a substantial cost. There are several uncertainties in this decision, such as predicting demand for the product, predicting the competitor's investment in

capacity, forecasting future prices for the product, and so on. Organizationally complex decisions require many people from different parts of the organization to be involved in the process since the choice will impact what they all do. For example, consider managers who are deciding on the features for the new version of a product. There may not be too many changes to the product's core features, but any change requires coordinated effort that means involving different parts of the organization, from taking into account the voice of customers by consulting the customer service department, the input from the distributors by consulting the sales division of the company, the cost of the new features by getting estimates from the accounting department, the compatibility and production capabilities by consulting the operations department, and so on.

When a business process is analytically and organizationally simple, there is no need for any investment in developing systems or competencies for handling these situations. Managers make the decisions promptly. If the business process is analytically complex but organizationally simple, then a specific tool to handle the nature of the analytical complexity should be deployed. These include specially designed models like forecasting models, risk analysis models, capacity planning systems, inventory management systems or other tools and techniques that address the special kind of analytical complexity associated with the business process and problem at hand. In the third case, if the business process is analytically simple but organizationally complex, then the best way to address it is through people-related methods – including facilitative leadership, training, re-designing organizational systems and structures to make communication easier, linking people across the various parts of the organization using ICTs, and so on. In the fourth situation where the business process is complex analytically as well as organizationally, there is a real need and potential for BA to make the biggest difference. It is in this situation that managers must make the investment in developing the BA capability. Having the right tools and techniques to deal with the analytical complexity as well as having the structures and systems that allow a better handling of organizational complexity will lead to the best outcomes for handling the business processes most efficiently.

In summary, there has been an evolution in managerial/organizational decision-making from an art to a science. This has been made possible with parallel evolutions in IS and DS that have made the tools and data available for scientific (hard evidence-based) decision-making. In addition, characteristics of certain decision-making contexts dictate whether BA will lead to success. Managers should develop BA capabilities for those contexts to maximize benefits. With increased managerial acceptance of analytical techniques for decision-making, it appears the time may be ripe for BA to succeed.

Information Systems Factors for BA Success

One necessary condition for BA success is the appropriate IT that supports the data, quantity, quality and availability, and analysis tools needs, availability and ease-of-use. Evolution in IT has made it possible for organizations to have access to massive amounts of useful data, internal as well as external, for BA use. With computerized record-keeping, organizations can access reports about customer demand, in different time periods, order size and content, customers quantities in different locations, segments of the market, account receivables, detailed inventory, and other such information that was much harder to track or consolidate without technology. The cost of data storage over this same time period has decreased at an exponential rate, thus making it possible for organizations to store more data that may be useful. There is also a trend toward sharing massive amounts of data with external entities, like Nielsen, that aggregate data from several sources

to make it available to any organization that wishes to purchase it. In addition, massive amounts of demographic and related data are available from sources such as the U.S. Census Bureau.

Organizations are also able to collect and store transaction data more easily due to the availability and development of standard, off-the-shelf enterprise-wide software packages that address specific business needs, e.g. enterprise resource planning (ERP) systems, customer relationship management (CRM) systems, and supply chain management (SCM) systems. When these systems are well implemented, they force users to input good quality data and assist in maintaining good data integrity.

The evolution of data management technology from file management systems (of the 1960s and 1970s) to database management systems (DBMS) to data warehouses and data marts has created easier access to well integrated data with good integrity.

In a related development, IT tools that assist organizations in analyzing the data have also become easier to access and use. The evolution has taken us from custom built packages for specific analysis and specific organizational decision contexts to standard off-the-shelf analysis packages and tool kits included as part of database packages. This has resulted in analysis tools that are better integrated with data sources and with interfaces that are easier to use. Another development in BA tools, BA capability as a Web service (as opposed to a product), has made it possible for organizations to benefit from BA without the need for an upfront investment in BA tools implementation. Business Analytics Online (BAO), a service offered by the Environmental Systems Research Institute (ESRI) of Redlands, CA, is an example of this development.

Thus, IT evolution has made it easier for organizations to succeed in their BA efforts as they pertain to data and IT tools for analysis. This, in essence, has provided a necessary condition for BA success. However, BA success for any organization initially depends on the extent to which the organization has capitalized on the IT evolution in the areas discussed. For example, there are many organizations in the process of implementing enterprise-wide systems and data warehouses and data marts. As a consequence, BA success for these organizations will be limited due to data access issues.

Though some organizations have good data access and, hence, a potential for BA success, many other organizations encounter data access issues. Even with the available data, the use could be limited. In a recent study by Davenport *et al* (2001), the authors found that less than 10% of the firms that had ERP data could cite examples of the data use for BA. They also found that few retail businesses that collect scanner data use much of that data for BA.

In summary, it is clear that there are many IS-related factors that are critical for BA success. Evolution in a variety of (information) technologies has made it possible for organizations to access massive amounts of good quality data for BA success. Analysis tools have evolved from stand-alone tools with limited capability into highly sophisticated ones integrated with tools for data access. These developments enhance the possibility of BA success.

Decision Sciences Factors for BA Success

One key factor that is critical for BA success is the use of the right quantitative analysis. This involves the application of sophisticated models, algorithms, and heuristics to solve complex business problems in various domains such as capacity planning, demand-supply matching, location planning and analysis, scheduling, and supply chain and logistics optimization. With the evolution of algorithms and computing machinery, prohibitively expensive computation times are a thing of the past. Davenport and Harris (2007) list combinatorial optimization,

constraint analysis, Monte Carlo simulation, multiple regression analysis, risk analysis, price optimization, etc. as some analytical applications for various business processes. It is pertinent to mention here that all these applications belong to the broader domain of DS. Most DS models are amenable to the performance of sensitivity analysis that allows a decision-maker to simulate various alternative scenarios. Simulation models (Conchran, Mackulak, and Savory, 1995; Hwarng, 2001; Nance and Sargent, 2002) are widely used for industrial problem-solving and analysis. In several instances, sub-problems of complex industrial problems can be formulated as network optimization models.

In several instances, however, a well-established model cannot be forced to fit into an actual industrial problem due to associated problem complexities. In such cases, it usually takes a substantial amount of imagination and modeling skill on the part of the management scientist, teamwork, and communication to transform a particular "real-life" industrial problem description to a well-defined problem which can then be solved using analytical tools or techniques, special purpose algorithms or heuristics, or by the use of software. The importance of creativity in modeling and MS overall has been highlighted in Evans (1991, 1992, 1993a, 1993b) and Tsoukas and Papoulias (1996).

Hillier and Lieberman (2005) state that it is almost impossible for a single individual to be an expert in all aspects of MS. Therefore, for a full-fledged DS study, a group comprised of individuals with diverse skills and backgrounds must collaborate. Clearly virtualization can play a key role in fostering teamwork and communication among modeling associates, especially when individuals can span space and time.

Another important characteristic of DS is the search for an optimal solution, loosely defined as the best solution under the given circumstances. When the search for optimal solutions often becomes prohibitively expensive (in terms of computation time) because industrial problems are simply too complex (too many variables, and/or too many constraints/relationships), heuristic approaches are employed which provide a "near-to" optimal solution. It is pertinent to mention here that top-level management, keeping in mind broader organizational targets and objectives, often decides the optimality gap. With recent advances in computing hardware and software, however, the search for an optimal solution has become faster. Bixby (2002) contains an account on how computation times of various test problems have improved over the last decade, and how the notion of "large" problem instances has evolved over the years. Bixby reports that several test problems were solved in computation times that were 52 times faster when using newer versions of the same commercial solver. The author further adds that a model that might have taken a year to solve could be solved in less than 30 seconds by 2002 due to an increase of several orders of magnitude of computing speed and algorithmic power.

DS problems have always been amenable to spreadsheet modeling. Bodily (1986) suggests the use of spreadsheets to solve DS problems in 1986. Since then, spreadsheets and MS have both evolved to the extent that DS practitioners are solving problems in many functional areas using spreadsheets. Leon, Przasnyski, and Seal (1996) report that some areas of DS such as linear programming, simulation, project management, and forecasting use spreadsheet modeling more than some other areas such as network models and queuing. Dhebar (1993) states that systematic spreadsheet development and documentation of logic are critical in any quantitative analysis and sounds a note of caution related to the accuracy of spreadsheet models.

A key step in the quantitative analysis of a problem through the development of a model is the availability and preparation of data required by the model. Data is often referred to as "uncontrollable inputs" and must be specified before analysts can feed the data to a model, specify a

solution methodology and obtain meaningful outputs (often decisions). Many quantitative analysts believe that problem definition and development of a model essentially means problem solution and that data collection and preparation are trivial steps in the overall analysis framework. Nothing can be further from the truth, and the importance of data in relation to business analytics cannot be overstated. Often a large database is required to support a quantitative model, and information systems experts may become involved with the data preparation step.

There are several other key modeling issues as well. One pertains to the ease of use or flexibility. The models developed in a business analytics framework must have the ability to access data from many different sources such as databases, spreadsheets, or the Internet, giving the user the flexibility to choose the most efficient and convenient way to incorporate data into the model. Another pertains to the issues of interfaces that should be straightforward and intuitive enough such that users can begin building models within minutes of installation; yet the modeling interfaces must possess depth of features to handle the most difficult problem scenarios. The scalability of models —in other words, their ability to handle and analyze huge volumes of data—is another pertinent issue. To that end, data mining is one of the most general approaches utilized to reduce data in order to explore, analyze and understand it. Several goals that are uniquely addressed by data mining have been identified in Fayyad and Uthurusamy (2002) and include scaling analysis to large databases and scaling to higher-dimensional data and models.

In summary, it is clear that many diverse factors related to DS are critical to BA success. The specific factors that will have an impact on BA success are context specific, organizational as well as decision-making. A summary (that presents the current context of BA) of BA-related evolution in the field is presented in Table 2.

Table 2. BA-related evolution

Evolution of the developments in management, IS, and DS that relate to BA	Current status of BA	The gap	What is possible
Management • Progress from rational decision-making to boundedly rational models of managerial decisions. • Management awareness of analytical and computational tools and techniques that can assist decision-making. Going beyond IT as a support function to ICTs as a source of sustainable competitive advantage. • Better understanding of the impact of technology on organizational structure, culture and form. • Organizational boundaries becoming blurred with rise of ICTs and virtualization of many teams and outsourcing of many functions. **IS** • Data management technologies —file management systems to DBMS to data warehouses and data marts • Increased availability of external data integrated from many different sources • Enterprise-wide systems that integrate & standardize organizational data • Better understanding of factors related to IT implementation success • Computing speed – Ability to actually solve very large and complex problems within reasonable time has increased tremendously due to (i) advances in computing machinery (hardware and software), and (ii) algorithmic improvements. **DS** • Evolution in modeling tools – For example, evolution in simulation from FORTRAN-based programming to visual interactive modeling using icons, graphical depictions of scenarios, and actual pictures of system elements. • Advances in analysis methodologies – For example variance reduction techniques, and extensive input data analysis. • Algorithmic improvements – For example, the dual simplex algorithm with steepest edge can help solve complex optimization problems much faster. • Popularity of spreadsheets has increased – due to their user friendliness, interactive nature, ability to support what-if analysis, and built-in presentation features. • Paradigm shift in industry – decision-making based on hard numbers as more and more data has become available.	Managerial acceptance of technology as being central to business success, not just a support function. Extensive availability of analysis tools Potential for extensive data availability Success in BA use by early adopters	Lack of a good understanding of factors, organizational/managerial, IT, and MS, that lead to BA success.	Widespread BA use and success in organizations.

FRAMEWORK FOR BA SUCCESS

Development

The framework for BA success has been developed over the past year. The authors began with a broad survey of existing literature in the field of business analytics in order to better understand this emerging area and the phenomena. Academic articles related to theory and practice in the area as well as trade press reports on the companies adopting and using business analytics were collected and studied. Early on in the process it was clear that the theory and academic research in the area was lagging behind practice. The cases and stories about the various companies' experiences with adopting business analytics were not described or explained adequately with any theories from the existing literature (For a list of examples of successful BA applications in businesses, please see Table 1). Initially, we derived a list of factors/variables related to BA success from the case material. Next the authors attempted a categorization of these variables, and during the process it was clear that the variables could be classified into three broad categories: managerial/organizational, information systems (IS), and decision sciences (DS).

Once it was clear to us that these factors had not been identified in the BA literature because these were traditionally studied in three separate disciplines, we returned to do a more in-depth literature review by searching for articles in each of these three disciplines. We used keywords related to the business analytics success factors. For example, we searched articles on modeling, decision-making, data integrity, decision support systems, data mining, business intelligence, etc. Though we could develop a more exhaustive list of factors that could impact BA success, it became clear that the interactions between the factors (within and among disciplines) played a critical role. We have presented this idea in a simple model in Figure 2.

To operationalize the model into a useable framework for BA success, we developed a list of factors/variables under each of the three disciplines. The framework consists of the dependent variable set (i.e., BA success factors/variables), the three sets of independent variables (i.e.,

Figure 2. Model of business analytics success in organizations

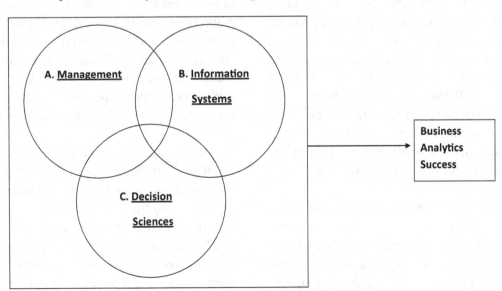

managerial/organizational, IS, and DS variables), and the relationships between the variables (i.e., relationships between independent variables, the interactions, and relationships between dependent and independent variable sets).

In the remainder of this section, we present this framework. First, we present our conceptualization of BA success (the dependent variable for our framework). Second, we present the discipline-specific factors with justification for including each of them. We then explore some interactions, both two-way and three-way, between the three sets of discipline-specific factors that have been discussed in some case studies of successful BA applications. Finally, we conclude this section by presenting the application (or implications) of the framework to managers and researchers.

Components

Motivation for any initiative that requires some expenditure (classified either as cost or investment) in an organization usually comes from survival, efficiency, or effectiveness. An initiative with the main motivation as survival usually deals with an organizational capability/need that is necessary just to stay in business. For example, an ATM network for a bank is the cost of doing business (i.e., cost of survival). Efficiency is a measure of output/input – i.e., the efficiency increases as more output is produced with the same level of input. Effectiveness, on the other hand, is a measure of market relevancy of the business. Defined differently, efficiency is "doing the thing right" and effectiveness is "doing the right thing." Success of an initiative is a measure of how well the (survival, efficiency, or effectiveness) objectives are met. Success of BA initiatives can also be measured in this way.

Methodologies/procedures for justifying initiatives vary depending on the context. Some common approaches are net present value (NPV), internal rate of return (IRR), return on investment (ROI), and total cost of ownership (TCO). On the cost side of the computations, there could be one-time or recurring costs or fixed and variable costs. On the benefits side there could be one-time and/or recurring benefits from an initiative. These concepts can also be applied to BA initiatives.

Our analysis of some successful BA applications (as listed in Table 1) yields the following success measures that have been used: customer retention rate, cost of customer acquisition, reduction in cost of operations, growth in market capitalization, revenue growth, growth in market share, and growth in profit. The first three measures are clearly efficiency measures. It is important to note that efficiency is necessary but not a sufficient condition for continued success. For example, the customer retention rate may not be good if the kind of customers a business is retaining is not value producing. Efficiency combined with effectiveness is a desirable condition always. The last three measures are clearly effectiveness measures. The fourth measure listed is most likely an effectiveness measure. Measures like the one listed are very appropriate for the BA success framework we have developed. These form the dependent variables set for our framework.

The independent variables for the framework of BA success are categorized into three disciplines: management, IS, and DS. Most of the variables in each category were either derived from the literature discussed in the previous section ("related developments" section) or from the reported case studies of successful BA applications in organizations (as listed in Table 1). As BA as a field is fairly new, academic research is sparse. Hence some variables were derived through conceptual reasoning.

Many of the factors/variables we have listed, in Tables 3A through 3C, can be assigned values on a Likert-type scale (an ordinal scale) or can be explicitly quantified. For example, factors such as level of availability of models and tools (C1 and C2) can be rated on an ordinal scale, while factors such as the amount of per capita investment in modeling infrastructure (factor C3) and

Table 3A.

	Factors/Variables—*Management*	Source
A1	Level of commitment of senior management to analytics and fact/data driven organizational decision-making—Rational Decision-making	Neo-classical economics.
A2	Level of flexibility in localized decision-making (for example, do regional managers have the ability to override system recommendations)—Organizational Structure and Culuture	Chandler 1962
A3	Level of comfort with models/modeling (mathematical, statistical, etc.) in the organization—Organizational capability	Barney 1991, Teece *et al* 1997
A4	Per capita investment in training employees to enhance their skills with models/modeling—Organizational resources	Barney 1991
A5	Level of ability of managers to implement analytical decisions	Mintzberg 1973, Cohen *et al* 1972
A6	Level of teamwork, communications and partnering skills of employees—Organizational capability	Barney 1991, Janis 1972
A7	Extent of end-user compliance with (and acceptance of) analytical decisions	
A8	Level of rewards for employees who support the analytics focus/mission and to insure data integrity (in data input for BA use)	
A9	Level of investment in tools, techniques and employees in order to build Business Analytics capability	Teece *et al* 1997
A10	Level of politics in organizational decision-making and trade-offs in individual versus group decisions	Allison & Zelikow, 1999
A11	Level of bounded rationality and satisficing mentality in organizational decisions	Cyert & March 1992, Kahnemann *et al* 1982

Table 3B.

	Factors/Variables—*Information Systems (IS)*	Source
B1	Level of availability of internal data	Davenport & Harris, 2007; Davenport *et al*, 2001; Ferguson *et al*, 2005; Vesset & McDonough, 2007
B2	Level of availability of external data	Davenport & Harris, 2007; Ferguson *et al*, 2005
B3	Level of access of internal data	Corstjens & Merrihue, 2003
B4	Level of access of external data	
B5	Level of quality of internal data	Davenport & Harris, 2007; Davenport *et al*, 2001
B6	Level of quality of external data	Davenport & Harris, 2007
B7	Level of integration of internal data (from numerous sources)	Corstjens & Merrihue, 2003
B8	Level of integration of internal & external data	
B9	Level of availability of tools for analysis	Ferguson *et al*, 2005; Kohavi *et al*, 2002
B10	Level of ease-of-use of analysis tools	
B11	Level of integration of data (internal & external) with analysis tools	Davenport & Harris, 2007
B12	Level of computing power available for BA use	
B13	Amount of per capita investment in computer hardware	

Table 3C.

	Factors/Variables—*Decision Sciences (DS)*	Source
C1	Level of availability of analytical models (such as scheduling, inventory management, forecasting, vehicle routing, site location, spatial analysis, etc.)	Labe *et al.* (1999)
C2	Level of availability of analytical problem-solving tools such as statistical software, simulation packages, decision analysis software, mathematical programming software, etc.	Labe *et al.* (1999)
C3	Amount of investment in modeling infrastructure (could be human resources investment or investment in tools/software, etc.) per capita.	Davenport (2006), Davenport & Harris, 2007
C4	Level of use of MS-Excel in the organization.	Leon *et al.* (1996), Dhebar (1993)
C5	Level of ease of use of models.	Bodily (1986), Weigel and Cao (1999)
C6	Level of ease of use of tools.	Bodily (1986), Weigel and Cao (1999)
C7	Extent of data compatibility of existing models/tools (for example, whether a mathematical programming software can read data from spreadsheets, databases, or data stored as text, and can also write output results to spreadsheets and databases).	Weigel and Cao (1999)
C8	Level of integration between different modeling tools (for example, whether a statistical sub-routine can be called upon from within a simulation package).	Weigel and Cao (1999)
C9	Given size and scale of organizational problems, what is the likelihood that models and tools will solve problems efficiently?	Bixby (2002)
C10	Percentage of employees with advanced degrees (graduate and beyond) in disciplines such as operations research, computer science, mathematics, and statistics (this is a metric of technical expertise, more specifically statistical modeling and analytical problem-solving skills, and also creativity in modeling).	Davenport, 2006, Davenport & Harris, 2007, Davenport *et al.* (2001), Cochran *et al.* (1995)

Table 3D. Interactions between factors

Example #	Organization	Table 3A factors	Table 3B factors	Table 3C factors
1	Capital One	A1	B1, B2, B8	C10
2	Netflix	A1	B1	C3
3	Progressive		B1, B2, B8, B4	C2
4	Marriott	A1, A2	B1	C1
5	Harrah's	A1, A5, A8	B1	C10
6	Proctor and Gamble	A1, A6	B2	C1, C8, C10
7	Sears, Roebuck, and Co.	A4, A5, A7, A8	B1, B2, B8, B12, B13	C1, C5, C8
8	Burlington Motor Carriers	A7, A8	B5, B6	C1
9	Merrill Lynch	A6	B7, B8	C10

percentage of employees with advanced degrees in computational areas (factor C10) can be unequivocally measured. We will discuss managerial implications of such factor definitions later in this section under implications for practitioners. It is also important to note that the objective of this work is neither to build an exhaustive list of factors that is critical to BA success, nor to study relative importance of the factors with respect to each other. (We discuss these issues later in this section under implications for researchers.) Hence the factors are not ranked in Table 3A -3C in order of importance. Let's examine each set of variables.

Management factors (or variables) that are critical to BA success in organizations are listed in Table 3A. In tracing the history of business analytics and its predecessors, the computerized modeling-based decision systems, we see that rapid rise and changes in technology have forced management to look at these tools and techniques rather differently today than they did even a decade or two ago. The most important change in management factors responsible for BA success has been this shift in managerial attitude towards evidence, data and analysis-based decision-making (A1, A10, A11). While the economics-based assumption of a rational economic agent was being challenged and replaced with the assumption of a boundedly rational economic agent who satisfices instead of optimizing every economic decision, the progress in technology was offering more sophisticated tools to allow individuals to make more rational choices in their business decisions. Once the senior managers were engaged with the technology and started to see it as central to success of their organizations, they began to hire, train and promote other managers who were computer/modeling savvy (A3, A4 and A5). The acceptance of rational decisions based on data and analysis using models began to spread across the different hierarchical levels within the organization.

Many cases mentioned how CEO or top management commitment was crucial to BA success because they drove all the other decisions within the organizations and could influence attitudes towards BA across the organization. They controlled the resources and made investments in technology, training, rewards and teamwork that were needed to set the organization up to succeed in adoption of BA (A6, A7, A8, A9). These changes added up to a change in organizational culture in some places, and there was also a corresponding shift in formal structure (A2, A8 and A10) with more decentralized decisions, better teamwork and changed organizational politics.

Information systems factors (or variables) that are critical to BA success in organizations are listed in Table 3B. The variables are in the following categories: data, tools, and computing power. Variables B1 and B2 address the availability of internal and external data for BA applications. Availability, the collection and storage or purchase of data, is the necessary condition for BA success. However, access to these data by anyone interested in using it for a BA application is more important for BA success. Access many times could be restricted by turf battles in an organization or by a lack of IT support for proper access. Variables B3 and B4 address this. In addition, it is also important to have data that is of good quality, and this can either be ensured by managing internal data collection and storage well or through quality assurance from the vendor supplying the external data. This issue is addressed by variables B5 and B6. For many BA applications it is necessary to have data from a variety of sources (both internal and external) that are well integrated. It is always likely that these integration efforts will lead to discovery of inconsistencies in data from different sources. Variables B7 and B8 address these issues. It is intuitively obvious that well integrated good quality data be available and easily accessible to end-users for their BA applications. Any one of the issues—access, availability, data quality, and/or integration—could dampen the spirit of the end-user if not addressed properly.

Mathematical and statistical tools that are used to perform analysis on the data play a critical role in the success of BA applications. For the end-user, who may not be very sophisticated in quantitative analysis or IT, the availability of the right tools for analysis and the ease-of-use of those tools play an important role in the actual use of the BA application. Variables B9 and B10 address these. In addition, for most users, it is also important to have a seamless integration of data with the tools they are using for their BA applications. Variable B11 addresses this issue.

Most BA applications use massive amounts of data and fairly sophisticated mathematical/ statistical analysis. This requires a good level of computing power available to the end-users so as to perform the analysis in a timely manner. Variables B12 and B13 address these.

Table 3C includes several DS factors that are critical to BA success. While the relevance of the factors is intuitively understood, the following discussion attempts to justify the importance of the factors relative to BA success by grounding them in literature and/or (justifying their importance as illustrated by) business applications.

Well-defined, easy-to-use, canned models exist in DS for many BA applications. From an end-user's perspective it is important to have a good set of canned models readily available in order to increase the likelihood of applying those models to potential BA situations. Similarly, it is also important to have readily available, easy-to-use tools (statistical and mathematical) available in order to increase the likelihood of use. These are captured in variables C1 and C2. Factor C3 is intuitively understood. The importance of investment in modeling and human resources (factor C3) infrastructure has been highlighted repeatedly by Davenport (2006) and Davenport and Harris (2007). Bodily (1986) reports that practitioners were adopting spreadsheets (factor C4) as a decision-making tool because (a) of their

ease-of-use (factors C5 and C6) in data input, solution and report generation, (b) spreadsheets provide a natural interface for model building (factor C1), and (c) their ability to perform what-if analysis. The pervasive use of spreadsheets in modeling and problem-solving (in varying degrees) is documented by Leon *et al.* (1996). Dhebar (1993) has identified systematic spread-sheet development as one of the ingredients of a sound quantitative analysis methodology. Ease of use of tools and models (factors C5 and C6) can also impact implementation and user compliance (factors A5 and A7 in Table 3A), both critically important to the success of BA. Such issues have been discussed by Weigel and Cao (1999) and Powell *et al.* (2002).

Complex business problems often require the integration of tools and models (factor C8). Very often business analysts/data modelers are hamstrung by the incompatibility of tools/models to data stored in specific storage formats. Seamless data communication between tools/models and data storage interfaces (factor C7) can also help facilitate the validation and implementation of complex customized models. The DS literature is replete with such examples. In one such instance, Weigel and Cao (1999) describe the integration of vehicle routing models within a GIS framework in Sears' Enhanced Home Delivery System, which allows Sears to develop efficient solutions for constrained routing problems in extremely dense street networks. Solution efficiency (in terms of optimality gap and computation time) is a function of the efficacy of available models and tools (factor C9) (Bixby, 2002) and computing horsepower (factor B13 in Table 3B). Finally, Willemain (1994, 1995), and Powell and Baker (2007) identify technical skills and craft skills as key characteristics of good modelers (in relation to factor C10). In a survey conducted by Cochran, Mackulak, and Savory (1995), 21% of the practitioners identified lack of technical background as an obstacle to in-house quantitative (in this case, simulation) analysis. In fact, Davenport *et al.* (2001) identify regression, data mining, data presentation and report preparation as some of the statistical modeling and analytical skills desirable of business analysts. The importance of factor C10 is clearly established.

Interactions Between Components

As stated earlier, our model is based on the premise that BA success hails from distinctive competencies in three broad business disciplines—management, IS, and decision sciences, and also as a result of the interaction between the disciplines. In the following discussion, we illustrate the use of IS in conjunction with decision-making tools and techniques, and aided by analytics-friendly management policies in organizations that have achieved a high level of BA success. More specifically we identify specific management, IS, and DS variables (listed earlier in Tables 3A, 3B, and 3C) and also study interactions between those variables in different organizational contexts. The purpose is to describe and validate our model using exemplars of several successful analytically competitive organizations. Note that while the following discussion pertains to the exemplars tabulated earlier in Table 1, we sometimes supplement our discussion with new examples.

One key factor for BA success (identified in Table 3A) is the level of commitment of senior management to analytics and fact/data-driven organizational decision-making (item A1 in Table 3A). Capital One and Netflix (examples 1 and 2, respectively, in Table 1) are classic examples where the founder(s) had the vision to be analytically driven when the company was a startup. Capital One annually collects data of millions of customers pertaining to spending rates, timely installment payments, credit scores, and various other parameters, and integrates (item B8 in Table 3B) these internal data (item B1 in Table 3B) with external data (item B2 in Table 3B) pertaining to conditions of general economic prosperity. Using these disparate data from various sources,

Capital One uses analytical models to calculate customers' willingness to repay loans/balances, maximize customer retention, and minimize the cost of acquiring a new account. The organization also actively recruits analysts who possess a high level of analytical aptitude and the ability to use software applications proficiently (item C10 in Table 3C). This example clearly highlights several discipline-specific variables of consequence to Capital One and also interactions between all three disciplines that lead to BA success.

The thrust in analytics at Netflix (example 2 in Table 1) comes from its founder (item A1 in Table 3A). The main objective of analytics at Netflix is to predict customer movie preferences. To that end, Netflix collects data about customers' rental history and film ratings (item B1 in Table 3B) and has created an overall IS environment with analytics in mind. Moreover Netflix recruits mathematicians with programming experience (item C3 in Table 3C) to write code and devise algorithms to define clusters of movies and then connect customer preference (data) with the movie clusters (based upon customer data collected).

Progressive (example 3 in Table 1) is a pioneer in the insurance industry in providing policies at competitive rates to "high-risk" customers. Progressive's internal customer data (item B1 in Table 3B) captures a wide range of attributes such as customer's age, level of education, credit scores, participation in high-risk activities (such as skydiving) and is integrated (item B8 in Table 3B) with widely available insurance industry external data (item B2 in Table 3B). It is pertinent to note here that pharmaceuticals and other such regulated industries are often hamstrung by the lack of availability and sometimes access to external industry data (item B4 in Table 3B). Progressive then employs regression analysis (item C2 in Table 3C) to determine customers with low credit scores who might actually be risk worthy and also identify those customer attributes that are better predictors of risk than other attributes. High-risk customers are a constituency that is typically neglected by

Progressive's competitors and hence provides competitive advantage. While this example illustrates the IS and DS factors/variables which are key to Progressive, and also illustrates their interaction, it is pertinent that senior management at Progressive chose analytics as a strategic focus (variable A1 in table 3A).

An overall culture of analytics perpetrates the entire organization at Marriott (example 4 in Table 1) comprising its employees, regional property managers, vendors, and senior management (item A1 in Table 3A). The focus is on fact-based decision-making, which is embedded in the corporate culture since Marriott's inception. The concept of revenue management, more specifically the revenue opportunity model (item C1 in Table 3C), originated in the hotel part of Marriott's business and now spans across its restaurants, catering services, and conference facilities. Flexibility in decision-making is a key at Marriott, where regional property managers have the ability to override system recommendations to account for localized events (item A2 in Table 3A). Internal customer data consists of attributes ranging from the type of service a particular customer prefers to the frequency of visits. Using this data (item B1 in Table 3B), promotions are designed and marketed to online and traditional travel agencies and major corporate customers to help them make informed travel management decisions. While this clearly exemplifies superior management practices at Marriott, the role played by IS and DS towards BA success at Marriott is also immense.

At Harrah's (example 5 in Table 1), CEO Gary Loveman brought with him a customer analytics drive (like Netflix and Capital One) which was broadly distributed but centrally driven (item A1 in Table 3A). Harrah's, like Marriott, focused on employing analytics at increasing customer loyalty, customer service, pricing, and promotions. The CEO made sure that individual casino property managers implemented (item A5 in Table 3A) the company's marketing and customer service programs in a uniform fashion. However

unlike Marriott, hotel managers are not allowed to override automated analytical decisions since evidence-based decisions outperform those made by individuals. Harrah's also introduced a novel method to collect customer behavior data via loyalty cards which captured gaming preferences, spending rates, etc. all collected in real time. These internal data (item B1 in Table 3B) were extensively used for a variety of purposes, for example to locate slot machines and guide customers to slower parts of the casino with added incentives during peak business hours. The organizational culture underwent a paradigm shift from paternalism and tenure to one based upon meticulous numbers-driven performance evaluation and customer service (item A8 in Table 3A). Notice that new management impacted overall organizational culture at Harrah's. However, a new culture of analytics, while necessary, was not sufficient. To that end, the CEO hired a group of statistical experts (item C10 in Table 3C) who designed and implemented quantitatively grounded loyalty programs and marketing campaigns and hence played a significant role at Harrah's in achieving BA excellence.

At Proctor and Gamble (P&G, example 6 in Table 1), the primary thrust for analysis comes from two vice-chairpersons (item A1 in Table 3A). P&G uses analytical software and databases to intensively analyze sales data obtained from external sources such as ACNielsen (item B2 in Table 3B) and accordingly designs promotions for its customers. Dozens of analytical professionals (items C10 in Table 3C) support various organizational functions such as operations, supply chain management, and marketing, and report directly to the CIO. During the mid-90s, P&G streamlined its North American product sourcing and distribution systems by successfully blending operations research models and techniques (item C1 in Table 3C) within a GIS framework (item C8 in Table 3C). The importance of teamwork (item A6 in Table 3A) vis-à-vis successful BA initiatives is also highlighted in this application in which over 500 P&G employees worked in approximately 30 teams to complete the supply-chain restructuring.

The vehicle routing and scheduling system developed by Sears, Roebuck and Company (example 7 in Table 1) is a perfect example for our model where an optimal marriage between IS, DS, and management resulted in a tremendously successful BA application. To develop the system, internal customer data such as location of customers, type of service required, products to be delivered, delivery time windows, etc. (item B1 in Table 3B) available from mainframe based databases was integrated (item B8 in Table 3B) with commercially available external data such as street networks, congestion, etc. (items B2 in Table 3B) within a geographical information systems (GIS) framework. The problem was modeled as a vehicle routing problem with time windows (item C1 in Table 3C) within a GIS framework (to accurately estimate travel distances) thereby highlighting the integration of modeling tools and software (item C8 in Table 3C). Sears' investment in hardware (item B13 in Table 3B) is apparent as the home delivery and routing systems developed are UNIX-based and operate on either a central server or distributed workstations. Their investment in developing computing horsepower (item B12 in Table 3B) is also apparent; vehicle routing problem instances with approximately two million street network arcs could be solved in less than 20 minutes of computing time. All the IS and DS investments would have proven futile if Sears employees were not trained (item A4 in Table 3A) by an outside firm to overcome difficulties associated with (1) shifting from text-driven terminals to mouse-based GUIs, a fundamental IT paradigm shift, and also (2) to overcome unfamiliarity problems with the various model input parameters (item C5 in Table 3C). Managers in charge of regional routing offices encountered implementation difficulties as technicians and truck drivers resented the online tracking by the systems. However the problem was overcome as field managers gained

more confidence in the system and were able to communicate its benefits to truck drivers (end users in this case) and encouraged them to follow the routes the automated systems suggested (items A5, A7, A8 in table 3A).

On a related note, but in a different context, Burlington Motor Carriers encountered user compliance (item A7 in Table 3A) problems while assigning drivers to its fleet of 1200 trucks (Powell, Marar, Gelfand, and Bowers, 2002). Fleet planners who were used to doing things in a different way complained vaguely about difficulties encountered in using the assignment model. To overcome these behavioral hazards, management implemented a system that monitored individual user compliance, which was then correlated with monthly bonuses (item A8 in Table 3A). As a result, user compliance rose by 20% over a five-month period. However the organization was still plagued by problems of imperfect, sometimes incomplete, data - clearly data quality issues (items B5 and B6 in Table 3B), and also end-user compliance issues (item A7 in Table 3A) where drivers often deviated from routes suggested by planners, costing Burlington several thousand dollars in recruiting and training new drivers.

Interestingly, some of the key traits of the management science group at Merrill Lynch are technical expertise (item C10 in Table 3C), objectivity, communication skills, proactivity, teamwork (item A6 in Table 3A), integration of various data (items B7 and B8 in Table 3B), data integrity, careful attention to implementation issues (item A5 in Table 3A), and focus on goals of the firm rather than goals of the department. (Labe *et al*, 1999). Notice that all of these are crucial and relevant for BA success in organizations. Through the examples described earlier, we have attempted to highlight key management, IS and DS factors/variables and explicitly identify interactions between those factors/variables (and disciplines themselves) that have led to BA success in a cross-section of very large organizations. It is pertinent to note that if organizations choose to outsource certain BA specific tasks such as modeling, IT infrastructure development and support, advanced communication technologies can still ensure BA success. In a later section of this chapter, we discuss virtualization and as a special case BA implementation in virtualized settings.

In summary, the discipline-specific (management, IS, and DS) variables/factors that interacted in each of the previous examples to ensure BA success have been tabulated in Table 3D. Admittedly the examples did not illustrate the relevance of each and every factor/variable listed in Tables 3A, 3B, and 3C (we have justified each variable in an earlier section). Also the objective of this chapter is not to construct an exhaustive set of variables/factors that lead to BA success and hence that particular task is outlined as a future research direction. Moreover, it is pertinent to observe here that there are too many possible interactions, two-way as well as three-way, between the three sets of factors (listed in Tables 3A, 3B, 3C). Table 3D tabulates only a sample of these interactions, and the previous discussion substantiates them with the aid of concrete examples found in a variety of industrial settings. Further, we note that the management, IS, DS variables/factors, and interactions between those discipline-specific factors which lead to BA success are purely contextual, almost industry specific. The interactions that cause casinos to attract more customers in gaming may not necessarily be identical to the interactions that help major retailers deliver products/services to customers more efficiently. Finally we recognize that BA success is clearly a function of the strength of the discipline-specific factors and their interactions. This work has not attempted to evaluate the strength of the various factors and their interactions vis-à-vis BA success.

Framework Use: Practice

In the previous discussion, we described the conceptualization and development of the BA

success framework. Discipline-specific factors were tabulated, and factor interactions were illustrated using exemplars from the literature. In this section, we outline the procedure to use the framework in practice and also discuss implications for researchers.

The framework presented will be useful to practicing managers to evaluate whether a new BA application contemplated by their organization is likely to succeed and/or to assess what needs to be done by the organization to make the initiative succeed. To illustrate the usage of our framework, let us consider a Sears-like scenario where a business manager of a major retailer is attempting to streamline product/service delivery and technician dispatching and routing functions. Let us assume that the Sears-specific success factors (listed in Table 3D) apply in this case, too. The business manager can assign ratings to all these factors on an ordinal scale. For example, factors such as A4 and A5 (management), B1 and B2 (IS), and C1 and C8 (DS) are assigned the highest ratings, factors such as A7 (management), B8, and B13 (IS), and C8 (DS) are assigned medium ratings, and the remaining factors A8 and B12 are assigned low ratings. Such a scenario will encourage a practitioner to invest in BA to meet the specified objective. It also helps to highlight the weaker factors, and corrective strengthening measures can be initiated to maximize chances of BA success.

Admittedly, such a paradigm to use the BA success framework is simplistic. Also, developing consistent ordinal scales for all factors is a challenging task. Finally, one immediate drawback of this approach is the fact that all factors are considered equally important. To that end, in order to refine usage of the framework, practitioners can also assign weights to the factors which are organizationally or contextually more important. This can facilitate the development of a factor rating approach, a technique that is widely used in personal as well as professional decision-making. Its application in a BA context is outlined as follows:

1. Determine which management, IS, and DS factors are relevant.
2. Assign a weight to each factor which indicates its relative importance. Whether to assign weights on a discipline-specific basis or irrespective of the discipline a factor belongs to is an open-ended question.
3. Decide a common ordinal scale for all factors (e.g. 0 to 100) and set a minimum acceptable threshold score for each factor, if necessary.
4. Multiply each factor's weight by its score and sum the results to develop a composite score.
5. If the composite score is above a threshold (to be decided organizationally), the chances of BA initiative success are maximized, ceteris paribus.

Clearly both approaches described for evaluating potential for BA success are somewhat simplistic. While the second approach refines the first one, several issues such as assigning weights to factors and developing thresholds (for individual factors and also a composite threshold) are distinctly tricky. Some sensitivity analysis can be performed to identify factors that are clearly critical to BA success.

Framework Use: Research

The conceptual framework of BA success developed in this work is based on the premise that BA success results not only from the individual factors but also from the interactions between three broad disciplines – management, IS, and DS. More specifically, BA success results due to the interactions between several discipline-specific factors which were earlier listed in Tables 3A, 3B, and 3C. The concept of BA success has not been formally defined until now, and the framework

presented in this chapter is a novel beginner in that regard. Researchers can further consolidate several aspects of the framework, and some are outlined below.

1. The factors in the tables are illustrative in nature; as a result each discipline-specific table can be populated further. The factors listed are either conceptual or their genesis lies in the literature (case examples from industry). Today BA is a growing phenomenon that is increasingly used in a variety of industrial sectors including retail, healthcare, financial institutions, manufacturing, petroleum, and also by government at various levels for several purposes, including homeland security. A thorough review of the literature for applications in each of these areas will yield several more discipline-specific factors that will consolidate the factor tables, and perhaps help to identify factors that are industry- or domain-specific.
2. Most of the factors listed in the tables are universal in relation to BA success. For example, senior management commitment, availability, access, and quality of internal data, and investment in quantitatively proficient analysts are all factors that are critical to BA success irrespective of industry sector, for-profit or government, and any such criterion. However, factors such as availability and perhaps access to external data (for highly regulated industries such as pharmaceutical) and level of organizational politics are arguably industry-specific. It would be worthwhile to categorize the management, IS, and DS discipline-specific factors as either universal or industry-specific. This will certainly aid researchers and practitioners understand the relevance of the factors more in depth. Moreover it can be conjectured that small and medium-sized enterprises (SMEs) are often constrained in relation to several of the factors already listed, for example ac-

cess to industry-wide external data. Hence classifying the factors with respect to size of organizations is another interesting avenue for future research.

3. As mentioned earlier, the factors listed in the tables have not been ranked in importance. It can be argued that senior management buy-in would perhaps be one of the most important management-specific factors, while employing analysts with advanced computational proficiency would be a key DS factor. Ranking the factors within disciplines (and then perhaps across disciplines) would be valuable. This will help researchers and practitioners alike understand the importance of specific factors and aid in predicting the chances of success of BA initiatives.

4. As the factor tables are consolidated, the scope of interactions increases polynomially. Previous discussion in this section (summarized in Table 3D) has highlighted several such interactions in successful BA applications. Clearly the interactions identified in the exemplars are by no means exhaustive, and more such interactions can be identified by thorough literature reviews and by conducting industry surveys.

5. Analogous to ranking the individual factors, studying the strength of factor interactions is also valuable. For example, a review of the interactions in Table 3D reveals that interaction between factor A1 (senior management commitment) and factors B1 and B2 (availability of internal and external data) is commonly reported to have contributed to BA success. Such an interaction can hence be defined as a strong interaction. Identifying such interactions and developing an allied framework to measure the strength of the interactions (followed by rank ordering them) will supplement the existing literature

and would also be meaningful to managers on the threshold of BA initiatives.

We have attempted to outline possible research implications of this work. Clearly research into BA issues such as understanding of BA success – the contributing factors and their interactions is still at a nascent stage, and our framework can be considered part of a growing body of literature. In the following section, we apply our framework to a special case—that of virtual organizations—and discuss how the framework can be adapted for virtual organizing.

VIRTUAL ORGANIZING: APPLICATION OF FRAMEWORK

Continued developments in information and communication technologies (ICT) have made it possible to distribute organizational processes/work spatially and temporally. This phenomenon is often called virtual organizing, and the organizations that use this extensively are called virtual organizations. We witness this through the revolution of the global marketplace for outsourcing of information and knowledge work (Friedman, 2007). One such process or knowledge work that can be distributed is organizational/managerial decision-making. Decision-making using analytics, i.e., business analytics, is by extension a good candidate for virtual organizing.

The costs and benefits of outsourcing/offshoring knowledge work also apply to virtualizing BA work in organizations. The opportunities and challenges are also similar. In this section we will first present a discussion on virtual organizing (and virtual organizations) and a discussion of the relationship between virtual organizing and BA. We will then discuss how the framework for BA success (presented in the previous section) can be applied to virtual BA work.

Emerging Organizations and Virtualization

Extensive availability of reasonably cost-efficient ICT to facilitate collaboration between entities separated spatially and temporally has made it possible for organizations or organizational work/ processes to become somewhat virtual. Though virtualization was possible before the widespread availability of the Internet platform, it became less expensive and easier to develop and use since the development of the World Wide Web.

Research on the move towards this virtualization in organizations has been discussed under virtual organizations (Bleecker, 1994; Chesbrough & Teece, 1996; Coyle & Schnarr, 1995; Davidow & Malone, 1992; Dutton, 1999; Fulk & DeSanctis, 1995; Goldman, Nagel, & Preiss, 1995; Hedberg, Dahlgren, Hansson, & Olve, 1997) as a form of organizational structure or under virtual organizing (Negroponte, 1995; Quinn, Anderson, & Finkelstein, 1996; Venkataraman & Henderson, 1998) as an organizational characteristic. However, the essence of virtualization appears to be similar between the two views.

According to DeSanctis and Monge (1999), virtualization in organizations implies the following: "(a) highly dynamic processes, (b) contractual relationships among entities, (c) edgeless, permeable boundaries, and (d) reconfigurable structures." A few of the other researchers who have contributed to the development of the concept of virtual organizations are Galbraith (1995), who presented the concept of "company without walls;" Clancy (1994) and Barner (1996), who discussed the concept of "employees who are physically dispersed from one another;" Coyle and Schnarr (1995), who discussed "organizations replete with external ties;" Grenier and Metes (1995) and Lipnack and Stamps (1997), who described virtual organizations consisting of "teams that are assembled and disassembled according to need;" and Bleecker (1994), Grenier and Metes (1995), and Hedberg *et al* (1997), who discussed

the concept of "people working together, regardless of location or who owns them." .

The degree of virtualization varies among organizations depending on their needs. For example, Cisco has developed a virtual relationship with its suppliers that results in their suppliers shipping 70% of the customers' orders directly without Cisco receiving them at their locations. What aspects of an organization's processes are virtualized depend on an organization's need. In the case of Cisco, manufacturing and shipping are highly virtualized and R&D is not as virtualized. The degree of virtualization of any organization is also dynamic. For example, Amazon.com had a vision to be a total virtual organization, i.e., an organization that does not take possession of any of the items it sells. Through the use of ICT, Amazon.com was designed to be an intermediary between the buyers and sellers. However, as the business slowly took shape it became clear that 100% virtualization will not work and Amazon. com had to become partly non-virtual by building warehouses and taking possessions of goods. On the other hand, half.com (now a part of eBay) started out as 100 percent virtual and has stayed that way. Another example of a company that is 100 percent virtual is threadless.com.

Virtualization in organizations opens up some opportunities and also results in some challenges as they pertain to BA. The availability of somewhat inexpensive global talent leads to better success in BA analytics. It is also possible to divide BA work in organizations to suit local conditions and still derive the benefits of BA. On the other hand the challenges posed through the use of communication technologies and differences in cultures of virtual participants in BA work could pose significant challenges to BA success in organizations.

Early work related to virtualization of organizational work and BA has focused on decision-making and problem-solving through the use of ICT, the group decision support systems (GDSS) (Armstrong, 1994; Chidambaram & Tung, 2005;

DeSanctis & Gallupe, 1987; Fjermestad & Hiltz, 1998; Hiltz, Johnson, & Turoff, 1986; Rao & Jarvenpaa, 1991). The work has focused on the role of technologies, task characteristics, and group dynamics/behavior on the success of problem-solving in a virtualized context.

Though the role of appropriate ICT in the success of virtualized BA work is important, we contend that success is also dependent on choosing the right aspects of BA work to virtualize, including the consideration of different phases of problem-solving (see Simon, 1977), the consideration of knowledge transfer needs between members separated by space and time, and on the nature of the BA work that is virtualized (whether it is autonomous where there is very little need for dynamic interactions between members or systemic where dynamic interactions are absolutely necessary).

As BA as a concept is fairly recent, very little research exists in the area. However, there is some research related to the issues we have identified for success of virtualized BA work. Chesbrough and Teece (1996) report that (1) virtualization and incentive to take risks are positively related, (2) virtualization and the ability to settle conflicts and coordinate activities are negatively related, and (3) BA work that can be autonomous is more likely to succeed in a virtualized context. In addition, they also point out the need to consider the type of knowledge transfer (tacit or explicit) needed for success of virtualized BA work. Majchrzak, Malhotra, and John (2005) report that lack of face-to-face cues creates challenges in developing collaborative know-how and that these challenges can be overcome by communicating not just content, but also context. Schmidt, Montoya-Weiss, and Massey (2001) report from their research that virtual teams are the most effective compared to other types of teams in making decisions.

Technological factors make it possible for organizations to virtualize BA work. The availability of global talent pools to better address certain aspects of BA work makes it more beneficial for

organizations to virtualize the work. However, much more research is necessary to develop a better understanding of the success of virtualized BA work.

Application of the Framework to Virtual BA Work

The framework for BA success presented has three sets of independent variables (one set each in management, IS, and DS disciplines) and a set of dependent variables (i.e., measures of BA success – these would usually be context specific for any organization/application). When we apply this framework to virtual settings it is very important to redefine these sets to suit the virtual context. It is possible some of the variables in the four sets could be the same for the new context and some could be different (some eliminated and some added). For example, the typical dependent variable set (as derived from successful BA applications and presented in the previous section) could be customer retention rate, reduction in cost of operations, revenue growth, growth in market share, etc. In a virtual BA setting an additional success measure could be how well organizational intellectual capital has been utilized. In independent variable sets, it is possible that we may need to add the following variables: extent of team members' comfort in working across spatial and temporal boundaries (an addition to variables listed in Table 3A), level of access of internal/external data across spatial and temporal boundaries (variables B1 and B2 modified from Table 3B set or an addition to the existing set), level of availability of analytical models (variable C1 in table 3C) that could be modified to reflect an added set of dimensions, temporal and spatial, etc.

Some of the BA work that could be straightforward in a one-location setting could pose a challenge for virtualized settings. Some aspects of the work such as problem definition and preliminary model building would involve considerable interactions between team members, and some activities such as model validation and solving may need lot less interactions. Thus it is important for organizations considering virtual BA work to break down the work to smaller parts and identify the best candidates for distributed work.

The following process (modified from the previous section titled "Framework Use: Practice") could be used by organizations considering virtual BA work:

1. Identify which variables are relevant as success measures for the application (i.e., identify and specify the dependent variable set).
2. Identify which variables from Tables 3A – 3C are relevant to the virtual BA context, make any changes to the specification of variables, and add any new variables to address the changed context (i.e., identify and specify independent variable set).
3. Assign weights in both sets of variables to indicate their importance to the context.
4. Identify variable interactions (within and among discipline-specific sets) that are believed to have a significant impact on the dependent variables set (i.e., success measures).
5. Assign weights to the interactions identified in the previous set.
6. Assign values to the variable sets (on an ordinal scale).
7. Use a composite score approach or judgment in deciding whether the BA application is likely to succeed in the virtual context.

The process is intentionally simplistic as this is the first attempt at using the new framework developed. As more research validating the framework becomes available and more and more organizations use this approach it is likely that more sophisticated processes for evaluating success will emerge.

CONCLUSION

This chapter presents a framework for business analytics success. BA is a novel data-driven quantitative analysis-based capability available to organizations. It is being increasingly used in diverse industry sectors such as retail, insurance, telecommunications, healthcare, financial services, sports and entertainment, manufacturing, and several others. Anecdotal evidence reported in the literature points to cost savings of millions of dollars and increased revenues and profits. Academic research in BA is lagging behind practice and is limited. It is mostly built on the basis of reports on successful business applications in the business and trade press. The limited literature, practitioner accounts, and documentation of BA usage have simply alluded to the fact that data-fueled developments in information systems, large scale quantitative analysis, and senior management buy-in have acted as catalysts in successful BA applications in organizations. However, what constitutes BA success is not very well documented and what specific factors result in BA success are not well laid out. The interactions between these factors, if any, are mostly not considered. The framework for BA success that is presented in this chapter is the first attempt, to our knowledge, to address this gap in BA research.

We consolidate the existing knowledge from reports of BA success in different applications. We review BA-related academic literature that discusses and explains what BA is and how companies are using it to become successful. We integrate the two aspects, accounts of practitioner-based experiences and the current academic thinking to develop a comprehensive framework. This framework offers a definition of BA success, identifies the various factors that have led to BA success in different situations. This chapter goes further to ground this framework in academic theoretical traditions by classifying and grounding these BA success factors under the academic literatures where these have been studied previously. This theoretical grounding reveals how practice has evolved with no regard to our disciplinary boundaries, and how managers have used whatever it takes to achieve business success. The chapter thus makes a call for inter-disciplinary research in the area of BA success. We believe that one of the novelties of this research is its inter-disciplinary nature.

The framework developed proposes that BA success comes from an optimal blend of factors in three key business disciplines – management, information systems (IS), and decision sciences (DS). We consider both the technological and organizational factors which contribute to and impact BA success. Three tables with details of factors by each of the three disciplines have been explicitly identified (see tables 3A, B and C for management, DS and IS-related factors for BA success). We take this one step further by making the first attempt to define these factors as measurable variables. By using the existing cases of successful BA applications, we demonstrate how BA success results from careful consideration of individual variables and also the critical interactions between these variables. The interactions between the various factors are also explicitly spelled out to the extent that we could make these connections based on the examples of BA success that we analyzed.

In addition to the list of factors important for BA success and their interactions, we lay out a roadmap for managers on how to use this framework to guide their own efforts at implementing BA in their organizations. While the press offers examples of tremendous savings and competitive advantages to be gained from implementing BA in organizations, urging managers to jump on this bandwagon, we actually take a more reasoned approach. We lay out a way to help managers decide if adopting BA is the right solution for their organization or not. In certain business situations, the more appropriate tools may be pure decision models or organizational interventions. BA is

not a solution to all problems but is suitable for a subset of specific situations characterized by both organizational and analytical complexity. Once managers decide to adopt BA, they can also use this chapter as a starting point to review all the factors to be considered for BA success and the interactions between these factors.

For the academics interested in this area, we draw out the implications of this work. Starting with a call for more inter-disciplinary research, we also have made a call for other researchers to build on this framework further. Since this is the first comprehensive attempt to consolidate the state-of-the-art research and practice in this emerging area, we feel that other researchers have an opportunity to develop further, refine, and validate the framework that has been presented here.

The final and perhaps the most crucial contribution of this chapter is to show both academics and managers how to use this framework by discussing in detail one specific application. Virtual organizations are becoming increasingly common. Virtualization offers contemporary challenges for both managers and researchers, and in discussing how to apply our BA success framework in this context, we demonstrate the utility of this work. By walking through an in-depth application in a virtually organized context, a relatively novel phenomenon that allows organizations to distribute work spatially and temporally, we show how BA works in a manner that is most likely to yield successful outcomes.

While BA applications are proliferating, BA as a research domain is sparsely populated. This work can hence be considered to be one of the first attempts at truly understanding BA success. Practitioner implications of such understanding followed by successful employment and use of BA can be potentially enormous. Clearly a lot more can be achieved given the nascent stage of BA research. The framework can be further consolidated by identifying newer factors, understanding newer interactions, and by classifying the factors so that organizations in various industry domains can explore the use of BA and derive the most value (and perhaps develop competitive advantage) through its extensive adoption and usage.

REFERENCES

Allison, G. T. & Zelikow, P. (1999) *Essence of decision: Explaining the Cuban missile crisis.* New York, NY: Addison-Wesley Longman.

Apte, C., Liu, B., Pednault, E. P. D., & Smyth. P. (2002). Business applications of data mining. *Communications of the ACM*, 45(8): 49-53.

Armstrong, M. P. (1994). Requirements for the development of GIS-based group decision support systems. *Journal of the American Society for Information Science.* 45(9), 669-677.

Ayers, I. (2007). *Super Crunchers.* New York: Bantam Books.

Bachani, J. (2005). Building decision quality in organizations. *California Journal of Operations Management*, 3 (1), 12-16.

Barner, R. (1996). The new millennium workplace: Seven changes that will challenge managers and workers. *The Futurist*, 30, 14-18.

Barney, J. B. (1991). Firm resources and sustained competitive advantage, *Journal of Management*, 17, 99-120.

Bixby, R. E. (2002). Solving real-world linear programs: A decade and more of progress. *Operations Research*, 50(1), 3-15.

Bleecker, S.E. (1994). The virtual organization. *The Futurist*, 28(2), 9-14.

Bodily, S. (1986). Spreadsheet modeling as a stepping stone. *Interfaces*, 16(5), 34-52.

Camm, J. D., Chorman, T. E., Dill, F. A., Evans, J. R., Sweeney, D. & Wegryn, G. W. (1997). Blending OR/MS, judgment, and GIS: Restructuring P&G's supply chain. *Interfaces*, 27(1), 128-142.

Chandler, A. D. (1962). *Strategy and structure: Chapters in the history of the industrial enterprise.* Cambridge, MA: MIT Press.

Chesbrough, H. W. & Teece, D. J. (1996) When is virtual virtuous? *Harvard Business Review.* January-February, 65-71.

Chidambaram, L. & Tung, L. L. (2005). Is out of sight, out of mind? An empirical study of social loafing in technology-supported groups. *Information Systems Research*, 16(2), 149-168.

Clancy, T. (1994). The latest word from thoughtful executives - the virtual corporation, telecommuting and the concept of team. *Academy of Management Executive*, 8(2), 8-10.

Cochran, J. K., Mackulak, G. T., & Savory, P. A. (1995). Simulation project characteristics in industrial settings. *Interfaces*, 25(4), 104-113.

Cohen, M. D., March, J. G., & Olsen, J. P. (1972). A garbage can model of organizational choice. *Administrative Science Quarterly.* 17(1), 1-25.

Corstjens, M., & Merrihue, J. (2003). Optimal marketing. *Harvard Business Review*, October, 114-121.

Coyle, J. & Schnarr, N. (1995). The soft-side challenges of the "virtual corporation." *Human Resource Planning*, 18, 41-42.

Cyert, R. M. & March, J. G. (1992). *A behavioural theory of the firm.* Cambridge, MA: Blackwell.

Davenport, T., Harris, J., De Long, D., & Jacobson, A. (2001). Data to knowledge to results: Building an analytic capability. *California Management Review*, 43(2), 117-138.

Davenport, T. (2006). Competing on Analytics. *Harvard Business Review*, 84(1), 99-107.

Davenport, T. & Harris, J. (2007). *Competing on Analytics.* Boston, MA: Harvard Business School Press.

Davidow, W. H., & Malone, M. S. (1992). *The virtual corporation*. New York, NY: Harper Business.

DeSanctis, G. & Gallupe, R. B. (1987). A foundation for the study of group decision support systems. *Management Science*, 33(5), 589-609.

DeSanctis, G. & Monge, P. (1999). Communication processes for virtual organizations. *Organization Science*, 10(6), 693-703.

Dhebar, A. (1993). Managing the quality of quantitative analysis. *MIT Sloan Management Review*, Winter, 69-75.

Dutton, W.H. (1999). The *virtual organization: Tele-access in business and industry*. In G. DeSanctis and J. Fulk (Eds), Shaping organizational form: Communication, connection, and community. Newbury Park, CA: Sage.

Evans, J. R. (1991). Creativity in OR/MS: Creative thinking, a basis for OR/MS problem solving. *Interfaces*, 21(5), 12-15.

Evans, J. R. (1992). Creativity in OR/MS: Improving problem solving through creative thinking. *Interfaces*, 22(2), 87-91.

Evans, J. R. (1993a). Creativity in OR/MS: The multiple dimensions of creativity. *Interfaces*, 23(2), 80-83.

Evans, J. R. (1993b). Creativity in OR/MS: Overcoming barriers to creativity. *Interfaces*, 23(6), 101-106.

Fayyad, U. & Uthurusamy, R. (2002). Evolving data mining into solutions for insights. *Communications of the ACM*, 45(8), 28-31.

Ferguson, G., Mathur, S., & Shah, B. (2005). Evolving from information to insight. *MIT Sloan Management Review*, Winter, 51-58.

Fjermestad, J. & Hiltz, S. T. (1998). An assessment of group decision support systems experimental research: Methodology and results. *Journal of Management Information Systems*, 15(3), 7-149.

Friedman, T. (2007). *The world is flat*. New York: Farrar, Straus and Giroux.

Fulk, J. & DeSanctis, G. (1995). Electronic communication and changing organizational forms. *Organization Science*, 6(4), 337-349.

Galbraith, J.R. (1995). *Designing organizations*. San Francisco, CA: Jossey-Bass.

Goldman, S. L., Nagel, R. N, & Preiss, K. (1995). *Agile competitors and virtual organizations: strategies for enriching the customer*. New York, NY: Van Nostrand Reinhold.

Grenier, R. & Metes, G. (1995). *Going virtual: Moving your organization into the 21st century*. New Jersey, NJ: Prentice Hall.

Hedberg, B., Dahlgren, G., Hansson, J. & Olve, N-G. (1997). *Virtual organizations and beyond: Discover imaginary systems*. New York, NY: Wiley.

Henderson, J. C. & Nutt, P. (1980). The influence of decision style on decision making behavior. *Management Science*, (26(4), 371-386.

Hillier, F. S. & Lieberman, G. J. (2005). *Introduction to Operations Research*. New York, NY: McGraw Hill.

Hiltz, S. R., Johnson, K., & Turoff, M. (1986). Experiments in group decision-making: Communication process and outcome in face-to-face versus computerized conferences. *Human Communication Research*, 13(2), 225-252.

Hwarng, H. B. (2001). A modern simulation course for business students. *Interfaces*, 31(3), 66-75.

Ittner, C. D. & Larcker, D. F. (2003). Coming up short. *Harvard Business Review*. November, 88-95.

Janis, I. L. (1972). *Victims of groupthink: a psychological study of foreign-policy decisions and fiascoes*. Boston, MA: Houghton Mifflin.

Jessup, L. & Valacich, J. (2007). *Information systems today.* Upper Saddle River, New Jersey: Prentice-Hall.

Kahneman, D., Slovic, P. & Tversky, A. (1982). *Judgment under uncertainty: Heuristics and biases.* Cambridge, MA: Cambridge University Press.

Kepner, C. & Tregoe, B. (1965). *The rational manager.* New York, NY: McGraw-Hill.

Kohavi, R., Rothleder, N., & Simoudis, E. (2002). Emerging trends in business analytics. *Communications of the ACM,* 45(8), 45-48.

Labe, R., Nigam, R., & Spence, S. (1999). Management science at Merrill Lynch Private Client Group. *Interfaces,* 29(2), 1-14.

Lawrence, P. R. & Lorsch, J. (1967). *Organization and Environment.* Cambridge, MA: Harvard University Press.

Leon, L., Przasnyski, Z., & Seal, K. C. (1996). Spreadsheets and OR/MS models: An end-user perspective. *Interfaces,* 26(2), 92-104.

Lipnack, J. & Stamps, J. (1997). *Virtual teams: Reaching across space, time and organizations with technology.* New York, NY: John Wiley.

Luecke, R. (2006). Make better decisions. *Harvard Management Update,* 11(4), 3-5.

Majchrzak, A., Malhotra, A. & John, R. (2005). Perceived individual collaboration know-how development through information technology-enabled contextualization: Evidence from distributed teams. *Information Systems Research,* 16(1), 9-27.

Mintzberg, H. (1973). *The nature of managerial work.* Englewood Cliffs, NJ: Prentice-Hall.

Mintzberg, H., Raisinghani, D. & Theoret, A. (1976). The structure of "unstructured" decision processes. *Administrative Science Quarterly,* 21, 246-275.

Nance, R. E., & Sargent, R. G. (2002). Perspectives on the evolution of simulation. *Operations Research,* 50(1), 161-172.

Negash, S. & Gray, P. (2003). Business intelligence. In Proceedings of *Ninth Americas Conference on Information Systems.*

Negroponte, N. (1995). *Being digital.* New York, NY: Knopf.

Powell, S. G., & Baker, K. R. (2007). *Management science: The art of modeling with spreadsheets.* New York, NY: Wiley.

Powell, W. B., Marar, A., Gelfand, J., & Bowers, S. (2002). Implementing real-time optimization models: A case application from the motor carrier industry. *Operations Research,* 50(4), 571-581.

Power, D. J. (2001). Supporting Decision-Makers: An Expanded Framework, In A. Harriger (Ed.), *Informing Science Conference, Krakow, Poland,* 431-436.

Power, D. J. (2002). *Decision Support Systems: Concepts and resources for managers.* Westport, CT: Greenwood/Quorum.

Power, D. J. (2004). Decision Support Systems: From the Past to the Future, In Proceedings of the *2004 Americas Conference on Information Systems,* New York, NY, 2025-2031.

Quinn, J.B., Anderson, P. & Finkelstein, S. (1996). Managing professional intellect: Making the most of the best. *Harvard Business Review,* 74(2), 71-80.

Rao, V. S. & Jarvenpaa, S. L. (1991). Computer support of groups: Theory-based models for SDSS research. *Management Science,* 37(10), 1347-1362.

Schmidt, J. B., Montoya-Weiss, M. M., & Massey, A. P. (2001). New product development decision-making effectiveness: Comparing individuals, face-to-face teams, and virtual teams. *Decision Sciences,* 32(4), 1-26.

Scott, W. R. (2003). *Organizations: Rational, natural, and open systems (5th ed.).* Upper Saddle River, NJ: Prentice Hall.

Simon, H. A. (1977). *The new science of management decision.* New York, NY: Harper & Row.

Simon, H. A. (1997). *Models of Bounded Rationality.* Cambridge, MA: MIT Press.

Teece, D. J., Pisano, G. & Shuen, A. (1997). Dynamic capabilities and strategic management. *Strategic Management Journal.* 18(7), 509-533.

Thompson, J. D., (1967, 2003). *Organizations in Action: Social Science Bases of Administrative Theory.* New Brunswick, NJ: Transaction Publishers.

Tsoukas, H., & Papoulias, D. B. (1996). Creativity in OR/MS: From technique to epistemology. *Interfaces*, 26(2), 73-79.

Tydeman, J., Lipinski, H. & Sprang, S. (1980). An interactive computer-based approach to aid group problem formulation. *Technological Forecasting and Social Change*, 16, 311-320.

Venkatraman, N. & Henderson, J. C. (1998). Real strategies for virtual organizing. *Sloan Management Review*, Fall, 33-48.

Vesset, D., & McDonough, B. (2007). The next wave of business analytics. *DM Review*, accessed from http://www.dmreview.com/issues/20070301/1076572-1.html on 1/21/08.

Weigel, D. & Cao, B. (1999). Applying GIS and OR techniques to solve Sears technician-dispatching and home-delivery problems. *Interfaces*, 29(1), 112-130.

Willemain, T. R. (1994). Insights on modeling from a dozen exerts. *Operations Research*, 42, 213-222.

Willemain, T. R. (1995). Model Formulation: What experts think about and when. *Operations Research*, 43(6), 916-932.

Woodward, J. (1975). *Management and Technology.* London: HMSO.

Chapter XIV
The Evolution from Data to Wisdom in Decision–Making at the Level of Real and Virtual Networks

Andrew Targowski
Western Michigan University, USA

ABSTRACT

This chapter provides theoretical analysis and synthesis of how computer applications are applied in problem-solving and decision-making in practice of real and virtual networks. The defined semantic ladder of cognition units provides the background for the analysis of the evolution of Knowledge Management technology and its applications in problem-solving and decision-making processes. The defined categories of decision-making tasks allow for the categorization of activities in network-oriented collaboration and the review of knowledge technology application in their implementations. Based upon this approach, the review of Knowledge Management technology is synthesized in real and virtual networks. Eventually both kinds of networks are compared by the Knowledge Management application criterion. However, Knowledge Management technology, despite its growing popularity is not the ultimate application, since wisdom not knowledge is the ultimate unit of cognition. Its structure in the civilization context is synthesized. Conclusions for theoreticians and practitioners are offered.

INTRODUCTION

The purpose of this chapter is to provide the theoretical background for the computer-driven applications in problem-solving and decision-making in practice of real and virtual networks. The main premises of this study are as follows:

1. So far Knowledge Management systems (KMS) were limited to data and information processing, but with the dawn of data mining, they should be very useful in elaborating *rules* of *knowledge* of a given business or organizational unit, which should enhance problem solving and decision-making in practice.

2. The KMS can be useful but is not the ultimate feature in problem-solving and decision-making, since the ultimate factor is wisdom, which is very difficult to automate. Hence the wisdom-oriented approach towards problem solving and decision-making is defined in this chapter.

3. The evolution approach towards *knowledge* and *wisdom* applications in problem-solving and decision-making is applied in this study in order to understand stages (and their possible success/failure factors) of information technology applications in applying these units of cognition.

The decision-making process is predominantly a cognition-oriented process. Cognition as a process is mostly associated with thinking, which processes information either stored in human memory or just fed into it from external sources. The "source material" in cognition-oriented processes is *information*. However nowadays, information can be treated as a colloquial term, which must be decomposed into more elementary, quanta kind of units, which will be called cognition units, such as; data, information, concept, knowledge, and wisdom. They convey the essence of thinking and decision-making under the form of message semantics. Of course there is a question of how do they sent it through several gates of mind, and external channels of communication. This flow reflects the syntax aspect of cognition units processing and handling. In this study this aspect is limited to networks, either real or virtual. Another aspect of messaging in decision-making is the pragmatic aspect of cognition which deals

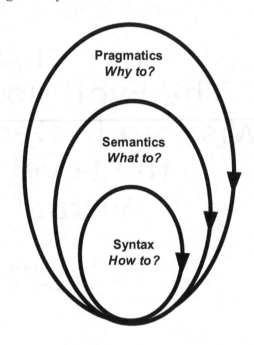

Figure 1. The cross-sections of knowledge management systems

with the question: Why is a decision made? This aspect is not considered in this study. These three cross-sections of cognition are treated under the framework of Knowledge Management systems as shown in Figure 1.

Knowledge management systems' technological tools are closely related to information technology as well as to organizational learning initiatives. Knowledge management may be distinguished from organizational learning by its greater focus on the management of specific knowledge assets and development and cultivation of the channels through which knowledge flows for the purpose of decision-making, supported by information technology.

This study will look how cognition units can be applied in the problem-solving/decision-making processes in order to make these processes more information-concept-knowledge intensive. The evolution of KMS will provide some suggestions for the limits of technology applications in management. This technology will be allocated in various processes taking place in real and virtual networks in order to evaluate its usefulness for decision-makers.

Since the potential of KMS seems to be endless, there is a question: How far can this technology automate decision-making? The answer will be provided after reviewing a concept of wisdom, which is one of the cognition units with the highest complexity. Based on these considerations some suggestions for practitioners and researchers as well as for developers will be provided.

THE SEMANTIC LADDER OF COGNITIVE UNITS

The process of communication in decision-making, as the main process of KMS, conveys meaning through five units of cognition:

- **Datum (D)**
  It is a measuring unit of cognition that describes transactions between natural, artificial, or semantic systems. In businesses, data can measure performance characteristics of production, distribution, transportation, or service. For example, a manufacturing process produces 3.4 defects per million units. An automobile company ships 200 vehicles per day. A JIT inventory system requires an average of one delivery every sixteen seconds. A help desk receives 100 calls per day.
- **Information (I)**
  It is a comparative unit of cognition that defines a change between the previous and present state of natural, artificial, or semantic systems. Businesses often compare data from two different periods of operations. Accounting systems often compare actual performance with standards. Continuing with the previous examples, the manufactur-

ing process decreased defects during the past year by 18 percent. Automobile shipments have increased an average of 2 vehicles per day. A supplier improved its "on-time" delivery performance by 20 percent over six months. Calls to the help desk decrease 20 percent during the summer months.

- **Concept (C)**
  It is a perceptive unit of cognition that generates thoughts or ideas that create our intuition and intention—a sense of direction. Concepts from the previous examples: Manufacturing quality is improving. Automobile demand is picking up. Suppliers are adjusting to JIT. Help desk call volume is seasonal.
- **Knowledge (K)**
  It is a reasoning unit of cognition that creates awareness based on facts, rules, coherent inferences, and well-defined methods. Knowledge provides a point of reference, a standard for analyzing data, information, and concepts. Knowledge can be categorized in four ways:
  - Personal knowledge (Kp)
  - Domain knowledge (Kd)
  - Societal knowledge (Ks)
  - Moral knowledge (Km)
  Once again elaborating on the previous examples: quality training is reducing product defects and should reduce customer complaints. The company should begin planning production schedules to meet increased demand. JIT works for suppliers and customers. Fewer resources are needed on the help desk during June through August.
- **Wisdom (W)**
  It is a pragmatic unit of cognition that generates volition—a chosen way of acting and communicating. Wisdom is the process of choosing ordered routines, intended to achieve success and eliminate obstacles. According to Marunama (1987) there are two types of wisdom. The first is the wisdom

Figure 2. The semantic ladder (the Targowski model)

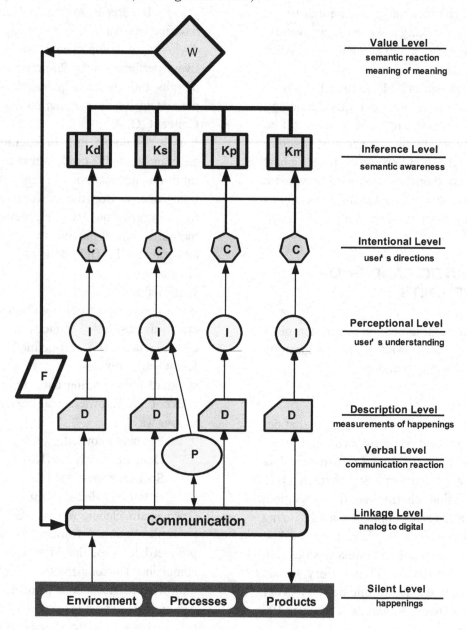

that exists in specific cultures or disciplines. This type is often taken for granted within the culture or discipline, and little or no explanation is needed for insiders. The other type of wisdom is gained through epistemological understanding. It concerns the limits of applicability of theories, logic, epistemologies, and culture-specific or discipline-specific wisdom. It is meta-wisdom. Concluding our examples: Quality training should be expanded throughout the company to improve performance on an enterprise-wide basis. All assembly lines in the Ohio plant should be brought on-line to meet higher demand. Supply chain planning and scheduling should be expanded to include distributors as well as suppliers. Fifteen percent of people currently assigned to the help desk will work on software implementation during the summer months.

The cognitive units can be structured from simplest to most complex in the Semantic Ladder, shown in Figure 2. Events occur at the silent level that are communicated as data (D) and inserted into the linkage of the human communication system. These data are subsequently processed into information (I) and concepts (C). People (P) who create information occupy the verbal level, which contains the communicators' intentions. The interaction of processed data and human information creates the intentional level of cognition where the information receiver assigns significance to the silent and verbal levels. As a result, other alternatives are considered and new concepts are created. The four types of knowledge previously discussed (Kp, Kd, Ks, Km) emerge from collections of alternative concepts. At this level of cognition, reasoning takes place. Wisdom occupies the value level of the semantic ladder where reasoning is used to make a choice among available courses of action. Cognitive wisdom is a pragmatic apparatus, formulating a communication frame (F) containing a message that reflects information and intentions. That frame enters the cognitive communication process and interacts at the verbal and silent levels with natural and artificial systems.

This feedback frame closes the loop of the cognition process causing two events:

- Choices are linked to silent level of events
- Learning patterns are established.

The semantic process is important because the patterns of analyzing happenings and events in human environments existed for millennia only in the human mind. As computer processing gets more powerful and programming techniques become more sophisticated, some of those analysis paradigms can be put into computer programs.

THE APPLICATIONS OF THE SEMANTIC LADDER OF COGNITIVE UNITS IN PROBLEM-SOLVING AND DECISION-MAKING

A number of frameworks have been proposed to describe the phases of decision-making. Perhaps the best known is Simon's (1965) intelligence-decision-choice triad. Simon simply asks, "What is the problem? What are my alternatives? What shall I do?" Ackoff (1978) perceives the decision-making process as a function of a problem-solving process. Mintzberg, Resinghani, and Theoret (1976) use terms like identification, development, and selection in seven central routines of decision-making. They also recognize the role of decision control, communication, and politics in reaching decisions. However, the most comprehensive model of decision-making must include units of cognition. Such a model, called a generic business problem-solving model, including the cognitive units and the routines of Mintzberg *et al* (1976), appears in Figure 3.

The problem-solving cycle-driven by cognitive units consists of five phases, as is shown in Figure 3:

1. **Problem identification:** Applies decision recognition and diagnosis to analyze problem symptoms and stimuli to determine a moment of action. That moment of action occurs when the cumulative effects of the stimuli exceed a user-defined threshold limit for action. The symptoms and stimuli are data.

2. **Problem diagnosis:** Involves an analysis of problem history in order to allocate resources required to determine implications of events

associated with the problem. It addresses the following questions (Wales et al):

- Who is involved?
- What things are involved?
- What happened?
- Where did it happen?
- Why did it happen?
- How serious is it?

3. **Decision conceptualization:** It is the heart of the problem-solving cycle and the most creative part of decision-making. It begins

Figure 3. Generic phases of problem solving and decision-making in the realm of cognition units

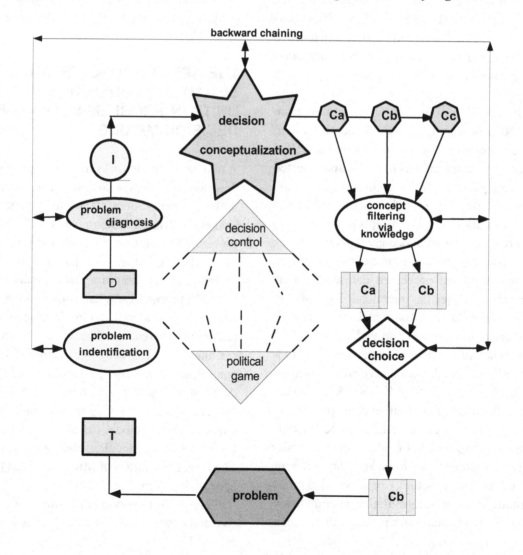

by defining a goal and search routine for historic solutions that fit the problem. If that search is unsuccessful, a customized routine must be created either from scratch, or by modifying an appropriate historic activity. The result of this phase is a concept of the problem solution—a direction for action and expected outcomes of that action. Automation of this phase is very difficult, but increased computer processing power and improvements in programming techniques make it possible to entertain the idea that computerized knowledge engineering will generate new concepts.

4. **Concepts filtering through knowledge:** Screen solutions eliminate those that are unfeasible. This phase challenges the appropriateness of alternatives that have never been used before. Facts and rules are the basis for the filtering process, which occurs before selecting an action. The question is: Do we have a correct decision? The field of knowledge engineering provides good tools for automating this phase.

5. **Decision rational choice:** Uses routines of evaluation-choice to select and authorize the best decision. Selection utilizes three modes:
   - **Judgment:** Mind-based individual choice
   - **Bargaining:** Group choice with various goals
   - **Analysis:** Factual technocratic techniques followed by managerial choice through judgment or bargaining.

Decision authorization occurs when a decision-maker lacks implementation authority and must obtain approval for an action from higher levels of management.

The main phases and central routines of the problem-solving cycle are guided by decision control support routines – operating systems that plan the cycle (schedules, strategies, resources) and switch the decision-maker from one phase to another. Transfer of intermediary results between phases is the function of communication routines that link cycle phases, managerial attention, and goals of individuals or groups involved in problem solving. Implementation of selected decisions depends on organization power structure and consensus of people affected by the decision. Forces of resistance are generally addressed through negotiation.

The problem-solving cycle incorporates a backward path in the event that feedback indicates the need to correct, clarify, or repeat a previous phase or routine. Different types of decisions flow in the pipeline of the problem-solving cycle, but all are rational and subject to the application of formal rules. Each has a different potential for automation.

THE EVOLUTION OF KNOWLEDGE MANAGEMENT TECHNOLOGY

Knowledge management technology attempts to manage the process of creation or identification, accumulation, and application of knowledge or intellectual capital across an organization. Knowledge management, therefore, attempts to bring under one set of practices relating to:

- Intellectual capital and the knowledge worker in the knowledge economy,
- The idea of the learning organization through knowledge/skills development,
- Various *enabling technologies* such as knowledge bases and expert systems, help desks, corporate intranets and extranets, content management, wikis and document management

Knowledge management may be viewed from each of the following perspectives:

- **Communication-centric:** Focus on technologies, ideally those that enhance knowledge sharing/growth within an enterprise: How does the enterprise need to be premeditated to facilitate knowledge processes implementation?
- **Computer-centric:** Any technology that does fancy stuff with information.
- **Cognition-centric:** Rules and laws which govern a given organization or its process.

The cognition-centric approach is analyzed in Table 1.

The evolution of Knowledge Management technologies permits for the following conclusion:

1. In the early days of business computing (1960-1970) Knowledge Management tools were limited to data and information processing, which measured the business performance and defined a change, however

conceptualization, knowledge filtering and solution choice were left to humans.

2. Some ambitious attempts have been undertaken under the forms of decision support systems (in 1980s), when the creeping revolution of microcomputers put personal computers in hands of millions of decision-makers and their staffers, who tried to apply management science techniques allowing for optimization of decisions through quantitative methods – leading to good conceptualizations of their options and clear choices. However, this kind of tool was more popular in the Academia than in business practice, because they looked too complicated for practitioners.

3. The application of expert systems (EXS) in the 1990s was the Academia's response to the failure of DSS. These systems were designed to automate decisional judgment and remove decisional burdens from managers. This idea was great on paper, however

Table 1. The evolution of cognitive units processing technologies

EVOLUTIONARY STEPS	COGNITIVE UNITS	DECISION QUESTIONS	ENABLING TECHNOLOGY
Data Processing (1960s)	Data	"How much to pay?"	Mainframe, tapes
Data Collection (1960s)	Data	"How fast to replenish a stock?"	Remote Data Entry
Data Access & Retrieval (1970s)	Data, Information	"What products have been sold in Michigan in 2006?"	Database
DSS (1980s)	Data, Information, Concept	"What is the optimal product mix?"	PC and management science software
EXS (1990s)	Wisdom (based on knowledge-oriented rules) for structured and preprogrammed decisions	"Which option should be accepted?"	Artificial Intelligence
ERP (1990s)	Data, Information	"What is the status of production in March 2007?"	Enterprise Systems
Data Mining (2000s)	Generation of business Knowledge (rules)	"What are new business rules on Mondays?"	Data Warehouse
EIP (2000s)	Structured & Unstructured Data and Information	"Who said that our product is bad?"	WWW
Web 2.0 (2010s)	All semantic-cognitive units	"What is an opinion of teenagers about our product XYZ?	Social software

was only applicable to a narrow scope of well structured decisions, while business practice is mostly based on ill structured decisions, particularly in the emerging global economy.

4. The emergence of enterprise resource planning (ERP) systems in the 1990s was only the response to the legacy systems chaos, bringing better organized and integrated systems, but still processing data and information only. To the same category of solutions one can include enterprise information portals (EIP) popular since the 2000s, through which Web technology expanded gateways to enterprise reservoirs of data and information.

5. The application of data mining tools in the 2000s radically changed the possibility of applying the great premises ideas of Knowledge Management technology. On the other hand, the Web 2.0 technology opens organizations to wide social networks, which bring a new "knowledge" to decision-makers, but it can be tented by untested knowledge, rather chaotic than truthful.

In the following considerations let's characterized the recent trends in Knowledge Management technology:

1. Data mining technology can generate new business opportunities by (Alexander 2007):

    *   **Automated prediction of trends and behaviors:** Data mining automates the process of finding predictive information in a large database. Questions that traditionally required extensive hands-on analysis can now be directly answered from the data. A typical example of a predictive problem is targeted marketing. Data mining uses data on past promotional mailings to identify the targets most likely to maximize return on investment in future mailings. Other predictive problems include forecasting bankruptcy and other forms of default, and identifying segments of a population likely to respond similarly to given events.

    *   **Automated discovery of previously unknown patterns:** Data mining tools sweep through databases and identify previously hidden patterns. An example of pattern discovery is the analysis of retail sales data to identify seemingly unrelated products that are often purchased together. Other pattern discovery problems include detecting fraudulent credit card transactions and identifying anomalous data that could represent data entry keying errors.

2. Alluding to the version-numbers that commonly designate software upgrades, the phrase "Web 2.0" hints at an improved form of the World Wide Web; advocates suggest that technologies such as Weblogs, social bookmarking, wikis, podcasts, RSS feeds (and other forms of many-to-many publishing), social software, Web APIs, Web standards and online Web services imply a significant change in Web usage. As used by its proponents, the phrase "Web 2.0" can also refer to one or more of the following (O'Reilly 2004):

    *   The transition of Web sites from isolated information silos to sources of content and functionality, thus becoming computing platforms serving Web applications to end-users,

    *   A social phenomenon embracing an approach to generating and distributing Web content itself, characterized by open communication, decentralization of authority, freedom to share and

re-use, and "the market as a conversa-tion,"

- Enhanced organization and categori-zation of content, emphasizing deep linking,
- A rise or fall in the economic value of the Web, possibly surpassing the impact of the dot-com boom of the late 1990s,
- Earlier users of the phrase "Web 2.0" employed it as a synonym for "Semantic Web," and indeed, the two concepts complement each other. The combination of social-networking systems such as FOAF and XFN with the development of tag-based folkson-omies, delivered through blogs and wikis, sets up a basis for a semantic Web environment [citation needed],
- The Web as a platform,
- Other.

THE TASKS OF DECISION-MAKING IN NETWORKS

The networks whether face-to-face (F2F) or computer-mediated-communication (CMC) oriented, secure *collaboration* among their par-ticipants. Most group tasks can be classified into the six categories; (1) *diagnose (information)*, (2) *generate (concept)*, (3) *negotiate (knowledge)*, (4) *choose (wisdom)*, (5) *execute (environment, events, processes, and products)*, and (6) *control (data)*, as depicted in Figure 4. This systematiza-tion is based on a problem-solving model, shown in Figure 3. The tasks in the *diagnose* category include information generation which tells about the state of the organization/problem/process, and looks for eventual changes. The *generate* category includes such tasks as; brainstorming and devis-ing potential solution's options – concepts. The *negotiate* category filters new and old concepts through their eventual knowledge-oriented rules

and tries to motivate those who will implement these concepts or tries to resolve-conflicts if these concepts causes some problems for the implementators. The *choose* category select the right or the best opinion and as well as directing option-concept, via a very complex processes of wisdom. The *execute* category communicate commanding (top-down) tasks or exchange tasks which are based on bottom-up execution. The last task category is the *control* one, which measures performance of routine and exceptional tasks via data.

As shown in Figure 4, these tasks can be related to one another within a two-dimensional space when the horizontal axis reflects either increase of cognitive complexity or behavioral one. The more a cognitive process is engaged in group col-laboration, the smaller is behavioral complexity, which leads to the fames rule that says: a form is more important than a substance of a decision. The vertical axis represents the information process-ing and collaboration complexities, which define the following rule; if information is limited then collaboration is more complex.

The application of KMS technology in col-laborative tasks is shown in Figure 5. It looks that from the network-oriented collaboration point of view, the most collaboration intensive tasks are: generate, negotiate, execute, and con-trol. The KMS-IT-driven systems, which are the best implemented in practice of decision-making are those which support control and diagnose-oriented tasks. Very promising is data mining system which makes decision-makers more and more knowledgeable and aware of their deci-sions' consequences. The applications of expert systems in generate and choose-oriented tasks are possible but very limited to these tasks huge cognitive complexity.

The analysis presented in Figure 5 indicates that network-oriented collaboration should be very useful in four (out of six tasks), namely in; gener-ate, negotiate, execute, and control categories.

Figure 4. Tasks types in network-oriented collaboration

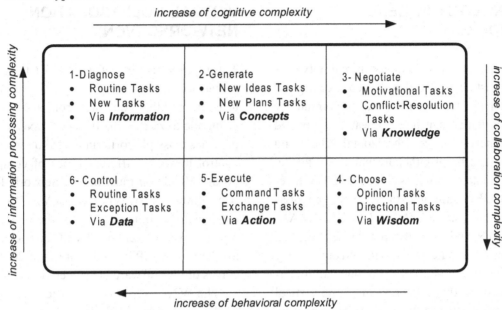

Figure 5. Tasks types in network-oriented collaboration and supporting information technology systems at the dawn of the 21ˢᵗ century

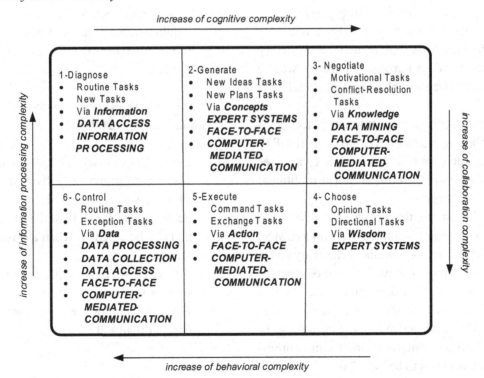

THE APPLICATION OF TECHNOLOGY IN REAL NETWORKS

The application of technology in real networks (RLN) must be analyzed at the scope of intraorganizational, interorganizational and community networks, which can be of upward, downward (vertical networks), and horizontal kinds, and each one can be of either formal and informal in nature. These networks can be based on face-to-face (F2F) communication and on computer-mediated-networks (CMN) such as; LAN, MAN, WAN, GAN, and VAN, where the user is limited in handling computerized inputs and outputs. By examining horizontal networks one can understand networks that cut across lines into vertical workplaces networks (teams, groups, reporting relationships, memberships, etc.). Communities practice this way. This kind of networks differs from matrix organizations where an individual wears two hats and reports to two different supervisors. Communities of practice cut across project or job-assignment lines to confab with peers who have similar professional/social expertise.

Inside a vertical network, we are limited in what we can learn, who we can relate to, and how we will grow. Inside a horizontal network we are unlimited and free to explore, choose, and change our minds.

Table 2 specifies main traditional technologies applied in collaborative tasks in the F2F networks, such ones as bureaucratic techniques and telephone-driven tools, as well as traditional meetings and events.

Table 3 illustrates the application of KMS technology in computer-mediated- networks (CMN) in the 2000s. The most popular technology tool is e-mail. In downward networks, the most popular technology tools are classic enterprise systems (ERP, SCM, and CRM). The most promising system in vertical networks is data mining. In informal and horizontal networks the most promising system seems to be Web 2.0.

THE APPLICFATION OF KMS IN VIRTUAL COLLABORATION NETWORKS (VCN)

Through the use of software – VNC acronym for *virtual network computing*, makes it possible to interact with a computer from any computer or mobile device on the Internet. VNC software provides cross-platform support allowing remote control between different types of computers. To use VNC you must have a network TCP/IP connection, a VNC server and a VNC viewer to connect to the computer running the VNC server. The open source version of VNC has been freely available since 1998, and more than 20 million copies of the software have been downloaded.

The VNC support activities in modern workplaces under the form of *virtual collaboration networks* (VCN). It means that people who collaborate with each other are geographically dispersed, and rely on mediated, rather than F2F communication. Virtual collaboration takes place via the following systems:

- Videoconferencing (VC)
- Audioconferencing (AC), and
- Computer-mediated-communication (CMC).

Virtual meetings bring in the following benefits (Wainfan & Davis 2004):

1. *Broadening reach* by including participants who are geographically dispersed,
2. *Responsiveness,* since virtual meeting can be organized faster than the physical ones and can be essential when a crisis must be met,
3. *Adaptiveness,* new people can be invited as soon as they are needed,
4. *Time and money,* the virtual meetings are cheaper than F2F ones.

Table 4 characterizes the main virtual meetings' tools.

Table 5 illustrates the application of virtual communication technology in Virtual Collaboration Networks. In general this kind of networks is similar to the F2F and CMN but limited mostly to specific technology tools, such as VC, AC, and CMC.

The application of virtual technologies does not improve decision-making completely, since it is based mostly on personal touch of communicating participants. This kind of technology should be treated as the complementary technology to CMN. In fact, the virtual technology makes distance unimportant in F2F communication.

OPERATIONAL DIFFERENCES BETWEEN REAL AND VIRUAL NETWORKS FROM THE DECISION-MAKING POINT OF VIEW

In general, F2F networks are less structured and more subjective in verbal discussion and rich in body language expressions than any of virtual networks, particularly AC-oriented ones. However, negotiation outcomes are more positive in the latter, leading more to win-win solutions.

According to Morley and Stephenson (1970) hypothesis:

The more formal the communication system the greater the emphasis will be placed on interparty rather than interpersonal aspect of interaction.

Table 2. The application of technology in face-to-face (F2F) networks

Networks Types	Face-To-Face					
	Upward		Downward		Horizontal	
	Formal	Informal	Formal	Informal	Formal	Informal
Intraorganizational	Diagnose Generate Negotiate **Bureau-cracy**	Diagnose Generate Negotiate "Control" **Cafeteria Telephone**	Control Diagnose Generate Negotiate Choose Execute **Bureau-cracy**	Diagnose Generate Negotiate "Control" **Country Club Telephone**		Diagnose Generate Negotiate "Control" **Cafeteria Telephone**
Interorganizational	Diagnose Generate Negotiate **Corporate Bureau-cracy**	Diagnose Negotiate "Control" **Events Telephone**	Diagnose Generate Negotiate Choose Execute Control **Corporate Bureau-cracy**	Diagnose Generate Negotiate **Events Telephone**		Diagnose Generate Negotiate "Control" **Events Telephone**
Community						Diagnose Generate Negotiate Choose "Execute" "Control" **Events Telephone Media**

Table 3. The application of technology in computer-mediated-networks (CMN) in the 2000s

| Networks Types | Face-To-Face | | | | | |
| | Upward | | Downward | | Horizontal | |
	Formal	Informal	Formal	Informal	Formal	Informal
Intraorganizational	Diagnose Generate Negotiate **Data & Information Processing and Access ERP Data Mining Web 2.0**	Diagnose Generate Negotiate "Control" **Cafeteria Telephone e-mail Web 2.0**	Control Diagnose Generate Negotiate Choose Execute **Data & Information Processing and Access ERP, EIP Data Mining**	Diagnose Generate Negotiate "Control" **Country Club Telephone e-mail blogs**		Diagnose Generate Negotiate "Control" **Cafeteria Telephone e-mail blogs Web 2.0**
Interorganizational	Diagnose Generate Negotiate **Data & Information Processing and Access SCM, CRM Data Mining**	Diagnose Negotiate "Control" **Events Telephone e-mail blogs**	Diagnose Generate Negotiate Choose Execute Control **Data & Information Processing and Access ERP, EIP, SCM, CRM Data Mining**	Diagnose Generate Negotiate **Country Club Telephone e-mail blogs**		Diagnose Generate Negotiate "Control" **Events Telephone e-mail blogs**
Community						Diagnose Generate Negotiate Choose "Execute" "Control" **Events Telephone Media e-mail blogs Web 2.0**

Table 4. The characteristics of virtual networks

Mode	Defining Characteristics	Examples
Videoconferencing (VC)	Useful real-time images, and voices of other participants; may include other share images/text.	Group videoconferencing in dedicated rooms; desktop conferencing.
Audioconferencing (AC)	Voice communication, but no useful real-time video images of other participants; may include other shared images, data, and text.	Phone calls, conference calls, or conference calls where people are also sharing views of images or documents.
Computer-mediated-conferencing (CMC)	Text, images, and other data received via computer, without effective voice or other participants.	E-mail, chat rooms, discussion boards, text messaging, instant messaging, shared databases, application-specific groupware.

Source: Wainfan & Davis 2004, p. 4.

In the more formal audioconference, the more likely the settlement will be in accordance with the merits of the case.

In an audioconference situation, researchers found (Wainfan & Davis 2004, p. 37) that participants exhibit delayed and fragile trust in comparing to VC, which impacts cooperation among involved parties. The less structured VC provides more comfort for participants than more formal AC. Also in a scope of choice shifts, AC discussions provide more shifts than F2F discussions (Reid 1977, Short, Williams, and Christie 1976).

Wainfan and Davis 2004 states that:

Whether the cause is more-negative participant impressions of each other, reduces occurrences of social interaction, or delayed and fragile trust, it is generally agreed that AC reduces interpersonal considerations and can produce better outcomes.

The removal of the voice and real-time video channel may significantly degrade participants satisfaction with CMC. In summary, Wainfan and Davis (2004, p. 64) found following outcomes effects:

CMC-specific collaboration in brainstorming produces more results than real networks. More choices shift than with other media. Shift toward risky or extreme options. Some cognition biases mitigated: social group membership bias, availability bias, representative bias. Some biases exacerbated: biased discussion, fundamental attribution error, sinister attribution bias. Deindividuation increased, polarization increased, local coalition form around real or hypothetical outgroups. Cohesiveness lower than in other tools.

The same authors found following process effects:

Subcommittee structure is more agile, longer time is for discussion, consensus is less likely, and status inequality is reduced. Leadership is more decentralized and less stable. More explicit proposals are offered and more sanctioning statement is issued.

In conclusion one can say that:

1. *Virtual networks* in comparison to *real networks* provide a good technological solution for efficient decision-making in the collaborative environment.
2. However, despite of the great progress in processing cognitive units, the human factor must be secure in choosing solutions, since wisdom is still and will be for some time very difficult to automate. Even if in some cases it is or will be possible, the question is: Why do it?

WISDOM IS STILL HUMAN RESPONSIBILITY IN CIVILIZATION

Based on research on wisdom (Targowski 2007) one can define the following hypothesis:

1. There is no one universal wisdom, unless we speak about civilization wisdom
2. Every kind of wisdoms has different characteristics and paradigms;
   a. SOCIAL WISDOM (religion, law, medicine) is in morality and prudence
   b. REFLECTIONAL WISDOM (great philosophers, writers and intellectuals) is in knowing through reasoning
   c. INDIVIDUAL'S WISDOM (great politicians, generals, businessmen, scientists, engineers, and so forth) is in concept choices

Table 5. The application of virtual communication technology in virtual collaboration networks (CMN) in the 2000s

Networks Types	Face – To - Face					
	Upward		Downward		Horizontal	
	Formal	Informal	Formal	Informal	Formal	Informal
Intraorganizational	Diagnose Generate Negotiate **CMC**	Diagnose Generate Negotiate "Control" **CMC**	Control Diagnose Generate Negotiate Choose Execute **VC, AC, CMC**	Diagnose Generate Negotiate "Control" **CMC**		Diagnose Generate Negotiate "Control" **CMC**
Interorganizational	Diagnose Generate Negotiate **CMC VC, AC**	Diagnose Negotiate "Control" **CMC**	Diagnose Generate Negotiate Choose Execute Control **CMC VC, AC**	Diagnose Generate Negotiate **CMC**		Diagnose Generate Negotiate "Control" **CMC**
Community						Diagnose Generate Negotiate Choose "Execute" "Control" **CMC**

d. METHODICAL WISDOM (management science, operation research, semantics, and so forth) is in balancing interests

3. Wisdom is time-oriented, hence it can be; universal, contingent, and pseudo-universal (partially universal and somehow time-oriented, like in science)

4. Wisdom is contextual, which means that cannot be analyzed without the understanding of human, society, culture, as well as infrastructure developmental stages and status.

In consequence, just based on the presented empiric review of wisdoms, we cannot perceive that wisdom has only one definition, unless we assume civilization's wisdom, then its definition is as follows:

Civilization wisdom is a combination of social, reflectional, individual's methodical wisdoms which strategize societal and individuals' judgment and actions through the composition of morality, prudence, conceptualization and balanced choices of interests in the context of civilization development, status, universality, pseudo-universality, and contingency, (time-oriented).

The architecture of civilization wisdom is depicted in Figure 6.

The presented model of human-civilization wisdom is very difficult to automate, if wisdom is treated comprehensively, not just a simple choice in a very well structured decisional situation.

CONCLUSION FOR PRACTITIONERS

1. The application of information technology in decision-making progresses from simple data mining to advanced data mining significantly improves knowledge about a given organization/business operations, which dramatically enhances decision reliability and quality.
2. The virtual collaboration, particularly in larger groups improves efficiency of decision-making process and in some circumstances also improves decision reliability and quality.
3. However, F2F communication should be maintained, since the full automation of human judgment has no civilization purpose, as long as we are not going to replace humans by machines. The latter should rather support human effort but not remove us from civilization, since such civilization won't be our civilization.

CONCLUSION FOR RESEARCHERS

1. The potential of information technology in developing info-communication system look alike is never saturated and ready to solve any challenge of complex systems. However, the role of researchers is to support the balance between technological solutions and the human factor. It should be always on

Figure 6. The composition of civilization wisdom (the Targowski model)

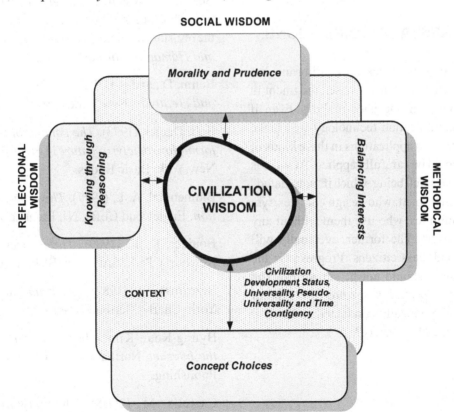

researchers/developers' minds that technology serves humans not vice versa.

2. The research potential of Knowledge Management systems (MSS) is in investigating and developing management support systems, which apply data mining techniques DMT) for specific industry/organization/problem/issue. Up till now DMT are of general kind, which supposedly can be applied in any situation. However, this last statement certainly is not correct and needs to turn research directions toward specialized solutions than to more general ones.

3. The research and developmental efforts should look for a more integrated environment of MSS, which steadily is moving into a so called "management dashboard." KMS should find a strong place in the management dashboard as the most advanced management tool.

FUTURE RESEARCH DIRECTIONS

Further research may seek an equilibrium between automated and human-based judgment in problem-solving and decision-making. Even if artificial/communication technology will make strong progress, its applications in these kinds of processes should be carefully applied. At stake is the human race's well being, which if "automated" may lead to supermen, who design complex systems, and dummies, who use them without any intellectual effort. The former, eventually will become second class citizens. Progress for the sake of progress should not be supported. The further research should define how this kind of progress can be ethically conducted and how it can be controlled by Society?

REFERENCES

Aleksander, D. Data mining. http://www.eco.utexas.edu/~norman/BUS.FOR/course.mat/Alex/, retrieved April 11, 2007.

Ackoff, R. L. (1967). Management misinformation systems. *Management Science,* (Nov):147-156.

Ackoff, R. L. (1978). *The art of problem solving.* New York: J. Wiley.

Ahtiuv, N., & Newmann, S. (1986). *Principles of information systems.* Dubuque, Iowa: William C. Brown Publishers.

Anthony, R. (1965). *Planning and control systems: a framework for analysis.* Boston: Harvard University.

Barber, B.R. (1992). Jihad vs. McWorld. *The Atlantic Monthly.* March. pp. 53-63.

Beach, L. R., Mitchell, T. R., *et al.* (1997). Information relevance, content, and source credibility in the revision of opinions. *Organizational Behavior and Human Performance*, (21), 1-16.

Behm, D., and F. D. Peat. (1978). *Science, order and creativity.* New York: Bantam Books.

Bell, Daniel. (1973). *The coming of the post-information society: a venture in social forecasting.* New York: Basic Books.

Blumenthal, A. L. (1977). *The process of cognition.* Englewood Cliffs, NJ: Prentice-Hall, Inc.

Boulder, K. E. (1989). *Three faces of power.* Newburry Park: SAGE PUBLICATIONS.

Brzezinski, Z. (1982). *The grand failure.* New York: Charles Scribner's Sons.

Byung-Keun-Kim (2005). *Internationalizing the Internet.* Northampton, MA.: Edward Elgar Publishing.

Castells. M. (2005). The network society. Northampton, MA.: Edward Elgar Publishing.

Chomsky, A. (1965). *Aspects of the theory of syntax.* Cambridge, Mass: MIT Press.

Coakes, E., & Clarke, S. (2006). *Encyclopedia of communities of practice in information and knowledge management.* Harrisburg, PA.: Idea Group Inc.

Cyert, R. and J. March. (1963). *A behavioral theory of the firm.* Englewood Cliffs, NJ: Prentice-Hall.

Dearden, J. (1972). MIS is a mirage. *Harvard Business Review.* February, pp. 90-99.

Denning, P. J., D. E. Comer, D. Gries, M. C. Mulder, A. Tucker, A. J. Turner, and P. T. Young. (1989). Computing as a discipline. *Communications of the ACM.,*32 (1), 9-23.

Dewhirst, H. D. (1971). Influence of perceived information-sharing norms on communication channel utilization. *Academy of Management Journal*, (14), 305-315.

Dodd, D. H, and White, R. M. (1980). *Cognition mental structures and processes.* Boston, Mass: Allyn and Bacon Inc.

Draft, R. L., and R. H. Lengel. (1984). *Information richness: a new approach to managerial behavior and organizational design.* Greenwich, Conn: JAI Press.

Drucker, Peter F.M. (1988). The coming of the new organization. *Harvard Business Review*, 88(1), 45-53.

Ekecrantz, J. (1987). The sociological order of the new information society. In *The ideology of the information age.* In Slack, J. D., & Fejes, F. (Ed.), Norwood,NJ: Ablex Publishing Corp.

Galbraith, J. (1973). *Strategies of organization design.* Reading, Mass: Addison-Wesley.

Gilder, George. (1992). A major work in the making: into the fibersphere. *Forbes ASAP*, December 7, 111-123.

Gore, Al. (1991). Information superhighways: the next information revolution. *The Futurist*, January-February, 21-23.

Gottschalk, P. (2007). *Knowledge management systems.* Harrisburg, PA.: Idea Group Inc.

Handzic, M. (2007). *Socio-technical knowledge management: studies and initiatives.* Harrisburg, PA.: Idea Group Inc.

Hartley, R. V. L. (1928). Transmission of information. *Bell System Tech Journal*, (7), 535.

Hicks, J. O. (1988). *Management information systems: a user perspective.* St. Paul, Minn.

Karraker, R. (1988). Highways of minds. *Whole Earth Review*, Spring, 4-15.

Laszlo, Ernst. (1972). *Introduction to systems philosophy.* New York: Harper and Row.

Leavitt, H. J. (1979). Beyond the analytic manager. *California Management Review*, (3), 5-12.

Lengel, R. H. (1984). *Management information processing and communication-media source selection behavior.* Unpublished doctoral dissertation, Texas A & M University.

Lubbe, S. (2007). *Managing information communication technology investments in successful enterprise.* Harrisburg, PA.: Idea Group Inc.

Man, de, A-P. (2006). *The network economy.* Northampton, MA.: Edward Elgar Publishing.

Maruyama, M. (1987). Communication between mindscape types. In *Decision Making About Decision Making, Metamodels, and Metasystems.* J. P. van Gigch, J. P. (Ed.), Cambridge, Mass: Abacus Press, p. 91.

Marvin, C. (1987). Information and history. In *The Ideology of the Information Age.* Slack, J. D., & F.Fejes, F. (Ed.), Norwood, NJ: Ablex Publishing Corp.

McWhirter, B. (1993). Disposable Workers of America. *Time*, March 29, 41-43.

Mintzberg, H., D., Raisinghani, & A. Theoret, A. (1976). The structure of unstructured decision processes. *Administrative Science Quarterly*, (21), 246-275.

Monge, P., J. Edwards, and K. Kirste. (1978). The determinants of communication structure in large organizations: a review of research. In *Communication Yearbook*. Ed. B. Ruben. New Brunswick, NJ: Transactions Books, 311-331.

Moreley, I. E. & Stephenson, G. M. (1969). Interpersonal and interparty exchange: a laboratory simulation of an industrial negotiations at the plant level. *British Journal of Psychology*, 60, 543-545.

Moreley, I. E. & Stephenson, G. M. (1970). Iformality in experimental negotiations: a validity study. *British Journal of Psychology*, 61, 383.

Mowshowitz, A. (1981). On approaches to the study of social issues in computing. *Communications of the ACM*, 24, (3), 146.

Naylor, J.,(1964). Accuracy and variability of information sources of determiners. *Journal of Applied Psychology*, (48), 43-49.

Nonaka, I. & Nishiguchi, T. (2000). *Knowledge emergence: social, technical, and evolutionary dimensions of knowledge creation*. New York: Oxford Press.

Nowell, A. (1973). Production systems: models of control structures. In *Visual Information Processing*. Ed. W. Chase. New York: Academic Press.

Nowell, A., A. Perils,A. & Simon, H. (1987). What is computer science? *Science,* (157), 1373-1374.

O'Reilly, C. A., J., Chatman, J. A. & J. C. Anderson, J. C. (1978). Message flow and decision making. In *Handbook of Organizational Communication*. Joblin, F. M., *et al.* (Ed.) Newbury Park, CA: SAGE.

O'Reilly, C. A. (1982). Variations in decision makers' use of information sources: the impact of quality and accessibility of information. *Academy of Management Journal*, (25), 756-771.

O'Riley on Media 2004, http://en.wikipedia.org/wiki/Web_2, Retieved on April, 11, 2007.

Parker, E. (1976). Social implications of computer/telecoms systems. *Telecommunications Policy*, 1, (December), 3-20.

Peat, F. David. (1987). *Synchronicity: the bridge between matter and mind*. New York: Bantam Books.

Porat, Marc. (1977). *The information economy*. Washington, DC: US Office of Telecommunications.

Poster, M. (1990). *The mode of information*. Chicago: The University of Chicago Press.

Powers, W. T. (1973). *Behavior: the control of perception*. Chicago: Aldine Publishing Company.

Pricher, W. (1987). Tours through the back-country of imperfectly informed society. In *The Ideology of the Information Age*. Slack, J. D., & Fejes, F.(Ed.). Norwood,NJ: Ablex Publishing Corp.

Quatroop, L. (1987). The information age: ideal and reality. In *The Ideology of the Information Age*. Ed. J. D. Slack, D. J. & Fejes, F. (Ed.). Norwood, NJ: Ablex Publishing Corp.

Roberts, K., and C. O'Reilly. (1978). Organization as communication structures: an empirical approach. *Human Communication Research*, (4),283-293.

Sadowski-Rasters, G., Duysters, G. & Sadowski, B. M. (2007). *Communication in the virtual workplace, teamwork in computer-mediated-communication*. Northampton, MA.: Edward Elgar Publishing.

Scott, M. M. S. (1986). The state of the art of researching management support systems. In *The Rise of Managerial Computing*. Rockart, J. F.& Charles V. B. (Ed.). Homewood, IL: Dow Jones-Irwin, p. 325.

Scovell, P. (1993). Assembling the building blocks for the networks of the future. *Telesis*, (96), 23 - 31.

Schwartz, D. G. (2006). *Encyclopedia of knowledge management*. Harrisburg, PA.: Idea Group Inc.

Shannon, C. E. (1948). A mathematical theory of communication. *Bell Systems Tech Journal*, (3-4).

Shannon, C. E., & Weaver, W. (1949). *The mathematical theory of communication*. Urbana, IL: University of Illinois Press.

Short, J., Williams, E., & Christie, B. (1976). *The social psychology of telecommunications*, London: John Wiley & Sons.

Simon, H. A. (1965). *The shape of automation*. New York: Harper and Row.

Simon, H. A. (1976). *Administrative behavior*. New York: Free Press.

Slack, J.D. (1987). The information age as ideology: an introduction. In *The Ideology of the Information Age*. Slack, J. D. & and F. Fejes, F. (Ed.). Norwood,NJ: Ablex Publishing Corp.

Stahl, C., & Redding, W. C. (1987). Message and message exchange process. In *Handbook of Organizational Communication: An Interdisciplinary Perspective*. F. M. Jablin, F. M. *et al*. Newbury Park, CA: SAGE.

Starr, M. K. (1971). *Management: a modern approach*. New York: Harcourt Brace Jovanovich, Inc.

Tapscott, D. & Willimas, A.D. (2006). *Wikinomics: how mass collaboration changes everything*. On-line: Portfolio Hardcover.

Tapscott, D. (1999). *Growing up digital: the rise of the net generation*. New York: McGraw-Hill.

Targowski, A. & Bowman, J. (1986). Generic elements of communication frames: toward the quantum theory of communication. *Proceedings of the 51st Association for Business Communication Convention*, Los Angeles, CA, November 12-16, p. 1.

Targowski, A., J. & Bosman, J. (1988). The layer-based pragmatic model of the communication process. *The Journal of Business Communication,* 25 (1).

Targowski, A. (1990). *The strategy and architecture enterprise-wide information management systems*. Harrisburg, PA.: Idea Group Publishing.

Targowski, A. (1996). *Global information infrastructure*, Harrisburg, PA.: Idea Publishing Group

Targowski, A. (1998). A definition of the information management discipline. *The Journal of Education for MIS*. 5. (1).

Targowski, A. (2007). *Wisdom explained*. Unpublished manuscript. Kalamazoo, MI: Western Michigan University.

Thieauf, R. J. & Hoctor, J. J. (2006). *Optimal knowledge management: wisdom management systems concepts and applications*. Harrisburg, PA.: Idea Group Inc.

Toffler, Alfred. (1980). *The third wave*. New York: Bantam Books.

Turiel, A., and P. Davidson. (1996). Heterogeneity, inconsistency and asynchrony in the development of cognitive structures. *In State and Structures*. Levin, I. (Ed.). Norwood, NJ: Albex Publishing Co.

Wales, Ch., & et al. (1986). *Professional decision-making*, West Virginia University.

Wainfan, L. & Davis, P. K. (2004). Challenges in virtual collaboration. Santa Monica, CA. RAND.

Weick, K. E. (1979). *The social psychology of organizing*. Reading, Mass: Addison-Wesley.

Wojciechowski, J. (1989). Progress of knowledge and right-left dichotomy: are existing ideologies adequate? *Man & Development*, 11(1).

Young, T.R. (1987). Information, ideology and political reality. In *The Ideology of   the Information Age*. Slack, J. D., & Fejes, F. Norwood, NJ: Ablex Publishing Corp.

ADDITIONAL READING

Abel, M. J., (1990). Experiences in exploratory distributed organization. In J. Galegher and R. Kraut (Eds.), *Intellectual teamwork: social and technological foundation of cooperative*. Hillside, NJ: Lawrence Erlbaum Associates, 111-146.

Adrienssen, J.H.E., & van der Velden, J.M. (1993). Teamwork supported by interaction technology: the beginning of an integrated theory. *European Work And Organizational Psychologis*, .3(2),129-144.

Anderson, A. H., Newlands, A. & Mullin, J. (1996). Impact of video-mediated communication on simulated service encounters. Interacting with computers, 8 (2), 193-206.

Bales, R. F. (2001). *Interaction process analysis: a method for the study of small groups*. Cambridge, MA: Addison-Wesley.

Berkowitz, B. (2003). Failing to keep up with the information revolution. *Studies in Intelligence*, 47(1), May 6.

Boland, R, J., Jr. & Tenkasi, R. V. (2001). Communication and collaboration In distributed cognition. In Olson, G. M., Malone, T. W. & Smith, J. B. (Eds.), Coordination theory and collaboration technology, Mahwah, NJ: Lawrence Erlbaum Associates, 51-66.

Carless, S. A. & DePaola, C. (2000). The measurement of cohension in work teams. *Small Group Research*, 31, 71-88.

Cornelius, C. & Boos, M. (2003). Enhancing mutual understanding in synchronous computer-mediated communication by training: trade-offs in judgment tasks. *Communication Research*, 30(2), 147-177.

Draft, R. L. & Lengel, R. H. (1986). Organizational information requirements, media richness, and structural design. *Management Science*, 32, 554-571.

Dennis, A. R. & Wixom, B. H. (2002). Investigating the moderators of group support system use. *Journal of Management Information Systems*, 18(3), 235-258.

Ferran-Urdaneta, C. (2001). The effects of videoconferencing on persuasion. *Dissertation Abstracts International, Section A: Humanities and Social Science*, 61(8), 3239.

Fjermestad, J. (2004). An analysis of communication mode in group support systems research. *Decision Support Systems*. 37(2), 239-263.

Gale, S. (1990). Human aspects of interactive multimedia communication. *Interacting with Computers*, 2, 175-189.

Hightower, R. & Sayeed, L. (1995). Effects of communication mode and prediscussion information distribution characteristics on information exchange in groups. *Information Systems Research*, 7(4), 451-464.

Janis, I. (1972). *Victims of groupthinking*. Boston, MA: Houghton-Miffin.

Kock, N. (2004). The psychological model: towards a new theory of computer-mediated communication based on Darwinian evolution. *Organizational Science*, 15(3), 327-248.

Martin, J. (1990). *Future Developments in Tele-communications*. New York: Telecom Library.

McGrath, J. E. (1984). *Groups: interaction and performance*. Englewood Cliffs, NJ: Prentice Hall.

Morris, M. W., Nadler, J., Kurtzberg, T., & Thompson, L. (2002). Schmooze or lose: social friction and lubrication in e-mail negotations. *Group Dynamics*. 6(1).

O'Hara-Deveraux, M., & Johansen, R. (1994). *Global work: bridging distance, culture, and time*. San Francisco, CA: Jossey-Bass.

Palme, J. (1995). *Electronic mail*. Norwood, MA: Artech House Publishers.

Rheingold, H. (2002). *Smart mobs: the next social revolution*. New York: Perseus Publishing.

Rice, R. (1984). *Mediated group communication*. In Rice, R. & Associates (Eds). The new media. New York: Academic Press.

Thompson, L. & Nadler, J. (2002). Negotiating vis information technology, theory and applications. *Journal of Social Issues*. 58(1).

Wilson, E. V. (2003). Perceived effectiveness of interpersonal persuasion strategies in computer-mediated communication. *Computers in Human Behavior*, 19(5), 537-552.

Zielinski, D. (2000). Face value. *Presentations*, 14(6), 58-64.

Chapter XV
Editor Conclusions

Cesar Camison
Universitat Jaume I, Spain

Daniel Palacios
Universitat Jaume I, Spain

Fernando Garrigos
Universitat Jaume I, Spain

Carlos Devece
Universitat Jaume I, Spain

The study of virtual organizations encompasses several research fields, and the variables involved in each of them are sometimes closely related. This represents a challenge for managers, since the decision taken about the technical tools to use, the organizational structure, incentives or procedures, for example, are tightly linked, and this represents a complex problem in itself. Nevertheless, the biggest challenge in virtual organization management is the lack of experience. Although the phenomenon is not new- there are plenty of successful communities of practice in the net- most of the managers and professionals have limited experience in networking, and only as users in specific areas of knowledge or business activities, and are not fully aware of networking possibilities and limitations. This lack of experience implies a big trial when facing the problems involved in virtual organizations management.

But this lack of experience is only relative. Information technology is not new. Nowadays, every manager has an extensive experience, at least as a user, in business processes that are partially or totally done by electronic means. The inexperience lies in the virtuality of the organization in itself, not the business processes. But the management of an organization completely virtual poses a set of complex decisions completely new in respect to traditional IS management. In the new virtual organization, some powerful social mechanisms for motivation and control disappear, the human resources techniques cannot be fully applied, and some essential ways of knowledge transmission and innovation are impossible. The advantage of a boundless space organization with workers and partners at hand no matter the place they live has disadvantages, too. Only when these disadvantages are mitigated with the right managerial decisions and it is possible to take the full advantage of virtuality, virtual organizations make sense.

In our opinion, virtual organization study must rely on some basic pillars. Perhaps, the most important is Knowledge Management. This is because the real power of networking is the access to highly qualified professionals and communities of practice. But it is not always easy to pump that knowledge out, and Knowledge Management offers a solid framework to approach the problem. Nevertheless, some specific limitations and considerations must be applied when considering the special case of Knowledge Management in virtual communities and organizations. Traditionally, networking has been considered in KM as a great advantage to add to other managerial

techniques, but in virtual organizations all goes around networking. Then, new specific studies in KM are necessary when dealing with virtual organizations. Most of the chapters of this book deal with this problem from different perspectives, and offer, as a whole, a complete vision of Knowledge Management in virtual organizations.

The second pillar is participation and motivation in virtual organization, or more generally, in communities of practice. It can be studied as a part of KM, but several studies state it is convenient to separate it from KM. The third pillar is the technical tools at hand for efficient problems like technical tools and classifications, and practical experiences. In this sense we assume it is impossible to offer a general formula to obtain the best results for a specific virtual organization. The structure of the organization, the size, objectives and activity of the organization must shape the best managerial solution for each case.

Section VI
Selected Readings

Chapter XVI
A Complex Adaptive Systems–Based Enterprise Knowledge Sharing Model

Cynthia T. Small
The MITRE Corporation, USA

Andrew P. Sage
George Mason University, USA

ABSTRACT

This chapter describes a complex adaptive systems (CAS)-based enterprise knowledge-sharing (KnS) model. The CAS-based enterprise KnS model consists of a CAS-based KnS framework and a multi-agent simulation model. Enterprise knowledge sharing is modeled as the emergent behavior of knowledge workers interacting with the KnS environment and other knowledge workers. The CAS-based enterprise KnS model is developed to aid Knowledge Management (KM) leadership and other KnS researchers in gaining an enhanced understanding of KnS behavior and its influences. A premise of this research is that a better understanding of KnS influences can result in enhanced decision-making of KnS interventions that can result in improvements in KnS behavior.

CAS-BASED MODELING OF ENTERPRISE KNOWLEDGE SHARING

The enterprise KnS model developed here models enterprise knowledge sharing from a complex adaptive systems perspective. Hypothetical con-cepts that are fundamental to the development of this CAS-based model and to this research include:

1. Knowledge sharing is a human behavior performed by knowledge workers;

2. Knowledge workers are diverse and heterogeneous;
3. Knowledge workers may choose to share knowledge; and
4. The KnS decision is influenced by other knowledge workers and the KnS environment.

Enterprise knowledge sharing is the result of the decisions made by knowledge workers, individually and as members of teams, regarding knowledge sharing. As depicted in *Figure 1*, there are two major decisions (rectangles) that a knowledge worker makes: "Share Knowledge?" and "Type of Knowledge to Share?" This research models the KnS decisions as being influenced by the attributes of the individual knowledge worker, the KnS behavior of other knowledge workers, and the state of the KnS environment. Previous

KnS studies and research identify factors that influence KnS behavior. However, few address the heterogeneity of knowledge workers and how the attributes of the individual knowledge worker, and knowledge worker teams, impact KnS behavior. The emergent enterprise KnS behavior, noted by the diamond shape in *Figure 1*, is the result of the interactions of the knowledge worker with the KnS environment and other knowledge workers. Relevant aspects of enterprise KnS behavior and the associated KnS influences are discussed in the sections that follow.

Enterprise KnS behavior takes on many forms. It can be a conversation around a water fountain, e-mail sent to a co-worker or a group forum, a presentation to a small group, an enterprise "best-practice" forum, or documents published to a corporate repository. Murray (2003) categorizes KnS activities into technology-assisted commu-

Figure 1. Enterprise KnS influence diagram

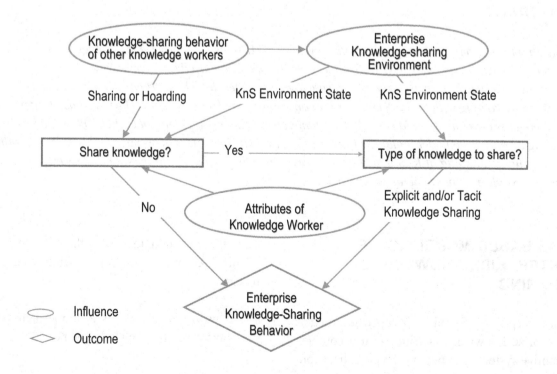

nication (videoconferencing, databanks/intranet, e-mail, and teleconferencing), meetings (face-to-face interaction, seminars and conferences, social events, and retreats), and training and development (mentoring, instructional lectures, video tapes, and simulation games). This research combines the two types of knowledge (tacit and explicit) and the ontological dimension (individual, group, and organization) of knowledge creation presented by Nonaka and Takeuchi (1995) to derive the types of KnS behavior for the model. The KnS behaviors investigated and incorporated in the enterprise KnS model are as follows:

1. **Individual tacit:** This behavior includes sharing tacit knowledge with an individual or individuals, such as face-to-face interactions in informal or formal meetings.

2. **Individual explicit:** This behavior includes sharing explicit knowledge with an individual or individuals, such as through sending e-mail or hard copy material to select individual(s).

3. **Group tacit:** This behavior includes sharing tacit knowledge with a group, such as face-to-face interactions with a community of interest, community of practice (CoP), or organizational unit.

4. **Group explicit:** This behavior includes sharing explicit knowledge with a group, such as posting or contributing to a community of interest, CoP, or organizational unit repository, Web site, or mailing list server.

5. **Enterprise tacit:** This behavior includes sharing tacit knowledge in an enterprise-wide forum, such as presenting at a technical exchange meeting or other forum that is open to the entire enterprise.

6. **Enterprise explicit:** This behavior includes sharing explicit knowledge in a manner that makes it available to anyone in the enterprise, such as publishing in a corporate-wide repository or enterprise-wide intranet.

While we investigate KnS behavior as being comprised of six different types, both tacit and explicit knowledge are often shared in a given situation. For example, in an enterprise KnS forum, tacit knowledge, such as unrehearsed oral presentations and responses to questions, and explicit knowledge, such as hard copy presentations, are generally both shared.

We investigate three major KnS influences on the associated sharing of knowledge:

1. The enterprise KnS environment,
2. KnS behavior of other knowledge workers, and
3. Attributes of the knowledge workers.

The KnS literature, such as reviewed in Small and Sage (2006), identifies many factors that influence KnS behavior. A discussion of each of the major influences is provided in the sections that follow.

The enterprise KnS environment is closely aligned to the Japanese concept of "ba" which translates into English as "place." Nonaka and Konno (1998) adapted this Japanese concept for their knowledge creation theory. "Ba," as described by Nonaka and Konno (1998), is the shared space for emerging relationships that can be physical, virtual, mental, or any combination of these. It is the place where knowledge is created, shared, and exploited. The "ba" is comprised of the knowledge resources and the people who own and create the knowledge. The KnS environment or "ba" is comprised of many factors that influence KnS behavior. There are at least six important influence factors in the KnS environment modeled and investigated here. A brief description of each of these factors is appropriate here:

1. **KnS technology:** KnS technologies are those technologies that allow knowledge workers to share tacit or explicit knowledge. Technologies and tools reported (APQC, 2000) as critical to knowledge sharing at best

practice firms included: e-mail, intranets, document sharing systems, collaboration tools, and video conferences. Chu (2003) included e-mail, Internet, intranet, databases, and teleconferences in his listing of these. With the advent of Web 2.0, wikis, blogs, and social networking applications are being used to enable enterprise knowledge sharing (APQC, 2008)

2. **Leadership:** Leaders and managers in an organization impact KnS behavior by directing behavior, rewarding or recognizing behavior, and by setting KnS behavior examples. Many studies indicate that organizations with appropriate KnS leadership behavior have more instances of appropriate KnS behavior than others.

3. **KnS culture:** Culture is an organization's values, norms, and unwritten rules. Most existing KM models and KnS investigations include culture as a critical enabler or influence on KnS behavior. Additionally, cultural issues are regularly cited as one of the concerns held by those implementing KM initiatives.

4. **Human networks:** This factor includes processes, technology, and resources that help to connect knowledge workers or support knowledge networks. Support for human networks, which includes informal and formal forums, is widely practiced among best practice organizations. They are often referred to as communities of practice or community of interests. Organizations can enable these networks with knowledge stewards, online collaboration tools, and tools to facilitate easy publishing.

5. **Rewards and recognition:** This factor includes the approaches organizations use to encourage or reinforce the discipline of knowledge sharing. Approaches include rewards, recognition, alignment with performance assessment and promotion, and conducting visible KnS events. When

establishing rewards, organizations must consider the generic type of behavior they are trying to stimulate. Many organizations have instituted reward and award programs for knowledge sharing and/or have integrated incentives for knowledge sharing with performance appraisals and promotions.

6. **Alignment with strategy:** This refers to the alignment of knowledge sharing with business strategy. Best practice organizations do not share knowledge for the sake of knowledge. Rather, knowledge sharing is deemed critical to achieving business goals and is linked to the business strategy (APQC, 1999). The alignment of knowledge sharing to business strategy can be either explicit or implicit. When organizations have explicit alignment, language regarding knowledge sharing can be found in documents such as strategic business plans, vision or mission statements, or performance measures. Organizations with implicit alignment are evidenced by knowledge sharing embedded in business practices. Fifty percent of the best-practice firms that participated in the APQC benchmarking study (APQC, 1999) on knowledge sharing were explicitly aligned, while the other half were implicitly aligned. Findings of two APQC benchmarking studies found that organizations where knowledge workers understood how knowledge sharing supported the business strategy had stronger KnS behavior.

The behavior of other knowledge workers within an organization affects the KnS decisions of a specific knowledge worker in many ways. Ford (2003) describes sharing knowledge as a risky behavior because the individual does not know how the shared knowledge will be used by the party who obtains it. Trust in, and some knowledge of, what the recipient of the shared knowledge will do with the shared knowledge are critical to knowledge sharing. From an enterprise perspective, knowledge workers must trust the organization not to cast them aside after the knowledge is harvested. From a peer interrelationship perspective, a knowledge worker must trust that the knowledge recipient will make ethical use of the shared knowledge (Bukowitz & Williams, 1999). If a knowledge worker shares and the knowledge recipient misuses the shared knowledge, from the perspectives of the intended purposes for sharing, then the knowledge worker may be reluctant to share knowledge in the future.

The KnS influence of individual knowledge workers attributes is very important because knowledge sharing is a human behavior in which the knowledge worker chooses to share. The decision to share is influenced by interactions. Leonard and Straus (1997), for example, assert that individuals have preferred habits of thought that influence how they make decisions and interact with others. Knowledge workers have many diverse attributes, some of which are fixed and others of which are variable. Some of the individual attributes or human factors identified in the KM and KnS literature include employees' means, ability, and motivation (Ives et al., 2000); job characteristics including workload and content (Chu, 2002); feelings of being valued and commitment to the project (Ipe, 2003); and conditions of respect, justice perception, and relationships with superiors (Liao et al., 2004).

Here, we model enterprise knowledge sharing as emergent behavior that is the result of decisions made by knowledge workers. The decisions, "Share Knowledge?" and "Type of Knowledge to Share?" depicted in *Figure 1* are based on dynamic interactions and are influenced by factors in the KnS environment, KnS behaviors of other knowledge workers, and the individual attributes and perspectives of the knowledge worker. The CAS-based enterprise KnS model integrates the knowledge worker, KnS decisions, and the KnS influences into a CAS-based framework, which consists of two major components:

1. CAS-based enterprise KnS framework
2. Enterprise KnS simulation model (e-KnS-MOD).

A detailed discussion of each of the components is provided in the sections that follow.

CAS-BASED KNS FRAMEWORK

The CAS-based KnS framework is the most critical element of our CAS-based KnS model and distinguishes it from other KM models, such as those described in Small and Sage (2006). The CAS-based KnS framework describes enterprise knowledge sharing from a complex adaptive systems perspective. The properties of a CAS, as described by Holland (1995), are aggregation, diversity, internal models, and non-linearity. Axelrod and Cohen (1999) identify variation, interaction, and selection as the hallmark of complex adaptive systems. Other important concepts of complex adaptive systems include the agent, strategy, population, type, and artifacts. For simplicity, the following constructs of a complex adaptive system have been addressed at the highest level of the enterprise KnS framework: agent, agent attributes, interactions, artifacts, and rules.

The CAS-based KnS framework, illustrated in *Figure 2*, is comprised of the following elements: knowledge worker(s); KnS environment (comprised of KnS influences/enablers and barriers); KnS behaviors; KnS rules; and attributes of the knowledge worker. The KnS behavior results from the interactions of the knowledge workers with each other and the KnS environment. The decision to share is influenced by individual attributes, KnS behavior of other knowledge workers, and the KnS environment. A mapping of the KnS influence diagram in *Figure 1* to the CAS concepts used in the CAS-based framework of *Figure 2* is as follows:

Figure 2. Major elements of the CAS-based KnS framework

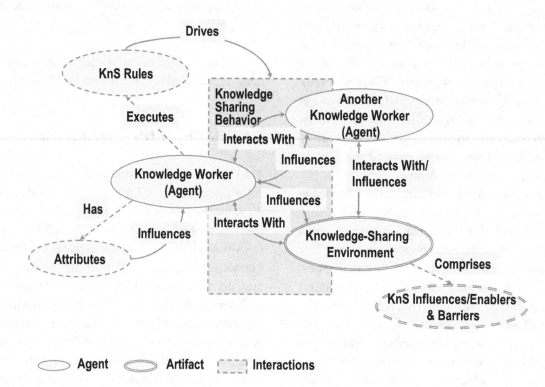

Figure 3. Investigated attributes of knowledge worker

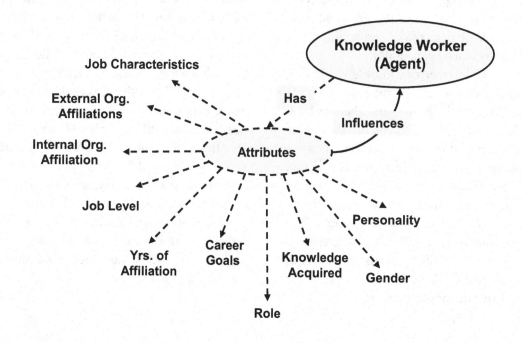

- **KnS influence diagram elements**
  - Knowledge workers
  - KnS environment
  - KnS decisions
  - Enterprise knowledge sharing
  - Knowledge worker attributes
- **CAS-based KnS framework elements**
  - KnS agents
  - KnS environment (artifacts)
  - KnS rules
  - KnS behaviors (interactions)
  - KnS agent attributes

The knowledge worker is the KnS agent within the CAS-based model. Critical to this concept is the diversity and heterogeneity of this KnS agent. The knowledge worker within an enterprise is diverse in many ways: personality, gender, role, and job level. *Figure 3* associates this segment of the KnS framework with the attributes of the knowledge worker. The KnS decisions (execution of rules) of a KnS agent depend on the agent's attributes and are influenced by the agents' interactions with other knowledge workers and the KnS environment.

The attributes of the knowledge worker investigated here include: personality, gender, level of knowledge acquired, years of affiliation, role, career goals, job level, internal organizational affiliation, external organizational affiliation, and job characteristics. These attributes are described as follows:

1. **Personality:** Such as introvert, extrovert, or a combination.
2. **Gender:** Male or female.
3. **Level of knowledge acquired:** The level of knowledge acquired over time (related to competency) by the knowledge worker.
4. **Years of affiliation:** The number of years a knowledge worker has been affiliated with the enterprise (i.e., number of years at the company).

5. **Role:** The role (s) the knowledge worker has within the enterprise, organization, or project. Examples include manager, technical leader, or technical contributor.
6. **Career goals:** The job or career-related goals possessed by the knowledge worker. Goals investigated as part of this research include: career growth (promotion), knowledge growth opportunities, satisfying customers, satisfying management, recognition, and reward.
7. **Job level:** The job level that is assigned by the company to a given knowledge worker, ranging from entry/junior level people to executive management.
8. **Internal organizational affiliation:** An enterprise usually consists of many organizations. This is the internal organization to which the knowledge worker is assigned.
9. **External organizational affiliations:** The number of external professional organizations with which the knowledge worker is affiliated.
10. **Job characteristics:** This includes number of tasks supported, workload, pace, and content of work.

KnS rules drive the decisions the knowledge worker makes. A knowledge worker has two fundamental KnS decisions: "Share Knowledge?" and "Type of Knowledge to Share?" The KnS rules are the same for all KnS agents. They are parameterized based on the attributes of the agents, behavior or other knowledge workers, and the state of the KnS environment.

An enterprise KnS environment consists of many factors that influence or enable KnS behavior. A KnS artifact is an entity in the enterprise (not a person) with which the knowledge worker interacts that either influences or enables their KnS behavior. An enterprise has many KnS artifacts, including information technology, performance and reward systems, knowledge repositories, and information help desk. The KnS influences or enablers examined here and illustrated in *Figure 4* include: KnS linked to corporate strategy, alignment of rewards and recognition, KnS embedded with work processes, KnS aligned with core values, enabling of human networks, and KnS technology (availability and ease of use). The artifacts that exist in an environment can have different enabling characteristics. A five-state characterization instrument was developed to characterize the KnS environment.

A knowledge worker (KW) gains or acquires knowledge by interacting with the environment and other knowledge workers. Knowledge sharing results in and from a KW interacting with another KW and/or with the KnS environment. Enterprise knowledge sharing is the result of knowledge workers interacting with other knowledge workers and the enterprise KnS environment. Included in the CAS-based framework are the following KnS behaviors: individual tacit, group tacit, enterprise tacit, individual explicit, group explicit, and enterprise explicit.

MULTI-AGENT ENTERPRISE KNS SIMULATION MODEL (E-KNSMOD)

The enterprise KnS model (e-KnSMOD) simulates enterprise knowledge sharing as the emergent behavior of knowledge workers, represented as agents, interacting with the KnS environment and other knowledge workers. The design of the e-KnSMOD is based on the CAS-based KnS framework described here. All of the constructs of the framework (KnS agent, agent attributes, KnS behavior, KnS environment, and rules) are implemented in the simulation model. For simplicity, the simulation model implements a subset of the attributes (level of knowledge, role, career goals, job level, and internal organizational affiliation) of the knowledge worker included in the CAS-based framework. The purpose of the model is to examine the effects of the KnS enterprise environment and behavior of other knowledge workers on the KnS behavior of a heterogeneous population of knowledge workers. Epstein and Axtell (1996) refer to agent-based models of so-

Figure 4. KnS influences/enablers investigated

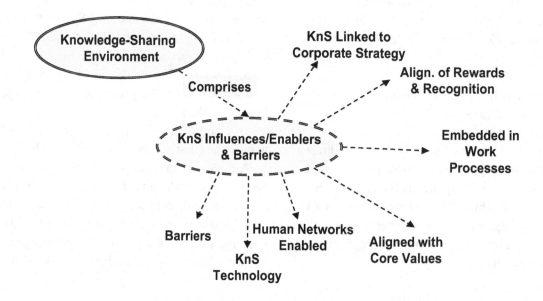

cial processes as artificial societies. The design and implementation of this model leverages the agent-based computer modeling of the artificial society known as The Sugarscape Model (Epstein & Axtell, 1996) and the Sugarscape source code developed by Nelson and Minar (1997) using Swarm (Minar et al., 1996; Johnson & Lancaster, 2000; Swarm Development Group, 2004).

The e-KnSMOD model simulates a population of knowledge workers that work in an artificial enterprise. As with Sugarscape (Epstein & Axtell, 1996), the e-KnSMOD leverages the research results that have been obtained using cellular automata (CA) for agent-based modeling. KnS agents represent the knowledge workers, and the CA represents the artificial enterprise, KnS-scape. The KnS agents interact with each other and their environment as they move around the enterprise gaining valuable knowledge (a goal of many knowledge workers). Agents acquire

knowledge by engaging in a knowledge creation opportunity or by receiving knowledge shared by other knowledge workers. In order to satisfy their goals, they must continue to generate new knowledge. As conceptually depicted in *Figure 5*, the e-KnSMOD consists of three major elements:

1. KnS agents ("knowledge workers")
2. The artificial enterprise or KnS-scape
3. Interactions (driven by rules).

Each of these elements, as implemented in the e-KnSMOD, is described in the following subsections.

KnS Agent

A KnS agent represents a knowledge worker in the artificial enterprise. The KnS agents are heterogeneous. This implementation of e-KnSMOD

Figure 5. Major elements of the e-KnSMOD

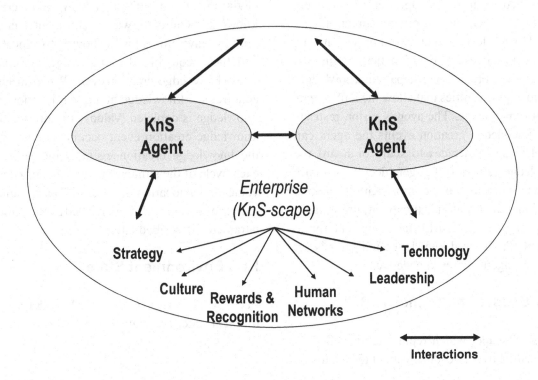

models the following subset of attributes included in the CAS-based KnS framework: level of knowledge acquired, role, job level, and organization affiliation. Each KnS Agent is characterized by a set of fixed and variable states that vary among the agents. The fixed states include:

1. Level of knowledge acquired (competency)
2. Job level (vision is based on job level) in organization (e.g., Jr. Analyst, Sr. Analyst, Principal, Director)
3. Role in organization (manager, non-manager)
4. Organizational affiliation.

Each agent has the following variable states:

- New knowledge gained
- Location on the KnS-scape
- KnS indicator (indicates if the agent shared in the previous run cycle).

The KnS agent comes to the KnS-scape with a specified competency. Upon entry, the agent is assigned a vision and organizational affiliation. The job level is then based on vision. The KnS agent moves (changes location) around the enterprise in order to participate in knowledge-creation opportunities that allow the KnS agents to gain knowledge. The agent's vision restricts what knowledge creation events the agent can see. The agent decides to share or hoard the knowledge gained. If the agent decides to share, it can participate in one or more KnS behaviors: individual tacit, individual explicit, group tacit, group explicit, enterprise tacit, and enterprise explicit. The shared knowledge indicator is set when the agent shares knowledge.

KnS-Scape: The Artificial "Ba"

The KnS-scape, which represents the "Ba," is represented by a two-dimensional (50 x 50) co-ordinate grid. The grid is built using the Swarm tool set. The grid has multiple views. Each point (x, y) on the grid has a knowledge-creation opportunity, an organization identifier, and a KnS environment state. The information needed by the model to create these views is read from data files, which can be specified at run time. A KnS agent is randomly placed on the KnS-scape. The organizational unit associated with the agent's initial location on the KnS-scape determines an agent's organizational affiliation. When a KnS agent engages in a knowledge-creation opportunity, it acquires the knowledge associated with the opportunity. An organization view of the KnS-scape would indicate that there are four different organizations within the enterprise. The KnS agents are colored by the organizational affiliation of their initial location on the KnS-scape.

Knowledge-Creation Opportunity

Each location on the KnS-scape, represented by an (x, y) coordinate, has a knowledge-creation event or opportunity. KnS agents interacting with their environment and with other KnS agents create knowledge. One of the ways a KnS agent interacts with the environment is by moving to a location and then acquiring the knowledge associated with a knowledge-creation event. When an agent acquires the knowledge at a given location, the knowledge is depleted (value = 0) until another knowledge creation event occurs. The value of the knowledge creation event is increased on each cycle of the simulation until the maximum value for that location is achieved. The amount of increase on each cycle is controlled by the "alpha" parameter, described later.

KnS Environment State

Each location on the KnS-scape has a KnS environment state. The states are as follows:

1. **Barrier:** KnS environment has a negative impact on KnS behavior.
2. **Neutral:** KnS environment has no or minimum impact on KnS behavior.
3. **Enabled:** KnS environment enables KnS behavior.
4. **Encouraged:** KnS environment encourages KnS behavior.
5. **Aligned:** KnS environment positively influences KnS behavior.

KnS Organization View

Each location on the KnS-scape, represented by an (x, y) coordinate, has an organizational identifier. When an agent enters the KnS-scape, it is given the organizational identifier of the location where it is placed. The organizational identifier is used in group KnS behaviors.

Interactions: Acquiring and Sharing Knowledge

The KnS agent interacts with the KnS-scape and with other KnS agents. As previously described, each KnS agent comes to the KnS-scape with a vision that allows it to see knowledge-creation opportunities. During each simulation cycle, an agent looks out over the KnS-scape and determines the location of the best knowledge-creation opportunity. It then moves there and acquires the knowledge. If the KnS agent acquires enough knowledge to share, the KnS agent then chooses to share or not to share. The KnS agent can participate in six types of KnS behaviors: individual tacit, individual explicit, group tacit, group explicit, enterprise tacit and enterprise explicit. The impact of each of these KnS interactions is briefly described as follows:

1. Tacit individual: Results in the "current knowledge" attribute of the recipient KnS agent being increased. The physical vicinity of KnS agents restricts this interaction.

2. Tacit group: Results in the "knowledge acquired" attribute of the recipient KnS agents being increased. The "current knowledge" attribute restricts this interaction.

3. Tacit enterprise: Results in the "current knowledge" attribute of all KnS agents being increased. The "organizational affiliation" attribute restricts this interaction.

4. Explicit individual: Results in the "current knowledge" attribute of the recipient KnS agent being increased.

5. Explicit group: Results in an increase of knowledge in the organizational or group repository.

6. Explicit enterprise: Results in an increase of knowledge in the enterprise repository.

The most important aspect of "ba" is interaction. Important to this research is that knowledge is created by the individual knowledge worker as a result of interactions with other knowledge workers and with the environment.

Rules for the KnS-Scape

Eptein and Axtell (1996) describe three types of rules: agent-environment rule, environment-environment rule, and agent-agent rule. There are three types of similar rules in the KnS-scape model:

1. Agent movement rule;
2. Generation of new knowledge creation events rule;
3. KnS rule.

A brief description of each rule is provided here:

- **Agent movement rule:** The KnS agent uses the movement rule to move around the KnS-scape. The movement rule processes local information about the KnS-scape and returns rank ordering of the state according to some criteria. The rules and functions used by the agents are the same for all agents. The values of the parameters change based on the attributes of the agent and the state of the environment. A summary of the movement rule is as follows:

1. Look out as far as vision (an agent attribute) permits and identify the unoccupied site(s) that best satisfies the knowledge acquisition goal.
2. If goals can be satisfied by multiple sites, select the closest site.
3. Move to the site.
4. Collect the knowledge associated with the knowledge-creation opportunity of the new position.

-   **Generation of new knowledge creation events:** A knowledge creation event has a knowledge value. After the knowledge is collected from the site on the KnS-scape, the value goes to zero (it no longer exists). The frequency of new events is driven by the "alpha" parameter. At the end of each cycle, each location on the KnS-scape is incremented by the "alpha" value until it reaches its maximum value.

-   **KnS Rule:** After an agent completes the move to the new location and acquires the knowledge there, the KnS rule is executed. The decision to share and the type of knowledge to share is dependent on the KnS behavior of other agents, the KnS environment state, and the "level of knowledge acquired" attribute.

-   **E-KnSMOD—Simulation of enterprise knowledge sharing:** Enterprise knowledge sharing is simulated by the e-KnSMOD. Enterprise knowledge sharing is measured by the number of KnS agents participating in one of the six KnS behaviors, the percent of KnS agents that share, the frequency that KnS agents share, and the number of items deposited into the group or enterprise repositories.

Initializing the e-KnSMOD environment properly is important here. E-KnSMOD, built using the Swarm tool set, has two basic components: the Observer Swarm, and the Model Swarm. Swarms are objects that implement memory allocation and event scheduling. Upon execution of the e-KnSMOD, two probes and a program control panel are displayed. The observer (ObserverSwarm) and model (ModelSwarm) probes consist of default parameters that are modifiable by the user. After the parameters for the Observer Swarm and Model Swarm are processed, the e-KnSMOD environment is established by creating the Observer and Model objects and building the Scheduler. The Observer objects consist of the windows used to display the KnS-scape and KnS agents and other graphs specified by the user. The Model objects consist of the KnS-scape and the KnS agents. These steps are described next:

1. **Creation of the KnS-scape:** The KnS-scape, a 50 x 50 lattice, represents the KnS enterprise environment. Each location (x,y) on the KnS-scape has a knowledge creation opportunity, an organization identifier, and a KnS environment state. The KnS_event, organization, and KnS_environment data-files (specified in the ModelSwarm probe) are used to build the characteristics of each (x,y) location, respectively. The knowledge creation events, which have a value of 1 through 5, are observable by the user of the KnS model from the KnS-scape window. The value of a knowledge creation (KC) event is distinguishable by color as represented in the KnS-scape window illustrated in *Figure 6*.

2. **Creation of the KnS agents:** After the KnS-scape is created, the KnS agents are created and randomly placed on the KnS-scape. The "KnSnumAgents" parameter is used to determine how many KnS agents are created. The model creates a heterogeneous population of KnS agents. Some of the at-

Figure 6. Knowledge creation (KC) events on the KnS-scape

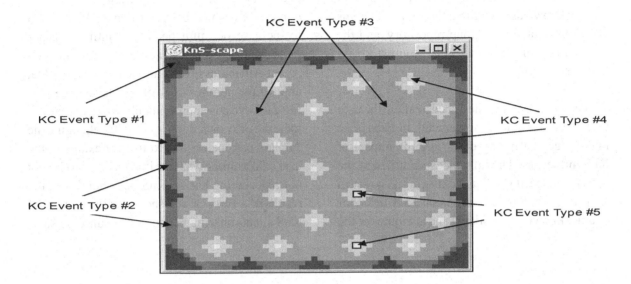

tributes are randomly generated, and others are based on where the agent is placed on the KnS-scape. The agents organizational affiliation is determined by the organization associated with the (x, y) coordinate at which the agent is placed. The initial value of current knowledge is based on the vision, which is randomly generated.

3. **Creation of the scheduler:** The observer swarm and the model swarm create a schedule for activities to be performed during each cycle of the model. The model swarm schedules the actions to be performed by the KnS agents and the actions to be performed on the KnS-scape. The actions include:

   1. **KnS agent:** Move and acquire knowledge.

   2. **KnS agent:** Execute KnS behavior rule.

   3. **KnS-scape:** Update KnS-scape (Knowledge Creation Event View).

   4. **KnS repositories:** Update group and enterprise repositories.

   5. **Display:** Update KnS-scape display window.

   6. **Display:** Update knowledge distribution graph.

   7. **Display:** Update KnS attributes over time.

   8. **Summary File:** Update KnS summary (metrics) file.

4. **Model Output:** The e-KnSMOD has three primary output windows that are updated after each cycle. The windows include: KnS agent attributes over time, agent knowledge distribution, and the KnS-scape. Additionally, the model maintains a KnS summary data file that captures the KnS metrics of the KnS agents. This data file is used for additional data analysis outside the e-KnSMOD environment. The following KnS metrics are captured by the model: the number of KnS

agents that shared, the number of agents that shared by organization, the average amount of knowledge acquired, the number of items contributed to a group repository, and the number of items contributed to an enterprise repository.

The e-KnSMOD is designed to allow the user to explore possible improvements in enterprise knowledge sharing by observing the impact of KnS influences. The influences identified in the enterprise sharing influence diagram, shown in *Figure 1*, are: KnS environment, KnS behavior of other knowledge workers, and attributes of the

knowledge workers. *Figure 7* shows the results of a 10-cycle run using the default "alpha" value (alpha = 1), which causes a depleted KC event to increase one unit per cycle until it reaches its maximum capacity. Examination of the KnS Agent Attributes Over Time window shows that an average number of KnS agents sharing during each cycle is approximately 50, with a steady increase of knowledge acquired. By changing the "alpha" parameter to zero (0), for example, the user can examine what the impact of the KC event not reoccurring has on KnS behavior. Here, the results of a 10-cycle run show that the number of KnS agents sharing began to drop until no shar-

Figure 7. Example run – recurring rate for KC events = 1

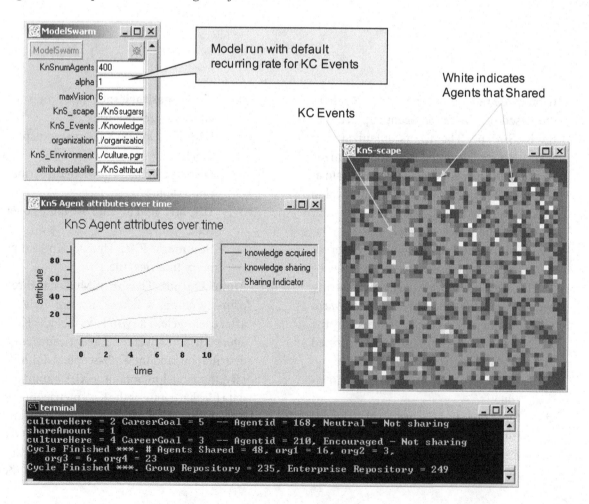

ing occurred. The resulting KnS-scape window shows that there are no KC events.

Sensitivity analysis may be performed on e-KnSMOD by executing the model of several varying conditions in order to determine if small changes to the parameters resulted in unexpected results. Analysis may be performed on the parameters that are used in either the KnS rule or the environment rules. A summary of the findings are:

1. **Number of agents:** the model was tested with the number of agents ranging from 100 to 500 with varying conditions. In most cases, the percent of agents sharing increases slightly (< 1.5%) as one increases the number of agents in increments of 50. The number of agents was more sensitive in the range of 100-300 than in the range of 200-500.

2. **Behavior influence:** the model was tested by setting this parameter to 0 and 1. In all the tests conducted the percent of agents sharing decreased in the range of 1.7 to 4.0 percent when the parameter was changed from 0 to 1.

3. **Max vision:** The maximum vision was tested with the values 7, 14 and 28. In most cases, as the vision increased (7 to 14 to 28) the resulting knowledge sharing increased ~ 1 %. However, the percent was higher when the knowledge creation events with high value (part of the KnS_scape) were further apart.

4. **KnS_scape:**– the percent of agents sharing is impacted most by this parameter. The KnS agents acquire knowledge from the KnS_scape and if the agent does not have knowledge, it does not share.

5. **KnS_environment:** the percent of agents sharing is impacted greatly by this parameter. A difference of one state (i.e., barrier to neutral or neutral to enable) can change the percent of agent sharing from 5 % to 14 %.

Much more detailed discussions of the construction of this simulation model are presented in Small (2006).

As described in this article, the e-KnSMOD, is a simple multi-agent simulation based on simple environment and KnS rules. The environment is represented by three 2-dimentional (50 by 50) lattices: one for the knowledge creation events, one for the organization affiliation, and one for the state of the KnS environment. Many complex relationships among the KWs and the KnS environment are not included in the implementation of e-KnSMOD. The objective of the model is not to predict enterprise KnS behavior, but to be used with the other CAS-based tools to enhance the understanding of enterprise knowledge sharing.

One major use of this KnS model is to improve enterprise knowledge sharing. The CAS-based enterprise KnS model can assist enterprise KM leadership, managers, practitioners, and others involved in KM implementation to characterize the current KnS environment, identify influences of KnS behavior, and better understand the impact of KnS interventions. This model can be applied to enterprises that are about to embark on KnS initiatives, as well as those that have a rich KnS portfolio.

The CAS-based characterization instruments allow a practitioner to characterize enterprise KnS from the perspective of the KW and from that of KM Leadership. Both instruments characterize the frequency of KnS behaviors, the extent of influence of KnS influences and barriers, and the state of the KnS environment. The data gathered using these instruments provide the information needed to characterize and model an enterprise from a CAS perspective.

The KW Profiling Questionnaire is a critical element here. The purpose of the KW Profiling Questionnaire is to determine, from an individual knowledge worker perspective, the answers to four questions:

1. What are your attributes?
2. What is your KnS behavior?
3. What influences your KnS behavior?
4. What is the state of the KnS environment?

The answers to these questions allow a KM practitioner to investigate the extent of KnS influences on the heterogeneous knowledge worker populations. Addressing the attributes of the knowledge worker is a critical aspect of this CAS-based methodology.

The focus of the KM Leadership Characterization Questionnaire is to determine, from the perspective of KM leadership and implementers, the answers to the following four questions:

• Part I: What is the understanding of the KM Leadership Team regarding the KnS needs (mission perspective) and KnS behavior within the organization?

• Part II: What are the KnS influences and the extent of the influences within your enterprise?

• Part III: What is the state of the KnS enablers/influences within your enterprise?

• Part IV: What is the KnS Strategy for Improvement?

Part I and Part IV of the KM leadership characterization instrument relates to the KnS improvement strategy. Part I addresses the importance of KnS to support mission needs, and whether KnS is occurring at the right level (individual, group, enterprise) and frequency. Part IV addresses the KnS strategy, which includes areas of improvement and the priority for achievement. The relationships of these questions to the CAS-based KnS framework are depicted in *Figure 8*.

Figure 8. KM leadership characterization and the CAS-based KnS framework

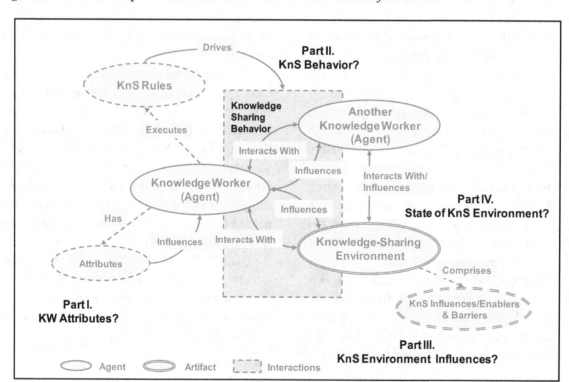

The CAS-based KnS improvement methodology can be used by either an enterprise about to embark on KnS improvement activities for the first time (Initial Stage) or an enterprise that has a KnS strategy and robust KnS portfolio (Learning Stage). The tools described here can be used to identify and prioritize KnS improvement courses of action. The CAS-based methodology consists of five primary steps:

1. **Step 1—Determine KnS needs in context of mission effectiveness:** During this step, the KM practitioner determines the importance of KnS to the organization and assesses whether KnS is occurring at the appropriate frequency to support mission needs. Part I of the KM Leadership Characterization Questionnaire is used to gather this information.

2. **Step 2—Characterize current state of KnS:** During this step, the KW profiling instrument is used to characterize KnS in the organization from a CAS perspective. The frequency of KnS behavior, KnS influences, and the state of the KnS environment are characterized from the individual knowledge worker perspective.

3. **Step 3—Establish KnS target state:** During this step, Part III of the KM Leadership Characterization Questionnaire is used to capture the target state of the KnS environment, identify factors in the KnS environment that need improvement, and to establish priority of their implementation.

4. **Step 4—Perform CAS-based analysis:** During this step, population analysis is performed based on KW attributes of interest to the organization. A gap analysis is performed on areas targeted for improvement against the extent of influence of the KnS factors identified by the KWs.

5. **Step 5—Develop KnS improvement strategy:** During this step, the results of the CAS-based analysis are used to develop

or align the KnS strategy. The current state of the KnS environment (KW perspective), the target state of KnS environment (KM leadership), and the extent of KnS influence (KW perspective) are used to identify areas of improvement and their priority. The CAS-based simulation model can be used to model the planned improvements to gain insight into the possible impacts on KnS behavior.

The steps of the CAS-based KnS methodology should be integrated into the organizational improvement framework. We describe the CAS-based KnS improvement methodology in the context of the IDEAL^{SM} (SEI, 1996) model, an improvement process originally designed for software process improvement. The IDEAL^{SM} model consists of five phases:

1. **Initiating:** This phase lays the groundwork for a successful KnS improvement effort. It includes setting the context and sponsorship, and establishing the improvement infrastructure (organizations). Step 1 is conducted during this phase.

2. **Diagnosing:** Assessing the current state of KnS in the enterprise and determining where the organization is relative to the target state. Step 2, 3, and 4 are conducted during this phase.

3. **Establishing:** Developing strategies and plans for achieving the KnS target state. Step 5 is conducted during this phase.

4. **Acting:** Executing the plan to improve KnS.

5. **Learning:** Learning from the KnS experience and feedback from mission stakeholders, KM leadership, and knowledge workers.

As shown in *Figure 9*, Step 1 occurs during the Initiating phase. Step 2, 3, and 4 occur during the Diagnosing phase, and Step 5 concurs during the Establishing phase.

Figure 9. CAS-based methodology: An IDEAL^{SM} perspective

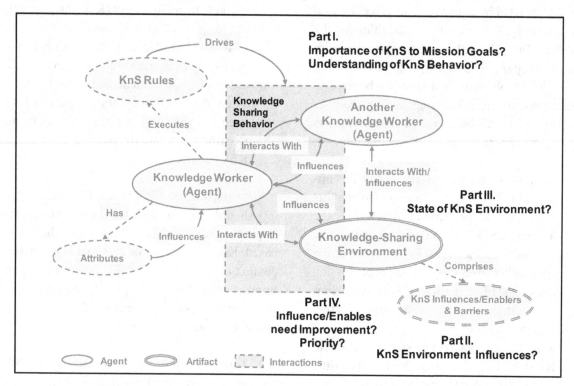

SUMMARY

A CAS-based enterprise KnS model is described in this article. The model was evaluated for validity and effectiveness in two case studies. The premise of our research was that modeling enterprise knowledge sharing from a complex adaptive systems (CAS) perspective can provide KM leadership and practitioners with an enhanced understanding of KnS behavior within their organization. This research found that the CAS-based enterprise KnS model and methodology provides KM leadership with an enhanced understanding of KnS behavior and the KnS influences. In the two case studies conducted in operational environments, members of the KM leadership teams indicated that they had gained a better understanding because of the CAS-based

modeling approach. Enhanced understanding of the following was indicated: KnS behavior in their organization; KnS influences in their organization; and the extent of the KnS influences within their organization. KM leadership also indicated that because of the CAS-based modeling, they would either change the target KnS state of the KnS environment or the priority for achieving that state.

The CAS-based enterprise KnS model developed as part of this research was found to be valid. The CAS-based enterprise KnS model was exercised in two case studies. The results of the case studies (Small, 2006) provided support for the validity of the assumptions on which the CAS-based enterprise KnS model was developed. The claims associated with the validity of the CAS-based enterprise KnS model are as follows:

1. **Claim 1 (C1):** The KnS behavior of other KWs is a significant influence on KnS behavior.
2. **Claim 2 (C2):** The KnS environment factors are a significant influence on KnS behavior.
3. **Claim 3 (C3):** The attributes of the KW are related to the frequency of KnS behavior (how often a KW engages in a KnS behavior).
4. **Claim 4 (C4):** Enterprise KnS behavior can be characterized using a multi-agent CAS model, with a few basic rules that drive agent behavior.

REFERENCES

American Productivity & Quality Center (APQC). (1999). *Creating a knowledge-sharing culture.* Consortium Benchmarking Study—Best-Practice Report.

American Productivity & Quality Center (APQC). (2000). *Successfully implementing knowledge management.* Consortium Benchmarking Study—Final Report, 2000.

Anderson, P. (1999). Complexity theory and organization science. *Organization Science, 10*(3), 216-232.

Axelrod, R. (1997). *The complexity of cooperation: Agent-based models of competition and collaboration.* New Jersey: Princeton University Press.

Axelrod, R., & Cohen, M. (1999). *Harnessing complexity: Organizational implications of a scientific frontier.* New York: The Free Press.

Bukowitz, W., & Williams, R. (1999). *The knowledge management fieldbook.* London: Financial Times Prentice Hall.

Epstein, M., & Axtell, R. (1996). *Growing artificial societies: Social science from the bottom up.* Washington D.C.: The Brookings Institution.

Ford, D. (2003). Trust and knowledge management: The seeds of success. In *Handbook on Knowledge Management 1: Knowledge Matters* (pp. 553-575). Heidelberg: Springer-Verlag.

HBSP. (1998). *Harvard Business review on knowledge management.* Cambridge, MA: Harvard Business School Press.

Holland, J. (1995). *Hidden order: How adaptation builds complexity.* MA: Perseus Books Reading.

Holsapple, C.W. (Ed.). (2003). *Handbook on knowledge management 1: Knowledge matters.* Heidelberg: Springer-Verlag.

Holsapple, C.W. (Ed). (2003). *Handbook on knowledge management 2: Knowledge directions.* Heidelberg: Springer-Verlag.

Ipe, M. (2003). *The praxis of knowledge sharing in organizations: A case study.* Doctoral dissertation. University Microfilms.

Ives, W., Torrey, B., & Gordon, C. (2000). Knowledge sharing is human behavior. In *Knowledge management: Classic and contemporary works* (pp. 99-129).

Johnson, P., & Lancaster, A. (2000). *Swarm users guide.* Swarm Development Group.

Leonard, D., & Straus, S. (1998). Putting your company's whole brain to work. In *Harvard Business Review on Knowledge Management* (pp. 109-136). Boston: Harvard Business School Press.

Liao, S., Chang, J., Shih-chieh, C., & Chia-mei, K. (2004). Employee relationship and knowledge sharing: A case study of a Taiwanese finance and securities firm. *Knowledge Management Research & Practice, 2,* 24-34.

Minar, N., Burkhar, R., Langton C., & Askemnazi, M. (1996). *The Swarm Simulation System: A toolkit for building multi-agent simulations.* Retrieved from http://alumni.media.mit.edu/~nelson/research/ swarm/.

Murray, S. (2003). *A quantitative examination to determine if knowledge sharing activities, given the appropriate richness lead to knowledge transfer, and if implementation factors influence the use of these knowledge sharing activities.* Doctoral dissertation. University Microfilms.

Nonaka, I., & Konno, N. (1998). The concept of Ba: Building a foundation for knowledge creation. *California Management Review (Special Issue on Knowledge and the Firm), 40*(3), 40-54.

Nonaka, I., & Takeuchi, H. (1995). *The knowledge-creating company: How Japanese companies create the dynamics of innovation.* New York: Oxford University Press.

O'Dell, C. (2008). *Web 2.0 and knowledge management.* American Productivity & Quality Center (APQC). Retrieved from http://www.apqc.org.

Small, C. (2006). *An enterprise knowledge-sharing model: A complex adaptive systems perspective on improvement in knowledge sharing.* Doctoral dissertation, George Mason University. University Microfilms.

Small, C., & Sage, A. (2006). Knowledge management and knowledge sharing: A review. *Information, Knowledge, and Systems Management, 5*(3), 153-169.

Software Engineering Institute (SEI). (1996). *IDEAL^{SM}: A user's guide for software process improvement* (Handbook CMU/SEI-96-HB-001). Pittsburgh, PA: Software Engineering Institute, Carnegie Mellon University.

Swarm Development Group. (2004). *Chris Langton, Glen Ropella.* Retrieved from http://wiki.swarm.org/.

Chapter XVII
Developing a Telecommunication Operation Support Systems (OSS):
The Impact of a Change in Network Technology

James G. Williams
University of Pittsburgh, USA

Kai A. Olsen
Molde College and University of Bergen, Norway

ABSTRACT

The Telecommunications Act of 1996 opened competition in the telecommunications market in the U.S. and forced the incumbent telecommunications companies to open both their physical and logical infrastructure for competitive local exchange carriers (CLECs). In this case study we focus on the problems that face a CLEC with regard to designing an information system and getting a back office system, called an operations support systems (OSS), operational in a highly competitive, complex, fast-paced market in a compressed time frame when a change in a critical telecommunications network component, namely the central office switch, is made after 75% of the system implementation was completed. This case deals with the factors that led to this change in central office switches, its impact on the IT department, its impact on the company, and the alternatives considered by the IT department as possible solutions to the many problems created by this change.

ORGANIZATIONAL BACKGROUND

Starting in the 1970s, there have been many deregulation efforts in many sectors of the U.S. economy as well as internationally. The basic objectives have been to increase competition, improve service, and lower prices (Perez, 1994).

In the telecommunications sector, an abundance of new firms have emerged since the Telecommunications Act of 1996, both to provide new services such as data networks and wireless, but also to compete with established wire line telephone services. While deregulation opened the telecommunications sector for competition in these areas, many of the new services were made possible by the advent of new technologies: wireless services, broadband on a twisted wire pair (DSL), optical fiber, digital switchboards, the Internet and the Web standards. In many cases, the new entrants (CLECS) were the first to apply these newer technologies.

In the telecommunications sector, the Telecommunications Act of 1996 opened up competition for local voice and data services. The incumbents in the U.S., the Regional Bell Operating Companies (RBOC) called Incumbent Local Exchange Carriers (ILECs), were forced to lease infrastructure to the new entrants, namely, Competitive Local Exchange Carriers (CLECs). Many CLECs managed to get their business and associated networks installed and running in a remarkably short period of time. However, as Martin F. McDermott discusses in his book *CLEC* (McDermott, 2002), problems occurred primarily in other areas. One area that caused major problems was operations support systems (OSS) and its associated provisioning and billing related functions.

Thus, by 1999, there were political rulings, court rulings, and FCC orders that laid a foundation for competition in the local exchange (CLEC) telecommunications sector in the U.S. This was a go-ahead signal for many new companies. By 2000, there were more than 700 CLECs. Some of these were sales only companies (Total Resale)

and owned no infrastructure but used the ILEC infrastructure to sell telecommunications services using different market plans and lower prices since the ILECS had to sell services to the CLECS at a discounted (wholesale) price. Other CLECs were facility based and developed a network and switching infrastructure; in many cases using new types of equipment and technologies. For example, they used DSL (digital subscriber line) to provide both data and phone services on the standard local loop (2-wire pair).

Broadstreet Communications, Inc., an entrant into the facilities based CLEC arena in February, 2000, was formed by eight individuals who had experience working for ILECS, CLECS, cable companies, or teaching and consulting for the telecommunications industry. The founders determined that there was a reasonable market for combined voice and data services for small and medium sized businesses over broadband facilities using DSL technology and formulated a business plan based on this technology as a foundation for the company. Small and medium sized businesses were defined as having between 1 and 100 employees. Based on the business plan, the founders were able to acquire 62 million dollars in venture capital from 3 different venture capitalist companies. In addition, Lucent Technologies provided $120 million dollars in financing for a total of $182 million dollars of available capital. The company was headquartered in an industrial park about 30 miles southeast of Pittsburgh, Pennsylvania and established its service area as the mid-Atlantic states of Pennsylvania, Maryland, and Virginia, as well as Washington, DC.

A major part of the business plan was the utilization of information technology to contain costs and provide a high level of service to internal users as well as customers. This was the ultimate goal of the information system design but with the need to remain within the boundaries of the business plan. The difficulties of building an information system that would integrate all aspects of the highly complex telecommunications industry are well known but the task becomes even more difficult when, after 9 months of system development on a 12 month completion schedule, a major change is made in the most critical component of the telecommunications network, namely the central office switch. The impact of this change in network components is the focus of this case study and includes the technological, organizational, managerial, industry, and economic issues that all interact in making system design decisions when a major change occurs in the environment that impacts many of the originally envisioned system requirements. This includes issues related to hardware, system software, application software, networking, scalability, reliability, buy vs. make decisions, requirements engineering, Flow through Provisioning, interfaces with the public telephone network (PSTN), reciprocal relationships with other telephone companies, and the difficulties associated with adopting new packet switched technologies for voice.

Products/Services Provided

Broadstreet Communications, Inc. was a telecommunications company offering voice and data services to small and medium sized businesses employing packet switched, broadband, digital subscriber line (DSL) technologies. This technology offered significant cost and service advantages over the traditional analog loops and leased lines traditionally used to provide voice and data services to a customer's premise.

BroadStreet provided an integrated suite of business communications services including high-speed data, local and long distance voice, voice messaging, e-mail, Internet, as well as Web and application hosting. Through the development of a next generation network, BroadStreet was among the first service providers to deliver voice and data solutions over an Internet Protocol (IP) network, and leverage digital subscriber line (DSL) technologies for last mile connectivity to customers. Local and long distance voice services

included all the services provided by a commercial central office switch such as caller ID, call forwarding, conference calling, voice messaging, E911, 800 numbers, and so forth. Data services included Local Area Network (LAN) services, Internet access, e-mail, Web site hosting, and application hosting.

Management Structure

Broadstreet Communications had a fairly flat but hierarchical organizational structure as shown in Figure 1.

The board of directors was composed of representatives from the Venture Capitalist groups (3) and 2 members of Broadstreet Communications, namely, the CEO and president, plus one outside members agreed upon by those members. The CEO was also the Chairman of the Board of Directors. The two anomalies in the structure were that the CIO and the VP of Sales had junior VPs for information systems and regional sales offices based on the demands of the individuals who fulfilled those roles.

Financial Status

At startup, Broadstreet Communications had $62 million dollars of venture capital from three different venture capital firms and $120 million dollars of financing from Lucent Technologies. The original business plan called for Broadstreet to begin delivering services and realizing revenue after one year of development. But, it took Broadstreet approximately 18 months to become fully operational and during that time it operated on the venture capital and finance funding provided with no revenue from products or services. After 18 months of developing an infrastructure of personnel, sales offices, networks, and information systems; Broadstreet began to offer products and services to small and medium sized business customers. This began in the Pittsburgh, Pennsylvania area and then expanded to Baltimore,

Figure 1.

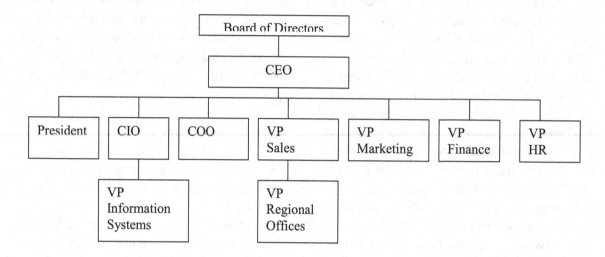

Maryland; Washington, DC; Richmond, Virginia; and Norfolk, Virginia. Within 7 months of offering services to customers, Broadstreet had approximately 1,400 customers with revenues of slightly over $1 million per month. Broadstreet was growing at approximately 20% per month. Based on covenants agreed to between Lucent Technologies and Broadstreet, as well as operating costs, the company needed to have revenues of approximately $2 million per month to cover costs. It was quite clear that had Broadstreet started offering services and realizing revenue 4 to 6 months earlier, the finance covenants and operating costs could have been met. Had the Back-office OSS system been operational 4 to 6 months earlier, Broadstreet would have survived the economic downturn that began in 2000, but the delay caused by the introduction of a new central office switch did not make this possible. It was late in 2001 when the "dot com" bust and the telecom sector's severe downturn caused Lucent Technologies to terminate the financing agreement based on the covenants, and one of the venture capitalist that suffered large losses in the "dot com" bust also decided to terminate

their investment. This made operating impossible due the lack of resources and Broadstreet made a decision to close the business after approximately 2 ½ years. At that point in time Broadstreet had over 180 employees as well as a number of subcontractors who were dependent upon BroadStreet for their livelihood.

Strategic Planning

In early 1999, the VP of operations for Adelphia Business Solutions decided that the Telecom Act of 1996, the advent of DSL technologies, and the telecommunications needs of small and medium sized businesses made the telecommunications market an attractive investment with large revenue opportunities (New Paradigm Resources Group, Inc., 2002). He contacted individuals who had special expertise in the areas of telecommunications technologies and networking, sales, marketing, finance and accounting, human resources, and information systems and technologies (IT). He asked the IT expert to gather data related to potential customers in major cities along the east coast of the U.S. as well as data on ILECS and other CLECs serving the same region. This data was used to determine the potential revenue for offering telecommunications services. At a meeting convened by this individual, all of the recruited individuals expressed an interest in leaving their current positions and forming a startup company to offer voice and data services over DSL to small and medium sized businesses

Each individual in this group was assigned the task of documenting a plan for getting their area of responsibility operational. This included the activities that needed to be accomplished, the schedule for completing the activities, the resources required to become operational, the cost of operating, and policies and procedures that would be followed in their area of responsibility. The marketing individual was tasked with defining the products and services, market service areas, the expected number of customers, and the estimated revenue. The individual in charge of sales was tasked with determining where sales offices would be located, the staffing required for each office, the sales methods to be used, and the policies and procedures from the time a sales order was acquired, to provisioning the service, to billing, and finally to customer follow-up. The telecommunications technology expert was tasked with determining what technologies would be used to offer the DSL service and interface with the Public Switched Telephone Network, how these technologies would be networked together, how the network would be monitored and controlled, how the products and services would be provisioned after a sale, and how repairs would be made when an outage occurred. The Human Resources expert was charged with determining the policies and procedures for managing the personnel issues related to hiring, termination, benefits, payroll, expense reimbursement, and work place safety and health issues. The finance and accounting expert was tasked with exploring sources of revenue including venture capitalists, bank loans, and other financing options, as well as establishing an accounting system with appro-

priate policies and procedures. The information systems expert was tasked with developing a plan for what information technologies were required to support and integrate all the other plans. This, of course, meant that the IT plan could not be fully formulated until all the other plans had been developed and required working closely with all the other groups to assess needs and offer advice as to what technologies could be used to support their areas. While others were getting started on their plans, the IT expert began to examine what operations support systems other CLECs and ILECS had either developed or acquired from software vendors. A major effort was to evaluate how competitors were offering converged local voice, long distance voice, data, and Internet services (Emre, 2001).

One of the strategic decisions made by the IT expert was to minimize the number of hardware, software, and network vendors involved and attempt to make sure that the interfaces between information system components were at the database level and minimize application program interfaces (APIs) at the program module level. This would provide flexibility in acquiring the best of breed or developing applications in-house, since the data needed by an application was available at the database level. Another strategic decision was to only use technologies that adhered to standards such as SQL compliant databases, TCP/IP protocols, telecommunications industry standard formats, and so forth. Outsourcing was also considered and rejected as an approach to getting the OSS functional, (Bhandari & Mania, 2005).

The decision to buy or build applications was decided by several factors:

1. The amount of time available to build an application that was known and controlled vs. the amount of time to install, configure, and learn a purchased application.
2. The level of knowledge required to build an application such as billing that was reliable and stable vs. the amount of time to install,

configure, and learn how to control a purchased application.

3. The resources required to build, operate, and maintain an application vs. the resources required to purchase, install, configure, operate, and maintain a purchased application.

4. Whether the functional capabilities as determined by the organization could be fulfilled by a purchased application or whether the application needed to be built with desired customized features.

Organizational Culture

The organization had a culture where micromanagement was typically not done and where individuals were valued for their capabilities and the results produced. Of course, there were exceptions. The CEO was a charismatic person who liked people but also valued hard work and honesty. He was a good motivational leader and knew all aspects of the telecommunications business better than anyone else in the organization. His charisma was demonstrated by getting personnel who were well established in their careers with established companies to take a career risk by resigning their position and joining a startup company. He also had the ability to boost employee morale when situations became difficult by giving highly motivational speeches and offering sound advice and additional resources where needed. The turnover in personnel was nearly zero. The CEO had many years of experience in the telecommunications business and had started two other telecommunications companies before joining Adelphia Cable's Business Solutions division after one of the companies he started was purchased by Adelphia Cable. Broadstreet had an executive committee that met on a weekly basis and made recommendations regarding resource allocations, policies and procedures, as well as business strategies.

The organization was driven by the sales and marketing people who were longtime friends of the CEO. This caused many IT decisions to be based on look and feel and resulted, in some cases, of selecting form over functionality. For example, the president spent over $400,000 on furniture and decorating the headquarters office so that customers would be impressed when they visited the company. Of course, this almost never happens with telephone companies. Another "form over functionality" decision that cost the IT department time and money was the president's decision to have the format of the customer bill changed so that it was more aesthetically pleasing since he viewed this as an important medium of communication from the company to the customer. Since the billing system was a purchased system, the vendor had to be contracted to make the changes. This took 60 days and $200,000. One other example of "form over functionality" was that the VP for marketing was determined to present the DSL technology model in sales presentations, service/product offerings, costing, and billing so as to impress the customers with this new broadband technology utilizing the standard telephone line. Nearly all the billing systems on the market had an underlying model of one line, one device (telephone, fax, PC) based on the old technology, and to make any of the billing systems accommodate the one line, multiple devices model of the DSL technology required either having the vendors modify their systems or finding work arounds in their models. This caused several months delay and nearly a million dollars in professional service charges from the billing system vendor.

Overall, the organizational environment was, on one hand, relaxed, but on the other hand, fast paced and highly stressful for task-oriented people like engineers and software developers. For example, it took over six months for marketing and sales to get the products and services defined and prices established which made order entry, flow through provisioning, and billing applications difficult to get underway by IT in a timely manner. Except for a few individuals, people cooperated with one another and strived to make the company a success. An example of the relaxed yet stressful nature of the company is that the entire headquarters staff frequently played softball on Friday afternoons but worked seven days a week, 12-16 hours a day. All employees were granted stock in the company and therefore had a vested interest in making the company successful.

Not all technology related decisions were made based on good technical criteria. For example, the central office switching technology initially selected by the Chief Technology Officer (CTO) was a new product from Lucent Technologies called a PathStar. This switch cost approximately 50% of the older, but proven, 5ESS switch used by other telephone companies. After nine months of struggling to get the PathStar switch to function correctly and reliably, Lucent decided to remove it as a central office replacement switch for the 5ESS due to lack of functionality, scalability, and reliability. After nine months, Broadstreet replaced the Pathstar switch with the 5ESS switch. The industry standard 5ESS switches were installed and functioning in approximately two months. This left Broadstreet's IT/IS department in the difficult position of having to completely reengineer, reconfigure, redesign, and rewrite software used to perform functions such as capturing call detail records for billing, controlling flow-through provisioning, performing network monitoring and control, as well as making changes to Order Entry, Sales Force Automation, inventory management, and other smaller applications.

Economic Climate

The economic climate going into 1999 appeared to be extremely good since the technology sector stocks were continuing to increase dramatically, and new technology based products and services in the e-commerce area were being created on an almost daily basis. Also, telecommunications was

a critical component of nearly all the new technology products and services and was growing in demand. Thus, in 1999, it was relatively easy to get the venture capital and financing necessary to start a company, especially with the experience and charisma of the CEO and highly experienced management team. By the time all the financing agreements had been signed in early 2000, the "dot com" crisis was starting to become a reality and the telecommunications industry was a prime victim of the overvalued companies and stocks. By mid-2001, CLECS were going bankrupt at an alarming rate, but Broadstreet was gaining momentum in terms of acquiring customers and increasing revenue.

By mid-2001, the company had grown to more than 160 employees in six markets and Broadstreet had become more proficient in its internal processes and dealing with its external partners and customers. Things were looking very positive for the company, but Lucent Technologies stock was decreasing in value at an alarming rate, and one of the venture capitalist who had invested in several of the overvalued "dot com" companies had taken large losses and was under pressure to get out of the telecommunications sector. Almost simultaneously, Lucent Technologies and this venture capitalist announced that they were terminating their agreements. The other venture capitalists could not provide additional funding and refused several others who wanted to invest because these potential investors wanted too large a share of the company.

After nine months of design, development, and testing of the telecommunications network, OSS software, and other software systems, a decision was made to change the central office switch because the one initially selected could not be made to function adequately and lacked many features needed by potential customers. This became a major factor in the survival of the company. The change in central office switches caused a nine month delay as network and software system personnel reworked all systems to accommodate the new central switch with its added capabilities and features. This delay consumed financial resources without the benefit of planned income and forced Broadstreet to close its doors in late 2001 because it could not meet the finance covenant agreements with Lucent Technologies and the declining confidence the investors had in the telecommunications industry.

Setting the Stage

While the U.S. Federal Communications Commission (FCC) orders based on the Telecommunications Act of 1996 seemed reasonable enough from a CLEC's point of view, the implementation of these orders was not simple and straightforward. Telecommunications is an extremely complex business. On the plain old telephone network, customers expect to be able to pick up any phone, at any time, and call anybody, within the country or internationally, independent of which phone company they or the recipient uses. While the technical issues of this connection are most often handled by the central office switches and network routers of the incumbent telephone companies, the OSS system of the CLEC must at least handle the provisioning, 911 access, call detail record processing, network monitoring, controls, alarms, and repairs as well as billing. This is quite a complex matter as many different companies and an abundance of procedures, data exchanges, standards, service level agreements, and price policies are involved.

Billing is a critical and extremely complex part of the functionality that OSS systems must provide and CLECs must also have functionality in place for provisioning new customers (often customers that earlier were connected to an ILEC), or for de-provisioning, when they lose a customer to a competitor as well as monitoring and controlling telecommunications network components, switches, routers, circuits, and so forth. While deregulation has opened up competition, there are other regulations in place that must be followed.

For example, all telephone provider companies must provide 911 (emergency) services. This includes the ability to tell the emergency facility where the caller is located. Other services, such as "caller ID" and "800 numbers" also involve the ability to access and update national databases. This would be an easy task if all the standards were in place and followed, but the standards are compromised by the incumbents and the CLEC must accommodate many different formats and processes.

To perform all these services, a CLEC needs reliable back office systems. In principle, these can be developed in-house, or be leased or bought from vendors. In practice, only the latter two alternatives are feasible if a CLEC wants to be operational in a very short period of time. One of the keys to the success of a telecommunications company that offers a range of narrow and broadband voice and data services is how effectively and efficiently the back office operations support system functions. This system has been defined as the set of hardware, software, procedures, policies, and personnel that support the following main activities:

- Network Design and Inventory
- Network Monitoring and Control
- Provisioning and Activation of Services
- Service Assurance
- Interconnection Management
- Customer Care & Billing
- Work and Workforce Management

One of the more obvious characteristics that stand out from the list presented above is the widely diverse but highly interrelated nature of these activities. But there are many details associated with of each of these functions and their relationships. Understanding the technology of telecommunications is one thing, understanding the *business* of telecommunications is quite another. Appendix A illustrates the technology architecture for DSL technology and Appendix B illustrates the business of telecommunications.

The "natural monopoly" of telecommunications, that is, the idea that there are advantages to having only one company, has been challenged (Perez, 1994), and the business complexity of having many companies "sharing" parts of a common infrastructure has perhaps not been fully understood.

New entrants into the telecommunications market see the potential for using new technologies to take customers from the incumbents and make huge profits. The number of CLECs that have failed show that most of those who are involved with these new companies do not understand the details of the business and consistently underestimate the cost, time, skill, and knowledge that it takes to offer and maintain a wide array of telecommunications services with an adequate Quality of Service and fulfill Service Level Agreements.

CASE DESCRIPTION

In order to design, implement and operate an OSS, it is necessary to understand not only the technology of telecommunications and the technology of information systems, but the business of telecommunications as well. This includes understanding the requirements of every technology, function, service, and product involved and incorporating these requirements into every design, development, testing, and documentation decision. One of the critical components in a telecommunications network is the central office switch because it dictates the services and associated features that can be offered, how provisioning is done, how network monitoring and control is performed, the interconnection with the PSTN, and what data is collected about each call for rating and billing purposes. When a decision was made to change the type of central office switch after 75% of the OSS has been developed, tested, and documented, it caused a major disruption to the IT implementation plan.

Broadstreet Communications experienced such an event 9 months into a 12 month IT implementation schedule which caused IT to develop a new plan to evaluate what information system and associated OSS components were impacted and what measures were necessary to change its acquired and in-house developed software to be compatible with the new central office switch and the new services and features provided by the new switch that sales and marketing now wanted to offer potential customers. The issue facing IT was how to recover from such a decision and still try to meet budgetary and schedule constraints imposed by management.

Technology Concerns

In attempting to recover from a change in a critical component in the telecommunications network that not only provides services to customers and interfaces with trading partners (ILECS) but also captures critical data for billing, network monitoring, network control, and provisioning, a complete halt in current system development occurred. All components in the OSS and related systems had to be evaluated to determine what, if any, impact the new switch would have. But, of course, this change in central office switches also caused marketing, sales, engineering, help desk, and so forth to all reexamine how their functions would be impacted. The following describes some of the areas of concern related to the change in central office switches.

When a CLEC acquires a customer from an incumbent (ILEC), an exchange of information between the incumbent's OSS and the competitor's OSS must take place to order facilities. The ordering process (Local Service Request [LSR] and Access Service Request [ASR]) requires knowledge of how the telephone business operates, the business rules used by the incumbent, and the special language used by the ILEC and the industry as a whole (Garifo, 2001). For instance, when ordering a local loop, you must know the

CLLI (Common Language Location Identifier) code of the central office to which the customer will be connected (Telcordia Technologies, Inc., 2000). A new switch introduces new terminology as well as new port and jack labels which are critical for the ILEC to connect a local loop to the CLECs switch.

The ordering of Unbundled Network Elements (UNE's), their installation by the incumbent, the installation of equipment at the customer's premise, disconnecting the current incumbent's service, and the testing and activation of the new service must be scheduled and monitored carefully so as not to leave a customer without any service. For example, a telephone service must provide 911 capabilities. This requires a trunk from a telephone company's local central office to a 911 center (called a PSAP—Public Safety Answering Point) and this, in turn, requires that the telephone company maintain a database of addresses where telephone lines are terminated along with the telephone number associated with each line. Since telephone numbers can be "ported" (i.e., customers can take their telephone numbers with them when they move within a region), there is a national database that must be updated with this porting information. If a customer wants an 800 number (dial free), this also requires interactions with other vendors and updating a national database. Likewise, if caller ID is desired by the customer, this requires yet another national database be updated as well. A new switch changes the flow-through provisioning components of an OSS to accommodate these features.

If a calling card service is to be offered to customers, then an agreement with the Centralized Message Distribution Service (CMDS) must be established and Call Detail Records (CDR) or billing records must be exchanged on a timely basis. Since most customers want a long distance service, interconnection arrangements must be made with the long distance carriers and if convergent billing is offered, the ability to acquire and exchange CDRs with the inter-exchange carriers (IXC or long distance—LD) is a must. Likewise, the equal access regulation requires the exchange of CARE information (Customer Account Record Exchange) to notify the LD carriers when they are losing or gaining a customer. This provisioning of services is one of the most complex components for an OSS to accommodate (Jethi, 2005) and a new switch can change the procedures and data formats necessary for this provisioning.

Although there are data exchange standards for the format of these records, every vendor has its own interpretation or use of various fields within the record which causes back office systems to have many translation software packages for transforming call detail and billing records into a format that can be processed by their own OSS. A new switch can have a different format and data element interpretation that have to be accommodated.

When a service is sold to a customer, the network devices and associated logical attributes must be installed or allocated, interconnected, configured, activated, and tested. This is the service provisioning and activation process. Any specific attributes associated with these components must also be tracked, for example, data speed, and calling features. Tracking what has been allocated to a customer and being able to trace the path from the customer premise is critical to managing and maintaining the service. A new switch can differ considerably from the previous switch in terms of components, labels, functionality, and terminology.

One of the most complex aspects of an OSS is billing. It is complex because rating calls (determining the class of call and associated billing rate) accurately can be a logical nightmare because a caller can theoretically call from anywhere in the world to anywhere in the world at anytime. The second is that the United States has divided its geographical area into LATAs (Local Access Transport Areas) over which a call is considered a long distance call. Unfortunately, LATAs cross state boundaries which make determining the type of call more difficult. Then, there are the message unit charges for local calls that extend over certain distances (zones) from the caller's central office. A call may come from a ship at sea, an airplane, a hotel, a prison, a pay phone, an educational institution, and so forth, all of which are rated differently. The billing system must not only determine what type of call was made but also what plan a customer has and how the charge must be computed, for example, was it a week day or weekend day, after 9:00 pm, over 1,000 minutes of usage, and so forth? This data is derived from the Call Detail Records (CDRs) captured at the central office switch, and a new switch may differ significantly in terms of the data it captures about calls and the format of the data as well as the procedures needed to bring this data into a billing system.

In order to configure and activate services for a customer, local loops must be acquired and installed, devices such as switches, multiplexers, routers, and customer premise interface access devices must be configured by setting device parameters to meet the attributes of the services purchased; and databases must be updated for porting numbers, 800 numbers, caller ID, 911, and so forth. For example, a last mile DSL provider of voice and data may need to access and configure the following devices to activate the service for a customer:

1. Interface Access Device (IAD) at the customer premise
2. DSL Multiplexer at the Local Service Office
3. ATM Router at the Central Office
4. Internet Router at the Central Office
5. Switch at the Central Office
6. Internet server
7. VPN server
8. Voice Mail server

Entering any local telecommunications market is not a simple thing to do, and a change in the central office switch may cause unforeseen problems (The Competitive Telecommunications Association, 2005).

Technology Components

Many of the OSS components run on systems with clustering capabilities, a database management system, and application software written in a programming language such as C or C++. The system architecture is usually client server where the desktop client uses TCP/IP over an Ethernet network. The Server CPUs are networked for high availability and reliability with multiple network connections. The network disk storage is usually RAID 5 or higher to guarantee data integrity. The database is replicated to ensure a fault tolerant data environment. A hot backup or a cluster is used to guarantee continuous operation. A disaster recovery plan and associated resources are in place. The internal network has redundant paths between remote offices and the OSS system location as well as the disaster recovery location.

Much of the OSS software commercially available does not scale, is not reliable, and is not flexible which, in turn, can cause a new company to struggle with commercial OSS software. It is important to balance what services and functions the Back-office system will provide (Tombes, 2003).

The basic system design for Broadstreet's OSS is shown in the diagram in Figure 2. It is obvious that the OSS is comprised of many different DBMSs, software packages, hardware platforms, operating systems, and networking components. The introduction of a new switch has side effects on many of these components.

Scalability and Reliability

To be successful, a telecommunications company needs to acquire customers and lots of them. The capital, circuit, and labor cost for a telecommunications company is very high and therefore the

Figure 2. OSS software architecture

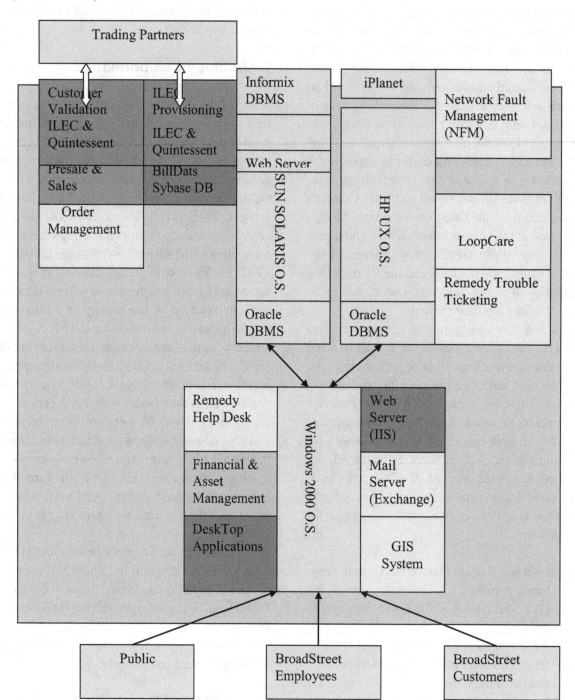

need to utilize the available capacity to produce revenue is essential for survival. The OSS, like the customer service network, must be highly reliable. The OSS must be able to scale with the business and must be available at all times. The scaling can only be accomplished by using efficient application software, database management systems, operating systems, and hardware as well as adequate network bandwidth for users of the OSS.

Management

The management of such a diverse set of technology resources and the people who design, implement, operate and use them requires a formal set of policies and procedures such as strict change control and a team of talented individuals who are not only dedicated but loyal, motivated, and able to withstand high levels of stress. The difficult management issue related to personnel is that it is very rare to find all these traits in a single individual. The management approach at Broadstreet was to have a detailed model of the systems and processes needed to design, code, test, install, implement, and operate either purchased or developed software. The management challenge was to make sure everyone involved understood the technologies, the business model, the busi-

ness rules, the technology models, the policies, procedures, and to implement systems within time and budget constraints. The IT department was organized around major functionality components as shown in Figure 3.

Advisory Committee

The advisory committee was composed of representatives from each of the major components of the organization such as sales, marketing, finance, provisioning, engineering, human resources, and so forth. This committee met once a week and was provided updates on progress, asked for advice on implementation and operational issues, and helped defined requirements for functionality, interfaces, and interrelationships. There was an attempt to use sound software engineering principles based on those in publications such as Thayer (2005).

The CIO was part of an executive management committee that met each week to discuss issues, schedules, plans, and resource allocation. The CIO expressed concern with many of the delays and mid-stream changes that marketing and sales advocated since it not only caused delays, consumed unplanned-for resources, and required reworking or acquiring new software, but it also caused

Figure 3.

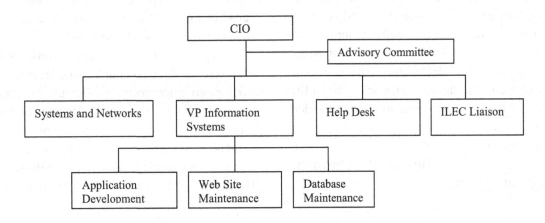

morale issues among the IT and engineering staff who seemed to never get anything completed. Typically, the CTO and engineering were aligned with the CIO in objecting to requested changes or lack of specificity in requirements for new features, functionality, or services. The question typically posed by these concerned individuals was: Will this change significantly to improve the service or the revenue stream? The answer was usually, "we don't know for sure but it will make us look good." For example, marketing wanted to significantly change the Web site with more graphics and animation so they could compete for an award for the most attractive Web site. The CIO objected because it would take personnel resources away from more critical software development areas such as billing, provisioning, sales force automation, and so forth. The project was approved anyway. This was a typical pattern at the management meetings.

The fact that sales personnel did not have any customers to call on meant that they had plenty of time to think up interesting data analysis, data presentation, order entry, customer care, and product and service packaging schemes which impacted many parts of the back-office system. The software was under continual enhancement and revision, which made it difficult to complete software to meet the unmet functional requirements of the originally designed OSS and information systems.

Eventually, the CIO was only invited to management meetings where there were technical issues that needed his expertise, and requests for changes, enhancements, and additional functionality were sent to him via e-mail or paper documents. The CIO then implemented an on-line service request system that not only guided the requestor through a set of questions that detailed the requirements for the requested change or enhancement but also required schedule, cost, and benefit estimates. This quickly reduced the number of requests.

When it was announced, after nine months of system development, that the current PathStar central office switch was being replaced by the 5ESS switch, everything came to a halt, and the CIO was invited to all the management meetings once again because the central office switch impacted nearly everything. The CIO and CTO presented a plan for accommodating the new switch into the physical network and the software environment. The impact on the physical network was much less than the impact on the software since the 5ESS switch was not only a well known device but the network engineers were experienced in its installation, configuration, usage, and provisioning. That was not the case for the software engineers who now had to reexamine nine months of software development and software configurations for purchased packages. This also meant that the professional services personnel who had helped configure purchased software had to be called back.

Technology Resources and Constraints

The major constraints for overcoming the introduction of a new switch were time, budget, and finding highly competent personnel and consultants (professional service personnel) who had the interests of the organization's success as a priority rather than their own personal benefit. Budgetary constraints placed limits on hiring more high priced personnel, equipment with capacity for the future, and software packages to perform every needed function.

Every individual in the organization had either a laptop or desktop computer. All sales personnel had laptop computers and most management personnel had both a laptop and a desktop computer. Each of the six regional offices had two servers, namely, a primary and a backup, with a DS1 channel back to the headquarters in Pittsburgh. Headquarters had two servers for the billing, provisioning, and ILEC interface systems and two servers for network monitoring and diagnosis. There were also two systems running purchasing, accounting, human resources and other business functions, two systems running order entry, customer relations, marketing, helpdesk, inventory control, GIS, Web Site, and interfaces to the provisioning, order management, billing, trading partners (for ordering lines, 800 numbers, etc.), and 911 centers and one e-mail server. The servers were all connected via an Ethernet network using Ethernet switches as well as routers for the regional offices. The Internet connection was a DS1 line connected via a router to the internal network and was available to every user.

The OSS and other application software was a combination of purchased packages and in-house developed packages. There were four different database management systems involved with the purchased software. The constraints associated with purchased software are simply those of control over how they function and the interfaces they provide. Some software systems provide configuration model parameters but once they are established and used to initialize the system, they cannot be easily changed. In many cases, the configuration must be done by professional services personnel from the provider since they provide little or no documentation on how to configure the software.

Since more full-time personnel could not be hired, the IT department had to approach the new switch problem using existing personnel, professional service personnel from the providers of the purchased software, and some contract programmers. The problem with contract programmers is that they typically have a long learning curve concerning the application's policies, procedures, and business rules. Professional service personnel also have some learning time about the particular configuration parameters used at an installation. Their services are also quite expensive and the budget for this new development was not extensive.

Organizational Concerns

The concerns that the organization had as the OSS was developed and put into operation were inadequate documentation, failure to follow standards, reliability, stability, configuration limitations, limited integration of components, and adequate functionality to provide flow-through provisioning. Of course, the integrity of data and the security aspects of the OSS were major concerns as well. Hiring experienced IT personnel in adequate numbers who had a wide range of skills was a primary concern. The most personnel IT ever had during the two and a half years of Broadstreet's existence was nine people serving over 180 personnel at six locations. This was due to budgetary constraints as well as the inability to find highly qualified, experienced, and motivated personnel.

With the introduction of a new switch, it was necessary to evaluate its impact on all the Back-office (OSS) software already developed as well as the physical network and determine what changes were necessary. It also was necessary to determine the impact on software not yet completely developed. This caused major concerns among everyone including Broadstreet personnel, the venture capitalists, and the financier, Lucent Technologies.

The major concerns revolved around resources and schedules. It was quite clear that the 12 months originally estimated in the business plan to start selling services to customers was never going to be met. The question was whether the resources that remained would be enough to allow Broadstreet to start realizing revenue, not only to meet its financial covenants, but to remain a viable company capable of meeting its operating cost obligations. It was estimated by the CTO and his network engineers that once the 5ESS switches were on-site it would take about 30-45 days to get them installed and configured and about 30-45 days before the 5ESS switches could be delivered to Broadstreet.

The software effort was estimated to take much longer than the switch installations since marketing and sales now had a much wider array of services than the PathStar switch offered, and they wanted to incorporate them into the products and services offered. Marketing and sales estimated it would take about 30 days to redesign their service and product packages. The CIO estimated it would take about 30-45 days to evaluate the impact the new switch had on existing purchased and developed software and another 10 days to evaluate the impact of the new switch on the redesign of software not yet developed. The CIO would then be in a position to provide a time and resources estimate for changing the existing software and completing the development of the unfinished software. Asked to give a ballpark estimate of time, the CIO estimated it would take another four to six months to complete the Back-office system if adequate resources were available.

Challenges/Problems Facing the Organization

The major challenge facing Broadstreet at the point when a new switch was introduced was the impact it had on operational functionality such as processing orders; provisioning customers; installing devices; configuring devices and software; testing devices and software; activating devices and software; collecting and processing call detail records; calculating and sending bills; monitoring and controlling the physical networks; answering help desk calls; paying personnel; paying taxes; paying for purchases; reconciling reciprocal billing with trading partners; distributing 911 address changes; acquiring 800 numbers; acquiring and managing telephone numbers; managing and distributing IP addresses; as well as acquiring, processing, and presenting sales and marketing data.

Another problem that became evident early in the development of the OSS was that the purchased software configured by the vendor's professional service personnel did not always work correctly because the model that the software was built around was not based on DSL technology where 1 line is used for multiple services, for example Voice and Data but was based on the typical 1 line 1 service model. This, of course, caused a number of last minute changes to make it work correctly. This, in turn, affected many other software packages that either used the data or that provided data feeds to such a package. The vendor, of course, recommended that more professional service personnel needed to be brought on board that had special, niche expertise needed to configure the system. The concern was whether the underlying models for the OSS components were configured incorrectly and were producing incorrect data and interfaces to other system components.

In evaluating the OSS purchased software it was discovered that the product/system documentation was poorly done, was incorrect in many instances, and outdated. Broadstreet had sent IT personnel to training classes on all the purchased software so that the IT personnel who attended the classes would be able to support, maintain, and change the configuration of the system. It was discovered that the training, for the most part, was superficial and introductory. In fact, the trainers, in some cases, were not technically trained but simply followed a lesson plan with canned examples that teach the students how to navigate menus and complete data fields for the simplest cases. The concern was that reliance on a vendor's professional service personnel was not only expensive but unreliable.

Since the OSS must interface with many external systems for exchanging Call Detail Records, 911 data, 800 numbers, porting numbers, SS7 services, and so forth, it was important that standards were followed so that data exchanges occurred flawlessly. It became evident during the evaluation for the new switch that participants in the industry compromise the standards to meet their legacy systems or for other unexplained reasons. The concern was whether billing data, customer data, 911 and other crucial data were being transferred correctly so as to avoid loss of service or liability issues.

The ability to account for every CDR in the billing process without losing potential revenue is critical. Billing is complex because all calls must be typed/classed and rated correctly and unfortunately there are hundreds of call types. The concern was whether or not call records for the new switch were formatted and data elements defined in the same way as the PathStar switch so that calls could be rated and billed correctly.

The new 5ESS switch had a much greater capacity than the PathStar switch. The OSS, like the customer service network, must be highly reliable. The OSS must be able to scale with the business and must be available at all times. The concern was whether or not the systems would scale with the capacity of the new switch.

The requirement for a Web site that allows marketing and sales to advertise products and services, provide customer care, take orders online, track the status of orders, track the status of installation, and allows human resources to provide information to employees and prospective employees was also a major initiative for the company. Marketing wanted changes to the Web site almost every other day to incorporate a great new marketing idea, which consumed valuable resources that were needed for more problem and operationally oriented functions. The concern was that the IT resources consumed by Marketing and Sales reduced the IT resources available for other aspects of the OSS that were in need of changes.

Hiring the right kind of IT personnel and enough of them was a major concern of the organization. Because of limited budget, there were not enough resources to hire another 5-10 personnel and because of the need to have personnel with multiple areas of expertise and with the appropriate experience, work ethic and motivation, it was difficult to find personnel to complete the needed work on the OSS.

Of course, the overwhelming challenge was to recover from the change in the central office switches so that Broadstreet could begin acquiring customers, realizing revenue, and meeting its covenants with its funding partners and financier.

Possible IT Options

The options identified by the IT department when a decision was made to replace all the central office switches with a different switch after 75% of the system had been developed and implemented were:

1. Make a case to management for keeping the existing central switches for a period of time and only installing the new switches in new central offices, thus preserving the back-office systems that had already been developed and would permit acquiring customers, offering services, and realizing income from the existing central offices while performing a redesign, reconfiguration, and rewrite of systems for the new switch which would not only be placed in new central offices but eventually replace the old switches

2. Evaluate the impact that the new switch would have on the existing back-office system and develop a new plan for retrofitting the back-office systems already developed by either:
   a. using only existing IT resources at Broadstreet
   b. using existing IT resources plus professional services from vendors
   c. using existing IT resources and vendor professional services personnel plus outsourcing work to a professional programming services company
   d. outsource the entire back-office application to an Application Service Provider (ASP) firm that supports DSL network technology and the new switch technology until the IT department

can redesign, reconfigure, rewrite, and implement a back-office system

e. partner with an ILEC or other CLEC who has a back-office system using the new switch (5ESS) (which nearly all of them have) while the IT department can redesign, reconfigure, rewrite, and implement a back-office system

REFERENCES

Bhandari, N., & Mania, V. (2005). Business process outsourcing for telecom service providers. Retrieved April 29, 2006, from http://www.dmreview.com/whitepaper/WID527.pdf

Emre, O. (2001). Delivering converged services. Retrieved April 29, 2006, from http://infocus.telephonyonline.com/ar/telecom_delivering_converged_services/index.htm

Garifo, C. (2001). A pain in the ASOG: Managing changes in ordering guidelines presents challenges. Retrieved April 29, 2006, from http://www.xchangemag.com/articles/171back1.html

Jethi, R. (2005). Getting what you wish for: New OSS keeps Northpoint on top Of DSL demand. Retrieved April 29, 2006, from http://www.xchangemag.com/articles/0a1sec8.html

McDermott, M. F. (2002). *CLEC: An insiders look at the rise and fall of competition in the local exchange competition.* Rockport, ME: Penobscot Press.

New Paradigm Resources Group, Inc. (2002). *Measuring the economic impact of the Telecommunications Act of 1996: Telecommunication capital expenditures.* Chicago: Author.

Perez, F. (1994). The case for a deregulated free market telecommunications industry. *IEEE Communications Magazine, 32*(12), 63-70.

Telcordia Technologies, Inc. (2000). *COMMON LANGUAGE(R) general codes—telecommunications service providers IAC Codes, exchange carrier names, company codes - Telcordia and region number: BR-751-100-112.* Morristown, NJ: Author.

Thayer, R.H. (2005). *Software engineering project management* (2nd ed.). Alamitos, CA: IEEE Computer Society Press.

The Competitive Telecommunications Association. (2005). *Entering the local market: A primer for competitors.* Retrieved April 29, 2006, from http://www.comptelascent.org/public-policy/position-papers/documents/CLECPrimerReport.pdf

Tombes, J. (2003, October). Cooking up OSS: Balancing your Back-office diet. *Communications Technology.* Retrieved May 8, 2006, from http://www.ct-magazine.com/archives/ct/1003/1003_oss.html

KEY TERMS

Asynchronous Transfer Mode (ATM): A high-speed small packet based method of transferring digital data between two digital devices such as a DSLAM and a router.

Digital Subscriber Line Access Multiplexer (DSLAM): A device that receives data from many devices over many telephone lines and transmits them in a sequential manner over a single high-speed communication line to another switching center for transfer the PSTN or Internet.

Generic Requirement-303 (GR303): A Telcordia standard interface to a Class 5 telephone switch from a digital loop carrier such as DSL. This is the primary interface to the telecommunications central office switch from the outside world. In order to connect directly to the PSTN, IP phones and IP telephony gateways must adhere to GR-303.

Interface Access Device (IAD): Connects the devices at the customer site to the telephone line by transforming the data when necessary to a form and format compatible with the DSLAM.

Local Serving Office (LSO): A switching center where local loops connect customer telephones, fax, PC, and so forth to the central office switch.

Network Operations Center (NOC): The place where all network components are monitored and troubleshooting of network malfunctions takes place.

PacketStar Access Concentrator (PSAX): Acts as a concentrator and router for digital data using an incoming ATM format.

Public Switched Telephone Network (PSTN): The Plain Old Telephone network that connects calls on a worldwide basis.

Simple Network Management Protocol (SNMP): The software standard used to detect network related errors and report them to the NOC.

Springtide Router—A device used to route packets of data through an Internet Protocol network.

APPENDIX A. TECHNOLOGY ARCHITECTURE

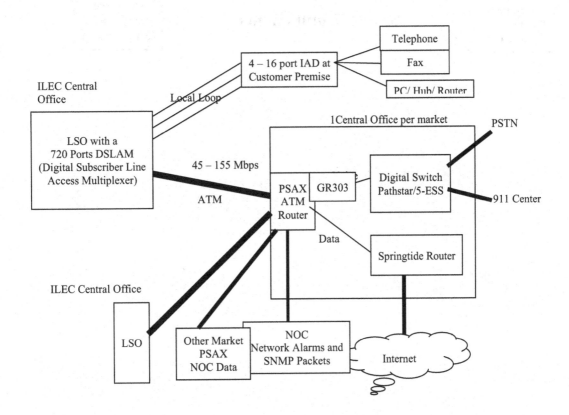

APPENDIX B

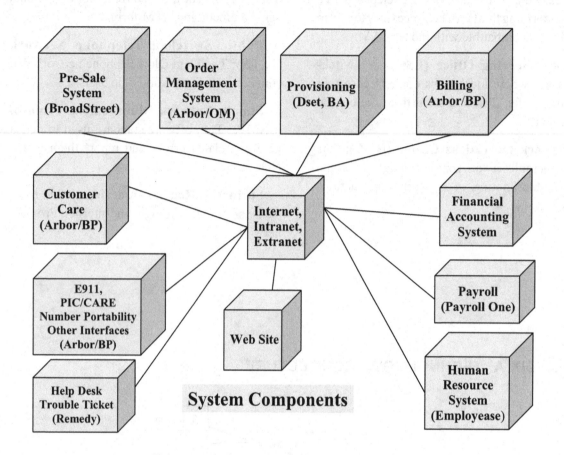

System Components

Chapter XVIII
Enabling the Virtual Organization with Agent Technology

Tor Guimaraes
Tennessee Tech University, USA

ABSTRACT

Emerging agent-based systems offer new means of effectively addressing complex decision processes and enabling solutions to business requirements associated with virtual organizations. Intelligent agents can provide more flexible intelligence/expertise and help the smooth integration of a variety of system types (i.e., Internet applications, customer relationship management, supplier network management, enterprise resources management, expert systems). This chapter presents an overview of expert systems as the most widely-used approach for domain Knowledge Management today as well as agent technology, and shows the latter as a superior systems development vehicle providing flexible intelligence/expertise and the integration of a variety of system types. To illustrate, a system developed first by using an expert system approach and then by an agent-based approach is used to identify the strengths and weaknesses of the agent-based approach. Last, the practical implications of a company adoption of agent-based technology for systems development are addressed.

INTRODUCTION

As we enter the 21st century, organizations are faced with extremely difficult challenges in a hyper-competitive world. As posited by Khalil and Wang (2002), to remain competitive they must simultaneously be efficient on a global scale, be responsive to local needs and wants, and continuously learn and adapt to changes in their environment. To accomplish such daunting requirements, organizations must focus on what they do best and find reliable partners to do the rest. Thus, Donlon (1997) stated that being virtual is about having allies to bolster an organization's weaknesses. According to Carlsson (2002), there are a number of reasons for the emergence of the virtual organization, including: (1) to make products and services available at the moment of need, at the right place, tailored and built according to quality standards, and at a competitive price; (2) to enable customers to help design and produce their own products; and (3) to enable suppliers to plan and execute their own part of the production process. The most effective way to eliminate the oscillating variations of demand in the supply chain was to build a good interface for the actors of the supply chain to share their planning.

Rahman and Bhattachryya (2002) propose that virtual organizations provide an effective vehicle to integrate a company's operations with those of other enterprises, to work with customers and create a better product or service, to achieve a faster time to market, and to acquire a higher degree of product customization. Further, these authors observed that virtual organizations seem to have five main characteristics in common: (1) They have a shared vision and goal with their partners and a common protocol of cooperation; (2) they cluster activities around their core competencies; (3) they work jointly in teams of core competence groups, to implement their activities in a holistic approach throughout the value chain; (4) they process and distribute information in real-time throughout the entire network, which allows them to make decisions and coordinate actions quickly; and (5) they tend to delegate from the bottom up whenever economies of scale can be achieved, new conditions arise, or a specific competence is required for serving the needs of the whole group.

According to Khalil and Wang (2002), the management of a virtual organization involves essential functions that are unique when compared to the traditional management practices: (1) much greater need for mechanisms useful for information filtering and knowledge acquisition to assist managers with information overload, a common problem in the new environment; (2) increased need to generate and use knowledge faster and more effectively; further, organizational knowledge needs to be captured, stored, and made available where it is needed; thus, organizations will have to treat human knowledge as a key component of their asset base, and create knowledge bases or repositories that enable workers to shorten learning curves by sharing each other's experience; and (3) management has to be based on trust and minimal supervision since it is very difficult to supervise and control in geographically-dispersed units; managers and workers who are comfortable in a traditional workplace may find the new environment difficult to live with.

THE IMPORTANCE OF IT FOR VIRTUAL ORGANIZATIONS

Needless to say, the price of "virtuality" is also paid as an increased need for intelligence and communication. Indeed, Carlsson (2002) recognized that a virtual organization could not exist without an effective information exchange between all the actors and stakeholders. Over the years, organizations have used a wide variety of mechanisms to keep in contact with their partners, from couriers to the telegraph and telephone, to today's electronic communication systems such as electronic data interchange (EDI), imaging systems, and the Internet. As competition and business globalization increases, so does the need for creating more virtual organizations, for more effective communication systems, and for more intelligent information systems as essential enablers. As discussed in more detail later, expert systems and agent technology are the most important tools to enable the increasing levels of system intelligence required by today's virtual organizations. Besides the more traditional information systems, the Internet provides the ubiquitous global communications infrastructure required, and Martin

(1999) observed that the Internet would enable business processes to change in dramatic ways: (1) New ways of buying and selling will create a new breed of online consumer, who will expect faster delivery, easier transactions, and more fact-based information; (2) the intranet will put more information in employees' hands and create virtual work communities; (3) boundaries between the corporation and the outside world, including suppliers and customers, will be erased; (4) new interactive dynamics will change how value is established for products; real-time, flexible pricing as value is established moment-by-moment; (5) new technologies for analyzing and predicting customer behavior in real-time will require companies to organize differently in order to move to a new Internet-version of customer-centric; (6) people will harness instant global communications, aggregating knowledge in real-time; collective experience will play a larger role in collecting information and in decision-making; and (7) the new means of networking will create a new generation of empowered and independent learners.

Khalil and Wang (2002) have proposed ways for IT to enable the management of virtual organizations by providing: (1) Web-based information systems, which enable uniform coupling of transactions within the organization for business-to-business (B2B) and business-to-consumer (B2C) applications; (2) sophisticated customer databases, which enable data mining to inform individual customers when new products become available and to create customized products and services; the main goal is to identify trends and turn consumer statistics into long-term customer relationships; (3) support for organizational learning by storing both structured and unstructured documents; this IT capability integrates, supports, and automates the acquisition, retention, maintenance, and sharing of information/expertise in a multimedia environment; and (4) groupware-supported coordination and decision-making so people from diverse cultures can work together effectively.

The Need for More Flexible and Integrative Intelligence

Carlsson (2002), while discussing the cyber trends proposed by Martin (1999) as the drivers for business in the Internet era, has prescribed the following focus points for IT: (1) intelligent transactions and logistics support, and providing customers with intelligent fact-finding methods and tools "on the run"; (2) intelligent support for virtual teams in planning, problem solving, and decision-making; (3) effective, interactive, and intelligent human-computer interaction; (4) support for products and services customization, continuous scanning of competitors with intelligent fact-finding and comparisons, and intelligent support for dynamic pricing decisions; (5) intelligent analysis and interpretation of customer data in online mode; (6) instant summarizing and synthesis of customer experience and feedback, and effective distribution and sharing of key insights; and (7) collecting, evaluating, and synthesizing insights for new value-adding products and services. Khalil and Wang (2002) confirm the importance of greater system intelligence when proposing that Knowledge Management support systems can help meet the managerial challenges posed by virtual organizations in the areas of system coordination and decision support for ill-structured tasks in a more loosely-structured organization. Besides the need for greater intelligence, Kishore and McLean (2002) have identified the integration of new information systems and technologies with the existing ones as more critical than ever before, as newer and newer pervasive and mobile information technologies are implemented.

Expert systems (ES) became the most important Artificial Intelligence technology since the early 1980's. Today, ES applications are found widely in business and government as ES development techniques and tool kits have multiplied. ES technology provides a software representation of organizational expertise dealing with specific problems, and it will remain a useful mechanism to accomplish the Knowledge Management. However, as an enabler of virtual organizations, which require a more flexible and integrative type of intelligence, traditional ES technology has several shortcomings: (1) ES are typically brittle, dealing poorly with situations that "bend" the rules; ES components typically are not intelligent enough to learn from their experiences while interacting directly with users; thus, the rules encoded initially do not evolve on their own but must be modified directly by developers to reflect changes in the environment; (2) ES are typically isolated, self-contained software entities; very little emphasis is placed on tool kits that support interaction with other ES or external software components; (3) as the ES develops, functionality increases are accompanied by an ever-growing knowledge base in which inconsistencies and redundancies are difficult to avoid; and (4) over time, portions of the process that initially required human intervention become well understood and could be totally automated, but there is no mechanism in place to support the transition from human-activated objects to autonomous objects.

These are exactly the types of shortcomings agent technology (AT) was developed to address. According to Carlsson (2002), ES technology is now being replaced by intelligent systems built to provide two key functions: (1) the screening, sifting and filtering of a growing overflow of data, information and knowledge, and (2) the effective decision support. When discussing the evolution of the Internet as a world where humans are quickly becoming a minority overwhelmed by intense communication between devices and services, Waldo (2002) suggests that the very evolution of Internet usage is exacerbating the need for more intelligent systems: "Humans are quickly becoming a minority on the Internet, and the majority stakeholders are computational entities that are interacting with other computational entities without human intervention. When services must be recognized and used by other computational

entities, no such assumption can be made. Traditional techniques used in the development of distributed systems can be combined with agent technologies to produce networks that are self-administering and allow the kinds of rapid change and evolution that will be required if the Internet is to continue to grow and thrive as a business vehicle" (p. 9). The objective of this study is to identify AT's characteristics which will make it the most powerful enabler for managing the knowledge flows and system integration required by virtual organizations. To accomplish that we first discuss what distinguishes it from widely-implemented ES technology, and its strengths and weaknesses in systems development. The discussion is further illustrated through a case study in which the specific tradeoffs between these technologies are explored.

USING AGENT TECHNOLOGY

While no standard definition of an agent has yet emerged, most definitions agree that agents are software systems that carry out tasks on behalf of human users. Intelligent agents generally possess the three properties: autonomy, sociability, and adaptability.

Autonomy means that an agent operates without the direct intervention of humans and has some control over its own actions and internal state. It is capable of independent action (Wooldridge & Jennings, 1995). An agent does not simply act in response to its environment; it is able to exhibit goal-directed behavior by taking the initiative.

Sociability refers to an agent's ability to co-operate and collaborate with other agents and possibly human users to solve problems. Agents share information, knowledge, and tasks among themselves and cooperate with each other to achieve common goals. The capability of an agent system is not only reflected by the intelligence of individual agents but also by the emergent behavior of the entire agent community. The infrastructure for cooperation and collaboration includes a common agent communication language like the Knowledge Query Manipulation Language (KQML) (Finin, Labrou, & Mayfield, 1998) or the Foundation for Intelligent Physical Agent (FIPA) (FIPA, 2000).

Finally, *adaptability* refers to an agent's ability to modify its own behavior as environmental circumstances change. An agent learns from experience to improve its performance in a dynamic environment. That learning can be centralized, as performed by a single agent without interaction with other agents, or decentralized, as accomplished through the interaction of several agents that cooperate to achieve the learning goal (Cantu, 2000).

Agent technology represents a new and exciting means of decomposing, abstracting, and organizing large complex problems. Agents, as autonomous, cooperating entities, represent a more powerful and flexible alternative for conceptualizing complex problems. As attention is increasingly placed on distributed applications like mobile and Web-based systems, applications will not necessarily run from a central location. Communications can be costly in such environments. Direct routing of data to the recipient must be fast and efficient to make additional bandwidth available to others. Agent architectures provide a template for a distributed architecture that lends itself to many of these emerging applications. Agents can be used as mediators between heterogeneous data sources, providing the means to interoperate, using ontologies for describing the data contained in their information sources, and communicating with the others via an agent communication language (Broome, Gangopadhyay, & Yoon, 2002).

For problems characterized by dynamic knowledge, it is infeasible to predict and analyze all possible interactions among modules at design time. Flexible interaction among agents at runtime enables an agent-based system to effectively handle dynamic, unpredictable knowledge. Al-

though knowledge of some problems is dynamic, the change is often local, affecting a subset of requirements. Therefore, some agents can be designated to deal with the dynamic knowledge of a problem, and the functionality of those agents can evolve, reflecting the changes which are encountered.

The inherent autonomy of agents enables the agent-based system to perform its tasks without direct external intervention. Agents can not only react to specific events but can also be proactive, polling the environment for events to determine the proper action in a given circumstance. Despite the increased level of autonomy in an agent-based system, however, the system itself may not be able to automate all levels of intelligent activity. Human users may be required to perform higher-level intelligent tasks. An intelligent distributed agent architecture that allows flexible interactions among participating agents maps well to applications, like expert systems, that require seamless integration with humans. Further, agent technology offers mechanisms for knowledge sharing and interoperability between autonomous software and hardware systems characterized by heterogeneous languages and platforms. Agents can be used as mediators between these various systems, facilitating interoperability.

ENHANCING EXPERT SYSTEMS WITH AGENT-BASED SYSTEMS

One way to better understand AT is to compare it with the more widely-used expert systems. This does not imply that ES technology is obsolete or that ES development has nothing in common with agent-based system development. Nevertheless, in general there are some important distinctions between ES and agent-based systems, which make the latter ideal for integrating individual ES with other ES and other system types. Probably the most important distinction is that expert systems rely on the user to initiate the reasoning process and to accomplish any action associated with the recommendations provided by the system (Yannis, Finin, & Peng, 1999). The integration of human interaction, then, is assumed and has been greatly facilitated by development tool kits and environments. Agents, on the other hand, are inherently autonomous. That does not mean that the integration of human interaction is necessarily complex. The human is simply another agent in the society of agents. While the user roles vary dramatically between the two paradigms, both readily accommodate human interaction.

Another important distinction is that expert systems have a fixed set of rules that clearly define their reasoning process, while agents interact with their environment and adapt to new conditions. Thus, an application that characteristically incorporates dynamic changes in its data and rules is more naturally accommodated by agent-based techniques. Further, the expert system's knowledge base impacts the modularity and scalability of the system. As new functions are introduced into the system, the central knowledge base grows increasingly large. New rules risk conflicts with old, and changed rules potentially impact more functions than the developer may have planned. Agents, on the other hand, are extremely modular, like self-contained programs that can readily be reused across applications.

Finally, the social interaction inherent in agents facilitates mobile and distributed systems, with formal standards in place outlining interfaces between agents assumed to be heterogeneous in design. Expert systems, on the other hand, are fundamentally built as a cohesive product with a single overarching goal. Despite early emphasis on linking knowledge bases and integrating expertise, those goals are rarely achieved, perhaps because of the issues of combining knowledge bases without the benefit of a standard interface technique. Further, the system components are rarely reused outside the system for which they were built. In fact, it is quite common to throw away one prototype and completely rebuild the

next version from scratch. Thus, tools are built with an emphasis on rapid prototyping rather than on facilitating component reuse.

AT Weaknesses

Most AT weaknesses can be traced back to its lack of maturity. While agent concepts were under discussion as far back as 1985 (Minsky, 1985), applications have been slow to develop, due in part to a lack of mature system development tool kits that enable agents to represent and reason about their actions. A number of systems are now available or under development (Barbaceanu, 2001; Traverse, 2001), but they still suffer from a general immaturity. A second weakness is the lack of software engineering techniques specifically tailored to agent-based systems. Although there are software development techniques such as object-oriented analysis and design, the existing approaches fail to adequately capture an agent's flexible, autonomous problem-solving behavior, the richness of an agent's interactions, and the complexity of an agent system's organizational structures; thus they are unsuitable for agent-based systems. If agents are to realize their potential, it is necessary to develop software engineering methods appropriate for developing such systems (Wooldridge, Jennings, & Kinny, 2003). A third weakness is the general difficulty associated with decomposing goals and tasks in ways that balance the computation and communication requirements, avoid or reconcile conflicts, and still achieve the initial objective. Finally, the issue of privacy is particularly relevant for a system in which software components act independently across a distributed environment. While standards are under development for insuring that agents are locked out of systems where they are unwelcome, such standards generally require cooperative agents that do not intentionally attack an unreceptive host.

As discussed by other authors, (Lu & Guimaraes, 1989) whether or not to use ES technology in systems development is one major consideration. Once that decision has been made, various ES development approaches must also be considered (Yoon & Guimaraes, 1993).

Last, as the previous discussion indicates, the software developer must consider numerous issues in determining whether an agent-based approach is appropriate for a given application. In the final analysis, the system requirements must drive these choices. To illustrate the choice of using an agent-based approach over a strictly ES-based approach, a case study is presented next.

THE REVERSE MORTGAGE ADVISOR (REMA) CASE STUDY

REMA Background

A reverse mortgage is a special type of home loan that allows a homeowner to convert the equity in his or her home into retirement income. The equity, built up over years of home mortgage payments, can be paid to the homeowner in a lump sum, in a stream of payments, or a combination of the two. Unlike a traditional home equity loan or second mortgage, repayment is not required as long as the borrowers continue to use the home as their principal residence (HUD, 2001). While reverse mortgages have long been seen as a means of increasing the income of the poor or elderly, they have more recently been proposed as a mechanism for tapping home equity for a variety of options and at various stages in the life cycle (Rassmussen, Megbolugbe, & Morgan, 1997). In either case, "because each reverse mortgage plan has different strengths—and because fees and fraud can catch unsuspecting customers—experts say seniors should either shop smart with these tricky loans or not shop at all" (Larson, 1999, p.12). The Internet already plays an important role in supporting the dissemination of information about reverse mortgages. In an effort to increase public awareness of this unique loan opportunity, federal regulators, consumer advocates, and loan companies have all developed Web sites (AARP, 2001; FannieMae, 2001; HUD, 2001; Reverse, 2001) to supplement the publications and training currently available through more traditional media. Such Web sites provide information on mortgage options and sources, answers to frequently-asked questions, and even "calculator" functions to help "shoppers" estimate the amount of loan for which they are eligible. The use of Web sites, however, can be quite daunting, particularly for the potential reverse mortgage client who is over 62 and of limited income. The REMA project was initiated to increase the accessibility of reverse mortgage information.

REMA I, A Traditional Expert System Approach

REMA I is an expert system designed to provide a structured approach to determining whether an individual qualifies for a reverse mortgage. Unlike the traditional Web site, users are not left to their own devices as they sort through information to better understand their loan options. Instead, REMA I provides advice on Web sites to visit and recommended loan types. It is meant to supplement the Web-based technologies that precede it.

- **System architecture:** REMA I was developed using Multilogic's Resolver® and Netrunner® tools. Resolver® is a knowledge-based system development tool that combines a powerful rule editor with a flexible visual decision tree interface and inference engine. While it supports backward and forward chaining, linear programming, fuzzy logic, and neural net reasoning, REMA used the default goal-driven backward chaining technique. Resolver® greatly facilitated the coding process, supporting not only the encoding of the initial logic representation, but the debug process as well.

Once REMA was developed, the executable was ported to Netrunner®, the engine that supports Web-top publication of Resolver® applications. Figure 1 provides a conceptual illustration of the final application, though, in fact, the knowledge base and inference engine are located in Resolver® and their output is located in Netrunner® at the time the application runs.

The decision process was initially represented as a decision tree. The decision tree was then converted into a series of 34 "if-then" statements. Each of the 34 rules resulted in the recommendation of one or more of 16 possible outcomes. The knowledge base represents the 34 rules the experts follow when providing advice to potential reverse mortgage consumers. Queries provide links to local Hypertext Markup Language (HTML) files that provide reverse mortgage training. Those files may, in turn, reference additional information in HTML files at other sites provided by government agencies, consumer advocates, or loan companies. Those links are provided to the Web server through Netrunner®.

- **System interface:** In addition to providing answers to fixed questions, the user may choose to view hypertext about home ownership issues, view the rules associated with the question (by clicking on "Why are you asking this question?"), or return to a previous state by undoing the last answer. The UNDO option is useful if, for example, users find they are not old enough to qualify for a loan but would still like to continue the analysis. The user must backtrack and modify the age answer to continue.

- **REMA I shortcomings:** As is common in the life cycle of an expert system, upon completing REMA I, the current system's shortcomings were identified for improvement in future iterations. The current version is clearly at an early stage of development,

Figure 1. REMA architecture

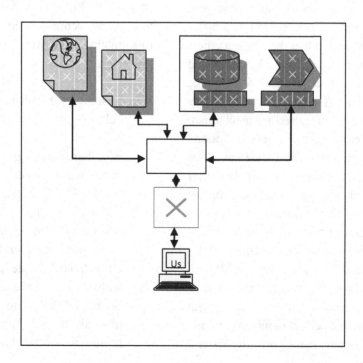

so it was expected that the developer would want to "grow the system" by incorporating more than the initial three loan companies selected for Phase 1. However, several of the problems identified indicate that the expert system design may not be best for meeting overall project objectives. The "build a little, test a little" approach associated with expert systems was quite useful in facilitating discussions with experts, but the outcome of those discussions indicates an alternative design option should at least be considered before moving to the next development phase.

First, beyond the original assessment of loan qualifications, a cost-benefit analysis is the primary basis for selecting the optimal loan type. While many of the rules for determining whether a user qualifies for a given loan are easily expressed in symbolic terms, the cost-benefit analysis is a computational rather than symbolic algorithm. In order to take full advantage of the Resolver® tools, the cost-benefit analysis was replaced with a number of rules-of-thumb. For example, if the applicant's home is very expensive, the Freedom plan is usually best. Otherwise, the HUD and FannieMae options are best. One problem is that the concept of "expensive" varies from state to state. The REMA I rules were stated crisply (with "expensive" arbitrarily set to $400,000, for example), and at a minimum should be replaced with fuzzy rules. Ideally, however, the exact loan size, interest rates, application fees, and so forth, should be used to provide accurate assessments. These inaccuracies must be avoided in future developments. In some cases, systems (like FannieMae's MorNet) are available to compute exact costs and benefits. While the original objective of the project was not to replace these previously developed computational systems but to augment them with a training system, the longer term objective should most assuredly move toward a combination of the two types of systems. Otherwise, the advice

portion of REMA will be inaccurate, which could have adverse legal implications. An agent-based design would more naturally accommodate the seamless integration of other software packages, while expert systems have very little support for interfacing with other expert systems.

Next, in generating REMA I, the developers discovered that both the rules for providing recommendations and the Web sites used for training users were extremely dynamic. A complete redesign of the decision tree and training files was required between building the baseline system, based on books and Web site information, and the current iteration, based on discussions with the experts. It was not just because tables of costs and benefits changed, though that did cause some system reconfiguration. Additionally, over a very brief period, Congress passed new regulations regarding applicant qualification requirements; companies opted out of the list of reverse mortgage providers; other companies restructured their programs to focus on different target audiences; and, as always, Web pages appeared and disappeared across the Internet without notice to the sites that referenced them. Again, expert systems technology was not meant to accommodate such a dynamic environment.

Finally, the training aspect of the system was not as powerful as one might hope. This is due, in part, to the fact that the training simply took the form of instructional text. It certainly was an improvement over the baseline, in which users were on their own to wander the Web looking for relevant documentation. Instead, REMA I focused the Web searches addressing those specific issues of which a prospective applicant should be aware. An online system of this sort, however, has the potential of being a tutor, keeping up with the users' previous searches and expressed preferences to even further tailor the training process. It has a potential for notifying the user as better options arise in this dynamic loan environment. But reaching this potential requires greater autonomy than is typical of expert systems.

The easiest choice for Phase II of system development would be to continue building the next iteration of the current expert system. The next iteration would require: (1) an update of references to outside Web sites; (2) current system assessments from experts; (3) correction of any recently modified data for the HUD, FannieMae, and Freedom Plan options currently represented; (4) incorporation of at least one new loan source; (5) fuzzification of current crisp rules-of-thumb for loan source selection; and (6) incorporation of the MorNet expert system for calculating costs and benefits for those companies it covers. The general system architecture would continue as depicted in Figure 1. However, for the reasons outlined above, instead of enhancing the current ES-based REMA, a decision was made to first explore the use of an agent-based approach to the problem.

REMA II, an Agent-Based Approach

System Architecture: Agents are specific, goal-oriented abstractions of task requirements in systems. From the discussion of the current REMA I system presented in this chapter, we derive a set of system requirements that agents must implement. These are:

1. **Mediating** between multiple external agencies including HUD and Fannie Mae, to ensure that external information contained in the system remains current
2. **Translating** between external information collected by the mediation with the external agencies (above) and the internal information on user characteristics and goals
3. **Recommending** the appropriate course of action to the user based on rules and expertise contained in the system
4. **Interfacing** with the user to guide them through collection of user characteristics and present the system recommendations to them

5. **Supervision** of the entire process to ensure that the asynchronous collection of information from external agencies is assimilated and incorporated in the recommendations of the system and the information presented to the user

The above system requirements, as derived from the design of the existing system, form the basis for an agent-based approach. The agent-based approach to REMA consists of multiple mediator agents, tutor agent, user interface agent, recommender agent, and supervisor agent, as shown in Figure 2.

Individual *mediator agents* are responsible for maintaining the most current information for calculating the costs and benefits of an individual company's reverse mortgage plan. These agents are responsible for interfacing with the external agencies that provide critical information about the programs available for REMA users and ensure that such information is available to the users of REMA. *User interface agents* collect and maintain information on the user's goals and personal characteristics, required for a reverse mortgage application. They are responsible for interaction with the user and provide guided input of user goals and characteristics in addition to presenting users with the final results and recommendations of the REMA system. The user agent receives information from the user, through the user interface, and presents user characteristics and goals to the *tutor agent* to determine which internal and external information is most required to teach the principles of reverse mortgages. A *recommender agent* incorporates user characteristics and the most recent loan company information in performing a cost-benefit analysis to determine the best loan source of those available. This information is passed back to the user interface agent with information on options that are available to the user given their characteristics and goals. Finally, a *supervisor agent* is responsible for the overall

Figure 2. Agent architecture for REMA

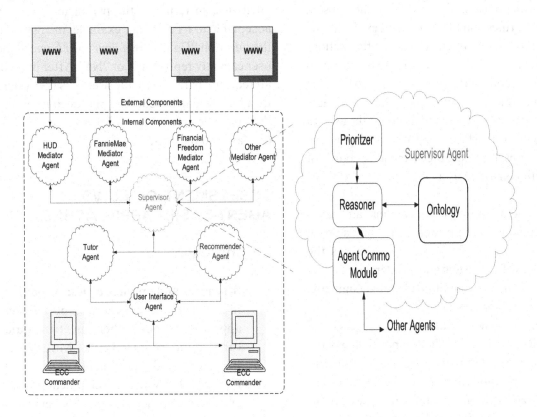

function of the agent system and performs critical meta-functions to prioritize data requests, supply the most recent loan company data, and interpret terminology from heterogeneous sources to consistent internal agents by providing and interpreting a shared ontology of concepts contained in the REMA system.

- **System interface:** REMA II is initialized with the user being assigned representation in the system through a user interface agent. This agent interacts with the user and collects information about the user through an interactive questionnaire. Information about the user is passed to the tutor agent who is responsible for matching the goals and characteristics of the user with information from the mediator agents to find

the appropriate agency that may fulfill user needs. The mediator agents, under supervision of the supervisor agent, constantly and asynchronously, update their information of the most current programs that are available from the various agencies they interface with. Upon performing the matching, the tutor agent generates a match between the internal information provided by the user and the external information available from the financial agencies, through the mediator agents. These results are transferred to the recommender agent, which maintains the knowledge about courses of action based on specific information received by the tutor agent. The recommender agent maintains an active, in-memory representation of the decision tree illustrated in Figure 2. Upon receiving user-specific information, it can select the rules that are fired and present those rules and the associated explanations for the recommendations as the action-specific knowledge that is pertinent given the users' characteristics and goals. The recommender agent sends this knowledge, as specific recommendations for the user, to the user interface agent who is responsible for presenting the recommended course of action(s) to the user.

The overall flow of information and user-system interaction is presented in the use-case diagram in Figure 3. The diagram shows the boundaries of the system and its interactions with external agencies, in addition to the oversight role of the supervisory agent.

Figure 4 shows a sample screen generated for the REMA II user. The top panel shows the rules that are part of REMA II, allowing the user to gain more knowledge about the explanations offered. Each rule, as illustrated in Figure 5, contains a set of conditions and a matching result, or decision value, for the REMA application. Each rule also contains a user-friendly explanation to provide textual explanation of the rule to the user in a human-interpretable manner. The user agent

interface takes input from the user on various attributes, in terms of the parameters that are acceptable to REMA. For example, in answer to the question "*Do you own your own home?*" the user can only reply "Yes" or "No". After input of all required parameters, the user asks the system to advise them by clicking the decide button; then the rule space is searched and the result is displayed to the user.

ASSESSMENT OF ES VS. AGENT-BASED APPROACHES

ES Approach

- **Strengths and opportunities:** As outlined in Table 1, the enhanced expert system approach is best when meeting quick turnaround requirements. Multilogic's Resolver® and Netrunner® tools greatly facilitate the system development process, and the consistency of design further insures efficiency. The resulting system will most certainly continue to support faster decision-making and improved consistency, less demand on experts, and improved public understanding of the reverse mortgage

Figure 3. Use case diagram for agent-based REMA

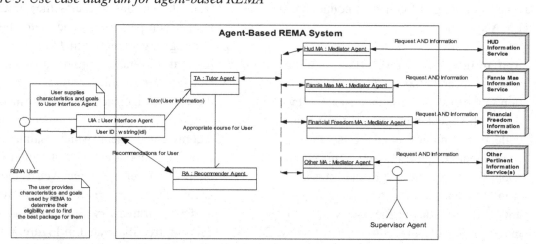

Figure 4. Sample interface screen of agent-based REMA

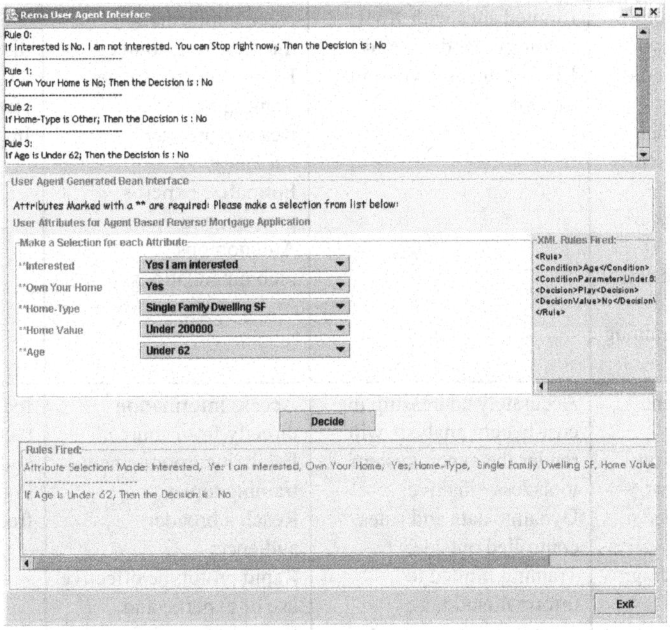

Figure 5. REMA II Rule in eXtended Markup Language (XML) format

Table 1. Analysis of the strengths, weaknesses, opportunities, and threats

	Strengths	Weaknesses	Opportunities	Threats
Agent-Based Approach	Faster decision-making; Improved consistency; Less demand on experts; Improved reverse mortgage understanding; Supports better focused Web searches; Rules reflect changes in the environment; Other ES work more easily incorporated; and Recommendations/training adapt to user.	Limited sites with XML/ ontology standard; and Limited agent development tool kits.	Access information directly from source; Easily incorporate new training topics; Reach a broader audience; Formalize expert's process; and Autonomous recommendations.	Web sites volatile, with distributed control; Changing interface standards; and Insufficient training data.
Enhanced ES Approach	Effective development tools; Faster decision-making; Improved consistency; Less demand on experts; Improved reverse mortgage understanding; and Supports better focused Web searches.	Accurately addressing the cost-benefit analysis will render the expert system tools less effective; Dynamic data and rules, controlled outside; Training limited to informational text; Knowledge base isolated from Web data; and Does not incorporate other ES work.	Access information directly from source; Easily incorporate new training topics; Reach a broader audience; Rapid prototype effective use of experts; and Formalize expert's process.	Inaccurate recommendations costly; and Potential legal impact from misinformation.

process. Further, it will continue to support direct access local HTML files or inserting new ones. Because of its Web emphasis, the system continues to broaden the audience for reverse mortgage training over previous brochure and booklet techniques. Finally, its "build a little, test a little" techniques have been shown to make effective use of the limited time of experts in the field, while essentially serving to formally document a process that is not currently well documented.

- **Weaknesses and threats:** The major shortcoming of this approach, however, is that it fails to resolve the three problem issues identified in developing REMA I. While a link to MorNet will improve the computational component of system recommendations as

new loan companies are added, those insertions will continue to be computational, rather than symbolic, in nature. The value of the more established tool sets associated with expert systems will be less noticeable than if the entire task were heavily symbolic in nature. Further, while this approach will incorporate changes to the current data and rules, bringing the system up-to-date, it does not address the fact that the rules and data will change again. The static nature of the expert system limits its ability to adapt to the dynamic reverse mortgage process it represents or the dynamic Web environment in which it resides. Its lack of advanced communication or interoperability tools limits its ability to incorporate the functionality of other expert systems or Web sites into its knowledge base. As a result, the system will require frequent manual updates or risk providing inaccurate information that could cost its users money. Such losses may, in turn, carry negative legal implications. Finally, its lack of autonomy restricts the training function to the display of informational text rather than a full-blown tutor that learns about the user as it progresses or, on its own initiative, notifies the user of changes in loan options.

Agent-Based Approach

- **Strengths and opportunities:** Possessing the properties of autonomy, social ability, and adaptability, agent technology provides the potential for greatly enhancing the capabilities of the REMA system. As illustrated in Table 1, the strengths and opportunities of an agent-based system parallel in many ways those of the expert system approach. The system will most certainly continue to support faster decision-making, improved consistency, less demand on experts, and improved public understanding of the reverse mortgage process. Further, it will continue to support direct access to a variety of loan sources by linking into their Web sites. Because of its Web emphasis, it continues to broaden the audience for reverse mortgage training over previous brochure and booklet techniques. The agent-based approach, however, has several additional strengths. First, it more specifically addresses the three problem areas identified at the end of Phase I: (1) Agent-based systems deal equally well with problems of a computational or symbolic nature; (2) it better addresses the dynamic nature of the reverse mortgage process; rather than establishing fixed rules that must be intentionally modified by the developer at regular intervals, information agents are established to seek and substitute relevant parameters from regulated Web-sites as appropriate; and (3) the learning component of agent-based systems supports incorporating a well-designed tutoring system that is both diagnostic, discovering the nature and extent of the user's knowledge, and strategic, planning its responses based on its findings about the learner. Also, while the three alternative loan sources are, in fact, representative of the available alternatives, future work must incorporate more companies. The agent-based approach provides a natural mechanism for incorporating new loan companies with minimal impact on previous software components. The ontology component of the supervisor agent would require updates as new loan sites are added, but it minimizes the effort in mediating between heterogeneous data sources. Finally, the autonomous nature of the agent facilitates an ongoing search for the best possible loan. Thus, the agent can provide information about a new or improved loan source without waiting for the user to think of querying for improvements.

- **Weaknesses and threats:** While agent development environments are available, they are generally not as mature as those for expert systems, so system development will generally be more time-consuming. The interface to remote Web sites could be facilitated by the use of the XML standard and an ontology to resolve varied terminology across heterogeneous formats; however, these standards are relatively new, and most of the sites of interest are HTML-based instead. It will, therefore, be important to establish a working relationship with sites across which data is shared; otherwise, the volatility of the data and the distribution of control will render the project ineffectual. Since the standards are relatively new and not widely in force, the developer risks having a new standard move in and replace the one on which the system is based. Finally, while the agent-based approach supports the development of an adaptive tutor/advisor, most learning algorithms require large amounts of data, which may be initially difficult to obtain.

RECOMMENDATION FOR NEXT PHASE OF DEVELOPMENT

Because of the dramatic increases in functionality associated with the agent-based approach, it is recommended that the fully functional system be built on the agent-based prototype, REMA II, rather than on the REMA I expert system. The only reason for selecting to an expert system approach would be to support a fast turnaround incremental improvement on the current system. Given current availability of a prototype system for immediate use, the plan that best incorporates the dynamic and heavily computational components of the advisor and the user-adaptive, self-initiating components of the tutor is preferred.

Practical Implications

A critical question for system development managers is, Under what circumstances would it likely be better to use AT instead of the presently more widely-used ES technology for the development of specific applications? AT is extremely promising, and it behooves all system development managers to understand its potential and limitations and perhaps begin to experiment with AT for possible adoption in the future. However, there are limitations. There are situations where the use of AT will not be efficient in terms of system development cost and implementation time. Systems development managers must remember that presently AT is still at a relatively early stage of adoption in industry at large. The availability of systems developers competent with the technology is relatively scarce. Also, there is a lack of

systems development tool kits and shells, which today are commonly found for the development of ES. As discussed previously in the chapter, the fact that AT is useful for addressing relatively more complex application requirements makes the systems development analysis and design tasks correspondingly more complex and requiring software engineering methods that are still under development. In a similar fashion, the ability of AT to bridge the gap between distributed application components may raise questions about user privacy, data integrity, and human control over the agent-based system. Nevertheless, increasingly there are applications which will require the use of AT. The following conditions are likely to call for the use of AT in system development: (1) applications requiring flexible decision-making beyond fuzzy logic and/or the relatively strict rules required by ES; (2) applications which require enough intelligence for direct system interaction with end users and for system learning from the experience itself, whereby the rules will evolve on their own without the need for modification by systems developers; and (3) applications that require a flexible and complex integration of two or more ES and/or systems of other types.

As the business community puts greater importance on the role of Knowledge Management in capturing collective expertise and distributing it in a manner that produces a payoff, the use of agent-based technology will have increasingly significant business implications. With the dramatic increase in Internet activity over the past five years, agents can play an important role in monitoring, filtering, and recommending information, using user profiles to personalize their support. Agent mediators can facilitate the exchange of data among heterogeneous sites, maintaining an ongoing record of variable site formats and mapping information seamlessly into a format more easily understood by their users. Network management agents can focus on increasing throughput and minimizing delay by adapting protocols to the current hardware and workload environment. In general, complex problems can be decomposed into smaller, segmented problems that can be more easily resolved. All of these advances open decision support and e-commerce opportunities to a wider community and facilitate tapping more widely-distributed knowledge bases to improve quality. Such advances are already within reach for many application areas. However, the ability to reach the full potential of these advances relies on continued development of software engineering methods specifically tailored to agent-based systems, software development tools, and security mechanisms that accommodate a widely-distributed, mobile computing environment.

The effective use of agent technology enables developers to gain significant advantages over existing technologies in achieving their Knowledge Management goals. An increased level of software system autonomy limits the user burden for direct intervention and can relieve communication requirements in a bandwidth-limited environment. The distributed decision-making process can increase robustness and, because tasks are performed in parallel, overall system efficiency increases. The approach facilitates developing mediators that can integrate heterogeneous and legacy systems without requiring a single data representation structure. Further, the techniques support incremental development of complex systems via independent reusable components.

The REMA case illustrates some of the many powerful enhancements achieved by using agent techniques where expert systems were originally envisioned. To system designers/developers, one of the most compelling arguments for using only ES is the ready availability of software development tools to support this more mature development technique. Although there are many issues to be addressed for agent technology to realize its full potential, the technology has advanced at a fast rate due to the significant research effort in both academia and industry. Many of the components to build effective agents are moving beyond research communities and coming into common use in the immediate future. With their arrival, we now have a powerful integrator for Web-based systems with the more traditional types of systems (including ES), thus providing a strong infrastructure for managing corporate knowledge.

ACKNOWLEDGMENT

The author is grateful to the Fannie Mae Foundation for the grant that supported the development of the REMA I prototype, to Dr. J. Liebowitz who led that prototype development effort, to Mr. Ed Szymanoski for his constructive review and comments on the REMA I effort, and to Ms. Judy Hees for her assistance with this project.

REFERENCES

AARP. (2001). Reverse mortgage. Retrieved 2001, from http://www.aarp.org

Barbaceanu, M. (2001). *The agent building shell: Programming cooperative enterprise agents.* Retrieved 2001 from http://www.eil.utoronto.ca/ABS-page/ABS-overview.html

Broome, B., Gangopadhyay, A., & Yoon, V. (2002). *CAER: An ontology-based community of agents for emergency relief.* Paper presented at the 6th World Multi-Conference on Systemics, Cybernetics, and Informatics, July, Orlando, FL.

Cantu, F. (2000). *Reinforcement and Bayesian learning in multiagent systems: The MACS project* (Tech.Rep.No. CIA-RI-042). Center for Artificial Intelligence, ITESM

Carlsson, C. (2002). Decisions support in virtual organizations: The case for multi-agent support. *Group Decision and Negotiation, 11*(3), 185-221.

Donlon, J. P. (1997, July). The virtual organization. *Chief Executive*, (125), 58-66.

FannieMae (2001). *Our business is the American dream*. Retrieved 2001, from: http://www.fanniemae.com

Finin, T., Labrou, Y., & Mayfield, J. (1998). KQML as an agent communication language. In J. M. Bradshaw (Ed.), *Software agents* (p. 28). Boston: MIT Press.

FIPA. (2000). *FIPA specification repository*. Retrieved 2001, from www.fipa.org/repository

HUD. (2001). *Homes and communities*. Retrieved 2001, from http://www.hud.gov

Khalil, O., & Wang, S. (2002). Information technology enabled meta-management for virtual organizations. *International Journal of Production Economics, 75*(1), 127-134.

Kishore, R., & McLean, E. (2002). The next generation enterprise: A CIO perspective on the vision, its impacts, and implementation challenges. *Information Systems Frontiers, 4*(1), 121.

Larson, M. (1999). *Shopping for a reverse mortgage: Few products, lots of tricky choices*. Retrieved 2001, from http://www.bankrate.com/brm/news/loan

Lu, M., & Guimaraes, T. (1989). A guide to selecting expert systems applications. *Journal of Information Systems Management*, (Spring), 6(2), 8-15.

Martin, C. (1999). *Net future*. New York: McGraw-Hill.

Minsky, M. (1985). *The society of mind*. New York: Simon and Schuster.

Rahman, Z., & Bhattachryya, S. K. (2002). Virtual organisation: A stratagem. *Singapore Management Review, 24*(2), 29-45.

Rassmussen, D., Megbolugbe, I., & Morgan, B. (1997). The reverse mortgage as an asset management tool. *Housing Policy Debate, 8*(1), 173-194.

Reverse. (2001). *Independent information on reverse mortgages for consumers, their families, professional advisors, and nonprofit counselors*. Retrieved 2001, from http://www.reverse.org

Traverse, M. (2001). *Agent-based programming environments*. Retrieved 2001, from http://xenia.media.mit.edu/~mt/childs-play-pp.html

Waldo, J. (2002). Virtual organizations, pervasive computing, and an infrastructure for networking at the edge. *Information Systems Frontiers, 4*(1), 9.

Wooldridge, M., & Jennings, N. R. (1995). Intelligent agents: Theory and practice. *The Knowledge Engineering Review, 10*(2), 115-152.

Wooldridge, M., Jennings, N. R., & Kinny, D. (2000). The Gaia methodology for agent-oriented analysis and design. *International Journal of Autonomous Agents and Multi-Agent Systems, 3.3*(28), 285.

Yannis, L., Finin, T., & Peng, Y. (1999). Agent communication languages: The current landscape. *IEEE Intelligent Systems and Their Applications, 14*(2).

Yoon, Y., & Guimaraes, T. (1993). Selecting expert system development techniques. *Information and Management*, (24), 209-223.

Chapter XIX
Virtual Communities of Practice:
A Mechanism for Efficient Knowledge Retrieval in MNCs

Jens Gammelgaard
Copenhagen Business School, Denmark

Thomas Ritter
Copenhagen Business School, Denmark

ABSTRACT

In geographically dispersed organizations, like multinational corporations (MNCs), contextual gaps exist between senders and receivers of knowledge. Employee socialization resulting from physical proximity facilitates contextualization of the transferred knowledge. However, in MNCs most knowledge transfers take place through virtual communication media. We investigate the phenomenon of virtual communities of practice, and propose them to be efficient for individual's knowledge retrieval as participation in such communities reduces the contextual gaps between senders and receivers of knowledge. However, the organization must provide a knowledge-sharing friendly culture, and an institutional protectionism, in order to establish the required level of swift trust within the virtual community.

INTRODUCTION

This article focuses on virtual communities of practices, and whether participation in such forums improves knowledge retrieval processes by overcoming problems of contextual gaps between the sender and the receiver of knowledge. Most multinational corporations (MNCs) have invested heavily in computer systems that help employees to easily download documents, but problems still arise when the searched knowledge is removed from its context and thereby loses some or all of its meaning to the reader. This article, though, differentiates the conventional wisdom that employee socialization, resulting from physical proximity that facilitates contextualization and trust building processes allows transfer of complex and tacit knowledge, (Cohendet, Kern, Mehmanpazir, & Muier, 1999; Constant, Kiesler, & Sproull, 1994; Granovetter, 1972; Hansen, 1999; Nonaka & Takeuchi, 1995) as in the case of communities of practice (Brown & Duguid, 1991, Wenger, 1998). Here, we point to the fact that proximity is seldom the case of the MNC—having operations spanning the globe—which makes most communication "global rather than local" (Li et al., 2007). This article, therefore, questions whether knowledge retrieval can be efficient in a virtual setting, given the context of an MNC. The description of knowledge retrieval, and knowledge transfer processes in general, are well established, and likewise the analyses and surveys of these processes in communities of practices. However, this article contributes by investigating these matters in the context of the *MNC* and the impact of knowledge retrieval processes when they take place in a *virtual* context.

The topic of knowledge retrieval is central to MNCs when they, to give one example, intend to implement best practices throughout the organization as it requires the application of knowledge from one context to another (Grant, 2005; Hornett & Stein, 2007). The question is which Knowledge Management strategy best fits knowledge retrieval. Typically, MNCs either practices socialization or codification strategies (Hansen, 1999). Hornett and Stein (2007) confirm this established fact because their survey company focused on the social or the technological part respectively, but seldom the combination of the two, that is, the sociotechnical orientation. Hornett and Stein further vary the debate with the finding of the company's attention paid to the knowledge transfer *per se* more than the usefulness of the transferred knowledge. Adding to this finding, we believe that MNC managers can benefit from this article, as we theorize on the underlying mechanism for efficient utilization of

transferred knowledge, that is, the establishment of a forum where knowledge is retrieved correctly. This issue has been investigated in proxy environments, but we discuss the efficiency of a sociotechnical Knowledge Management strategy, in this case a virtual communities of practice. This contributes to a recent debate in this journal, where Bartczak, Turner, and England (2007) survey of the Knowledge Management strategy of the US Air Force Material Command showed the difficulties of leveraging the otherwise efficient communities of practice in a virtual context, and Vizcaino, Soto, Portillo-Rodriguez, and Piattini (2007) arguing that technological solutions seldom take into account the fundamental problems of transferring knowledge. Contrarily, Cheuk (2007) reports how the British Council has established sense-making processes in a virtual context by initiating social networks. This article taps into this debate and contributes to this area of research because it examines the pros and cons of virtual communities of practice in regard to knowledge retrieval.

The article proceeds in the following order: Section Two provides an overview of the knowledge retrieval process, followed by discussions of communities of practice and virtual communities of practice in the next two sections. Thereafter, knowledge retrieval is analyzed in the context of virtual communities and this discussion leads to the formulation of propositions. Conclusions are drawn in the final section.

THE KNOWLEDGE RETRIEVAL PROCESS

Retrieval of knowledge takes place in a two step process: one employee acquires, encodes and stores knowledge in the corporate memory, after which another employee retrieves (finds, reads, and decodes) the knowledge and then subsequently applies it in a certain setting (Alavi & Leidner, 2001; Holzner & Marx, 1979; Krippendorff, 1975; Pentland, 1995; Stein & Zwass, 1995). Therefore, retrieval processes begin when an individual requires knowledge stored in the organizational memory in order to meet a specific goal (a consultant meeting a client's request, for example). Krippendorff (1975, p. 19) defines *retrieval* as "processes by which information is reconstituted or reconstructed and made available, by, for example, 'reading documents for what is encoded in them.'" Knowledge retrieval can be seen as a two-stage process that starts by identifying specific, relevant knowledge stored in the organizational memory and continues with its decodification. Although these two stages are related, we focus on the second, with an emphasis on the interpretation of the knowledge (Paepcke, 1996). The research question we address is: How can the MNC employee decode knowledge stored in document, and written by a colleague working in a distant organizational unit when this distance often creates a contextual gap?

If we are to fully understand the retrieval process, we first require clarification of what "knowledge," "memory," "document," and "contextual gap" mean. Normally, distinctions are made between data, information and knowledge. Zack (1999, p. 46) provides the following definition: "data represent observations or facts out of context that are, therefore, not directly meaningful. Information results from placing data within some meaningful context, often in the form of a message. Knowledge is that which we come to believe and value on the basis of the meaningfully organized accumulation of information (messages) through experience, communication or inference." This indicates a hierarchy of complexity with knowledge at the top, making it hardest to retrieve. Here, Tiwana (2000) views knowledge as actionable information, which further puts an emphasis on efficient retrieval processes, as utilization of transferred knowledge depends on this condition.

Memory refers to all knowledge-storage media, encompassing a varied range of concepts

beginning with the "individual brain," including "routines and learning practices" and ending with such media as documents and databases. The act of retrieval depends on the particular medium used for knowledge access. Our article focuses on the retrieval of knowledge from the shared pool of available *written information* (possible actionable information), the MNC organizational memory. In Krippendorff's (1975) words, this is a memory that involves a record, that is, "a medium which thereby carries into the present some information about its past history" (p. 22). This article chooses the written *document* as the media for investigation. A document contains information and knowledge and is the actual product of writing; it stores collection of data and refers to something physical like printed pages, or to a virtual document in an electronic format. An example of a document could be a written report, which contains the findings of an individual.

A context is a "set of premises used in interpreting an utterance" (Sperber & Wilson, 1995, p. 15). A context is, therefore, a psychological construct, based on the retriever's assumption about the world. These assumptions are not only based on information or "pure facts" but can be influenced by, as Sperber and Wilson write (p. 16) "expectations about the future, scientific hypotheses or religious beliefs, anecdotal memories, general cultural assumptions, beliefs about the mental state of the speaker." Secondly, assumptions relate to the situation in which knowledge was acquired or need to be applied; such as a customer relationship (Alavi & Leidner, 2001; Alvesson & Kärreman, 2000), a representation that will be included in the final document reporting these findings. Encoding, therefore, accounts for the way records come into being in a medium, whereas decoding refers to the act of retrieving (Krippendorf, 1975). Senders will typically design text (encode) to give meaning within their own context, and receivers will likewise retrieve knowledge in their context in order to apply it in a specific situation (Shotter, 1993; Wenger, 1998), like a customer relationship relevant to the receiver. Therefore, a contextual gap exists between the sender and the receiver, keeping them apart (Nahapiet & Ghoshal, 1998). Contextual gaps in communication emanate from lack of mutual knowledge. If sender and retriever share mutual knowledge, every piece of contextual information in a message must be mutually known by the sender and retriever, and both actors must know that they *do* share mutual knowledge (Sperber & Wilson, 1995). However, this hypothetical state of symmetric information seldom exists, even in the case of actors with very tight relationships.

Furthermore, when interpreting written utterances, imperfections in language (Alvesson & Kärreman, 2000) and translation problems (Welch, Welch, & Piekkari, 2005) complicate retrieval processes. Further, written language is often imperfect in order to make accurate representations of perceived objects. One example is provided by Alvesson and Kärreman (2000) showing how an expression like "very little" can be measured and interpreted differently. Palmer (1993) provides another example showing how the use of different punctuations in the same sentence changes the meaning considerably. Using Barthes' words (1997, p. 272): "The text is plural. This does not mean just that it has several meanings, but rather that it achieves plurality of meaning, an *irreducible* plurality." Large amounts of situated verbal interaction, where the sender controls for correctly comprehended retrieval—is as pointed out by Reddy (1979)—needed to reduce plurality, because the sender helps the receiver to remove limitations to her or his own understanding (Deetz, 1992), and alignment of meaning is based on negotiation processes between the two actors (Shotter, 1993; Wenger, 1998). Face-to-face conversation and socialization is then often required to transfer knowledge (Nonaka & Takeuchi, 1995). However, meaningful communication, further, requires a shared context of codes and language (Boland & Tenaski, 1995). Codification, in itself, is not sufficient for minimizing contextual gaps. As Cowan,

David, and Foray (2000, p. 225) write: "what is codified for one person or group may be tacit for another and an utterly impenetrable mystery for a third." Encoding might even impede retrieval, because the use of, for example, a metaphor creates ambiguity. *Shared* context and frequent communication diminishes, on the other hand, the distance between encoding and decoding. Shared contexts can be face-to-face or virtual, where past interpretations may, in fact, be documented (Kogut & Zander, 1992; Krippendorff, 1975). Lave and Wenger (1991) and Brown and Duguid (1991, 2000) observe that shared codes and language bring people together and further shape members perceptions. The importance of shared narratives has also been emphasized (Wenger, 1998). Communities of practice encapsulate this situation, where common sense is build through mutual engagement in a geographically proxy environment, and will be the focal point for our further investigations.

COMMUNITIES OF PRACTICE

A community of practice is an informal group of people sharing common concerns or expertise, strengthening its bonds through ongoing interaction (McDermott, 1999; Wenger, McDermott, & Snyder, 2002; Wenger & Snyder, 2000). The group aims to develop practices and domains of knowledge with a unique perspective. Each community member has a distinctive identity and finds a unique place in the group (Wenger, 1998). Both the possession and contribution of knowledge are distributed asymmetrically, although knowledge is available to all members. This shared knowledge pool lets individuals work without having to know everything (Brown & Duguid, 2001; Wenger, 1998). On the other hand, individuals are aware of the others' membership, that is, they know who is who (Brown & Duguid, 1991; Lave & Wenger, 1991) and what different people know. The shared codes and language are most important, turning the community of practice into an effective means of communication. Brown and Duguid (1991) point to the sharing of practices as leading to common tacit knowledge, engendering knowledge transfers, communication and learning within the community. As such, information travels fast within real communities and is readily accessible to other members. Gertler (2003) views communities of practice as facilitators of tacit knowledge transfers through collaborative problem solving assisted by storytelling. In general, communities of practice provide their members with the opportunity for conversation, experimentation and sharing expertise with colleagues (Pan & Leidner, 2003). The sharing of practice establishes one shared context that might overcome other contextual differences (Alvesson & Kärreman, 2000). Giving the receivers appropriate historical and social contexts assists the group's knowledge-decoding processes.

The creation of meaning is of particular relevance discussing communities of practice. Wenger (1998, p. 47, italics added) explains:"Communities of practice are the prime context in which we can work out *common sense* through mutual engagement." Hereby, the interpretation of the term "common sense" goes beyond its meaning in colloquial English referring to "sound and prudent judgment," that is some fact or interpretation everybody can agree upon. Wenger refers explicitly to the shared understanding of participants in a community and the development of individual viewpoints. In Wenger's (1998, p.48) words: "We all have our own theories and ways of understanding the world, and our communities of practice are places where we develop, negotiate, and share them." Therefore, participation in a community of practice leads to a social production of meaning, because the community members negotiate meaning through the reification processes, through which they produce shared understandings of, for example, symbols, stories, and metaphors. As such, common sense does not refer in this context to "minimal joint

agreement" or "general fact of life" but to common sense-making, common sense-development and common sense-negotiation. The activities in communities of practice are, therefore, not centered around the identification and defense of one "common sense" (universal agreement) but are focused to offer members ample opportunity to develop their own thinking based on "common sense" (mutual understanding). According to Stein (2005), communities of practice, therefore, specify a knowledge domain of interest, within ongoing processes of sense-making, knowledge sharing and discovery take place among interested and interconnected participants.

Within communities a relationship become idiosyncratic and meaning is based in a detailed, complex, embedded shared understanding (Wenger, 1998). Consequently, personal and social relationships within the community are essential to sense-making processes. The concept of "social capital" is useful in this context as it helps to clarify the value of the resources that are embedded in the network of relationships extending from a particular individual or social unit (Burt, 1997; McElroy, 2002; Nahapiet & Ghoshal, 1998). Additionally, "social capital" expresses the sense of trust that develops from continued interpersonal connections, bridging cultural differences and creating a shared context of meaning (Daniel, Schwier, & McCalla, 2003).

A community of practice has a flexible structure with no precise termination date. Numbers and intensity of participation fluctuate as people move in and out, but the group normally includes tens or even hundreds, although only a few take social and intellectual leadership (Lesser & Everest, 2001; Wenger, 1998; Wenger & Snyder, 2000). Participants seldom pursue an agreed, shared end goal. They are instead connected through a joint interest in a particular topic. Evolving without constraint of authority, the group is self-organized (Creplet, Dupouet, Kern, Mehmanpazir, & Munier, 2001; Lesser & Everest, 2001). Unlike informal networks of people who share information and build relationships, the community of practice focuses on something specific (Lave & Wenger, 1991; Nonaka, Toyama, Konno, 2001). Furthermore, its informality and focus on knowledge-building and sharing distinguishes it from formal workgroups and project teams that concentrate instead on final products or services. Early studies assume communities of practice form spontaneously. More recent work describes far more management-governed processes (Soo, Devinney, Midgley, & Deering, 2002; Storck & Hill, 2000; Swan, Scarbrough, & Robertson, 2002). An example of this is the "epistemic community" where members accept the presence of a procedural authority, urging fulfillment of a specified goal (Cowan et al., 2000; Creplet et al., 2001). When members of a community of practice pay attention to the increasing performance of a given practice, members of epistemic communities are cautious about peers' orders and rewards (Cohendet & Llerena, 2003). A reason is that communities of practice may have broadly intrinsic motivation, while epistemic communities are more likely to be defined by extrinsic incentives.

This literature review clearly points out a range of factors that minimizes the contextual gap between senders and receivers of knowledge. In practice it also covers the situation where the reader of a written document either contact the original informant personally for additional information, or automatically are aware of the premises of decoding based on a prior process of negotiated meaning, and by the use of a shared set of resources such as methods, tools, theories and practices, as stated by Stein (2005). However, the same author opposes the electronic information exchange to the far much richer concept of proxy sense-making (p. 3). It is, therefore, reasonable to discuss the efficiency of virtual information retrieval, and whether communities of practice are replicable in a virtual context.

VIRTUAL COMMUNITIES OF PRACTICE

Virtual communities are, at first sight, very near to communities of practice, a group of frequently interactive individuals sharing a practice. What is different is that communication and coordination of work takes place in cyberspace through information technology. The community is, therefore, relational without reference to a specific location (Ahuja & Carley, 1999). Koh and Kim (2004) speak of *distributed community of practices,* and refer to a group of geographically distributed individuals who are informally bound together by shared expertise and shared interest of work. Like communities of practice, they operate with informal goals, common language, shared understanding and reasonable levels of trust.

Two factors stand out as being significantly different for communities established in a virtual context: (1) communication takes place in cyberspace, and (2) the lack of physical proximity between sender and receiver. With regard to the online communication, MNCs usually establish an "Intranet" as an essential part of their Knowledge Management system: a replication of Internet technology that uses a firewall to prevent external access (Boettcher, 1998; Bowman, 2002). An intranet allows establishment of discussion forums where the receiver taps into written database documents describing, for example, best practice and, subsequently, has the opportunity to discuss their reapplication with the original creators (Zack, 1999). In general, information technologies are cost-efficient instrument for information exchange over a geographical distance (Huber, 1991) by linking organizational units and individuals through standardized information flows (Bowman, 2002; Ensign, 1998) and established repositories of codified knowledge (Constant, Sproull, & Kiesler, 1997; Pickering & King, 1995; Purvis, Sambamurthy, & Zmud, 2001). In fact, by using databases, more people—or at least their written documents—serve the individual as information sources. MNC computer networks present the opportunity to ask (a large number of) strangers for advice and people can respond without having to know their colleagues and without having to travel. Such networks connect those who do not enjoy physical proximity, shared histories or demographics. Communities are connected primarily by e-mail networks (Wenger & Snyder, 2000) and overcome spatial distance by using collaborative groupware technologies (McKnight & Bontis, 2002). Members of "online communities" feel part of a larger Web of relationships in which there are ongoing exchanges of commonly-valued items together with long-lasting, maintained interactions and a developed shared history (Figallo, 1998). Online communities not only offer the possibility for information exchange, but also enable people to socialize (Preece, 2000). The computer system thus supports and mediates social interaction, facilitating a sense of togetherness.

To distinguish between intranet, newsgroups, and chat rooms on one side and virtual communities on the other, the former ones describe tools by which persons can be found and contacted but no long-term interest is needed, nor a strong common sense. The main purpose is provision of data and "ready made" knowledge, which can be retrieved without further interaction or any longer term interactions. By contrast, virtual communities of practice do have a common topic and a long-term working history, even though individual members may have joined recently. The common theme unites the members and they jointly are working to improve and develop the field of their interest. Thus, the demarcation between the two concepts is duration of membership (long for virtual communities), direction of communication (two-sided in virtual communities) and finally, the level of joint interests (high for virtual communities). However, despite the joint interest, the lack of physical proximity, through which people meet face-to-face and which provides the opportunity of warmth, attentiveness and other interpersonal

affections, is expected to lead to a situation where trust may be unlikely to develop (Jarvenpaa & Leidner, 1999; Wenger et al., 2002). In decentralized and dispersed organizational structures, employees can—through the use of IT—work anytime and anywhere, but the fraying of ties between people impedes trust-building, which again affects the extent of knowledge transfers and the kind of information the sender is willing to share (Wiesenfeld, Raghuram, & Garud, 1999). The next section, therefore, describes the circumstances in which knowledge retrieval can be efficient in a virtual community.

VIRTUAL COMMUNITIES AND KNOWLEDGE RETRIEVAL

Because of the doubts about trust mentioned earlier, the virtual community's efficacy as an information-retrieval medium is not clear. We must ask whether the lack of geographical proximity, the difficulty in building strong ties and the general rootlessness of social relationships severely hampers retrieval processes. Communities of practice normally rely on social capital rather than on techno structures (Alvesson & Kärreman, 2001) or the overall organizational Knowledge Management strategies emphasizing economic aspects (Davenport & Prusak, 1998). The distance between scattered groups of employees means people do not meet by chance and face-to-face contact is rare. Participants, therefore, remain in separate national and company cultures representing organizational units that possess different capabilities.

The question is whether members of virtual communities do retrieve knowledge effectively. A literature review by Huysman et al. (2003) reveals that virtual teams generally solve such problems as lack of trust, lack of shared background knowledge, and coordination, behavior and interaction issues: however, these problems were in this case mostly solved using a combination of video conferencing and communication through e-mail. Cramton (2001) opposes this view and finds in her survey that mutual knowledge is a problem of geographical dispersed groups due to failures in communicating, retaining and updating contextual information. Lea and Spears (1991) provide one explanation, namely that computer-mediated communication reduces the number of cues available to the receiver relative to face-to-face communication. Conversely, the feeling of solidarity and mutual interest in communities of practice should increase the will to retain and update contextual information and minimize polarization effects.

Strong ties among individuals are also seen as necessary for transferring complex knowledge, one reason being the awareness of contextual backgrounds (Granovetter, 1972; Hansen, 1999). Whether it is possible to establish strong ties between actors in a virtual setting (Preece, 2000) is questionable. Virtual strong ties are typically founded on initial face-to-face meetings that are then later maintained virtually (McDermott, 1999). Thus, computer-mediated communication supports *existing* ties, whether weak or strong (Pickering & King, 1995; Preece, 2000). The establishment of new online weak ties typically results from newsgroup and chat room participation, often organized around specific topics or demographics, and not necessarily involving proxy social relationships (Kraut et al., 1998).

The virtual context addresses the question of whether or not the lack of face-to-face interaction in online relationships hinders or at least limits the retrieval processes that are otherwise characterized by frequent, long-lasting voluntary information transfer, where both partners are willing to develop companionship and accept mutual needs (Wellman & Gulia, 2000). However, different surveys suggest the possibility to build close online social relationships. With asynchronous and necessarily verbal information, this is more difficult and time-consuming to achieve (Walther, 1995). Other surveys indicate that group newcom-

ers readily participate actively in online groups because the medium affords greater anonymity, thus actually lowering barriers to enter a group (Ahuja & Galvin, 2003). Gertler (2003) claims that even tacit knowledge will flow across regional and national boundaries if the virtual community is "strong enough." Nonaka and Takeuchi (1995) see the need of transferring knowledge through proxy socialization mechanisms. However, this claim should not be misread as a ply for face-to-face relationships because virtual socialization media do exist. In addition, through a combination of narratives or storytelling techniques and with the use of boundary objects such as documents (Boland & Tenkasi, 1995), the virtual community of practice is useful for retrieval processes. Studies by Yates, Orlikowski, and Okamura (1999) reveal that communities develop "genres," that is "socially recognized types of communicative actions … that are habitually enacted by members of a community to realize particular social purpose" (p. 84) and further particular forms (e.g., choice of media), structural features (like formatting) and linguistic features (specialized vocabulary) are developed in communities, all in all helping receivers to retrieve knowledge correctly. A survey by Zucchermaglio and Talermo (2003) also showed how informality in communication was reached over time, even in the context of using electronic mail systems. This study also proves that sense-making processes can be established, but further, that the time aspect should be integrated into the analyses. Therefore, if the receiver is provided with the contextual background, and if codes and language can be aligned, the same degree of retrieval should be achievable even in a virtual context. As Wenger (1998, p. 74) writes: "Given the right context, talking on the phone, exchanging electronic mail, or being connected by radio can all be part of what makes mutual engagement possible." One has also to remember that physical proximity also triggers personality clashes and, as such, a community of practice might be less effective than a virtual community.

The remaining factor to stress is the issue of trust. Dirks and Ferrin (2001) emphasized its importance through a literature review, pointing out that trust within a group had a significant positive effect on openness in communication (Zand, 1972). However, as Mayer, Davis, and Schoorman (1995, p. 712) write, information transfers depends on the sender's willingness "to be vulnerable to the action of another party based on the expectation that the other will perform a particular action important to the trustor, irrespective of the ability to monitor or control the other party." The question, here, is whether or not a sender will provide contextual information to a receiver whom he has never met and perhaps only has communicated with via e-mail. Regardless the media, it requires repeated interactions to build up a feeling of confidence in the other party's value and trustworthiness (Jones & George, 1998). This supports our argument that a virtual community of practice is a forum for repeated interaction and thus, enables the necessary feeling of confidence in a virtual environment. Further, the degree of trust needed for transfer depends on the "criticalness" of the transferred information (Bhattacharya, Devinney, & Pillutla, 1998). One example is the case where an employee assesses his "market value" and bargaining power within the company, aiming for future career building, in respect to the uniqueness of the knowledge he possess. Such kinds of knowledge are very critical and demands high levels of trust before it will be transferred (Constant et al., 1999; Husted & Michailova, 2002). However, communicating with the "unknown" do take place in the initial phase of a relationship that simultaneously is the most critical phase for trust building (as documented by Constant et al., 1999; see also McKnight, Cummings, & Chervany, 1998). Trust in this stage is based on calculation, and, therefore, depends on the availability of relevant information (Lane, 1998). Trust can only proceed on the basis of institutionalized protection or the reputation of the receiver (Child, Faulkner, & Tellman, 2005). The question is when the corporation can provide the needed institutional protection in the beginning of the relationships between sender and receiver, where trust is to be characterized as fragile. Here, the organization can build up a knowledge-sharing friendly culture and, in general, align corporate norms and values through proper communication, which again increases the possibility of shared contextual backgrounds (Wiesenfeld et al., 1999). Second, trust can be established in virtual communities. Meyerson, Weick, and Kramer (1996) operate with the term *swift trust* in describing the creation of trust in temporary teams. When trust cannot be established through frequent face-to-face contact, group members instead *import* expectations of trust from other familiar settings. Likewise, the community's genre repertoire (i.e., the types of communicative actions and the forms it takes) typically reflects the organizational cultural context (Yates et al., 1999).

Subsequent trust retaining then depends on the ongoing activity in the group. Virtual communities thereby establish swift trust *if* the organization in which the community is embedded has implemented a trust-based knowledge-sharing culture, and as Constant et al. (1999, p. 400) write: "a belief in organizational ownership of work encourages and mediates attitudes favoring sharing." In this respect, Jarvenpaa and Leidner (1999) test the swift trust framework and find that dispersed teams do experience "swift trust," although such trust is fragile and only temporal. Kasper-Fuehrer and Ashkanasy (2001) also find that a common business understanding and strong business ethics are needed to establish trust in virtual organizations. Meyerson et al. (1996) provide three reasons for an initial high level of trust in interaction between individuals without any prior relationships (e.g., trusting a newcomer to a virtual community and vice versa): a) implicit threat within the organization that inefficient managed communities at the end of the day harm the organization; b) the prospects of future interaction between sender and receiver;

and c) role clarity where individuals rather act as role models. This effect is also described by Dawes (1994, p. 24): "we trust doctors because we trust modern medicine, and we have evidence that it works when antibiotics and operations cure people." If the trustworthiness and reputation of a particular group (e.g., engineers or business development team) in a particular organization is high, it will, following the line of thoughts from Meyerson et al. (1996), generate swift trust even in newly established virtual communities.

In fact, virtual communities, or at least geographically dispersed groups—like scientific communities—have existed for centuries and have been able to establish new paradigms despite the disadvantage of distance (Kuhn, 1962). Their use of conferences, sabbaticals and virtual communication as sense-making media (Pickering & King, 1995) leads us to question whether any opportunity to establish a common sense through mutual engagement can overcome problems such as the lack of geographical proximity (Wenger, 1998). CERN (The European Nuclear Research Centre) and the establishment of the World Wide Web (WWW) are relevant examples. The Web was conceived by Tim Berners-Lee to solve problems of a dispersed group of scientist, all of whom were paying CERN short visits. They still needed to communicate with colleagues after their temporary assignments. Even though the coding problem among physicists seems manageable, there was no documentation of what happened during each individual's stay. In general, employees entering the organization were only given a few hints of whom to address (Naughton, 1999). The situation inspired Tim Berners-Lee to design the basic structure of the WWW, which primarily began as a search opportunity, not particularly helpful for decoding, even though the initial idea was that entered documents should be editable by the receiver (Naughton, 1999). On the other hand, the WWW is forceful as it makes it possible to create and share not only written text, but also multimedia by combining transfers of hypertext

with transmissions of images and audio/video versions (Abbate, 1999). The story is similar to the invention of the telegraph and how it enabled industries like the railway (Chandler, 1990) or a company like Reuters (Witzel, 2003) to develop into geographical dispersed entities.

Today, IT is an integrated means to communicate among geographical dispersed actors. Pan and Leidner (2003) use a case study of Buckman Labs—a chemical company with operations in 21 different countries—to show how IT supports knowledge sharing within and between communities of practice. Furthermore, Ryssen and Godar (2000) provide an example of students working in virtual teams communicating by e-mail and the Web. Lee and Cole (2003) give a recent example, describing the development of the Linux operating system. In the improvement of this system, thousands of volunteers dispersed among both *organizational* and *geographical* boundaries collaborated via the Internet. Criticism impelled learning processes, review processes and error corrections, which enforced correct retrieval of written documents. Linux successfully uses culture as a social control mechanism to solve trust (and property rights) problems and as such illustrates that trust can be developed and maintained in virtual settings.

To conclude the above discussion we propose that knowledge retrieval–between a sender and a receiver communicating in a far distant context within an MNC–can be more efficient in virtual communities of practice than compared to transfer activities outside such communities. By formulating propositions, we intent to put an emphasis on those factors that *initially* in the communication process are going to (1) minimize contextual gaps between sender and receiver, and (2) increase the likelihood of communication among "stranger," that is, a situation without trust building in a proxy environment, given the context of transfers and retrieval of written reports within a virtual community of an MNC. Over time, virtual communities of practices are anticipated to mirror the characteristics from proxy communities of practices, in cases where negotiation of meaning takes place among participants (such as asking for additional information via a phone call) and contextual gaps are minimized via experience. Huysman et al. (2003) have here demonstrated that a combination of using e-mail and video-conferencing solved retrieval problems. Therefore, if "negotiation of meaning" processes are established, virtual communities will contain the same characteristics as proxy communities, showing distinctive identities, full information availability, high level of "knowing who" information, including contextual background information, and in general that conversation, experimentation and shared expertise or passion overcome contextual differences.

However, the question is what makes an initial retrieval of a written document more efficient in a virtual community of practice compared to reading documents—accessed from the corporate intranet—in general. From our perspective, there are various points why the existence of virtual communities leads to more efficient retrieval processes: First, it is easier for the receiver to search a particular piece of information from the sender through a virtual community, because the amount of entries is less and more relevant as compared to a general database. Second, swift trust is easier to establish if other group members act as role models: this does not help the receiver to retrieve *per se,* but it increases the acceptance and the acknowledgement of the relevance of the information. Third, sharing a practice means shared codes because members often possess the same theoretical and practical background (Håkanson, 2007). Writings in the concept of absorptive capacity also advocate for more fluently communication and retrieval when members share a professional and theoretical background (Cummings & Teng, 2003; Lane & Lubatkin, 1998; Reagans & McEvily, 2003; Schultz, 2003): to exemplify, shared theoretical and professional background will lead to shared

vocabulary (Yates et al., 1999). This approaches the situation described by Sperber and Wilson (1995), where contextual information is mutually known, and actors are aware (because of the shared practice) that contextual information is shared. Therefore, we propose:

- **P1:** Individuals participating in virtual communities of practice more efficiently retrieve knowledge from written documents in this forum than from the corporate database, because senders and receivers of knowledge more often will share a theoretical and professional background.

Still, what really drives people apart in MNCs, even in cases of shared practice, are obviously national cultures. Hofstede (1980) is famous for his research and publications on national culture characteristics. However, a recent survey by Li et al. (2007) showed that individual hostility rather than national cultural-related factors impacted knowledge sharing through online communities of practice. One reason could be the anonymity that the virtual setting offers the individual, which brings all participants on the same ground, compared to a "face to face" meeting, where participants bring their national identity with them (Ahuja & Galvin, 2003). These assumptions are similar to the swift trust situation, where the "role the sender can play in relation to his practice" becomes more important than what he or she represents in relation to national background. Secondly, we argue that there will be less knowledge sharing hostility if members identify themselves with the community in which they participate. Even though that Fiol and O'Connor (2005) demonstrate ambiguous findings in the literature up to now, they still argue that members will be motivated to identify with the group because of the relatively high degree of uncertainty that participation in such a virtual group produced. Therefore, swift trust—importing trustworthiness from the organizational setting—and providing the initial institutional protection, is a key factor to overcome problems of knowledge sharing hostility and uncertainty. We propose that lack of institutional protection will lead to failures in communicating, retaining and updating contextual information. The corporate culture is for that reason a crucial player for efficient knowledge retrieval. This produces our second proposition:

- **P2:** Individuals' willingness to share knowledge through virtual communities of practice increases when the MNCs culture, and in relation hereto its norms and values, establish the needed institutional protection to establish swift trust.

CONCLUSION

This article discusses conceptually the phenomenon of communities of practice when established in a virtual context by MNCs. Our specific focus is on the outcome for the individual employee to retrieve knowledge efficiently when participating in such a group. Communities of practice are recognized as being efficient for knowledge transfers in general. The aim of the article was a discussion of whether this comes true in an intra-organizational virtual setting as well. Based on findings from the existing literature, we suggest that individual members will share knowledge more efficiently in a virtual context, if the organization provides institutional protection to establish swift trust situations. Furthermore, similarities in practice and theory initially minimize contextual gaps. Over time, negotiation of meaning processes needs to be established to copy the success of proxy communities of practice. In this case, the virtual community must be rich in its use of media, opening up the possibility of negotiation of meaning processes to supply members with other members' contextual background. Further, shar-

ing practices, in the sense of a jointed professional and theoretical background, is further helpful for information retrieval, and it helps the receiver of information to acknowledge the sender as a relevant informant.

Referring to retrieval of written documents, the receiver often deals with text written by a "stranger" with whom the sender could not establish face-to-face contact. A weaker tie between the actors is foreseeable when compared to a local community of practice. The members are not "colleagues," in the sense that daily operations beyond the community area were to be fulfilled. To put the discussion in perspective, it is worthwhile to address whether a combination of the two community forms would be effective, such as a virtual community of practice, including regular face-to-face meetings. We suggest that business (or virtual communities within MNCs) get inspired by the structure from scientific communities where members occasionally meet at conferences or pay each respective organization short visits and, subsequently, cooperate. As a part of that process they retrieve knowledge from written documents in a virtual context. A combination may encompass the positive sides but also carries costs and risks of inefficient resource allocation. We suggest that the evaluation of relative importance of these two mechanisms should form the basis for further research.

REFERENCES

Abbate, J. (1999). *Inventing the Internet.* Cambridge, MA: The MIT Press.

Ahuja, M.K., & Carley, K.M. (1999). Network structure in virtual organizations. *Organization Science, 10,* 741-757.

Ahuja, M.J., & Galvin, J.E. (2003). Socialization in virtual groups. *Journal of Management, 29,* 161-185.

Alavi, M., & Leidner, D. (2001). Review: Knowledge management and knowledge management systems: Conceptual foundations and research issues. *MIS Quarterly, 25*, 107-136.

Alvesson, M., & Kärreman, D. (2000). Taking the linguistic turn in organizational research: Challenges, responses, consequences. *The Journal of Applied Behavioral Science, 36*, 136-158.

Alvesson, M., & Kärreman, D. (2001). Odd couple: Making sense of the curious concept of knowledge management. *Journal of Management Studies, 38*, 995-1018.

Bartczak, S.E., Turner, J.M., & England, E.C. (2007). Challenges in developing a knowledge management strategy: A case study of the Air Force Material Command. *International Journal of Knowledge Management, 4*(1), xx-xx.

Barthes, R. (1997). *From work to text*. In S. L. Feagin & P. Maynard (Eds.), Aesthetics. Oxford University Press.

Bhattacharya, R., Devinney, T.M., & Pillutla, M.M. (1998). A formal model of trust based on outcomes. *Academy of Management Review, 23*, 459-472.

Boettcher, S. (1998). *The Netscape intranet solution: Deploying the full-service intranet*. New York: John Wiley and Sons.

Boland, R.J, & Tenkasi, R.V. (1995). Perspective making and perspective taking in communities of knowing. *Organization Science, 6*, 350-372.

Bowman, B.J. (2002). Building knowledge management systems. *Information Systems Management, 19*, 32-40.

Brown, J.S., & Duguid, P. (1991). Organizational learning and communities-of-practice: Toward a unified view of working, learning and innovation. *Organization Science, 2*, 40-57.

Brown, J.S., & Duguid, P. (2001). Knowledge and organization: A social-practice perspective. *Organization Science, 12*, 198-213.

Burt, R.S. (1997). The contingent value of social capital. *Administrative Science Quarterly, 42*, 339-365.

Chandler, A.D. (1990). *Scale and scope - the dynamics of industrial capitalism*. Cambridge, Ma: Belknap Press.

Cheuk, B.W. (2007). Using social networking analysis to facilitate knowledge sharing in the British Council. *International Journal of Knowledge Management, 2*(4), 67-76.

Child, J., Faulkner, D., & Tallman, S. (2005). *Cooperative strategy: Managing alliances, networks, and joint ventures*. Oxford University Press.

Cohendet, P., Kern, F., Mehmanpazir, B., & Munier, F. (1999). Knowledge coordination, competence creation and integrated networks in globalised firms. *Cambridge Journal of Economics, 23*, 225-241.

Cohendet, P., & Llerena, P. (2003). Routines and incentives: The role of communities in the firm. *Industrial and Corporate Change, 12,* 271-297.

Constant, D., Kiesler, S., & Sproull, L. (1994). What's mine is ours, or is it? A study of attitudes about information sharing. *Information System Research, 5*(5), 400-421.

Constant, D., Sproull, L., & Kiesler, S. (1997). The kindness of strangers: On the usefulness of electronic weak ties for technical advice. In S. Kiesler (Ed.), *Culture of the Internet*. Mahwah, NJ: Lawrence Erlbaum Associates.

Cowan, R., David, P.A., & Foray, D. (2000). The explicit economics of knowledge codification and tacitness. *Industrial and Corporate Change, 9*, 211-253.

Cramton, C.D. (2001). The mutual knowledge problem and its consequences for dispersed collaboration. *Organization Science, 12*, 347-371.

Creplet. F., Dupouet, O., Kern, F., Mehmanpazir, B., & Munier, F. (2001). Consultants and experts in management consulting firms. *Research Policy, 30*, 1517-1535.

Cummings, J.L., & Teng, B. (2003). Transferring R&D knowledge: The key factors affecting knowledge transfer success. *Journal of Engineering and Technology Management, 20*, 39-68.

Daniel, B., Schwier, R.A., & McCalla, G. (2003). Social capital in virtual learning communities and distributed communities of practice. *Canadian Journal of Learning and Technology, 29*, 113-139.

Davenport, T.H., & Prusak, L. (1998). *Working knowledge: How organizations manage what they know.* Boston: Harvard Business School Press.

Dawes, R.M. (1994). *House of cards: Psychology and psychotherapy built on myth.* New York: Free Press.

Deetz, S.A. (1992). *Democracy in an age of corporate colonization: Developments in communication and the politics of everyday life.* Albany, NY: State University of New York Press.

Dirks, K.T., & Ferrin, D.L. (2001). The role of trust in organizational setting. *Organization Science, 12*, 450-467.

Ensign, P.C. (1998). Interrelationships and horizontal strategy to achieve synergy and competitive advantage in the diversified firm. *Management Decision, 36*, 657-668.

Figallo, C. (1998). *Hosting Web communities: Building relationships, increasing customer loyalty, and maintaining a competitive edge.* New York: John Wiley and Sons.

Fiol, C.M., & O'Connor, E.J. (2005). Identification in face-to-face, hybrid, and pure virtual teams: Untangling the contradictions. *Organization Science, 16*, 19-32.

Gertler, M.S. (2003). Tacit knowledge and the economic geography of context or the undefinable tacitness of being (there). *Journal of Economic Geography, 3*, 75-99.

Grant, R. M. (2005). *Contemporary strategy analysis (5th ed).* Malden, MA: Blackwell Publishing.

Granovetter, M.S. (1972). The strength of weak ties. *American Journal of Sociology, 78*, 1360-1380.

Hansen, M.T. (1999). The search-transfer problem: The role of weak ties in sharing knowledge across organization subunits. *Administrative Science Quarterly, 44*, 82-111.

Holzner, B., & Marx, J. (1979). *The knowledge application: The knowledge system in society.* Boston: Allyn-Bacon.

Hofstede, G. (1980). *Culture's consequences: International differences in work-related values.* Beverly Hills, CA: Sage.

Hornett, A., & Stein, E.W. (2007). Mapping the knowledge management domain of ideas: Evidence from a practice group. *International Journal of Knowledge Management, 3*(3), 1-25.

Huber, G.P. (1991). Organizational learning: The contributing process and the literatures. *Organization Science, 2*, 88-115.

Husted, K., & Michailova, S. (2002). Diagnosing and fighting knowledge sharing hostility. *Organizational Dynamics, 31*, 60-73.

Huysman, M., Steinfield, C., Jang, C., David, K., Huis In 'T Veld, M., Poot, J., & Mulder, I. (2003). Virtual teams and the appropriation of communication technology: Exploring the concept of media stickiness. *Computer Supported Cooperative Work, 12,* 411-436.

Håkanson, L. (2007). Creating knowledge–the power and logic of articulation. *Industrial and Corporate Change, 16*(1), 51-88.

Jarvenpaa, S.L., & Leidner, D.E. (1999). Communication and trust in global virtual teams. *Organization Science, 10,* 791-815.

Jones, G.R., & George, J.M. (1998). The experience and evolution of trust: Implications for cooperation and teamwork. *Academy of Management Review, 23,* 531-546.

Kasper-Fuehrer, E.C., & Ashkanasy, N. (2001). Communicating trustworthiness and building trust in interorganizational virtual organizations. *Journal of Management, 27,* 235-254.

Kogut, B., & Zander, U. (1992). Knowledge of the firm: Combinative capabilities, and the replication of technology. *Organization Science, 3,* 383-397.

Koh, J., & Kim, Y.-G. (2004). Knowledge sharing in virtual communities: An e-business perspective. *Expert Systems with Applications, 26,* 155-166.

Kraut, R., Patterson, M., Lundmark, V., Kiesler, S., Mukopadhyay, T., & Scherlis, W. (1998). Internet paradox. *American Psychologist, 53,* 1017-1031.

Krippendorff, K. (1975). Some principles of information storage and retrieval in society. *General Systems, 20,* 15-35.

Kuhn, T.S. (1962). *The structure of scientific revolutions.* The University of Chicago Press.

Lane, C. (1998). Introduction. In C. Lane & Backmann (Eds.), *Trust within and between organizations.* Oxford University Press.

Lane, P.J., & Lubatkin, M. (1998). Relative absorptive capacity and interorganizational learning. *Strategic Management Journal, 19,* 461-477.

Lave, J., & Wenger, E. (1991). *Situated learning: Legitimate peripheral participation.* New York: Cambridge University Press.

Lea, M., & Spears, R. (1991). Computer-mediated communication, deindividuation and group decision-making. *International Journal of Man-machine Studies, 34,* 283-301.

Lee, G.K., & Cole, R.E. (2003). From a firm-based to a community-based model of knowledge creation: The case of the Linux kernel development. *Organization Science, 14,* 633-649.

Lesser, E., & Everest, K. (2001). Using communities of practice to managing intellectual capital. *Ivey Business Journal, 65,* 37-41.

Li, W., Ardichivili, A., Maurer, M., Wentling, T., & Studemann, R. (2007). Impact of Chinese culture values of knowledge sharing through online communities of practice. *International Journal of Knowledge Management, 3,* 46-59.

Mayer, R.C., Davis, J.H., & Schoorman, F.D. (1995). An integrative model of organizational trust. *Academy of Management Review, 20,* 709-734.

McDermott, R. (1999). Why information technology inspired but cannot deliver knowledge management. *California Management Review, 41,* 103-117.

McElroy, M. (2002). Social innovation capital. *Journal of Intellectual Capital, 3,* 30-39.

McKnight, B., & Bontis, N. (2002). E-improvisation: Collaborative groupware technology expands the reach and effectiveness of organizational improvisation. *Knowledge and Process Management, 9,* 219-227.

McKnight, D.H., Cummings, L.L., & Chervany, N.L. (1998). Initial trust formation in new organizational relationships. *Academy of Management Review, 23,* 473-490.

Meyerson, D., Weick, K.E., & Kramer, R.M. (1996). Swift trust in temporary groups. In R.M. Kramer & T.R. Tyler (Eds.), *Trust in organizations: Frontiers of theory and research*. Thousands Oaks, CA: Sage Publications.

Nahapiet, J., & Ghoshal, S. (1998). Social capital, intellectual capital, and the organizational advantage. *Academy of Management Review, 23*, 242-266.

Naughton, J. (1999). *A brief history of the future: The origins of the Internet*. London: Weidenfield and Nicholson.

Nonaka, I., & Takeuchi, H. (1995). *The knowledge-creating company - how Japanese companies create the dynamic of innovation*. Oxford University Press.

Nonaka, I., Toyama, R., & Konno, N. (2001). SECI, Ba and leadership: A unified model of dynamic knowledge creation. In I. Nonaka & D. J. Teece (Eds.), *Managing industrial knowledge: Creation, transfer and utilization*. London: Sage Publications.

Paepcke, A. (1996, May). Digital libraries: Searching is not enough. *D-Lib Magazine*.

Palmer, R. (1993). *Write in style – a guide to good English*. London: E and FN Spon.

Pan, S.L. & Leidner, D.E. (2003). Bridging communities of practice with information technology in pursuit of global knowledge sharing. *Journal of Strategic Information Systems, 12*, 71-88.

Pentland, B.T. (1995). Information systems and organizational learning: The social epistemology of organizational knowledge systems. *Accounting, Management and Information Technologies, 5*, 1-21.

Pickering, J.M., & King, J.L. (1995). Hardwiring weak ties: Interorganizational computer-mediated communication, occupational communities, and organizational change. *Organizational Science, 6*, 479-486.

Preece, J. (2000). *Online communities: Designing usability, supporting sociability*. Chichester: John Viley and Sons.

Purvis, R.L., Sambamurthy, V., & Zmud, R.W. (2001). The assimilation of knowledge platforms in organizations: An empirical investigation. *Organization Science, 12*, 117-135.

Reagans, R., & McEvily, B. (2003). Network structure and knowledge transfer: The effects of cohesion and range. *Administrative Science Quarterly, 48*, 240-267.

Reddy, M.L. (1979). The conduite metaphor: A case of frame conflict in our language about language. In A. Ortony (Ed.), *Metaphor and thought*. Cambridge University Press.

Ryssen, S.V., & Godar, S.H. (2000). Going international without going international: Multinational virtual teams. *Journal of International Management, 6*, 49-60.

Schultz, M. (2003). Pathways of relevance: Exploring inflows of knowledge into subunits of multinational corporations. *Organization Science, 14*, 440-459.

Shotter, J. (1993). *Conversational realities: Constructing life through language*. London: Sage Publications.

Soo, C., Devinney, T., Midgley, D., & Deering, A. (2002). Knowledge management: Philosophy, processes and pitfalls. *California Management Review, 44*, 129-150.

Sperber, D., & Wilson, D. (1995). *Relevance: Communication and cognition*. Oxford, UK: Blackwell.

Stein, E.W. (2005). A qualitative study of the characteristics of a community of practice for knowledge management and its success factors. *International Journal of Knowledge Management, 1*, 1-24.

Stein, E.W., & Zwass, V. (1995). Actualizing organizational memory with information systems. *Information Systems Research, 6*(2), 85-117.

Storck, J., & Hill, P.A. (2000). Knowledge diffusion through "strategic communities." *Sloan Management Review, 41*, 63-74.

Swan, J., Scarbrough, H., & Robertson, M. (2002). The construction of "communities of practice" in the management of innovation. *Management Learning, 33*, 477-496.

Tiwana, A. (2000). *The knowledge management toolkit.* Upper Saddle River, NJ: Prentice Hall.

Vizcaino, A., Soto, J.P., Portillo-Rodríguez, J., & Piattini, M. (2007). Developing knowledge management systems from a knowledge-based and multi-agent approach. *International Journal of Knowledge Management, 3*(4), 67-83.

Walther, J.B. (1995). Relational aspects of computer-mediated communication: Experimental observations over time. *Organization Science, 6*, 186-203.

Welch, D., Welch, L., & Piekkari, R. (2005). Speaking in tongues: The importance of language in international management processes. *International Studies of Management and Organization, 1*, 10-27.

Wellman, B., & Gulia, M. (1999). Virtual communities as communities: Net surfers don't ride alone. In M. A. Smith & P. Kollock (Eds.), *Communities in cyberspace.* London: Routledge.

Wenger, E. (1998). *Communities of practice: Learning, meaning, and identity.* Cambridge University Press.

Wenger, E., McDermott, R., & Snyder, W.M. (2002). *Cultivating communities of practice: A guide to managing knowledge.* Boston: Harvard Business School Press.

Wenger, E.C., & Snyder, W.M. (2000). Communities of practice: The organizational frontier. *Harvard Business Review, 78*, 139-145.

Wiesenfeld, B.M., Raghuram, S., & Garud, R. (1999). Communication patterns as determinants of organizational identification in a virtual organization. *Organization Science, 10*, 777-790.

Witzel, M. (2003). The world's first virtual business organization. *European Business Forum,* (13), 72-74.

Yates, J., Orlikowski, W., & Okamura, K. (1999). Explicit and implicit structuring of genres in electronic communication: Reinforcement and change of social interaction. *Organization Science, 10*(1), 83-103.

Zack, M.H. (1999). Managing codified knowledge. *Sloan Management Review, 40*, 45-58.

Zand, D.E. (1972). Trust and managerial problem solving. *Administrative Science Quarterly, 17*, 229-239.

Zucchermaglio, C., & Talamo, A. (2003). The development of a virtual community of practice using electronic mail and communicative genres. *Journal of Business and Technical Communication, 17*, 259-284.

Compilation of References

AARP. (2001). Reverse mortgage. Retrieved 2001, from http://www.aarp.org

Abbate, J. (1999). *Inventing the Internet*. Cambridge, MA: The MIT Press.

Abel, M. J., (1990). Experiences in exploratory distributed organization. In J. Galegher and R. Kraut (Eds.), *Intellectual teamwork: social and technological foundation of cooperative*. Hillside, NJ: Lawrence Erlbaum Associates, 111-146.

Ackoff, R. L. (1967). Management misinformation systems. *Management Science*, (Nov):147-156.

Ackoff, R. L. (1978). *The art of problem solving*. New York: J. Wiley.

Adrienssen, J.H.E., & van der Velden, J.M. (1993). Teamwork supported by interaction technology: the beginning of an integrated theory. *European Work And Organizational Psychologis*, .3(2),129-144.

Aguilar Bustamante, M.C., Martínez, A., Fandiño, A. & Fajardo, S.C. (2007). A retrospective vision of the formation process in the organizations. *Revista Diversitas: Perspectivas en Psicología, 3 (1)* ,151-174.

Ahtiuv, N., & Newmann, S. (1986). *Principles of information systems*. Dubuque, Iowa: William C. Brown Publishers.

Ahuja, G. (2000). Collaboration Networks, Structural Holes and Innovation: a Longitudinal Study. *Administrative Science Quaterly, 45*, 425-455.

Ahuja, G. (2000). The duality of collaboration: inducements and opportunities in the formation of inter-firm linkages. *Strategic Mangement Journal*, 21(3), 317-343.

Ahuja, M.J., & Galvin, J.E. (2003). Socialization in virtual groups. *Journal of Management, 29*, 161-185.

Ahuja, M.K., & Carley, K.M. (1999). Network structure in virtual organizations. *Organization Science, 10*, 741-757.

Aladwani, A. M. (2002). An empirical examination of the role of social integration in sytem development projects. *Information Systems Journal*, 12(4), 339-353.

Al-Alawi, A.I., Al-Marzooqi, N.Y., & Mohammed, Y.F., (2007). Organizational culture and knowledge sharing: critical success factors. *Journal of Knowledge Management, 11* (2), 22-42.

Alavi, M. & Leidner, D.E. (2001). Review: Knowledge Management and Knowledge Management Systems: Conceptual Foundations and Research Issues. *MIS Quarterly, 25*, 107-136.

Alavi, M. (1994). Computer-mediated collaborative learning: an empirical evaluation. *MIS Quarterly, 18*(2), 159-174.

Alavi, M., & Leidner, D. (2001). Review: Knowledge management and knowledge management systems: Conceptual foundations and research issues. *MIS Quarterly, 25*, 107-136.

Alberts, D.S. & Hayes, R.E. (2003). *Power to the Edge* Washington, DC: CCRP.

Albrecht, K., & Zemke, R. (2002). *Serviço ao Cliente – A Reinvenção da Gestão do Atendimento ao Cliente*, Rio de Janeiro, Editora Campus.

Aleksander, D. Data mining. http://www.eco.utexas.edu/~norman/BUS.FOR/course.mat/Alex/, retrieved April 11, 2007.

Algesheimer, R., Dholakia, U.M., and Herrmann, A. (2005). "The Social influence of Brand Communities: Evidence from European Car Clubs," *Journal of Marketing* (59:3), pp. 19-34.

Allen, D., Colligan, D. & Finnie, A. (1999) "Trust, Power and Inter-Organizational Information Systems: The Case of the Electronic Trading Community TransLease". *The 7th European Conference on Information Systems* (pp. 834-849). Copenhagen, Denmark: Copenhagen Business School.

Allison, G. T. & Zelikow, P. (1999) *Essence of decision: Explaining the Cuban missile crisis*. New York, NY: Addison-Wesley Longman.

Almeida, P.; Phene, A. & Grant, R. (2003). Innovation and Knowledge Management: Scanning Sourcing and Integration. In M. Easterby-Smith & M.A. Lyles (eds.), *Handbook of Organizational Learning and Knowledge Management* (pp. 356-371). Oxford, UK: Blackwell Publishing.

Al-Sebie, M. & Irani, Z. (2003). E-Government: Defining Boundaries and Lifecycle maturity. In *Proceedings of the 3rd European Conference on e-Government*, (pp. 19-29) Ireland: Trinity College of Dublin,.

Alton, C & Wing L. (2007). Quality assurance in online education: The Universitas 21 Global approach. *British Journal of Educational Technology 38 (1)*, 133–152

Álvarez, M. (1998). *El liderazgo de la Calidad Total*. Madrid: Escuela Española. S.A.

Alvesson, M., & Kärreman, D. (2000). Taking the linguistic turn in organizational research: Challenges, responses, consequences. *The Journal of Applied Behavioral Science, 36*, 136-158.

Alvesson, M., & Kärreman, D. (2001). Odd couple: Making sense of the curious concept of knowledge management. *Journal of Management Studies, 38*, 995-1018.

American Productivity & Quality Center (APQC). (1999). *Creating a knowledge-sharing culture.* Consortium Benchmarking Study -- Best-Practice Report.

American Productivity & Quality Center (APQC). (2000). *Successfully implementing knowledge management.* Consortium Benchmarking Study -- Final Report, 2000.

Anand, V., Manz, C.C. & Glick, W.H. (1998). An organizational memory approach to information management. *Academy of Management Review, 23*(4), 796-809.

Andersen, P.H. (2005). "Relationship marketing and brand involvement of professionals through web-enhanced brand communities: The case of Coloplast," *Industrial Marketing Management* (34), pp. 39-51.

Anderson, A. H., Newlands, A. & Mullin, J. (1996). Impact of video-mediated communication on simulated service encounters. Interacting with computers, 8 (2), 193-206.

Anderson, E. and Weitz, B. (1989). "The Use of Pledges to Build and Sustain Commitment in Distribution Channels," *Journal of Marketing Research* (29), pp. 18-34.

Anderson, J., and Gerbing, D. (1988). "Structural Modeling in Practice: A Review and Recommended Two-Step Approach," *Psychological Bulletin* (103:3), pp. 411-423.

Anderson, J.C., and Narus, J.A. (1990). "A Model of Distribution Firm and Manufacturer Firm Working Partnerships," *Journal of Marketing*, (54:1), pp. 42-58.

Anderson, P. (1999). Complexity theory and organization science. *Organization Science, 10*(3), 216-232.

Andreassen, T.W. (1999). "What Drives Customer Loyalty With Complaint Resolution?," *Journal of Service Research* (1:4), pp. 324-332.

Anthony, R. (1965). *Planning and control systems: a framework for analysis.* Boston: Harvard University.

Apostolou, D., Mentzas, G. & Maas, W. (2003). *Knowledge Networking in Extended Enterprise.* Espoo, Finland :ICE, 9th. Int. Conference on Concurrent Engineering.

Apte, C., Liu, B., Pednault, E. P. D., & Smyth. P. (2002). Business applications of data mining. *Communications of the ACM,* 45(8): 49-53.

Argote, L.; McEvily, B. & Reagans, R. (2003). Managing Knowledge in Organizations: An Integrative Framework and Review of Emerging Themes. *Management Science,* 49, 571-582.

Argyris, C. & Schon, D.A. (1978). *Organizational Learning* Reading, MA: Addison-Wesley.

Argyris, C., & Schön, D. (1978). *Organizational learning: a theory of action perspective.* Mass: Addison-Wesley, Reading.

Argyris, C., & Schon, D. (1996). *Organizational learning II. Theory, method and practice.* Mass: Addison-Wesley, Reading.

Armstrong, M. P. (1994). Requirements for the development of GIS-based group decision support systems. *Journal of the American Society for Information Science.* 45(9), 669-677.

Arthur, M.B., & Defillippi, R.J. (1994). The boundaryless career: A competency-based perspective. *Journal of Organizational Behavior, 15*(4), 307-324.

Atuahene-Gima, K. (1992). Inward Technology Licensing as an Alternative to Internal R&D in New Product Development: A Conceptual Framework. *Journal of Product Innovation Management, 9*(2), 156-167.

Augustyn, M. M., & Knowles, T. (2000). Performance of tourism partnerships: A focus on York. *Tourism Management,* 21, 341-351.

Austin, J. E. (2002). *Meeting the Collaboration Challenge Workbook: Developing Strategic Alliances Between Nonprofit Organizations and Businesses.* New York: Peter F. Drucker Foundation for Nonprofit Management.

Axelrod, R. (1997). *The complexity of cooperation: Agent-based models of competition and collaboration.* New Jersey: Princeton University Press.

Axelrod, R., & Cohen, M. (1999). *Harnessing complexity: Organizational implications of a scientific frontier.* New York: The Free Press.

Ayers, I. (2007). *Super Crunchers.* New York: Bantam Books.

Bachani, J. (2005). Building decision quality in organizations. *California Journal of Operations Management,* 3 (1), 12-16.

Bacharach, S., & Lawler, K.(1980). *Power and politics and organizations.* San Francisco, CA: Jossey-Bass.

Bagnasco, A. (1977). *Tre Italie: la problematica territoriale dello sviluppo economico italiano.* Bolonia: Il Mulino.

Bagozzi, R.P. and Dholakia, U.M. (2006). "Open Source Software Communities: A Study of participation in Linux User Groups," *Management Science* (52:7), pp. 1099-1115.

Baker, D., Georgakopoulos, D., Schuster, H. & Cichocki, A. (2002), Awareness provisioning in collaboration management. International Journal of Cooperative Information Systems, 11(1-2), 145-173.

Baker, W. E. (1992) The network organization in theory and practice. In Nohria, N. and R. Eccles (Eds.), *Networks and Organizations.* (pp 397-429). Boston, MA: Harvard Business School Press.

Balasubramanian, S., & Mahajan, V. (2001). The economic leverage of the virtual community. *International Journal of Electronic Commerce, 5(3),* 103-138.

Bales, R. F. (2001). *Interaction process analysis: a method for the study of small groups.* Cambridge, MA: Addison-Wesley.

Bandura, A. (1989). Social Cognitive Theory. In R. Vasta (Ed.), *Annals of Child Development* (pp. 1-60). Greenwich, CT: Jai Press LTD.

Barabasi, A-L. (2002). *Linked: The New Science of Networks*. Persues Publishing.

Barbaceanu, M. (2001). *The agent building shell: Programming cooperative enterprise agents*. Retrieved 2001 from http://www.eil.utoronto.ca/ABS-page/ABS-overview.html

Barber, B.R. (1992). "Jihad vs. McWorld." *The Atlantic Monthly*. March. pp. 53-63.

Barberá, E. (2001). *La incógnita de la educación a distancia*. Barcelona: Editorial Horsori, S.L.

Barbera, E. (2004). Quality in virtual education environments. *British Journal of Education Technology 35 (1)*, 13-20.

Barca, C. & Cordella, A. (2004). Seconds out, round two: Contextualising e-Government projects within their institutional milieu – A London local authority case study. In *ECIS: The European Information Systems Profession in the Global Networking Environment*, Turku, Finland.

Barner, R. (1996). The new millennium workplace: Seven changes that will challenge managers and workers. *The Futurist*, 30, 14-18.

Barney, J (1991). Firm resources and sustained competitive advantage. *Journal of management*, 17 (1), 99-120.

Barney, J. B. (1991). Firm resources and sustained competitive advantage, *Journal of Management*, 17, 99-120.

Barney, J.B. (1991): Firm Resources and Sustained Competitive Advantage: A Comment. *Journal of Management*, *17*(1), 99-120.

Bartczak, S.E., Turner, J.M., & England, E.C. (2007). Challenges in developing a knowledge management strategy: A case study of the Air Force Material Command. *International Journal of Knowledge Management*, *4*(1), xx-xx.

Barthes, R. (1997). *From work to text*. In S. L. Feagin & P. Maynard (Eds.), Aesthetics. Oxford University Press.

Bassi, L.J. & Van Buren, M.E. (1999). Valuing investments in intellectual capital. *International Journal of Technology Management, 18,* 414-432.

Bates, A.W. (1999). Research and Evaluation. In A.W. Bates. *Managing Technological Change*, 198-210. California: Jossey-Bass.

Batt, P.J. (2003). "Building Trust between Growers and Market Agents," *Supply Chain Management: And International Journal* (8:1), pp. 65-78.

Bauer, H. H., Grether, M. and Leach, M. (2002). "Building customer relations over the Interntet," *Industrial Marketing Management* (31), pp. 155-163.

Baumgartner, P. $ Payr, S. (1997). *Methods and practice of software evaluation. The case of the European Academic Software Award*. Proceedig of ED-MEDIA 97 & ED-TELECOM 97, AACE.

Baumgartner, P. & Pays, S. (1997). *Methods and practice of software evaluation. The case of the European Academic Software Award*. Proceeding of ED-MEDIA 97. ED-TELECOM 97, ACCE.

Beach, L. R., Mitchell, T. R., *et al.* (1997). Information relevance, content, and source credibility in the revision of opinions. *Organizational Behavior and Human Performance*, (21), 1-16.

Becattini, G. (1987). *L'unità d'indagine / Mercato e forze locali: Il distretto industriale*. Bolonia: Il Mulino.

Becattini, G. (1990). The marshallian industrial district as a socio-economic notion. In Pyke, F., Becattini, G. & Sengenberger,W. (Eds.), *Industrial Districts and Local Economic Regeneration*, Geneva: International Institute for Labor Studies.

Becker, J.; Algermissen, L. & Niehaves, B. (2003). Implementing e-Government Strategies. A procedural model for process oriented e-Government projects. In K. Soliman (Ed.), *Proceedings of the 2003 International Business Information Management Conference (IBIMA): "E-Business and organisations in the 21st Century"*, El Cairo, Egypt.

Becker, W., & Peters, J. (2000). *Technological Opportunities, Absorptive Capacities and Innovation.* Paper presented at the Eighth International Joseph A. Schumpeter Society Conference, Centre for Research in Innovation and Competition (CRIC), Manchester.

Beerli, A., & Martin, J. D. (2004). Tourists' characteristics and the perceived image of tourist destinations: a quantitative analysis – a case study of Lanzarote, Spain. *Tourism Management*, 25(5), 623-636.

Behm, D., and F. D. Peat. (1978). *Science, order and creativity.* New York: Bantam Books.

Belanger, F. & Jordan, D.H. (2000). *Evaluation and Implementation of Distance Learning: technologies, tools and techniques.* London: Idea Group Publishing.

Belanguer, F. & Jordan, D.H. (2000). *Evaluation and Implementation of Distance Learning. Technologies, tools and techniques.* London: Idea Group Publishing.

Bell, Daniel. (1973). *The coming of the post-information society: a venture in social forecasting.* New York: Basic Books.

Bellanger, F., & Hiller, J.S. (2006). A framework for e-government: privacy implications. *Business Process Management Journal, 12* (1), 48-60.

Bendapudi, N. and Berry, L.L. (1997). "Customer's Motivations for Maintaining Relationships with Service Providers," *Journal of Retailing* (73:1), pp. 15-35.

Benko, G. & Lipietz, A. (1994). *Las regiones que ganan.* Valencia: Ed. Alfons el Magnànim.

Benson, J. K. (1975). The inter-organizational network as a political economy. *Administrative Science Quarterly*, 20(2), 229-249.

Berk, J. (2003). Learning Measurment: It's Not How Much You Train, But How Well. *The E-learning Developer' Journal*, 11, 1-8

Berkowitz, B. (2003). Failing to keep up with the information revolution. *Studies in Intelligence*, 47(1), May 6.

Beyerlein, M., Johnson, D. & Beyerlein, S. (1994). *Theories of self-managing work teams (Advances in Interdisciplinary Studies of Work Teams).* Stamford, CT: JAI Press.

Bhandari, N., & Mania, V. (2005). Business process outsourcing for telecom service providers. Retrieved April 29, 2006, from http://www.dmreview.com/white-paper/WID527.pdf

Bhattacharya, R., Devinney, T.M., & Pillutla, M.M. (1998). A formal model of trust based on outcomes. *Academy of Management Review, 23*, 459-472.

Bieber, M., Engelbart, D., Furuta, R., Hiltz, S. Noll, J., Perece, J., Stohr, E., Turoff, M., & Van de Walle, B. (2002). Toward virtual community knowledge evolution. *Journal of Management Information Systems, spring, 18* (4), 11-35.

Bieber, M., Engelbart, D., Furuta, R., Hiltz, S. Noll, J., Perece, J., Stohr, E., Turoff, M. & Van de Walle, B. (2002). Toward Virtual Community Knowledge Evolution. *Journal of Management Information Systems, spring, 18(4),* 11-35.

Bixby, R. E. (2002). Solving real-world linear programs: A decade and more of progress. *Operations Research*, 50(1), 3-15.

Bjork P. & Virtanen H. (2005). What Tourism Project Managers Need to Know about Co-operation Facilitators, *Scandinavian Journal of Hospitality and Tourism*, vol. 5(3), 212-230.

Black, J. & McClintock, R. (1995). An Interpretation Construction Approach to Constructivist Design. In B. Wilson (Ed.), *Constructivist learning environments.* NJ: Englewood Cliffs.

Blanchard, A. L. & Horan, T. (1998): Virtual communities and social capital. *Social Science Computer Review, 1(3)*, 293-307.

Bleecker, S.E. (1994). The virtual organization. *The Futurist*, 28(2), 9-14.

Blumenthal, A. L. (1977). *The process of cognition.* Englewood Cliffs, NJ: Prentice-Hall, Inc.

Blumentritt, R. & Johnston, R. (1999). Towards a Strategy for Knowledge Management. *Technology Analysis and Strategic Management, 11,* 287-300.

Bock, G. & Marca, D. (1995). *Designing Groupware.* New York, McGraw-Hill.

Bodily, S. (1986). Spreadsheet modeling as a stepping stone. *Interfaces,* 16(5), 34-52.

Boettcher, S. (1998). *The Netscape intranet solution: Deploying the full-service intranet.* New York: John Wiley and Sons.

Boland, R, J., Jr. & Tenkasi, R. V. (2001). Communication and collaboration In distributed cognition. In Olson, G. M., Malone, T. W. & Smith, J. B. (Eds.), Coordination theory and collaboration technology, Mahwah, NJ: Lawrence Erlbaum Associates, 51-66.

Boland, R.J, & Tenkasi, R.V. (1995). Perspective making and perspective taking in communities of knowing. *Organization Science, 6,* 350-372.

Bonham, G., Seifert, J. & Thorson, S. (2001). The transformational potential of e-government: the role of political leadership, In *Proceedings of the 4th Pan Euroepan International Relations Conference,* Kent, UK.

Bontis, N. (1999). Managing Organizational Knowledge by Diagnosing Intellectual Capital: Framing and Advancing the State of the Field. *International Journal of Technology Management, 18,* 433-462.

Bontis, N.; Crossan, M.M.; Hulland, J. (2002), "Managing an organizational learning system by aligning stocks and flows". *Journal of Management Studies,* 39 (4), pp. 437-469.

Bordas, E. (1994) La Calidad de los Servicios Turísticos: De la Teoria a la Prática, *WTO Seminar on "Quality - A Challenge for Tourism"* (pp. 133-159). Madrid: World Tourism Organization.

Bos, N., Olson, J., Olson, G., & Wright, Z. (2002). Effects of four computer-mediated communications channels on trust development. In *Proceedings of the SIGCHI conference on Human factors in computing systems: Changing our world, changing ourselves. Confidence and Trust* (pp. 237-288). New York: Association for Computing Machinery Press.

Boshyk, Y. (1999): "Beyond knowledge management: how companies mobilise experience", Financial Times, 8 February, pp.12-13.

Boulder, K. E. (1989). *Three faces of power.* Newburry Park: SAGE   PUBLICATIONS.

Bouncken, R. B. (2000) The Effect of Trust on Quality in the Culturally Diverse Tourism Industry, *Journal of Quality Assurance in Hospitality & Tourism,* 1(3), 85-104.

Bowman, B.J. (2002). Building knowledge management systems. *Information Systems Management, 19,* 32-40.

Bowman, C. (2001), "tacit knowledge: some suggestions for operationalization". *Journal of Management Studies,* 38 (6), pp. 811-829.

Boxall, P. (1996). The strategic HRM debate and the resource-based view of the firm. *Human Resource Management Journal, 6(3),* 59-75

Bradbury, H., & B.M. Bergmann Lichtenstein (2000). Relationality in organizational research: Exploring the space between. *Organization Science, 11*(5). 551-564.

Braden R. (1989). RFC 1122: Requirements for Internet Hosts: Communication Layers. *Information Sciences Institute (ISI) at University of Southern California.* Retrieved September 15, 2007, from http://www.isi.edu/in-notes/rfc1122.txt

Bradner, E. (2002). Computer mediated communication among teams: what are "teams" and how are they "virtual"?. In C. & D. FISHER (Eds). *From UseNet to CoWebs: interacting with social information spaces* (pp. 135-152). London: Springer-Verlag.

Bramwell, B., & Lane, B. (2000). Collaboration and partnership in tourism planning. In B. Bramwell, & B. Lane (Eds.), *Tourism collaboration and partnerships: Politics, practice and sustainability* (pp. 143-158). Clevedon, Uk: Channel View Publications.

Brandenburger, A.M., & Nalebuff, B.J. (1996). *Co-opetition*. New York: Doubleday.

Brathwaite, R. (1992). Value-Chain Assessment of the Travel Experience, *Cornell Hotel and Restaurant Administration Quarterly*, 33(5), 41-49.

Bresnen, M. & Marshall, N. (2000). Building partnerships: case studies of client-contractor collaboration in the UK construction industry. *Construction Management and Economics*, 18: 819-832.

Bressler, S. (2000). *Communities of Commerce: Building Internet Business Communities to Accelerate Growth, Minimize Risk, and Increase Customer Loyalty*. New York: McGraw-Hill.

Bressler, S.E. (2000). *Communities of Commerce: Building Internet Business Communities to Accelerate Growth, Minimize Risk, and Increase Customer Loyalty*. New York: McGraw-Hill.

Brockman, B. (1998). "The influence of affective state on satisfaction ratings," *Journal of Consumer Satisfaction, Dissatisfaction and Complaining Behavior* (11), pp. 40-50.

Broome, B., Gangopadhyay, A., & Yoon, V. (2002). *CAER: An ontology-based community of agents for emergency relief*. Paper presented at the 6th World Multi-Conference on Systemics, Cybernetics, and Informatics, July, Orlando, FL.

Brown, J. & Duguid, P. (1998). Organizing Knowledge. *California Management Review*, 40(3), 90-111.

Brown, J. y Duguid, P. (1998), "Organizating knowledge". *California Management Review*, 40 (3), pp. 90-111.

Brown, J.S. & Duguid, P. (1991). Organizational Learning and Communities of Practice: Towards a Unified view of Working, Learning and Innovation. *Organization Science, 2*, 40-57.

Brown, J.S. & Duguid, P. (1998). Organizing Knowledge, *California Management Review, 40*, 90-111.

Brown, J.S., & Duguid, P. (1991). Organizational learning and communities-of-practice: toward a unified view of working, learning, and innovation. *Organization Science*, 2 (1), 40-57.

Brown, J.S., & Duguid, P. (1991). Organizational learning and communities-of-practice: Toward a unified view of working, learning and innovation. *Organization Science, 2*, 40-57.

Brown, J.S., & Duguid, P. (2001). Knowledge and organization: A social-practice perspective. *Organization Science, 12*, 198-213.

Brown, S.L., & Eisenhardt, K.M. (1998). *Competing on the Edge: Strategy as Structured Chaos*. Boston, MA.: Harvard Business School Press.

Browne, J. & Zhang, J. (1999). Extended and Virtual Enterprises: Similarities and differences. *International Journal of Agile Management Systems*, 1(1), 30-39.

Brusco, S. (1982). The Emilian model: Productive descentralisation and social integration. *Rev. Cambridge Journal of Economics*, 6.

Brzezinski, Z. (1982). *The grand failure*. New York: Charles Scribner's Sons.

Buckley, P. J. (1987). Tourism - an economic transactions analysis, *Tourism Management*, 8(3), 190-194.

Buckley, P.J., & Casson, M. (1988). A theory of cooperation in international business. In F.J. Contractor, & P. Lorange (eds.), *Cooperative strategies in international business* (pp. 31-54). Lexington: Lexington Books.

Bueno García, O. (2002). Modernización de la AAPP, líneas estratégicas para la e-Administración. Retrieved from http://www.lawebmunicipal.com

Bueno, E. & Plaz, R. (2005). Desarrollo y Gobierno del Conocimiento Organizativo: Agentes y procesos. *Boletín Intellectus, 8*, 16-23.

Bueno, E. & Salmador, M.P. (eds.) (2000). Perspectivas sobre Dirección del Conocimiento y Capital Intelectual. Madrid: Instituto Universitario Euroforum Escorial.

Bueno, E. (2002). Dirección estratégica basada en conocimiento: Teoría y práctica de la nueva perspectiva. In P.

Morcillo & J. Fernández Aguado (eds.), *Nuevas claves en la Dirección Estratégica* (pp. 91-166), Madrid: Ariel.

Bueno, E. (2003). Enfoques principales y tendencias en dirección del conocimiento (Knowledge Management). In R. Hernández (ed.), *Dirección del conocimiento: Desarrollos teóricos y aplicaciones* (pp. 21-54). Trujillo, Spain: Ediciones La Coria.

Bueno, E. (2005). Fundamentos epistemológicos de dirección del conocimiento organizativo: Desarrollo, medición y gestión de intangibles. *Economía Industrial* [Spanish Ministry for Industry, Tourism y Trade], *357*, 13-26.

Buhalis, D. (2000). Marketing the competitive destination of the future, *Tourism Management, 21*(1), 97-116.

Bukowitz, W., & Williams, R. (1999). *The knowledge management fieldbook*. London: Financial Times Prentice Hall.

Bultje, R., & Van Wijk, J. (1998). Taxonomy of virtual organisations, based on definitions, characteristics and typology. *Virtual-organization.net, Newsleter 2*(3), 7-21.

Burnett, G., (2000). Information exchange in virtual communities: a typology. *Information Research*, 5(4). Retrieved January 18, 2007, from http://informationr.net/ir/5-4/paper82.html.

Burt, R.S. (1997). The contingent value of social capital. *Administrative Science Quarterly, 42*, 339-365.

Burt, R.S., R.M. Hogarth, & C. Michaud (2000). The social capital of French and American managers. *Organization Science 11*(2),123-147.

Butler, R., (1980). The concept of a tourist area cycle of evolution: implications for management of resources. *Canadian Geographer* 24(1), 5-12.

Byrne, J. & Davis, G. (1998). *The Australian Policy Handbook*. Sydney, Australia: Allen & Unwin, 3rd edition.

Byrne, J. (1993), "The virtual corporation", Business Week, pp. 36-41.

Byrne, J. (1993). The virtual corporation. *Business Week,* 8, 98-102.

Byung-Keun-Kim (2005). *Internationalizing the Internet.* Northampton, MA.: Edward Elgar Publishing.

Cabero, J. (2001). La evaluación e investigación sobre los medios de enseñanza. In J. Cabero, *Tecnología Educativa. Diseño y utilización de medios de enseñanza.* Barcelona: Ediciones Paidós Ibérica, S.A., 447-490.

Cabrera, A. & Cabrera, E. (2002). Knowledge-sharing dilemmas. *Organization Studies*, 23(5), 687-710.

Caloghirou, Y., Kastelli, I., & Tsakanikas, A. (2004). Internal capabilities and external knowledge sources: complements or substitutes for innovative performance. *Technovation, 24*(1), 29-39.

Camagni, R. P. (1992). Development Scenarios and Policy Guidelines for the Lagging Regions in the 1990s. *Regional Studies*, 26(4).

Camarinha-Matos, L.M. (2002). *Collaborative Business Ecosystems and Virtual Enterprises.* Kluwer Academic Publishers.

Camillus, J. (1993). Crafting the competitive corporation: Management systems for the future organizations. In P. Lorange, B. Chakravarthy, J. Roos, & A. Van De Ven (Eds), *Implementing strategic process: Change, learning, and cooperation* (pp. 313-328). Oxford, Uk: Blackwell.

Camisón, C. (2000): "La empresa valenciana ante la sociedad del conocimiento: situación actual y retos de futuro". *Revista Valenciana de Estudios Autonómicos*, (32), pp. 3-28.

Camisón, C., & Forés, B. (2007). *Factores antecedentes de la capacidad de absorción de conocimiento: un estudio teórico.* Paper presented at the XXI AEDEM Annual Congress, Madrid.

Camm, J. D., Chorman, T. E., Dill, F. A., Evans, J. R., Sweeney, D. & Wegryn, G. W. (1997). Blending OR/MS, judgment, and GIS: Restructuring P&G's supply chain. *Interfaces*, 27(1), 128-142.

Campbell, A. (1999). Knowledge management in the web enterprise: exploiting communities of practice. In P. Jackson,. (Ed.), *Virtual Working: Social and Organisational Dynamics* (pp. 21-32). London, UK: Routledge.

Cannon, J.P., Achrol, R.S., & Gundlach, G.T. (2000). Contracts, norms, and plural form governance. *Journal of the Academy of Marketing Science, 28*(2), 180-194.

Cantu, F. (2000). *Reinforcement and Bayesian learning in multiagent systems: The MACS project* (Tech.Rep. No. CIA-RI-042). Center for Artificial Intelligence, ITESM

Cap, Gemini, Erst & Young. (2002). Summary Report: Web-based Survey on Electronic Public Services. Results of the second measurement. Retrieved from http://europa.eu.int/information_society/eeurope/ benchmarking

Car A.A. (2005). Global Perspectives On E-Learning: Rhetoric And Reality. Sage Publications.

Carbo, J., Molina, J. M. & Davila, J. (2003). Trust management through fuzzy reputation. *International Journal of Cooperative Information Systems*, 12(1), 135-155.

Carless, S. A. & DePaola, C. (2000). The measurement of cohension in work teams. *Small Group Research*, 31, 71-88.

Carlsson, C. (2002). Decisions support in virtual organizations: The case for multi-agent support. *Group Decision and Negotiation, 11*(3), 185-221.

Carr, N.G. (2006). The Sixth Force: Strategy and the Public Interest. Retrieved from http://www.nicholasgcarr.com/digital_renderings/archives/the_sixth_force_strategy.shtml

Carvalho, R. & Araújo, M. (2002).Using information technology to support knowledge conversion processes. *Information Research, 7*(1).

Cashion, J. & Palmieri, P. (2002). *Evaluation of Quality in On-line Learning*. TAFE School of Social Sciences. Swinburne University of Technology. From http://www.tafe.swin.edu.au/ncver/

CastelFranchi, C. (2002). The social nature of information and the role of trust. *International Journal of Cooperative Information Systems*, 11(3-4), 381-403.

Castells, M. (1996). The Information Age: Economy, Society, and Culture. Volume I: *The Roise of the Network Society*. Oxford: Blackwell

Castells. M. (2005). The network society. Northampton, MA.: Edward Elgar Publishing.

Chandler, A. D. (1962). *Strategy and structure: Chapters in the history of the industrial enterprise.* Cambridge, MA: MIT Press.

Chandler, A.D. (1990). *Scale and scope - the dynamics of industrial capitalism.* Cambridge, Ma: Belknap Press.

Chang, C. (2004). The Determinants of Knowledge Transfer through Strategic Alliances". *Academy of Management Proceedings*, pp. H1-H6.

Chen, Y.C. & Perry, J. (2003). Outsourcing for e-Government. Managing for success. *Public Performance and Management Review, 26* (4), 404-421

Chesbrough, H. W. & Teece, D. J. (1996) When is virtual virtuous? *Harvard Business Review*. January-February, 65-71.

Chesbrough, H. W. (2003). *Open Innovation: The New Imperative for Creating and Profiting from Technology.* Harvard Business School Press.

Cheuk, B.W. (2007). Using social networking analysis to facilitate knowledge sharing in the British Council. *International Journal of Knowledge Management, 2*(4), 67-76.

Chidambaram, L. & Tung, L. L. (2005). Is out of sight, out of mind? An empirical study of social loafing in technology-supported groups. *Information Systems Research*, 16(2), 149-168.

Child, J. & Faulkner, D. (1998), *Strategies of co-operation. Managing alliances, networks, and joint ventures.* New York: Oxford University Press.

Child, J., Faulkner, D., & Tallman, S. (2005). *Cooperative strategy: Managing alliances, networks, and joint ventures.* Oxford University Press.

Chiou, J.S., Hsieh, C.H. and Yang, C.H. (2004). "The effect of franchisors' communication, service assistance, and competitive advantage on franchisees' intentions to remain in the franchise system," *Journal of Small Business Management* (42:1), pp. 19-36.

Chiu, C., Hsu, M. & Wang, E. (2006). Understanding knowledge sharing in virtual communities: An integration of social capital and social cognitive theories. *Decision Support Systems, 42(3),* 1872-1888

Chiu, C., Hsu, M., & Wang, E. (2006). Understanding knowledge sharing in virtual communities: An integration of social capital and social cognitive theories. *Decision Support Systems, 42,* 1872-1888.

Choi, B., & Lee, H. (2003). An empirical investigation of KM styles and their effect on corporate performance. *Information and Management, 40*(5), 403-417.

Chomsky, A. (1965). *Aspects of the theory of syntax.* Cambridge, Mass: MIT Press.

Choo, C.W. (1998). *The Knowing Organization.* Oxford University Press.

Choo, C.W., Detlor, B. & Turnbull, D. (2000). *Web Work: Information Seeking and Knowledge Work on the World Wide Web.* Dordrecht, Kluwer Academic Publishers.

Christensen, P.H. (2007). Knowledge sharing: moving away form the obsession with best practices. *Journal of Knowledge Management, 11*(1), 36-47.

Christopher, M. (1992). *Logistics and supply chain management.* London: Pitman Publishing.

Chua, A. (2004). Knowledge management system architecture: a bridge between KM consultants and technologists. *International Journal of Information Management, 24,* 87-98.

Churchill, G. A. (1979). "A Paradigm for Developing Better Measures for Marketing Constructs," *Journal of Marketing Research* (16:1), pp. 64-73.

Ciborra, C.U. & Andreu, R. (2001). Sharing knowledge across boundaries. *Journal of Information Technology,* 16: 73-81.

Ciborra, C.U., & Andreu, R. (2001). Sharing knowledge across boundaries. *Journal of Information Technology, 16,* 73-81.

Clancy, T. (1994). The latest word from thoughtful executives - the virtual corporation, telecommuting and the concept of team. *Academy of Management Executive,* 8(2), 8-10.

Clark, R. (1989). *Developing Technical Training: A Structured Approach for the Development of Classroom and Computer-Based Instructional Materials.* Reading, MA: Addison-Wesley

Clark, R. (2002). *Putting Learning Standards into Practice. ASTD E-learning Hanbook.* McGraw Hill.

Clark, R. (2002). *Putting Learning Standards into Practice.* ASTD E-learning Hanbook. McGraw Hill.

Claver-Cortés, E., de Juana-Espinosa, S. & González, R. (2005). Local e-Government strategies in Spain: an empirical survey. In *Proceedings of the 2005 BAM Conference,* Oxford, UK.

Claver-Cortés, E., de Juana-Espinosa, S. & Tari, J. (2006). e-Government maturity at Spanish local levels. In *Proceedings of the 2006 EMCIS Conference,* Alicante, Spain.

Clift, S. (2003). *Public Network On-line Information Exchange in Pursuit of Public Service Goals.* OCDE E-Government Project.

Coakes, E., & Clarke, S. (2006). *Encyclopedia of communities of practice in information and knowledge management.* Harrisburg, PA.: Idea Group Inc.

Cochran, J. K., Mackulak, G. T., & Savory, P. A. (1995). Simulation project characteristics in industrial settings. *Interfaces,* 25(4), 104-113.

Cohen, E. B. & Nycz, M. (2006). Learning Objects and E-Learning: an Informing Science Perspective. Interdisciplinary Journal of Knowledge and Learning Objects, 2.

Cohen, M. D., March, J. G., & Olsen, J. P. (1972). A garbage can model of organizational choice. *Administrative Science Quarterly.* 17(1), 1-25.

Cohen, W.M. & Levinthal, D.A. (1990). Absorptive Capacity: A New Perspective on Learning and Innovation. *Administrative Science Quarterly, 35,* 128-152.

Cohen, W.M., & Levinthal, D.A. (1989). Innovation and learning: The two faces of R&D. *Economic Journal, 99,* 569-596.

Cohen, W.M., & Levinthal, D.A. (1990). Absorptive capacity, a new perspective on learning and innovation. *Administrative Science Quarterly,* 35 (1), 128-152.

Cohen, W.M., & Levinthal, D.A. (1990). Absorptive capacity: A new perspective on learning and innovation. *Administrative Science Quarterly, 35,* 128-152.

Cohen, W.M., & Levinthal, D.A. (1994). Fortune favours the prepared firm. *Management Science, 40,* 227–251.

Cohen, W.S., & Levinthal, D.A. (1990). Absorptive capacity: A new perspective on learning and innovation. *Administrative Science Quarterly,* 35, 128-152.

Cohendet, P., & Llerena, P. (2003). Routines and incentives: The role of communities in the firm. *Industrial and Corporate Change, 12,* 271-297.

Cohendet, P., Kern, F., Mehmanpazir, B., & Munier, F. (1999). Knowledge coordination, competence creation and integrated networks in globalised firms. *Cambridge Journal of Economics, 23,* 225-241.

Colace, F., DeSanto, M.& Vento, M. (2003). Evaluating On-line Learning Platforms: a Case Study. In Proceedings *36th Hawaii International Conference on System Science.* Hawaii: IEEE Press

Commission Européenne (1999). *Pour un tourisme urbain de qualité – La gestion integrée de la qualité (GIQ) des destinations touristiques urbaines.* Bruxelles: Commission Européenne.

Conole G. & Oliver, M. (2006). Contemporary Perspectives in E-learning Research (Themes, Methods And Impact on Practice). Routledge.

Constant, D., Kiesler, S., & Sproull, L. (1994). What's mine is ours, or is it? A study of attitudes about information sharing. *Information System Research, 5*(5), 400-421.

Constant, D., Sproull, L., & Kiesler, S. (1997). The kindness of strangers: On the usefulness of electronic weak ties for technical advice. In S. Kiesler (Ed.), *Culture of the Internet.* Mahwah, NJ: Lawrence Erlbaum Associates.

Cook, S.D. y Brown, J.S. (1999), "Bridging epistemologies: The generative dance between organizational knowledge and knowing". *Organization Science,* 10 (4), pp. 381-400.

Cook, S.D. y Yanow, D. (1993), "Culture and organizational learning". *Journal of Management Inquiry,* 2 (4), pp. 373-390.

Cook, S.D.N. & Brown, J.S. (1999). Bridging Epistemologies: The Generative Dance between Organizational Knowledge and Organizational Knowing. *Organization Science, 10*(4), 381-400.

Cooke, P. (2002). *Knowledge economies. Clusters, learning cooperative advantage.* London: Routledge

Cornelius, C. & Boos, M. (2003). Enhancing mutual understanding in synchronous computer-mediated communication by training: trade-offs in judgment tasks. *Communication Research,* 30(2), 147-177.

Corritore, C.L., Kracher, B., and Wiedenbeck, S. (2003). "On-Line Trust: Concepts, Evolving Themes, a Model," *International Journal of Human-Computer Studies* (58:6), pp. 737-758.

Corstjens, M., & Merrihue, J. (2003). Optimal marketing. *Harvard Business Review,* October, 114-121.

Corvelo, S., Moreira, P. S. & Carvalho, P. S. (2001). *Redes Interorganizacionais.* Lisboa: Inofor.

Costa, C. (1996). Towards the Improvement of the Efficiency and Effectiveness of Tourism Planning and Development at the Regional Level – Planning and Networks. The case of Portugal. Unpublished doctoral dissertation, University of Surrey, Guildford.

Cowan, R., David, P.A., & Foray, D. (2000). The explicit economics of knowledge codification and tacitness. *Industrial and Corporate Change, 9*, 211-253.

Coyle, J. & Schnarr, N. (1995). The soft-side challenges of the "virtual corporation." *Human Resource Planning, 18*, 41-42.

Cramton, C.D. (2001). The mutual knowledge problem and its consequences for dispersed collaboration. *Organization Science, 12*, 347-371.

Cravens, D. W., Piercy, N. F., Shipp, S.H (1996). New Organizational Forms for Competing in Highly Dynamic Environments: the Network Paradigm. *British Journal of Management, 7*, 203-218.

Cravens, D.W., & Piercy, N.F. (1994). Relationship marketing and collaborative networks in service organizations. *International Journal of Service Industry Management, 5*, 39-53.

Creplet. F., Dupouet, O., Kern, F., Mehmanpazir, B., & Munier, F. (2001). Consultants and experts in management consulting firms. *Research Policy, 30*, 1517-1535.

Criado Grande, J.I. & Ramilo Araujo, M.C. (2003). E-Government in practice. An analysis of web site orientation to the citizens in Spanish municipalities. *The International Journal of Public Sector Management, 126* (3), 191-218.

Croitts, J. C. & Wilson, D. (1995). An integrated model of buyer-seller relationship in the international travel trade. *Progress in Tourism and Hospitality Research,* 1(2), 125-140.

Cronbach, L.J. (1970). *Essentials of psychological testing,* New York: Harper and Row.

Crosby, L. and Stephen, N. (1987). "Effects of Relationship Marketing on Satisfaction, Retention, and Prices in the Insurance Industry," *Journal of Marketing Research* (24), pp. 404-411.

Crossan, M.M., & Inkpen, A.C. (1994). Promise and reality of learning through alliances. *The International Executive,* 36 (3), 263-274.

Cummings, J.L., & Teng, B. (2003). Transferring R&D knowledge: The key factors affecting knowledge transfer success. *Journal of Engineering and Technology Management, 20*, 39-68.

Curran, J., Jarvis, R., Blackburn, R., & Black, S., (1993). Networks and small firms: constructs, methodological strategies and some findings. *International Small Business Journal* 11(2), 13-25.

Cushman, M. (2001). *Action research in the UK construction industry - the B-Hive Project.* IFIP 8.2, Boisit USA.

Cyert, R. and J. March. (1963). *A behavioral theory of the firm.* Englewood Cliffs, NJ: Prentice-Hall.

Cyert, R. M. & March, J. G. (1992). *A behavioural theory of the firm.* Cambridge, MA: Blackwell.

D'Aveni, R. (1994). *Hypercompetition: Managing the Dynamics of Strategic maneuvering.* Free Press, New York.

D'Aveni, R.A. (1994). *Hyper-Competition: Managing the dynamics of strategic manoeuvring.* New York: Free Press.

Daft, R.L., & Lengel, R.H. (1986). Organisational information requirements, media richness and structural design. *Management Science, 32*(5), 554-571.

Daghfous A. (2004). Absorptive Capacity and the implementation of Knowledge-Intensive Best Practices. *SAM Advanced Management Journal,* pp.21-27.

Dahlstrom, R., & Nygaard, A. (1995). An exploratory investigation of interpersonal trust in new and market economies. *Journal of Retailing, 71*(4), 339-361

Daniel, B., Schwier, R.A., & McCalla, G. (2003). Social capital in virtual learning communities and distributed communities of practice. *Canadian Journal of Learning and Technology, 29*, 113-139.

Daniels, M. (1998). Focussing in a fuzzy world: trading in the networking world. *Journal of Information System,* 24 (6), 451-456.

Dankbaar, B. (1998). Technology Management in technology contingent SMES. *International Journal of Technology Management*, 15(1-2), 70.

Das, T.K., & Teng, B. (2000). A resource-based theory of strategic alliances. *Journal of Management*, 26 (1), 31-61.

Davenport, T. & Harris, J. (2007). *Competing on Analytics*. Boston, MA: Harvard Business School Press.

Davenport, T. & Prusak, L. (1998). *Working Knowledge: how organizations manage what they know*. Boston, Harvard Business School Press.

Davenport, T. (1999). *Ecología de la Información*. Oxford University Press,

Davenport, T. (2006). Competing on Analytics. *Harvard Business Review*, 84(1), 99-107.

Davenport, T., Harris, J., De Long, D., & Jacobson, A. (2001). Data to knowledge to results: Building an analytic capability. *California Management Review*, 43(2), 117-138.

Davenport, T., Prusak, L. (1998). *Working Knowledge. How Organizations Manage What They Know*. Boston: Harvard Business School Press.

Davenport, T.; Prusak, L. (1998): "Working Knowledge: How Organizations Manage What They Know", Harvard Business School Press.

Davenport, T.H. & Prusak, L. (1998). *Working Knowledge. How Organizations What They Know*. Harvard, US: Harvard Business School Press.

Davenport, T.H. & Prusak, L. (1998). *Working Knowledge: How Organizations Manage what they Know* Harvard Business School Press: Boston, MA.

Davenport, T.H., & Prusak, L. (1998). *Working knowledge: How organizations manage what they know*. Boston: Harvard Business School Press.

Davenport, T.H., Eccles, R.G., Prusak, L. (1992): "Information politics". *Sloan Management Review*, 34(1), pp. 53-65.

Davidow, W. H., & Malone, M. S. (1992). *The virtual corporation*. New York, NY: Harper Business.

Davidow, W., & Malone, M. (1992). *The virtual corporation: structuring and revilatizing the corporatin for the 21st Century*. New York: Harper Collins.

Davidow, W.H. & Malone, M.S. (1992). *The Virtual Corporation* New York, NY: Harper Business.

Davidow, W.H. & Malone, M.S. (1992). *The Virtual Corporation: Structuring and Revitalising the Corporation for the 21st Century*. Harper Collins Publishers.

Davidson, R. & Maitland, R. (1997). *Tourism Destinations*. London: Hodder & Stoughton Educational.

Davies, G. & Stancey, E. (2003). *Quality education a distance*. Kluwer Academy Publishers. This book contains the papers presented at the working conference on Quality Education

Dawes, R.M. (1994). *House of cards: Psychology and psychotherapy built on myth*. New York: Free Press.

De la Rica, E. (2000). *Marketing en internet y e-business*. Madrid, Anaya Multimedia.

de Michelis, G. (2001). Cooperation and Knowledge Creation. In I. Nonaka & T. Nisiguchi (Ed.), *Knowledge Emergence. Social, Technical and Evolutionary Dimensions of Knowledge Creation* (pp.124-144). Oxford: Oxford University Press.

De Moor, A. & Weigand, H. (2007). Formalizing the evolution of virtual communities. *Information Systems*, 32(2), 223-247.

Dearden, J. (1972). MIS is a mirage. *Harvard Business Review*. February, pp. 90-99.

Deeds, D.L., Decarolis, D., & Coombs, J. (2000). Dynamic capabilities and new product development in high technology ventures: An empirical analysis of new biotechnology industry. *Journal of Business Venturing*, *12*, 31–46.

Deetz, S.A. (1992). *Democracy in an age of corporate colonization: Developments in communication and the politics of everyday life*. Albany, NY: State University of New York Press.

Delclós, M. (2003). Una herramienta para la productividad. *Automática e Instrumentación*, 343.

Denmann, R. (1998). *Integrated quality management of rural tourist destinations*. Paper presented at the European Tourism Forum of the Austrian Presidency of the Council of the European Union and the European Commission, Mayrhofen.

Denning, P. J., D. E. Comer, D. Gries, M. C. Mulder, A. Tucker, A. J. Turner, and P. T. Young. (1989). Computing as a discipline. *Communications of the ACM.*,32 (1), 9-23.

Dennis, A. R. & Wixom, B. H. (2002). Investigating the moderators of group support system use. *Journal of Management Information Systems*, 18(3), 235-258.

DeSanctis, G. & Gallupe, R. B. (1987). A foundation for the study of group decision support systems. *Management Science*, 33(5), 589-609.

DeSanctis, G. & Monge, P. (1999). Communication processes for virtual organizations. *Organization Science*, 10(6), 693-703.

DeSanctis, G., & Monge, P. (1999). Introduction to the special issue: communication processes for virtual organizations. *Organization Science*, *10*(6), 693-703.

Desouza, K.C. (2002): Barriers to effective use of knowledge management in software engineering. ACM 46, 1.

Dess, G., & Beard, D. (1984). Dimensions of Organizational Task Environments. *Administrative Science Quarterly*, 29(1), 52-73.

Devaraj, S., Kohli, R. (2003):"Performance Impacts of Information Technology: Is Actual Usage the Missing Link?", Management Science, 49(3), pp. 273-289.

Devine, M. & Filos, E. (2000). Erastos. Virtual teams and the organisational gravepine. In Kluwer Academic Publishers (Ed.), *International Federation for Informa-*

tion Processing; Working Conference on Infrastructures for Virtual Organisations, Florianopolis.

Dewhirst, H. D. (1971). Influence of perceived information-sharing norms on communication channel utilization. *Academy of Management Journal*, (14), 305-315.

Dewhurst, F., Martínez Lorente, A.R., & Dale, B.G. (1999). TQM in public organisations: an examination of the issues. *Managing Service Quality, 9*(4), 265-273.

Dhebar, A. (1993). Managing the quality of quantitative analysis. *MIT Sloan Management Review,* Winter, 69-75.

Dibella ,A.J., Nevis, E.C. (1998): "How organization learn. An integrated strategy for building learning capability". Jossey-Bass. Inc. California.

Ding, H.B. & Peters, L.S. (2000). Inter-firm knowledge management practices for technology and new product development in discontinuous innovation. *International Journal of Technology Management*, 20(5-8): 588-600.

Dingsoyr, T.; Djarraya, H. K. and Royrvik, E. (2005): Practical knowledge management tool use in a software consulting company. Communications of the ACM, 48(12), pp. 96-100.

Dirks, K.T., & Ferrin, D.L. (2001). The role of trust in organizational setting. *Organization Science, 12*, 450-467.

Dixon, N. (2000). *El conocimiento común.* Oxford University Press.

Djordjevic, I., Dimitrakos, T., Roman N., Mac D., & Ritrovato, P. (2007). Dynamic security perimeters for inter-enterprise service integration. *Future Generation Computer Systems, 23,* 633-657.

Djordjevic, I., Dimitrakos, T., Roman N., MacD. & Ritrovato, P. (2007). Dynamic security perimetes for inter-enterprise service integration. *Future Generation Computer Systems 23(4),* pp. 633-657.

Dodd, D. H, and White, R. M. (1980). *Cognition mental structures and processes.* Boston, Mass: Allyn and Bacon Inc.

Doney, P., and Cannon, J. (1997). "An Examination of the Nature of trust in the Buyer-Seller Relationship," *Journal of Marketing* (61:2), pp. 35-51.

Donlon, J. P. (1997, July). The virtual organization. *Chief Executive*, (125), 58-66.

Donlon, J.P. (1997). The virtual organization. *Chief Executive* 125, 58-66.

Dosi, G. (1988). Sources, procedures and microeconomic effects of innovation. *Journal of Economic Literature, 26*, 1120-1171.

Draft, R. L. & Lengel, R. H. (1986). Organizational information requirements, media richness, and structural design. *Management Science*, 32, 554-571.

Draft, R. L., and R. H. Lengel. (1984). *Information richness: a new approach to managerial behavior and organizational design.* Greenwich, Conn: JAI Press.

Dredge, D. (2006). Policy networks and the local organisation of tourism. *Tourism Management*, 27(2), 269-280.

Drucker, P. (2001): The Next Society. *The Economist*, November 3rd, 3-22.

Drucker, Peter F.M. (1988). The coming of the new organization. *Harvard Business Review*, 88(1), 45-53.

Duncan, R. B. (1972). Characteristics of organizational environments and perceived environmental uncertainty. *Administrative Science Quarterly, 17*, 313-327.

Duncan, T. and Moriarty, S. (1998). "A Communication-Based Marketing Model for Managing Relationships," *Journal of Marketing* (62), pp. 1-13.

Dutton, W.H. (1999). The *virtual organization: Teleaccess in business and industry.* In G. DeSanctis and J. Fulk (Eds), Shaping organizational form: Communication, connection, and community. Newbury Park, CA: Sage.

Dwyer, F. R., Schurr, P. H. and Oh, S. (1987). "Developing Buying-Seller Relationships," *Journal of Marketing* (51), pp. 11-27.

Dyer J.H. & Singh, H. (1998). The relational view: Cooperative strategy sources of interorganisational competitive advantage. *Academy of Management Review*, 23, 660-679.

Dyer, J.H., & Nobeoka, K. (2000). Creating and managing a high-performance knowledge-sharing network: The Toyota case. *Strategic Management Journal, 21*, 45–367.

Dyer, J.H., & Singh, H. (1998). The relational view, Cooperative strategy and sources of interorganizational competitive advantage. *Academy of Management Review*, 23 (4), 660-679.

Dyer, J.H., & Singh, H. (1998). The relational view: Cooperative strategy and sources of interorganizational competitive advantage. *Academy of Management Review*, 23(4), 660-679.

Earl, M (2001). Knowledge management strategies: toward a taxonomy. *Journal of Management Information Systems, 16*(1), 215-233.

Easterby-Smith, M. & Lyles, M.A. (Eds.) (2003). *The Blackwell Handbook of Organizational Learning and Knowledge Management.* Oxford: Blackwell.

Easton, G. (1992). Industrial Networks: A Review. In B. Axelsson & G. Easton (Eds.), *Industrial Networks: A new View of Reality*, London: Routledge.

Ebrahim, Z. & Irani, Z. (2005). E-government adoption: architecture and barriers. *Business Process Management Journal, 11* (5), 589-611.

EFQM (1999). *Eight Essentials of Excellence*, Brussels: European Foundation for Quality Management.

Egbu, C. & K. Botterill (2001). *Knowledge Management and Intellectual Capital: Benefits for project based industries.* CoBRA.

Ehlers, U.D., Goertz, L & Hildebrant, B. (2005). Use and dissemination of quality approaches in European e-learning. A study by the European Quality Observatory. Cedefop Panorama series, 116.

Eisenhardt, K.M., & Schoonhoven, C.B. (1996). Resource-based view of strategic alliance formation, Strategic and social effects entrepreneurial firms. *Organization Science*, 7 (2), 136-150.

Ekecrantz, J. (1987). The sociological order of the new information society. In *The ideology of the information age*. In Slack, J. D., & Fejes, F. (Ed.), Norwood,NJ: Ablex Publishing Corp.

Ellis, N., & R. Mayer (2001). Inter-organisational relationships and strategy development in an evolving industrial network: Mapping structure and process. *Journal of Marketing Management, 17*, 183-222.

Emden, Z., Yaprak, A., & Cavusgil, S.T. (1998). Learning from experience in international alliances, antecedents and firm performance implications. *Journal of Business Research*, 58 (7), 883-892.

Emre, O. (2001). Delivering converged services. Retrieved April 29, 2006, from http://infocus.telephonyonline.com/ar/telecom_delivering_converged_services/index.htm

Endres, M., Endres, S. Chowdhury, S., & Alam, I. (2007). Tacit knowledge sharing , self-eficacy theory, and application to the open source community. *Journal of Knowledge Management, 11*(3), 92-103.

Endres, M., Endres, S., Chowdhury, S. & Alam, I. (2007). Tacit knowledge sharing , self-eficacy theory, and application to the Open Source community. *Journal of Knowledge Management, 11(3),* 92-103.

Eng, T-Y. (2004). Implications of the Internet for Knowledge Creation and Dissemination in Clusters of Hi-tech firms. *European Management Journal, 22*(1), 87-98.

Ensign, P.C. (1998). Interrelationships and horizontal strategy to achieve synergy and competitive advantage in the diversified firm. *Management Decision, 36*, 657-668.

Epstein, M., & Axtell, R. (1996). *Growing artificial societies: Social science from the bottom up.* Washington D.C.: The Brookings Institution.

Erramilli, M.K., Agarwal, S., & Dev, C.S. (2002). Choice between non-equity modes: An organizational capability perspective. *Journal of International Business Studies, 33*, 223–242.

Escorsa, P. & Maspons, R. (2001). De la Vigilancia Tecnológica a la Inteligencia Competitiva. *Financial Times.* Madrid: Prentice Hall.

European Union (2007). Breaking barriers to e-government. Retrieved from http://www.egovbarriers.org

Evans, J. R. (1991). Creativity in OR/MS: Creative thinking, a basis for OR/MS problem solving. *Interfaces*, 21(5), 12-15.

Evans, J. R. (1992). Creativity in OR/MS: Improving problem solving through creative thinking. *Interfaces*, 22(2), 87-91.

Evans, J. R. (1993a). Creativity in OR/MS: The multiple dimensions of creativity. *Interfaces*, 23(2), 80-83.

Evans, J. R. (1993b). Creativity in OR/MS: Overcoming barriers to creativity. *Interfaces*, 23(6), 101-106.

Evans, P., & Wolf, B. (2005). Collaboration rules. *Harvard Business Review, July–Aug*, 1–10.

Ewt, N. & Ewc, C. (2005). Evaluation of knowledge management tools using AHP. *Expert Systems with Applications, 29*(4), 889-899.

Eyob, E. (2004). E-Government: breaking the frontiers of inefficiencies in the public sector. *Electronic Government, 1*(1), 107-114

FannieMae (2001). *Our business is the American dream.* Retrieved 2001, from: http://www.fanniemae.com

Fayos-Solá, E. & Moro, J. R. (1995). Calidad Ecoturística para el Desarrollo Sostenible, *Conferencia Mundial de Turismo Sostenible* (pp. 33-42). Islas Canarias.

Fayyad, U. & Uthurusamy, R. (2002). Evolving data mining into solutions for insights. *Communications of the ACM, 45*(8), 28-31.

Ferguson, G., Mathur, S., & Shah, B. (2005). Evolving from information to insight. *MIT Sloan Management Review*, Winter, 51-58.

Ferran-Urdaneta, C. (2001). The effects of videoconferencing on persuasion. *Dissertation Abstracts International, Section A: Humanities and Social Science*, 61(8), 3239.

Figallo, C. (1998). *Hosting Web communities: Building relationships, increasing customer loyalty, and maintaining a competitive edge.* New York: John Wiley and Sons.

Filos, E. & Banahan, E. (2000). Will the organization disappear? The challenges of the new economy and future perspectives. In Kluwer Academic Publishers *(Eds.)*, *International Federation for Information Processing; Working Conference on Infrastructures for Virtual Organisations*, Florianopolis.

Finin, T., Labrou, Y., & Mayfield, J. (1998). KQML as an agent communication language. In J. M. Bradshaw (Ed.), *Software agents* (p. 28). Boston: MIT Press.

Fiol, C.M., & O'Connor, E.J. (2005). Identification in face-to-face, hybrid, and pure virtual teams: Untangling the contradictions. *Organization Science, 16*, 19-32.

FIPA. (2000). *FIPA specification repository.* Retrieved 2001, from www.fipa.org/repository

Fitzpatrick, W.M., & Burke, D.R. (2000). Form, functions, and financial performance realities for the virtual organization. *SAM Advanced Management Journal,* 65 (3), 13-22.

Fjermestad, J. & Hiltz, S. T. (1998). An assessment of group decision support systems experimental research: Methodology and results. *Journal of Management Information Systems*, 15(3), 7-149.

Fjermestad, J. (2004). An analysis of communication mode in group support systems research. *Decision Support Systems.* 37(2), 239-263.

Flavián, C., and Guinalíu, M. (2005). "The influence of virtual communities on distribution strategies in the Internet," *International Journal of Retail & Distribution Management* (33:6), pp. 405-425.

Foray, D. (2000). *L'économie de la connaisance.* París: La Découverte.

Ford, D. (2003). Trust and knowledge management: The seeds of success. In *Handbook on Knowledge Management 1: Knowledge Matters* (pp. 553-575). Heidelberg: Springer-Verlag.

Fosfuri, A., & Tribó, J.A. (2008). Exploration the antecedents of potential absorptive capacity and its impact on innovation performance. *Omega, 36,* 173-187.

Fosler, R., & Berger, R. (1982). Public-private sector partnership in American cities: Seven case studies. Lexington: Heath.

Foss, N. (2006): The Emerging Knowledge Governance Approach: Challenges and Characteristics, DRUID Working Paper, no. 06-10.

Foss, N.J. (1996), "Knowledge-based approaches to the theory of the firm: Some critical comments". *Organization Science*, 5 (7), pp. 470-476.

Framke, W. (2001). The Destination: a problematic concept. IPaper presented at the *10th Nordic Tourism Research Conference*, Vasa, Finland.

Franke, U.J. (2002). The competence-based view on the management of virtual web organizations. In U.J. Franke (Ed.), *Managing virtual web organizations in the 21st century: issues and challenges* (pp. 1-27). London: Idea Group Publishing.

Frenkel, A., Afsarmanesh, H., Garita, C. & Hertzberger, L. (2000). Supporting information access rights and visibility levels in virtual enterprises. In Kluwer Academic Publishers *(Ed.)*, *International Federation for Information Processing; Working Conference on Infrastructures for Virtual Organisations*, Florianopolis.

Friedman, T. (2007). *The world is flat.* New York: Farrar, Straus and Giroux.

Frochot, I. & Hughes, H. (2000). Histoqual: the development of a historic houses assessment scale, *Tourism Management*, 21(2), 157-167.

Frydenberg, J. (2002). Quality Standards in e-learning: A matrix of analysis. *International Review of Research in Open and Distance Learning, 3,2*.

Fulk, J. & DeSanctis, G. (1995). Electronic communication and changing organizational forms. *Organization Science*, 6(4), 337-349.

Fulk, J. and DeSanctis, G. (1995). Electronic communication and changing organizational forms. *Organization Science* 6(4), 1-13.

Fyall, A., & Garrod, B. (2004). *Tourism marketing: A collaborative approach*. Cleveland: Channel View Publications.

Fyall, A., Callod, C. & Edwards, B. (2003). Relationship marketing: The challenge for Destinations. *Annals of Tourism Research*, 30 (3), 644-659.

Galbraith, J. (1973). *Strategies of organization design*. Reading, Mass: Addison-Wesley.

Galbraith, J.R. (1995). *Designing organizations*. San Francisco, CA: Jossey-Bass.

Gale, S. (1990). Human aspects of interactive multimedia communication. *Interacting with Computers*, 2, 175-189.

Gallié, E.P., & Guichard, R. (2002). *The impact of ICT sophistication on geographically distant networks: the case of space physics as seen from France*. Paper presented at the Workshop TIC et réorganisation spatiale des activités économiques, Brest.

Garbarino, E., and Johnson, M.S. (1999). "The Different Roles of Satisfaction, Trust, and Commitment in Customer Relationships," *Journal of Marketing* (63:2), pp. 70-87.

Garifo, C. (2001). A pain in the ASOG: Managing changes in ordering guidelines presents challenges. Retrieved April 29, 2006, from http://www.xchangemag.com/articles/171back1.html

Garlasu, D., Dumitrache I., & Mihai A. (2005) A new approach for e-learning in collaborative networks. *Proc. of 6th Conference on Virtual Enterprises. Collaborative Networks and Their Breeding Environments* (pp. 243-248). New York: Springer

Garrigos, F. (2002). *Análisis del Papel Contingente De La Percepción Directiva Sobre El Desempeño Empresarial: Un Estudio En El Sector Hotelero*. Doctoral Thesis. Castellón, Spain: Universitat Jaume I.

Gefen, D. (2000). "E-commerce: the Role of Familiarity and Trust," *OMEGA: The International Journal of Management Science* (28), pp. 725-737.

Geisler, E. (2007). A typology of knowledge management: strategic groups and role behavior in organizations. *Journal of Knowledge Management, 11*(1), 84-96.

George, G., Zahra, S.A., Wheatley, K.K., & Khan, R. (2001). The effects of alliance portfolio characteristics and absortive capacity on performance. A study of biotechnology firms. *Journal of High Technology*, 12, 208-226.

Georgiev, T., Georgieva, E., & Smrikarov, A. (2004, June). M-Learning - a New Stage of E-Learning. Paper presented at International Conference on Computer Systems and Technologies - CompSysTech'2004, Rousse, Bulgaria.

Gertler, M.S. (2003). Tacit knowledge and the economic geography of context or the undefinable tacitness of being (there). *Journal of Economic Geography, 3*, 75-99.

Geyskens, I., Steenkamp, J. and Kumar, N. (1999). "A Meta-Analysis of Satisfaction in Marketing Channel Relationships," *Journal of Marketing Research* (36:2), pp. 223-238.

Geyskens, I., Steenkamp, J.E.M., Scheer, L.K. & Kumar, N. (1996). The effects of trust and interdependence on relationship commitent: a trans-atlantic study. *International Journal of Research in Marketing, 13*, 303-317.

Gibson, L., Lynch, P. A. & Morrison, A. (2005). The Local Destination Tourism Network: Development Issues, *Tourism and Hospitality Planning & Development,* 2(2), 87-99.

Gilder, George. (1992). A major work in the making: into the fibersphere. *Forbes ASAP,* December 7, 111-123.

Girard, J.P. (2006). Where is the knowledge we have lost in managers?. *Journal of Knowledge Management,* 10(6), 22-38.

Glaister, K.W., & Buckley, P.J. (1996). Strategic motives for international alliance formation. *Journal of Management Studies,* 33 (3), 301-332.

Glazer, R., & Weiss, A. (1993). Marketing in Turbulent Environments: Decision Processes and the Time-Sensitivity of Information. *Journal of Marketing Research,* 30(November), 509-521.

Glendinning, C. (2003). Breaking down barriers: integrating health and care services for older people in England. *Heath Policy,* 65(2), 139-151.

Goh, S. y Richards, G. (1997), "Benchmarking the learning capacity of organizations". *European Management Journal,* 15 (5), pp. 575-583.

Goldman, S. L., Nagel, R. N, & Preiss, K. (1995). *Agile competitors and virtual organizations: strategies for enriching the customer.* New York, NY: Van Nostrand Reinhold.

Goldman, S., Nagel, R., & Preiss, K. (1995). *Agile competitors and virtual organizations.* New York, Van Nostrand Reinhold.

Goldman, S., Nagel, R., & Preiss, K. (1995). *Agile competitors and virtual organizations: Strategies for enriching the customer.* New York: Van Nostrand Reinnhold.

González, T. (2000). Evaluación y gestión de la calidad educativa. In T. González (coord.): *Evaluación y gestión de la calidad educativa. Un enfoque metodológico.* Málaga: Ediciones Aljibe, 49-80.

Goranson, H. T. (2000). Infrastructure for the advanced virtual enterprise: a report using a Brasilian-based example. In Kluwer Academic Publishers (Ed.), *Interna-tional Federation for Information Processing; Working Conference on Infrastructures for Virtual Organisations,* Florianopolis.

Gore, Al. (1991). Information superhighways: the next information revolution. *The Futurist,* January-February, 21-23.

Gorey R.M. & Dovat D.R. (1996). *Managing on the Knowledge Era.* New York: Harper and Row.

Gottschalk, P. (2007). *Knowledge management systems.* Harrisburg, PA.: Idea Group Inc.

Govindarajan V. & Gupta, A. (2001). Strategic innovation: a conceptual road map. *Business Horizons, 44* (4), 3-12.

Grabher, G. (1993). The weakness of strong ties: the lock-in of regional development in the Ruhr area, in G. GRABHER, (Ed.). *The embedded Firm: on the Socioeconomics of Industrial Networks.* London: Routledge.

Grabowski, M., & Roberts, K.H. (1999). Risk mitigation in virtual organizations. *Organization Science,* 10, 704-721.

Graf, S. & List, B. (2005). An Evaluation of Open Source E-Learning Platforms Stressing Adaptation Issues. In Proceedings of the *Fifth IEEE International Conference on Advanced Learning Technologies (ICALT'05),* (pp. 163 – 165). Washington: IEEE Computer Society.

Granovetter, M. (1973). The strength of weak ties. *American Journal of Sociology, 78*(6), 1360-1380.

Granovetter, M.S. (1972). The strength of weak ties. *American Journal of Sociology, 78,* 1360-1380.

Grant (1996). Prospering in dynamically-competitive environments: organizational capability as knowledge integration. *Organization Science, 7,* 375-387.

Grant, R. M. (2005). *Contemporary strategy analysis (5th ed).* Malden, MA: Blackwell Publishing.

Grant, R. M., & Baden-Fuller, C. (2004). A knowledge accessing theory of strategic alliances. *Journal of Management Studies,* 41(1), 61-85.

Grant, R.M. (1991). A Resource Based Theory of Competitive Advantage: Implications for Strategy Formulation. *California Management Review, 33*(3), 114-135.

Grant, R.M. (1996) Toward a Knowledge-based Theory of Firm. *Strategic Management Journal, 17*, 109-122.

Grant, R.M. (1996). Prospering in Dynamically-Competitive Environments: Organizational Capability as Knowledge Integration. *Organization Science, 7*(4), 375-387.

Grant, R.M. (1996). Toward a Knowledge-Based Theory of the Firm. *Strategic Management Journal* 17, Special Issue: Knowledge and the Firm, 109-122.

Grant, R.M. (1996). Towards a knowledge-based theory of the firm. *Strategic Management Journal 17*(10), 109-122.

Grant, R.M. (2001). Knowledge and Organization, Nonaka, I. and Teece, D.J. (eds) (2001): *Managing industrial knowledge: Creation, transfer and utilization.* London: Sage.

Grantham, C.E. & Nichols, L.D. (1993). *The digital workplace: Designing groupware platform.* New York: Van Nostrand-Reinhold Grau, America.

Grau, A. (2001). Herramientas de Gestión del Conocimiento. Retrieved February 19, 2007, from http://www.gestiondelconocimiento.com/documentos2/america/herramientas.htm

Gray, B. (1985). Conditions facilitating interorganizational relations. *Human Relations, 38*(10), 911-936.

Greis, N.P., & Kasarda, J.D. (1997). Enterprise logistics in the information era. *California Management Review, 39* (3), 55-78.

Greitzer FL, DM Rice, SL Eaton, MC Perkins, RT Scott, and JR Burnette. (2003). A Cognitive Approach to e-Learning. *In Proceedings of the Interservice/Industry Training, Simulation, and Education Conference (I/ITSEC).* Orlando, Florida.

Greitzer, F. L. (2002). A cognitive approach to student-centered e-Learning. Proceedings Human Factors and Ergonomics Society 46th Annual Meeting, (pp. 2064-2068).Baltimore, Maryland, USA.

Grenier, R. & Metes, G. (1995). *Going virtual: Moving your organization into the 21ˢᵗ century.* New Jersey, NJ: Prentice Hall.

Guibilato, G. (1983). *Economie Touristique*, Suisse: Delta & Spes.

Gulati, R. (1999). Network location and learning, the influence of network resources and firm capabilities on alliance formation. *Strategic Management Journal, 20*, 397-420.

Gulati, R., Nohria, N., & Zaheer, A. (2000). Strategic networks. *Strategic Management Journalk,* vol. 21, n.3, 203-217.

Gummesson, E. (1994). Service Management: An Evaluation and the Future. *International Journal of Service Industry Management, 5*(1), 77-96.

Gummesson, E. (1994). Service Management: An Evaluation and the Future. *International Journal of Service Industry Management, 5*(1), 77-96.

Gundlach, G.T., and Murphy, P.E. (1993). "Ethical and legal foundations of relational marketing exchanges", *Journal of Marketing* (57:4), pp. 35-46.

Gunn, C., (1993). Tourism Planning. London: Taylor & Francis.

Gupta, A., & Govindarajan, V. (2000). Knowledge flows within MNCs. *Strategic Management Journal, 21*, 473-496.

Gupta, A.K. & Govindarajan, V. (2000). Knowledge Management's Social Dimension: Lessons from Nucor Steel. *Sloan Management Review*, fall issue, 71-80.

Hackney, R.A, & Jones, S. (2002). Towards e-Government in the Welsh (UK) Assembly: an information systems evaluation. In *Proceedings of the ISOne World Conference*, Las Vegas, US.

Hagel, J. & Armstrong, A. (1997). *Net Gain: Expanding Markets Through Virtual Communities.* Boston, MA: Harvard Business School Press.

Hagel, J. III, and Armstrong, A.G. (1997). *Net Gain: Expanding Markets through Virtual Communities*, Harvard Business School Press, Boston, MA.

Hagel, J., III, & Armstrong, A.G. (1997). *Net Gain: Expanding Markets Through Virtual Communities*. Boston, M.A.: Harvard Business School Press.

Hair, J., Anderson, R., Tatham, R.; & Black, W. (1999). *Multivariant Analysis*. Boston, US: Prentice Hall, 5°ed.

Hair, J.F. Jr., Anderson, R.E., Tatham, R.L. and Black, W.C. (1998). *Multivariate Data Analysis*. Prentice Hall.

Håkanson, L. (2007). Creating knowledge–the power and logic of articulation. *Industrial and Corporate Change, 16*(1), 51-88.

Hakansson, H. & Johanson, J. (1992). A model of industrial networks. In B. Axelsson & G. Easton (Eds.) *Industrial Networks: A New View of Reality*, (pp. 28-34), London: Routledge.

Hakansson, H. & Snehota, I. (1989) No business is an island: The network concept of business strategy. *Scandinavian Journal of Management*, 5(3), 187-200.

Hall, C. M. (1999). Rethinking collaboration and partnership: A public policy perspective. *Journal of Sustainable Tourism*, 7(3/4), 274-289.

Hall, C. M. (2000). Rethinking collaboration and partnership: A public policy perspective. In B. Bramwell, & B. Lane (Eds.), *Tourism collaboration and partnerships: Politics, practice and sustainability* (pp. 143-158). Clevedon, Uk: Channel View Publications.

Hamel, G. (1991). Competition for competence and inter-partner learning within international strategic alliances. *Strategic Management Journal*, vol. 12, 83-103.

Hamel, G., & Prahalad, C.K (1988). *When Competitors Collaborate*. London, UK: London Business School.

Hamel, G., Doz, Y.L., & Prahalad, C.K. (1989). Collaborate with your competitors and win. *Harvard Business Review*, 67 (1), 133-139.

Hammer, M. & Champy, J. (1993). *Reengineering the corporation: A manifesto for business revolution.* New York: Harper Collins.

Handzic, M. (2007). *Socio-technical knowledge management: studies and initiatives.* Harrisburg, PA.: Idea Group Inc.

Hansen, M., Nohria, N., & Tierney, T. (1999). What's your strategy for managing knowledge?. *Harvard Business Review, March-April*, 106-116.

Hansen, M.T. (1999). The search-transfer problem: The role of weak ties in sharing knowledge across organization subunits. *Administrative Science Quarterly, 44*, 82-111.

Harris, L. (2002). The future for the HRM function in local government: everything has changed- but has anything changed?. *Strategic Change, 11*, 369-378.

Harris, L.C. and Goode, M.M.H. (2004). "The four levels of loyalty and the pivotal role of trust: a study of online service dynamics," *Journal of Retailing* (80), pp. 139-158.

Harrison, J.S., Hitt, M.A., Hoskisson, R.E., & Ireland, R.D. (2001). Resource complementarity in business combinations, extending the logic to organizational alliances. *Journal of Management, 27*, 679-690.

Hartley, R. V. L. (1928). Transmission of information. *Bell System Tech Journal*, (7), 535.

Hasman, A., Albert, A., Wainwright, P., Klar, R., & Sosa, M. (Ed.) (1995). *Education and Training for Health Informatics in Europe: State of the Art - Guideline - Applications.* Amsterdam, Netherlands: IOS Press.

Hawes, J.M., Mast, K.E. and Swan, J.E. (1989). "Trust earning perceptions of sellers and buyers," *Journal of Personal Selling and Sales Management* (9), pp. 1-8.

Haywood, K. M. (1993). The Price-Value Relationship: Perspective and Definitional Issues. *World Travel and Tourism Review*, 3, 213-217.

HBSP. (1998). *Harvard Business review on knowledge management.* Cambridge, MA: Harvard Business School Press.

Hedberg, B., Dahlgren, G., Hansson, J. & Olve, N-G. (1997). *Virtual organizations and beyond: Discover imaginary systems.* New York, NY: Wiley.

Hedberg, B., Dahlgren, G., Hansson, J., & Olve, N. G. (1997). *Virtual Organizations and Beyond: Discover Imaginay Systems.* Chichester, UK: John Wiley & Sons.

Heide, J.B., & John, G. (1992). Do norms matter in marketing relationship?. *Journal of Marketing*, **56**, 32-44.

Helgensen, S. (1995). *The web of Inclusion: Building an Organization for Everyone.* Currency Doubleday.

Henderson, J. C. & Nutt, P. (1980). The influence of decision style on decision making behavior. *Management Science*, (26(4), 371-386.

Henderson, R., & Cockburn, I. (1996). Scale, Scope, and Spillovers: The Determinants of Research Productivity in Drug Discovery. *RAND Journal of Economics*, *27*(1), 32-59.

Hicks, J. O. (1988). *Management information systems: a user perspective.* St. Paul, Minn.

Hightower, R. & Sayeed, L. (1995). Effects of communication mode and prediscussion information distribution characteristics on information exchange in groups. *Information Systems Research*, 7(4), 451-464.

Hillier, F. S. & Lieberman, G. J. (2005). *Introduction to Operations Research.* New York, NY: McGraw Hill.

Hillman, A.J., Jr. A.A. Cannella, & R.L. Paetzold (2000). The resource dependence role of corporate directors: Strategic adaptation of board composition in response to environmental change. *Journal of Management Studies*, *37*(2). 235-255.

Hiltz, S. R., Johnson, K., & Turoff, M. (1986). Experiments in group decision-making: Communication process and outcome in face-to-face versus computerized conferences. *Human Communication Research*, 13(2), 225-252.

Hitt, M.A., Hoskisson, R.E., Johnson. R.A. & Moesel, D.D. (1996). The Market for Corporate Control Firm Innovation. *Academy of Management Journal*, 36, 1084-1119.

Ho, V.Y., Ang, S. & Straub, D. (2003). When subordinates become IT contractors: persistent managerial expectations in Outsourcing. *Information Systems Research*, *14* (1), 66-86.

Hofstede, G. (1980). *Culture's consequences: International differences in work-related values.* Beverly Hills, CA: Sage.

Hofstede, G. (1999). *Culturas y Organizaciones. El Software Mental. La Cooperación Internacional y su Importancia para la Supervivencia.* Madrid: Alianza Press.

Holden, S.H. (2003). The new e-Government equation: ease, engagement, privacy and protection. *The Council for Excellence in Government.* Retrieved from: http://www.excelgov.org

Holland, J. (1995). *Hidden order: How adaptation builds complexity.* MA: Perseus Books Reading.

Holsapple, C.W. (Ed). (2003). *Handbook on knowledge management 2: Knowledge directions.* Heidelberg: Springer-Verlag.

Holsapple, C.W. (Ed.). (2003). *Handbook on knowledge management 1: Knowledge matters.* Heidelberg: Springer-Verlag.

Holzner, B., & Marx, J. (1979). *The knowledge application: The knowledge system in society.* Boston: Allyn-Bacon.

Hope, C. A. & Muhlemann, A. P. (1998). Total quality, human resource management and tourism. *Tourism Economics*, 4(4), 367-386.

Hornett, A., & Stein, E.W. (2007). Mapping the knowledge management domain of ideas: Evidence from a practice group. *International Journal of Knowledge Management, 3*(3), 1-25.

Horrigan, J. B.; Rainie, L. & Fox, S. (2001). *Online communities: networks that nurture long-distance relationships and local ties.* Washington, DC: Pew Internet and American Life Project.

Horton, W. (2000). *Designing Web-Based Training.* New York: John Wiley

Horton, W. (2001). *Evaluating e-learning.* California. ASTD (American Society for Training and Development).

Housel, T. & Bell, A. (2001). *Measuring and Managing Knowledge.* New York, McGraw-Hill.

Howlet M. & Ramesh, M. (1995). *Studying public policy: policy cycles and policy subsystems.* Toronto: Oxford University Press.

Hsu, M., Ju, T., Yen, C. & Chang, C. (2007). Knowledge sharing behavior in virtual communities: The relationship between trust, self-efficacy, and outcome expectation". *International Journal of Human-Computer Studies, 65(2),* 153-169.

Hsu, M., Ju, T., Yen, C., & Chang, C. (2007). Knowledge sharing behavior in virtual communities: The relationship between trust, self-efficacy, and outcome expectation. *International Journal of Human-Computer Studies,* 65, 153-169.

Hu, Y.S. (1995), "The international transferability of the firm's advantages". *California Management Review,* 37 (4), pp. 73-88.

Huber, G. (1991), "Organizational learning: the contributing processes and the literatures". *Organization Science,* 2 (1), pp. 88-115.

Huber, G.P. (1991). Organizational learning: The contributing process and the literatures. *Organization Science, 2,* 88-115.

HUD. (2001). *Homes and communities.* Retrieved 2001, from http://www.hud.gov

Huete, L. M. (1994). Factores que infuyen en la calidad del producto, In World Tourism Organization (Ed.), *WTO Seminar on Quality - A Challenge for Tourism* (pp. 53-55). Madrid.

Hughes, G. & Hay, D. (2001). Use of concept mapping to integrate the different perspectives of designers and other stakeholders in the development of e-learning materials. *British Journal of Educational Technology 32* (5), 557–569.

Hughes, J.A., O'Brien, J., Randall, D., Rouncefield, M., & Tolmie, P. (2001). Some 'real' problems of 'virtual' organization. *New Technology Work Employ, 16*(1), 49-64.

Hurst, D.K. (1997). When it comes to real change, too much objectivity may be fatal to the process. *Strategy and Leadership, 25,* 7-11.

Huselid, M.A.(1995). The impact of human resource management practices on turnover, productivity, and corporate. *Academy of Management Journal, 38*(3), 635-643.

Husted, K., & Michailova, S. (2002). Diagnosing and fighting knowledge sharing hostility. Organizational Dynamics, 31, 60-73.

Huysman, M., Steinfield, C., Jang, C., David, K., Huis In 'T Veld, M., Poot, J., & Mulder, I. (2003). Virtual teams and the appropriation of communication technology: Exploring the concept of media stickiness. *Computer Supported Cooperative Work, 12,* 411-436.

Hwarng, H. B. (2001). A modern simulation course for business students. *Interfaces,* 31(3), 66-75.

IADE-CIC (2003). *Modelo de medición y gestión del capital intelectual: Modelo Intellectus.* Madrid: Universidad Autónoma de Madrid: CIC-IADE.

ICMA (2002). e-Government survey. Retrieved from: http://www.icma.org

Inkpen, A. & Ross, J. (2001). Why do some strategic alliances persist beyond their useful life?. *California Management Review,* 44(1), 132-148.

Inkpen, A.C. (1996). Creating knowledge trough collaboration. *California Management Review,* 39 (1), 123-140.

Ipe, M. (2003). *The praxis of knowledge sharing in organizations: A case study.* Doctoral dissertation. University Microfilms.

Irani, Z., Khoumbathi, K., & Themistocleous, M. (2003). Conceptual Model for the Adoption of Enterprise Application Integration in Healthcare Organizations. In *Proceedings of the America's Conference on Information Systems,* Tampa (Florida), US.

Ireland, R.D., Hitt, M.A., & Vaidyanath, D. (2002). Alliance management as a source of competitive advantage. *Journal of Management,* 28 (3), 413-446.

Itami, H. & Roehl (1987). *Mobilizing Invisible Assets.* Cambridge, MA: Harvard University Press.

Itami, H. & Roehl, T.W. (1987). *Mobilizing invisible assets.* Harvard University Press, Cambridge.

Itami, H. (1987). *Mobilizing Invisible Assets.* Boston, Harvard University Press.

Ittner, C. D. & Larcker, D. F. (2003). Coming up short. *Harvard Business Review.* November, 88-95.

Ives, W., Torrey, B., & Gordon, C. (2000). Knowledge sharing is human behavior. In *Knowledge management: Classic and contemporary works* (pp. 99-129).

Jägers, H., Jansen, W., & Steenbakkers, W. (1998). Characteristics of virtual organizations. In P. Sieber & J. Griese (Ed.), *Organizational virtualness* (pp. 65-76). Bern: Simona Verlag Bern.

Jamal, T. & Getz, D. (1995). Collaboration theory and community tourism planning. *Annals of Tourism Research,* 22(1), 186-204.

James, E.H. (2000). Race-related differences in promotions and support: Underlying effects of human and social capital. *Organization Science, 11*(5), 493-508.

Janis, I. (1972). *Victims of groupthinking.* Boston, MA: Houghton-Miffin.

Janis, I. L. (1972). *Victims of groupthink: a psychological study of foreign-policy decisions and fiascoes.* Boston, MA: Houghton Mifflin.

Jansen, J., Van Den Bosch, F., & Volberda, H. (2005). Managing Potential and Realized Absorptive Capacity: How Do Organizational Antecedents Matter?. *Academy of Management Journal, 48*(6), 999-1015.

Janssen, M., Gortmaker, J. & Wagenaar, R.W. (2006). Web service orchestration in public administration: challenges, roles and growth stages, *Information Systems Management, 23* (2), 44-55.

Jara, M. & Mellar, H. (2006). Exploring the mechanism for assuring quality of e-learning courses in UK higher education institutions. *European Journal of Open Distance and E-learning.*

Jarvenpaa, S., & Leidner, D. (2002). Communication and trust in global virtual teams. *Organization Science, 10*(10), 791-815.

Jarvenpaa, S.L., & Leidner, D.E. (1999). Communication and trust in global virtual teams. *Organization Science, 10,* 791-815.

Jarvenpaa, S.L., & Tanriverdi, H. (2003). Leading virtual knowledge networks. *Organizational Dynamics, 31*(4), 403-412.

Jérez, P.; Céspedes, J.; Valle, R. (2005), "Organizational learning capability: A proposal of measurement". *Journal of Business Research,* 58 (6), pp. 715-725.

Jessup, L. & Valacich, J. (2007). *Information systems today.* Upper Saddle River, New Jersey: Prentice-Hall.

Jethi, R. (2005). Getting what you wish for: New OSS keeps Northpoint on top Of DSL demand. Retrieved April 29, 2006, from http://www.xchangemag.com/articles/0a1sec8.html

Johnson, P., & Lancaster, A. (2000). *Swarm users guide.* Swarm Development Group.

Joia, L.A. (2004). Developing Government-to-Government enterprises in Brazil: a heuristic model drawn from multiple case studies. *International Journal of Information Management, 24* (2), 147-166.

Jones, G.R., & George, J.M. (1998). The experience and evolution of trust: Implications for cooperation and teamwork. *Academy of Management Review, 23*, 531-546.

Jöreskog, K. (1971). "Statistical analysis of sets of congeneric tests," *Psychometrika* (36), pp. 109-133.

Jöreskog, K., and Sörbom, D. (1993). *LISREL 8 Structural Equation Modeling with the SIMPLIS Command Language*, Scientific Software International, Chicago-Illinois.

Jornet, J., Suarez, J. & Perales, M.J. (2001). Evaluación de la Formación Ocupacional y Continua. *Revista de Investigación Educativa, 19 (2)*.

Kahneman, D., Slovic, P. & Tversky, A. (1982). *Judgment under uncertainty: Heuristics and biases.* Cambridge, MA: Cambridge University Press.

Kakabadse, A. & Kakabadse, N. (2001). Outsourcing in the public services: a comparative analysis of practice, capability and impact. *Public Administration and Development, 21* (5), 401-413.

Kale, P., Singh, H., & Perlmutter, H. (2000). Learning and protection of proprietary assets in strategic alliances, Building relational capital. *Strategic Management Journal,* 21, 217-237.

Kalpic, B. and Bernues, P. (2006): "Business process modelling through the knowledge management perspective". Journal of Knowledge Management, 10 (3), pp. 40-56.

Kalpic, B., & Bernus, P (2006). Business process modeling through the knowledge management perspective. *Journal of Knowledge Management, 10*(3), 40-56.

Kamara, J.M., Anumba C.J., & Carrillo, P.M. (2002). A clever approach to selecting a knowledge management strategy. *International Journal of Project Management,* 20, 205-211.

Kamara, J.M., Anumba C.J., & Carrillo, P.M. (2002). A clever approach to selecting a knowledge management strategy. *International Journal of Project Management,* 20, 205-211.

Kamoche, K. & Mueller, F. (1998). Human Resource Management within a Resource-Capability View of the Firm. *Journal of Management Studies, 33 (2),* 213-233.

Kamoche, K. (1996). Strategic Human Resource Management within a resource-capability view of the firm. *Journal of Management Studies, 33,* 213-233.

Kandampully, J. (2000). The impact of demand fluctuation on the quality of service: a tourism industry example. *Managing Service Quality,* 10(1), 10-18.

Kanter, R.M. (1988). When a thous flowers bloom: Structural, collective, social conditions for innovation in organizations, in B. M. STRAW, L. L. CUMMINGS (Eds). *Research in organizational behavior,* 169-211. Greenwich, CT: JAI Press.

Kaplan, R.S. & Norton, D.P. (1992). The Balanced Scorecard Measures that Drive Performance. *Harvard Business Review,* 70(1), 71-79.

Karraker, R. (1988). Highways of minds. *Whole Earth Review,* Spring, 4-15.

Kasper-Fuehrer, E.C., & Ashkanasy, N. (2001). Communicating trustworthiness and building trust in interorganizational virtual organizations. *Journal of Management, 27,* 235-254.

Kasper-Fuehrer, E.C., & Ashkanasy, N.M. (2004). The interorganizational virtual organization. *International Studies of Management and Organization,* 33 (4), 34-64.

Katzenbach, J.R., & Smith, D.K (1993). The discipline of teams, *Harvard Business Review, 17*(2), 111-120.

Keller, J. (1983). Motivational Design of Instruction. In Reigeluth, C. (Ed.). *Instructional-design theories and models: an overview of their current status.* Mahwah, NJ: Lawrence Erlbaum.

Keller, J. (1983). Motivational Design of Instruction. In Reigeluth, C. (Ed.). *Instructional-design theories and models: an overview of their current status.* Mahwah, NJ: Lawrence Erlbaum.

Kepner, C. & Tregoe, B. (1965). *The rational manager.* New York, NY: McGraw-Hill.

Khalil, O., & Wang, S. (2002). Information technology enabled meta-management for virtual organizations. *International Journal of Production Economics, 75*(1), 127-134.

Khan, Badrul, H. (eds.) (2007). *Flexible learning in an information society.* Hershey, P.A.: Information Science Publishing.

Khanna, T., Gulati, R., & Nohria, N. (1998). The dynamics of learning alliances: Competition, Cooperation, and relative scope. *Strategic Management Journal*, vol. 19, n.3, 193-212.

Kim, D.H. (1993), "The link between individual and organizational learning". *Sloan Management Review*, fall, pp. 37-50.

Kim, L. (1998). Crisis construction and organizational learning: Capability building in catching-up at Hyundai Motor. *Organization Science, 9*(4), 506-521.

Kim, W.G., Lee, C. and Himstra, S.J. (2004). "Effects of an online virtual community on customer loyalty and travel product parchases," *Tourism Management* (25), pp. 343-355.

Kirkpatrick, D.L. (1999). *Evaluación de acciones formativas: los cuatro niveles.* Barcelona: EPISE-Barcelona: Edicions Gestió 2000, S.A.

Kishore, R., & McLean, E. (2002). The next generation enterprise: A CIO perspective on the

Klein, R. (2000). EU activities to improve the quality of European tourist products, In *Workshop on Quality in Tourism: from Patterns to indicators.* Faro: Universidade do Algarve.

Kluber, R. A. (1998). A framework for virtual organizing. In Sieber, P. & Griese J. (Eds), *Organizational Virtual-ness. Proceedings of the VoNet* – Workshop (pp. 9-24). Bern: Simona Verlag Bern.

Knoke, D., & Kuklinski, J. (1983). *Network Analysis.* Beverly Hills: Sage.

Koch, M.J. & McGrath, R.G. (1996). Improving labor productivity: human resource management policies do matter. *Strategic Management Journal, 17*, 335-354.

Kock, N. (2004). The psychological model: towards a new theory of computer-mediated communication based on Darwinian evolution. *Organizational Science, 15*(3), 327-248.

Kodama, M. (2005). New knowledge cration through leadership-based strategic community—a case of new product development in IT and multimedia business fields. *Technovation, 25*(8), 895-908.

Kodama, M. (2005). New knowledge creation through leadership-based strategic community—a case of new product development in IT and multimedia business fields. *Technovation, 25*, 895-908.

Kogut (2000). The network as knowledge: Generative rules and the emergence of structure. *Strategic Management Journal, 21*, 405-425.

Kogut, B. & Zander, U. (1992). Knowledge of the Firm, Combinative Capabilities and the Replication of Technology. *Organization Science, 3*, 383-397.

Kogut, B. & Zander, U. (1992). Knowledge of the firm, combinative capabilities, the replication of technology. *Organization Science, 3*, 383-397.

Kogut, B. (1988). Joint ventures: theoretical and empirical perspectives. *Strategic Management Journal, 9* (4), 319-333.

Kogut, B. and Zander, U. (1992). Knowledge of the Firm, Combinative Capabilities, and the Replication of Technology. *Organization Science 3*(3), 383-397.

Kogut, B. y Kulatilaka, N. (2001), "Capabilities as real options". *Organization Science, 12* (6), pp. 744-758.

Kogut, B. y Zander, U. (1992), "Knowledge of the firm, combinative capabilities, and the replication of technology". *Organization Science*, 3 (3), pp. 383-397.

Kogut, B. y Zander, U. (1996), "What firms do? Coordination, identity and learning". *Organization Science*, 7 (5), pp. 502-518.

Kogut, B., & Zander, U. (1992). Knowledge of the firm, combinative capabilities, and the replication of technology. *Organization Science, 3*, 383-397.

Kogut, B., & Zander, U. (1992). Knowledge of the firm, combinative capabilities, and the replication of technology. *Organization Science, 3* (3), 383-397.

Kogut, B., & Zander, U. (1992). Knowledge of the firm: Combinative capabilities, and the replication of technology. *Organization Science, 3*, 383-397.

Koh, C.E., Prybutok, V.R., Ryan, S., & Ibragimova, B. (2006). The importance of strategic readiness in an emerging e-government environment. *Business Process Management Journal, 12* (1), 22-33.

Koh, J. & Kim, Y. G. (2004). Knowledge sharing in virtual communities: an e-business perspective. *Expert Systems with Applications*, 26(2), 155-166.

Koh, J., & Kim, Y.-G. (2004). Knowledge sharing in virtual communities: An e-business perspective. *Expert Systems with Applications, 26*, 155-166.

Koh, J., and Kim, D. (2004). "Knowledge sharing in virtual communities: an e-business perspective," *Expert Systems with Applications* (26), pp. 155-166.

Kohavi, R., Rothleder, N., & Simoudis, E. (2002). Emerging trends in business analytics. *Communications of the ACM*, 45(8), 45-48.

Koka, B., & Prescott, J. (2002). Strategic Alliances As Social Capital: A Multidimensional View. *Strategic Management Journal, 23*, 795–816.

Koschatzky, K. (2002). Networking and knowledge transfer between research and industry in transition countries: empirical evidence from the Slovenian InnovationSystem. *Journal of Technology Transfer, 27*(1), 27-38.

Kozinets, R.V. (1992): E-tribalized marketing? The strategic implications of virtual communities of consumption. *European Management Journal, 17(3)*, 252-264.

Kozinets, R.V. (2002). "The Field Behind the Screen: Using Netnography for Marketing Research in Online Communities," *Journal of Marketing Research* (39:1), pp. 61-72.

Krackhard, D. & Hanson, J. (1993). Informal networks: The company behind the chart. *Harvard Business Review, 71*(4), 104-111.

Kraut, R., Patterson, M., Lundmark, V., Kiesler, S., Mukopadhyay, T., & Scherlis, W. (1998). Internet paradox. *American Psychologist, 53*, 1017-1031.

Krippendorff, K. (1975). Some principles of information storage and retrieval in society. *General Systems, 20*, 15-35.

Krugman, P. (1991). Increasing returns and economic geography. *The Journal of Political Economy, 99*, 483-499.

Kuhn, T.S. (1962). *The structure of scientific revolutions*. The University of Chicago Press.

Kumar, N., Scheer, L., and Steenkamp, J.B. (1995). "The Effects of Supplier Fairness on Vulnerable Resellers", *Journal of Marketing Research* (32:1), pp. 42-53.

Kumar, R., & Nti, K. (1998). Differential Learning and Interaction in Alliance Dynamics: A Process and Outcome Discrepancy Model. *Organization Science, 9*(3), Special Edition: *Managing Partnerships and Strategic Alliances*, 356-367.

Labe, R., Nigam, R., & Spence, S. (1999). Management science at Merrill Lynch Private Client Group. *Interfaces*, 29(2), 1-14.

Ladkin, A. & Bertramini, A. M. (2002). Collaborative tourism planning: Case study of Cusco, Peru. *Current Issues in Tourism*, 5(2), 71-93.

Lähteenmäki, S.; Toivonen, J.; Mattila, M. (2001), "Critical aspects of organizational learning research and proposals for its measurement". *British Journal of Management*, 12 (2), pp. 113-119.

Lambert, D., Cooper, M. & Pugh, J. (1998). Supply Chain Management. *International Journal of Logistics Management*. 9(2), 1-19.

Lane, C. (1998). Introduction. In C. Lane & Backmann (Eds.), *Trust within and between organizations*. Oxford University Press.

Lane, P.J. & Lubatkin, M. (1998). Relative absorptive capacity interorganisational learning. *Strategic Management Journal*, 19, 461-477.

Lane, P.J., & Lubatkin, M. (1998). Relative absorptive capacity and interorganizational learning. *Strategic Management Journal, 19*, 461-477.

Lane, P.J., & Lubatkin, M. (1998). Relative absorptive capacity and interorganizational learning. *Strategic Management Journal*, 19 (5), 461-477.

Lane, P.J., & Lubatkin, M. (1998). Relative absorptive capacity and interorganizational learning. *Strategic Management Journal, 19*, 461-477.

Lane, P.J., Salk, J.E. & Lyles, M.A. (2001). Absorptive Capacity, Learning, And Performance In International Joint Ventures. *Strategic Management Journal*, 22(12), 1139–1161.

Lane, P.L., Koka, B. & Pathak, S. (2006). The reification of absorptive capacity: a critical review and rejuvenation of the construct. *Academy of Management Review, 31*(4), 833-863.

Lant, T. & Shapira, Z. (2001). *Organizational Cognition: Computational and Interpretation* Mahwah, NJ: Lawrence Erlbaum Associates.

Lant, T.K. y Mezías, S.J. (1992), "An organizational learning model of convergence and reorientation". *Organization Science*, 3, pp. 47-71.

Lapre, M., & Van Wassenhove, L. (2001). Creating and transferring knowledge for productivity improvement in factories, *Management Science, 47*(10), 1311-1325.

Lara, J.L. (2000). *Diez respuestas a las preguntas más frecuentes sobre gestión del conocimiento.*

Larson, A. (1992). Networks dyads in entrepreneurial settings: a study of governance of exchange relationships. *Administrative Science Quarterly, 37*(1), 76-104.

Larson, M. (1999). *Shopping for a reverse mortgage: Few products, lots of tricky choices.* Retrieved 2001, from http://www.bankrate.com/brm/news/loan

Laszlo, Ernst. (1972). *Introduction to systems philosophy*. New York: Harper and Row.

Lave, J. and Wenger, E. (1992). *Situated Learning: Legitimate Peripheral Participation*. Mass: Harvard U. Press.

Lave, J., & Wenger, E. (1991). *Situated Learning: Legitimate Peripheral Participation*, New York, NY: Cambridge University Press.

Lave, J., & Wenger, E. (1991). *Situated learning: Legitimate peripheral participation*. New York: Cambridge University Press.

Lawrence, P. R. & Lorsch, J. (1967). *Organization and Environment*. Cambridge, MA: Harvard University Press.

Laws, E., (1995). Tourism Destination Management: Issues, Analysis and Policies. London: Routledge.

Layne, K. & Lee, J. (2001). Developing fully functional E-Government: A four stage model. *Government Information Quarterly, 18*(2), 122-136.

Lazlo, G. P. (1999). Implementing a quality management program- three Cs of success: commitment, culture, cost. *The TQM Magazine*, 11(4), 231-237.

Lazzarini, S.G., Chaddad, F.R. & Cook, M.L. (2001). Integrating supply chain and network analyses: the study of netchains. *Journal on Chain and Network Science*, 1(1), 7-22.

Lea, M., & Spears, R. (1991). Computer-mediated communication, deindividuation and group decision-making. *International Journal of Man-machine Studies, 34*, 283-301.

Leavitt, H. J. (1979). Beyond the analytic manager. *California Management Review*, (3), 5-12.

Lee, G.K., & Cole, R.E. (2003). From a firm-based to a community-based model of knowledge creation: The case of the Linux kernel development. *Organization Science, 14*, 633-649.

Lee, S., Tan, X. & Trimi, S. (2006). Current practices of leading e-government countries. *Communications of the ACM, 48* (10), 99-104.

Lei, D, & Hitt, M. A. (1995). Strategic restructuring and outsourcing: The effect of mergers, acquisitions and LBOs on building firm skills and capabilities. *Journal of Management, 21*, 835–859.

Lei, D., Slocum, J.W. & Pitts, R.A. (1999). Designing organizations for competitive advantage: the power of unlearning and learning. *Organizational Dynamics, 37 (3)*, 24-38.

Lei, D.; Slocum, J.W.; Pitts, R.A: (1999), "Designing organizations for competitive advantage: The power of unlearning and learning". *Organizational Dynamics*, 37 (3), pp. 24-38.

Lei,, D.; Hitt, M.A.; Bettis, R. (1996), "Dynamic core competence through meta-learning and strategic context". *Journal of Management*, 22 (4), pp. 549-569.

Lengel, R. H. (1984). *Management information processing and communication-   media source selection behavior.* Unpublished doctoral dissertation, Texas A & M University.

Lenox, M., & King, A. (2004). Prospects For Developing Absorptive Capacity Through Internal Information Provision. *Strategic Management Journal, 25*, 331–345.

Leon, L., Przasnyski, Z., & Seal, K. C. (1996). Spreadsheets and OR/MS models: An end-user perspective. *Interfaces*, 26(2), 92-104.

Leonard, D., & Straus, S. (1998). Putting your company's whole brain to work. In *Harvard Business Review on Knowledge Management* (pp. 109-136). Boston: Harvard Business School Press.

Leonard-Barton, D. (1992). Core capabilities and core rigidities: A paradox in managing new product development. *Strategic Management Journal, 13*(Summer special number), 111–125.

Leoni, P. (1999). *La città ospitale*, Paper presented at the International Conference "From Destination to Destination Marketing and Management", Venice.

Les Pang (2001). Understanding Virtual Organizations. *Information Systems Control Journal*, 6.

Lesser, E., & Everest, K. (2001). Using communities of practice to managing intellectual capital. *Ivey Business Journal, 65,* 37-41.

Levitt, B. & March, J.G. (1988). Organizational Learning. *Annual Review of Sociology,* 14, 319-340.

Levitt, B. y March, J. (1988), "Organizational learning". *American Review Of Sociology*, 14, pp. 319-340.

Levy, M., Loebbecke, C. & Powell, P. (2003). SMES, co-opetition and knowledge sharing: the role of information systems. *European Journal of Information Systems*, 12(1), 3-17.

Lévy, P. (1996). *O que é o virtual*, São Paulo: Editora 34.

Li, F. & Stevenson, R. (2003). Implementing e-government strategy in Scotland: current situation and emerging issues. In *Proceedings of the 2nd European Conference on e-Government*, Oxford, UK.

Li, F. (2003). Implementing E-Government strategy in Scotland: current situation and emerging issues. *Journal of Electronic Commerce in Organizations, 1* (2), 44-65.

Li, F. (2006). *What is e-Business? How the Internet transforms organisations.* Oxford, UK: Blackwell.

Li, H. (2004). "Virtual Community Studies: A Literature Review, Synthesis and Future Research," *Proceedings of the Americas Conference on Information Systems*, New York, August 2004.

Li, W., Ardichivili, A., Maurer, M., Wentling, T., & Studemann, R. (2007). Impact of Chinese culture values of knowledge sharing through online communities of practice. *International Journal of Knowledge Management, 3*, 46-59.

Liao, J., Welsch, H., & Stoica, M. (2003). Organizational Absorptive Capacity and Responsiveness: An Empirical Investigation of Growth-Oriented SMEs'. *Entrepreneurship: Theory & Practice, 28*(1), 63-86.

Liao, S., Chang, J., Shih-chieh, C., & Chia-mei, K. (2004). Employee relationship and knowledge sharing: A case study of a Taiwanese finance and securities firm. *Knowledge Management Research & Practice, 2*, 24-34.

Lichtenstein D.R., Netemeyer R.G., and Burton S. (1990). "Distinguishing coupon proneness from value consciousness: an acquisition—transaction utility theory perspective," *Journal of Marketing* (54:3), pp. 54– 67.

Lin, F. & Hsueh C. (2006). Knowledge map creation and maintenance for virtual communities of practice. *Information Processing and Management, 42*, 551-568.

Lin, F., & Hsueh, C. (2006). Knowledge map creation and maintenance for virtual communities of practice. *Information Processing and Management 42(2)*, pp. 551-568

Lin, F., Lin, S., & Huang, T. (2007). Knowledge sharing and creation in a teachers' professional virtual community. *Computers & Education*, xxx. Article in press.

Lindvall, M., Rus, I. & Suman, S. (2002). *Technology Support for Knowledge Management.* Paper presented at 4th International Workshop on Learning Software Organizations (LSO'02). Chicago, Illinois, EEUU.

Lipnack, J. & Stamps, J. (1997). *Virtual teams: Reaching across space, time and organizations with technology.* New York, NY: John Wiley.

Lipnack, J. S. (1993). *Rede de Informações.* Rio de Janeiro: Makron Brooks.

Lockee, B., Moore, M. & Burton, J. (2002). Measuring Success: Evaluation Strategies for Distance Eduaction. Educase Quaterly, 1, 20-26.

Looney, J.P. & Nissen, M.E. (2006). Computational Modeling and Analysis of Networked Organizational Planning in a Coalition Maritime Strike Environment. In *Proceedings* 2006 Command and Control Research and Technology Symposium, San Diego, CA.

Looney, J.P. & Nissen, M.E. (2007). Organizational Metacognition: the Importance of Knowing the Knowledge Network. In *Proceedings* Hawaii International Conference on System Sciences, Waikoloa, HI.

Lowe, J., & Taylor, P. (1998). R&D and technology purchase through licence agreements: complementary strategies and complementary assets. *R&D Management,* 28(4), 263-278.

Loyarte, E., & Rivera, E. (2007). Communities of practice: a model for their cultivation. *Journal of Knowledge Management 11*(3), 67-77.

Lu, M., & Guimaraes, T. (1989). A guide to selecting expert systems applications. *Journal of Information Systems Management,* (Spring), 6(2), 8-15.

Lubbe, S. (2007). *Managing information communication technology investments in successful enterprise.* Harrisburg, PA.: Idea Group Inc.

Luecke, R. (2006). Make better decisions. *Harvard Management Update*, 11(4), 3-5.

Lundgren, A. (1995). *Technological Innovation and Network Evolution.* London: Routledge.

Lutz, J. & Ryan, C. (1993). Hotels and the businesswoman - An analysis of businesswomen's perceptions of hotel services. *Tourism Management*, 14(5), 349-356.

Lytras. M.D., & Pouloudi, A. (2006). Towards the development of a novel taxonomy of knowledge management systems form a learning perspective: an integrated approach to learning and knowledge infrastructures. *Journal of Knowledge Management, 10*(6), 64-80.

Madhok, A., & Tallman, S. (1998). Resources, transactions and rents, managing value through interfirm collaborative relationships. *Organization Science*, 9 (3), 326-339.

Maguire, S., Koh, S.C. and Magrys, A. (2007): "The adoption of e-business and knowledge management in SMEs". Benchmarking, an International Journal, 14(1), pp. 37-58.

Maguire, S., Koh, S.C.L, & Magrys, A. (2007). The adoption of e-business and knowledge management in SMEs. *Benchmarking. An International Journal, 14*(1), 37-58.

Majchrzak, A., Malhotra, A. & John, R. (2005). Perceived individual collaboration know-how development through information technology-enabled contextualization: Evidence from distributed teams. *Information Systems Research*, 16(1), 9-27.

Malhotra, Y. (1997). Knowledge management in Inquiring Organizations, in the *Proceedings of 3rd Americas Conference on Information Systems*. Philosophy of Information Systems Mini-track (pp. 293-295). Indianapolis.

Man, de, A-P. (2006). *The network economy.* Northampton, MA.: Edward Elgar Publishing.

Manente, M. & Furlan, M. (1998). Quality in the Macroeconomics System of Tourism. *Revue de Tourisme*, 2, 17-28.

Manju K. Ahuja & Kathleen M. Carley (1992). Network structure in Virtual Organizations. *Journal of computer-Mediated Communication, 3, 4.*

Mantyla, K. (2000). Evaluating Program Success. En K. Mantyla, *Distance Learning Yearbook* (pp. 259-287). New York: McGraw-Hill,

Marcelo, C. (2000). Formación, empleo y nuevas tecnologías. In C. Marcelo (coord), D. Puente, M.A. Ballesteros & A. Palazón. *E-learning-Teleformacion,*

Diseño, desarrollo y evaluación de la formación a través de Internet (pp. 9-18). Barcelona: Ediciones Gestión 2000, S.A.

March, J.G. (1991), "Exploration and exploitation in organizational learning". *Organization Science*, 2 (1), pp. 71-87.

March, J.G. (1991). Exploration and exploitation in organizational learning. *Organization Science, 2*, 71-87.

Markus, M. L. (2001): "Toward a theory of knowledge reuse: Types of knowledge reuse situations and factors in reuse success". *Journal of Management Information Systems*, 18(1), pp. 57-93.

Mars, D. (1998). *Comparing policy networks.* Buckingham: Open University Press.

Martin, C. (1999). *Net future.* New York: McGraw-Hill.

Martín, D. (2000). Metodología de Calidad en Turismo, in Turismo: comercialización de productos, gestión de organizaciones, aeropuertos y protección de la naturaleza. In Tirant lo Blanch (Ed.), *II Congreso Universidad y Empresa, Turismo: comercialización de productos, gestión de organizaciones, aeropuertos y protección de la naturaleza* (pp. 429-447), Benicasim.

Martin, J. (1990). *Future Developments in Telecommunications.* New York: Telecom Library.

Martínez, I; Ruiz, J. & Ruiz, C. (2001). *Aprendizaje organizacional en PYMES.* Paper presented at the XI ACEDE National Congress, Zaragoza.

Martínez, M.T., Fouletier, P., Park, K.H. & Favrel, J. (2001). Virtual enterprise: organisation, evolution and control. *International Journal of Production Economics,* 74.

Martínez, M.T., Fouletier, P., Park, K.H., Favrel, J. (2001). Virtual enterprise: organisation, evolution and control. *International Journal of Production Economics, 74,* 225-238.

Maruyama, M. (1987). Communication between mindscape types. In *Decision Making About Decision Making,*

Metamodels, and Metasystems. J. P. van Gigch, J. P. (Ed.), Cambridge, Mass: Abacus Press, p. 91.

Marvin, C. (1987). Information and history. In *The Ideology of the Information Age.* Slack, J. D., & F.Fejes, F. (Ed.), Norwood, NJ: Ablex Publishing Corp.

Massy, J. (2002). Quality and e-learning in Europe. Bizmedia.

Mateo, J. (2000). La evaluación del profesorado y la gestión de la calidad de la educación. Hacia un modelo comprensivo de evaluación sistemática de la docencia. *Revista de Investigación Educativa, 18 (1),* 7-34

Matusik, S., & Heeley, M. (2005). Absorptive Capacity in the Software Industry: Identifying Dimensions that Affect Knowledge and Knowledge Creation Activities. *Journal of Management, 31,* 549-572.

Mayer, R., Davis, J., and Shoorman, F. (1995). "An Integrative Model Of Organizational Trust," *Academy Of Management Review* (20:3), pp. 709-734.

Mayer, R.C., Davis, J.H., & Schoorman, F.D. (1995). An integrative model of organizational trust. *Academy of Management Review, 20,* 709-734.

McAdam, R. & Walker, T. (2004). Evaluating the best value framework in UK local government services. *Public Administration and Development, 24* (3), 183-196.

McArdle, G.E. (1999). *Training Design and Delivery.* Alexandria: V.A. American Society for Training and Development

McCLure, D. (2000). Electronic government: federal initiatives are evolving rapidly but they face significant challenges. Retrieved from: http://www.gao.gov/new.items/a200179t.pdf

McDermott, M. F. (2002). *CLEC: An insiders look at the rise and fall of competition in the local exchange competition.* Rockport, ME: Penobscot Press.

McDermott, R. (1999). Why information technology inspired but cannot deliver knowledge management. *California Management Review, 41,* 103-117.

McDonald, D. W. and Ackerman, M.S. (1998). Just talk to me: A field study of expertise location. Proceedings of the 1998 ACM Conference on Computer Supported Cooperative Work (CSCW).

McElroy, M. (2002). Social innovation capital. *Journal of Intellectual Capital, 3,* 30-39.

McEvely, B., & Zaheer, A. (1999). Bridging ties: A source of firm heterogeneity in competitive capabilities. *Strategic Management Journal, 20,* 1133-1156.

McEvily, B. & Zaheer, A. (1999). Bridging ties: A source of firm heterogeneity in competitive capabilities. *Strategic Management Journal, 20,* 1133-1156.

McGill, M.E. & Slocul, J.W. (1993). Unlearning the organization. *Organizational Dynamics, 22 (2),* 67-79.

McGill, M.E. y Slocum, J.W. (1993), "Unlearning the organization". *Organizational Dynamics,* 22 (2), pp. 67-79.

McGrath, J. E. (1984). *Groups: interaction and performance.* Englewood Cliffs, NJ: Prentice Hall.

McGrath, J.E. & Argote, L. (2002). Group Processes in Organizational Contexts. In M.A. How & R.S. Tindale (eds.). *Blackwell Handbook of Social Psychology.* Oxford, UK: Blackwell.

McHugh, P., Merli, G. & Wheeler III, W. (1995). Beyond *Business Process Reengineering – Towards the Holonic Entreprise.* Chichester: John Wiley & Sons.

McIvor, R., McHugh, M., and Cadden, C. (2002). "Internet Technologies: Supporting Transparency in the Public Sector," *The International Journal of Public Sector Management* (15:3), pp. 170-187.

McKnight, B., & Bontis, N. (2002). E-improvisation: Collaborative groupware technology expands the reach and effectiveness of organizational improvisation. *Knowledge and Process Management, 9,* 219-227.

McKnight, D.H., Cummings, L.L., & Chervany, N.L. (1998). Initial trust formation in new organizational relationships. *Academy of Management Review, 23,* 473-490.

McMillan, K., Money, K., Money, A. and Downing, S. (2005). "Relationship marketing in the not-for-profit sector: an extension and application of the commitment-trust theory," *Journal of Business Research* (58), pp. 806-818.

McWhirter, B. (1993). Disposable Workers of America. *Time*, March 29, 41-43.

MCYT & MAP (Ministerio de Ciencia y Tecnología & Ministerio de Administración Pública) (2003). Plan de Choque para el Impulso de la Administración Electrónica en España. Retrieved from http://www.csi.map.es/csi/pdf/plan.pdf

Merali, Y. (2002). The role of boundaries in knowledge process. *European Journal of Information Systems*, 11(1), 47-60.

Merino, C. (2004). La Inteligencia Organizativa como Dinamizador del Capital Intelectual. *Revista Puzzle*, 3(14), 4-10.

Meroño-Cerdan, A.L., Lopez-Nicolas, C., & Sabater-Sánchez, R. (2007). Knowledge management strategy diagnosis from KM instruments use. *Journal of Knowledge Management, 11*(2), 60-72.

Metcalf, J. & Shimamura, A. (Eds.). (1994). *Metacognition: Knowing about Knowing* Cambridge, MA: MIT Press.

Meyer-Krahmer, F., & Schmoch, U. (1998). Science-based technologies: university-industry interactions in four fields. *Research Policy, 27*(8), 835-851.

Meyerson, D., Weick, K.E., & Kramer, R.M. (1996). Swift trust in temporary groups. In R.M. Kramer & T.R. Tyler (Eds.), *Trust in organizations: Frontiers of theory and research*. Thousands Oaks, CA: Sage Publications.

Michaud, J.-L., Planque, V. &. Barbaza, Y. (1991). Tourisme qualitatif - Ses Conditions et ses Chances Futures sur le Plan Economique, Social et Ecologique. In AIEST (Ed.), *41ème Congrès de l'Association International d'Experts Scientifiques du Tourisme* (pp. 63-78), Mahé, Seychelles.

Middleton, V. T. (1994). The marketing and Management of Tourism destinations: research directions for the next decade, In AIEST (Ed.) *44ème Congrès de l'Association International d'Experts Scientifiques du Tourisme* (pp. 115-141), Vienne, Austria.

Miguéns, J. & Costa, C. (2006). Tourism Network: new methodologies, potential approach to tourism analysis. In School of Management, University of Surrey (Ed.), Proceedings of *Cutting Edge Research in Tourism: New directions, Challenges and Applications*, School of Management, University of Surrey, UK.

Mills, D. (1991). *Rebirth of the corporation*. New York: John Wiley and Sons, Inc.

Minar, N., Burkhar, R., Langton C., & Askemnazi, M. (1996). *The Swarm Simulation System: A toolkit for building multi-agent simulations*. Retrieved from http://alumni.media.mit.edu/~nelson/research/swarm/.

Miner, A.S. y Mezías, S.J. (1996), "Ugly duckling no more: Past and futures of organizational learning research". *Organization Science*, 7 (1), pp. 88-99.

Minsky, M. (1985). *The society of mind*. New York: Simon and Schuster.

Mintzberg, H. (1973). *The nature of managerial work*. Englewood Cliffs, NJ: Prentice-Hall.

Mintzberg, H., D., Raisinghani, & A. Theoret, A. (1976). The structure of unstructured decision processes. *Administrative Science Quarterly*, (21), 246-275.

Mintzberg, H., Raisinghani, D. & Theoret, A. (1976). The structure of "unstructured" decision processes. *Administrative Science Quarterly*, 21, 246-275.

Mitchell, V. (1999). "Consumer Perceived Risk: Conceptualisations and Models," *European Journal of Marketing* (33:1/2), pp. 163-195.

Mitchell, W., & Singh, K. (1996). Survival of business using collaborative relationships to commercialize complex goods. *Strategic Management Journal*, 17, 169-195.

Mohr, J.J., & Spekman, R.(1994). Characteristics of partnership success: partnership attributes, communication behaviour, and conflict resolution techniques. *Strategic Management Journal, 15*, 135-152.

Molina, A. & Flores, M. (2000). Exploitation of business opportunities: the role of the virtual enterprise broker. In Kluwer Academic Publishers (Ed.), *International Federation for Information Processing; Working Conference on Infrastructures for Virtual Organisations*, Florianopolis.

Monge, P., J. Edwards, and K. Kirste. (1978). The determinants of communication structure in large organizations: a review of research. In *Communication Yearbook*. Ed. B. Ruben. New Brunswick, NJ: Transactions Books, 311- 331.

Montes, J.M., Pérez, S. & Vázquez, C.J. (2002). *Influencia de la cultura organizativa sobre el aprendizaje: Efectos sobre la competitividad*. Paper presented at XII ACEDE National Congress, Palma de Mallorca.

Montes, J.M.; Pérez, S.; Vázquez, C. (2006), "Managing knowledge management: The link between culture and organizational learning". *Journal of Knowledge Management* (forthcoming).

Moon, M.J. & Norris, D.F. (2005). Does managerial orientation matter? The adoption of reinventing government and e-government at the municipal level. *Information Systems Journal, 15* (1), 43-60.

Moon, M.J. (2002): The evolution of E-Government among municipalities: Rhetoric or reality?. *Public Administration Review, 62* (4), 424-433.

Moor, A., & Weigand, H. (2007). Formalizing the evolution of virtual communities. *Information Systems, 32(2)*, 223-247.

Moor, A., Weigand, H. (2007). Formalizing the evolution of virtual communities. *Information Systems, 32*, 223-247.

Moran, K. & Ghoshal, S. (1996). Value Creation by Firms. *Academy of Management Best Paper Proceedings*, 41-45.

Moreley, I. E. & Stephenson, G. M. (1969). Interpersonal and interparty exchange: a laboratory simulation of an industrial negotiations at the plant level. *British Journal of Psychology*, 60, 543-545.

Moreley, I. E. & Stephenson, G. M. (1970). Iformality in experimental negotiations: a validity study. *British Journal of Psychology*, 61, 383.

Morgan, R., and Hunt, S. (1994). "The Commitment - Trust Theory of Relationship Marketing," *Journal of Marketing* (58:3), pp. 20-38.

Morris, M. W., Nadler, J., Kurtzberg, T., & Thompson, L. (2002). Schmooze or lose: social friction and lubrication in e-mail negotations. *Group Dynamics*. 6(1).

Mowery, D.C., Oxley J. & Silverman, B.S. (1996). Strategic alliances and interfirm knowledge transfer. *Strategic Management Journal, 17*(Winter special number), 77–91.

Mowshowith, A. (1986). Social dimensions of office automation. In M. Yovitz, *Advances in Computers (v.25)*. New York: Academic Press.

Mowshowitz , A. (1997). *Virtual organization*. Communications of the ACM. 40(9), 30-37.

Mowshowitz, A. (1981). On approaches to the study of social issues in   computing. *Communications of the ACM*, 24, (3), 146.

Mowshowitz, A. (1997). Virtual organization. *Communications of the ACM* 40(9), 30-7.

Mundim, A. P. & Bremer, C. F. (2000). Design of a computer-supported cooperative environment for small and medium enterprises. In Kluwer Academic Publishers *(Ed.), International Federation for Information Processing; Working Conference on Infrastructures for Virtual Organisations*, Florianopolis.

Muniz, A., and O'Guinn, T.C. "Brand Communities," *Journal of consumer research* (27), 2001, pp. 412-432.

Murray, S. (2003). *A quantitative examination to determine if knowledge sharing activities, given the appropriate richness lead to knowledge transfer, and if implementation factors influence the use of these knowledge sharing activities*. Doctoral dissertation. University Microfilms.

Muthusamy, S. K.; Palanisamy, R. and MacDonald, J. (2005). "Developing knowledge management systems (KMS) for ERP implementation: A case study from service sector". *Journal of Services Research*, pp. 66-92.

Nahapiet, J. & Ghoshal, S. (1998). Social Capital, Intellectual Capital, and the Organizational Advantage. *Academy of Management Review, 23*, 242-266.

Nahapiet, J., & Ghoshal, S (1998). Social capital, intellectual capital, and the organizational advantage. *The Academy of Management Review, 23*(2), 242-266.

Nahapiet, J., & Ghoshal, S. (1998). Social capital, intellectual capital, and the organizational advantage. *Academy of Management Review, 23*, 242-266.

Nance, R. E., & Sargent, R. G. (2002). Perspectives on the evolution of simulation. *Operations Research*, 50(1), 161-172.

Naughton, J. (1999). *A brief history of the future: The origins of the Internet*. London: Weidenfield and Nicholson.

Naylor, J.,(1964). Accuracy and variability of information sources of determiners. *Journal of Applied Psychology*, (48), 43-49.

Neff, D. (2007). Local wireless networks- a prerequisite for the future. *Public Management, 89* (2), 10-14.

Negash, S. & Gray, P. (2003). Business intelligence. In Proceedings of *Ninth Americas Conference on Information Systems*.

Negroponte, N. (1995). *Being digital*. New York, NY: Knopf.

Nelson, R.R. and Winter, S. (1982). *An Evolutionary Theory Economic Change* Cambridge, MA: Harvard University Press.

Nevis, E.C., Dibella, A.J. & Gould, J.M. (1995). Understanding organizations as learning systems. *Sloan Management Review, 36 (2)*, 73-85.

Nevis, E.C.; Dibella, A.J.; Gould, J.M. (1995), "Understanding organizations as learning systems". *Sloan Management Review*, 36 (2), pp. 73-85.

New Paradigm Resources Group, Inc. (2002). *Measuring the economic impact of the Telecommunications Act of 1996: Telecommunication capital expenditures*. Chicago: Author.

Nicolini, D. y Meznar, M.B. (1995), "The social construction of organizational learning: concepts and practical issues in the field". *Human Relations*, 48 (7), pp. 727-746.

Nielsen, A. P. (2006). Understanding dynamic capabilities through knowledge management. *Journal of Knowledge Management, 10*(4), 59-71.

Nieto, M., & Quevedo, P. (2005). Variables estructurales, capacidad de absorción y esfuerzo innovador en las empresas manufactureras españolas. *Revista Europea de Dirección y Economía de la Empresa, 14*(1), 25-44.

Nissen, M.E. (2002). An Extended Model of Knowledge-Flow Dynamics. *Communications of the Association for Information Systems, 8*(18), 251-266.

Nissen, M.E. (2006a). Dynamic Knowledge Patterns to Inform Design: A Field Study of Knowledge Stocks and Flows in an Extreme Organization. *Journal of Management Information Systems*, 22(3), 225-263.

Nissen, M.E. (2006b). *Harnessing Knowledge Dynamics: Principled Organizational Knowing & Learning* Hershey, PA: Idea Group Publishing.

Nissen, M.E. (2007). Knowledge Management and Global Cultures: Elucidation through an Institutional Knowledge-Flow Perspective. *Knowledge and Process Management* 14(3), 211-225.

Nissen, M.E., Kamel, M.N. & Sengupta, K.C. (2000). Integrated Analysis and Design of Knowledge Systems and Processes. *Information Resources Management Journal, 13*(1), 24-43.

Nonaka I. & Takeucki H. (1995). *The Knowledge-creating Company: How Japanese Companies Create the Dynamics of Innovation*. New York: Oxford University Press.

Nonaka, I . (1994), "A dynamic theory of organizational knowledge creation". *Organization Science*, 5 (1), pp. 14-37.

Nonaka, I. & Nishiguchi, T. (2000). *Knowledge emergence: social, technical, and evolutionary dimensions of knowledge creation*. New York: Oxford Press.

Nonaka, I. & Takeuchi, H. (1995). *The Knowledge Creating Company: How Japanese Companies Create the Dynamics of Innovation. Oxford University Press, Nueva York*

Nonaka, I. & Takeuchi, H. (1995). *The Knowledge-Creating Company: How Japanese Companies Create the Dynamics of Innovation*. New York: Oxford University Press.

Nonaka, I. (1988), "Creating organizational order out of chaos: Self-renewal in Japanese firms". *California Management Review*, 30 (3), pp. 57-73.

Nonaka, I. (1991), "The knowledge-creating company". *Harvard Business Review*, 69 (6), pp. 96-104.

Nonaka, I. (1991). *The knowledge creating company*. Massachusettes: Harvard Business Review.

Nonaka, I. (1991). The Knowledge-creating Company. *Harvard Business Review*, *69*, 96-104.

Nonaka, I. (1991). The Knowledge-Creating Company. *Harvard Business Review, 69 (6)*, 96-105.

Nonaka, I. (1994). A dynamic theory of organizational knowledge creation. *Organization Science, 5*(1), 14-37.

Nonaka, I. (1994). A dynamic theory of organizational knowledge creation. *Organization Science, 5*, 14-37.

Nonaka, I. (1994). A dynamic theory of organizational knowledge creation. *Organization Science, 5* (1), 14-37.

Nonaka, I. (1994). A Dynamic Theory of Organizational Knowledge Creation. *Organization Science, 5*(1), 14-37.

Nonaka, I. (1994). A Dynamic Theory of Organizational Knowledge Creation. *Organization Science, 5*(1), 14-37.

Nonaka, I., & Konno, N. (1998). The concept of Ba: Building a foundation for knowledge creation. *California Management Review (Special Issue on Knowledge and the Firm), 40*(3), 40-54.

Nonaka, I., & Takeuchi, H. (1995). *The Knowledge-Creating Company: How Japanese Companies Create the Dynamics of Innovation*. New York: Oxford University Press.

Nonaka, I., & Takeuchi, H. (1995). *The knowledge-creating company*. New York: Oxford University Press.

Nonaka, I., & Takeuchi, H. (1995). *The Knowledge-creating Company: How Japanese Companies Create the Dynamics of Innovation*. New York: Oxford University Press.

Nonaka, I., & Takeuchi, H. (1995). *The knowledge-creating company: How Japanese companies create the dynamics of innovation*. New York: Oxford University Press.

Nonaka, I., & Takeuchi, H. (1995). *The knowledge-creating company - how Japanese companies create the dynamic of innovation*. Oxford University Press.

Nonaka, I., Takeuchi, H. (1995): "The knowledge-Creating Company. How Japanese Companies Create the Dynamics of Innovation". Oxford University Press, New York.

Nonaka, I., Toyama, R. & Cono, N. (2000). SECI, Ba and Leadership: a Unified Model of Dynamic Knowledge Creation. *Long Range Planning*, 33: 5-34.

Nonaka, I., Toyama, R., & Konno, N. (2001). SECI, Ba and leadership: A unified model of dynamic knowledge creation. In I. Nonaka & D. J. Teece (Eds.), *Managing industrial knowledge: Creation, transfer and utilization*. London: Sage Publications.

Nonaka, I., Toyama, R., & Nagata, A. (2000). A firm as a knowledge creating entity: a new perspective on the theory of the firm. *Industrial and Corporate Change*, 9 (1), 1-20.

Nonaka, I.; Byosiere, P.; Borucki, C.; Konno, N. (1994), "Organizational knowledge creation theory: A first comprehensive test". *International Business Review, 3* (4), pp. 337-351.

Nonaka, I.; Toyama, R. & Cono, N. (2000). SECI, Ba and Leadership: A Unified Model of Dynamic Knowledge Creation. *Long Range Planning, 33*, 5-34.

Nonaka, I.; Toyama, R.; Knno, C. (2000), "SECI, ba and leadership: A unified model of dynamic knowledge creation". *Long Range Planning*, 33 (1), pp. 5-34.

Nooteboom, B., Van Haverbeke, W., Duysters, G., Gilsing, V., & Van den Oord, A. (2007). Optimal cognitive distance and absorptive capacity. *Research Policy, 36*, 1016-1034.

Norris, D.F.; Fletcher, P.D. & Holden, S.H. (2001). *Is your local government plugged in? Highlights of the 2000 electronic government survey.* Maryland, US: International City/County Management Association (ICMA) and Public Technology, Inc. (PTI).

Nowell, A. (1973). Production systems: models of control structures. In *Visual Information Processing.* Ed. W. Chase. New York: Academic Press.

Nowell, A., A. Perils,A. & Simon, H. (1987). What is computer science? *Science,* (157), 1373-1374.

Nunnally, J.C. (1978). *Psychometric Theory*, McGraw-Hill, 2ª ed., New York.

Nunnaly, J.C., and Bernstein, I.H. (1994). *Psychometric theory*, McGraw-Hill, New York.

Nurosis M.J. (1993). *SPSS. Statistical Data Analysis*, Spss Inc.

O'Dell, C. (2008). *Web 2.0 and knowledge management.* American Productivity & Quality Center (APQC). Retrieved from http://www.apqc.org.

O'Hara-Deveraux, M., & Johansen, R. (1994). *Global work: bridging distance, culture, and time.* San Francisco, CA: Jossey-Bass.

O'Neill, M. , Watson, H. & Mckenna, M (1994). Service Quality in the Northern Ireland Hospitality Industry. *Managing Service Quality*, 4(3), 36-40.

O'Reilly, C. A. (1982). Variations in decision makers' use of information sources: the impact of quality and accessibility of information. *Academy of Management Journal*, (25), 756-771.

O'Reilly, C. A., J., Chatman,J. A. & J. C. Anderson, J. C. (1978). Message flow and decision making. In *Handbook of Organizational Communication.* Joblin, F. M., *et al.* (Ed.) Newbury Park, CA: SAGE.

O'Riley on Media 2004, http://en.wikipedia.org/wiki/Web_2, Retrieved on April, 11, 2007.

Okkonen, J. (2007). Democracy in management – the new coming of MBO via organisational dialogue. *Benchmarking: An International Journal, 14*(1), 7-21.

Oliver, A.L. (2001), Strategic alliances and the learning lifecycle of biotechnology firms. *Organization Studies, 22*, 467–489.

Oliver, M. (1998) (Ed.) Innovation in the Evaluation of Learning Technology. London. University of North London.

Oltra, M. J., & Flor, M. (2003). The impact of Technological Opportunities and Innovative Capabilities on Firms. *Creativity & Innovation Management, 12*(3), 137-144.

Ordoñez, P. (2001). Relevant Experiences on Measuring and Reporting Intellectual Capital in European Pioneering Firms. In N. Bontis & C. Cheng (eds.) *World Congress on Intellectual Capital Reading.* New York: Butterworth-Heinemann.

Ordóñez, P. (2004). Knowledge flow transfers in multinational corporations: knowledge properties and implications for management. *Journal of Knowledge Management, 8*(6), 105-116.

Ordóñez, P. (2004). Knowledge flow transfers in multinational corporations: knowledge properties and implications for management. *Journal of Knowledge Management*, 8(6), 105-116.

Otto, J. E. & Ritchie, J. R. (1995). Exploring the Quality of the Service Experience: A Theoretical and Empirical Analysis. *Advances in Services Marketing and Management*, 4, 37-61.

Otto, J. E. & Ritchie, J. R. (1996). The service experience in tourism. *Tourism Management*, 17(3), 165-174.

Ouchi, W.G. (1981). *Theory Z: How American business can meet the Japanese challenge*. Reading, MA: Addison-Wesley.

Paauwe, J., & R. Williams (2001). Seven key issues for management development. *The Journal of Management Development, 20*(2), 90-105.

Paepcke, A. (1996, May). Digital libraries: Searching is not enough. *D-Lib Magazine*.

Palacios, D., & Garrigós (2003). Validating and measuring IC in the biotechnology and telecommunication industries. *Journal of Intellectual Capital, 4*(3), 332-347.

Palme, J. (1995). *Electronic mail*. Norwood, MA: Artech House Publishers.

Palmer, R. (1993). *Write in style – a guide to good English*. London: E and FN Spon.

Pan, S.L. & Leidner, D.E. (2003). Bridging communities of practice with information technology in pursuit of global knowledge sharing. *Journal of Strategic Information Systems, 12*, 71-88.

Papadopoulos, S. I. (1989). Greek Marketing Strategies in the European Tourism Market. *The Service Industries Journal*, 9(2), 297-314.

Parker, E. (1976). Social implications of computer/telecoms systems. *Telecommunications Policy*, 1, (December), 3-20.

Passiante, G., & Andriani, P., (2000). Modelling the learning environment of virtual knowledge networks: some empirical evidence. *International Journal of Innovation Management, 4*(1), 1-31.

Pávez, A. A. (2000). Modelo de implantación de gestión del conocimiento y tecnologías de la información para la generación de ventajas competitivas. Retrieved April 1, 2007, from http://www.gestiondelconocimiento.com/documentos2/apavez/gdc.htm

Pavlin, S. (2006). Community of practice in a small research institute. *Journal of Knowledge Management, 10*(4), 136-144.

Pavlin, S. (2006): Community of practice in a small research institute. *Journal of Knowledge Management, 10(4)*, 136-144.

Pavlovich, K. (2003). The evolution and transformation of a tourism destination network: the Waitomo Caves, New Zealand. *Tourism Management*, 24(2), 203-216.

Pearce, D., (1989). Tourism Development. New York: Longman.

Peat, F. David. (1987). *Synchronicity: the bridge between matter and mind*. New York: Bantam Books.

Pentland, B.T. (1995). Information systems and organizational learning: The social epistemology of organizational knowledge systems. *Accounting, Management and Information Technologies, 5*, 1-21.

Perez, F. (1994). The case for a deregulated free market telecommunications industry. *IEEE Communications Magazine, 32*(12), 63-70.

Pérez-Soltero, A. (1997). Modelo para la representación de una memoria organizacional utilizando herramientas computacionales de Internet. Doctoral dissertation, University of Monterrey, Mexico.

Perrin, A., Rolland, N., & Stanley ,T. (2007). Achieving best practices transfer across countries. *Journal of Knowledge Management, 11*(3), 156-166.

Peteraf, M.A. (1993). The Cornerstone of Competitive Advantage: A Resource-Based View. *Strategic Management Journal*, 14, 179-191.

Phan, D.D. (2003). E-business development for competitive advantages: a case study, *Information & Management, 40*, 581-590.

Phene, A., Fladmoe-Lindquist, K. & Marsh, L. (2006). Breakthrough innovations in the U.S. biotechnology industry: the effects of technological space and geographic origin. *Strategic Management Journal, 27*(4), 369-388.

Pickering, J.M., & King, J.L. (1995). Hardwiring weak ties: Interorganizational computer-mediated communication, occupational communities, and organizational change. *Organizational Science, 6*, 479-486.

Pieterson, W., Ebbers, W., & Van Dijk, J. (2005). The opportunities and barriers of user profiling in the public sector. In *Proceedings of the 2005 EGOV*, Copenhagen, Denmark.

Pine II, B. J. & Gilmore, J. H. (1999). *The Experience Economy – work is theatre & every business a stage*, Boston: Harvard Business School Press.

Pineda, P. (2002). Formació, transferència i avaluació: un triangle complex. *Revista Econòmica de Catalunya, 44*, 79-89.

Pitta, D.A. and Fowler, D. (2005). "Online consumer communities and their value to new product developers," *Journal of Product & Brand Management* (14:5), pp. 283-291.

Pizam, A. (1991). The Management of Quality Tourism Destinations, In AIEST (Ed.) *41ème Congrès de l'Association International d'Experts Scientifiques du Tourisme* (pp. 79-87), Mahé, Seychelles.

Pizam, A., Neumann, Y. &. Reichel, A. (1978). Dimensions of Tourist Satisfaction with a Destination Area, *Annals of Tourism Research, 5*(3), 314-322.

Plaz, R. & González, N. (2005). La gestión del conocimiento organizativo: dinámicas de agregación de valor en la organización. *Economía Industrial, 357*, 41-62.

Poler R., & Tormo G. (2003, November). Business Process Integration, Knowledge Management and Decision Support Tools in Supply Chain of Industrial SMEs. Paper presented at CONex, Donostia.

Poler, R. & Sanchis, R. (2006). Deliverable D10.4. Dissemination of courses on Interoperability. Version 1. *IST-1-508011: Interoperability Research for Networked Enterprises Applications and Software (INTEROP)* Retrieved April 5, 2007, from http://interop-noe.org/backoffice/workspaces/Reviewers/documents/M36/dtg10.4/

Poler, R. (2006). Deliverable D10.3. Training courses on Interoperability. *IST-1-508011: Interoperability Research for Networked Enterprises Applications and Software (INTEROP)* Retrieved March 2, 2007, from http://interop-noe.org/backoffice/deliv/D10.3/

Poon, A. (1993). Tourism, technology and competitive strategies. UK: Cab International.

Porat, Marc. (1977). *The information economy*. Washington, DC: US Office of Telecommunications.

Porter, M. E. (1994). The role of location in competition. *Journal of the Economics of Business*, 1(1).

Porter, M.E. (1980). *Competitive Strategy: Techniques for Analysing Industries and Competitors*. New York: Free Press.

Porter, M.E. (1990). The competitive advantage of nations. *Harvard Business Review*, March-April 1990.

Porter, M.E. (1998). *On Competition*. Harvard Business School Press.

Poster, M. (1990). *The mode of information*. Chicago: The University of Chicago Press.

Powell, S. G., & Baker, K. R. (2007). *Management science: The art of modeling with spreadsheets*. New York, NY: Wiley.

Powell, W. B., Marar, A., Gelfand, J., & Bowers, S. (2002). Implementing real-time optimization models: A case application from the motor carrier industry. *Operations Research*, 50(4), 571-581.

Powell, W.W. (1998). Learning from collaboration: knowledge and networks in the biotechnology and pharmaceutical industries. *California Management Review, 40*(3), 228–240.

Powell, W.W., Koput K.W., & Smith-Doerr, L. (1996). Interorganizational collaboration and the locus of innovation, networks of learning in biotechnology. *Administrative Science Quarterly*, 41 (1), 116-145.

Powell, W.W., Koput, K.W. & Smith-Doerr, L. (1996). Interorganizational collaboration and the locus of innovation: Networks of learning in biotechnology. *Administrative Science Quarterly, 41*, 116–145.

Power, D. J. (2001). Supporting Decision-Makers: An Expanded Framework, In A. Harriger (Ed.), *Informing Science Conference, Krakow, Poland*, 431-436.

Power, D. J. (2002). *Decision Support Systems: Concepts and resources for managers.* Westport, CT: Greenwood/ Quorum.

Power, D. J. (2004). Decision Support Systems: From the Past to the Future, In Proceedings of the *2004 Americas Conference on Information Systems*, New York, NY, 2025-2031.

Powers, W. T. (1973). *Behavior: the control of perception.* Chicago: Aldine Publishing Company.

Prahalad, C.K. & Hamel, G. (1990). The Core Competence of the Corporation. *Harvard Business Review*, 86.

Preece, J. (2000). *Online communities: Designing usability, supporting sociability.* Chichester: John Viley and Sons.

Preece, J. (2000). *Online Communities: Designing Usability, Supporting Sociability.* New York, NY: John Wiley & Sons.

Pricher, W. (1987). Tours through the back-country of imperfectly informed society. In *The Ideology of the Information Age.* Slack, J. D., & Fejes, F.(Ed.). Norwood,NJ: Ablex Publishing Corp.

Prokopiadou G., Paptheodorou C. & Moschopoulos D. 2004. Integrating knowledge management tools for government information. *Government Information Quarterly, 21*, 170-198.

Prokopiadou, G.; Papatheodorou, C. and Moschopoulos, D. (2004). "Integrating knowledge management tools for government information". *Government Information Quarterly*, 21(2), pp. 170-198.

Pucik, V. (1988). Strategic alliances, organizational learning and competitive advantage: the HRM agenda. *Human Resource Management*, vol. 27, n. 1, 77-94.

Pundt, H. and Bishr, Y. (2002): "Domain ontologies for data sharing: An example from environmental monitoring using field GIS". *Computers and Geosciences*, 28, pp. 95–102.

Purvis, R.L., Sambamurthy, V., & Zmud, R.W. (2001). The assimilation of knowledge platforms in organizations: An empirical investigation. *Organization Science, 12*, 117-135.

Putnam, R. (2000). *Bowling Alone: The Collapse and Revival of American Community.* New York: Touchstone.

Putnam, R. (2000). *Bowling alone: the collapse and revival of American community.* New York: Simon and Shuster.

Pyke, F. & Sengenberger, W. (1992). *Industrial districts and Local Economic Regeneration.* Geneve: International Institute for Labour Studies.

Pyöriä, P. (2007). Informal organizational culture: The foundation of knowledge workers' performance. *Journal of Knowledge Management, 11*(3), 16-30.

Quatroop, L. (1987). The information age: ideal and reality. In *The Ideology of the Information Age.* Ed. J. D. Slack, D. J. & Fejes, F. (Ed.). Norwood, NJ: Ablex Publishing Corp.

Quin, J.B., Anderson, P., & Finkelstein, S. (1996). Managing professional intellect: Making the most of the best, *Harvard Business Review, 72*(2), 71-81.

Quinn, C.N. (2006). Making It Matter to the Learner: e-Motional e-Learning. *Practical Applications of Technology for Learning.* Retrieved January 13, 2007, from http://www.quinnovation.com/eMotional-eLearning.pdf

Quinn, J. B. (1992). *Intelligence Enterprise.* New York: Free Press.

Quinn, J.B., Anderson, P. & Finkelstein S. (1996). Managing professional intellect: making the most of the best. *Harvard Business Review, 74*(2), 71-80.

Quinn, J.B., Anderson, P. & Finkelstein, S. (1996). Managing professional intellect: Making the most of the best. *Harvard Business Review, 74*(2), 71-80.

Rahman, Z., & Bhattachryya, S. K. (2002). Virtual organisation: A stratagem. *Singapore Management Review, 24*(2), 29-45.

Ramussen, K. & Davidson, G.V. (1996). *Dimensions of learning styles and their influence on performance in hypermedia lessons.* CD-ROM Proceedings from the annual ED-MEDIA/ED-TELECOM conference. Article n° 385.

Randeree, E. (2006). Knowledge management: securing the future. *Journal of Knowledge Management, 10*(4), 145-156.

Rao, V. S. & Jarvenpaa, S. L. (1991). Computer support of groups: Theory-based models for SDSS research. *Management Science, 37*(10), 1347-1362.

Rasmussen, L.B., & Wangel, A. (2007). Work in the virtual enterprise – creating identities, building, trust, and sharing knowledge. *AI & Soc, 21*, 184-199.

Rassmussen, D., Megbolugbe, I., & Morgan, B. (1997). The reverse mortgage as an asset management tool. *Housing Policy Debate, 8*(1), 173-194.

Rastogi, P.N. (2000). "Knowledge Management and Intellectual Capital. The new virtuos reality of Competitiveness". Human Systems Management, 19.

Reagans, R., & McEvily, B. (2003). Network structure and knowledge transfer: The effects of cohesion and range. *Administrative Science Quarterly, 48*, 240-267.

Reddy, M.L. (1979). The conduite metaphor: A case of frame conflict in our language about language. In A. Ortony (Ed.), *Metaphor and thought.* Cambridge University Press.

Reed, R., & DeFillippi, R.J. (1990). Causal Ambiguity, Barriers to Imitation, and Sustainable Competitive Advantage. *Academy of Management Review, 15*(1), 88-102.

Reverse. (2001). *Independent information on reverse mortgages for consumers, their families, professional advisors, and nonprofit counselors.* Retrieved 2001, from http://www.reverse.org

Revilla, E. (1996): "Factores Determinantes del Aprendizaje Organizativo. Un Modelo de Desarrollo de Productos". Club Gestión de Calidad, Madrid.

Rheingold, H. (1993). *The Virtual Community: Homestanding on the Electronic Frontier,* New York: Addison-Wesley.

Rheingold, H. (2002). *Smart mobs: the next social revolution.* New York: Perseus Publishing.

Rhodes, R. A. (1997). *Understanding governance: policy networks, governance, reflexivity and accountability.* Buckingham: Open University Press.

Ricci, A., Omicini, A. & Denti, E. (2002). Virtual enterprises and workflow management as agent coordination issues. *International Journal of Cooperative Information Systems, 11*(3-4), 355-379.

Rice, R. (1984). *Mediated group communication.* In Rice, R. & Associates (Eds). The new media. New York: Academic Press.

Richarson, J. (2001). An evaluation of Virtual Learning Environments and their learners: do individual differences effect perception of virtual learning environments. Interactive. *Educational Multimedia, 3.*

Ridings, C.M., Gefen, D., and Arinze, B. (2002). "Some antecedents and effects of trust in virtual communities," *Journal of Strategic Information Systems* (11), pp. 271-295.

Ridley, S. (1995). Towards a new business culture for tourism and hospitality organizations. *International Journal of Contemporary Hospitality Management, 7*(7), 36-43.

Riege, A. & Lindsay, N. (2006). Knowledge management in the public sector: stakeholder partnerships in the public policy development. *Journal of Knowledge Management, 10* (3), 24-39.

Riempp, G. (1998). *Wide area workflow management:* creating partnerships for the 21st century. London: Springuer-Verlag London.

Ring, P., & Van de Ven, A. (1994). Development processes of cooperative interorganizational relationships. *Academy of Management Review, 19*(1), 90-118.

Rita, P. (1995). O Turismo em Perspectiva: Caracterização e Tendências do Mercado Internacional. *Revista Portuguesa de Gestão,* II/III, 7-18.

Ritchie, J. R. B. &. Crouch, G. I. (1997). Roles and contributions to destination competitiveness, In AIEST (Ed.), *47th Congress of the Association International d'Experts Scientifiques du Tourisme* (pp. 117-139), Cha-Am, Thailand.

Ritchie, J. R. B. &. Crouch, G. I. (2000). The competitive destination: a sustainability perspective. *Tourism Management,* 21(1), 1-7.

Roberts, J. (2000). From know-how to show-how: Questioning the role of information and communication technologies in knowledge transfer. *Technology Analysis and Strategic Management,* 12(4), 429-443.

Roberts, K., and C. O'Reilly. (1978). Organization as communication structures: an empirical approach. *Human Communication Research,* (4),283-293.

Robins, J.A., Tallman, S., & Fladmoe-Lindquist, K. (2002). Autonomy and dependence of international cooperative ventures: an exploration of the strategic performance of U.S. ventures in Mexico. *Strategic Management Journal, 23,* 881-901.

Rocco, E., Finholt, T.A., Hofer, E.C., & Herbsleb, J.D.(2001). *Out of sight, short of trust.* Paper presented at the Conference of the European Academy of Management, Barcelona, Spain.

Rodríguez, A., & Ranguelov, S. (2004). Knowledge Networks: A Key Element for University Research and Innovation Process. *The ICFAI Journal of Knowledge Management,* 2(4), 78-85.

Rory, C. (2000). La gestión del conocimiento. La herramienta del futuro. *Trend Management, 2* (3), 83-107.

Rosenberg, M. (2001). *E-learning: Estrategias para transmitir conocimiento en la era digital.* Bogotá: McGraw-Hill Intramericana.

Rothaermel, F.T. (2001). Incumbent's advantage through exploiting complementary assets via interfirm cooperation. *Strategic Management Journal,* 22, 687-699.

Rowley, T. J. (1997). Moving beyond dyadics ties: a network theory of stakeholder influences. *Academy of Management Review,* 22(4), 887-910.

Roy, M., Dewit, O. and Aubert, B. (2001). "The Impact of Interface Usability on Trust in Web Retailers," *Internet Research: Electronic Networking Applications and Policy* (11:5), pp. 388-398.

Rubio, M.J. (2003). Enfoques y modelos de evaluación del e-learning. *Revista electrónica de Investigación y Evaluación Educativa, Relieve,* 9 (2).

Rubio, M.J. (2003). Enfoques y modelos de evaluación del e-learning. *Relieve,9,2,* 101-120

Ruggles, R. (1997). *Knowledge management tools.* Oxford: Butterworth-Heinemann.

Rumelt, R.P. (1984). The evaluation of business strategy, in Glueck, W.F., (ed) *Business policy and strategic management,* New York: Mc Graw Hill.

Ryan, C. (1995). Learning about tourists from conversations: the over - 55s in Majorca, *Tourism Management,* 16(3), 207-215.

Ryssen, S.V., & Godar, S.H. (2000). Going international without going international: Multinational virtual teams. *Journal of International Management, 6,* 49-60.

Saabeel, W., Verduijn, T.M., Hagdom, L., & Kumar, K. (2002). A model of virtual organisation: a structure and process perspective. *Electronic Journal of Organizational Virtualness, 4*(1), 1-16.

Sabel, Ch. (1992). Studies Trust: Building New Forms of Cooperation in a Volatile Economy. In Pyke, F. & Sengenberger, W. (Ed.) *Industrial Districts and Local Economic Regeneration.* Geneve: International Institute for Labour Studies, International Labour Office.

Sadowski-Rasters, G., Duysters, G. & Sadowski, B. M. (2007). *Communication in the virtual workplace, teamwork in computer-mediated-communication.* Northampton, MA.: Edward Elgar Publishing.

Sáez Vacas, F. (1991). La sociedad informatizada: Apuntes para una patología de la técnica, Claves de la Razón Práctica. *Colección Impactos. Ed. Funesco*

Saint-Onge, H, & Wallace, D (2003). *Leveraging Communities of Practice for Strategic Advantage.* Amsterdam, Netherland: Butterworth-Heinemann.

Saint-Onge, H. , & Wallace, D. (2003). *Leveraging Communities of Practice for Strategic Advantage.* Amsterdam: Butterworth-Heinemann.

Sakakibara (1997). Heterogeneity of firm capabilities and cooperative research an development: an empirical examination of motives. *Strategic Management Journal,* vol. 18, n. 6, 143-165.

Sancho, A. (1993). Calidad Y Educación: Un reto para el Sector Turístico. *Estudios Turísticos,* 119/120, 23-28.

Santoro, M.D., & Gopalakrishnan, S. (2001). Relationship Dynamics between University Research Centers and Industrial Firms: Their Impact on Technology Transfer Activities. *Journal of Technology Transfer, 26,* 163-171.

Sanzo, M., Santos, M., Vázquez, R., and Álvarez, L. (2003). "The Effect of Market Orientation on Buyer-Seller Relationship Satisfaction," *Industrial Marketing Management* (32:4), pp. 327-345.

Sarkar, M.B., Echambadi, R., Cavusgil, S.T., & Aulakh, P.S. (2001). The influence of complementary compatibility and relationship capital on alliance performance. *Journal of the Academy of Marketing Science, 29*(4), 358-373.

Saviotti, P.P. (1998). On the Dynamics of Appropriability, of Tacit and of Codified Knowledge. *Research Policy* 26, 843-856.

Schein, E.H. (1993), "How can organizations learn faster? The challenge of entering the green room". *Sloan management Review,* winter, pp. 85-92.

Schmidt, J. B., Montoya-Weiss, M. M., & Massey, A. P. (2001). New product development decision-making effectiveness: Comparing individuals, face-to-face teams, and virtual teams. *Decision Sciences,* 32(4), 1-26.

Schmoll, G. (1977). *Tourism Promotion. Marketing Background, Promotion Techniques and Promotion Planning Methods.* London: Tourism International Press

Schubert, P. & Ginsburg, M. (2000). Virtual communities of transaction: the role of personalization in electronic commerce. *Electronic Markets,* 10(1), 45-55.

Schultz, M. (2003). Pathways of relevance: Exploring inflows of knowledge into subunits of multinational corporations. *Organization Science, 14,* 440-459.

Schultze, U. (2000). A confessional account of an ethnography about knowledge work. *MIS Quarterly, 24*(1), 3-41.

Schultze, U., Boland, R. J. (2000). Place, space and knowledge work: a study of outsourced computer systems administrators. *Accounting Management and Information Technologies,* 10(3), 187-219.

Schwartz, D. G. (2006). *Encyclopedia of knowledge management.* Harrisburg, PA.: Idea Group Inc.

Scott, B. R. (1989). Competitiveness: Self Help for a Worsening Problem. *Harvard Business Review,* 67 (4), 115 - 121.

Scott, M. M. S. (1986). The state of the art of researching management support systems. In *The Rise of Managerial Computing.* Rockart, J. F.& Charles V. B. (Ed.). Homewood, IL: Dow Jones-Irwin, p. 325.

Scott, M.; Golden, W. & Hugues, M. (2004). Implementation strategies for e-Government: a stakeholder analysis approach. In *Proceedings of ECIS: The European Information Systems Profession in the Global Networking Environment,* Turku, Finland.

Scott, W. R. (2003). *Organizations: Rational, natural, and open systems (5th ed.).* Upper Saddle River, NJ: Prentice Hall.

Scovell, P. (1993). Assembling the building blocks for the networks of the future. *Telesis*, (96), 23 - 31.

Selin, S, & Chavez, D. (1995). Developing an evolutionary tourism partnership model, *Annals of Tourism Research*, 22(4), 844-856.

Selin, S. & Myers, N. (1998) Tourism marketing alliances: member satisfaction and effectiveness attributes of a regional initiative. *Journal of Travel and Tourism Research*, 7, 79-94.

Selin, S. (2000). Developing a Typology of Sustainable Tourism Partnerships. In B. Bramwell, & B. Lane (Eds.), *Tourism collaboration and partnerships: Politics, practice and sustainability* (pp. 143-158). Clevedon, Uk: Channel View Publications.

Selin, S., & Myers, N. (1995). Correlates of partnership effectiveness: the coalition for unified recreation in the Eastern Sierra. *Journal of Recreation Administration*, Winter, 13(4), 37-46.

Senge, P. (1990). *The Fifth Discipline: The Art and Practice of the Learning Organization*. New York, Doubleday Currency.

Severt, E. (2002). *The Customer's Path to loyalty: A Partial Test of the Relationships of Prior Experience, Justice, and Customer Satisfaction*, Doctoral Thesis, Faculty of the Virginia Polytechnic Institute and State University (EEUU), 2002.

Shan, W., & Song, J. (1997). Foreign Direct Investment And The Sourcing Of Technological Advantage: Evidence From The Biotechnology Industry. *Journal of International Business Studies*, 28(2), 267-284.

Shankar, V., Smith, A. and Rangaswamy, A. (2003). "Customer Satisfaction and loyalty in online and offline environments," *International Journal of Research in Marketing* (20), pp. 153-175.

Shannon, C. E. (1948). A mathematical theory of communication. *Bell Systems Tech Journal*, (3-4).

Shannon, C. E., & Weaver, W. (1949). *The mathematical theory of communication*. Urbana, IL: University of Illinois Press.

Shekhar, S. (2006). Understanding the virtuality of virtual organizations. *Leadership & Organization Development Journal* 27(6), 465-483.

Shenk, D. (1998). *Data smog: Surviving the information glut*. San Francisco, Harper.

Shenkar, O., & Li, J. (1999). Knowledge Search in International Cooperative Ventures. *Organization Science*, 10(2), 134-143.

Sherif, K. (2006). An adaptive strategy for managing knowledge in organizations. *Journal of Knowledge Management*, 10(4), 72-80.

Shin, M.; Holden, T. & Schmidt, R.A. (2001). From Knowledge Theory to Management Practice: Towards an Integrated Approach. *Information Processing and Management*, 37, 335-355.

Short, J., Williams, E., & Christie, B. (1976). *The social psychology of telecommunications*, London: John Wiley & Sons.

Shotter, J. (1993). *Conversational realities: Constructing life through language*. London: Sage Publications.

Shrader, R.C. (2001). Collaboration and performance in foreign markets, the case of young high-technology manufacturing firms. *Academy of Management Journal*, 44 (3), 45-60.

Shumar, W. & Renninger, K. A. (2002). On conceptualizing community. In K. Renninger & W. Shumar (Ed.) *Building virtual communities: learning and change in cyberspace*. Cambridge: Cambridge University Press.

Sieber, P. (1997). Virtual organizations: static and dynamic viewpoints. *Virtual-organization.net, Newsletter*, 1(2), 3-9.

Siebert, P. (2000). Virtual organizations: static and dynamic viewpoints. *VoNet: The Newsletter*.

Silva, J. A. (1991). *O Turismo em Portugal – Uma Análise de Integração Micro-Macroecómica*, Unpublished doctoral dissertation, Universidade Técnica de Lisboa, Lisboa, Portugal.

Silva, J. A., Mendes, J. & Guerreiro, M. M. (2001). A Qualidade dos Destinos Turísticos: dos Modelos aos Indicadores. *Revista Portuguesa de Gestão*, III(1), 65-81.

Silver, C.A. (2000). Where technology and knowledge meet. *Journal of Business Strategy,* 21(6), 28-33.

Simchi-Levi, D., Kaminski, P. & Simchi-Levi, E. (2000). *Designing and Managing the Supply Chain: Concepts, Strategies, and Case Studies*. New York: McGraw-Hill.

Simmons, D. E. (2002). The forum report: E-learning adoption rates and barriers. In A. Rossett (Ed.), *The ASTD e-learning handbook* (pp. 19-23). New York: McGraw-Hill.

Simon, H. A. (1965). *The shape of automation*. New York: Harper and Row.

Simon, H. A. (1976). *Administrative behavior*. New York: Free Press.

Simon, H. A. (1977). *The new science of management decision*. New York, NY: Harper & Row.

Simon, H. A. (1997). *Models of Bounded Rationality*. Cambridge, MA: MIT Press.

Simon, H.A. (1991). Bounded Rationality and Organizational Learning. *Organization Science* 2, 125-134.

Simonin, B.L. (1997). The importance of collaborative know-how, an empirical test of the learning organization. *Academy of Management Journal,* 4 (5), 1150.

Simpson, J.M., & Mayo, D.T. (1997). Relationship management: a call for fewer influence attempts?. *Journal of Business Research, 39*, 209-218.

Skyrme, D.J. (1999). *Knowledge networking. Creating the collaborative enterprise*. Oxford: Butterworth-Heinemann.

Skyrme, D.J. (1999). *Knowledge networking. Creating the collaborative enterprise*. Oxford: Butterworth-Heinemann.

Slack, J.D. (1987). The information age as ideology: an introduction. In *The Ideology of the Information Age*.

Slack, J. D. & and F. Fejes, F. (Ed.). Norwood,NJ: Ablex Publishing Corp.

Small, C. (2006). *An enterprise knowledge-sharing model: A complex adaptive systems perspective on improvement in knowledge sharing*. Doctoral dissertation, George Mason University. University Microfilms.

Small, C., & Sage, A. (2006). Knowledge management and knowledge sharing: A review. *Information, Knowledge, and Systems Management, 5*(3), 153-169.

Smith, J., and Barclay, D. (1997). "The effects of Organizational Differences and Trust on the Effectiveness of Selling Partner Relationships," *Journal of Marketing* (61), pp. 3-21.

Smith, K.W. (1974). "On estimating the reliability of composite indexes through factor analysis," *Sociological Methods & Research* (2), pp. 485– 510.

Smith, M. (2002). Tools for navigating large social cyberspaces, *Commun. ACM, 45(4),* 51-55.

Smith, S. L. (1994). The Tourism Product, *Annals of Tourism Research*, 21(3), 582-595.

SOCITM (2006). Modern public services: a role for change. The CIO as agent of transformation. Retrieved from: http://www.socitm.gov.uk/socitm/Services/Socitm+Insight/News/Role+of+CIO.htm

Software Engineering Institute (SEI). (1996). *IDEAL^{SM}: A user's guide for software process improvement* (Handbook CMU/SEI-96-HB-001). Pittsburgh, PA: Software Engineering Institute, Carnegie Mellon University.

Soo, C., Devinney, T., Midgley, D., & Deering, A. (2002). Knowledge management: Philosophy, processes and pitfalls. *California Management Review, 44*, 129-150.

Spence, M. (1984). Cost reduction, competition, and industry performance. *Econometrica, 52*, 101-122.

Spender, J.C. (1996). Making knowledge the basis of a dynamic theory of the firm. *Strategic Management Journal*, 17 (Winter Special Issue), 45-62.

Spender, J.C. (1996). Making Knowledge the Basis of a Dynamic Theory of the Firm. *Strategic Management Journal, 17*, 45-62.

Sperber, D., & Wilson, D. (1995). *Relevance: Communication and cognition.* Oxford, UK: Blackwell.

Spreng, R. A. and Chiou, J. (2002). "A cross-cultural assessment of the satisfaction formation process," *European Journal of Marketing*, (36:7/8), pp. 829-839.

Stahl, C., & Redding, W. C. (1987). Message and message exchange process. In *Handbook of Organizational Communication: An Interdisciplinary Perspective.* F. M. Jablin, F. M. *et al.* Newbury Park, CA: SAGE.

Stanoevska-Slabeva, K. (2002): Toward a community-oriented design of Internet platforms. *International Journal of Electronic Commerce, 6*(3), p. 71-95.

Staples, D.S.; Greenaway, K. & Mckeen, J. (2001). Opportunities for Research about Managing the Knowledge-based Enterprise. *International Journal of Management Reviews, 3*, 1-20.

Starr, M. K. (1971). *Management: a modern approach.* New York: Harcourt Brace Jovanovich, Inc.

Stata, R. (1989): Organizational learning: the key to management innovation. *Management Review, 30,1,* 63-74.

Stauss B. &. Weinlich, B. (1997). Process-oriented measurement of service quality. *European Journal of Marketing*, 31(1), 33-55.

Steenkamp, J.B.E.M. and Geyskens, I. (2006). "How Country Characteristics affect the perceived value of a website," *Journal of Marketing* (70:3), pp. 136-150.

Stein, E.W. & Zwass, V. (1995). Actualizing Organizational Memory with Information Systems. *Information Systems Research, 6*(2).

Stein, E.W. (2005). A qualitative study of the characteristics of a community of practice for knowledge management and its success factors. *International Journal of Knowledge Management, 1*, 1-24.

Stein, E.W., & Zwass, V. (1995). Actualizing organizational memory with information systems. *Information Systems Research, 6*(2), 85-117.

Stewart T.A. (1997): "Intellectual Capital: The New Wealth of Organizations". New York: Doubleday Currency.

Stewart, K.J. (2003). "Trust Transfer on the World Wide Web," *Organization Science* (14:1), pp. 5-17.

Storck, J., & Hill, P.A. (2000). Knowledge diffusion through "strategic communities." *Sloan Management Review, 41*, 63-74.

Strausak, N. (1998). Resumée of Vo Talk. In Sieber, P & Griese J. (Eds). *Organizational Virtualness. Proceedings of the VoNet* – Workshop (pp. 9-24), Simona Verlag Bern.

Stufflebeam, D.L. (2000). *The CIPP model for evaluation.* In Stufflebeam, D.L., Madaus & G.F., Kellaghan, T. (ed.): Evaluation Models. Boston.

Sunassee N. N., & Sewry, D.A.(2002). A Theoretical Framework for Knowledge Management Implementation. *Proceedings ACM International Conference Proceeding Series; Vol. 30.* (pp. 235 – 245). Port Elizabeth, South Africa.

Swan, J., Scarbrough, H., & Robertson, M. (2002). The construction of "communities of practice" in the management of innovation. *Management Learning, 33*, 477-496.

Swarm Development Group. (2004). *Chris Langton, Glen Ropella.* Retrieved from http://wiki.swarm.org/.

Sweeney, G. (1991). Technical culture and the local dimension of entrepreneurial vitality. *Entrepreneurship and Regional Development*, 3.

Szulanski, G. (1996). Exploring internal stickiness: Impediments to the transfer of best practice within the firm. *Strategic Management Journal, 17*, 27-43.

Szulanski, G. (2000). The Process of Knowledge Transfer: A Diachronic Analysis of Stickiness. *Organizational Behaviour and Human Decision Processes, 82*, 9-27.

Szulanski, G. and Winter, S. (Jan 2002). Getting it right the second time. *Harvard Business Review* 80(1), 62-69.

Tapscoot, D. &. Caston, A. (1993). *Paradigma Shift*, McGraw-Hill.

Tapscoot, D. (1995). *The Digital Economy,* Richard D. Irwin.

Tapscott, D. & Willimas, A.D. (2006). *Wikinomics: how mass collaboration changes everything.* On-line: Portfolio Hardcover.

Tapscott, D. (1999). *Growing up digital: the rise of the net generation.* New York: McGraw-Hill.

Targowski, A. & Bowman, J. (1986). Generic elements of communication frames: toward the quantum theory of communication. *Proceedings of the 51st Association for Business Communication Convention*, Los Angeles, CA, November 12-16, p. 1.

Targowski, A. (1990). *The strategy and architecture enterprise-wide information management systems.* Harrisburg, PA.: Idea Group Publishing.

Targowski, A. (1996). *Global information infrastructure,* Harrisburg, PA.: Idea Publishing Group

Targowski, A. (1998). A definition of the information management discipline. *The Journal of Education for MIS.* 5. (1).

Targowski, A. (2007). *Wisdom explained.* Unpublished manuscript. Kalamazoo, MI: Western Michigan University.

Targowski, A., J. & Bosman, J. (1988). The layer-based pragmatic model of the communication process. *The Journal of Business Communication,* 25 (1).

Teece, D. J., Pisano, G. & Shuen, A. (1997). Dynamic capabilities and strategic management. *Strategic Management Journal.* 18(7), 509-533.

Teece, D.J. (1998). Capturing value from knowledge assets: The new economy, markets for know-how, and intangible assets. *California Management Review,* 40(3), 55-79.

Teece, D.J. (1998). Research Directions for Knowledge Management. *California Management Review, 40,* 289-292.

Teece, D.J. (2000). Strategies for managing knowledge assets: the role of firm structure and industrial context. *Long Range Planning, 33,* 35-54.

Teece, D.J. (2000). Strategies for Managing Knowledge Assets: The Role of Firm Structure and Industrial Context. *Long Range Planning, 33,* 509-533.

Teece, D.J., Pisano, G., & Shuen, A. (1997). Dynamic capabilities and strategic management. *Strategic Management Journal, 18,* 509-533.

Teicher, J.; Hughes, O. & Dow, N. (2002). E-Government: a new route to public sector quality. *Managing Service Quality, 12* (6), 384-393.

Telcordia Technologies, Inc. (2000). *COMMON LANGUAGE(R) general codes—telecommunications service providers IAC Codes, exchange carrier names, company codes - Telcordia and region number: BR-751-100-112.* Morristown, NJ: Author.

Thayer, R.H. (2005). *Software engineering project management* (2nd ed.). Alamitos, CA: IEEE Computer Society Press.

The Competitive Telecommunications Association. (2005). *Entering the local market: A primer for competitors.* Retrieved April 29, 2006, from http://www. comptelascent.org/public-policy/position-papers/documents/CLECPrimerReport.pdf

Thieauf, R. J. & Hoctor, J. J. (2006). *Optimal knowledge management: wisdom management systems concepts and applications.* Harrisburg, PA.: Idea Group Inc.

Thompson, J. D., (1967, 2003). *Organizations in Action: Social Science Bases of Administrative Theory.* New Brunswick, NJ: Transaction Publishers.

Thompson, L. & Nadler, J. (2002). Negotiating vis information technology, theory and applications. *Journal of Social Issues.* 58(1).

Tiemessen, I., Lane, H.W., Crossan, M., & Inkpen, A.C. (1997). Knowledge management in international joint ventures. In P. W. Beamish & J. P. Killing (Ed.), *Cooperative strategies: North American perspective* (pp. 370–399). San Francisco: New Lexington Press.

Timothy, D. J. (1998). Co-operative tourism planning in a developing destination. *Journal of sustainable Tourism*, 6(1), 52-68.

Tinsley, R., & Lynch, P. (2001). Small tourism business networks and destination development. *International Journal of Hospitality Management*, 20(4), 367-378.

Tiwana, A. (2000). *The knowledge management toolkit.* Upper Saddle River, NJ: Prentice Hall.

Toffler, Alfred. (1980). *The third wave.* New York: Bantam Books.

Toledo, L. A., & Loures, C. A. (2006). Organizações Virtuais. *Cadernos EBAPE. BR.* IV(2), 1-17.

Tomás, J.V., Poler, R., Capó J., & Expósito, M. (2004, September). *Las herramientas de gestión del conocimiento. Una visión integrada.* Paper presented at Congreso de Ingeniería de Organización, Leganés, Spain.

Tombes, J. (2003, October). Cooking up OSS: Balancing your Back-office diet. *Communications Technology.* Retrieved May 8, 2006, from http://www.ct-magazine.com/archives/ct/1003/1003_oss.html

Traverse, M. (2001). *Agent-based programming environments.* Retrieved 2001, from http://xenia.media.mit.edu/~mt/childs-play-pp.html

Trend (2000). La gestión del conocimiento. La herramienta del futuro. *Trend Management*, 2(3), 83-107.

Trienekens, J.H. & Beulens, A.J.M. (2001). Views on inter-enterprise relationships. *Production Planning & Control*, 12(5), 466-477.

Tsai, W. (2002). Social structure of "coopetition" within a multiunit organization: coordination and intraorganizational knowledge sharing. *Organizational Science,* 13(2), 179-190.

Tsai, W., & Ghoshal, S. (1998). Social capital and value creation: an empirical study of intrafirm networks. *Academy of Management Journal, 41*(4), 464-476.

Tsang, E.W.K. (1997), "Organizational learning and the learning organization: A dichotomy between descriptive and prescriptive research". *Human Relations,* 50 (1), pp. 73-89.

Tsoukas, H. & Vladimirou, E. (2001). What Is Organizational Knowledge? *Journal of Management Studies, 38*, 973-993.

Tsoukas, H. (1996). The firm as a distributed knowledge system: a constructionist approach. *Strategic Management Journal*, 17 (Winter Special Issue), 11-25.

Tsoukas, H. (1996). The Firm as a Distributed Knowledge System: A Constructionist Approach. *Strategic Management Journal, 17*, 11-25.

Tsoukas, H., & Papoulias, D. B. (1996). Creativity in OR/MS: From technique to epistemology. *Interfaces*, 26(2), 73-79.

Tsui, E. (2000). Exploring the KM toolbox. *Knowledge Management*, 4.

Tsvetozar Georgiev, T., Georgieva, E., & Smrikarov, A. (2004). *E-Learning, a New Stage of E-Learning.* *Paper* presented at International Conference on Computer Systems and Technologies - CompSysTech'2004, Rousse, Bulgaria.

Tuomi, I. (1999). Data is More than Knowledge: Implications of the Reversed Knowledge Hierarchy for Knowledge Management and Organizational Memory. *Journal of Management Information Systems,* 16(3), 103-117.

Turiel, A., and P. Davidson. (1996). Heterogeneity, inconsistency and asynchrony in the development of cognitive structures. *In State and Structures.* Levin, I. (Ed.). Norwood, NJ: Albex Publishing Co.

Tydeman, J., Lipinski, H. & Sprang, S. (1980). An interactive computer-based approach to aid group problem formulation. *Technological Forecasting and Social Change*, 16, 311-320.

Tyndale, P. (2002). A taxonomy of knowledge management tools: origins and applications. *Evaluation and Program Planning 25* (2), 183-190.

Ulrich, D.; von Glinow, M.A.; Jick, T. (1993), "High-impact learning: building an difussing, learning capability". *Organizational Dynamics*, 22 (2), pp. 52-66.

Uslaner, E. (2000). Social capital and the Net. *Communications of the ACM, 43*(12), 60-65.

Uzzi, B., & Lancaster, R. (2003). Relational embeddedness and learning: the case of bank loan managers and their clients. *Management Science, 49*(4), 383-399.

Valles, D. M. (1999). Calidad en los Servicio. Una aproximación metodológica. *Estudios Turísticos*, 139, 15-33.

Van De Berghe, W. (1997). *Aplicación de las Normas ISO 9000 a la enseñanza y la formación. Interpretación desde una perspectiva europea.* Luxemburgo. CEDEFOP.

Van De Bergue, W. (1997). *Aplicación de las Normas ISO 9000 a la enseñanza y la formación. Interpretación desde una perspectiva europea.* Luxemburgo: CEDEFOP.

Van de Ven, A. H. & Ferry, D. L. (1980). *Measuring and Assessing Organizations.* New York, John Wiley.

Van den Bosch, F., Van Wijk, R., & Volberda, H. (2003). Absorptive capacity: antecedents, models and outcomes. In the M. Easterby-Smith and M.A. Lyles (Ed.), *The Blackwell Handbook of Organizational Learning and Knowledge Management* (pp.278-301). Malden, MA: Blackwell.

Van den Bosch, F.A.J., Volberda, H.W., & de Boer, M. (1999). Coevolution of firm absorptive capacity and knowledge environment: Organizational forms and combinative capabilities. *Organization Science, 10*, 551-568.

Van den Bosch, F.A.J., Volberda, H.W., & de Boer, M. (1999). Coevolution of firm absortive capacity and knowledge environment: organizational forms and combinative capabilities. *Organization Science*, 10 (5), 551-568.

Van Slyke, C., Kittner, M. & Belanguer, F. (1998). *Identifying Candidates for Distance education: A telecommuting*

perspectiva. Proceedings of the America's Conferencie on Information Systems (pp. 666-668). Baltimore

Van Waarden, F. (2001). Institutions innovation: the legal environment of innovating firms. *Organization Studies*, 22 (5), 765-795.

Vassiliadis, S.; Seufert, A.; Back, A. & Von Krogh, G. (2000). Competing with Intellectual Capital: Theoretical Background. Institute for Information Management and Institute of Management, University of St. Gallen.

Vega, A. V. R., Casielles, R. V. & Martín, A. M. D. (1995). La Calidad Percibida Del Servicio en Establecimientos Hoteleros de Turismo Rural. *Papers de Turisme*, 19, 17-33.

Venkatraman, N. & Henderson, J. C. (1998). Real strategies for virtual organizing. *Sloan Management Review*, Fall, 33-48.

Venkatraman, N., & Henderson, J.C. (1998). Real strategies for virtual organizing. *Sloan Management Review*, Autumn, 33-48.

Vermeulen, F., & Barkema, H. (2001). Learning through acquisitions. *Academy of Management Journal, 44*, 457–476.

Vernadat, F.B. (1996). *Enterprise modelling and integration: principles and applications.* Chapman & Hall.

Vesset, D., & McDonough, B. (2007). The next wave of business analytics. *DM Review*, accessed from http://www.dmreview.com/issues/20070301/1076572-1.html on 1/21/08.

Veugelers, R. (1997). Internal R&D expenditures and external technology sourcing. *Research Policy, 26*, 303-315.

Veugelers, R., & Cassiman, B. (1999). Make and buy in innovation strategies: Evidence from Belgian manufacturing firms. *Research Policy, 28*, 63–80.

Vishanth, W. & Jyoti, C. (2004). Exploring e-Government: challenges, issues and complexities. In *Proceedings of the European and Mediterranean Conference on Information Systems (EMCIS)*, Tunisia, Tunez.

vision, its impacts, and implementation challenges. *Information Systems Frontiers, 4*(1), 121.

Vizcaino, A., Soto, J.P., Portillo-Rodríguez, J., & Piattini, M. (2007). Developing knowledge management systems from a knowledge-based and multi-agent approach. *International Journal of Knowledge Management, 3*(4), 67-83.

Von Friedrichs Grangsjo, Y. (2002). Marketing equilibrium in entrepreneurial cluster: An idea of a dynamic relationship between co-operation, competition and institutions. Paper presented at the 11th Nordic Symposium in Tourism and Hospitality Research, Goteborg, Sweden.

von Hippel, E. (1994). 'Sticky Information' and the Locus of Problem Solving: Implications for Innovation. *Management Science, 40*(4), 429-439.

Von Hippel, E. (1994). Sticky information and the locus of problem solving: Implications for innovation. *Management Science, 49*, 429-439.

Von Hippel, E., von Krogh, G. (2003): "Open Source Software and the Private-Collective Innovation Model: Issues for Organization Science". Organization Science, 14 (2), pp. 209-223.

Von Krogh, G. & Ross, J. (1995). *Organizational Epistemology.* New York: MacMillan and St Martin's Press.

von Krogh, G., Ichijo, K. & Nonaka, I. (2000). *Enabling Knowledge Creation: How to Unlock the Mystery of Tacit Knowledge and Release the Power of Innovation* New York, NY: Oxford University Press.

Von Krogh, G.; Nonaka, I.; Ichijo, K. (1997), "Develop knowledge activists". *European Management Journal,* 15 (5), pp. 475-483.

Wabad, S., & Cooper, C. (2001). *Tourism in the age of globalization.* London: Routledge.

Wainfan, L. & Davis, P. K. (2004). Challenges in virtual collaboration. Santa Monica, CA. RAND.

Waisanen, B. 2002. The future of E-government: Technology fuelled management toll. *Public Management, 84* (5), 6-9.

Waldo, J. (2002). Virtual organizations, pervasive computing, and an infrastructure for networking at the edge. *Information Systems Frontiers, 4*(1), 9.

Wales, Ch., & et al. (1986). *Professional decision-making,* West Virginia University.

Walsh, J.P. & Ungson, G.R. (1991). Organizational Memory. *Academy of Management Review,* 16(1), 57-91.

Walsh, J.P. & Ungson, G.R. (1991). Organizational Memory. *Academy of Management Review, 16,* 57-91.

Walther, J. (1996). Computer-mediated communication: Impersonal, interpersonal and hyperpersonal Interaction. *Communication Research, 23(*1), 3-43.

Walther, J. (1997). Group and interpersonal effects in international computer-mediated collaboration. *Human Communication Research, 19,* 50-88.

Walther, J.B. (1995). Relational aspects of computer-mediated communication: Experimental observations over time. *Organization Science, 6,* 186-203.

Wang, Y., & Fesenmaier, D. (2005). Towards a theoretical framework of collaborative destination marketing. In *Proceeding of the 36th travel and tourism research association annual conference.* New Orleans, USA.

Wang, Y., Yu, Q. and Fesenmaier, D.R. (2002). "Defining the virtual Tourist Community: Implications for Tourism marketing," *Tourism Management* (23), pp. 407-417.

Wanhill, S. (1995). Some Fundamentals of Destination Development. *Revista Portuguesa de Gestão,* II/III, 19-33.

Ward, M. (2006). Information Systems Technologies: a public-private sector comparison. *The Journal of Computer Information System, 46* (3), 50-56.

Warner, A. (2003). Buying Versus Building Competence: Acquisition Patterns in the Information and Telecommunications Industry 1995–2000. *International Journal of Innovation Management, 7*(4), 395–415.

Wasko, M., & Faraj, S. (2005). Why should I share? Examining social capital and knowledge contribution in electronic networks of practice. *MIS Quarterly, 29*(1), 35-57.

Watkins, M. & Bell, B. (2002). The experience of forming business relationships in tourism. *International Journal of Tourism Research,* 4(1), pp. 15-28.

Weber, M.M. (2002). Measuring supply chain agility in the virtual organization. *International Journal of Physical Distribution & Logistics Management,* 32 (7), 577-590.

Weick, K. E. (1979). *The social psychology of organizing.* Reading, Mass: Addison-Wesley.

Weick, K.E. & Roberts, K.H. (1993). Collective Mind in Organizations: Heedful Interrelating on Flights Decks. *Administrative Science Quarterly,* 38, 357-381.

Weiermair, K. (2000b) Quality Assessment and Measurement in Tourism: Issues and Problems, Paper presented at the *Workshop Quality in Tourism: from Patterns to Indicators,* Universidade do Algarve, Faro, Portugal.

Weiermair, K. (1994) Quality Management in Tourism: Lessons from the Service Industries? In AIEST (Ed.) *44éme Congrès de l'Association International d'Experts Scientifiques du Tourisme* (pp. 93-113), Vienne, Austria.

Weiermair, K. (2000a) Tourist's perceptions towards and satisfaction with service quality in the cross-cultural service encounter: implications for hospitality and tourism management, *Managing Service Quality,* 10(6), 397-409.

Weigel, D. & Cao, B. (1999). Applying GIS and OR techniques to solve Sears technician-dispatching and home-delivery problems. *Interfaces,* 29(1), 112-130.

Weisenfeld, U., Olaf, F., Alan, P., & Klaus, B. (2001). Managing technology as a virtual enterprise. *R & D Management, 31*(3), 323-334.

Welch, D., Welch, L., & Piekkari, R. (2005). Speaking in tongues: The importance of language in international management processes. *International Studies of Management and Organization, 1,* 10-27.

Wellman, B. (2001). Computer networks as social networks. *Science,* 293(5537), 2031-2034.

Wellman, B., & Gulia, M. (1999). Virtual communities as communities: Net surfers don't ride alone. In the M.A. Smith and P. Kollock (Ed.),*Communities in cyberspace* (pp. 167–194). London: Routledge.

Wellman, B., & Gulia, M. (1999). Virtual communities as communities: Net surfers don't ride alone. In M. A. Smith & P. Kollock (Eds.), *Communities in cyberspace.* London: Routledge.

Wellman, B., Quan-Haase, A., Witte, J., & Hampton, K. (2001). Does the Internet increase, decrease, or supplement social capital? Social networks, participation, and community commitment. *American Behavioral Scientist,* 45(3), 437-456.

Wenger, E. (1999). *Communities of practice, learning, meaning and identity.* US: Cambrige University Press.

Wenger, E. (2001). Comunidades de práctica aprendizaje, significado e identidad. Barcelona: Paidós.

Wenger, E., McDermott, R., & Snyder, W. (2002). *Cultivating Communities of Practice: A Guide to Managing Knowledge.* Boston, MA: Harvard Business School Press.

Wenger, E., McDermott, R., & Snyder, W. (2002). *Cultivating Communiteis of Practice: A Guide to Managing Knowledge.* Boston, MA: Harvard Business School Press.

Wenger, E., McDermott, R., & Snyder, W.M. (2002). *Cultivating communities of practice: A guide to managing knowledge.* Boston: Harvard Business School Press.

Wenger, E.C., & Snyder, W.M. (2000). Communities of practice; the organizational frontier. *Harvard Business Review, 78*(1), 139-145.

Wernerfelt, B. (1984), A resource based view of the firm. *Strategic Management Journal*, 5(2), 171-178.

White, G. & Hutchison, B. (1996). Local Government. In Farnham D. Hortorn (eds.), *Managing People in the Public Services* (pp. 185-224). Basingstoke: Macmillan Press.

Wiesenfeld, B.M., Raghuram, S., & Garud, R. (1999). Communication patterns as determinants of organizational identification in a virtual organization. *Organization Science, 10*, 777-790.

Wiig, K.M. (1993): "Knowledge Management Foundations. thinking about thinking - How People and Organizations Create, Represent and Use Knowledge". Schema Press, Arlington Texas.

Willemain, T. R. (1994). Insights on modeling from a dozen exerts. *Operations Research*, 42, 213-222.

Willemain, T. R. (1995). Model Formulation: What experts think about and when. *Operations Research*, 43(6), 916-932.

Williamson, O. (1990). *Comparative economic organization: The analysis of discrete structural alternatives.* Working paper presented at the law and economics workshop, the University of Michigan.

Wilson, E. V. (2003). Perceived effectiveness of interpersonal persuasion strategies in computer-mediated communication. *Computers in Human Behavior*, 19(5), 537-552.

Wind, Y. (1976). "Preference of relevant others in individual choice models," *Journal of Consumer Research* (3:1), pp. 50-57.

WISE Consortium. (2002). Deliverable D1.3: Review of KM Tools. IST-2000-29280, Web-enabled Information Services for Engineering. Retrieved March 26, 2002, from http://www-eurisco.onecert.fr/Wise/Publication/WISEReviewKMtoolsVA4.pdf

Witzel, M. (2003). The world's first virtual business organization. *European Business Forum*, (13), 72-74.

Wojciechowski, J. (1989). Progress of knowledge and right-left dichotomy: are existing ideologies adequate? *Man & Development*, 11(1).

Woods, R. (2005). *Trident Warrior Experiment Series*, Unpublished briefing by Space and Naval Warfare Systems Command (SPAWAR); http://enterprise.spawar.navy.mil/UploadedFiles/TridentWarriorExperimentSeries.pdf .

Woodward, J. (1975). *Management and Technology.* London: HMSO.

Wooldridge, M., & Jennings, N. R. (1995). Intelligent agents: Theory and practice. *The Knowledge Engineering Review, 10*(2), 115-152.

Wooldridge, M., Jennings, N. R., & Kinny, D. (2000). The Gaia methodology for agent-oriented analysis and design. *International Journal of Autonomous Agents and Multi-Agent Systems, 3.3*(28), 285.

Wright, P.M., McMahan, G.C. & McWilliams (1994). Human resources and sustained competitive advantage: a resource based perspective. *The International Journal of Human Resource Management,* 5,301-326

Wright, W. F., Jindanuwat, N. and Todd, J. (2004): "Computational Models as a Knowledge Management Tool: A Process Model of the Critical Judgments Made during Audit Planning". *Journal of Information Systems*, 16(1), pp. 23-33.

WTO (2000). Global Tourism Forecast to the Year 2000 and Beyond : The World, WTO, Madrid.

Yannis, L., Finin, T., & Peng, Y. (1999). Agent communication languages: The current landscape. *IEEE Intelligent Systems and Their Applications, 14*(2).

Yao, L.J., Kam, T.H.Y & Chan, S.H. (2007). Knowledge sharing in Asian public administration sector: the case of Hong Kong. *Journal of Enterprise Information Management, 20* (1), 51-69.

Yates, J., Orlikowski, W., & Okamura, K. (1999). Explicit and implicit structuring of genres in electronic communication: Reinforcement and change of social interaction. *Organization Science, 10*(1), 83-103.

Yli-Renko, H., Autio, E., & Sapienza, H. (2001). Social capital, knowledge acquisition, and knowledge exploitation in young technology-based firms. *Strategic Management Journal, 22*(6), 587-613.

Yoon, Y., & Guimaraes, T. (1993). Selecting expert system development techniques. *Information and Management,* (24), 209-223.

Young, T.R. (1987). Information, ideology and political reality. In *The Ideology of the Information Age.* Slack, J. D., & Fejes, F. Norwood, NJ: Ablex Publishing Corp.

Yuksel, A. & Yuksel, F. (2005). Managing relations in a learning model for bringing destinations in need of assistance into contact with good practice. *Tourism Management,* 26(5), 667-679.

Zack, M. (1999). Developing a Knowledge Strategy. *California Management Review, 41,* 125-145.

Zack, M. (2003). Rethinking the Knowledge-Based Organization. *MIT Sloan Management Review,* summer issue, 67-71.

Zack, M.H. (1999). Managing codified knowledge. *Sloan Management Review, 40,* 45-58.

Zaheer, A., & Geoffrey G. B. (2005). Benefiting from Network Position: Firm Capabilities, Structural Holes, and Performance. *Strategic Management Journal, 26,* 809-825.

Zahra, S. A., & George, G. (2002). Absorptive capacity: A review, reconceptualization, and extension. *Academy of Management Review, 27*(2), 185-203.

Zaichkowsky, J.L. (1985). "Measuring the Involvement Construct," *Journal of Consumer Research* (12:4), pp. 341-352.

Zand, D.E. (1972). Trust and managerial problem solving. *Administrative Science Quarterly, 17,* 229-239.

Zander, U., & Kogut, B. (1995). Knowledge and the speed of the transfer and imitation of organizational capabilities: An empirical test. *Organization Science, 6,* 76-92.

Zander, U., & Kogut, B. (1995). Knowledge and the speed of the transfer and imitation of organizational capabilities: an empirical test. *Organization Science, 6,* 76-92.

Zenger, T.R., & Hestley, W.S. (1997). The disaggregation of corporations: selective intervention, high-powered incentives and molecular units. *Organisation Science,* 8(3), 209–222.

Zielinski, D. (2000). Face value. *Presentations,* 14(6), 58-64.

Zimmerman, F. O. (1997). Structural and managerial aspects of virtual enterprises. In *Proceedings of the European Conference on Virtual Enterprises and Networked Solutions - New Perspectives on Management, Communication and Information Technology* (pp. 7-10). Germany: Paderborn.

Zimmermman, F. (2000). *Structural and Managerial Aspects of Virtual Entreprises.* University of Bamberg, Business Information Systems, Germany. Retrieved May 7, 2000, from http://www.seda.sowi.uni-bamberg.de/persons/zimmermann.html

Zollo, M. y Winter, S.G. (2002), "Deliberate learning and the evolution of dynamic capabilities". *Organization Science,* 13 (3), pp. 339-351.

Zucchermaglio, C., & Talamo, A. (2003). The development of a virtual community of practice using electronic mail and communicative genres. *Journal of Business and Technical Communication, 17,* 259-284.

About the Contributors

Cesar Camison holds a PhD in economic and business sciences. He is the principal professor at University Jaume I (Spain). He has been visiting professor at the University of Texas, the Universitá Commerciale Luigi Bocconi de Milán, the University of Surrey, the University of Vienna, and the Université de Montpellier I. He is Director of the Strategy, Knowledge Management and Organizational Learning Research Group (GRECO). His specialization areas are strategic management and competitiveness, entrepreneurship (SME and familiar enterprises), knowledge management, strategic alliances and industrial districts.

Daniel Palacios has a PhD in Management and Assistant Professor in the Department of Business Administration and Marketing, Universitat Jaume I (Spain). MSc in Control and Quality Management, Polytechnic University of Valencia. Degree in Computer Science from the Polytechnic University of Valencia. He has touch or researched in universities of Germany, USA, UK, or Thailand. His primary areas of research include Tourism Management and Knowledge Management. He has published in international books and journals such as *Annals of Tourism Research, International Journal of Contemporary Hospitality Management, International Journal of Innovation Management, International Journal of Technology Management, Journal of Intellectual Capital, Journal of Knowledge Management, Management Research, or Tourism Management.*

Fernando Garrigos has a PhD in Management and Assistant Professor in the Department of Business Administration and Marketing, Universitat Jaume I (Spain). Dr. Garriogos has a MSc in Tourism Management and Planning from Bournemouth University and a degree in Economics from the University of Valencia. He has touch or researched in universities of France, Germany, USA, UK, or Thailand. His primary areas of research include Tourism Management and Knowledge Management. He has published in international books and journals such as *Annals of Tourism Research, International Journal of Contemporary Hospitality Management, International Journal of Innovation Management, International Journal of Technology Management, Journal of Intellectual Capital, Journal of Knowledge Management, Management Research, or Tourism Management.*

Carlos Devece is an Assistant Professor in Department of Business Administration and Marketing at the Universitat Jaume I of Castellon (Spain). His research interests are Knowledge Management and the role of Information Technology as a source of competitive advantage. He has been a consultant in an engineering consulting firm. He has a bachelor's degree in Electronics and Communication Engineering from the Polytechnic University of Valencia and a PhD in management from the Universitat Jaume I. He has participated as software developer in several projects funded by government agencies and private companies.

* * *

Mr. Bachani PhD in Management and Assistant Professor in the Department of Business Administration and Marketing. He has taught or researched in universities of Germany, USA, UK, or Thailand. His primary areas of research include Tourism Management and Knowledge Management. He has published in international books and journals such as Annals of Tourism Research, International Journal of Contemporary Hospitality Management, International Journal of Innovation Management, International Journal of Technology Management, Journal of Intellectual Capital, Journal of Knowledge Management, Management Research, or Tourism Management.

Eduardo Bueno Campos —Professor on Business Economics in the Autonomous University of Madrid, Head of the University Institute for Research (IADE) and Managing Director for Innovation of the Scientific Park of Madrid— is one of the Spanish authors with greatest prestige within the field of business organization, especially in what refers to strategic management and its approach based on knowledge, having numerous research publications and projects with public and private organizations

Carles Camisón Haba Bachelor of Business Management (2008) by Polytechnic University of Valencia. Member of Research Group on Strategy, Competitiveness and Knowledge and Innovation Management (GRECO). His field of expertise is strategic management and firm as a knowledge organization.

Josep Capó-Vicedo is currently an associate professor at Polytechnic university of Valencia (Spain). M.Sc. in Industrial Engineering from Polytechnic University of Valencia (Spain); PhD in Management from Polytechnic University of Valencia (Spain).His research has been focus on Industrial districts; Inter and intra organizational relationships and Knowledge Management. Researcher of several Research Programs and many publications in journals and international conferences.

Luis Casaló is assistant professor at the University of Zaragoza (Spain). His main research line is focused in the analysis of online consumer behaviour in the context of virtual communities. His work has been presented in national and international conferences, and has been published in several journals, such as *Journal of Marketing Communications, Computers in Human Behaviour, Online Information Review*, and books, such as *Mobile Government: An Emerging Direction in E-Government and Encyclopedia of Networked and Virtual Organizations*.

Enrique Claver *is a* full Professor in Business Management at the University of Alicante, Spain. His PhD dissertation was an analysis of Strategy Management. His current research includes Strategy Management, Competitiveness and Quality.

Júlio da Costa Mendes has a degree in Business, Master of Business, PhD in Management – Strategy and Organizational Behaviour. Assistant Professor at the Faculty of Economics, University of Algarve, Portugal. Coordinator of the PhD programme in Tourism and in some Master and Post-Graduation Degrees.Synopsis of the current research interests: Integrated Quality Management in Tourism Destinations, Competitiveness, Events Management, Tourism Destinations Image, Branding, Marketing Strategies, Customer Satisfaction.Supervision of some academic research studies. Several presentations made at conferences both in Portugal and abroad. Professional experience in public and private companies.

Susana de Juana-Espinosa Assistant Lecturer in Business Management at the University of Alicante (Spain). Her PhD consisted in the analysis of the e-Government strategies carried out by Spanish councils. Her current research includes e-Business strategy and management in public and private sectors.

Manuel Expósito-Langa is currently an associate professor at Polytechnic university of Valencia (Spain). MSc in Computers Engineering from Polytechnic University of Valencia (Spain). His research has been focus on Industrial districts; Inter and intra organizational relationships; Technology Management and Innovation. Researcher of several Research Programs and many publications in journals and international conferences.

MªEugenia Fabra is associate professor of the Department of Applied Economics of the University of Valencia (Spain). She is doctor of Economics from the same University. Her main research interest centre on aspects related to human capital and the value of education and training as comparative advantages. She has participated in different projects and investigations on models for measuring distinctive competences in the Department of Business Administration of the Faculty of Economics and Law Sciences of the Universitat Jaume I (Castellón, Spain). She is currently working on job quality and effects of education on job satisfaction.

Carlos Flavián holds a Ph.D in Business Administration and is Professor of Marketing in the Faculty of Economics and Business Studies at the University of Zaragoza (Spain). His research has been published in several academic journals, specialized in marketing (*European Journal of Marketing, Journal of Consumer Marketing, Journal of Strategic Marketing, International Journal of Market Research,* etc.) and new technologies (*Information & Management, Industrial Management and Data Systems, Internet Research, Online Information Review,* etc.). He is a member of the Editorial Board of the Industrial Marketing Management, the *Journal of Retailing and Consumer Services,* the *International Journal of Services and Standards and the Journal of Marketing Communications.*

Beatriz Forés Julián holds a Business Administration and Management Degree (2004, Universitat Jaume I, Castellón). She was awarded a prize for the best academic record of the Business Administration and Management Degree at Universitat Jaume I (2004, Castellón Business Association). She obtained a diploma of advanced studies in 2006 (first stage of doctoral studies). She is currently preparing her PhD dissertation. She is a member of the GRECO Research Group on Strategy, Competitiveness and Knowledge Management (www.greco.uji.es), in the Business Administration and Marketing Department. She currently has a research fellowship from the Generalitat Valenciana. She also participates in three investigation projects, whose principal investigators are Professor César Camisón (Universitat Jaume I, Castellón) and Sonia Cruz, PhD (Universitat de València). Her research interests coincide with the GRECO line of investigation which focuses on the study of the firm as a knowledge and learning organisation.

Jens Gammelgaard is associate professor of international business at the Department of International Economicsa and Management at the Copenhagen Business School. He joint the Copenhagen Business School in April 1998. His main research interest is knowledge management practices of multinational corporations, international mergers and acquisitions, and subsidiary development. His work has been widely published in journals like *Journal of International Management, Journal of Knowledge Management,* and edited volumes. Jens Gammelgaard has taught various courses on bachelor, MSc, and MBA, and is currently Deputy Head of the Bachelor of International Business program at Copenhagen Business School.

Miguel Guinalíu holds a PhD in Business Administration and is assistant professor in the Faculty of Economics and Business Studies (University of Zaragoza, Spain). Previously, he worked as an e-business consultant. His main research line is online consumer behaviour, particularly the analysis of online consumer trust and virtual communities. His work has been presented in national and international conferences, and has been published in several journals, such as *Journal of Marketing Communications, Information & Management, Industrial Management & Data Systems, Internet Research, Journal of Retail & Consumer Services, International Journal of Bank Marketing or International Journal of Retail & Distribution Management,* and books, such as *Advances in Electronic Marketing, Mobile Government: An Emerging Direction in E-Government, Encyclopedia of Networked and Virtual Organizations and Encyclopedia of E-Commerce, E-Government and Mobile Commerce.*

Carlos Merino Moreno is currently responsible for research projects in the University Institute for Research (IADE) and Coordinator of Innovation Services in the Scientific Park of Madrid. His specialization fields are centred on intangible-asset management, paying special attention to innovation, organizational intelligence, intellectual capital and knowledge governance, transferring research results into realities of technical assistance for different kinds of organizations and institutions.

Montserrat-Boronat Navarro is a lecturer in Strategic Management and Operations Management at Jaume I University, in Castellón, Spain. She received her PhD in November 2007. Her research interests are related to knowledge integration, dynamic capabilities, innovation, strategic alliances, organizational structure. She has published articles in Organization Studies and also in Spanish academic publications. She has presented her research in some international conferences such as EURAM and EGOS.

Mark E. Nissen is Chair Professor of Command & Control, and Professor of Information Science and Management, at the Naval Postgraduate School. His research focuses on dynamic knowledge and organization for competitive advantage. He views work, technology and organization as an integrated design problem, and has concentrated recently on the phenomenology of knowledge flows. Mark's extensive publications span information systems, project management, organization studies, knowledge management, counterterrorism and related fields. Before his information systems doctoral work at the University of Southern California (PhD in 1996), he acquired over a dozen years' management experience in the aerospace and electronics industries.

Kai A. Olsen is a professor of Informatics (Computing Science) at Molde College and at the University of Bergen, Norway. He is an adjunct professor at the School of Information Sciences, University of Pittsburgh. His main research interests are user interfaces, man-machine communication, and logistic systems. He has been a pioneer in developing software systems for PCs, information systems for primary health care, and systems for visualization. He acts as a consultant for Norwegian and U.S. organizations. He is the author of a recent book for Scarecrow Press, The Internet, the Web and eBusiness: Formalizing Applications for the Real World.

Reinaldo Plaz Landaeta is currently responsible for the area of technological development of the University Institute for Research (IADE). His speciality is focused on technological applications for knowledge creation, development and management and has developed numerous projects of technical assistance for the configuration of collaboration platforms and virtual-environments within the support initiatives for knowledge-governance strategies.

Raúl Poler is Associate Professor in Operations Management and Operations Research at the Polytechnic University of Valencia. He is Deputy Director of the Research Centre on Production Management and Engineering (CIGIP) in which he has developed R & D Projects in the areas of Industrial Management and Supply Chain Management for companies from the metallurgic, textile, footwear, toy and automotive sectors. He works as researcher in several Spanish Government Projects (CICYT, GV, etc.) and European Projects (ESPRIT, IST, GROWTH, etc.). He has published a hundred of research papers in a number of leading journals such as Production Planning and Control, Computers in Industry, European Journal of Operational Research, International Journal of Business Performance Management, International Journal of Production Research, Fuzzy Sets and Systems, etc., and in several international conferences (ECKM, ETFA, EURO, INFORMS, EurOMA, EUROSIM, EUSFLAT, ICMS, IEPM, IESM, POM, etc.). He has been member of the scientific committee of several international conferences and chairman of several sessions. He is member of the European Operations Management Association (EurOMA), the Production and Operations Management Society (POMS) and the Association for the Organization Engineering (ADINGOR). His key research topics include Enterprise Modelling, Knowledge Management, Production Planning and Control and Supply Chain Management.

Alba Puig-Denia has a degree in Business Administration from University Jaume I of Castellón. Currency, she has a grant as research assistant and is member of GRECO (Research Group on Strategy, Competitiveness and Innovation and Knowledge Management).

Hindupur Ramakrishna is an associate professor of information systems at the University of Redlands School of Business where he teaches undergraduate and Graduate courses in MIS. He earned his Ph.D. from Georgia State University. His research interests focus on Information Systems personnel, IS curriculum, intellectual property, and IS project success issues. He has taught in a variety of business schools in the US during the past 29 years. He is a member of the DSI, and AIS. He has published in the Interfaces, Journal of CIS, Omega, Information and Management, Human Performance, Human Resource Development Quarterly, Computer Personnel, and other journals.

Thomas Ritter is professor of business market management and research director at the Center for Applied Market Science at the Copenhagen Business School. He joint the Copenhagen Business School in January 2001 after holding academic positions in Germany and the UK. His main research interests are in business relationship and inter-firm network management, collaborative value creation and segmentation. His work has been widely published in journals including International Journal of

Research in Marketing, Journal of Business Research, Industrial Marketing Management and Journal of Business and Industrial Marketing. He has also written a book on network competence and edited a volume on international relationships and networks. Thomas Ritter has taught various courses on bachelor, MSc, MBA and executive level and consults firms on business marketing and strategy issues. He is a regular speaker at industry gatherings.

Andrew P. Sage is the founding dean emeritus university professor and First American Bank professor in the systems engineering and operation research department at George Mason University in USA. Professor Sage is recognized as one of the shapers of Systems Engineering discipline by his important academic, scientific and consulting contributions for advancing the scientific knowledge and the practice of Systems Engineering from 1960s in the topics of: Systems integration and architecting, complex adaptive systems and knowledge management, economic systems analysis, and systems management. Professor Sage is author or co-author from several books on systems engineering and a plethora of papers in journals. Professor Sage has been editor in chief of the IEEE Transactions on Systems, Man, and Cybernetics (January 1972 - December 1998), editor of Automatica (July 1981 - June 1996) and co-editor in chief (with W. B. Rouse) of Information, Knowledge, and Systems Management, IOS Press, from April 1999 at present. Currently, Professor Sage is the editor in chief of the International Council on Systems Engineering Journal Systems Engineering from, January 1998. He has received several international awards for his academic and professional activities such as: the International Council on Systems Engineering (INCOSE) Pioneer Award (2002), the Eta Kappa Nu Eminent Member Award (2002) and the Third Millennium Medal IEEE (2000), the IEEE Simon Ramo Medal (2000). His formal education is a BSEE (The Citadel, 1955), a SMEE (Massachusetts Institute of Technology, 1956), a PhD (Purdue University, 1960), a DEngr (University of Waterloo, 1987, Honoris Causa) and a DEngr (Dalhousie University, 1997, Honoris Causa).

Raquel Sanchis Gisbert is an Engineer of Industrial Management at the Polytechnic University of Valencia. She has obtained the Diploma of Advanced Studies in the Doctorate Program of Textile Engineering and nowadays she is attending the Doctorate Program of Advanced Models for Operations and Supply Chain Management in the Department of Organizational Matters of Enterprises. She does research work in the fields of Knowledge Management and Business Process Modelling in the Research Centre on Production Management and Engineering (CIGIP). She has participated in different National and European projects: 'Integration of Business Processes, Knowledge Management and Decision Support Tools in Supply Chain of Industrial SMEs (GNOSIS)', 'Interoperability Research for Networked Enterprises Applications and Software (INTEROP)'and 'High Performance Manufacturing (HPM)'.

Avijit Sarkar is an Assistant Professor in the School of Business, University of Redlands since July 2005. Avijit comes to Redlands from The University of Toledo where he taught in the Mechanical, Industrial and Manufacturing Engineering Department as a visiting faculty (2004-05). He received his PhD (2004) and MS (2002) degrees in Industrial Engineering from the State University of New York at Buffalo. His research interests are in business analytics, applied GIS, and congestion in facilities location and layout and his research articles have been published in Journal of Geographical Systems, IIE Transactions, European Journal of Operational Research, Computers and Operations Research, and Socio-Economic Planning Sciences. At Redlands, Avijit teaches management science and operations management courses at both the graduate and undergraduate level.

Cynthia T. Small is department head of the information and knowledge management department at The MITRE Corporation. Since joining MITRE in June 1997, Dr. Small has supported the Intelligence Community in a variety of technical and leadership roles in the areas of knowledge management (KM), IT service management and governance, performance management, and collaboration. Dr. Small was a key innovator in the initial stages of MITRE's Corporate Knowledge Management Program for which she was instrumental to the development of a holistic KM model which enabled a sound foundation in learning theory and organizational aspects which cause knowledge sharing to flourish. Prior to joining MITRE, Small held several senior leadership positions including program manager, technical director, and vice president at a rapidly growing IT enterprise. In 2001, Small received the Woman of Color Government and Defense Technical Innovation Award. Dr. Small received her PhD in information technology with a specialization in Knowledge Management from George Mason University, her MS in technology of management from American University and a BA in mathematics/government from The College of William and Mary. She participates in a variety of academic, industry, and government forums, authoring articles and presentations in the area of knowledge management (KM). Her research interests include knowledge capture and representation, knowledge sharing, KM measurement, and complex adaptive systems.

Juan José Tarí Senior Lecturer in Business Management at the University of Alicante, Spain. His Ph. D. dissertation was an analysis of Quality Management. His current research includes Total Quality Management and the relationship between Quality Management and Environmental Management.

Prof. Dr. Andrew Targowski was engaged in the development of social computing in totalitarian Poland (INFOSTRADA and Social Security # PESEL-1972) and received political asylum in the U.S. during the crackdown on Solidarity in 1981. He has been a professor of Business Information Systems at Western Michigan University since 1980. He published 21 books on information technology, history, and political science (Red Fascism-1982) in English and Polish. During the 1990s he was a Director of the TeleCITY of Kalamazoo Project, one of the first digital cities in the U.S. He investigates the role of info-communication in enterprise, economy, and civilization. He is a President of the International Society for the Comparative Study of Civilizations and a former Chairman of the Advisory Council of the Information Resources Management Association (1995-2003).

José V. Tomás-Miquel is Assistant Professor in Operations Management of the Department of Business Management at the Polytechnic University of Valencia since 2005. During his PhD research he is working in different national and European research projects resulting in several international scientific publications. He is a member of the Production & Operations Management Society (POMS) and the European Operations Management Association (EurOMA).

Ana Villar-López is a lecturer in Strategic Management at Jaume I University, in Castellón, Spain. She is currently developing her thesis about organizational forms and innovation. Her research interests are related to innovation, strategic alliances, organizational structure, organizational forms, internationalization. She has published articles in several Spanish academic publications. Her research has been presented in some international conferences such as EURAM, EGOS and IAM.

James G. Williams is professor emeritus in the School of Information Sciences at the University of Pittsburgh and an adjunct professor at Molde College in Norway and Siam University in Thailand. He was the CIO of Broadstreet Communications, Inc.; a broadband telecommunications company from 1999-2002. He is also president of Automated Systems Research and Development, Inc., which develops software systems for hospitals, courts of law, manufacturers, libraries, educational institutions, and retailers. Dr. Williams has authored or co-authored eight books and nearly 100 journal articles and conference proceedings.

Index